117350

JI

EXPOSITION
OF
PROVERBS

George Lawson

KREGEL PUBLICATIONS
Grand Rapids, MI 49501

Exposition of Proverbs by George Lawson.
Copyright © 1980 by Kregel Publications
a division of Kregel, Inc. All rights reserved.

Library of Congress Cataloging in Publication Data

Lawson, George, 1749-1820.
    Exposition of Proverbs.

  (Kregel timeless classics)
  Reprint of the 1829 ed. *Expositions of the Book of
Proverbs* published by W. Oliphant, Edinburgh.
    1. Bible. O.T. Proverbs—Commentaries. I. Title.
BS1465.L34   1980   223'.707   80-8070
ISBN 0-8254-3123-9

Printed in the United States of America

Contents

Foreword

The brilliant English Bible student and bibliographer, Dr. Thomas Hartwell Horne (1780-1862), in compiling a list of the best books written up to his time — books which he chose to recommend to readers of his now famous *Introduction to the Scriptures* — selected for inclusion Dr. George Lawson's *Exposition of the Book of Proverbs*. Of this work, he wrote:

This exposition, as well as those of the *History of Joseph** and the *Book of Ruth,** were chiefly intended for the instruction of Christians in the ordinary walks of life. They are pious and sensible, full of sound doctrine, and salutary admonition and instruction. There is rarely anything of a critical nature to be found in them, which indeed was not the writer's object; but they everywhere discover a minute acquaintance with the Bible and the human heart, and reflect a deep concern to profit the reader. The style is plain, and the illustrations [are] very brief.

George Lawson (1749-1820) was a Scottish clergyman. His father was a carpenter as well as a farmer, and through his personal industry was able to give George a good education. Upon graduating from the University of Edinburgh, Lawson was licensed to preach and began his ministry in a seccession church in Selkirk.

A learned exegete, Lawson could quote extensive portions of the Bible from memory. He frequently spoke without the use of notes, and was loved by his congregation for his clear, practical exposition of the Word.

In 1787 George Lawson was called to Edinburgh

to succeed his former mentor, John Brown, as Professor of Theology, which position he held for the next thirty-three years. The University of Aberdeen later honored him with the degree of Doctor of Divinity.

Dr. Lawson's literary efforts were significant. At the time of his death, he had authored numerous books and left behind him eighty large volumes in manuscript form. These comprised a commentary on the Bible, but regretfully these have never been published.

George Lawson's *Exposition on the Book of Proverbs* has been out-of-print and unobtainable for more than a century. Those who are fortunate enough to possess a copy will readily testify to the rich, rewarding insights to be found in this able Scot's warm, devotional exposition. He, in compnay with very few others, knew the human heart and had the ability to so teach the Word that his hearers and readers were continuously blessed by his messages.

It is a real delight to be able to welcome this new printing of these studies, now entitled *Exposition of Proverbs*. The publisher is to be commended for retrieving this work from oblivion.

CYRIL J. BARBER

*Kregel Timeless Classics, Kregel Publications 1981.

EXPOSITION
of
PROVERBS

Of Augustus Cæsar it is said, that when he read the works of men of learning and genius, he used to extract such precepts as might prove useful to him in his government. This part of his conduct manifested wisdom; the precepts thus collected, served to assist him and his ministers in managing the affairs of the empire. But the necessity of our imitating this part of his conduct, has been in a great measure superseded by that Spirit of truth, under whose guidance Solomon wrote his Proverbs, and transmitted them to future ages for their instruction in righteousness. In this little book there appears more wisdom than in the combined monuments of Greek and Roman learning. The wisest of men wrote it, and his object is to make us wise :—But a greater than Solomon is here, for Wisdom speaks in her own person.

The first nine chapters are a preface to the book. In it Solomon recommends to our study, that wisdom which he designs to teach, and insists on some of her most useful precepts.

Proverbs 1

In this chapter, Solomon gives us an account of the writer, and the design, of this book; recommends the fear of the Lord, a dutiful regard to the instructions of parents, and diligence in guarding against the temptations of bad company, as principal parts of wisdom. It is concluded with an earnest call to the unwise to learn wisdom.

Let us hear, first, what Solomon has to say, for recommending this much neglected book to our attention.

Verse 1. *The Proverbs of Solomon, the son of David, King of Israel.*

This book consists of proverbs, which are wise, and short sayings of great use to direct us in the conduct of life. Proverbs were much valued in ancient times. But no proverbs deserve so much esteem and attention as these, for they are the proverbs of Solomon, another name almost for wisdom. In his days he was honoured like angel of God, for his understanding. All kings that heard of him, admired him, and thought themselves happy if they could hear some of his wise instructions. The Queen of Sheba came from the uttermost parts of the earth to hear his wisdom; although she had not heard the one half of what she found to be true concerning him, yet even these imperfect accounts were such as to exceed her belief. Did she come so far, upon uncertain reports, to hear his wisdom? and shall not we receive with gladness his instructions, since he is come to us, to be our teacher? We have no need to cross dangerous seas, and travel into distant

countries, to hear the lectures of this divine teacher,—
he cries to us in our streets, he talks with us in our
closets. He died some thousands of years ago, but he
yet speaks.

Though Solomon had been the son of an Ahaz, or
of some poor herdsman, his wisdom would have entitled him to our respect. But this wisest of men was
the son of the best of men. He that was raised on
high,—the anointed of the God of Jacob,—the man
after God's own heart,—was his father. This wise son
enjoyed all the advantages to be expected from the instructions and the example, the prayers and the blessings, of so good a father. Solomon was a prophet,
and the son of a prophet,—he was the son of the best
of kings; and of the many sons whom God had given
to David, he was chosen to fill his father's throne.

Great men are not always wise, and except from
their own subjects, the words of kings are seldom entitled to more regard than those of other men. But it
was in Israel, where God was well known, that Solomon was king; and he was advanced to that dignity,
because he was the worthiest of it in the kingdom.

These words are the instructions of that king, who
excelled in wisdom and grandeur all the kings of the
earth. This great prince is our teacher; but not he
alone,—the only wise God here condescends to become
our instructor;—he, then, who disregards this book,
despises a greater than Solomon.

This book is the work of a noble writer, and truly it
was written with a noble design—

Ver. 2. *To know wisdom and instruction, to perceive
the words of understanding—*

To give us the knowledge of wisdom, and that instruction by which knowledge is conveyed into our
minds; for man is born without wisdom, and without
instruction must continue foolish all his days.

The words of understanding are the instruction of wisdom, and this book will lead the simple and inexperienced to perceive these words. But what sort of wisdom is it that Solomon means to teach in this book ? The best kind of wisdom—

Ver. 3. *To receive the instruction of wisdom ; justice, and judgment, and equity.*

The careful reader of this book will receive the instructions of that wisdom which directs men to practise justice, regulated by discretion, and tempered by moderation and mercy. It teaches us our duty to God and man, and leads us in every good path. Solomon could have given us lectures on Astronomy and Poetry, on the nature of birds and beasts, and every thing that attracts the curiosity of men ; but as the wisdom of the prudent is to understand his way, he is directed by the Spirit of God to give us in this book the instructions of divine and moral wisdom, to remain for the use of men till the latest posterity.

They thought themselves happy that were admitted to hear the discourses of this great philosopher, while he lived among men. But the best of his instructions are left on record for our benefit. The best knowledge is the knowledge of God, and of Christ, who is his representing image to men, and holiness, which is the image of God in men. The most necessary truths are first to be learned, and these are clearly represented in this little book.

But who are the persons that may receive benefit from it ? . This you may learn from the next verse—

Ver. 4. *To give subtilty to the simple, to the young man knowledge and discretion.*

Plato wrote on the door of his Academy, " Let no man unskilled in Geometry come hither." Solomon writes the very reverse on the door of his school : " Let the simple man who is easily deceived come hither, and he shall learn that subtilty which is necessary to preserve him from the snares of the destroyer, and is yet fully consistent with integrity. Let the young and inexperienced come and learn knowledge and discretion."

Which of us does not need subtilty to preserve us from the wiles of the great deceiver and his agents? This book not only teaches, but gives subtilty to the simple. When its truth enters into the soul, and takes possession of the heart through the grace of the Spirit who dictates the Scriptures, and makes use of them as his instrument of illumination, then the simple are made wise, and the hearts of the rash understand knowledge.

It were our happiness if we understood our own simplicity, that we might thankfully receive the instructions of wisdom, and fervently pray for the Spirit of God to open our ears and seal our instructions. If any man would be wise in this world, let him become a fool, that he may be wise.

Persons to whom books are dedicated, may be expected to give them a careful perusal. Solomon dedicates this book to the young, as well as to the simple. He knew that young people stand in great need of advice and direction, and earnestly desired to do them good; and could they be persuaded to accept of Solomon as their teacher, he will speak to them with the kindness of a father, and communicate to them knowledge and discretion.

But is this book of no use but to the unwise and the untaught?—It is of great use to the wise also; and if men are truly wise, they will value it above much fine gold, and by the diligent use of it, will greatly improve in wisdom.

Ver. 5. *A wise man will hear, and will increase learn-*

ing ; and a man of understanding shall attain unto wise counsels.

This book contains wise counsels for directing a man under every perplexing difficulty in the way of peace and safety, and enabling him to give the most season-able and prudent counsels to others.

How precious are wise counsels ! and what a treasure is a wise counsellor to his friends and neighbours !— This book will also enable a wise man,

Ver. 6. *To understand a proverb, and the interpre-tation thereof; the words of the wise, and their dark sayings.*

The dark sayings of fools and triflers are not worth a thought ; but the dark sayings of the wise are worthy to be studied till we obtain a complete knowledge of their meaning ; for they are dark at first hearing only, on account of the sublimity of their views, and the force of their manner of expression, which contains much useful instruction in small compass.

Are we old or young, wise or unwise? Here is milk for babes, and strong meat for those that are of full age. Here are plain instructions for the ignorant, and depths of wisdom proper to exercise and enrich the minds of the most intelligent.

Let us attend, and learn, and practise. It is Solo-mon the son of David, and king of Israel, that speaks. He speaks to the simple and inexperienced, and to the wise. He speaks of the most important points of truth, and a greater than Solomon is here. Christ spoke by his Spirit in the prophets, and he still speaks from heaven to us. He speaks by his word and by his Spirit. He opens the understandings of men, that they may understand the Scriptures. Christ is the Word and the Wisdôm of God, and he is made to us wisdom. Let us depend upon him as our wisdom, that his Spirit may write in our hearts the things written in this book : so shall we be the epistle of Christ, written not with pen and ink, but with the Spirit of the living God, and our conversations will be living commentaries on the proverbs of Solomon.

Some of the most necessary parts of wisdom are explained and enforced from the 7th to the 17th verse. The first of these is, that—

Ver. 7. *The fear of the Lord is the beginning of knowledge.*

The fear of the Lord, so often recommended in this book, is not that fear which hath torment in it, and is excluded by love ; but that fear which is joined with faith, and keeps it from degenerating into presumption, whilst faith keeps fear from sinking into despondency. It is a lively impression of the excellency of God upon the soul, whereby a man is disposed to walk before him unto all pleasing, and to put far away every thing provoking and offensive to the eyes of his glory. It is therefore justly made to signify the whole of religion in the heart and life of man.

Great commendations are bestowed on this grace in Scripture. It makes a chief part in the noble characters of Abraham and Job, and here Solomon tells us that it is the *beginning*, the ground-work, and the comprehensive sum of all true knowledge.

He that wants the fear of the Lord does not know him ; and he that knows not God, knows nothing as he ought to know it. He knows neither his business in life, nor his happiness. A rational creature without the fear and knowledge of God, is like a soldier that never saw a sword, or a lawyer that never read an act of parliament. But he that knows the Lord so as to fear him, knows Christ, through whom we see those glorious perfections that are the object of our reverence. He knows his duty and happiness, and he is on the plain road to the knowledge of every thing necessary to make the man of God perfect.

Let no man say that this kind of knowledge deserves not our study, because it is generally despised ; it is indeed despised, but by whom ? The wise man tells us,

—*But fools despise wisdom and instruction.*

Who would despise a pearl because an idiot would not give his rattle for it ? It is no dishonour to the divine wisdom to be despised by any man ; but it is the utmost dishonour to any man to despise the wisdom of God. He is an unreasonable and foolish man that has not the faith of Christ and the fear of the Lord *.

The next part of doctrine taught by the wise man, respects the reverence due to the instructions of parents.

Ver. 8. *My son, hear the instruction of thy father, and forsake not the law of thy mother.*

This exhortation speaks to us as unto children ; Solomon is entitled to the authority, and addresses us with the tenderness of a father. If such, then, be the affection with which he addresses us, surely we owe him the reverence of children. God is our heavenly Father. All his precepts are the expressions of divine goodness, and we are unnatural to our Maker if we forget them.

It is here supposed that parents will instruct their children. They are monsters rather than parents, who do not love the fruit of their own bodies. Love will dispose persons to do all the good they can to the objects of it ; and the best thing that can be done for children, is to teach them the fear of the Lord. To be careful about providing the supports of life, or raising portions for children, without taking care of their souls, is like taking care of the clothes, and being indifferent about the body that wears them. " O ye people,"

*2 Thess. 3:2

cried an ancient philosopher, " why do ye toil in raising estates for your children, and neglect to prepare
them by needful instructions for enjoying them ?"

Mothers are to instruct their children, as well as
fathers. Solomon gratefully remembered the instructions he received in his younger years from Bathsheba ;
and the last chapter of this book contains the noble
instructions which a wise king had learned from his
mother.

Perhaps the reason why the names of the mothers of
the kings of Judah are recorded along with their characters is, because the lessons and example of their
mothers had a considerable influence in forming their
behaviour.

Children are required to hear, and reverence, and
obey the instructions of their fathers. Next to the
duties we owe immediately to God, the commandments
require us to obey our parents in the Lord *. He that
despiseth his earthly father, is no doubt a despiser of
the Father of spirits. A proper regard to the wise
and godly instructions of parents, gives a happy presage of good behaviour in after life. Vice and ruin, on
the other hand, are the ordinary consequences of irreverence to these natural guardians of our tender years.

The sages of heathen antiquity, though themselves
born of women, usually held them in such small respect, that they almost confined to the father precepts
that regarded filial duty. The more enlarged wisdom
of Solomon, however, pleads the cause of the mother
in forcible words. The instructions of a mother are to
be considered by us as a law that we are never to forsake. When old, she is still entitled to our respect ;
and we are never to leave those good paths into which
her affectionate care has directed our steps.

---

*Exod. 20

But what advantage is proposed to us by attending to the voice of parental admonition ?

Ver. 9. *For they shall be an ornament of grace unto thy head, and chains about thy neck.*

Young people are generally fond of fine clothes, and of ornaments to their bodies ; but with regard to this, Solomon here sets their notions right. Reverence to parents, a dutiful regard to their instructions, and the wisdom which is learnt from them, is by far the most beautiful ornament. It will make the face to shine ; it will be a chain to the neck ; it will be a graceful ornament, more beautiful than a crown of gold, to the head. With such ornaments was our Lord himself arrayed, while he dwelt among us. He was subject to his parents, though himself their Maker and Saviour *.

Young people are generally disposed to hearken to advice ; but because human nature is in a corrupt state, they are generally more prone to follow bad advice than good. Having therefore exhorted them to reverence and to obey God and their parents, he now proceeds to warn them against hearkening to the enticing words of seducers to sin, ver. 10.—19.

Ver. 10. *My son, if sinners entice thee, consent thou not.*

Sinners have generally so much of the venom of the old serpent in them, that they do not wish to go unattended to hell, but desire to make others as much the children of the devil as themselves. Sinners, after complying with the suggestions of their tempter, generally proceed from evil to worse, till they become devils themselves, and aid their master in ruining others.

The young ought to remember, that they will meet with ill advisers ; and if so, how firmly should they resolve, through the grace of God, to hold on in the

---

*Luke 2:51,52

way of virtue, and to refuse the least compliance with that advice which causeth to err from the words of knowledge!

Solomon arms us against these deceivers, by making us acquainted with their devices.

Ver. 11. *If they say, Come with us, let us lay wait for blood, let us lurk privily for the innocent without cause.*—

These are not the express words of seducers, but a translation of them into the language of truth. They will say, ' Come let us pick the pocket of some covetous miser, who has made himself rich by cunning, and scraped money together by such cowardly practices, as cannot expose him to the vengeance of the law.' Solomon tells us not the express words of the tempter, but puts into his mouth such language as expresses the real meaning and tendency of his solicitations. When transgressors varnish over their crimes, it is our part to pluck off the false covering, and to represent sin to ourselves in its true colours, and in its tendency to other iniquities of higher aggravation. When the drunkard invites us to go to the tavern, and drink a cheerful glass with him, let his words sound in our ears as if he had said, ' Let us go to the tavern, and there drown our reason, and make ourselves monsters.' When another desires us to take a hand at cards, let us take his meaning to be, ' Come, let us rob our friend of his money, without incurring the pains of law.'

Perhaps those men whom the tempters here spoken of wish to rob or kill, may be like themselves, strangers to every good way ; but they are innocent in comparison with those pests of society, who plot against their property or their lives. The treasons of Abner and Amasa, did not exempt Joab, their murderer, from the guilt of innocent blood.

These tempters to iniquity will try to persuade the inexperienced, that there is no danger of being detected.

Ver. 11. *Let us swallow them up alive as the grave, and whole as those that go down to the pit.*

We shall manage matters in such a manner, as that there cannot be even the possibility of detection. So well concerted shall our plans be, that the thing will be as effectually concealed from public view, as those bodies which are covered by the grave. Vain hopes! can men flatter themselves that they shall escape the righteous judgment of God? Even in this life, murderers seldom escape punishment. But what though men neither see nor suspect? conscience sees, angels see, the great Avenger of blood sees; the assembled world shall know their crimes, shall hear their sentence, and witness their punishment.

The devil told our Lord, that he would give him all the kingdoms and glories of the world, if he would comply with his persuasions. The ministers of Satan in like manner endeavour to persuade men that they will obtain much advantage by sin, that the gains of it shall fill all their treasures, and every corner of their houses.

Ver. 13. *We shall find all precious substance, we shall fill our houses with spoil.*

These promises are lies; or if such treasures be procured, they will last but for a moment. What profit had Judas the traitor in his thirty pieces of silver, though paid him to the last farthing? Though thirty thousand talents of gold had been his reward, they could not have soothed his racked conscience, they could not have retained his breath when his own hands had applied the halter, they could not have preserved his separated soul from going to its place. The profits of sin are the worst of losses *.

---

*Rev. 10:3, Matt. 16:26

These wretches, abandoned as they are, have yet the effrontery to pretend a regard to honesty, and a generous disinterestedness in their mutual dealings—

Ver. 14. *Cast in thy lot among us, let us all have one purse.*

Let the security and profit of our way of living induce thee to join our society; we shall lead a merry life, we shall faithfully share our gains, and none shall want while another has.

In what manner ought a young man to act when offers so tempting are made to him?

Ver. 15. *My son, walk not thou in the way with them, refrain thy foot from their path.*

Let us attend with filial regard to the kind advice of a venerable father, who tells us, that we must not only shut our ears against these ensnaring words, and resolve to keep the path of innocence, but shun their company, and avoid those places which they haunt. If we knew a place that was said to be a haunt of ghosts and infernal spirits, we need not shun it, for these terrors are but creatures of fancy; but places frequented by men who have the devil in their hearts, and who hire him their tongues for the purpose of deceiving their fellow-men,—such places are dangerous indeed. All of us have corrupted natures ready to be inflamed; how infatuated the man who, carrying gunpowder, enters a smith's shop, where the sparks fly from the anvil in every direction!

But may we not take a single turn with them? No.

Ver. 16. *For their feet run to evil, and make haste to shed blood.*

Let us never forget the evil that is in sin. However men may dress it out in beautiful colours, it is the very quintessence of naughtiness. All men see a great deal of evil in some infernal crimes, but the God whose judgment is always true, sees more evil in the least sin, than we are able to do in the greatest. It is a dangerous and detestable thing for a man wilfully to transgress the smallest commandment of the law of God. But the men of whom we now speak, are desperately bent upon sin. Their feet run to evil, and that of the most damnable sort, for they make haste to shed blood.

Perhaps it will be said, that they have no design to load their souls with such bloody crimes, but only to cheat or rob somebody that well deserves to be plundered. But let us remember, that no man becomes desperate in wickedness all at once. Hazael had no intention to murder the king of Syria, or rip up women with child; he would have abhorred the thoughts of such wickedness, till interest and ambition uniting, gradually hardened his heart, and prepared him for perpetrating without remorse deeds of darkness and of horror. Young sinners are like travellers, who at first setting out cannot bear a speck of mud to alight upon their clothes, but who in the course of their journey become inured to bad roads, and can suffer themselves, without feeling uneasiness, to be all bespattered with mire.

They are like silly birds, who suffer themselves to be ensnared by the arts of the cunning fowler.

Ver. 17. *Surely in vain is the net spread in the sight of any bird.*

Birds have not the gift of reason, to warn them against the snares of the fowler. But how lamentable is it, that men, whom God hath made wiser than the fowls of heaven, should be as easily deceived as the silliest of these animals, and that in matters of greater importance! Do not reply, that the snares are set, not for the sinner himself, but for those whom he intends to destroy. It is for his *own* life that a sinner spreads his nets.

Ver. 18. *And they lay wait for their own blood, they lurk privily for their own lives.*

It is not the sufferer, so much as the doer of evil, that is hurt. Whom did Judas destroy by his treachery? The death to which Jesus was sold was glorious to himself; the treason which Judas wrought was his own destruction. Abel lives and speaks, and his name is embalmed in the memories of the good; the life which his murderer led was more miserable than death, and his name is remembered only to be execrated. The sinner designs mischief to his neighbour; but all things are under the direction of the just Lord, under whose administration mischief recoils upon its author, bringing him to the scaffold here, or to hell hereafter *.

But is such the natural tendency of covetousness ?— Yes.

Ver. 19. *So are the ways of every one that is greedy of gain, which taketh away the life of the owners thereof*

" Take heed and beware of covetousness," said he who knew the heart of man, and the native tendency of every vice. It is a mother of abominations and miseries. They that are determined to be rich, would have money by honest means if it could be got, but at any rate they must have it. If it cannot be had to fill their desires (which indeed are insatiable) by fair means, it must by chicanery and cunning. When the conscience has been brought to this, it is prepared for advancing in wickedness, till at last it offers but small resistance, even at the commission of crimes, from the very thought of which their author would once have shrunk. The last step in vice, is less painful to a man than the first departure from honesty †.

---

*Matt. 7:2, Ps. 7:11-17, 9:15,16   †1 Tim. 6:10

If the eyes of these pests of society were not altogether shut, they would see that a man's life depends not on the abundance of his wealth. In their own hands it becomes a sword to slay its owner ; and can they anticipate comfort in that ill-gotten wealth which has proved fatal to its honest possessor ?

We must therefore flee from unrighteousness, and stand at a distance from the way of sin. Every one that would tempt us to evil, is to be looked upon as a factor for Satan.

Sinners are addressed, through the remaining part of this chapter, by Wisdom herself, who speaks to men in solemn and awful language.

Ver. 20, 21. *Wisdom crieth without, she uttereth her voice in the streets. She crieth in the chief places of concourse, in the opening of the gates ; in the city she uttereth her words, saying,*

How can wisdom cry ? Is not wisdom a quality, and not a person ? Wisdom cries to men when God speaks to them for he is the fountain of wisdom. The words of men may be wise, but when God speaks, Wisdom itself addresses us. He opens his mouth in infinite wisdom, and speaks to us by him who is the Word and Wisdom of God. He who despiseth that wisdom which is from above, despiseth the Father and the Son, and brands with the imputation of folly the emanations of unsearchable wisdom.

Wisdom desires to be heard, and therefore speaks not in secret ; she whispers not in the ears of a few favourites, but in the public places of resort, she proclaims to every one that will listen her interesting truths. She crieth without, in every place where a crowd is likely to be collected, in the streets, in the chief place of concourse, in the gates, the place of judgment, and in every part of the city.

No disobedient sinner can make a valid excuse for

his conduct. The voice of wisdom is heard every where. It sounds from the pulpit. From every creature it is heard *. The word is in our very hearts, and conscience echoes the voice to our souls. Let us go where we will, we must hear it, unless we wilfully shut our ears. And what does she say?

Ver. 22. *How long, ye simple ones, will ye love simplicity, and the scorners delight in their scorning, and fools hate knowledge!*

'Had I a mountain for a pulpit, and a voice capable of reaching to the ends of the world, (said a venerable father), I would preach on that text, " O ye sons of men, how long will ye love vanity?" ' Wisdom proclaims the like words to all the world as far as her voice is heard.

If persons ruin themselves by their folly, it will be no excuse to them that they were cheated by the great deceiver. Who will excuse Eve for hearkening to the voice of the serpent, or Adam for hearkening to the voice of his wife, in opposition to the voice of God? The simpleton and the fool are justly condemned, because they love simplicity and hate knowledge. So strongly are they bent upon their foolish courses, that every suggestion of the devil meets with a cheerful compliance. Sin is loved with the whole heart, and those truths which might be the means of salvation, are the objects of extreme aversion.

Many are so mad upon their idols, that they take pleasure in scoffing at holiness, and at the preachers and professors of it ; some run to such a pitch in wickedness as to jest with the word of the Most High, though safer far it were to sport with fire and death.

Were the Physician of souls like earthly physicians, he would leave such creatures to pine away in their sins till their obstinacy terminate in eternal death. But

---

*Job 12:7,8

O how merciful is he! He is in earnest with them when he urges them to admit of his salutary medicines. It is a grief to him that they will not come to him for health. He cries to them,

Ver. 23. *Turn ye at my reproof; behold, I will pour out my Spirit unto you, I will make known my words unto you.*

The lovers of folly must turn or perish ; for Christ is an all-sufficient Saviour from sin and wrath, but he will deliver none to continue in abominations : " Except ye repent, ye shall all perish."

The lovers of sin, and those that delight in scorning, are graciously called by him to turn,—a plain evidence that there is pardoning and saving mercy for these worst of sinners *. Even scoffers at religion are among the number of those sinners whom the Son of Man called to repentance, when he came to seek and to save the lost.

Such profligates have for the most part an intention to turn from their evil ways at some future but indefinite period ; but if they turn not at present, they refuse to hear the voice of wisdom. " Turn ye," says the Wisdom of God, " at my reproof." " To day," says the Spirit, " if ye will hear my voice, harden not your hearts." We harden our hearts when we intend to take our pleasure in sin to-day, though we resolve to hear the voice of God to-morrow.

The reproof of wisdom is a means of alarming us, and of impressing our souls with a sense of the necessity of turning. If we harden our hearts against these reproofs while they are sounding in our ears, the impression is not likely to be deeper or stronger when the bustle and noise of the world have helped us to forget the awful admonition.

---

*Isa. 55:7

It is at the reproof of the word of God that we are called to turn. It is brutish for a son to despise the reproof of a parent. It is devilish for a creature to despise the reproof of its Creator. It is a sin which devils could never commit, for a guilty creature to shut his ears against the reproof of a Saviour, who addresses us in earnest and affectionate language, and calls us to turn our feet from the paths of death.

But how can fools turn ?—Are they not infatuated by sin ?—are not their affections possessed with the love of it ?—" Behold, I will pour out my Spirit unto you," says the Saviour. By his influences you shall be enabled to understand my words, and to comply with them.—Let not sinners imagine that it will excuse them to say, they had no ability to repent. They were not called to turn by any power of their own, but in the strength of divine grace. They were unwilling, and therefore unable. Their sins were so dear to them, that they disliked the reproofs of Christ, and resisted his Spirit. Our Lord does not make a jest of the lovers of sin, when he calls them to turn. His words do good even to sinners, or the fault is their own *.

Do we then feel the necessity of turning, and yet an unconquerable aversion to it in our hearts? Let us plead for the abundant communications of the enlightening and renewing Spirit. If persons are made heartily willing to submit to his influence, it is a happy presage that he will be granted, or rather a sign that he has already begun to work †.

But there are many so foolishly devoted to sin, that they reject the counsel of God, and instead of welcoming the good Spirit, resist his motions till they provoke him to depart. The doom of such persons will be very terrible, but very just.

---

*John 5:40, Matt. 23:37   †Jer. 31:18-20

Ver. 24—27. *Because I have called, and ye refused;
I have stretched out my hand, and no man regarded; but
ye have set at nought all my counsel, and would none of
my reproof: I also will laugh at your calamity; I will
mock when your fear cometh; when your fear cometh as
desolation, and your destruction cometh as a whirlwind;
when distress and anguish cometh upon you.*

Do none then, or next to none, regard the admonitions of wisdom? Strange. Are men enemies to
themselves? are they in love with destruction? Is it
their joy to please the devil, and to cross the benevo-
lent intentions of a Saviour? Was the devil crucified
for them? or do they think the burnings of eternity,
and the pain of condemnation, more tolerable than the
tears of repentance or the self-denial which Jesus prescribes?

John's disciples complained to him, that all men
went after Jesus, but John complained that so few
believed his report: " No man receiveth his testimony."
How wonderful is that grace, which continues to deal
with men when it is so ungratefully despised!

The sin of unbelief and impenitence is exceeding
great. Various are the forms of expression by which in
the passage before us the wickedness of it is inti-
mated, and the offence which it gives to him who
comes in the name of the Lord to save us, pointed out.
It is a refusal of divinely gracious offers and advices;
a disregard of the most earnest importunities of the
wisdom of God; a sovereign contempt of all the counsel
of that wonderful Counsellor who is given to be the
leader and commander of the people; a stubborn opposition of the will to the most needful and salutary
reproof. Hear, O ye heavens, and be horribly afraid!
Rational creatures rebel against the Father of spirits.
Diseased sinners scorn the great Physician, and refuse
to accept of that sovereign cure for all their maladies,

which he so graciously offers. Abhorring, as they do, the name of devils, they yet spurn at those compassions which devils can never experience.

But let sinners remember, that there is justice as well as grace in the Most High. Justice shall avenge the contempt of mercy. Sinners feel some presage of that vengeance in their own guilty conscience. Fears of punishment often make them uneasy. They would gladly persuade themselves that these are but the terrors of a distempered fancy; but the day is coming when they will find them to be terrible realities ; or if they want truth, it is because they are nothing to that vengeance which is their object. No passion is so tormenting as fear, but no fear can equal the power of God's anger.

The fear of sinners shall come upon them, and their feet shall slide in due time. It shall come like a desolating judgment, which with resistless violence lays waste a country. It shall come like a raging tempest, and a furious whirlwind, at once sweeping away every comfort and every hope. Then shall distress and anguish seize upon the mind of the stubborn transgressor, when he feels himself involved in remediless sorrow. This threatening will have its great accomplishment in the everlasting world, when the torrents of wrath shall swallow up the impenitent sinner, and the whirlwind of fury shall beat upon him with ceaseless violence. Wrath and indignation shall press him down in the lake of fire. Anguish and despair shall prey upon his soul, without the intermission of a moment; no ray of hope shall ever enter the abodes of darkness and of horror.

But will the poor victim of suffering find no pity from the Saviour of men ? No ! says the Spirit of God, " I will laugh at your calamity, and mock when your fear comes." With relentless eye shall he behold that

terrible vengeance which now overtakes the wicked.
God has no pleasure in the death of the wicked, but
rather that they should turn and live ; yet he will take
pleasure in the death of them that turn not, for in this
manner is his justice glorified, and the dishonours done
to his love repaired.   God sometimes laughs at the
trial of the innocent.   He took pleasure in bruising his
ownSon.   He is comforted in the ruin of the wicked *.

But may not prayer avail in this deplorable condition ? By no means.

Ver. 28. *Then shall they call upon me, but I will not
answer ; they shall seek me early, (i. e. earnestly,) but they
shall not find me.*

The prayer of faith is ever heard, and they that seek
God shall find him, when they seek him with all their
heart.   But the prayers of these desperate rebels,
are like the howlings of a dog.   They are cries
extorted by strong necessity, and intolerable anguish.
They are the cries of such as sought not the Lord
whilst he was to be found, nor called on him whilst
he was near.

Sinners miserably delude their own souls by proposing to live in the indulgence of their sins, and die in
the exercise of repentance.   True repentance is never
too late, but late repentance is seldom true.   Christ is
not every day hanging on the cross, nor are thieves
every day converted, and sent from the place of punishment to the paradise above.

Prayers are of no use in the eternal world.   The
day of grace is at an end, and the wretched shall cry
in vain to the rocks and mountains to fall upon them,
and hide them from the wrath of the Lord God and
of the Lamb.   Behold, now is the accepted time,

---

*Job 9:23, Isa. 53:10 and 1:24, Ezek. 5:13

now the Lord waits to be gracious; but the day is coming that is cruel with wrath and fierce anguish; no place shall then be found for mercy, though sought with an ocean of tears. But why does he who takes pleasure in the voice of prayer, and listen so graciously to the cry of the supplicant,—why does he refuse to accept the petitions of those who are reduced to such an extremity of distress? The reason is,

Ver. 29, 30. *For that they hated knowledge, and did not chuse the fear of the Lord. They would none of my counsel; they despised all my reproof.*

The punishment is indeed tremendous, but the sin that causes it is atrocious. It is no less than a contempt and hatred of the counsels of the Lord. What is this but an undeniable proof of enmity against God himself? and will not God ease himself of his adversaries, and avenge himself of his enemies?

When men do not chuse the fear of the Lord, but prefer to it the base pleasures of sin, they give plain proof of their hatred to every thing that is good, and how can they escape the damnation of hell? If we think that the punishment is greater than the sin, the reason is, that we are under the power of iniquity. Self-love disposes the malefactor to prescribe to his judge. Let us impartially consider what malignity lies in impenitence, and what a complication of wickednesses is contained in the rejection of the great salvation, and we must acknowledge that the ruin of sinners is entirely owing to themselves. God is not to be blamed, but on the contrary, he will be eternally glorious as their avenger. His insulted mercy will be glorious in the punishment of its despisers. His justice shall shine in dispensing to the workers of iniquity the reward of their works: " They despised all my reproof —

Ver. 31. *Therefore shall they eat of the fruit of their own way, and be filled with their own devices.*

They laughed at God's threatenings, as if they had been idle tales; and God shall laugh at them. They despised his counsels, and he shall despise their prayers. They were always the same, and continued unchanged after all admonition; and God will prove an immutable avenger, and will pay no regard to their cries for help. They took pleasure in sin, and God will take pleasure in punishing on account of it.

If a man plants and dresses a poisonous tree in his garden, it is just that he should be obliged to eat of its fruit. If our vine is the vine of Sodom, and our clusters the clusters of bitterness, we must leave our complaint on ourselves, if we must drink till we are drunken, and fall, and rise no more.

Sinners never think they have drunk deep enough of the poisoned cup of sin; but they shall at length be filled with it. Then shall it satiate them, when they find that intolerable misery is its native consequence. That cup which now delights the lover of evil, will then be found a cup of fury, and the wicked of the earth must drink it out to its bitterest dregs.

Ver. 32. *For the turning away of the simple shall slay them, and the prosperity of fools shall destroy them.*

The sins of men, unless pardoned through the blood of Christ, shall be their destruction; for he that turns away from God and his law, turns his back upon happiness; and he that cherishes iniquity, warms in his bosom the most venomous of serpents *. Sinners owe their ruin to their wilful hardness of heart, their abuse of mercy, and their indifference about salvation.

It may be alleged, that sinners often prosper; but their prosperity is a part of their misery, for it will in-

---

*Job 20:11 etc.

crease their guilt, and render their damnation terrible. It nourishes their vicious affections, and tends to inspire them with pride and insolence, with sensuality and earthliness of mind. It is so strong a temptation, that our Lord has declared it almost impossible for a rich man to enter into the kingdom of God. This saying has been justified by fact. In times of persecution, the prosperous have been ordinarily the apostates who made shipwreck of faith, while the poor loved the world less, and stood out more firmly against temptation

If the prosperity of fools leads them to the indulgence of sin, and the neglect of holiness, it renders their damnation more certain and more dreadful. Their provocations are like those of the Israelites, who provoked God, by turning the Egyptian gold and silver, which he had given them, into an idol of jealousy. They are like the impious ingratitude of Jeroboam the son of Nebat, whom God raised to a throne, but who degraded God into the image of a four-footed beast. When the favours of God are turned into means and instruments of unrighteousness, Oh! what wrath is then treasured up against the day of wrath, and revelation of the righteous judgment of God!

But the prosperity of the wise has a very opposite tendency. When they act like themselves, it excites their gratitude; it stimulates them to serve God more effectually, and to do good to men more diligently. Wisdom teaches those who hearken to her voice, to make to themselves friends of the mammon of unrighteousness; so that while riches serve to expose the folly of the foolish, they prove a crown to the wise. But though the disciples of Wisdom should never attain prosperity, they are happy; for says Wisdom,

Ver. 33. *But whoso hearkeneth unto me shall dwell safely, and be quiet from the fear of evil.*

They that love knowledge, and chuse the fear of the Lord, and value the instructions of wisdom more than thousands of gold and silver, are the men that hearken to Wisdom, ver. 29, 30. Many of these once loved folly, and took pleasure in scorning ; but they have received the atonement, and all their unrighteousnesses are blotted out. They now share in the privileges of the children of wisdom, and while prosperous sinners are set in slippery places, they dwell safely, for they dwell in God, and God dwelleth in them. They are safe from the devil, and from the power of sin, from death and from hell. They may endure tribulation in the world, but in Christ they shall have peace. They enjoy quiet consciences, and pleasant hopes. They are quiet, not only from evil, but from the fear of evil. They may indeed have fears, but they are clouds that shall soon be blown away, and succeeded by everlasting serenity. Even while these fears continue, they have a refuge where they can find safety, and hopes sufficient to give them such happiness as worldly men cannot enjoy amid their ill-grounded confidence. Paul had often fightings without, and fears within ; but this was his comfort, that nothing could separate him from the love of God, which is in Christ Jesus.

Let us examine ourselves impartially, whether we are the despisers or the lovers of wisdom. The question is not, whether we attend the means of grace, and make a profession of religion. Herod heard John gladly, and did many things. Ananias and Sapphira parted with a considerable share of their substance. But do we chuse the fear of the Lord? Do we value Christ above the whole world ? Do we prefer holiness, in its most painful exercises, to the most pleasant sins ?

Are we yet despisers of wisdom ? Let us tremble at the vengeance threatened. Let our prayers ascend up on high, that the Lord by his Spirit would open our hearts, that we may attend to the dictates of heavenly wisdom.

Are we lovers of wisdom? Let us bless God who hath opened our ears to discipline, and sealed our instruction. Let us thankfully rejoice in the blessings that Wisdom bestows. Let us testify our regard to Wisdom, in the manner directed in the succeeding chapter. In vain do we pretend to religion, unless that which we call by this honourable name, be approved by that word whereby we must be judged.

Proverbs 2

WISDOM is an excellent thing, therefore get wisdom. But how shall we get wisdom? or in what shall the attainment of it profit us? You have an answer to both these questions in this chapter.

How shall we get wisdom? The wise man answers,

Ver. 1.—7. *My son, if thou wilt receive my words, and hide my commandments with thee, so that thou incline thine ear unto wisdom, and apply thine heart to understanding; yea, if thou criest after knowledge, and liftest up thy voice for understanding; if thou seekest her as silver, and searchest for her as for hid treasure; then shalt thou understand the fear of the Lord, and find the knowledge of God; for the Lord giveth wisdom: out of his mouth cometh knowledge and understanding. He layeth up sound wisdom for the righteous.—*

It is not enough for us to attend the public ordinances of God, and to read a chapter or two of the Bible at home every day, but we are required to receive the words of wisdom, to keep them in our hearts, and to apply our souls to them.

We are to receive the words of our heavenly Father, with reverence and love, with faith and diligent attention. No gift is so precious as that knowledge which God imparts to us in the scriptures, and we ought to receive it with eagerness, like that which the covetous man shews for gold and silver ; and as he who receives money is careful to lay it up where he may find it when he has occasion to use it, so in like manner it becomes us to lay up in the midst of our heart the instructions of wisdom, collecting and hiding the precious treasure, till the word of Christ dwell in us richly in all wisdom. When we give due attention to the word of truth, it will dwell in our minds, dispelling ignorance and error, and communicating that light which is necessary to direct the whole of our conduct ; in our memories, affording a constant supply for spiritual meditation, ready for use on every emergency ; in our wills, to guide their choice and inclination ; in our affections, to direct their motions, to curb their extravagance, and to inflame their ardour towards spiritual objects ; and in our consciences, to preserve alive the impressions of the divine law, and to direct them in judging of the spiritual state of the soul.

The ear must be inclined to wisdom, that we may learn it. The senses of the body minister to the soul. The eye, surveying the wonders of God's hand, furnishes the soul with apprehensions of his power and wisdom ; but the ear is that learning sense by which the richest treasures of spiritual knowledge are admitted into the soul. As the mouth tastes the food of the body, so the ear receives and tries those words that nourish the soul. We attend to our friends or neighbours when they are informing us of some new thing ; we count it a piece of good manners to listen, when nothing is to be heard but dulness and insipidity : shall we not, then, attend to Him that made the ear, when he condescends to speak to us, and to disclose truths of eternal moment ?

Whilst our ears are attentive, our hearts must be applied to wisdom. Angels, who are so much our superiors, apply themselves to the learning of it. They are already replenished with the stores of truth, and yet they desire to pry deeper into the mystery of wisdom. Great as was the measure which Solomon had received, he still continued to apply his heart to it ; surely, then, the wisest of us ought to apply our whole hearts; for what is so needful to us, and so valuable in itself?

But after all our application, we have understandings so dark, that the Bible must remain a sealed book unto us, unless our eyes are enlightened to discern the wonders of God's law. With our instructions, therefore, earnest prayer must be mingled, that the Spirit of wisdom and revelation may illuminate our understandings, and fit our souls for receiving and retaining the truths of God. David was wiser than his teachers, and yet he still lifts up his voice for wisdom to the Father of lights, and pleads, with fervent importunity, that God would open his eyes, and not conceal his laws from him, nor take the word of truth out of his mouth. Let us, in imitation of such a holy example, earnestly pray that we may stand perfect and complete in all the will of God ; and particularly, that we may be furnished with all that wisdom and knowledge that is requisite for directing us in our respective stations and circumstances. Solomon was already a wise man, yet when commanded to chuse what he would have, he chose a greater measure of wisdom, of that wisdom especially which would be most useful for him in governing the kingdom of Israel. With this petition God was well pleased. He gave him not only what he requested, but everything most highly valued by men.

But while we cry after wisdom, and depend on God to bestow it on us, it would be presumptuous to neglect the means of obtaining it. We must seek it as silver, and search for it as for hid treasure. We every day see with what anxious diligence men seek for silver. They fatigue their bodies, and waste their spirits; they destroy their health, and expose their lives; they even wound their consciences, and expose themselves to shameful deaths and everlasting misery, that they may load themselves with shining clay. Shall the professed disciples of the great Teacher set less value upon knowledge, than other men set upon silver? David well knew the value of this knowledge, and esteemed it above thousands of gold and silver. Job prefers it to every thing that dazzles with its lustre the eyes of mortals *.

It is therefore highly reasonable, that we diligently and carefully use all those means which God hath appointed for this end; that we hear sermons with earnest attention; that we read and search the word of God, and make it the subject of our frequent meditation; that we make use of edifying conversation; that we go to the wise, who have the law of God in their hearts, so that their mouth speaks wisdom, and their tongue talks of judgment. To the use of such means of improvement as these, we must add prayer for the divine blessing, to render them effectual to our instruction and salvation. Truth is like a mine, more pre-

---

*Job 28

cious than that which is the depository of gold and of diamonds. Had any of us such a precious treasure as this in our garden, we would not travel over the ground for pleasure, but employ ourselves day and night in digging, till our houses should be enriched with the precious store. Why, then, are we careless about that which will enrich us to eternity, and fill all our treasures ?

You see the means to be used by us for attaining wisdom. Our ears and hearts must be employed in the search. We must lift up our voices to the Author of wisdom, and seek for it with all the desire of our souls, and with such earnest endeavours as men use in digging for hid treasures. Through the blessing of God the search shall not be unsuccessful ; for " then shalt thou understand the fear of the Lord, and find the knowledge of God." It is plain that those who employ themselves in the diligent pursuit of wisdom, have been already blessed with some degree of true knowledge ; for how could they value so highly that with which they were altogether unacquainted ? He is already wise, who prefers wisdom to every earthly object ; and he shall be wiser still, for to him that hath shall be given, and he shall have more abundantly.

The fear of the Lord, and the sound knowledge of God, are inseparably connected. Religious fear is not a blind and tormenting passion of the soul, but a holy and delightful grace, founded in true apprehensions of the awful and lovely glories of the divine nature, and disposing him who possesses it, to walk with God. The knowledge of God regulates this fear, and preserves it from sinking into terror, or degenerating into superstition, but guides it to express its power in checking and subduing every corrupt affection, and animating the soul to every instance of obedience.

If men are careless about wisdom, and use no diligence in seeking it, they make it evident that they are destitute of the knowledge and fear of the Lord. They have not, and from them shall be taken even that which they seem to have.

The efficacy of every means of knowledge is from God, for " the Lord giveth wisdom ; out of his mouth cometh knowledge and understanding." Every beam of reason in men, is communicated from the wisdom of God *. The simplest of the mechanical arts cannot be acquired unless men are taught of God †. How, then, can we expect to understand the mystery of the divine will, without spiritual light communicated from that God who is the Father of lights, and the author of every good and perfect gift !

Knowledge and understanding cometh out of the mouth of God. By his Spirit he bestows upon us this blessing through his word, for it is the inspiration of the Almighty that giveth understanding to men. Experience, however long, observation, however close, human teaching, however skilful, can do nothing to supply us with true knowledge, without the influence of that Spirit which rested upon Christ as a Spirit of wisdom and understanding, and which is given by him to all his followers in their measure ‡.

The wisdom that God in his kindness bestows upon men, is sound and substantial. There are many kinds of knowledge of little importance. The knowledge which some possess tends only to vex and disquiet them, or to inspire them with vanity and self-conceit. How different the knowledge that God imparts to the diligent students of wisdom ! Far from perplexing or elating, it fills their understanding with the most pleasant truths, and directs them in the way ever-lasting.

---

*1 John 1:9   †Isa. 28:26   ‡Job 32:7,8, Matt. 16:17

But who are the blessed persons that are favoured with this divinely excellent wisdom ? " The Lord lays it up for the righteous."   God is said to teach sinners in the way * ; for man's unworthiness does not exclude him from divine mercy.   Saul the persecutor had the Son of God revealed in him by divine grace, and neither his stubborn prejudices, nor his cruelty to the church of Christ, could shut out the beams of heavenly light.   Sinners are invited to Christ as the light of the Gentiles, and the salvation of the lost † ; but here it is said, he lays it up for the righteous.   Sinners and fools *may* have it, but the righteous *shall* have it. They are already made sensible of their need of it, and desire it more than silver and gold.   They ask it from God, who giveth liberally to all men, and upbraideth not, and it shall be given them.   The Lord layeth up this wisdom for them.   There are infinite stores of it in his possession, and they are all treasured up in Christ, and out of his fulness shall the righteous receive supplies suited to their exigencies.

To encourage God's people to expect all needful supplies of wisdom from him, let them consider his peculiar regard to them, and the constant protection he has engaged to afford them.

Ver. 7, 8. *He is a buckler to them that walk uprightly. He keepeth the paths of judgment, and preserveth the way of his saints.*

Whoso hearkeneth unto wisdom shall dwell safely, for God is a sure defence to those that walk in wisdom's ways.   There are many adversaries that would destroy them if they could, and these are too strong for them ; but there is none like unto the God of Jeshurun, that rideth on the heavens in their help, and in his excel-

---

*Ps. 25:8   †Eph. 5:14

lency in the skies. While therefore they are walking to their eternal home, they may sing in the ways of the Lord. Mighty is their protector; in the shadow of his wings they may trust, and to his faithfulness they may look as their shield and buckler.

The most dreadful enemies of them that walk uprightly, are those that endeavour to turn aside the way of their paths; but against these enemies God is a mighty defence, for he keepeth the paths of wisdom and righteousness. He is a fence about their ways, and a wall of fire around those that walk in them. The devil casteth his fiery darts, but they are safe from the arrow that flieth by day, and from the noisome pestilence. No weapon formed against them shall prosper. They are commanded still to trust in the name of the Lord, and their faith is like a shield that will quench every fiery dart. The world displays its terrors and its charms to terrify or allure them into the paths of sin. Against this, as well as the adversary formerly mentioned, they must exercise vigilance. Still, however, in the hottest part of the combat they may be of good cheer, for the Captain of their salvation hath overcome the world, and shall make them through their faith to share in his victory *.

Their own remaining corruptions give them many alarms. Nor is it wonderful that they feel alarmed when ready to halt by its influence, or powerfully solicited to turn aside unto the flowery but destructive paths where poisons grow and serpents haunt. But their fears shall not overpower them, for the spirit lusts against the flesh, and shall prevail. What says their Almighty guide? " Sin shall not have dominion over you."

Those that walk in the paths of judgment are God's

---

*I John 5

saints. He has beautified them with holiness, and he acknowledges them as his own property. They are his portion and the lot of his inheritance, his treasure and his glory, and he will suffer none of them to be lost. Every one of them shall be hid in the day when he maketh up his jewels.

Let us ask for these good old ways, and walk in them, and we shall find rest and safety for our souls. They are safe paths when God guards them, and preserves the way of those that walk in them. No lion, no ravenous beast is found there ; and the wayfaring man, though a fool, shall not err therein. But it is our duty, while we trust in God to guide and preserve us, to make use of our eyes. None of Zion's travellers shall be found wanting in the end, but many too that thought themselves in the good way shall fail of the end of their hopes, because they entered not in at the gate, neither trod the narrow path. He that is born of God keepeth himself, that the wicked one toucheth him not. We cannot. by our utmost care keep ourselves in safety ; but a true dependance upon God will dispose us to be as sober and vigilant as if we had none else to keep us, while we yet trust entirely in God, and not in ourselves, knowing that if left to ourselves one hour, we must perish.

You see that the lovers of wisdom are furnished with the best wisdom, and led into those paths of holiness where safety is to be found. In order to persuade us to hearken to the instructions of wisdom, the wise man adds—

Ver. 9. *Then shalt thou understand righteousness, and judgment, and equity, yea, every good path.*

There is no end of the commendation of the ways of wisdom. The fear and knowledge of God is not only the beginning, but the perfection of wisdom. But the lovers of wisdom have those instructions also which

are necessary for guiding them in their behaviour toward men. They are taught how to walk justly and
wisely, and in what manner to behave in every affair.

When a traveller is going to a distant place, it is
pleasant to him to be informed that his way is safe,
and that it may be found without difficulty. Now, as
the way of holiness is the way of peace, so the scriptures
give us sufficient directions for every step of it. Are
we at a loss about our duty in any case? We may then
safely infer, either that we have forgotten what our
directory says, or that we are not skilful in applying it.
Our carelessness in the study of this rule of life may
often put us to a stand, therefore we ought to have
it daily in our hands, and to meditate on it day and
night, so shall we find it a counsellor in all our straits.

The Spirit is promised as our guide through this
world, and he directs us by his word, opening our
minds to understand it, and directing our conduct in
the way that it prescribes. Is the saint at a loss with
regard to the way of duty in any particular instance?
Let him pray, as David did in such cases, and like this
holy man, he shall be led in the way of truth *.

Solomon has instructed us how to obtain wisdom,
and in part shewn the advantages of it. He insists on
this last point through the remaining part of this chapter, telling us that it will preserve us from the snares
of wicked men and women, ver. 10—19. and lead us
in the way that has been traced by the saints in every
age, who have found it to be the way of happiness and
joy, ver. 20, 21, 22.

Wisdom will be a preservative from the worst dangers.

Ver. 10, 11. *When wisdom entereth into thine heart,
and knowledge is pleasant unto thy soul, discretion shall
preserve thee, understanding shall keep thee.*

---

*Ps. 25:4,5

That we may enjoy the advantages of wisdom, it must enter into our heart, which is naturally disposed to entertain sin and folly; for man, however fond he may be of the reputation of wisdom, is born like the wild ass's colt. Some receive the words of wisdom into their ears, but understand not what they hear; others hear, and form clear apprehensions of what they hear, so as to be able to talk of them, like Balaam or Judas, and instruct others. But the children of wisdom not only hear and understand, but love the truth. The Spirit of God writes it in the inward part; then it comes to them in power and in the Holy Ghost, and the testimonies of God are received by their spirits with pleasure and joy. Knowledge becomes sweeter than honey dropping from the comb, and is esteemed more than necessary food. Paul counted every thing but loss for the excellency of the knowledge of Christ Jesus. When Jeremiah found the word of God, he did eat it, and it was to him the joy and rejoicing of his heart.

The pleasure that saints take in knowledge, is very different from the transient affection experienced in the word by those hearers whom our Lord compares to stony ground. These false believers were moved and transported by the novelty of the truth, by the prospect of deliverance from hell and possession of heaven which it presented to them, but they had no spiritual apprehensions of its divine glory, nor any deep-rooted affection to it. They still loved the world more than the testimonies of God, and this reigning earthliness of spirit in time choked the beautiful springing of this seed in their souls. But those into whose hearts wisdom enters, have their eyes opened to see its glory, and their affections sanctified to relish its genuine sweetness. They rejoice in the truths that oppose their most darling corruptions. They take pleasure in the way of God's testimonies, as well as in the glorious prospects which they present. They heartily esteem all God's precepts concerning all things to be right, and delight in the law of God after the inward man, because it is pure and spiritual. They delight in it, though it forces them to confess that they are carnal, sold under sin.

This wisdom entering into their souls, furnishes them with understanding to see their way, and discretion to manage their affairs with prudence and judgment to the end *.

This understanding and prudence is an antidote aganst the poisonous infection of evil men and strange women.—It is, *first*, a means of preserving us from the snares of bad men.

Ver. 12—15. *To deliver thee from the way of the evil man, from the man that speaketh froward things ; who leave the paths of uprightness, to walk in the ways of darkness ; who rejoice to do evil, and delight in the frowardness of the wicked ; whose ways are crooked, and they froward in their paths.*

Such is the portrait drawn by Solomon of those bad men by whom his pupils are in danger of being seduced, unless furnished with wisdom to avoid the snare. They speak froward things; they pay no regard to truth, but bend their tongue like their bow for lies. Among these pests of men, none are such virulent pests of every thing that is good, as those that once made a profession of religion, but have left the way of uprightness to walk in those miserable and gloomy paths, which begin in the darkness of the mind, and end in the darkness of hell. The stings of conscience which such persons experience, instead of reclaiming them, tend only to irritate their spirits, and inflame them into fierce enmity against religion. If, instead of being

---

*Ps. 112:5

pierced with such stings, they are cursed with the conquest of their own consciences, they are hardened enough for the blackest sin, and prepared not only to do evil, but to work it with both hands greedily. They rejoice in the service of Satan,' and no greater pleasure do they know than that which arises from seeing that his interests flourish, that his kingdom prospers. Such persons are crooked in their ways. The only straight way is the way of uprightness, but that sinners leave, and wander into paths where they are bewildered and lost. They know not whither they go, because darkness hath blinded their eyes. One sin leads them on to another, and that to a third, till at length they run into wickednesses, of which they could not have thought without horror when first they set foot in these deceitful paths.

These miscreants are froward and stubborn in their ways; and why? Custom has become a second nature to them, their hearts are become impenetrably hard, and proof against admonition. Yet look back to their early days, and you shall find them to have evinced tempers and dispositions very different. They would then have abhorred gross impieties, and were not without impressions of the necessity of virtue and holiness. But the unwearied adversary of mankind spread his toils around them, and employed such men as they are now become, to efface every good impression, and to lead them on, by slow and imperceptible degrees, to those lengths in wickedness at which they have now arrived. Had they been armed with the instructions of wisdom, and employed these in their own defence, what different persons might they now have been! Whilst they would mislead us by their persuasions, let us learn instruction from their miserable situation, and thankfully improve those means which God has afforded, to keep us out of the paths of destruction.

God is our preserver, but he has been pleased to appoint the instructions of wisdom as our great defence against these instruments of mischief. The knowledge of the truth, and the cordial love of it, will open our eyes to our danger, and possess our hearts with a settled aversion to the practices of the ungodly. As our Lord repelled every temptation of the devil by the word of God, so when it abides in us, it will enable us to meet every temptation of the old serpent, and of his instruments, with safety and stedfast resolution *.

Grace in the soul is weak of itself, but the seed of God shall remain for ever. The powers of hell shall never be able to extinguish it utterly, for it receives new supplies from the fountain of grace †.

Secondly, Wisdom, by its instructions received into the heart, will preserve us also from the malignant influence of bad women.

Ver. 16.—19. *To deliver thee from the strange woman, from the stranger that flattereth with her lips ; which forsaketh the guide of her youth, and forgetteth the covenant of her God : For her house inclineth unto death, and her paths unto the dead : None that go unto her return again, neither take they hold of the paths of life.*

It is a great happiness for young people to escape the snares of the harlot, in which so many have been entangled and lost. A true love to the word of God is eminently fitted to secure such a happiness.

There is no viler object in nature than an adulteress. Her beauty is but a jewel of gold in a swine's snout. Though born and baptized in a Christian land, she is to be looked upon as a heathen woman and a stranger ; and as self-made brutes are greater monsters than natural brute beasts, so baptized heathens are by far the worst of pagans.

---

*Acts 20:32   †Jer. 32:40, Rev. 3:10

Her words may be sweet and soft to the inexperienced ear of a thoughtless youth, but she is only flattering with her lips. Honey and milk seem to be under her tongue, but it is the cruel venom of dragons.

She is a monster of ingratitude to that husband who was the guide and protector of her youth. All the fervours of her first love are forgotten. She returns the most cruel treatment for all that fond affection by which he bound her to him in the most endearing obligations.

But her profaneness is still more shocking ; for she violates that sacred bond which was instituted by him whom she presumes to call her God, and regards not the marriage-oath which she swore by his great and awful name.

Shall a woman unfaithful to the best and kindest of friends,—a wretch that commits perjury without remorse,—prove faithful to any man ? When she speaks fair, believe her not, for there are seven abominations in her heart.

Miserable are they who trust to her alluring professions, for there is scarcely a hope that they will recover themselves from the snare of the devil. Her house is full of the pestilence of sin, and will infect every one that enters with a mortal and almost incurable distemper. The mind is darkened, and the conscience deadened ; the affections, too, are by uncleanness sunk into sensuality. How then can they again take hold of the paths of life ? No doubt. there is virtue in the blood and Spirit of Christ for the remission of the greatest sins, and the purification of the most defiled souls. It is even admitted, that whoremongers have been made illustrious monuments of the power of divine grace *; but let it be remembered that these are miracles of grace. Who would cast himself into a deep pit, in the hopes of

*1 Cor. 6:11

coming out alive, when almost all that fell into it were dashed in pieces or buried alive !

Whosoever pleaseth God, shall escape from this devouring deep. Let us therefore cleave to God's judgments, and follow their direction, and keep at a distance from the place of temptation. How worthy of our imitation is the example of Joseph, who was tempted day by day, but hearkened not to his mistress to lie by her or to be with her, because he would not sin against God *.

But wisdom will not only keep us from the paths of the wicked, it will also lead us in the way of good men.

Ver. 20. *That thou mayest walk in the way of good men, and keep the path of the righteous.*

It is not enough to refrain from wickedness, we must also work righteousness. We profess to be the servants of God, and it will be no sufficient excuse for a servant that has slept all day, to say that he did no mischief. There are two ways, in one or other of which all men walk,—the narrow way that leads unto life, and the broad way that leads to destruction. In the former way few walk, but it has been trodden by the feet of all who are worthy of our imitation. In it Abraham, and Job, and David walked, whilst those whose memorials are now perished, or whose names are remembered only to be execrated, were travelling in the broad way that leads to destruction. Which of these classes of persons would we chuse to follow in our course of life ? If the former, we must take our directions from the wisdom taught by Solomon, and the other inspired writers. Those venerable men who have obtained a good report, and who through faith and patience inherit the promises, were close students

---

*Gen. 37

of the word of God, so far as they enjoyed the benefit
of its instructions; and by faith in its doctrines and
promises, and a constant regard to its precepts, they
obtained their good report. Happy shall we be if, like
them, we esteem the word of God more than our necessary food, and keep the judgments of God still in our
view ;

Ver. 21. *For the upright shall dwell in the land, and
the perfect shall remain in it.*

They shall enjoy a long and a prosperous life, as far
as it is for their real advantage, in that good land which
God bestowed on his people, and shall, even when
they are dead, possess it in the persons of their posterity, who are blessed for their sakes. Sinners enjoy
not this happiness,

Ver. 22. *But the wicked shall be cut off from the
earth, and the transgressors shall be rooted out of it.*

Must not the righteous leave the earth too? Yes:
But the earth is a very different thing to the righteous,
and to the wicked. To the latter it is all the heaven
they ever have; to the righteous it is a place of preparation for heaven. Death is a kind messenger sent
to the righteous by their heavenly Father, calling them
to the possession of their eternal inheritance; to the
wicked it is a messenger of wrath, summoning them to
the abodes of misery. It is almost the beginning of happiness to God's people, but the final conclusion of all
that the wicked counted their happiness. To the
righteous, death is a translation to a better life. To
the wicked, it is destruction and woe. And is it all
one to us whether we share with the wicked in the
miseries of their latter end, or with Zion's travellers in
those everlasting joys that shall crown them when they
attain the end of their faith * ?

*Ps. 37:36-40

Proverbs 3

THIS chapter contains a variety of useful precepts, enforced by the strongest motives.

First, To remember and keep in our hearts the things written in this book, ver. 1, 2.

Ver. 1. *My son, forget not my law, but let thine heart keep my commandments.*

This inspired teacher is to be reverenced as a spiritual father. His word is to be regarded as a law published by Solomon, but binding on us by the authority of God *. We must never forget this law, but make it familiar to our memories, that we may have a guide ready to direct us in every situation in which we may be placed ; and when we treasure it up in our memory, we are to keep it in our heart. Richly does it deserve to form the object of our constant love, and the subject of our meditation all the day. Our obedience to it must proceed from the heart. What is the difference between good men, and false pretenders to religion ? To the latter, the religion which they have is a burden, to the former a pleasure ; to the one the law is a disagreeable restraint, to the other God's commandments are not grievous, for they rejoice in the way of his testimonies, more than in all riches. Interest dictates to us the propriety of keeping God's commandments—

Ver. 2. *For length of days, and long life,* [*Heb.* years of life,] *and peace, shall they add to thee.*

A long and happy life is the desire of all men, and

---

*Mal. 4:4

riches and good physicians appear to them the most likely means of obtaining it. But religion is better than all the gold and physicians in the world, for it has the promise of this life, as well as of that to come. Solomon knew well that good men sometimes die young, while the wicked live, become old, yea, mighty in power ; but still he asserts and often repeats the promise of long life which belongs to godliness. Surely, then, it is not without meaning and truth. The godly shall enjoy life as far as it is really a blessing in their particular circumstances, and the meaning carried beyond this would convert the blessing into a threatening. Peace is enjoyed by the godly, even that peace of God which passeth all understanding, and it keeps their hearts and minds through Jesus Christ. Outward prosperity is enjoyed by them, as far as it is consistent with their spiritual interests. Tribulations and enemies they may meet with, but they live in peace. Though slaughtered by the hand of violence, or the sword of war, they die in peace ; and when they die, they enter into everlasting peace.

The *second* precept in this chapter, is one requiring us to live in the exercise of mercy and truth.

Ver. 3. *Let not mercy and truth forsake thee. Bind them about thy neck, write them upon the table of thine heart.*

Mercy and truth are to be exercised by us in every part of our intercourse with our fellow-creatures, however defective they may be in the practice of these virtues to us. They are to be tied about our necks as a precious ornament, to be worn through life, and made visible to all men. Our light should shine before men, not for our own praise, but for the glory of our heavenly Father.

But it is not enough to practise mercy and truth, so as to obtain a character for fidelity among men.

Our outward acts must proceed from the heart. As the law of commandments was written upon tables of stone, so is the law of Christ written on the fleshly tables of the Christian's heart, by the Spirit of the living God. As workers under the Spirit, we are required to write the law of kindness and of truth upon the tables of our heart, by maintaining deep impressions of it, by meditating upon the peaceful motives that should excite us to that virtue, and by endeavouring, through the grace of Christ, to have our hearts habitually disposed to all those duties which are the natural fruits of love and integrity.

Ver. 4. *So shalt thou find favour and good understanding in the sight of God and man.*

God is well pleased, not only with the reverence and love which his people shew to himself, but with that generosity and mercy, that sincerity and faithfulness, which they evince to their fellow-men. Mercy and truth are glorious perfections in the Deity,—perfections which shall be for ever praised as the springs of our felicity. Of these, the mercy and truth found in wisdom's disciples, are to be regarded as a faint imitation. To find in his children this his true, though imperfect image, the Deity is greatly delighted. To the merciful he will shew himself merciful, and they that deal truly are his delight. He not only smiles upon them with the light of his countenance, but gives them favour in the sight of men also. Kindness and truth are qualities so amiable as to engage the esteem even of those who are too selfish to practise them. They attract the good-will of men. They procure that good name which is better than precious ointment. For a good man some have even dared to die.

That understanding which is good in the sight of God and man, is another fruit of the constant practice of mercy and truth. A good understanding appears already in this behaviour, but it is also promoted by it; for the practice of what we know, tends greatly to render our knowledge more clear, and certain, and extensive *.

The next precept is, to depend on God, and not on our own understanding.

Ver. 5. *Trust in the Lord with all thine heart, and lean not to thine own understanding.*

To trust in God, is to depend on him for bestowing on us every needful blessing, and preserving us from all evil.

Faith in Christ for eternal life is included in this dependence on God, for by him we believe in God. But we are commanded to trust in God for every thing necessary for us in this life also ; for the Lord God is a sun and shield, he will give grace and glory, and every good thing. O Lord God of hosts, blessed is the man that trusteth in thee !

This dependence on God is to be exercised with all our hearts, our judgments being persuaded that God is the only and the all-sufficient object of confidence, and our souls resting with full satisfaction in his power and faithfulness. This holy exercise is fully and clearly exemplified to us in many of the psalms of David †.

Whilst we trust in the Lord, our hearts must cleave to him, and renounce every sublunary dependance. To divide our confidence between God and the creature, is to lean with one hand upon a rock, and with the other hand upon a broken reed. David charges his soul to wait upon God only, for his expectation was from him, and from none else.

We must not make our own understanding a staff to our hearts.—Dependance on our own wisdom, will

*Ps. 119:100 †Ps. 62 etc.

lead us from trusting in God, to make lies our refuge, and to adopt unhallowed means for the attainment of our wishes. When men reject the testimony of God concerning Christ, when they depend on their own righteousness and strength instead of Christ, or on creatures rather than on God for help in difficulty, or when they expect to obtain pleasure or profit by sinful means, it is evident that they are departing from God, through an evil heart of unbelief, and trusting for the direction of their behaviour to their own corrupted minds.

Do we trust in God, and not in ourselves? It will then give us much pleasure to know that we are directed and encouraged to make known all our affairs to God, according to the following words of the wise king,

Ver. 6. *In all thy ways acknowledge him, and he shall direct thy paths.*

God is well acquainted with all our affairs, and yet he graciously requires us to present them to him in prayer, and to ask from him direction in the management of them, that we may be guided by his providence and Spirit, according to his word. The saints have found much relief in their perplexities, by spreading their case before him, and petitioning his interposition for their help *. But times of distress are not the only seasons in which we ought to apply to him. "Be careful for nothing, (says Paul,) but in every thing, by prayer and supplication with thanksgiving, make known your requests unto him." We are every day to pray that our steps may be so ordered, as that we may not be led into temptation. Joshua in the midst of his prosperity erred, by neglecting to ask counsel at the mouth of the Lord, because he thought

---

*Ps. 14:2,3

the matter so clear, as that he might safely trust to his own understanding.

Our encouragement to this duty is a promise that our path shall be directed. Having shewed to God our way, we must wait on God for direction, not by a voice from heaven, or by a new inspiration, but by his Spirit enabling us to understand his word, and apply it to particular affairs, and by his providence making the way where we should walk clear before us. Thus will our path be so directed, as that we shall be preserved from falling into sin, from meeting with temptations that might prove too hard for us, and from being subjected to more than needful calamity.

What a pleasure is it to have a wise and kind friend to consult with in all our affairs! but how much sweeter the pleasure, that we know where to find God, that we are invited to go even to his seat, and to utter all our words before him! When we interest God in our affairs by prayer, we may cast away every care, and walk on cheerfully, believing that he will guide every step of our journey; for his eyes are not only upon the way of his people, but upon every step of it *.

But when we acknowledge the Lord in all our ways, let us be sure to do it with self-diffidence, and with sincere resolutions to adhere to that way that will be pleasing to God.

Ver. 7. *Be not wise in thine own eyes ; fear the Lord, and depart from evil.*

Vain man would be wise, although man is born like the wild ass's colt. The world is full of wise men, or of men that would be thought wise. But we cannot be truly wise unless we become fools, renouncing all dependance on our own wisdom, and depending with humility upon the Lord, for those supplies of wisdom that

*Ps. 37:23,31

are necessary for enlightening our minds and directing our paths. When we pretend to ask counsel from God, whilst we have a secret dependance upon ourselves, and a reserved determination to pay no regard to his word or providence if it should cross our own humours, we play the hypocrite with God, and cover over that self-confidence which he abhors, with false professions of faith and resignation to the will of God. Johanan and his proud companions were terribly threatened for this dissimulation by the prophet Jeremiah *.

A high opinion of men's own wisdom is so danger-ous, that Isaiah pronounces a heavy woe upon it. We are not indeed to pull out our own eyes, to re-nounce our own understandings, or to believe con-tradictions ; but we ought certainly to keep our rational powers in subjection to the word of God, to be sen-sible of our great liableness to err, and of our absolute need of the divine direction, especially in those mat-ters that concern religion †.

That we may have our paths made straight, we must also fear the Lord and depart from evil. To them that fear the Lord is addressed a promise of divine teach-ing ‡. This religious affection has a native tendency to prevent men from turning out of the way of truth : By the fear of the Lord, men depart from evil. It acts as a sentinel to the soul, which keeps temptation from entering. God makes use of the grace of fear, as well as that of faith, in repelling temptation, and in sub-duing corruption. " I will put my fear," says he, " into their hearts, and they shall not depart from me." Abraham displayed his fear of God, as well as his un-conquerable faith, when nothing could for one moment

*Jer. 42:19-22   †Jer. 10:23, 1Cor. 2:14,15   ‡Ps.25:12-14

withhold him from obeying the strangest command which mortal ever received. " Now I know that thou fearest God," said the angel, " seeing thou hast not withheld from me thy son, thine only son *."

The fear of God preserves men from bodily disease, as well as from sin.

Ver. 8. *It shall be health to thy navel, and marrow to thy bones.*

The navel is a useful part of the body, being a sort of ligament to knit the bowels together ;—the bones are the strength and fence of the body. The fear of God is health to the outward, as well as to the inward man. Health is an objeet of great desire to all, and the wise man will not only use medicines when sick, for the restoration of it, but will attentively consider what food and what exercise are the most proper for preserving health in the navel, and marrow in the bones. The spiritually wise will remember, that in God's hands is our life, and breath, and all our ways,—that diseases are his servants, which come and go at his pleasure,—and that the surest way to health is to walk before him unto all pleasing. Does he then enjoy health ? he has a blessing along with it. Is he the victim of disease ? it will be more beneficial to him than is to the wicked his unsanctified health.

Religion has a natural tendency to impart health and vigour to the body, because it preserves a man from those distempers which proceed from unsubdued lusts, and diffuses over the mind that calm serenity and heartfelt joy, which even upon the body exercise a medicinal influence.

We are next required to be liberal in the service of God.

---

*Gen. 22:12

Ver. 9, 10. *Honour the Lord with thy substance, and with the first fruits of all thine increase : So shall thy barns be filled with plenty, and thy presses shall burst out with new wine.*

Earthly substance is necessary for the use of our bodies, but we are called to make a nobler use of it than the mere service of the outward man. We are to honour the Lord with it, making no use of any part of our increase, till we have set apart a reasonable proportion of it for the service of God. God needs nothing at our hands ; but for our own benefit, he will have us to render back a part of all he gives us for the decent support of his worship, and for the maintenance of the poor. Is it any hardship to give a part to him from whom we have received all ? Can we make a better use of our wealth, which is often a snare and a trap to men, than by serving God, and thus making to ourselves friends of the mammon of unrighteousness ?

By this means we honour the Lord. He is the Creator and Redeemer of our souls and bodies, and therefore we are to glorify him with our bodies and our spirits, which are his. Our substance is his also, and we must honour him with it by a liberality in his service, proportioned to the extent of his bounty. By the practice of this duty, we shew our faith in his providence and promises, our love to God, our gratitude for his goodness, and our preference of his service to that of mammon. In this manner we justify our profession of the gospel of Christ, and others are made to glorify God, while they enjoy the benefit of our ministrations to this purpose.

By the neglect of this duty, we are guilty of robbing God himself of that rent which he requires from us as his tenants. We dishonour him by shewing that we love the world better than his service, and that we trust more to our chests, or to our bonds upon our fellow-

creatures, than to his promises ; for has he not assured
us, that instead of being losers, we shall be great gainers by what we bestow upon him ? Liberality on God's
account brings down the blessing of providence to such
a degree, that our barns shall be filled, and our presses
need enlargement. God has the sun, and winds, and
rain, and creatures of every description, in his hand ;
and these he manages in such a manner, as that none
shall be a loser by him, nor a gainer by withholding
from him. Robbers of God are visited with a curse,
which like a moth wastes, or like a fire destroys, their
substance *. Liberality opens the windows of heaven,
destroys the devouring locust, and turns the barren
field into a delightful land †.

Health and riches are the advantages that attend the
fear of the Lord, and liberality in his service ; but we
must not imagine that these blessings are promised
without a reservation of the cross, when God sees it
needful for us, nor suppose that God is unfaithful when
he administers correction to his children. This truth
is inculcated in the next instruction of the wise king,
which teaches us how to behave under afflictive providences.

Ver. 11. *My son, despise not the chastening of the
Lord, neither be weary of his correction.*

This exhortation, like many of the others, speaks to
us as unto children ; and it is a piece of ingratitude in
the children of wisdom to forget it, by suffering it to
be obliterated from their memories, or to produce no
practical influence ‡.

We are here warned against despising divine rebukes, or fainting under them. The rebukes of providence are despised, when persons regard not the supreme

---

*Hag. 1:6, 2:16   †Mal. 3:10-12   ‡Heb. 12:5

hand that afflicts ; when they consider not the design of God in afflicting ; or when, through stupidity of mind or hardness of heart, they neglect to comply with it. This is a great affront to God. It is as if a child should say to his father when he strikes him, ' I do not care, do with me what you will, I shall behave no better than I have done.' Ahaz was a very wicked man, but nothing shewed the stubbornness of his heart so much, as his walking contrary to God, when he sent sore distress upon him *.

God's people may fall into this sin, sleeping like Jonah amidst the storm that God sends to testify his displeasure with them. But those whom he loves, he will awaken out of their sleep ; and this he sometimes does by terrible tempests of outward calamity or of inward terror, sufficient to rouse them from the deepest slumber. As the lively Christian is thankful for the least mercy, so the afflictions which others despise are improved by him as calls to serious thought.

Afflictions may be despised in another sense, which seems to agree better with the argument used in the following verse. Men despise them, when they do not value them as necessary and useful. We need afflictions, and yet we are ready to think that they might be very well spared, and the work designed by them effected by gentler means. This notion is to be rejected by us with abhorrence, because it implies a reflection upon the wisdom and love of our heavenly Father, who does not afflict willingly, nor grieve the children of men ; though now for a season, if need be, he afflicts them, because the beneficial consequences are far more than sufficient to counterbalance the pain of it. The original word often signifies to abhor.

---

*2 Chron. 28:22

Weariness under the divine correction is another common fault, which we must avoid with care. Our hearts must not fret against the Lord, nor suffer reflecting thoughts to spring up, for God never exceeds the due measure in distressing us. No ingredient is poured into the cup of affliction, but by infinite wisdom and grace; nor shall the rod of Jehovah rest upon the lot of the righteous, longer than need requires. Weariness will make the heart to sink like a stone, and produce harsh suspicions of the divine goodness. It will disqualify the mind for relishing the consolations of God, and answering the designs of the Almighty.

To keep our minds from fainting, let us consider who it is that corrects us. It is the Lord, and all flesh must be silent before him, and receive what evils he is pleased to appoint, with reverence and resignation. It is the Lord, let him do unto us what seemeth good in his sight. He is excellent in judgment, and in plenty of justice, and cannot do wrong to any of his creatures. But it is a sweeter consideration, that he is a Father, and chastens us in love.

Ver. 12. *For whom the Lord loveth he correcteth, even as a father the son in whom he delighteth.*

He intends, not to destroy but to reform, and correction is one of those privileges that belong to the family of God. Christ himself, though a Son in an infinitely higher sense than we, though altogether free from the need of correction, yet learned obedience by the things which he suffered. Christ was the first-born among many brethren, and we are predestinated to be conformed to him in sufferings and in holiness, and the sorrows which we endure are means appointed for making us partakers of God's holiness. Earthly fathers correct their children, in order to drive away folly from them; and that misguided lenity which withholds the rod, is but cruelty in disguise. Now, we yield reverence and submission to earthly parents ; how much more do we owe it to that heavenly Father, who exercises love infinitely wiser and greater than theirs ! He knows the greatest afflictions have not so much bitterness as the least sin, and he loves his children too well to spare correction, when it is requisite to purge away their sin.

The best commentary we can have on this text, is that given by Paul in his epistle to the Hebrews *. Did we understand it aright, we should bless God for correction, as well as for smiles ; and the wormwood and the gall of our miseries would be turned into honey and the honey-comb.

Whatever corrections the children of God suffer, they are still happy, and it is our duty to believe them so. Behold, happy is the man whom God correcteth ! Nothing can make that person unhappy who is possessed of wisdom, as the inspired philosopher tells us in the next part of this chapter. In it he again recommends wisdom to our esteem and pursuit, ver. 13.—26.

Ver. 13. *Happy is the man that findeth wisdom, and the man that getteth understanding.*

Where shall wisdom be found, and who is the man that getteth understanding ? Wisdom is to be found in the Bible, and in Christ, who is revealed in it. The Scriptures are able to make us wise unto salvation, through faith which is in Christ Jesus. All the treasures of wisdom are hid in him, and he communicates this precious gift by his word and Spirit, to those who apply to him for this purpose. And while they diligently make use of the prescribed means, they increase in wisdom, and with it their happiness increases too.

---

*Heb. 12:5-11

None can tell how happy the man is that finds wisdom. They are accounted happy who possess large quantities of gold, or silver, or precious stones; but these lose all their value when brought into comparison with this heavenly treasure.

Ver. 14, 15. *For the merchandise of it is better than the merchandise of silver, and the gain thereof than fine gold. She is more precious than rubies, and all the things thou canst desire are not to be compared with her.*

Silver is much esteemed by men, and gold is almost adored by them. Rubies are still more precious, and perhaps there are some things still preferred to these shining stones. But none of them all are to be named in one day with wisdom; and he has no true judgment of the real value of things, who would give a grain of true wisdom for a mountain of diamonds.

Earthly riches are for the body, wisdom is for the soul; the former may enrich a man for the space of threescore and ten years, the latter for numberless millions of ages. Gold and rubies are the true riches in the eyes of erring mortals, wisdom and grace in the eyes of Christ; and if we follow his judgment, the diseased beggar Lazarus was incomparably happier than the rich man who was clothed with purple, and who fared sumptuously every day.

A venerable father, when he saw Rome in its splendour, took occasion to contemplate the ineffable glories of the celestial city, compared with which Rome itself was but a pitiful village. The Scripture teaches us, when we are charmed with the lustre of earthly riches, to consider how incomparably these are surpassed by the excellency of wisdom.

He is not a true Christian who would not wish to be rich in faith rather than in silver and gold; for every one that partakes of heavenly wisdom is enlightened by the Spirit of God, and disposed, in his judgment of the value of things, to listen to the instructions of God in his word.

The excellency of wisdom further appears in the gifts she bestows. She is a munificent princess, holding in both hands the richest presents, to be given to her servants.

Ver. 16. *Length of days is in her right hand ; and in her left hand riches and honour.*

A happy life extended to old age is given to the lovers of wisdom ; or if cut off in the midst of their days, they are no losers. They cannot even in this case complain that God is unfaithful to his promise, for in another world they enter on a state of life which excels the present as much in value as in duration. If a man promises to give us threescore and ten acres of ground in a barren country, and instead of them gives us ten thousand in a fruitful soil, watered by the river of God, and blessed by the smiles of heaven, he is not worse, but a great deal better than his word.

Riches and honour are given in the same sense as length of days. When Solomon testified his high regard for wisdom, God bestowed upon him the riches and glory of this world. But experience taught Solomon that these things did not make him wiser, or better, or happier. Let us, from the history of the wise man, learn to implore the accomplishment of this promise in a spiritual sense. There are eternal treasures and unfading diadems reserved for the wise in another world. There they will be so rich, that the streets of their city of habitation are paved with pure gold,—so honourable, that they shall sit with Christ himself on his throne.

But great as are the advantages, splendid as are the honours which wisdom confers, the world is generally prejudised against it, and prepossessed with the idea of

its being burdensome and unpleasant. Worldly pleasure appears so desirable, so essential indeed to human
happiness, that for this sole reason multitudes abhor
the thoughts of becoming religious. In order to remove this mischievous prejudice, Solomon assures us,
that religion is not less conducive to pleasure than it is
to honour and wealth.

Ver. 17. *Her ways are ways of pleasantness, and all
her paths are peace.*

Call not religion Marah, but call her Naomi, for she
is in every respect desirable. True, indeed, it is no rare
occurrence to find a religious man leading an unpleasant life, but this is to be ascribed to his own mistakes
and dispositions, and not to religion, than which nothing
tends so much to render the present life a scene of
happiness.

It is pleasant to enter into wisdom's ways by believing on Christ. It is pleasant to go on in these paths,
by walking in him who is the new and living way. In
God's presence is that fulness of joy into which those
travellers shall enter at the termination of their journey.
Even now some drops of those rivers of pleasure that
are with him enter into their souls, and give them more
delight than the highest earthly enjoyments can impart
to those whose portion is in this life.

It will readily be admitted, that some of wisdom's
ways are pleasant; but are they all so? Yes, all her
paths are peace itself, for the work of righteousness, as
well as the effect of it, is peace.

There is peace and pleasure in repentance, which is
sweetened by the apprehension of God's mercy in Christ;
so that the true penitent enjoys more satisfaction in one
hour's mourning, than the votary of worldly pleasure
in twenty years' carnal gratification. There is pleasure
in self-denial, for he that practises it knows that he is
the true self-seeker; and of this he is assured by the

word of Christ *. There is pleasure and peace in bearing the cross of Christ, for it is made light by the Spirit of Christ, and the prospect of sharing with him in his glory †. There is pleasure and peace in tribulations, because when they abound, consolations abound much more by Christ ‡. There is peace in fighting the Lord's battles against the mightiest enemies, for the Christian soldier fights under the banner of the Prince of Peace. His feet are shod with the preparation of the gospel of peace. The God of peace will bruise every enemy under his feet. More exquisite is that pleasure which the subjugation of one sinful affection produces, than that which results from the gratification of a thousand. —Should the Christian be called to die a violent death, there is peace in his latter end, as we find there was in the death of the good Josiah when he fell in battle.

The pleasures of the world are like the gleams of a wintry sun, faint, and feeble, and transient. The pleasures of religion are satisfying and eternal. The calamities of this life are not able to interrupt, far less to destroy them. This is verified in the experience of every one whose soul is under the lively influence of that faith which constitutes an essential part of religion. David, though in deep waters, yielded not to desponding thoughts, believing that the Lord would yet command his loving-kindness; though about to walk through the valley of the shadow of death, he saw no ground for the fear of evil.

All the exercises, all the privileges, all the hopes of religion, are full of pleasure. Even the trials to which religious men are exposed afford pleasure, if not whilst they are felt, at the farthest when they come to a period ||.

---

*Matt. 26:25   †1 Peter 4:13,14   ‡2 Cor. 1:5

||James 1:4, 12, I Peter 1:6,7, Isa. 49:10

Such is the pleasure and peace with which wisdom is attended, that,

Ver. 18. *She is a tree of life to them that lay hold upon her ; and happy is every one that retaineth her.*

Nothing in the present state of the creation is sufficient to furnish out a proper emblem of the happiness that wisdom affords, and therefore the wise man goes back to the state of the world under innocent Adam, comparing the delights of religion to the fruits of the tree of life. For the sin of Adam we were driven from Paradise, and our approach to the tree of life in the midst of the garden for ever prevented. But a second Adam has opened our way to a better paradise, in which is the tree of life that bears every month twelve manner of fruits. The branches of this wide-spreading tree bend down to this lower world, and those that are wise unto salvation sit under its shadow with great delight, while its fruit is sweet to their taste.

If we wish to eat of these delicious and soul-reviving fruits, we must take fast hold of wisdom, and keep that hold against all the enemies that would tear it from us. To wisdom we must cleave with purpose of heart, when the devil and the world would persuade us to forego some part of truth or duty, or to make some small compliance with sin, in order to serve some worldly end *. " To him that overcometh, [i. e. to him that keepeth Christ's works unto the end,] will he give to eat of the tree of life which is in the midst of the paradise of God †."

To all the great things that have been said of wisdom, let us add the glory which belongs to wisdom, as it appears in creation and providence.

Ver. 19, 20. *The Lord by wisdom hath founded the earth ; by understanding hath he established the heavens.*

---

*James 1:12   †Rev. 2:7

By his knowledge the depths are broken up, and the clouds drop down the dew.

Knowledge and wisdom belong to God in their highest perfection, and shine forth in all his works. By his wisdom he established the world, and formed every creature beautiful in its kind. By his knowledge, the heavens and the earth, and all their inhabitants, were formed into one universe, which incessantly proclaims the greatness of its Creator's wisdom. The language of every creature when considered by itself, and especially when viewed as part of the grand system, is, "We come forth from the Lord of Hosts, who is wonderful in counsel and excellent in wisdom." The world could never have afforded us a convenient dwelling-place, had not the depths by the knowledge of God been broken up, and the waters separated from the dry land, to be laid up in the vast repository of the sea, or to flow along in rivers for our benefit. It is wisdom that draws up the moisture from the earth in waters, and exhales it in vapours, forming them into clouds, and again distilling them in dew, or pouring them down in rain, that food may spring out of the earth for man and beast.

This wisdom calls for our gratitude, and praise, and imitation. We cannot pretend to make or govern a world, but we are enjoined to manage our own concerns with wisdom. The God whose understanding is infinite, hath dignified us with rational powers, and directed us to that wisdom which is proper for us. When he displayed the wonders of his infinite understanding at the creation of all things, he said unto man, "The fear of the Lord, that is wisdom, and to depart from evil is understanding." He is the giver of wisdom, and he gives it from his own exhaustless stores. Every beam of wisdom in man is a ray from that eternal Sun ; and the divine image, which we lost by our folly in departing from God, begins to be renewed in us when we attain that knowledge and wisdom so earnestly re-commended by the royal teacher.

Is wisdom so incomparably useful and excellent? let us then listen with reverence to the instruction that again speaks to us as unto children.

Ver. 21. *My son, let not them depart from thine eyes ; keep sound wisdom and discretion.*

There are some kinds of wisdom highly esteemed by the world, yet of these some are so far from being use-ful, that they are brutish folly. No wisdom is sound but that which is taught by the word of God, and ap-proved by him who is the Author of wisdom, and who has given us plain marks for distinguishing it from that which is earthly, sensual, and devilish *. This sound wisdom makes us discreet and prudent, and guards us against that selfish cunning which has so often assumed its name.

This sound wisdom and discretion must be like frontlets before our eyes, that we may keep them al-ways in our view. Then will our steps be ordered in God's word ; for by what means shall we purify our way ? By taking heed thereto, according to God's word.

There are many adversaries that would rob us of this treasure, and we are but too ready to let it slip out of our hearts. For this reason, we need to be frequently reminded of our duty to keep it. If we retain it on our minds and hearts, if we uniformly exhibit it in our practice, we shall certainly find that our labour is not in vain in the Lord.

Ver. 22. *So shall they be life unto thy soul, and grace to thy neck.*

Fools can scarcely be said to live ; they neither glo-rify God nor enjoy him, so that they are dead whilst

---

*James 3:17

they live. But the excellency of knowledge is, that
wisdom giveth life to them that have it. It imparts to
life that happiness which alone renders it worthy of
the name. True wisdom is real life, communicated
from him who is the quickening Spirit, to them that
were dead in trespasses and sins. It is an ornament
of grace to the neck, which renders the meanest beggar who possesses it more noble than the mightiest
monarch, who is acquainted with no brighter ornament
than his regal crown.

Safety is another of the great advantages which always attend wisdom.

Ver. 23, 24. *Then shalt thou walk in thy way safely,
and thy foot shall not stumble. When thou liest down,
thou shalt not be afraid ; yea, thou shalt lie down, and thy
sleep shall be sweet.*

Whilst we keep wisdom and discretion, we are safe
by the protection of the Almighty. We are safe
whether we walk in the way, or sit in the house, or repose on the couch. There shall no evil happen to the
just ; even those events which are evil to others, are
sanctified and blessed to them.

" He shall give his angels charge over thee to keep thee
in all thy ways, (says the scripture), lest thou shouldst
dash thy foot against a stone." Happy it is to be the
care of angels, but happier far to be under his protect-
ing eye who is the keeper of Israel.

We must remember, that this promise has a direction embodied with it, " Thou shalt walk in thy way."
Satan endeavoured to cheat our Saviour out of this important part of the promise, that he might cheat him
out of the benefit of it altogether. But Jesus knew
well the regard due to every jot and tittle of the word
of God. We are required still to keep the way of the
Lord, and in the affairs of life to attend to our own

concerns, shunning the character of busy-bodies, by not meddling in the affairs of others. In the calling wherewith we are called, let us abide with God, and we shall dwell in safety under the shadow of the Almighty.

Sleep commonly flies from the victims of wretchedness and calamity; but quiet and peaceful are the slumbers of those who can lie down in safety, because the Lord sustaineth them. Even in the prospect of danger and distress, they can repose in calm serenity, for Jehovah giveth his beloved sleep. Such were the calamitous circumstances of David, when exiled and pursued by the unnatural Absalom, that all the people who were witnesses of his banishment, wept for him. Yet what says David himself? " I laid me down and slept; I awaked, for the Lord sustained me." When the most prosperous sinners lie down to rest, they want covenant protection, and know not but they may open their eyes in hell. The servant of God knows, that when buried in the arms of " Nature's sweet restorer," he is under that guardian eye which neither slumbers nor sleeps.

There may be seasons in which the good man cannot enjoy pleasant slumbers. But what does he lose, if, by the thoughts that Wisdom suggests, he enjoys a feast of holy contemplation, more refreshing to him than sleep is to others * !

In order to enjoy this tranquillity of mind, we must believe the promises of God, and by the exercise of holy confidence, banish those fears that would distress the soul.

Ver. 25, 26. *Be not afraid of sudden fear, neither of the desolation of the wicked when it cometh. For the Lord shall be thy confidence, and shall keep thy foot from being taken.*

---

*Ps. 63:5

Sudden fears are attended with a stupifying influence upon those that want faith, but far different is the fact with regard to the righteous. The righteous man is bold as a lion, for he knows, like the three children in Babylon, that the God whom he serves is able to deliver him, or to render him happy, though the desolation of others should involve the destruction, not only of all his outward comforts, but of his mortal life *.

The Lord is a sure ground of confidence in the worst of times. Our proper exercise in such seasons, is to trust in the Lord, and to pour out our hearts before him, knowing that he will be a refuge for us. This comfortable doctrine is illustrated and enforced in almost every Psalm.

May not one, then, exclaim with the royal philosopher, " Happy is the man that findeth wisdom, and the man that getteth understanding !" The way in which wisdom leads us, is attended with every blessing, and free from every evil ; or if there be any evil in it, so wonderful is the providence of God, that it is turned into good. Thus is Sampson's riddle verified to every afflicted saint. May our lives be those of the righteous, and our last end their's !

The wise man next directs us, to make no unnecessary delay in the performance of any good work.

Ver. 27. *Withhold not good from them to whom it is due, when it is in the power of thine hand to do it.*

To do justly, is one great point of religion ; and we ought not unnecessarily to delay giving every man his due, for the delay of justice is temporary injustice. When we owe money to our neighbours, which they require from us at present, and we, though able, defer payment till afterwards, we are plainly guilty of injustice ; for a man has the same right to his property now,

---

*Hab. 3:17,18, Ps. 46

that he will have a year hence. We find men reproved and threatened for keeping in their own hands the hire of the labourer. The same censure may be applied to those who refuse to pay just debts, or to restore to its rightful owner any piece of lost property which they have found ; for we are not to do what we will with that which is not ours, nor are we to owe to another any thing but love.

We owe love and the proper fruits of it to our fellow-creatures, according to their necessities and characters, and our connection with them ; and we transgress the rule of righteousness, if we withhold even from our enemies that which is due to them by the law of Christ ; for many things are to be reckoned just debts from us on his account, which they have no title to claim for their own sakes. It may be difficult for us to render to others what is due to them by the laws of justice or charity ; but the question is not, whether it is easy, but whether it is in the power of our hands, to render unto others that good which is due to them. The fruits of love are often labours, but they are not such labours of love as those which our Redeemer cheerfully performed for us, nor is any man a loser by them *.

What is in the power of our hands to-day, may not be in our power to-morrow, and therefore we ought not to delay the performance of any good work †.

Ver. 28. *Say not unto thy neighbour, Go, and come again, and to-morrow I will give thee ; when thou hast it by thee.*

Delays in any part of duty, furnish a strong presumption that we do not perform it cheerfully. We are commanded, not only to do good works, but to be ready to every good work ; not only to shew mercy,

---

*Heb. 6:10   †Gal. 6:10

but to shew it with cheerfulness. He that gives speedily, gives twice ; but he that gives with slow reluctance, gives in part a denial. Much of the benefit is often lost to the receiver, and much of the gratitude to the giver, by telling our neighbour to go and come again.

There is a manner of giving that but ill accords with that humanity and mercy which should dispose us to give. Airs of superiority assumed even to the meanest of our fellow-creatures, are unbecoming ; for however inferior to us in point of station, they are still our neighbours, and God commands us to love them as ourselves. God often delays answering our prayers, but he is infinitely and essentially superior to us ; yet his delays are all in wisdom and love. When it is fit that his petitioners should receive what they ask, he gives before they ask, or whilst they are yet speaking he hears.

In one case, the wise man allows us to defer giving. When we have it not by us, and when we cannot give at all in a consistency with more urgent duties, we may refuse to give ; but still we must have hearts to give, were it in our power. And if there be first a willing mind, it is accepted according to what a man hath, and not according to what he hath not.

The next direction is against doing evil to our neighbours.

Ver. 29. *Devise not evil against thy neighbour, seeing he dwelleth securely by thee.*

Our fellow-men are our neighbours, and we are destitute of the love of God if we feel no love to them. If the practice be an index of what passes within, we must conclude that man to be wholly destitute of love, who can wilfully hurt those whom he is required to love as himself. Such a man cannot surely pretend to religion ; or if he does, he is at best like a tinkling brass, or a sounding cymbal, for his professions are emptiness and hypocrisy.

At the day of judgment, they shall be doomed to hell, who did not serve their neighbour in love ; where, then, must those appear whose practice was quite the reverse ?

All injurious persons are wicked, and the more con‑ trivance there is in any evil that we do, it has so much the greater malignity in it *. It is criminal to devise evil against any person ; but it is double iniquity to hurt those that dwell securely by us, for this in effect is a breach of trust, and an indication of a heart base and depraved beyond the common pitch of human wicked‑ ness. The meek and the quiet of the land are the persons who dread no injury from us, as they plot none against others ; and the Lord Jesus, to whom all judgment is committed, is the Redeemer of all such persons. He hath pronounced a blessing on them, and will avenge them of their enemies ; for with righ‑ teousness shall he judge the poor, and reprove with equity for the meek of the earth †.

We must not even contend with our neighbours by hard words, when they have done nothing to provoke us ; otherwise we are volunteers in the devil's service, sinning without putting him to the trouble of tempt‑ ing us.

Ver. 30. *Strive not with a man without cause, if he have done thee no harm.*

If a man has injured us, we ought to forgive him. Do we believe that God for Christ's sake hath for‑ given us ten thousand talents, and shall we reckon it a hard matter, at Christ's command, to forgive our brother a few pence ?

If the unforgiving shall never enter into heaven, what curses shall for ever lie upon those who are

---

*Mic. 2:1   †Isa. 11:4, Mic. 2:9, Ps. 72:12,14

guilty of unprovoked injuries? Railers and revilers
stand excluded from the kingdom of God, and the admission of injurious persons, like Saul the Pharisee,
into the kingdom of God, is to be regarded as a miracle
of mercy.

It may possibly be alleged, that injurious persons
are often prosperous in the world. It may be so in
some circumstances, yet,

Ver. 31. *Envy thou not the oppressor, and chuse none
of his ways.*

Imagine not that a man can be happy in the enjoyment of that which he has gained by dishonest means.
Envy or admiration of his success, might lead us to
imitate his unrighteous behaviour. Though his wine
sparkle, let us remember that there is poison in the cup.

Ver. 32. *For the froward is abomination to the Lord;
but his secret is with the righteous.*

That man who is detested by the Lord, is so far
from being happy, that he is miserable and accursed.
Can he know true happiness, who is looked upon with
an angry countenance by him whose smiles are heaven,
and whose frowns are hell? Such is the situation of
oppressors of every rank, from the mighty Nimrods of
the world, who employ themselves in general mas-
sacres and desolations, down to the petty parish oppressors, who grind the faces of their poor neighbours,
and by adding field to field, to the ruin of many families, endeavour to plant themselves alone in the country-
side *.

"But his secret is with the righteous." They enjoy a fellowship with God unknown to the world. He
discovers to them the secret mysteries of grace, refreshes their souls with the manifestations of his special love, and blesses their substance by the unper-

---

*Isa. 5:8-10, Hab. 2

ceived workings of his gracious providence *. God not only enriches them with his goodness, but treats them as friends, and to them all his paths are mercy and truth.

The blessing of God upon his people, and his indignation toward his enemies, spread through their dwellings, rendering them happy or miserable. The cottage of the just is a quiet and pleasant habitation. The palace of the wicked is blasted by a secret curse.

Ver. 33. *The curse of the Lord is in the house of the wicked, but he blesseth the habitation of the just ;*

And happiness or misery lies in the blessing or curse of God †. When you behold the magnificent structures in which sinners dwell, let not your thoughts be lost in wonder, or your hearts rankle with envy. They are fabrics, stately indeed, but not solid. You may pronounce them cursed. Eliphaz saw the wicked taking root, but suddenly he cursed his habitation, for his children are far from safety. The curse of God has often destroyed the timber and the beams of the most towering palaces ; often has it kindled a fire, by which they have been destroyed to the lowest foundation. Such dwellings as these are houses of infection, for the leprosy of sin has taken possession of them, and it can be ascribed only to wonderful mercy, if the children and servants in them escape the plagues prepared for their lords.

By the blessing of the Lord, the meanest cottage is converted into a dwelling of joy and praise. We read of whole houses that have been blessed for the sake of godly servants; how much more may the divine blessing be expected, where the masters are pious, and make their dwellings a little church, where the melody of

---

*Ps. 25:14, John 14:21-15:15, Hag. 2:19   †Ps. 37:22

thanksgiving and the voice of prayer are daily heard! The blessing of God, that is daily asked, shall not be refused; and the members of the family are blessed with instructions and examples that must produce good effects on them, unless they harden their hearts like an adamant. The holy conversation of good wives may be a means of winning their husbands; and many children and servants have found the greatest reason to thank God for the appointment of their dwelling in a family of saints.

From among the wicked, we find that proud and haughty scorners are singled out as signal monuments of the vengeance of God.

Ver. 34. *Surely he scorneth the scorners, but he giveth grace unto the lowly.*

It is pride that makes men scorners. When men have an overweening conceit of themselves, they are likely to behave insolently to others, and contemptuously to God himself*. But on such arrogant worms of the dust, Jehovah looks down with contempt, and makes them objects of derision to all men. We read in scripture of many, whom the pride of their heart and countenance brought to the lowest disgrace. Nebuchadnezzar, and Haman, and Herod, and the proud Pharisee, are set forth for examples, to shew us that these men stand not on an even place, whose hearts are not kept low by that grace which cherishes humility. That God whose eye turns away with disdain from the splendour of haughty princes, and the diadems of imperious kings, looks with kindness upon the meanest of those who walk humbly with their God †. He visits them in mercy, and refreshes their spirits with his love ‡. He gave them that grace which makes

---

*Compare 1 Peter v. 5 and James 4:6   †Isa. 66:2   ‡Isa. 57:15

them humble, and he giveth more grace. God bestows grace on men, that he may be glorified ; and the lowly, who are made sensible of their emptiness and guilt, are the persons who will ascribe praise to him, for the least of his favours : In them he will display the excellency of his love, and enrich them with his blessings in this, and in the everlasting world. " Blessed are the poor in spirit, for theirs is the kingdom of heaven." With the lowly is wisdom, and,

Ver. 35. *The wise shall inherit glory, but shame shall be the promotion of fools.*

Some by their birth and fortune inherit high sounding titles, and celebrated kingdoms. But if they are not wise, their lofty situation is the theatre of their dishonour. Those who are blessed with sound wisdom, have an inheritance of glory in reserve, compared with which the crowns and sceptres of the world deserve not a name. The prudent are even at present crowned with knowledge ; but the happy day is coming when they that are wise shall shine as the brightness of the firmament, and they that have turned others to the wisdom of the just, as the stars for ever and ever.

Fools are fond of honours, but all the honours they can enjoy are like bubbles when they glitter in the sun. They shall be promoted, indeed, but their exaltation shall be like that of Haman, who was exalted when he was hung upon a gallows fifty cubits high. Their shame shall be conspicuous to the world, when they shall be covered with everlasting disgrace, and become an abhorring to all flesh *.

---

*Luke 14:11

Proverbs 4

In this chapter, Solomon renews his exhortations to us to get wisdom, ver. 1—13, and to avoid temptations, ver. 14—19. The chapter concludes with a short sum of practical religion.

In his exhortation to wisdom, he makes use of many of the same motives by which he had already recommended it. Solomon had a heart filled with knowledge, beyond all the sons of men; and he could have charmed and astonished, by the discoveries of new truths in every sentence; but he had wisdom to manage his knowledge, and therefore prefers those discourses which are solid and useful, to those which, by their dazzling brilliancy, are fitted only to produce admiration and surprise. He desires not our applause, but our benefit; and his aim is not to shine, but to instruct. He was a wise householder, instructed into the mysteries of the kingdom of heaven, and brings out of his treasure things old as well as new.

God speaks to us more than once or twice by this inspired penman, and shall we not listen to his voice? We have precept upon precept, and line upon line; and if we do not receive instructions pressed upon us so warmly, we must go and fall backwards, and be broken, and snared, and taken. May God open our hearts to hear what is said by him who was the wisest of men, and who spoke under the guidance of unerring Wisdom.

Ver. 1. *Hear, ye children, the instruction of a father, and attend to know understanding.*

Our Lord teaches us to pray to God, as children to a father. Have we such confidence toward God, and shall we not attend with the reverence and love of children, to him who addresses us with the infinite tenderness of a heavenly Father?

Some have lost their fathers; some have fathers who give no food to the souls of their children. There is a Father who will take up these orphans, and supply them with the best and kindest instructions. He calls upon all of us to attend to his understanding, for he still opens his mouth in wisdom. That blessed God who makes the sun to shine upon our world, has caused this luminary still to shine for enlightening the souls of men. It was in mercy to Israel that the sun was made to stand still upon Gibeon, that the people might avenge themselves of their enemies; but it is a richer favour, that this light of his age still shines, to direct our paths in wisdom and safety. But let us hear what he can say in recommendation of what he inculcates upon us.

Ver. 2. *For I give you good doctrine, forsake ye not my law.*

The many say, " Who will shew us any good?" But they know not what is good for them, and suffer themselves to be deceived with shadows. Here God shews us what is good, and gives it to us. All the things that the sons of men can desire, are not to be compared to good doctrine.

But is it becoming in a wise man to commend his own discourses? Solomon might well commend them, for they are not his, but God's, and God is graciously pleased to commend them to our acceptance. He calls us to buy wisdom without price, and discovers as much earnestness in recommending this precious merchandize, as if he were to be enriched by the price.

Were a thousand volumes to be written in commendation of this book, they could not say so much for it, as it can say for itself in a few words. God is not only the author, but the recommender of it. He calls it good doctrine, and requires us not to forsake it in our practice. To despise it, is to despise the authority and love of him who guided the pen of Solomon in writing and commending it to us. To forsake his law is to forsake the king's highway, which is ever under his eye and protection, (chap. ii. 9.) and to turn into those paths which are haunted by ravenous beasts.

The words of Wisdom here sounding in our ears, are the words, not only of Solomon the wise, but of David, the man after God's own heart. He delivers to his children, what he heard from his blessed father, by whom also the Spirit of the Lord spake.

Ver. 3, 4. *For I was my father's son, tender and only beloved in the sight of my mother. He taught me also, and said unto me,—*

His parents had, in his tender years, instructed him in the principles of religion; and the reason why they did so, was, that they loved him; for the best evidence of parental love is to instruct, and when necessary, to correct children. Solomon was the best loved son in the family, and the greatest pains were employed in training him up in the way wherein he should go. Of him, accordingly, we find, that his parents had more joy than of all the rest.

His mother gave him instruction, as well as his father. Her crime had lost her a child, but her religious care was rewarded with double comfort in the best and dearest of her sons. Were there more women of the spirit of Bathsheba, and Lois, and Lemuel's mother, we might hope to see a greater number of Solomon's, and Timothy's, and Lemuel's in the world. Solomon was a wise and good king, but his mother's name was Bathsheba. Rehoboam was a bad king, and his mother's dame was Naamah, an Ammonitess. It was peculiarly creditable to Asa that he behaved well, though Abijah was his father, and Maacha his mother, or grandmother.

Solomon communicates to his children the instructions which his father had given him. We do injustice to our children, if we do not endeavour to leave them that estate which our forefathers acquired for their posterity. It is a more grievous iniquity, if the fathers transmit not to their children those pious instructions, which in their tender years they received from their own parents. Families are reckoned honourable, when a rich estate passes from father to son, through many generations ; but it is a far more lovely sight, to behold the same faith dwelling in a rising family, that dwelt in their mother, and father, and remote ancestors.

We have a specimen of David's instructions to Solomon in the twenty-eighth chapter of the first book of Chronicles. The reading of it is sufficient to warm our hearts, and make us wish to hear more of the venerable king's instructions to his son. Solomon, who did not forget what his affectionate father said, gives us more of them in this place. Let us hear them with reverence, that we may not be found despisers of him, by whose direction David spoke, and Solomon wrote.

Ver. 4. *Let thine heart retain my words : keep my commandments, and live.*

Children must attend to the words of their pious parents, and treasure them up in their hearts, to be observed in their lives ; for it is no vain thing, but their life, to which they are called to hearken *. When our fathers leave us money or land, we will not part with these gifts of their love; but the instructions of life are

---

*Deut. 32:46

more precious than any earthly heritage. The wisdom which Solomon learned by his father's counsels, was better than his kingdom. When proved by God, it appeared that he valued an increase of wisdom above an addition to his dominions, or his wealth, or even to the years of his life.

Ver. 5. *Get wisdom, get understanding ; forget it not, neither decline from the words of my mouth.*

How earnestly are we called to seek after wisdom, till we find it ! It would be a happy token of getting it, were we so deeply convinced of its value, as to make the attainment of it our grand concern; for blessed are they that hunger and thirst after righteousness, they shall be filled. If we cry for wisdom, and lift up our voice for understanding, our cries shall not remain unanswered. The success of Solomon's petition is recorded as an encouragement to our prayers and our hopes *.

It is not enough to get wisdom ; we must also use it, and walk in its ways. They are all pleasantness and peace, but pain and misery will meet us, if we turn either to the right hand or to the left.

Ver. 6. *Forsake her not, and she shall preserve thee : love her, and she shall keep thee.*

There are some who think it necessary, in particular cases, to forsake wisdom, lest their strictness should expose them to damage. But David here tells Solomon and us, that this must be a dangerous error. The way of duty and of safety is still the same. Those who walk by faith will believe this, though it appear to such as walk by sight, an absurdity contradicted by a thousand facts. It is incomparably safer and happier, to lose our credit and our life, by cleaving to the

---

*Chap. 2:1-5

truths and ways of Christ, than to preserve both by base compliances with the enemies of the truth *.

That we may not forsake wisdom, we must embrace and love her. A miser will never forget where his treasure lies, and he will lose his life sooner than be robbed of his precious store. The love of wisdom will in like manner induce us to lay it up in our hearts, and to keep fast hold of it in defiance of every danger. When persons receive not the truth in the love of it, they provoke God to leave them to the influence of strong and soul-ruining delusions. When we receive it into our hearts, it makes us strong and victorious over the wicked one †.

Ver. 7. *Wisdom is the principal thing; therefore get wisdom, and with all thy getting get understanding.*

David had got understanding by meditating on God's testimonies, and he found it the principal thing. His crown and palace were not comparable to it in his eyes. Setting so high a value upon it himself, it was his great desire that his beloved son should get it also. And those parents who are possessed of David's spirit, would rather see their children wise unto salvation, than rich and great in the world. Evil parents are not so bad as to refuse bread and fishes to their children. Good parents use every means to make them sharers of that wisdom, which they have found to be their own happiness.

Whatever we get, let us get wisdom. I remember to have read of two religious women in the reign of Queen Mary of England, who parted with a considerable portion of their estate, for a few leaves of the Bible. They who look upon the bargain as a foolish one, have little knowledge of the worth of the scriptures. If a man has acquired thousands of gold and

---

*Matt. 16   †2Thess. 2:10, 1 John 2:14

silver, and is without wisdom, he has gained thousands of shining nothings. If he has acquired wisdom, and nothing besides, he has gained the one thing needful*.

Having gained wisdom, we ought to value her as she deserves to be valued.

Ver. 8, 9. *Exalt her, and she shall promote thee; she shall bring thee to honour, when thou dost embrace her. She shall give to thine head an ornament of grace; a crown of glory shall she deliver to thee.*

All that truly know wisdom, must embrace and exalt her. The only reason why any treat her with indifference, is that they are entire strangers to her. None knew her better than David and Solomon, and we hear how eloquent in her praises they are.

We must prize wisdom as a pearl of inestimable value, and we must testify our regard for her, by growing in grace and in knowledge; by improving every means and opportunity afforded us of increasing this divine treasure; by valuing, for the sake of wisdom, the teachers and lovers of it; by earnest endeavours to make our friends and neighbours sensible of its value; and, in a word, by giving it the throne of our hearts, and the government of every action of our lives.

They who honour wisdom, obtain the noblest honours, for by wisdom they are promoted. Their heads are adorned with a diadem of beauty, and a crown of glory is delivered to them.

None are so apt to be vain of earthly honours as those who, like David, are unexpectedly raised to the possession of them, or who, like Solomon, surpass in majesty all their contemporaries. Yet we find, that neither David nor Solomon was greatly charmed with the lustre of a crown. The reason is obvious,—their eyes were open to the glories of true wisdom, and all

---

*Matt. 13:44-46

the glories of earthly kingdoms were lost in the superior brightness. They would rather have exchanged conditions with the poorest saint in Israel, than with the most magnificent monarch in a land where God was not known.

Solomon received and readily assented to his father's good doctrine; we need not wonder therefore that he prayed for wisdom rather than for long life, or glory, or power. He had learned not only that wisdom was a nobler possession than any of these things, but that it brings these along with it. If we receive in faith and love these instructions of the holy man, our desires will be like his. He that is told of a rich treasure hid in his ground, will soon make it appear whether he believes the report. He who believes the report of God concerning the excellency of wisdom, will dig for it as for hid treasure.

These are the instructions of David to Solomon, which he communicates to us. Solomon now appears again to address us in his own person.

Ver. 10. *Hear, O my son, and receive my sayings; and the years of thy life shall be many.*

Who is the man that desires to live long, that he may see good? Let him hear and receive the sayings of David * and of Solomon. There are few men that do not wish to live long, but there are few too that can trust as much to the counsels of the sovereign arbiter of life and of death, as to the counsels of a good physician; for all men have not faith. Many shorten their days by seeking to the physicians rather than to the Lord.

A wise man would not chuse, for the sake of a long life, to expose himself to guilt and misery. But Solomon, in his prescription, consults our innocence and happiness, as well as the length of our lives.

---

*Ps. 34:11-14

Ver. 11—13. *I have taught thee in the way of wisdom ; I have led thee in right paths. When thou goest, thy steps shall not be straitened ; and when thou runnest, thou shalt not stumble. Take fast hold of instruction ; let her not go : keep her, for she is thy life.*

In our journey through life we have great need of one to guide us, for it is not in man that walketh to direct his steps. God only can lead us in a safe way, and he does it by his Spirit through his word. This inspired writer does not only teach, but guide us. He is like a companion in our journey, who points out every step that we should take, and every step that we ought to avoid.

The way in which he leads us, is the way of wisdom, for we are taught to keep our great end constantly in view, and to adopt the proper methods for reaching it. It is a right way, for our interest and duty are jointly pursued ; and every point is gained, when these two most important objects are combined. Our duty to God and to man, and to ourselves, are all clearly explained by this divinely instructed teacher.

It is a straight way,—a way in which we shall not be straitened, and in which we shall not stumble. They that walk in the ways of sin and folly, imagine themselves the only persons that enjoy liberty. But how vain the thought ! They are very slaves, for they are in bondage to impetuous passions, which prescribe service hard and impossible to be performed. One of these tyrants contradicts the orders of another ; and though one should gain the sovereignty, and crush every insurrection of the rest, the servant of sin is still straitened, because conscience terrifies him, or divine providence crosses him in his pursuits. He, on the contrary, that walks in the way of God's precepts, walks at liberty ; for though he is in the strait way that leads to life, that way is broad enough to allow him all the room that a reasonable being can desire.

We are taught to manage our civil and spiritual business with ease and safety, and to avoid every thing that might encumber or ensnare us. Stumbling-blocks lie before us in our journey through life, and they that have not a skilful guide often fall upon them to their hurt. Sometimes we are under the necessity of running, and there is then most danger of falling into sin and mischief, when, without being allowed time to deliberate, we must instantly resolve upon one of two courses that lie before us, or must act with vigour and alacrity, at the risk of being by our passions hurried forcibly along, without time to take due care of our steps. In such cases as these, it is needful to have religious principles rooted in our hearts; and religious knowledge stored up in our minds, which through divine grace will prevent us from adopting any course of action displeasing to God, and enable us to determine by what means we may best consult the glory of God and our own real interest. When we act with resolution, and shew our fervent zeal in religion, this knowledge and wisdom will preserve us from those dangerous extremes which have so often brought dishonour on religion and the professors of it.

Many temptations surrounded David in the days of his youth, and he was sometimes ready to slip with his feet ; but he meditated on God's testimonies, and in all his ways acknowledged God, and the Lord directed his steps, and enlarged them under him. If at any time he stumbled, the reason was, that he lost sight of that word which was the light of his path, but he was never left to turn aside from following the Lord.

Let us therefore receive the instructions of life with

all the desire of our hearts. Let us value them as our life, and abhor sin and folly more than death.

That we may keep fast hold of instruction, and walk in this straight way in which we shall not stumble, it is necessary to keep out of the way of evil men.

Ver. 14, 15. *Enter not into the path of the wicked, and go not in the way of evil men. Avoid it, pass not by it, turn from it, and pass away.*

We must not have fellowship with bad men. Their course and company are to be avoided *. We must not so much as enter into their path, or if we have entered, we ought instantly to turn out of it. Their path is to be avoided by us when we are at a distance from it. It is unsafe to pass by it, lest we should be tempted to take a step or two in it. When we find ourselves near, it is our duty to hasten away till we get at a distance from danger.

This wise leader calls out to us with a loud voice, to keep at a great distance from the way of evil men. He calls as if it were a haunt of robbers and murderers; and so indeed he may, for they that would rob us of our innocence and peace, are more dangerous than those that would rob us of our money. The sins to which they would tempt us by their example and persuasions, may prove the destruction of our comforts and our souls.

We pray to be kept from temptation, and our practice ought not to contradict our prayers; otherwise it is evident, that as one man mocketh another, so we mock God, by asking from him what we wish not to have.

No wonder that the wise man is so peremptory in urging us to avoid the society of the wicked,

Ver. 16, 17. *For they sleep not, except they have done mischief; and their sleep is taken away, unless they cause*

---

*Eph. 5:13

some to fall. For they eat the bread of wickedness, and drink the wine of violence.

They are faithful servants of him who is a murderer from the beginning, and their pleasure lies in doing mischief. It is their meat and their drink to do the will of the wicked one. They subsist on robbery and spoil, and if they have not been eating he bread of wickedness, they retire to their beds with the reluctance of those who have been unable to procure for themselves necessary food

These wicked persons may teach us how zealous we ought to be of good works. Why should the servants of the best Master labour in his service with less fidelity and resolution than those that serve the devil, and work for his poor wages * ? If we have David's spirit, we will not give sleep to our eyes, nor slumber to our eye-lids, till we have done the work of the day for God. The faithful followers of Christ will count it their meat and their drink to do the will of their heavenly Father.

He was a heathen, but he had the soul as well as the purple of an Emperor, who said on the evening of a day in which he had not done any good, " Friends, I have lost a day."

There are many whom it would be difficult to persuade to manifest the same zeal in the service of righteousness, which these profligates discover in the service of iniquity ; but it may reasonably be expected that we should flee their company when their character is laid before us. Let us not form the mistaken idea, that the worse they are, we are in the less danger of imitating them, for the heart of man is deceitful above all things, and desperately wicked. Of little sins we are not afraid, but say within ourselves, " These sins are at-

---

*Rom. 6:23

tended with little danger, are they not little ones ? surely our souls shall not die though we fall into them." We are as little afraid of great sins, because we think them so shocking that we cannot fall into them. Frequently does it happen, that labouring under such misapprehensions as these, men lay down their heads upon the lap of temptation, and awake like Sampson in the hands of their enemies. By these enemies they are carried captive at their will, and to this punishment God has given them up for neglecting to follow his counsels, and preferring to them the instructions of those who cause to err.

There is as great a difference between the path of the just and that of the wicked, as there is between light and darkness.

Ver. 18, 19. *But the path of the just is as the shining light, that shineth more and more unto the perfect day. The way of the wicked is as darkness ; they know not at what they stumble.*

The righteous man possesses an understanding brightened by the rays of divine truth, for the Sun of righteousness hath shone into his soul. His heart is beautified by the light of purity, diffusing a pleasant lustre around him in his conversation ; and his spirit is cheered with the light of joy and consolation from the countenance of God.

This light is not like that of a taper which burns itself away into darkness, but like that of the morning sun, which shines brighter and brighter, till it blazes with meridian splendour.

Christians increase in knowledge, and grace, and happiness, in this world, and are perfected at death and the resurrection. Clouds may indeed obscure their brightness, and thick darkness may occasionally cover them. Their progress may be suspended, like that of the sun in the days of Joshua ; or they may go backward, as the same glorious luminary did in the days of Hezekiah, but these days of threatening aspect shall not extinguish their light. The Lord will make their light to spring forth speedily, and their darkness as the noonday. He will remove or turn back in their progress the causes that obstructed them, and he that began the good work in them will perform it until the day of Christ. Then shall they shine forth as the sun in the kingdom of their Father, for the Lord shall be to them an everlasting light. They shall see God as he is ; they shall love him to the utmost extent of their capacity, and enjoy full satisfaction in the presence of him with whom is the fountain of life.

The wicked travel in darkness all their days. This is true, not only of those rebels against the light who abandon themselves to all manner of wickedness, but of all who follow not him who is the light of the world, and live without that charity which is the distinguishing mark of the disciples of Christ *. Unbelievers may have some glimmerings of light in their minds and consciences, but these are not sufficient to keep them from walking in darkness; their eyes are evil, and their whole course of life is full of the darkness of ignorance and error, of misery and sin.

So great is this darkness, that they often stumble and wound themselves without knowing the cause of it, or even that they are wounded ; and hence arises their ignorance of their need of healing. The wise are not ignorant of Satan's devices, and when they fall they are instructed to avoid the stumbling-block by which their fall was occasioned ; but it is the misery of fools walking in darkness, that being insensible to the means of their seduction into sin, they fall again and again by the same instruments of temptation. Instead of learn-

---

*John 8:12, 1 John 2:11,12

ing caution by their sins, one fall is the occasion of another, and perhaps a worse.

There is indeed a great difference between the darkness of their path, and that region of darkness to which it leads. Their minds being blind, there is no light within them; still, however, the light of Christ shines around them, and they are called upon to give it admission *. Arise, shine, for thy light is come, O thou that long dwellest in darkness ! If you are deaf to the voice of him who has come to shed light into your souls, you know not when your feet may stumble upon the dark mountains, and your souls drop into the regions of eternal darkness, where there is not the light of a candle to mitigate the horrors of the gloom.

If, after all that our wise instructor says, we still chuse the path of evil men, let us hear the sentence of our Judge †.

This chapter is concluded with a short but comprehensive sum of practical directions; but before addressing them to us, the preacher again summons us to attend.

Ver. 20—22. *My son, attend to my words ; incline thine ear unto my sayings. Let them not depart from thine eyes ; keep them in the midst of thine heart. For they are life unto those that find them, and health to all their flesh.*

When a preacher has truths of great importance to communicate, and sees many of his hearers asleep, he endeavours to rouse them up ; so this wise man, knowing that we are dull of hearing, frequently renews his calls to us to hear and treasure up his words.

It is our duty to be frequently summoning the powers of our souls to attend with reverence to the words of God, our Maker and our Judge, and to pray

*John 7:33, Eph. 5:14, Matt. 8:16   †John 3:19,20

to God that he may open our ears to discipline, and seal our instruction.

He that hath ears, let him hear. Let him place these necessary instructions before his eyes, that they may be a rule to his life, and let him lay them up in the midst of his heart, believing them to be the faithful sayings of God, and loving them with a cordial affection, because they are more precious than gold, and sweeter than honey from the comb.

The motives that call for our attention are exceedingly powerful. It is a father that speaks. The things which are spoken are of quickening and invigorating virtue. They are life to such as find them, and health not only to the soul but to the body ; not to a particular part of it, but to all the flesh. A medicine effectual to the cure of a single member might soon enrich the inventor of it. Here is a medicine for all the flesh, and yet the physician that prescribes it without reward, finds so few willing to make use of it that he must proclaim its virtues again and again. He speaketh once and again, but man perceiveth it not. Are we then dead not only to every generous principle, but to every feeling of self-interest? Are life and death become matters of indifference to us ? Is it all one in our eyes whether we enjoy health in our bodies and spirits, or pine away under the power of deadly distempers ? Here is healing balm. Here is a physician of infinite value. Attend to the directions which he gives for the management of our whole life.

He that is born of God keepeth himself, and the wicked one toucheth him not. The Lord is our keeper ; and in the history of Peter we are furnished with a melancholy proof, that unless he keep us, our care of ourselves will be unavailing ; but if we commit the care of ourselves to God by a lively faith, it will not make us careless about ourselves, for God keeps us by his power through faith, by putting his fear into our hearts, and by exciting into activity those beneficial graces. If God keeps his fear alive in our hearts, we shall be powerfully disposed to guard our hearts and tongues, our eyes and feet from evil. We are here instructed by Solomon in what manner to manage this important affair.

Ver. 23. *Keep thy heart with all diligence, for out of it are the issues of life.*

The heart is the fountain of vital action. It is out of the good treasure of the heart that a good man brings forth good things, and out of the evil treasure of the heart that the evil man brings forth evil things. No actions can be good unless the heart be good, more than the fruit can be good when the tree is corrupt. The heart of Simon Magus was not right with God, and therefore his professions were hypocrisy. This corrupt fountain must be purified by the Spirit of Christ, or the streams issuing from it will be corrupt and poisonous. But even when purified by renewing grace, it is not altogether pure. Such is the remaining tendency to corruption, that the heart must still be kept with all diligence.

We ought carefully to keep our tongues and hands, our eyes and feet; but above all, we ought to keep our hearts. This will be the best means for keeping all the rest, and without this, however well our external behaviour is regulated, we are but corrupt and false-hearted professors of religion *.

That our hearts may be kept, we must observe them with a watchful eye, and endeavour to be well acquainted with their leading principles and their inward workings. It is a shame for one who knows many things

---

*Ps. 119:80

not to know himself, and the chief thing about our-selves to be known is the heart.

With a strong hand must the heart be ruled, and it ought to be our constant endeavour to subject to the word of God every imagination and reasoning, every opinion and thought, every inclination and affection· A neglected garden will not be so full of weeds, as a neglected soul of vain thoughts and exorbitant passions, hateful to God, and dangerous to our own happiness and peace.

The heart must also be guarded against those dan-gers that perpetually threaten our best interests. It is like a besieged city attacked by mighty and cunning enemies, and in danger of being betrayed by a trea-cherous party within.

It is a great encouragement to us in performing this difficult duty, that our labour shall not be in vain. Nu-merous are the promises made to us of assisting grace *; and if we suffer from a surprise of the enemy, Christ prays that our faith fail not.

The tongue is that member of the body which com-municates most readily with the heart. For this reason it is to be regarded as its most active instrument, either for good or evil service ; therefore, in the next place,—

Ver. 24. *Put away from thee a froward mouth, and perverse lips put far from thee.*

A wry mouth is a great deformity to the counte-nance ; a perverse tongue is a more ugly blemish to the conversation.

The tongue is a world of iniquity, and needs a world of care to manage it. We must not only refrain from evil discourse, but put it far from us, avoiding every thought and feeling that might set an evil tongue in motion, and refusing to listen to evil speakers, that we

---

*Ezek. 36:26, Jer. 32:40

may not be tempted by them to retail their infamous slanders.

It is a sad thing to think evil, for that corrupts ourselves ; but if we have done foolishly in thinking evil, let us lay our hands upon our mouths, lest we corrupt others also.

We must repent bitterly of evil imaginations, but the manifestations of pardoning grace restore complete comfort and calm serenity to the wounded spirit. But when we have given our tongues a license, whereby others also have been drawn into sin, we must remember that, though pardoning mercy may clear our consciences from the terrors of guilt, deep remorse must still be felt for the irreparable injury done to others. Who can tell how far its baneful influence may have spread ?

The commandment of God must also give direction to our eyes.

Ver. 25. *Let thine eyes look right on, and let thine eyelids look straight before thee.*

Sincere views in the course of our life to the great end of our being is a necessary part of religion, and without these there is no truth in our religious profession. The Pharisees abounded in prayers and giving of alms ; but the praise of men was in their eye, and our Lord tells us that they had their reward. Their desire was to be seen and honoured by men ; that they no doubt by their religion obtained, but it was all that they obtained by it. Jehu thought himself a very zealous man, but he took not heed to walk in the way of the Lord with all his heart ; and it is testified of him, that he departed not from the sins of Jeroboam all his days. He did many good things, but his eyes looked aside to his honour and profit. All the splendid actions he performed, were but so many splendid sins.

None of us liveth to himself, and none dieth to himself. The glory of God must be our great aim, otherwise it appears that redeeming grace has not taken effect upon us.

Heaven is in the Christian's eye, and from it his views must never be turned aside to the world *. No doubt the enjoyments of the world may be sought by us, but still in subordination to the hope of our calling. Heaven is our home, earth our inn. If the world be our home, we are not strangers and pilgrims here, neither are we citizens of heaven †.

We must not, under the pretence of serving God, make earthly motives our end, otherwise we are guilty of that kind of sacrilege which is of all others the worst, —that which consists in alienating God's own service from him. It is not less dishonourable to God, when in our zeal for the accomplishment of good ends, we have recourse to means disapproved by him, for the command of God combined with his glory must be kept in our eye ‡.

Our actions must be all ordered in the word of God.

Ver. 26, 27. *Ponder the path of thy feet, and let all thy ways be established. Turn not to the right hand nor to the left ; remove thy foot from evil.*

Consideration is one of those things in which man excels the irrational animals, and it is absolutely necessary in the religious life. If we shew not ourselves men, we can never please him, who made us wiser than the beasts of the earth! If we walk not circumspectly, we can with no propriety be numbered among the wise ||.

Our actions will be weighed by God in an even ba-

*Heb 11:25   †Phil. 3:18-20   ‡Job 13:7-9, Rom. 3:5
||Eph. 5:15

lance at last, and it is necessary for us to weigh them now in the same balance. As we ought to compare our past actions with the word of God, in order to know what occasion there is for repentance ; so in like manner those which we design to perform, that we may know whether it be lawful to perform them or not.

This is necessary for the direction and establishment of our ways. They that ponder not their paths are like a wave of the sea, driven by the wind and tossed ; but in the hearts of such as receive and apply it to the cleansing of their way, the word of God has an establishing efficacy *.

Our ways ought to be stable and consistent. It is disgraceful for men to have their religion modelled and varied by their company and circumstances of life. Let us resemble, not the osier, but the oak. Our goodness, if like the morning cloud, is no goodness at all, for the path of the just is as the morning sun. To be unstedfast in God's covenant, is to be treacherous to God. The truly righteous man is faithful unto death. His frames of mind may vary, and his steps may sometimes be seduced from the straight way, but the good Spirit of God will restore his soul, and make him again to walk in the paths of righteousness. David slipped with his feet, and he once turned aside, yet could he say in truth that he had not wickedly departed from his God. He finished his course with joy, and received the crown of life.

It is dangerous to turn either to the left hand or the right from the way of God's commandments. On each side of the King's highway are those crooked paths, which are full of precipices and pitfalls. Men may be destroyed by being righteous, as well as by being wicked overmuch. The Pharisees in the days of Christ's

---

*Ps. 119:9,11, Eph. 4:14

flesh, sinned as much by adding to God's law as by taking from it. To add to God's precepts, is a reflection upon the wisdom of the Lawgiver; to violate them, is an insult upon his authority. It commonly happens, that when men have the presumption to make some new articles of religion, they make compensation to themselves for their additional restraints on their liberty, by straitening the law of God in some other points, and thus make it on the whole much easier to flesh and blood, than it was made by God.

Our foot must be removed from all evil. Sin must not be indulged in thought, word, or action. No degree of this abominable thing is to be allowed in our practice. Saints have fallen into some of the greatest sins, but it is inconsistent with holiness to take liberty in the least *. Even the garment spotted by the flesh must be hated by us.

From this whole directory, we may see our need of pardoning mercy ; for which of us can say, " We have made our hands clean, or kept our tongues from every evil thing ?" But the blood of Jesus is a fountain opened to cleanse from all sin.

Without renewing grace, our labour in guarding our hearts, and restraining our tongues and feet from evil, will be as vain as to attempt washing an Ethiopian white. The old heart cannot be reformed, but God hath promised to give us a new heart, and to put a new spirit within us.

With our vigilance, faith and prayer must be joined †.

---

*Matt. 5:19   †Ps. 17:5, 56:12,13

Proverbs 5

The wise man gives us this chapter, as an antidote against those youthful lusts by which so many are ensnared. Let such as are tempted by their own hearts, or by the agents of Satan, to sins of uncleanness, seriously consider its contents, and pray that God may bless them for their benefit. None of us are superior to all temptations of this nature; let us therefore give heed to the things that are spoken, in order to represent the danger and mischief of impurity, and to shew us in what manner to avoid it.

Ver. 1, 2. *My son, attend unto my wisdom, and bow thine ear unto my understanding: That thou mayest regard discretion, and that thy lips may keep knowledge.*

The wisdom which Solomon teaches in this chapter cost him dear; but if we attend to his instructions, we shall have them at an easy rate. It may save us much bitter repentance, and preserve us from some of the most dreadful dangers; for it will teach us that spiritual subtilty and discretion, by which, like David, we shall become wiser than our enemies, and be enabled to escape their snares.

Attention will enable us to keep knowledge in our hearts, for a wanton imagination, ever dictating corrupt conversation to the lips, proves the beginning of ruin to many of the sons of men. They accustom themselves to speak of things not fit to be named among Christians; and from foolish talking, and impure jesting, by which they corrupt themselves and their companions, they proceed to the works of darkness.

When the word of God enters into our hearts, it will banish all pollution from the tongue, and dispose us to entertain our companions with that discourse which is good for the use of edifying. Thus our own hearts will be more deeply impressed, God will be honoured, and other men guarded against the snares of the destroyer.

Now it is of great importance for men, especially in their younger days, to furnish themselves with preservatives, from that word which is able to keep us, against the snares of the strange woman. Solomon had already warned us against her ; but he is directed by God to do it a second time at greater length.

Ver. 3. *For the lips of a strange woman drop as an honey-comb, and her mouth is smoother than oil.*

She talks of nothing but love, and pleasure, and perpetual delights. To hear her, one would suppose that she possessed the most generous and disinterested spirit. Her tongue is taught by him who betrayed Eve to paint the vilest sin with the most beautiful colours, and to conceal all its deformity and danger ; but it is the part of a reasonable creature to look beyond the present moment, and to consider the end of things, as well as their beginning. There is sweetness indeed in the mouth of this strange woman,

Ver. 4. *But her end is bitter as wormwood, sharp as a two-edged sword.*

The venom and sting of a serpent is concealed under the honey of her lips. Those who repent of their uncleanness will experience far more bitterness than ever they tasted pleasure, in their unlawful gratifications. But few get so well off, and if persons continue hardened, the end is more bitter than death. It is like a sharp two-edged sword, which wounds and destroys both soul and body at once.

Ver. 5. *Her feet go down to death, her steps take hold on hell.*

She is on the highway to eternal ruin, and thither she is carrying those that listen to her bewitching voice. Her house is in the suburbs of the place of destruction, and her steps take hold of hell. David was in great fear when he said to his friend, " As the Lord liveth, there is but a step between me and death." But there is not even this small interval between the steps of the strange woman and hell. They already take hold of it. But may not persons, when they see this danger before their eyes, make a timely retreat to the paths of life? No. In must cases this is not to be expected.

Ver. 6. *Lest thou shouldst ponder the path of life, her ways are moveable that thou canst not know them.*

When men enter into a course of sin, they have no intention to be damned. They intend only to indulge themselves in the pleasures of sin for a time, and then to return to the paths of life. Millions of souls have been seduced to everlasting destruction by this one temptation of the old serpent,—" Ye shall not die although you eat ; grace is free, and there is abundance of time to repent." The wise man gives what may repel this temptation, by letting us know how foolish it is for men to flatter themselves with the hope, that they shall be truly disposed and enabled to repent of their sin.

" Her ways are moveable, that thou canst not know them." She can form her mode of behaviour into a hundred different shapes, to entangle the heart of the lover. She spreads a thousand snares, and if you escape one of them, you will find yourself held fast by another. She knows well how to suit her words and behaviour to your present humour, to lull conscience asleep, and to spread before your eyes such a mist, as shall prevent you from being able to descry the paths of life. If you ever think of the danger of your course, and feel the necessity of changing it, she will urge you to spend a little time longer in the pleasures of sin. If her solicitations prevail, if you linger within the precincts of guilt, your resolutions are weakened, and your passions gain new strength. What is the awful result? The devil obtains more influence; conscience, forcibly repressed, ceases to reclaim with so loud a voice; God gives you up to the lusts of your own heart, and leaves you to chuse your own delusions. Attend, then, to the wisest of men, who instructs you to keep free of these dangerous temptations.

Ver. 7. *Hear me now, therefore, O ye children, and depart not from the words of my mouth.*

If a father saw his son walking on the edge of a precipice, how greatly would he be alarmed! how loud would be his cries! And if the adventurous youth still kept his dangerous post, he would fly to him, and try to force him from the brink of destruction. No less earnest is this kind instructor to save us from impending ruin. His words are cries; they have life and power in them. He is deaf who will not attend; he is stubborn who will not comply.

Ver. 8. *Remove thy way far from her, and come not nigh the door of her house.*

But what need is there for so much preciseness? May not a man be permitted to talk with her, merely by way of amusement? Is it unlawful to drink a glass in her house, and to satisfy our curiosity by observing what passes in it, and by what arts she contrives to seduce those who are less established in virtue than ourselves? Yes; it is unlawful to have the least correspondence with her. By the requirements of the ceremonial law, no man was to be in the same house with a leper. The moral law forbids us to enter into a house full of the leprosy of sin. Her house is full of snares, and her hands are as bands. The devil glances in her smiles, and lurks in her dress and in her motions. He is there, ready to discharge at you his fiery darts of temptation ; and to aid his efforts, you have much combustible matter about you. Dare you then promise yourself that the fire of licentious passion shall not be kindled, and blown up into a flame that you cannot quench. The devil will tempt you enough without your own help. To tempt is his business. As you love your life and your own soul, give him no assistance in the work of destruction.

Ver. 9—11. *Lest thou give thine honour unto others, and thy years unto the cruel ; lest strangers be filled with thy wealth, and thy labours be in the house of a stranger ; and thou mourn at the last, when thy flesh and thy body are consumed.*

A good name is better than precious ointment, but of a good name this abominable sin is the ruin. The credit of David and of Solomon was greatly sunk by it. By it has the honour of thousands been irrecoverably lost.

Life is a great blessing, and may be regarded as the foundation of every earthly blessing. But unclean persons part with every thing that renders life worthy of the name, and in a literal sense, they often give their years unto the cruel. Their lives are lost in the pursuit of this sin by the just vengeance of God, by its native consequences, or by the accidents to which it exposes those who practise it.

And for what are these years given away ? Did men generously part with their lives in the defence of their country, or for the sake of a generous friend, the loss would be amply compensated by honour, and by the pleasure of a good conscience. But how infatuated are they who give their years unto the cruel, who conceal a selfish and malignant heart under the mask of love! All unlawful love is hatred, and all tempters to it are cruel enemies to our happiness. Shall we then gratify inhuman enemies, at the expense of honour and life, and every thing dear to us?

These false friends and malicious enemies rob you of your honour and life, with as much eagerness as if they could enjoy these precious blessings of which you are deprived. Their real views, however, are directed to your money or estate, and why should men give away the fruits of their own labour and toil? or if they wish to be rid of them, why should strangers be filled with them, rather than friends?

Some are so foolish, as to live in the lust of uncleanness, to save the necessary expences of a family. But observation, as well as Scripture, might convince them of their error. The followers of vice are often attacked by poverty, that comes upon them like an armed man; and how distressing is poverty to those who have indulged themselves in lewd courses, contracted insatiable desires after carnal pleasure, deprived themselves of their friends, and disqualified themselves for any business that might retrieve their circumstances, or supply their wants!

Poverty is still more distressing when it is attended by weakness and disease, the natural consequences which Providence has annexed to those courses by which men dishonour God and themselves.

When the body is tortured, and the spirits dejected by the loathsome distempers which sin brings in its train, their conscience, which was formerly trampled under foot, rises up and regains its power, and inflicts severe vengeance for the injuries it has received. Then, O profligate sinner! thou wilt mourn—

Ver. 12—14. *And say, How have I hated instruc-*
tion, and my heart despised reproof ; and have not
obeyed the voice of my teachers, nor inclined mine ear to
them that instructed me ! I was almost in all evil in the
midst of the congregation and assembly.

Religion has received many testimonies in its favour
from enemies, whose hearts have at last forced them to
curse the day when they were so mad, as to turn a
deaf ear to its friendly voice.

The word of God read and preached, is God's appointed means of keeping or reclaiming men from sin,
and in a Christian land the votaries of vice are rebels
against the light.   They are, to their own loss, fatally
successful in fighting against that God who opposes
their wickedness by the sword of the Spirit, which is
the word of God, written by prophets and apostles,
and preached by the ministers of God.

It is not in vain for ministers, and parents, and tu-
tors, to use means for acquainting young persons with
the Scripture, and imprinting it upon their hearts.
The confession of profligates, when arrived at the end
of their career, makes it evident, that if any thing would
have proved effectual to preserve them from ruin, it
would have been the instructions and reproofs of
teachers.   Such means have no doubt been the instruments of preserving many, and reclaiming some.

The confession of the wretch tortured by his conscience, is not introduced by the inspired sage as the
humble confession of a penitent, who looks for pardon
through the merits of Christ.   How greatly are they
deluded who think that misery can produce true repentance, or that sorrow pressed out of the soul by distress of body and anguish of conscience, are signs of
real grace !   Persons may cry out of their folly, and
warn others, and beg others to pray for them ; and

yet, like Simon Magus, remain all the while in the gall of bitterness and in the bond of iniquity.

Sinners who will not comply with the calls of God, may now make them the object of their scorn ; but at the latter end, when conscience shall preach with a voice louder than any minister, sorrow shall be their inevitable portion. Then, in the breasts of desperate sinners, despised admonitions shall burn like raging fire. Then shall multitudes of iniquities, once over-looked, present themselves like so many dismal apparitions to the eyes of the sinner, and make him a terror to himself.

The pleasure derived from the present moment is nothing. Our enjoyment is derived from the recollection of the past, or from the prospect of what is to come. Sensualists cannot flatter themselves so grossly, as to fetch any pleasure from that part of life which they have already spent, but their hopes are ever on the wing to seize on anticipated pleasure. It frequently happens, that when their course is run, and hope can no longer be indulged, their attention is forced back on the scenes of life, through which they have already passed. When in this manner they are brought to recollect the numberless sins, to the commission of which their various dispositions have led them, and to forebode the punishments that await them, their souls are convulsed with remorse, and horror takes full possession of them : " Wretched creatures that we are ! Our impetuous passions have hurried us into all wickednesses, those only excepted which our powers were too feeble and narrow to add to the rest. Would to God we had been brutes, or could yet have our portion with them, to be turned for ever into earth and rottenness ! O that we had been heathens, and had never heard the gospel of Christ, and the law of the Most Holy ! Our abominable iniquities are dreadfully aggravated by the opportunities we have had of being present in the assemblies of Zion, and receiving the instructions and reproofs of life. Instead of deriving benefit from the ordinances of God's worship and the communion of saints, we have exposed ourselves to the reproach of the whole assembly of the pious. By our example we have grieved some, and caused others to stumble. Our hell must be heated seven times more than the hell of heathens !''

The words in the 14th verse may be translated, *In a moment I am in all evil, &c.* ' I am suddenly punished with all the plagues threatened by the ministers of God, and made a spectacle of misery and horror to the whole congregation.' It is an aggravation of that misery which is the fruit of a man's own ways, when publicity is one of its attendant circumstances *.

They who will not believe the threatenings of God shall feel them. There are no free-thinkers in hell, and but few on a death-bed. How happy are they who are preserved by the grace of God from laying up treasures of wrath against the last days, and planting thorns to line their death-bed pillows !

To avoid uncleanness, let every man have his own wife, and let him love her as himself. This remedy against such a vice Solomon illustrates in a beautiful allegory.

Ver. 15.—19. *Drink waters out of thine own cistern, and running waters out of thine own well. Let thy fountains be dispersed abroad, and rivers of waters in the streets. Let them be only thine own, and not strangers with thee. Let thy fountain be blessed, and rejoice with the wife of thy youth. Let her be as the loving hind and pleasant roe ; let her breasts satisfy thee at all times, and be thou ravished always with her love.*

---

*Isa. 66:24

Children are in the language of Scripture sometimes compared to waters *. We find Solomon in this passage comparing both wife and children to fountains; for there is as great a difference between the joys of lawful and unlawful love, as there is between the waters of a clear spring, and those which are drunk out of an impure and poisonous stream.

Let every man, to avoid fornication, have his own wife. Then may he reasonably expect to have children who shall be like olive plants around his table, or like fountains dispersed in the streets, pleasant to others, and likely to become one day comforts to their neighbours as well as to their parents. Is not this far better than to have a bastard progeny imposed on him, which he does not know, and yet cannot deny to be his own?

Husbands ought to praise God for virtuous wives, and to observe their good qualities, and call them blessed. They ought to love them as themselves, to wear a cheerful countenance in their company, to take pleasure in them as the companions of their youth, to rejoice in their love, and to treat them with the tenderest affection. They ought to view them with feelings of delight. The pleasant roes are the delight of their masters, who are charmed with that bland and insinuating manner of behaviour which nature teaches them. Much more may it be expected, that this human creature will be dear to our souls, whom God has given us to be the solace of our lives. In old age, when their beauty fades, the kindness of youth is to be retained for them, more especially if they retain those amiable virtues which fade not with the complexion of the countenance.

Wives are to be hated in comparison with Christ;

*Isa. 48:1

but for the sake of Christ, they are to be loved with an affection so ardent, that other women, however beautiful, may appear in their presence like painted flowers *.

It is the duty and the interest of wives, to be adorned with those beauties which will render easy the duties which their husbands owe them. It is indeed the duty of husbands to love their wives, for the sake of God's command, and Christ's example; but it is very difficult to love, where this pleasant affection is not engaged by lovely qualities in the object. Why should husbands and wives tempt one another to sin against God to their own prejudice?

This cordial love in the married state, will produce pleasures far sweeter than were ever found in unlawful love; and what chiefly recommends them is, that they have no sting attending them, and give no offence to God, our Witness and our Judge.

Ver. 20, 21. *And why wilt thou, my son, be ravished with a strange woman, and embrace the bosom of a stranger? For the ways of man are before the eyes of the Lord, and he pondereth all his goings.*

Is it a pleasure to men to affront their Judge, and to provoke the vengeance of an Almighty arm? Will they prefer these poor, and spiritless, and unsatisfying pleasures which he forbids, to those pure delights which are licensed by his goodness? Remember, sinners, that God is present in your close retreats of wickedness! You see him not, because you are blind, but your stupidity cannot banish an omnipresent Deity; your bars and bolts cannot exclude him who fills heaven and earth. Darkness hideth not from him of whom it is said, " The day is thine, the night also is thine." Why should men dare to affront Jehovah,

---

*Eph. 5:25-32

their Maker and their Judge, by doing that in his
presence, which they would be ashamed to do in the
presence of a child ? God will not be mocked. He
will punish the wanton glance, and the lascivious
thought. Where, then, shall they appear who indulge
themselves in acts of criminality ? Will a thief steal in
the presence of the judge, and yet hope to escape vengeance ? And shall abandoned sinners flatter themselves with the thought of escaping the damnation of
hell, from Him who will come to judgment, and will
be a swift witness against adulterers * ?

Sinners think that they will repent, after having for
a while enjoyed the pleasures of sin,—pitiable delusion !

Ver. 22. *His own iniquities shall take the wicked himself, and he shall be holden with the cords of his own sins.*

Sinners will find, when too late, if wonderful mercy
prevent not, that the sorrow which springs from self-
love, is a very different thing from repentance, and
that it is not so easy a matter as the devil told them,
to venture their salvation in the hands of a Redeemer.
They look upon saints as slaves who live an unpleasant
life, but time will convince them, since admonition cannot, that themselves are the slaves, bound in the strongest and most ignominious chains. They are fettered
by vicious affections, and they have neither power nor
will to assert their liberty. The cords of their own
sins shall hold them fast, till they are cast into that
prison from whence there is no release.

This is a wretched condition, but they may thank
themselves. Their own hands forged the chains which
are rivetted upon them. They refused that glorious
liberty proclaimed to them in the word of Christ.

The sinner flattered himself that he did not refuse
redemption, he only delayed the acceptance of it. But

---

*Mal. 3:5, Heb. 13:4

such delays are refusals in God's estimation. To the sinner they are for the most part fraught with ruin.

Ver. 23. *He shall die without instruction ; and in the greatness of his folly he shall go astray.*

He despised instruction during life, and he shall die without it. He expected, that when his mortal career should draw near its close, good ministers should attend him and pray with him. He shall either want that comfort, or it is to be feared that it will not be blessed to him. None but God can awaken a sleeping and stupified conscience ; and when it is awakened, its clamours drown the voice of him who says, " Believe in Christ, and thou shalt be saved."

In his amazing folly, he goes astray in his crooked ways, and is led forth in the first rank of the workers of iniquity *.

Let those who are not yet tainted by this vice bless God, and let them watch and pray. Let the guilty tremble and mourn ; yet despair not. The arm that rescued Solomon is not weakened. The blood that cleansed the Corinthian whoremongers has lost none of its virtue.

Proverbs 6

I N this chapter we are cautioned by the wise man, against rash suretiship, idleness, mischievousness, and especially against impurity, together with a variety of other sins, exceedingly hateful to God.

---

*2 Peter 2:11

The first five verses contain a warning against sure-tiship.

Ver. 1, 2. *My son, if thou be surety for thy friend, if thou hast stricken thy hand with a stranger, thou art snared with the words of thy mouth, thou art taken with the words of thy mouth.*

God graciously directs our temporal affairs by his providence, and condescends, in his word, to give us instructions concerning them. If we regard not these, we need not be surprised though his providence convince us, by dear-bought experience, of our folly and sin.

He forbids us to become surety, even for a friend, (except for some weighty reason,) and to strike hands with a stranger, in token of our becoming bound for our friend's debts. Men who think only of the present time, are generally too rash in undertaking; but they ought to remember, that the time to come is before them, and will be present time when the time now present is past. If the money were to be paid just now, they would hesitate and deliberate before acting, lest they should wrong their families; but Solomon tells them, that men may ensnare and entangle themselves with the words of their mouths, as well as with the works of their hands.

This consideration may alarm those who have already implicated themselves by such engagements. This kind teacher, therefore, puts them on a plan to get free.

Ver. 3. *Do this now, my son, and deliver thyself, when thou art come into the hand of thy friend : go, humble thyself, and make sure thy friend.*

By rash suretiship, you put yourself into the power, not only of the creditor, but of the debtor, for whom you are bound. You lie at his mercy. He has it in his power to make you smart severely for your foolish kindness to him. The world is full of complaints about ungrateful men, who have basely abused, to the prejudice of their benefactors, the goodness they have experienced. Endeavour, therefore, by the humblest behaviour toward your friend, to induce him to take the proper steps to bring you out of your present embarrassed situation ; for if you peevishly reflect on him as the means of bringing you into it, he may be provoked to use his advantage to your loss.

The wise man is very urgent with his scholars to take this step.

Ver. 4, 5. *Give not sleep to thine eyes, nor slumber to thine eye-lids. Deliver thyself as a roe from the hand of the hunter, and as a bird from the hand of the fowler.*

A roe and a bird are creatures destitute of reason, yet when entrapped by the arts of the sportsman, they will try every method of escape, and make no delay in using every effort for regaining their freedom. May not equal prudence and attention to their own interests, be expected from reasonable creatures !

But what is the great importance of this precept, that Solomon will not allow his disciple to rest till he is free from these rash engagements ? Has this precept any connection with our spiritual interest ? It has. It is a part of the eighth commandment, and though men regard it rather as a loss than a sin to endanger their outward estate, it is both a sin and a temptation. Men who once seemed upright in their dealings, have brought reproach upon religion, by living and dying in other men's debt, and by having recourse to unjustifiable methods, suggested by distress, to relieve themselves.

The effect of suretiship, even with the most upright men, has often proved hurtful to their souls, embittering their days, and unfitting them for the cheerful services of religion. It has not unfrequently rendered them unable to perform those services to God and to his church, for the sake of which a competency of the good things of life is to be valued. We are the servants of Christ, and must not disqualify ourselves for his service, by making ourselves needlessly the servants of men.

The precept here given may remind us, how foolish it is for us to make ourselves debtors to divine justice, to please any friend in the world. When one tempts you to commit any sin, however small, consider whether it would be wise in you to make yourselves debtors even to man on his account.

As we are all in debt to God, let us give no sleep to our eyes, till we implore his mercy. How powerful must be that lethargy which closes in sleep eyes that shall awake in hell, if another day of life is not granted by the abused long-suffering of God! We may be ashamed to humble ourselves to our friends, or our applications to them may be fruitless. But God is equally glorious in majesty and mercy. He delights in forgiving thousands of talents.

The wise man next proceeds to warn us against the vice of sluggishness, to which he was a constant enemy.

Ver. 6. *Go to the ant, thou sluggard; consider her ways, and be wise.*

God has taught us more than the beasts of the earth, and made us wiser than the fowls of heaven. But the sluggard equals not in wisdom the least of insects. He complains that he is not able to work, but has he less strength than an emmet? " The ants, (says another wise man), are a people not strong, yet they prepare their meat in the summer ;" they therefore shall be his judges.

Why has God made such a multitude of creatures, that are of no use to man? Why has he made some that destroy his property? This is a vain question. We are sure that God has made them all in wisdom, and that he has made some of them teachers of wisdom to us. The ant devours some part of our sustenance, but it will pay us well for it, if we are wise enough to improve by its lessons. Every ant-hill is a school, and the wisest of men gives these little animals a testimonial, recommending their instructions to us. That man makes a god of his belly, who thinks no creature of any use to us but such as gives us its flesh to eat, or its labour to provide for our sustenance or comfort. The wisdom which some of them teach is far more valuable than the food with which they supply us.

Other creatures are teachers to us as well as the ant. Look on the whole brutal creation, O atheist! and confess their Maker. Go to the oxen and the asses, O unthankful man! and be wise to acknowledge thy Benefactor. Consider the fowls of the air, ye that are of little faith, and trust the providence of God!

Why does the wise man single out the ant as a teacher of wisdom to the sluggard? Agur gives us one reason in the 30th chapter of this book,—their weakness, which may render the sluggard ashamed of his silly excuses. Another reason we find assigned by Solomon in this place.

Ver. 7, 8. *Which having no guide, overseer, or ruler, provideth her meat in the summer, and gathereth her food in the harvest.*

The bees are a very industrious people, but they have a queen to require their labour, and if she dies they will work no more. The ant has no guide to set her an example, no overseer to inspect her work, no ruler to exact her task ; and yet she neglects not a day in summer, when the roads are clean and the sky clear; or in harvest, when the grain can be had in plenty. She improves every opportunity to store up provisions, that she may spend in comfort the days of cold and scarcity. And what is the result of all her toil? In winter she enjoys plenty, when other creatures are pinched with poverty, or perish with cold and hunger.

We have guides to set us a good example. We have overseers and rulers appointed us by the King of nations, and the King of Zion. Yet how many sluggards are to be found among us, who spend their days in vanity! They are like butterflies, which wanton away the best days of their existence, when they ought to be like ants, suffering no summer day to pass unimproved.

These little animals have knowledge of the times, and are wise to improve opportunities. They join with the stork, and the crane, and the swallow, in reproving those who know not the judgment of the Lord, and neglect the duty of the day in its day.

There are sluggards who bring misery upon them. selves in this world. There are far more who bring eternal misery upon their souls, by neglecting the happy opportunities afforded them by the long-suffering of the Lord, for securing their everlasting interests. They see many days of the Son of man, and enjoy the beams of the Sun of righteousness. They are called with a loud voice to arise and shine, but they are less concerned about an everlasting duration of happiness or misery, than the despised ant about the provisions of a few months. How will they mourn at the last, and say, " The summer is past, and the harvest is ended, and we are not saved!"

The sluggard will not awake from his sleep to go and

learn wisdom, but the wise man goes to him to break his slumbers.

Ver. 9. *How long wilt thou sleep, O sluggard! when wilt thou awake out of thy sleep?*

It is a great waste of time, to spend in sleep more hours than are necessary. Yet from the practice of how many does it appear, that they have adopted the maxim of the Indians,—That rest is better than work, and lying better than sitting, and sleeping better than waking, and death better than life!

It is a shame for men to give up to sleep a third part of their time, but it is not less so to spend our waking hours in doing nothing, or in doing what is as unprofitable. All the world would despise a man who should keep his bed from morning till night, though in the possession of perfect health; but in what respect is he better employed, who trifles away in idleness every hour of the day? He is still worse, for want of employment and weariness of life will lead him to seek relief in impertinent and mischievous talk, or in sensual indulgencies, or in meddling with the matters of others.

If a man of rank should come to the sleeper's bedside, while he is dozing away the morning-hours, and should call him to rise, it might be expected that he would be covered with confusion, and instantly shake off the bands of slumber; but here the wise king comes and draws aside his curtains, and expostulates with him, —" How long wilt thou sleep, O sluggard!" The sluggard's ears are heavy with sleep, and cannot hear. Solomon cries again, " When wilt thou awake out of thy sleep?" Does the sluggard now hear? The voice is loud enough to pierce his ears, but he hears as if he heard not. He is nailed to his bed by sloth, and though conscious that he should arise and walk, he pleads hard for a little delay.

Ver. 10. *Yet a little sleep, a little slumber, a little folding of the hands to sleep.*

He forms some faint resolutions to awake, and it is only a short respite from that torment that he begs—" a little sleep." If that is too much—" a little slumber ;" or if even that cannot be granted, " a little folding of the hands to sleep," is but a moderate request.

The sluggard himself cannot vindicate his sloth, and is resolved to shake it off, only he will not do it presently. From time to time he defers the hated reformation, and what is the consequence ?

Ver. 11. *So shall thy poverty come as one that travelleth, and thy want as an armed man.*

The house of the sluggard is the haunt of poverty, and it comes not like an invited guest, whose visit is expected, but like a traveller, whose approach is unforeseen. It comes like an armed man, and gains an easy victory over the naked and slumbering sluggard. Had he been awake and busy, .he might easily have defended himself against its assaults.

Sleep, sloth, and delay, are the thieves of time. By them vigorous bodies have been often enervated, shining talents covered with rust, estates melted into nothing ; and what is a thousand times worse, millions of souls have been betrayed into perdition. The Spirit of God says, " To-day, if ye will hear his voice." The sluggard is not at leisure to-day, but he will hear it to-morrow. To-morrow comes, but the cause of this delay still exists. A thousand to-morrows pass away, and the sluggard is never awakened to wisdom. At last the king of terrors seizes him with irresistible violence, and hurries him to that place of darkness where there is no work, nor device, nor counsel. The soul must then appear before the awful Judge ; and what excuse can be made for these delays of complying with the voice of the great God ? If a king were to call us to

come to him, in order to receive some great favour at
his hands, we surely would not shew so little respect
to royalty, and so little regard to our own interest, as
to defer from day to day compliance with the kind invitation. Is the majesty of earthly princes so much
revered by us? Yet to the majesty of heaven's great
Lord, it bears only the same proportion that a spark
does to the sun.

The idle man is bad, but the mischievous man is still
worse; but indeed it generally happens, that he who
is enslaved by the one of these vices, becomes in pro-
cess of time the slave of the other also.

Ver. 12—15. *A naughty person, a wicked man, walketh
with a froward mouth. He winketh with his eyes, he
speaketh with his feet, he teacheth with his fingers: Frowardness is in his heart, he deviseth mischief continually;
he soweth discord. Therefore shall his calamity come
suddenly; suddenly shall he be broken without remedy.*

The mischievous person casts off the yoke of God,
but he remains the willing and active servant of the
devil. He rebels against God beyond his might, and
beyond nature presses the members of his body into
the service of iniquity. He not only speaks, but walks
with a froward tongue, making a constant trade of
slandering his neighbours, and spreading dissension.
His tongue is a world of iniquity, and yet it does not
serve him sufficiently for expressing the wickedness of
his heart. To supply its defects, therefore, he makes
artificial tongues of his eyes, his fingers, and his feet.
By winking with his eyes, by stamping with his feet,
and by pointing with his fingers, he shews the scorn
and the malice which he bears towards others, and
conveys his instructions to his accomplices in wickedness.

It is the malice of his heart that employs all the
members of his body, as the instruments of his un-

righteousness. His heart overflows with malignity, and is still running over into the words and works of mischief. The greatest miser takes some rest to his body, from the toils by which he expects to enrich himself; but the heart of this profligate wretch takes no rest from the contrivances of wickedness. He is perpetually torturing his own brain, in devising methods for destroying the happiness and the peace of others.

What will be the end of a fiend like this? He shall, while dreaming of success in his hellish plans, fall a prey to some unexpected calamity. He may possibly flatter himself with the intention of repenting of his misdeeds, before called to that war in which there is no discharge; but he is suddenly and irremediably broken. He lived like a devil clothed with flesh, and his soul shall be chased out of his body, to dwell with its kindred devils. He that does evil to others, does a thousand times greater hurt to himself.

O my soul! come not thou into the secret of such creatures. Blessed be God, who checks that corruption which abounds in the hearts of men, and makes the earth a habitable world. Who could live an hour in peace, if God did not provide for our safety, by his all-governing providence? To this must our safety be all ascribed, since evil spirits, numerous and crafty, constantly traverse our earth, and men whose hearts are filled with all iniquity, abound on the face of it *.

The mischievous man is a compound of vices abhorred by the Lord.

Ver. 16—19. *These six things doth the Lord hate; yea, seven are an abomination unto him: A proud look, a lying tongue, and hands that shed innocent blood: An heart that deviseth wicked imaginations, feet that be swift*

---

*Rom. 3:10-18

in running to mischief: *A false witness that speaketh lies, and him that soweth discord among brethren.*

Every sin is hateful to God. The sins enumerated in this passage are not mentioned, because there are not others as hateful to God, but because they are nearly allied to that vice which had been last reprobated by the wise man, and are generally found in the character of the mischievous person. They are all abhorred by him who is the guardian of his creatures, and the avenger of injuries done to his saints.

Pride leads the van of this troop of iniquities. Its palace is the heart, but its throne is erected in the eye, whence it looks with disdain upon men, and lours defiance towards Heaven. The proud man is not only a rebel to God, but a usurper of his dignity. He would be a God to men, but the living and true God looks upon him with contempt and indignation, and spurns him into hell *.

A lying tongue is abhorred by men, because it tends to the dissolution of society. The devil was a liar from the beginning, and is the father of lies. It is by means of lying that this adversary of man carries on his work. The God of truth hates liars. • He has barred the gates of heaven fast against them, for none of them are his people †.

Murder is a crime against which the first law enacted after the fall was passed ‡. Providence seldom suffers it to escape unpunished in this world. Mighty tyrants, who shed the blood of the innocent without fear of human vengeance, escape not punishment from the King of nations. The wicked Emperors of Rome, and many persecuting and bloody kings, are instances of this truth. They shed the blood of men, and God

---

*Chap. 3:32   †John 8:44, Rev. 21:27, Isa. 63:8   ‡Gen. 9:5

gave them blood to drink. That murder which lies hidden in the heart, or breaks forth only in the tongue, escapes not the eye and the vengeance of the Almighty *.

The first motions of sin in the hearts of men are offensive to God. How greatly then must he abhor that heart, which employs itself in contriving wickedness, and forms deliberate purposes of sin! A royal chamber, filled, like that of Pharaoh, with frogs and vermin, is not so loathsome as a human heart, that should be the residence of God, filled with evil imaginations and hellish contrivances. It may well be called, like Babylon in ruins, a habitation of devils, and a hold of every unclean and foul spirit.

Sin is bad enough when men venture upon it with reluctance and fear, but when they are cheerful in the practice of it, and thus run swiftly to mischief, it is a sign that they are veterans in the devil's army, and have in a great degree conquered their consciences. The feet of such transgressors shall slide in due time, for the things that shall come upon them make greater haste than their feet can possibly do, either to do evil, or to escape the punishment which is their due.

A false witness that speaketh lies, is the most dangerous pest of human society. Who can insure any man's life, or fortune, or character against his tongue, which is like a two-edged sword, or against his throat, which is an open sepulchre, to swallow up every thing dear to men? But the God whose awful name is profaned by these enemies of mankind, holds them in abhorrence, and will by no means permit them to escape punishment †.

The sowers of discord among brethren, are worse than those who set fire to the houses of their neighbours. They kindle flames which burn with unre-

---

*1 John 3:19, Matt. 5:22   †Ps. 36:4

lenting fury, and set on fire families and provinces, and sometimes even nations themselves. They not only sin, but, like Jeroboam the son of Nebat, they cause multitudes to sin, destroying that charity which is the soul of every commandment, and disseminating those corrupt passions, which prove incentives to all the works of mischief. The God whose commandments are all included in love, and who sent his Son to be our peace, cannot but abhor these sons of Belial. Surely he will make their mischiefs to recoil with an awful vengeance upon their own heads.

The wise man proceeds again to warn us against the snares of the strange woman ; but first he renews his call to attend to those instructions which are the only effectual preventives from her dangerous artifices.

Ver. 20—21. *My son, keep thy father's commandment, and forsake not the law of thy mother. Bind them continually upon thine heart, and tie them about thy neck.*

The inspired writer takes it for granted, that the instructions of parents will correspond with the law of God. Can it be supposed that parents will give stones instead of bread, or serpents instead of wholesome nourishment, to their children ? If they do, they are not to be obeyed, for they act not as parents, but as enemies.

The children of Jonadab denied themselves, for many generations, some of the pleasures of the land of Canaan. This they did from a regard to the advice of their progenitor. But when the commands of our earthly parents only enforce those laws of our heavenly Father which are designed for our own benefit, every motive of interest and duty, whether divine or human, concurs to enforce our obedience.

These laws ought to be bound continually upon our hearts, that they may be ever present to our souls. The ancient Israelites wore them on their garments, but let us wear them on our hearts, and tie them about our necks as the most precious ornament.

We must read the instructions of God, and hear the good instructions of men, with attention. We must transcribe them into our hearts, and meditate upon them, and make them the guide of our lives. Hereby much good shall come unto us.

Ver. 22. *When thou goest, it shall lead thee ; when thou sleepest, it shall keep thee ; and when thou awakest, it shall talk with thee.*

We derive much enjoyment and security from having a companion who can entertain us with agreeable conversation, direct us in doubtful paths, and protect us from impending dangers. All these valuable purposes are served by the word of God.

When we walk, it will be our guide, and enable us to avoid every bad step. It will lead us in safety to the land of uprightness, at which none can arrive, who walk according to the course of this world, fulfilling the desires of their flesh and their mind *.

When we sleep, it will keep us. There is nothing improbable in supposing that foolish and distressing dreams may be prevented, by the sweet composure which it imparts to the spirit. But be this as it may, we know well that the providence of God will perform the promises of the word of God. By it we shall be preserved from the pestilence that walketh in darkness, and from the malicious snares of those invisible enemies who wake when we sleep, and who, when not checked by the power of God, have methods of disquieting our minds and destroying our peace in the season of rest. Job's fancy was harassed by the devil in his sleep. That, however, was an extraordinary case, and

*Ps. 119:1

even then the rage of that cruel enemy was under restraints.

The word of God will be an entertaining and useful companion to us, when we awake from sleep. It will talk to us of the loving-kindness of the Lord, and the grace of our Redeemer. It will give us the best advices about the business of the day, and teach us to order every step with discretion. If we cannot sleep in the night, it will suggest meditations far more pleasant to our minds, than is refreshing sleep to the body of the worn-out labourer *.

How does the law of the Lord answer all these purposes ?

Ver. 23. *For the commandment is a lamp, and the law is light ; and reproofs of instruction are the way of life.*

It is necessary to have a lamp, when one is in a dark place. The law of God is a lamp to dispel the darkness of this world, and to guide our steps in safety. But as it may be compared to a lamp, because it gives us light in the night, so also to the sun, because it is the light of the world. Christ, who is the Sun of righteousness, shines upon us by the word of his grace, enlightening our minds in the knowledge of every useful truth, and guiding us in safety to a better world. If we shut our eyes on this light, we walk in darkness ; but those who walk under its beams, have the light of Heaven shining on their paths. The places that want it, are the dark places of the world ; and the souls that receive not the rays of this luminary, are but dungeons in which the day-star has not risen.

It will be allowed, that the doctrines and precepts of the word of God are useful and pleasant as the light ; but are not the reproofs of it very disagreeable ? No † ; the reproofs of it convey necessary and most bene-

---

*Ps. 63:5, 139:18   †Ps. 119:103

ficial instruction. They are like the admonitions of a kind father, who will not suffer his son to follow those courses which he knows would be his ruin. The reproofs of the law may alarm and terrify, but they are not to be less valued on that account. The threatenings of hell guard the way to heaven, and strongly urge us to keep the King's high-way, the only way of safety. The admonitions given us against sin, have a powerful tendency to keep us from the paths of the destroyer.

Ver. 24. *To keep thee from the evil woman, from the flattery of the tongue of a strange woman.*

The insinuating language of a bad woman is nothing but flattery. She professes the fondest love, but she designs the gratification of her own detestable passions, and the serving of her interests, at the expence of what is most valuable to her fond admirer. Her tongue is full of falsehood. By her fair speeches the unwary youth, whom she wishes to seduce, is in great danger of being entangled, and is therefore in great need of some effectual preservative. Now, the only effectual preservative against the dangers of temptation is the word of God. A good education, a sense of honour, the principle of self-interest,—may have some efficacy for this end ; but the great means blessed by God for this purpose is his own word, which is the sword of the Spirit, by which he enables us effectually to resist and baffle, not only flesh and blood, but principalities and powers. Every part of the word of God serves to promote purity in all its branches. No pasages of it are more effectual to preserve us from fleshly lusts, than the warnings of Paul to the Corinthians *, and those of Solomon in various parts of this book.

***

*1 Cor. 6

Solomon knew well from experience, that it is extremely dangerous to give sin indulgence in the heart, though we design not to practise it. He therefore warns us against lusting after the beauty of the strange woman in our heart.

Ver. 25. *Lust not after her beauty in thine heart; neither let her take thee with her eye-lids.*

The beauty that sparkles in the eye of a virtuous woman is a lovely ornament. The beauty of the strange woman is a temptation to the unwise, for to others it appears like a beautiful garment on a body covered with loathsome sores, or a jewel of gold in a swine's snout.

The lust of the heart is adultery in the sight of God, and it were better to have our eyes plucked out, than to have our hearts inflamed with lust *. But impure imaginations do not ordinarily rest in quiet. They push on the man that harbours them, to outward acts of sin. When lust hath conceived, it bringeth forth sin; and sin, when it is finished, bringeth forth misery.

Ver. 26. *For by means of a whorish woman a man is brought to a piece of bread; and the adulteress will hunt for the precious life.*

Poverty is the object almost of horror to the greater part of men. The desire of removing or preventing it, is the grand spring which keeps the world constantly in motion. But the adulterer drives on furiously towards it, for though as much afraid of it as other men, he is hurried along in his wild career by tyrannizing passions, that have blinded his eyes, and taken possession of his soul to such a degree, that he must have them gratified, though ruin be the inevitable consequence †.

Life is so precious, that a man will give for it all

---

*Matt. 5:29   †Luke 15

that he hath. Yet the infatuated whoremonger sells his life at a cheaper rate than a wise man would sell his dog. He flatters himself indeed that he shall escape vengeance ; but the scripture assures us that such hopes are self-delusions, and that a man may as well expect to remain unhurt though he take fire to burn himself, or walk on burning coals.

Ver. 27—29. *Can a man take fire in his bosom, and his clothes not be burnt? Can one go upon hot coals, and his feet not be burnt? So he that goeth in to his neighbour's wife; whosoever toucheth her shall not be innocent.*

Sodom and Gomorrah are standing illustrations of this awful truth. You say, " The burning of these cities was a strange act, scarcely any thing similar to it has happened since." But God hath set forth these cities as an example, making them to suffer the vengeance of eternal fire *, and impenitent sinners will find at the last, that they who despised the words of Solomon, and of Christ himself, shall suffer more severely than the cities of the plain, whose iniquities were not so terribly aggravated, by despised means of instruction and reformation.

Stealing is a detested sin, and exposes men to severe punishment ; but it is much less heinous than adultery, nor will the punishment of it be so great.

Ver. 30.—35. *Men do not despise a thief, if he steal to satisfy his soul when he is hungry: But if he be found, he shall restore seven-fold ; he shall give all the substance of his house. But whoso committeth adultery with a woman, lacketh understanding ; he that doeth it destroyeth his own soul. A wound and dishonour shall he get, and his reproach shall not be wiped away. For jealousy is the rage of a man, therefore he will not spare*

*Jude 6, Job 31:12

in the day of vengeance. He will not regard any ransom ; neither will he rest content, though thou givest many gifts.

Theft is a sin deservedly abhorred, and they who are guilty of it expose themselves to contempt and indignation. Yet when necessity tempts a man to steal, he is the object of pity rather than of scorn. No necessity can excuse any sin, but apparent necessity may extenuate it. This plea, however, cannot be urged to palliate the crime of adultery, which is always the effect of a wicked disposition, and an impure imagination.

When a man steals, it is perhaps to satisfy his soul, and to appease the cravings of hunger, which is an appetite too fierce for human nature to oppose. But unclean actions are the gratifications of brutal lust, and tend not to the preservation, but to the destruction of the life.

Yet a thief must suffer, although he is pitied when hunger urges him on to steal. He shall restore manifold, according to the law ; and if he cannot make the ample restitution required, he must give all the substance of his house. How then does the adulterer hope to escape a much more grievous punishment, for a crime which can admit of no reparation ? A thief may steal for want of bread, but the adulterer sins because he has no understanding. He exposes himself to a deadly wound from a jealous husband, or an avenging magistrate. He contracts a blot upon his name which adheres to it indelibly, and spreads itself even to his children *. He may give all the substance of his house to the man whom he has injured, but it will not be accepted as an atonement for his life ; for a fire of jealousy is kindled, which can be quenched only in his blood.

---

*Deut. 23:2

This argument may be supposed to have little weight among us, who punish theft more severely than adultery. But when crimes that deserve death escape punishment from men, God, the King of all nations, punishes them by his providence, and sometimes with greater severity, because his earthly ministers neglect to shew his resentment of them. Hophni and Phineas, Amnon and Absalom, gained nothing by the indulgence of their fond parents. David himself smarted severely under the rod for this sin, though divine mercy exempted him from death. Earthly magistrates often punish thieves and highwaymen more severely than adulterers, but whoremongers and adulterers God will judge. We may without presumption suppose, that even in this world he often brings them to a gibbet, by suffering them to imbrue their hands in blood, or to commit other capital crimes. The Bible assures us, that God often punishes one sin, by permitting the transgressor to fall into another ; and particularly, that God has given up men to uncleanness, for the indignities they have done to his own name *, and along with it, to other iniquities that bring vengeance in their train †.

If these sinners escape outward punishment, let them remember how terrible that destruction is, which God has designed for them, and how impossible it will be to escape from the Judge of all. They complain that they cannot extinguish their burning lusts, but it shall be more impossible to extinguish the fire that shall never be quenched ‡.

---

*Rom. 1:23   †Rom 1:29 etc.   ‡Job 31:3, Matt. 5:28

Proverbs 7

SOLOMON was deeply impressed with a sense of the evil of profligate courses. Nor was he less fully convinced of that danger to which young men are exposed, from the temptations presented by those factors for hell, who, lost to all sense of shame and interest, precipitate themselves, and as many along with them as they can, into an everlasting hell, and all for the momentary gratification of a base and brutal passion. On this subject he had already said as much as might have served to guard any man against this danger, who was not under the influence of a very dark mind, and a very depraved heart. But he wishes to penetrate the heart of the most hardened, to rouse to thought the most inconsiderate of the sons of men. He thinks that too much cannot be said on a matter of such concernment to us.

We have in this chapter an affecting illustration of the danger of youthful lusts. The mode of instruction to which our teacher in the present instance has recourse, is the narration of a piece of history or parable, (for it matters not which), of the most instructive kind. Will any one dare to venture on temptations that lead to impurity, after Solomon has set before his eyes in so lively a manner, the danger of so much as going near the harlot's house? Then is he as inexcuseable as the man who dances on the brink of a precipice, when he has just seen another, who ventured to display his courage in the same manner, fall headlong from his place, and dashed to pieces on the rocks below, perish the sad victim of his own rashness and folly.

The danger of vicious courses should mightily recommend to us the word of God, which is able to keep us from falling *, and to which self-ruined sinners give testimony, when they must acknowledge too late, that their misery began in their disregard to that blessed book. What would not men give for an antidote that could preserve them from every bodily disease? If any person, possessed of such a medicine, were to perish by some fatal distemper, in consequence of neglecting to have recourse to it, surely his fate would excite no commiseration.

Ver. 1.—5. *My son, keep my words, and lay up my commandments with thee. Keep my commandments, and live, and my law as the apple of thine eye. Bind them upon thy fingers, and write them upon the table of thine heart. Say unto wisdom, Thou art my sister ; and call understanding thy kinswoman : That they may keep thee from the strange woman, from the stranger which flattereth with her words.*

When a man has got possession of some precious jewel, he will deposit it in some place secured from the depredations of thieves. The words of God are infinitely more precious than diamonds, and ought to be laid up in our hearts, and kept with constant diligence and caution. They are to be kept as our life, for we are but dead men if we lose them, and they are the effectual instruments by which God is pleased to quicken men to newness of life, and to nourish, and strengthen, and preserve their souls. Without them,

---

*Acts 20:32

the life of the body is no better than a dream. It is our advantage that God has in view, in furnishing us with a rule of conduct. " Be holy," is the sum of the whole law ; and its excellency is, that it is as good as it is holy and just. Those, therefore, who neglect it, regard lying vanities, and despise their own mercy.

God expresses that regard which he has for his people, and that compassionate care which he exercises over them, by affirming that he who touches them touches the apple of his eye. No less regard is certainly due on our part to that divine word of his, without which our souls must remain in darkness. The eye is a most precious member, and the apple of the eye is its most precious part. The Author of the body has guarded that part of it with a natural fence, and no less vigilance is exercised by us in its protection. We will not, if possible, permit the smallest mote to fall into it. With equal care ought we to observe the law of God, and to avoid every temptation which might induce us in the smallest degree to transgress its commandments *.

The law is to be fixed as a ring upon our fingers, that it may constantly present itself to our view, and deeply impress our hearts. These are the living tables, on which the statutes of the Lord are to be inscribed, that every inward power may be wrought into a suitableness unto them †.

We take great pleasure in the society of amiable friends. Wisdom ought to be our most beloved friend, and our constant companion. With this best of friends let us daily converse, and thus shall we be preserved from the danger of infectious company,

---

*Matt. 5:19   †Rom. 6:16

and the allurements of seducers to vice. Those who love understanding, and call wisdom their sister, are acknowledged by our Saviour himself as his dearest relations *.

When we familiarize ourselves to wisdom, and treat her as a kinswoman, we shall find ourselves great gainers by it. She will preserve us from the strange woman, and from her flatteries. The charms of wisdom will sink her beauty into deformity. The music of wisdom's voice will render us deaf to the most inviting eloquence of her who would tempt us to forget the covenant of our God. Her lips drop as a honey-comb, but wisdom assures us that her end is bitter as wormwood †.

But those who reject wisdom, will find this tempter too cunning for them. Of this Solomon gives us a proof from his own observation. He was a wise observer of men and manners, and the result of his observation, as well as the wisdom which he learned by experience, he has communicated for our caution and instruction.

Ver. 6.—10. *For at the window of my house, I looked through my casement, and beheld among the simple ones, I discerned among the youths, a young man void of understanding, passing through the street near her corner ; and he went the way to her house, in the twilight, in the evening, in the black and dark night ; and, behold, there met him a woman with the attire of an harlot, and subtile of heart.*

Though this story were to be considered as a parable, the instruction it contains is grounded on the observation of Solomon. He was, no doubt, acquainted with many who owed their ruin to the arts which are here described.

---

*Matt. 12:46, 50   †Chap. 5:3,4

Persons of every age, and sex, and condition, ought to watch against the temptations incident to their particular situations, for the great master of deceit knows how to suit his temptations to the different circumstances of men. Young persons, whose passions are warm and whose experience is little, are easily seduced into those sins which gratify the lusts of the flesh. The man whom Solomon observed going towards the house of the strange woman, was a young, man. He was void of understanding, for he had not supplied the want of experience on his own part, by the instructions of the aged, or of the word of God. If young men would be prevailed on to read and study the Book of Proverbs, they would not deserve to be classed among the simple ones ; for it gives subtilty to the simple, to the young man knowledge and discretion.

This young man had no intention to pollute his body with acts of wickedness, (ver. 21.), but in the evening he wished to have a little amusement; and, forgetful of the danger of going near the dwellings of the wicked, he went in the way that leads to the harlot's house. We ought daily to pray that we may be preserved from running into temptation ; for if we invite our enemies to spread their snares for us, how can we expect to escape?

The time of work was over ; and for the purpose of recruiting our spirits, a little evening's relaxation is allowable. Those amusements, however, that lead us into the company of the wicked, are exceedingly dangerous. In our evening walks, let us avoid the places where we are likely to meet with devils, possessed indeed of human shapes, but not of human hearts. Isaac goes out at the evening-tide, to converse with himself and his God, and God sends him a virtuous wife. This poor simpleton goes out to walk in the purlieus of vice, and, behold, he meets with a common harlot, dressed out with that gaudiness of attire which befitted her wicked dispositions; for sometimes the dress of the female is like the sign-post hung out before the house, telling what is within. Her heart was subtle, for she possessed the art as well as the venom of the old serpent. Her manners accorded with her dress and her heart.

Ver. 11, 12. *(She is loud and stubborn; her feet abide not in her house: Now is she without, now in the streets, and lieth in wait at every corner.)*

Her obstreperous tongue is the token of her imperious and stubborn spirit. She loves to reign, and cannot brook subjection to the guide of her youth; thus exemplifying a spirit completely opposite to those godly women ·who call their husbands *lord*. But clamorous and stubborn as she is at home, (where indeed she is seldom to be found), she has the art, when she comes abroad, to fashion her speech to her designs. With soothing words and insinuating flattery, she seduces the unhappy victim of her wiles. She is fierce, like a tiger, but when a purpose is to be gained, can assume all the meekness of a lamb.

She hates her own house, because she abhors useful labour, and holds her husband in detestation; but she is still roaming about those places where she may meet unwary passengers. Like a wild beast of the desert, she constantly prowls about those places where a prey may be expected.

Let women that desire to be thought virtuous be keepers at home; and let them beware of eating the bread of idleness, which, though not always, is oftentimes the companion of profligacy, and never the attendant of virtue.

Thus was the unwary youth caught by one but too well versed in the arts of seduction.

Ver. 13.—20. *So she caught him, and kissed him, and with an impudent face said unto him, I have peace-offerings with me, this day have I paid my vows : Therefore came I forth to meet thee, diligently to seek thy face, and I have found thee. I have decked my bed with coverings of tapestry, with carved works, with fine linen of Egypt. I have perfumed my bed with myrrh, aloes, and cinnamon. Come, let us take our fill of love until the morning ; let us solace ourselves with loves. For the goodman is not at home, he is gone a long journey : He hath taken a bag of money with him, and will come home at the day appointed.*

Modesty is the lovely ornament of the female sex, and nothing can be more hateful than a woman that hath renounced it. When this fence of virtue is demolished, profligacy is the natural and unavoidable consequence.

The words and the behaviour of this abandoned creature are alike shameless. Yet, with marvellous inconsistency, she pretends to a sense of religion. The feast which she intends for her lover, is that part of the peace-offerings which, according to the law, she had reserved for herself and her friends, after paying her vows to the Lord. It is strange to tell, and yet certainly true, that there are persons who endeavour to join together the service of God and Belial. They must have their passions gratified, and in all other things they will be obedient to the dictates of conscience. But those who think that they may sometimes eat a little poison, provided they take wholesome food at other times, and yet live and enjoy tolerable health, are not more foolish. God is glorious in shewing mercy to sinners, but he will shew none to sin *.

She pretends a special and tender regard for this miserable youth, whom she wishes to draw into her snares, and has the address to avail herself of an accidental meeting for the proof of it. Words are very cheap, and the warmest professions of kindness are for the most part the most insincere. The old serpent made use of this artifice to deceive our common mother. There is nothing that renders the young a more easy prey to deceivers, than their inexperience of the emptiness of the professions of many.

This abandoned woman artfully entangles the heart of the simple youth, by promising him every thing that can afford delight to any of his senses. She will entertain him with the delicate provision of which feasts were made, after performing the ceremonies of religion. His eyes shall be entertained with the sight of furniture, equally valuable for its materials and workmanship. The bed is decked with the finest linen, and the whole house perfumed with odours, emitted by the most fragrant herbs. All these pleasures, she informs him, may be enjoyed in the most perfect security, for the goodman (she takes care not to call him husband,) is gone far from home; and it is certain that he will not return till the time appointed, for he has a great deal of business to transact, and has carried a great deal of money with him, to bear his expences, and to employ in trade.

Beware of those sins that are represented to you as pleasant sins. They are more dangerous than others, because they most easily gain the heart, and most powerfully guard it against repentance. Eve found

---

*Ps. 68:31, Zeph. 1:15

that the pleasure of forbidden fruit was only an introduction to horror and remorse.

Our hearts must be guarded against the admission
of sin, by stronger motives than the fear of detection
and disgrace; for artful solicitors to evil, will easily
baffle such restraints as these. Joseph might have
expected his master's favour by complying with the
desires of his mistress, but the motive that induced him
to decline her company was irresistible,—" How can
I do this great wickedness, and sin against God?"

But the unhappy subject of the wise man's story
was not a Joseph.

Ver. 21. *With much fair speech she caused him to
yield, with the flattering of her lips she forced him.*

There is a force in words, which it is often almost
impossible to resist. Good words have a wonderful
virtue in them to work upon the mind, and a great
part of the good which we are called to do in the
world, is to be accomplished by means of that little
member—the tongue. But corrupt minds are often
found to have greater influence in persuading men to
sin, because human nature is depraved, and needs only
a temptation to draw men to the practice of the worst
of evils.

No words have greater force in them to persuade
men to sin, than the flatteries of the strange woman;
and therefore the apostle Paul, who directs us to strive
against sin, calls loudly to us to flee youthful lusts.
Such lusts can scarcely be conquered but by flight,
because the temptations to them, when they meet
with a simple mind and an impure heart, are like
sparks of fire lighting upon stubble fully dry.

The force that is in the tongue of the strange woman, will not excuse the deluded youth; for his yielding to her is to be attributed to the depravity of his
own heart, which inclines him to prefer the advice of

a bad woman, to the counsels of the Supreme and Eternal Wisdom. When a thief is arraigned before a magistrate, he is not suffered to escape punishment, because it appears that he had such a propensity to steal, that he could not find in his heart to resist the influence of a temptation.

Ver. 22, 23. *He goeth after her straightway, as an ox goeth to the slaughter, or as a fool to the correction of the stocks : Till a dart strike through his liver, as a bird hasteth to the snare, and knoweth not that it is for his life.*

Poor deluded creature ! The cursed enchantress persuaded him that she would conduct him to a paradise ; but he soon finds his feet entangled in the stocks, and bound with fetters of iron. He is more brutish than the ox, which will not without reluctance go to the place of slaughter, but must be forced and goaded onward by its driver. He is sillier than a bird, which will not sit to be shot, but flies from the appearance of danger : Whereas he wilfully sets himself up as a mark for the arrows of justice. A bird may indeed fly into the snare, for it has not the gift of reason ; but for *men* to hasten into a snare, there is no excuse. God hath made *them* wiser than the fowls of heaven.

It was a good maxim, said to be delivered by an eastern sage,—Do nothing till thou hast well considered the end of it. The time to come will be soon present, and by the exercise of reason and faith, we should make it now present to us. The pleasures of sin will then be seen in a very different light. They will appear to be remorse and anguish, varnished over with a little transient pang of delight that never reaches the heart, or at least plays only on the surface of it. Were a man to live as long as Methuselah, and spend all his days in the highest delights of sin, one hour of the anguish and tribulation that must follow will far outweigh them.

What must we do in order to avoid that infatuation which is so common, and which is attended with consequences so awful?

Ver. 24, 25. *Hearken unto me now, therefore, O ye children, and attend to the words of my mouth. Let not thine heart decline to her ways, go not astray in her paths.*

Let us give the most earnest heed to these calls, that are addressed to us with such urgent and repeated importunity, and let us guard our hearts and ways with all diligence. Indulgence given to any impure imagination, is an indication of a sensual heart, and an introduction to a licentious behaviour, which will in all probability lead to a miserable end.

Ver. 26, 27. *For she hath cast down many wounded, yea, many strong men have been slain by her. Her house is the way to hell, going down to the chambers of death.*

When but one of the disciples was to betray Christ, all of them were anxious lest they should fall into such a horrid sin. When not a small number, but multitudes, have fallen by the force of temptations to impurity, and when the same depraved disposition continues in men, and the same temptations expose them to danger, shall we not fear, and depart from evil?

Men have been wounded and slain by the arts of the strange woman, who seemed to possess resolution and strength to support them against the most dangerous assaults. David was sore wounded; Sampson was slain; and when cedars are shaken and fall, it is time for the fir-trees to be afraid. It is a dangerous piece of self-confidence in us to imagine, that we are possessed of more strength than Sampson, or endowed with more steady virtue than David.

Uncleanness is not the blasphemy against the Holy Ghost, but it is ordinarily a sin unto death. He that has entered on a course of it, is on a staircase that leads down to death and hell ; and the descent makes the brain so giddy, that power is seldom left to make a timely retreat. They are gross self-flatterers, who imagine that they may go on for a time in sensuality, and stop short, and repent when they please. Who but God can say to the waves of sin, " Hitherto shall ye come, and no farther, and here shall your proud swellings be stayed ?"

David repented, and was pardoned, and so we hope was Sampson. The three children were cast alive into a burning fiery furnace, and came out unsinged ; but we will not cast ourselves into the fire, in hope that the same miracle will be wrought for our deliverance. May the Lord keep us from temptation, and pluck out hardened sensualists as brands out of the fire !

Proverbs 8

T HE grand question in this chapter is, What are we to understand by that wisdom which is here introduced, recommending her instructions to us ? The fear of the

Lord is said to be the beginning of wisdom *. But the wisdom that speaks in this passage appears to be a person ; and it is disputed whether we are to understand it of Christ, the great Fountain of wisdom, or of the noble quality of wisdom, represented by a strong eastern figure under a personal character.

This wisdom has been generally understood in the Christian church to mean the Lord Jesus Christ,—the Word (Logos) spoken of by John, who ascribes to him under that name several of those glories which are here ascribed to wisdom.

There are some things spoken of men in the prophetical passages of Scripture, too great to be understood in their full meaning of any of the sons of men, except the man Christ. These we are taught by the Scriptures of the New Testament, to understand of him who is the glory of our race, to whom all the prophets bare witness †. Now, if Solomon say concerning wisdom things that are true to their full extent of signification in Christ only, may we not with good reason conclude, that the Spirit who directed his pen, meant to lead our thoughts to the personal Word of God, in whom are all the treasures of wisdom, 'and to whom the church of Israelites and Christians is indebted for all the discoveries that were ever made? The voice of Christ is the voice of wisdom itself. The wise will hear, and will increase their learning, and fools only will despise this wisdom and instruction ; for surely they cannot be reasonable creatures, who resist the fervent eloquence and the persuasive arguments addressed to us in this chapter.

Ver. 1. *Doth not wisdom cry, and understanding put forth her voice ?*

---

*Chap. 9:10   †Heb. 1:5, Compare 2 Sam. 7:14

Our consciences bear testimony to this truth, that wisdom not only speaks, but cries to us with a voice like the sound of a trumpet. If we do not hear, it is because our ears are shut, or because we turn them away from the truth, to hear the alluring and enchanting voice of sin and its servants; and how shall they excuse themselves who give ear to the voice of the cunning serpent, rather than to the voice of the Eternal Wisdom? But where does wisdom put forth her voice?

Ver. 2, 3. *She standeth in the top of high places, by the way in the places of the paths. She crieth at the gates, at the entry of the city, at the coming in at the doors *.*

If we hear not the voice of wisdom, we have ourselves to blame. Her pulpit is erected in the high places, and her voice is heard from afar. She preaches at the places of concourse, the gates of the city, and in the places where roads meet. At our very doors we may hear her publishing her precious doctrines; and ignorance, when chosen and wilful, will by no means excuse us. If we are in darkness, it is not for want of light, but because we hate light, and by winking hard exclude its beams.

Why should we not use all due pains to find wisdom, when wisdom uses such pains to find us out, and to proclaim her necessary instructions in our ears? Surely our Lord Jesus was willing to communicate his saving instructions, when he preached in mountains and in fields, in public roads and in deserts, in synagogues and in ships, inviting men to receive his salvation, and pressing them to repent. Nor is the voice of wisdom in our days become more feeble, or heard

---

*See Chap. 1:21,22

in fewer places. Unless we are stupidly inattentive, we may still hear it sounding in our ears, whether we are at home or abroad, walking in the fields or sitting in the church. The voice of the gospel, the voice of providence, the voice of conscience, the voice of honest friends, is a cry of wisdom, to which we do well to take heed, for to all of us she speaks.

Ver. 4. *Unto you, O men, I call, and my voice is to the sons of men,*

The mercy of God is sovereign, and therefore the sons of Adam are called to repentance ; while by the angels that fell, no voice of mercy was ever heard. They were nobler in their origin, and more excellent in their natures. But the Son of God loved us because he loved us, and was made of God unto us, and not to them, wisdom and righteousness.

There are many of the sons of Adam, that never heard the calls of wisdom ; but all within hearing are called, and earnestly importuned to comply with the call. Let us not then give reason for that complaint, " Wherefore when I came was there no man, when I called was there none to answer." The disobedient and unbelieving shall be tormented in hell with a soul-rending remorse, which devils and heathens cannot feel.

Say not that the calls of wisdom are not to you, because ye are fools ; for to such she speaks—

Ver. 5. *O ye simple, understand wisdom ; and ye fools, be ye of an understanding heart.*

Those that are easily seduced, those that live under the power of error and sin, are here called to hear the wisdom which is from above. Your case, O ye simple ones ! is not hopeless. Eternal Wisdom is your teacher, and calls you to learn ; and to none does wisdom say, Seek ye me in vain. The teacher is the Lord our God ; and he teacheth to profit, because there is power and light in his words, and in the Spirit that accompanies them *.

Have you been foolish and disobedient? you are called to turn to the wisdom of the just; and there is pardoning mercy revealed to encourage you to turn to the Lord †, there is converting power in the words of wisdom ‡. Your situation is bad, but not desperate ||. Hear the words that are spoken to you, and let them sink into your souls; consider the excellencies of the words, and of the speaker of them.

Ver. 6. *Hear, for I will speak of excellent things; and the opening of my lips shall be right things.*

Where the words of a king are, there is power. The words of wisdom are the princely words of the eternal King. As the sun and moon, these works of God's hands, are more excellent than a machine or clock made by some curious artist, so is the word of God more excellent than the sayings of the wisest and greatest of men. The same divine excellency which appears to reason's eye in the works of God, appears to the eye of faith in the word of God. In the words of the wisest philosophers and most eloquent orators, there are some good and some bad things. There is dross mingled with their silver; but all the words of wisdom are right words, they are like silver seven times purified. They are spoken in perfect righteousness and faithfulness.

Ver. 7. *For my mouth shall speak truth, and wickedness is an abomination to my lips.*

Why do we not all believe the words of Christ? Heaven and earth shall pass away, but one jot or tittle shall not pass from his word. Let us never again be so impious as to suspect the faithfulness of his pro-

---

*Isa. 48:17, Prov. 1:23, Ps. 119:130   †Isa. 55:7   ‡Ps. 19:7
||Ezek. 33:11

mises, or the sincerity of his invitations, or the truth of his precious doctrines. We believe the word of an honest man ; but Christ is the Amen, the faithful and true Witness. All lying is wickedness in his esteem, and is abhorred by his heart. If we believe the word of a man who will not lie, shall we disbelieve the word of him that cannot lie, nor suffer liars to stand in his presence ?

We attend with diligence to the words of a man famous for wisdom and integrity ; but all the words of Christ are the words of wisdom itself, and the things spoken are uprightness, even words of truth.

Ver. 8. *All the words of my mouth are in righteousness, there is nothing froward or perverse in them.*

One of the characters which our Lord takes is, " I that speak in righteousness." Eternal righteousness is in our Lord Jesus Christ, and shines in all his administrations and in all his words. God has given us in his word a representation of the righteousness of his own nature and will, and framed it as a rule of righteousness to us. Those are froward and perverse who walk in ways not authorized by this rule *; and by the degree of our conformity to it, are our improvements in righteousness and true holiness to be estimated. There is righteousness in the promises and doctrines, as well as in the commands of it. God's words of grace are spoken by him in his holiness, and are therefore to be received with an unshaken confidence †. Hath God promised us eternal life, and called us by his word to depend on his Son for salvation ?—We may safely venture our souls upon the faithful word of Jehovah. To doubt whether these addresses to us are sincere or not, is to suspect that there is something crooked or perverse in the faithful sayings of God.

---

*Ps. 125:5 †Ps. 60:7

But is it possible for us to understand the words of wisdom? Yes.

Ver. 9. *They are all plain to him that understandeth, and right to them that find knowledge.*

The words of wisdom are a great depth. In them are mysteries which cannot be fully comprehended; for we find that the all-wise God has laid up in every part of Scripture, stores of wisdom too deep for mortal minds to fathom. There are some passages of Scripture, especially in that part of it which was written after the time of Solomon, in which are things hard to be understood; and yet all the words of wisdom are here said to be plain to him that understandeth. The meaning is, that every thing necessary for faith and practice is clearly revealed in the Bible by the great Author of it, who meant not to insult our ignorance, but to instruct our minds, by that sacred book. When we are puzzled with difficulties, we ought not to quarrel with the Bible, but to ascribe it to our own stupidity or sloth. If, after the due use of means, some parts of Scripture still continue dark to us, let us bless God that the needful doctrines contained in them are in other passages taught with sufficient plainness.

But if these words are plain only to him that understandeth, of what service can it prove for simple * and foolish persons to attend to them? Fools are called not only to hear, but to receive wisdom from our great Teacher, for none teaches like him. Socrates confessed that he could not make any man wise who was not furnished by nature with talents for acquiring wisdom, more than his mother Phœnareta could deliver a woman who was not pregnant. But the en-

---

*Verse 3

trance of God's word gives understanding to the simple, and the Spirit of Christ makes them wise unto
salvation, who were born like the wild ass's colt.

The words of God meet with reproach and banter
from some, who would found a reputation for wit
upon wickedness; but wisdom will be justified of
her children, and her words will be esteemed to be
right concerning all things by them that find knowledge.

What improvement should we make of these commendations given to the words of wisdom? We ought
to receive them with superlative esteem.

Ver. 10, 11. *Receive my instructions, and not silver;
and knowledge, rather than choice gold. For wisdom is
better than rubies, and all the things that may be desired
are not to be compared to it *.*

We profess to prefer wisdom in our judgment to the
most valued things upon earth; but we are hypocrites,
if there is not a consistency between our profession and
our practice. If wisdom is better than silver, we must
receive it rather than silver; and if it were put to our
choice whether to be rich or holy, we ought not for a
moment to hesitate in deciding.

It is actually put to our choice, whether we will seek
first the kingdom of God and his righteousness, or the
delights of sense, and the riches that shine to the eye
of flesh †. If we are resolved at any rate to be rich; if
we value the means of enriching ourselves with gold
above the means of grace; if we grudge the necessary
expence that may attend the means of religious instruction; then we receive gold, and not wisdom. The
truly wise have some degree of Paul's spirit in them,
and are taught by God to count every thing loss and

---

*See Chap. 3:14,15   †Deut. 30:15,19

dung for the excellency of the knowledge of Christ
Jesus their Lord *.

Silver and gold are good things, under the direction
of wisdom †. But they must not be the chief object
of our esteem ; for if any man love the world, the love
of the Father is not in him. Luther, having received
large presents from some princes of Saxony, protested
that he would not have them for his portion. If gold
or rubies are equal to wisdom in our judgment, we
have not the mind of Christ.

That we may be disposed heartily to prefer wisdom
to every thing that our eyes have seen, or our fancies
have imagined, let us hear and believe what more can
be said on wisdom's behalf.

Ver. 12. *I wisdom dwell with prudence, and find out
knowledge of witty inventions.*

For a man to search out his own glory, is no glory ;
but for the Son of God to discover his own glory to us,
is one of the innumerable instances of his condescend-
ing grace. Had he not manifested his own glory to us,
we should, to our loss, have remained for ever ignorant
of it.

Prudence is the companion of wisdom, and infinite
prudence was from eternity familiar to the personal
Wisdom of God, who abounded toward us in all prudence, in the contrivance of that glorious plan by
which the wisdom of God is raised to the highest pitch
in the salvation of men. For the Word was with God,
and was a sharer in the glory of his eternal purpose of
grace. Consummate prudence and divine invention
shine with illustrious splendour in the whole administration of our Lord Jesus Christ, and out of his treasures we receive all that prudence and skill that is ne-

---

*Phil. 3:8   †Ezek. 7:11

cessary for us, whilst sojourning in a world full of enemies and snares.

Who would not rather go for water to a fountain that ever flows, than to a brook that often disappoints the thirsty traveller? The Son of God has the fountain of life with him, and in his light shall we see light.

Perfect purity is another excellency of our divine Teacher, and his instructions have a sanctifying effect upon us.

Ver. 13. *The fear of the Lord is to hate evil. Pride and arrogancy, and the evil way, and the froward tongue, do I hate.*

Some men refrain from evil actions through fear of shame or punishment; but true wisdom teaches men not only to refrain from evil, but to hate it, through the fear of God. Then we are possessed of this gracious principle, when we abhor not only evil actions, but evil words and dispositions. Pride and arrogancy of spirit, wickedness in the course of the conversation, or frowardness in spirit, are equally abhorred by our Lord; and such as have received his instructions into their hearts, cannot love that which is declared in every part of his word to be utterly offensive to him *.

Were any thing deserving the name of wisdom to be found any where else, we might with less damage despise the word of exhortation; but Christ claims it as his peculiar excellency-

Ver. 14. *Counsel is mine, and sound wisdom: I am understanding, I have strength.*

Bildad had referred Job to the wise men that lived in the days of old, as the oracles of wisdom, for deter-

---

*Chap. 6:17-19

mining the disputes between Job and his friends. Job acknowledged that the ancients had some degree of wisdom, but would not implicitly submit his understanding to their maxims, because there was no comparison in this respect between the wisest sages and the Ancient of days *. What is the wisdom of philosophers, who frequently became vain in their reasonings, and spoiled men by their philosophy and vain deceit, to the wisdom of the Eternal Word ? But why should we speak of wise men, when the angels are charged with folly ?

There is no sound wisdom but in Christ, or from him, who is the Fountain of human reason, and the Author of that wisdom which has procured so high a reputation to some that were ignorant of the name of Christ. Whether these great men made their celebrated discoveries by the mere force of their own genius or by the help of tradition, it is plain that their light was but a beam from that true light that lighteth every man that cometh into the world †. Counsel is his, for he is the wonderful Counsellor, between whom and his eternal Father the council of peace was formed, and who by his counsel conducts us in the right way to happiness. The very quintessence of wisdom is his. He is understanding itself, and his eyes penetrate to the bottom of the deepest mysteries. Blessed be God that such a person is made to us wisdom !

Wisdom is better than strength, and yet wisdom needs strength to execute its plans. The eternal wisdom of God is joined with omnipotence. The eternal Word is the Almighty, by whom all things were made, and all the purposes of grace effected. He gives courage and power to all that learn wisdom from him, so

---

*Job 12:12,13,16   †John 1:9

that a man of understanding increaseth strength. Where counsel to contrive and wisdom to propose the noblest end, understanding to discern the true nature and tendencies of things, and strength to execute, concur, there can be nothing wanting.

The wisdom and power of kings, and of those that have power delegated from kings, is derived from him.

Ver. 15, 16. *By me kings reign, and princes decree justice. By me princes rule, and nobles, even all the judges of the earth.*

Eternal wisdom has devised magistracy, and determined the persons to be entrusted with it. From the same source is derived all the majesty, and wisdom, and righteousness which ever appeared in the world, to adorn the thrones of princes. When David governed the people of God according to the good skill of his hands and the integrity of his heart,—when Solomon governed the same nation with wisdom and righteousness, they were indebted for all their noble qualifications to that Word of God, by whom all creatures were formed, and from whom all light is derived *.

When magistrates of inferior rank distinguish themselves by their wise and righteous administration, they owe their glory and usefulness to the same fountain of wisdom †.

Those princes that are strangers to the name of Christ are the ministers of his providence, and are furnished from his treasures with every ornamental and useful qualification which they may possess. If we admire the courage and fortune, the generosity and wisdom of Cyrus king of Persia, we ought to give

---

*John 1:3,9   †Isa. 22:24, Prov. 21:1

glory to the King of Israel, by whom that heathen prince was guided *.

The histories of every nation, through the light of this text, may lead us to contemplate the excellency of the Son of God, from whom every good gift comes. All the wisdom in the world must be ascribed to him, but none of that folly which always attends wisdom in men. His treasures of wisdom are not diminished in the least degree. Let the simple ones apply to him with faith and importunity, and they shall be made wise unto holiness and salvation, for says Wisdom—

Ver. 17. *I love them that love me, aad they that seek me early shall find me.*

All of us profess to love wisdom, but few justify this profession. We do not truly love that person whose friendship we do not seek to share, and whose company we do not desire to enjoy. We do not love Christ if we do not seek him with our hearts, and with all earnestness of spirit desire fellowship with him in his wisdom, and righteousness, and sanctification, and redemption.

They that seek him are accounted by him lovers of his name, and this love to him is a proof that they are loved by him. He loved them before they loved him. His good-will disposed their hearts to love him, and he takes pleasure in that love which was kindled by himself, and will not disappoint those ardent desires which were excited by his Spirit. He has been found of them that sought him not, and will he hide himself from them that seek him ?

Young persons have good encouragement from this Scripture to seek wisdom. Christ was kind to those young children that were brought to be blessed by

---

*Isa. 46

him. He loved a young man who came to ask him
what he should do to inherit eternal life, although he
neither asked a right question, nor shewed a proper
regard to Christ's answer. It is mentioned as the honour of Josiah king of Judah, that when he was
young, he sought the God of his fathers. The word
translated *seek early*, may be rendered *seek earnestly*
or *diligently* *.

All the true lovers and seekers of Christ shall find
him, and find inexpressible happiness in him †. They
are sharers in his fulness, and he opens all his treasures to them.

Ver. 18, 19. *Riches and honour are with me, yea, durable riches and righteousness. My fruit is better than
gold, yea, than fine gold, and my revenue than choice
silver.*

On whom do the kings of this world bestow their
gifts? On their own friends, or on strangers and
enemies? On their friends, no doubt, unless they
are restrained by an interested policy. No motives of
that kind can direct the managements of the eternal
King. The silver is his, and the gold is his; and he
would give silver and gold to all that love him, if he
did not see it better for the greater part of them to
want these perishing riches. It is not for want of
riches and honours to bestow. It is not for want of
love to his people, that he does not bestow on every
one of them crowns of gold, and mines of precious
metals. The riches of Christ are incomparably more
valuable than gold and silver. His justifying righteousness, which is upon all them that believe, enriches
them for ever, though formerly they were indebted
millions of talents, and unable to pay one farthing to

---

*Chap. 7   †John 14:21,22

the justice of God. The grace of the Spirit enriches them above what the finest gold or the choicest silver could ever do. These shining metals glitter in the eye, but they cannot shed joy or contentment in the heart. The only use that riches can answer, is to help us to be content ; but even here riches can do little, whilst godliness does all, and is justly esteemed great gain *.

How wisdom enriches men, we are more clearly told in the next verse.

Ver. 20, 21. *I lead in the way of righteousness, in the midst of the paths of judgment ; that I may cause those that love me to inherit substance, and I will fill all their treasures.*

Great was the favour bestowed by God on the children of Israel, when he conducted them through the wilderness to the land of promise by a pillar of cloud and fire. Had he left them to their own conduct, they must have lost themselves, and perished in that land of desarts, of pits and serpents, of drought and of the shadow of death. Nor could we find the way to the celestial city without the Captain of salvation, who is given by God to be a Leader to the people. He leads us in the paths of righteousness for his own name's sake, and in the midst of the paths of judgment, keeping us from every dangerous mistake, and preserving us from the snares which on each side of our way are spread for our feet.

Our great Teacher leads us in this way, to enrich us with the most precious substance. The followers of Christ shall be no losers by him. They shall not inherit the wind, nor possess for their portion those unsubstantial things, of which it is said—*they are not* †, because they are not the true riches ; but they shall pos-

---

*1 Tim. 6:6   †Prov. 23:5

sess, by the right and tenure of the children of God, that which is durable and solid riches. The fashion of this world passeth away, but he that doth the will of God abideth for ever, and shall be for ever rich, for all his treasures are filled by the wisdom of God. In this world he receives every needful supply, and can say in truth that all things are his *. In the eternal world every craving shall be fully satisfied, and no uneasy desires shall remain.

Blessed are the lovers of wisdom, though the world may account them poor. Have they no silver or gold? The apostles for the most part had none, and yet they made many rich. The angels have none, and desire to have it as little as we desire to have our treasures filled with gravel. Saints are like angels, rich in heavenly treasure; and whilst God is rich, they shall not be poor. Here is a short way of becoming rich, and here covetousness is a virtue.

These blessed treasures of righteousness and glory were designed for the possessors of them before the foundation of the world, and God entered into a covenant of grace with his own eternal Son to provide them; for Christ existed from eternity, and before all worlds he was appointed to be the Author of our salvation, and rejoiced with his Father in the prospect of it.

Ver. 22. *The Lord possessed me in the beginning of his way, before his works of old.*

The Son of God was begotten by the Father before all worlds †; and if we may speak it with reverence, it was the unspeakable blessedness of the most holy God, that he possessed a Son the same in essence with himself, and the brightness of his glory, by whom he designed to make and govern the world, and to shew the

---

*1 Cor. 3:22 †Compare Gen. 4:1

glory of his wisdom in repairing the ruins of it. When the eternal decrees of God were framed in his infinite mind, before any of his creatures were made, the Word was with God, even in the bosom of the Father, and the purpose of God was purposed in him *.

Ver. 23. *I was set up from everlasting, from the beginning, or ever the earth was.*

It was a profane question which a philosopher once asked at a Christian, What God was doing before he made the world? But we have here a serious and delightful answer to it. The Son of God was ordained before the foundation of the world to be the Author of wisdom and salvation to us, and he accounted it his glory to be the foundation of the counsel of God about the administration of grace. The eternal power and Godhead of Christ, are enlarged upon by himself at great length in the following verses.

Ver. 24, 25. *When there were no depths I was brought forth, when there were no fountains abounding with water. Before the mountains were settled, before the hills was I brought forth.*

The antiquity of his existence, of his generation by the Father, and his appointment to be our Redeemer, are expressed in the same language in which the unbeginning duration of the Godhead is described †.

Ver. 26. *While as yet he had not made the earth, nor the fields, nor the highest part of the dust of the world.*

The Wisdom of the Father was in the beginning, but had no beginning to his own existence. The Father himself did not exist before the only-begotten Son, and he that spread abroad the earth by himself, without the assistance of other beings, or the agency of instruments, did not create the world without the everlasting Word.

*Eph. 3:11   †Ps. 90:2

Ver. 27. *When he prepared the heavens I was there, when he set a compass upon the face of the deep.*

Fashioning the great mass of earth and water by a divine architecture, into the most regular form.

Ver. 28, 29. *When he established the clouds above, when he strengthened the fountains of the deep : When he gave to the sea his decree that the waters should not pass his commandment, when he appointed the foundations of the earth. Then was I by him.*

The power and wisdom of God appeared in the order and stability which he gave to the various creatures, as well as in the formation of them. He separated the waters below from the waters above the firmament, and fixed both in their respective places. He confined the waters of the sea within their proper channels, and appointed foundations to the earth, that it might not be removed.

It is our duty to consider the works of God with attention, and to contemplate them in their different parts, which make one beautiful whole ; and every one of these parts is fitted to excite our veneration for the great Author of nature,—the three-one God.

When we survey the earth and the waters, the mountains and the valleys, and consider that they had a beginning, we are led by the Scripture to adore the Word which was with God, and was God, when these creatures that make so good a figure in our eyes were nothing.

When we consider the wisdom and power that shine with amazing lustre in the fabric of the world, let us raise our thoughts to the Son of God, by whom God made the world, and by whom he has now recovered it from the ruins that were the fruits of our sin.

If we reverence the wisdom of the aged, what reverence is due to the unbeginning Word, who condescends to reveal to us the Father, and to disclose the secrets of his wisdom!

When we behold the immense repository of waters, and the spacious earth, when we lift up our eyes to the lofty mountains, and to the immeasureable circuit of the heavens, can we forbear saying, What is man, that he who is before all these things, and by whom they all consist, should regard him with such astonishing favour! and how ungrateful must we be, if we turn a deaf ear to the merciful instructions of our Divine Teacher!

But let us admire, with increasing wonder, the glory and grace of Him who speaks to us from heaven, when we hear him declaring his infinite happiness in the bosom of his Father.

Ver. 30. *Then I was by him, as one brought up with him; and I was daily his delight, rejoicing always before him.*

The blessedness of rational creatures lies in their fellowship with God. Those are blessed whom God makes to approach to himself; and the nearer the approach, the greater the blessedness. But there is infinite blessedness in the Godhead itself, and in that divine and incomprehensible fellowship which the Son of God enjoyed from eternity, whilst he was in the Father's bosom, as his only-begotten Son. The Father was in the Son, and the Son in the Father, and both in the Spirit, and the Spirit in both, and they were infinitely blessed in one another. These things are so mysterious to us, that it is safer to adore and wonder, than to speak. But one thing we cannot overlook, that when we consider the infinite happiness of the Son of God, in his oneness of nature with the Father, and in that infinite nearness of person to him, which must be inferred from the unity of essence, and mutual relation of the persons, we must be a-mazed to think that he bestowed a thought upon men,—upon creatures whose apostacy and wickedness were foreknown by him. Before the world began, he thought upon men with compassion, and rejoiced in the purposes of his love concerning them. Then, (says he,) was I by him,

Ver. 31. *Rejoicing in the habitable part of his earth ; and my delights were with the sons of men.*

It was infinite goodness to rejoice in the prospect of those holy angels, whose dwelling was assigned them in heaven, beside the throne of God. But he delighted in the prospect of that grace and salvation that was de-signed for lost men, through the sufferings to be en-dured in that human nature which was pre-ordained for him.

Did our Lord Jesus think upon us with compassion and love, before the foundation of the world? Let our thoughts be often employed in contemplating that amazing goodness, and in tracing up redemption and the blessings of salvation, to the fountain whence they proceed. Shall we, from day to day, put off the thoughts of Christ, and defer that regard and obedi-ence which is so entirely his due, when he thought on us with pity, before we or the world in which we dwell had a being?

Ver. 32. *Now therefore hearken unto me, O ye chil-dren : for blessed are they that keep my ways.*

We must not give unto him the hearing of the ear only, but the hearing of faith and obedience also. The blessing is upon those that are not forgetful hear-ers, but observers of his word. We are under infinite obligations, from the greatness and the eternal grace of Christ, to hearken unto him ; and our duty and in-terest are here the same. Our observation of his ways is not the foundation or cause of our blessedness, for that was designed for us before we could do good or evil, and our holy dispositions are not the cause, but the effect of the purpose of grace in Christ Jesus * ; yet because they are the effect, they are also a proof of our happy interest in it.

Are they blessed that keep the way of wisdom ? Then,

Ver. 33. *Hear instruction, and be wise, and refuse it not.*

If we hear instruction with faith and reverence, we shall be wise. If we refuse it, we are fools, and must continue to be so. Christ is the only author of wisdom, and it is by the hearing of faith that he conveys it. The word is the good seed, and if it be not sown, how can we expect a harvest ? But it is not enough that the seed is sown. Should it be presently picked up, or should no fruit be brought forth to perfection, the sowing of it will be of no avail. We are required, not only to hear instruction, but to hold it fast in our hearts and practice; and the man that does so, is truly wise, and receives blessing from God †.

Ver. 34. *Blessed is the man that heareth me, watching daily at my gates, waiting at the posts of my doors.*

Those who desire favours from the great, attend their levees day by day, and think themselves happy if they can at length obtain a favourable answer to their suit. With how much greater reason do we wait at the posts of Wisdom's doors, in expectation of blessings the most necessary and important !

Happy were Solomon's servants, in the opinion of the queen of Sheba, because they enjoyed the privilege of daily hearing that celebrated prince. We are happy, if we knew our own happiness, who are admitted to hear the instructions of Him who is Wisdom it-

*2 Tim. 1:9, Eph. 1:4   †Matt. 13:1-20, James 1:23 etc.

self. His palace is erected amongst us, and it is a greater happiness to stand at the door of it, than to dwell in the tents of wickedness. David desired one thing, and what was it? Not that he might enjoy a long and undisturbed possession of his throne, but that he might dwell in the house of the Lord all the days of his life, and enjoy the blessed views and discoveries afforded in the sanctuary.

If we have long attended the instructions of Christ, and found little advantage from them, we must not say with the unbelieving prince, Why should I wait for the Lord any longer? The God of mercy waits to be gracious to us, and we ought to wait for him, attending those ordinances where he is pleased to display his glory and love, with unwearied diligence, earnest desire, and lively hope. The man that waited thirty-eight years at the pool of Siloam, was well rewarded at last, when he received vigour to his body. But they enjoy greater happiness, who wait for God in his appointed way. Christ is found of those that seek him, for to whom did he ever say, Seek ye me in vain? And blessed are they that find him,

Ver. 35. *For whoso findeth me findeth life, and shall obtain favour of the Lord.*

He that hath the Son hath life, and he that hath not the Son of God hath not life. The first man, Adam, was made a living soul, but by sin he died, and we all sinned and died in him, and must have continued for ever in a state of death, had not another Adam appeared who was made a quickening Spirit; and whosoever believeth in him shall not die, but have everlasting life. Even in this land of darkness and death, believers enjoy a true and happy life, for they are delivered from condemnation, and entitled to the heavenly life. They are made free from that principle of corruption, which is called the law of sin and death, and made alive unto God and holiness. They enjoy that which is better than life,—the loving-kindness of the Lord ; for through Jesus, the Father looks upon them with a pleasant countenance. The smiles of God make heaven, and they that obtain favour of the Lord have a heaven upon earth.

But miserable are the despisers of the wisdom and grace of Christ.

Ver. 36. *But he that sinneth against me wrongeth his own soul: all they that hate me love death.*

They that despise Christ's gospel, or reject his salvation, are sinners against him who is the Supreme Wisdom, and the fountain of happiness to men. They are haters of Him who is love itself. Such ungrateful rebels are as great enemies to themselves as to Christ. They murder their immortal souls ; they love those sins which are death and damnation in disguise.

Sinners against Christ shall receive a reward of vengeance suited to the blackness of their guilt, and shall, through eternity, have no room to complain of their Judge. Death and life were set before them, and they chose death, and shall for ever eat of the fruit of their own choice. Consider these things, O unbelievers ! If ye will not now consider them, in the latter days ye shall perfectly consider them.

Proverbs 9

T̲h̲e̲ happiness of the followers of Christ is not entirely reserved to another world. Even in this life they are admitted to a feast of fat things.

Ver. 1. *Wisdom hath builded her house, she hath hewn out her seven pillars.*

The church of Christ is a house, wherein he dwells and takes pleasure *. It must be a glorious edifice, for wisdom is the builder of it †. It is a strong and durable building, for it has many pillars, hewed out, not by the wisest of kings, but by the wisdom of God. Here there is abundance of soul-nourishing provision ; for,

Ver. 2. *She hath killed her beasts ; she hath mingled her wine ; she hath also furnished her table.*

We shall surely be satisfied with the fatness of God's house, with that flesh which is given for the life of the world, and with that spiced wine which is the blood of the New Testament. Does Christ give us his own flesh and blood, to nourish and refresh our souls ? what grace, what comfort, what privilege, will he withhold ? He is most willing to communicate this provision to us.

Ver. 3. *She hath sent forth her maidens ; she crieth upon the highest places of the city.*

The servants of Christ are called maidens, because Christ himself is spoken of under the character of Wisdom, which in the Hebrew language is of the feminine

---

*Ps. 132:13   †Matt. 16:18

gender. The followers of the Lamb are called virgins, to denote their purity *. Ministers also must be pure in their doctrine and behaviour. The voice of these maidens, is the voice of that wisdom which sends them. It is she that gives the invitation by their mouth ; and she does it in the most public and audible manner, crying with a voice like that of a herald from the highest places of the city. But who are invited to this feast?

Ver. 4, 5. *Whoso is simple, let him turn in hither ; as for him that wanteth understanding, she saith to him, Come, eat of my bread, and drink of the wine which I have mingled.*

The simple and unwise are welcomed to this feast. They are called not only by the servants, but by the master of the feast, to partake of these precious provisions. The poor, the maimed, the lame, and the blind,—they that have no money, and they that have spent all their substance for things that do not profit, are graciously invited to come, and eat and drink abundantly, by receiving Christ and his salvation, as they are freely offered in the gospel †.

But we cannot be partakers of the Lord's table, and the table of devils. When we come to Jesus by faith, and partake of his precious blessings, we must forsake the society and the course of the foolish.

Ver. 6. *Forsake the foolish, and live ; and go in the way of understanding.*

The companions of fools shall remain for ever in the congregation of the dead. But in the way of understanding there is life, and no death. Do we abhor death, and love life ? Then, if we believe the words of Christ, we will forsake the foolish, and go in the path of understanding ‡.

---

*Rev. 14   †Luke 14, Isa 55, 1-4   ‡Prov. 13:14, John 7:51

But may we not associate with the foolish, in order to reclaim them ? There are two sorts of foolish persons. Some have naturally a pliable and modest disposition ; though destitute of the grace of God, or though conversant in the ways of sin, they are not yet hardened in sin by long practice. There may be some hope of making good impressions on the minds of such persons as these. But there are others who are stubborn and determined sinners. To them, in ordinary cases, there is no hope of doing any good.

Ver. 7, 8. *He that reproveth a scorner getteth to himself shame ; and he that rebuketh a wicked man getteth himself a blot. Reprove not a scorner, lest he hate thee—* If we reprove the profligate sinners that mock at every thing sacred, we are not likely to benefit them, but to procure hurt to ourselves.

Such men, when we have irritated them by our admonitions, will pry into our characters with all the keenness of malice and revenge. Few characters can stand the scrutiny of a malicious eye ; so that instead of serving them, we shall be in danger of losing much of our usefulness to others, by making them our enemies *.

Yet reproofs are like pearls when they are administered with the meekness of wisdom, and met with an obedient ear †.

Ver. 8, 9.——*Rebuke a wise man, and he will love thee. Give instruction to a wise man, and he will be yet wiser ; teach a just man, and he will increase in learning.*

There is scarcely a man so wise and holy as not to need instruction and reproof. The difference between wise men and fools lies not in this, that the former are above reproofs, but that they know their need of them, and are disposed to receive them with meekness, and to improve by them, and to love and thank their re-

---

*Matt. 7:6   †Ps. 141:5

provers *. The wise and the just man are the same in the view of this wisest of men, for this is a fundamental maxim in his writings—

Ver. 10. *The fear of the Lord is the beginning of wisdom; and the knowledge of the holy is understanding.*

Solomon knew how to appreciate that wisdom which directs men in the prudent management of their own concerns, and in the wise administration of public affairs; but he rightly judged that religion is the true wisdom, and that, compared with it, all other kinds are vanity and folly. He examined with the eye of the prince of philosophers the objects of nature; but the knowledge of the most holy God, one in essence, but subsisting in three persons, was in his estimation true understanding. This kind of knowledge excels the other as much as the light of the sun the glimmer of a glow-worm. He that knows God in truth, is possessed of a never-ending life †.

Ver. 11. *For by me thy days shall be multiplied, and the years of thy life shall be increased.*

It is not for God's benefit, but for ours, that he invites us to receive wisdom ‡.

Ver. 12. *If thou be wise, thou shalt be wise for thyself; but if thou scornest, thou alone shalt bear it.*

God can receive no additions of blessedness by our wisdom, though he delights in it. He cannot lose his glory by our contempt of his gospel and laws ‖. The ministers of wisdom will rejoice in our compliance with their calls, but the profit or the loss of our behaviour under a dispensation of the gospel, must be felt by ourselves §. Life and death are set before us. May God grant us a disposition to chuse life.

---

*Ps. 141:5   †John 17:3, Phil. 3:8   ‡Prov. 3:2, Job 35:6
‖Ezek. 33:11, Rom. 9:22   §Isa. 49:4

Another offer is made us of entertainment, but alas ! of how different a kind ! It is made by the harlot, against whom we need to be often warned.

Ver. 13. *A foolish woman is clamorous ; she is simple, and knoweth nothing.*

She is foolish, ignorant, and stupid to the last degree, for she buys a moment of empty delight at the expense of everlasting burnings. She is impudent and clamorous. The damned in hell are afraid that their companions should come to their place of torment. But this shameless creature earnestly calls others to share with her in those pleasures which are followed by everlasting sorrows.

Ver. 14, 15. *For she sitteth at the door of her house, on a seat in the high places of the city, to call passengers who go right on their ways.*

They are evil times, when tempters to sin are permitted to hunt so avowedly for prey. Let well-meaning persons, in such a time, watch and pray against temptation. These are the persons whom the foolish woman solicits, and too often with success.

Ver. 16, 17. *Whoso is simple, let him turn in hither ; and as for him that wanteth understanding, she saith to him, Stolen waters are sweet, and bread eaten in secret is pleasant.*

They are surely stupid, who believe that there is any pleasure in those things that are forbidden by God, and afraid to appear in open day. Yet such is the corruption of the hearts of men, that they relish doctrines so contrary to reason, as well as to Scripture. We are naturally prone to things forbidden, and till our souls are renewed by the grace of God, can taste an unaccountable sweetness in that which is poison to the soul. But when we are restored to a sound mind, those delights only will be relished, which consist with a pure conscience, and the dignity of a rational and immortal soul.

It is through blindness and inconsideration that any man is entangled in the snares of the foolish woman—

Ver. 18. *But he knoweth not that the dead are there ; and that her guests are in the depths of hell.*

We are naturally starving creatures, and cannot find happiness within ourselves. As every man must have food to satisfy the natural cravings of hunger, so every soul must have some gratification to its desires of happiness. Wisdom and folly do each spread a feast for men. The question is, Whose guests shall we be ? And did we possess any wisdom, or any true and well-directed self-love, it might be easily decided. The entertainments of wisdom, are soul-quickening provision. They that hear her calls, shall eat that which is good, and their souls shall live for ever. The guests of wisdom are in the heights of heaven. They feast on the hidden manna, and on the fruits of the tree of life. The provisions of the foolish woman are a deadly, though perhaps a slow poison. Her guests have their portion with the wicked giants, who brought on the world a universal deluge, and with the inhabitants of Sodom and Gomorrah, who are set forth for an example, suffering the vengeance of eternal fire. Let us consider where Joseph now is, and what blessings are come upon the crown of the head of him, who so bravely resisted temptations the most alluring, and the most threatening. Let us, on the other hand, remember Sodom and Gomorrah, and chuse our portion with the one or the other. Be astonished, O heavens ! that men should be so cruel to their own souls, as to deliberate a moment in so clear a case. To-day let us hear the voice of wisdom.

Proverbs 10

SALVATION is by grace through faith; and this faith works by love, producing universal obedience to the law of our Creator and Redeemer. This law is summarily comprehended in the ten commandments, and published with more particularity in this divinely inspired body of Christian morality. Let us study it with attention, and pray that the Spirit of Jesus may enable us to understand and practise it.

Ver. 1. *The proverbs of Solomon. A wise son maketh a glad father : but a foolish son is the heaviness of his mother.*

The first nine chapters are a prefatory address. Now begin the proverbs, (or masterly sayings,) properly so called. Weighty sayings deserve and gain regard. But how shall we sufficiently esteem the proverbs left us by Solomon, which is almost another name for wisdom itself! By this inspired philosopher, Divine Wisdom speaks to every generation.

Were the first of these proverbs to have its due influence on mankind, the world would be greatly reformed and blessed by its efficacy. A great part of our race are parents,—all mankind are, or have been children ; and by it both parents and children are directed. Parents are instructed to use all possible means to make their children wise. But how shall they effect this? Is it not the prerogative of God to give wisdom ? No doubt. But he makes use of proper and appointed means for this purpose. Would you then derive com-

fort from your children? Instruct, reprove, exhort
them, pray for them, recommend religion to them by
your example; for thus saith the Author of wisdom,
" Train up a child in the way wherein he should go,
and when he is old he will not depart from it." But if
in some rare instance he should, your souls will not on
that account be stung with self-accusations.

Remember, ye that are children, how greatly you
are indebted to your parents, and how much their
comfort is bound up in you. Be wise, seek useful
knowledge, and search for it as for hid treasure. Walk
in the fear of the Lord. Let prudence and discretion,
(such as Solomon teaches,) appear in every part of
your conduct; so shall your father and mother greatly
rejoice, and bless the Lord on your account. But if
you are foolish and unruly, you grieve their spirits,
and wound the souls that love you with the dearest
affection. Consider that your mothers bore you with
sorrow. Why should your lives also be a continual
source of pain to their tender hearts! or why should
the anxieties of your fathers on your behalf, be rewarded with the cutting view of your ungodly lives!
" A wise son maketh a glad father, but a foolish man despiseth his mother *." Though he should in no other
way express his contempt for her, his foolish behaviour
is a plain proof that he values not her happiness.

Ver. 2. *Treasures of wickedness profit nothing—*

Ill-gotten riches are called treasures of wickedness.
It is an opinion generally held by men, that riches, in
whatever way procured, will do them great service.
If, therefore, they cannot come at the possession of them
by honest means, they will scrape them together by any
means in their power. But here the Spirit of God tells

---

*Chap. 15:20

us, that if a man should heap up immense riches to himself, they will profit him nothing. And how can they? They are cursed to him. If a moth in his substance, and stings in his conscience, and the damnation of hell, can bring any advantage to the robber and extortioner, let them rejoice in their portion.

———*But righteousness delivereth from death.*

No righteousness but that which is by the faith of Jesus Christ, delivers from eternal death. However, he is a gross deceiver of his own soul, who pretends to be clothed with it, while he continues to live unrighteously.

By righteousness, we give to every one his due; first to God, and next to men. This righteousness is a preservative from death and misery of every kind. How? Through the gracious protection of him that keepeth the path of the righteous, as the wise man tells us in the next words:

Ver. 3. *The Lord will not suffer the soul of the righteous to famish : but he easteth away the substance of the wicked.*

But was it never known that the just man perished by want? Are ravens always commissioned to feed the people of God in times of famine? God has them at his command, if he sees it proper to make use of them ; and when he pleases, he can administer to his people's necessities as easily by miracle as by the use of ordinary means. Let them, then, joyfully commit the care of their bodies to his mercy. So long as his infinite wisdom shall see their continuance in life meet for them, their bread and their water shall be sure ; and though their bodies should in some rare instances be pinched with hunger, he will nourish their souls with bread which the world knows not of.

But the wicked are not so. Whilst the righteous are sure of being satisfied in days of famine, they are near

to ruin in their greatest abundance; for the Lord
casteth away that which they call their substance.
Many of them will take care not to spend it upon riotous living, and harlots. None of them will part with
it, from motives of generosity and charity. But whilst
they grasp it fast with both hands, God will pull it
out from between their fingers, and toss it irrecoverably from them. Should they even be permitted to
hold it all their days, death, that terrible messenger,
shall at last drag them from it; nor shall their glory
descend after them to the grave, but that wickedness
by which they acquired it, shall lie down with them
in the dust, and torture their souls in hell.

You see from this verse, how it comes to pass, that
righteousness delivereth from death, and that treasures
of wickedness are so unprofitable. But let none from
these truths conclude, that honest labour is useless.
God takes care of his people, but he makes use of
their labours in the performance of his promise about
their provision, and whoever indulges himself in idleness, may expect poverty as a matter of course; for,

Ver. 5. *He becometh poor that dealeth with a slack
hand : but the hand of the diligent maketh rich.*

Idleness was never designed for man. Adam in
paradise, was to dress the garden. Why should men
expect any good from slothfulness, since that doom
was pronounced, " In the sweat of thy face shalt thou
eat bread !" Show me a slothful man, and I will show
you a wicked, a poor, and a miserable man.

" But the hand of the diligent maketh rich." Riches
are dispensed by God at his pleasure, and he commonly gives them to the man employed in honest industry.
How then do we see some men laborious, and yet poor !
Perhaps they trust too much to their own labour.
Perhaps they are earth-worms, abhorred by God. Or
if they fear the Lord, and look to him for a blessing

on the labour of their hands, he sees that riches are not convenient for them. To prevent pride and vanity from being increased in them by the wealth of the world, he keeps them poor, designing to bestow upon them the better and enduring substance. Would you complain of one, who promised you one acre of ground, and gave you instead of it an hundred in a better soil?

But are not some indolent persons enriched by unexpected means? No; at least their wealth is not substantial nor enduring. It is worse than poverty.

Let us, therefore, be at once fervent in spirit and diligent in business; and if we would deserve this character, we must carefully improve the proper seasons of profitable labour; for,

Ver. 5. *He that gathereth in summer is a wise son: but he that sleepeth in harvest is a son that causeth shame.*

Summer and harvest are the fit seasons for rearing and gathering in the fruits of the field. He who improves these and similar opportunities for honest gain, does honour to himself, and to those who had the care of his education. He who neglects them, is like one who sleeps all the time he should be working. It would be a shame for a man in health to spend all his days in bed. The idle man might as well be there, for any thing he does out of it. He brings disgrace to himself, and to his father, who ought to have trained him to habits of prudence and diligence.

Are prudence and diligence so commendable, when employed about the bread that perisheth? How much more necessary and profitable are they, when we are called to labour in the strength of divine grace, for the meat that endureth unto everlasting life! He that trifles away the acceptable time and the day of salvation, is a thousand times more distracted, than the man who defers the reaping of his fields till the end of December.

Riches are the ordinary fruit of labour, but the fruit of righteousness shall be peace and every good thing; for,

Ver. 6. *Blessings are upon the head of the just; but violence covereth the mouth of the wicked.*

The just man is not only commended by men, but by God. He not only expects, but possesses blessings. He is not only enriched, but crowned with blessings coming down from the Father of lights. He shall not be confounded, but his mouth is opened to bless the Author of his blessings.

" But violence covereth the mouth of the wicked." The covering of Haman's face, was a badge of his condemnation. The violent man is condemned already, and when the Judge of all shall return his violent dealings upon his own head, his face shall be covered with confusion, nor shall he be able to open his mouth in extenuation of his crimes.

The happiness of the just and the misery of the wicked is not confined to this life. The just man shall not all die. His spirit is life because of righteousness; his body shall sleep in Jesus; and,

Ver. 7. *The memory of the just is blessed.—*

His name shall live when he is dead. The remembrance of him is dear to his friends, and honoured by the wise. And what signifies an empty name? It brings honour to God, and prolongs the influence of his good example who has left it. His good works not only follow him, but live behind him. As Jeroboam made Israel to sin after he was dead, so the good man helps to make others holy whilst he is lying in the grave. Should it so happen that his character is mistaken in the world, or should his name die out among men, it shall yet be had in everlasting remembrance before God; for never shall those names be erased from the Lamb's book of life, which were written in it from the foundation of the world.

——*But the name of the wicked shall rot.* It shall either perish, or be covered with disgrace. Have they performed great actions, or built stately monuments to perpetuate their name? These may be useful, indeed, to keep up and to recal their infamy to recollection. The names of the Alexanders and Cæsars of the days of old, are honourable among bad judges of character. Among the wise, leopards and other voracious beasts are accounted no less deserving of glory and fame *.

Ver. 8. *The wise in heart will receive commandments; but a prating fool shall fall.*

All men desire to be accounted wise; but who is truly a wise man? Solomon being judge, the man is wise who receives commandments. He will not admit of any lord to his conscience, but the Judge of all; yet he hearkens to instruction from all who are authorized or qualified to give it. He receives with meekness the instructions of parents and teachers, and yields a cheerful submission to lawful authority. He is much readier to hear than to speak, and his feet stand upon an even place.

——"But a prating fool shall fall." Loquacity is a sure sign of vanity and folly. This kind of fool, in his endless talk, speaks many vain and sinful words, for which he must give an account; many proud and senseless words, which bring upon him contempt; many rash, malicious, and provoking words, which lay him open to hatred and mischief. Sooner or later, his ungoverned tongue must fall upon him with unsupportable weight, and hurl him to ruin.

---

*Dan. 8:6,7

Ver. 9. *He that walketh uprightly walketh surely;
but he that perverteth his ways shall be known.*

Men's characters are discerned by their conversation.
The good man walketh uprightly, for he regulates his
steps by the unerring rule, and constantly endeavours
to follow it, unbiassed by interest or honour, persuasion, terror, or example. He abhors dissimulation in
his dealings either with God or men, but speaks as
he thinks, acts as he speaks, and makes the example
of Christ his constant pattern. This man walks *surely*,
or *confidently*. None of his steps shall slide. If he
should fall, he shall not be utterly cast down. If he
meets with enemies, and tribulations, he receives joy
from the testimony of his conscience; and the name of
the Lord is a strong tower, to which he runs and is
safe.

The dissembler walks in crooked paths. Like Judas, who put on a cloak of charity to hide his covetousness *, he conceals the selfish principles which regulate his behaviour under the appearances of piety,
prudence, and other good qualities. But he cannot
hold the mantle so tight about him, as to conceal from
the wise observer his inward baseness. It will occasionally be shuffled aside, it will at length drop off,
and he shall be known for what he is, abhorred by all
men, and punished with other hypocrites.

Ver. 10. *He that winketh with the eye causeth sorrow;
but a prating fool shall fall.*

He that winketh with the eye, either in derision of
his neighbour, or to give a signal to his associate in
mischief, is the cause of sorrow to another, which shall
return upon himself; for he that does a bad thing to
others, in whatever way he does it, is doing a worse to
himself. Better to suffer an hundred wrongs, than to

---

*John 12

commit one. " And a prating fool shall fall." Such a fool is often boasting that he is no dissembler, and indeed he has no talent for dissembling and carrying on his schemes by policy ; but his plainness is no virtue, nor shall it make atonement for the follies of his mouth.   The scorner, the plotter of mischief, and the prating fool, shall be involved in equal misery.

Some ancient translations, particularly that of the LXX. read the verse thus : " He that winketh with the eye causeth sorrow ; but he that reproveth causeth safety."

In this contrast, winking with the eye is the gesture of one that hides his eyes from his neighbour's fault, because he is unwilling to risk his favour by administering necessary reproof.   Such a man is not a true friend, for he suffers sin upon his brother, when he might, by faithful admonition, have prevented it. And he that does not prevent sin when it is in his power, is the cause of grief, the sure consequence of sin ; but he who faithfully reproves, causes safety to his friend, and shall, in the end, receive more thanks than he that winked with the eye, and flattered with the mouth.

Ver. 11. *The mouth of a righteous man is a well of life ; but violence covereth the mouth of the wicked.*

Much is spoken by the wise man about the government of the tongue, but not too much, for he that learns effectually to bridle his tongue is a perfect man, and able also to bridle the whole body.

The mouth of a righteous man utters words which are refreshing to the mourners, as cold waters to a thirsty soul. His wise and edifying conversations, through the Divine blessing, promote the spiritual interests of the hearers. Let our speech, therefore, be always with grace, seasoned with salt.

The mouths of others are like a standing pool ; nothing but insipid trash is to be found in them.   They are too frequently like a poisoned fountain, tending to corruption and death.

But the violence breathed from the mouths, or executed by the hands of the wicked, shall bring upon them condemnation, or stop their mouths with shame *.

Ver. 12. *Hatred stirreth up strifes ; but love covereth all sins.*

Hatred is so hateful a thing, that no man will acknowledge it in himself ; but by its fruits ye shall know it. What else is it that induces men to provoke their neighbours to wrath and contention, by expressions of contempt, by base insinuations, by cutting reproaches, by opprobrious names, by recalling old faults to remembrance, and raising up to view what seemed buried in the grave of forgetfulness? Can the man who indulges in such practices, be justly regarded as a child of the God of peace, or a follower of Jesus, who shewed such love to his disciples, after all of them had forsaken, and one denied him in the day of his distress † ?

"But love covereth all sins."—All sins! What a strange word is that ! We think it a great deal to cast a mantle over seven offences of our brother : to hide from our eyes, and drop from our remembrance, not a few nor a great number of offences, but all sins, is a hard matter. Yet what are all the sins of our brother, by which he has offended us, compared with our sins against God ? Why should not he to whom ten thousand talents are remitted, readily forgive his brother a few pence ?

Examine yourselves, whether love or hatred reign in your souls.

Ver. 18. *In the lips of him that hath understanding*

---

*Verse 6 †1 John 2:9-11

178 / Exposition of Proverbs

wisdom is found ; but a rod is for the back of him that is void of understanding.

He that is wise in heart will receive commandment *. That is one mark of a wise man, but he shews his wisdom in speaking, as well as in hearing. Wisdom seals not up, but governs the mouth, and dictates to it useful words. On whatever occasion you consult the possessor of it, you will find wisdom, whether you want instruction, or direction, or comfort. Should you consult him about matters that come not within the compass of his talents, even then he will evince his wisdom, for it is the part of a wise man not to deal in things too high for him. The wisdom of his heart and tongue is his safety and honour, but a rod is for the back of him that is void of understanding. How can he escape an ignominious punishment, when by his unbridled mouth he makes both God and man his enemy ? " A whip for the horse, a bridle for the ass, and a rod for the fool's back †." A bridle was necessary to govern asses when men rode on them ; a rod is equally necessary for fools. It is not by words, but blows, that they must be managed. They deserve the scourge, and sooner or later they shall have it.

Ver. 14. *Wise men lay up knowledge ; but the mouth of the foolish is near destruction.*

Here we learn how the lips of the wise are furnished with wisdom. Their heart is a storehouse, in which they lay up a treasure of it. How do they come by it ? By reading the Bible, by meditating, by hearing sermons, by conversation, by observation and experience, by prayer, by faith in Christ, who is made of God unto us wisdom. And when they have found it, they take care not to lose it, but lay it up in their memories and hearts, where it is kept to be used by

---

*Verse 8   †Chap. 26:3

themselves, and communicated to others. Such men are in the way of happiness, but fools lay up lies and vanities, and idle, malicious stories, which furnish a large supply for their mischievous tongues, so that they are not far from destruction, for of the fruit of their mouths shall they eat.

Ver. 15. *The rich man's wealth is his strong city—*

Can this be true? Yes, if you will believe himself. The rich man's wealth is his strong city, and as an high wall in his own conceit *. It is not *a* strong city, but *his* strong city. He thinks it will prove a sufficient defence to him from that destruction which his mouth has merited. You see how justly the worldling is called an idolater, for he makes not God his confidence, but trusts to a thing of nought ; for his riches, if they are a city, are not a strong city, but a city broken down, and without walls. How hard is it for rich men to obtain an entrance into that city that hath foundations, when it is a miracle for a man that hath riches, not to trust in them ! But are we to suppose poor men exempt from the temptation to idolize gold and silver? No ; for

—*The destruction of the poor is their poverty.—* That was a good prayer, " Give me neither poverty nor riches." Poor men, by envying the rich, by cringing to them, by discontentment with their lot, by despondency and fear of ruin, do often make themselves as wretched and vile, as the rich who boast of their wealth.

Ver. 16. *The labour of the righteous tendeth to life ; the fruit of the wicked to sin.*

The advantage of diligence has been already explained, but there is a very great difference between the righteous and the wicked in this as in other things.

---

*Chap. 18:4

To the pure all things are pure, but to the defiled and unbelieving there is nothing pure. The labour of a righteous man is blessed by God, and tends, not only to procure the necessaries of life, but to make his life comfortable, and to lengthen its days. Nay, it has a favourable influence upon his eternal life, for it is a preservative from temptation, and the performance of a duty, part of the fruits of which are lent unto the Lord, to be repaid with abundant increase. The fruit of the wicked man's labours, on the contrary, tends to sin ; it does so, whether it be hoarded up by his covetousness, or spent in the gratification of vanity and luxury. With all your getting, get righteousness, which will make your labour pure and profitable. Without it, your ploughing is sin, your gains loss to your souls.

Ver. 17. *He is in the way of life that keepeth instruction ; but he that refuseth reproof erreth.*

A wise man will receive commandment, but it is not truly received if it is not kept. The instructions received from parents, ministers, and wise men, must be esteemed as a treasure, laid up in our memories, followed in our lives. He that keeps instruction, is in the way of happiness. His present life is safe and joyful ; his soul is prosperous ; death is his passage to eternal life. Hereby do we know that we know Christ, if we keep his commandments.

Reproofs are necessary for us on many occasions, and the wise man that keeps instruction, will receive them with meekness and thankfulness, and improve them for his humiliation and correction. But he that refuseth reproof erreth from the way of life. He is like a sick man to whom a kind physician prescribes some medicine of powerful virtue, but bitter to the taste ; so infatuated, however, is he, that he will rather risk his life, than follow the prescription.

Ver. 18. *He that hideth hatred with lying lips, and he that uttereth a slander, is a fool.*

He who indulges so wicked and dangerous a passion, is a fool, whether he conceals it under the mask of friendship, or discovers it by reproaches and calumnies. It must neither be concealed nor published, but suppressed and extinguished. To conceal it like Absalom, is to nourish a fire within us, that will consume our vitals, and prove mortal in the end. To utter it in slander, like Shimei, is to set on fire our dwelling, which may soon involve us in the flames.

Ver. 19. *In the multitude of words there wanteth not sin—*

And that of many different kinds. Expressions of vanity and pride, of ill-nature and impiety, of rashness and inconsideration, never fail to proceed from the lips of a man who loves to hear himself talk. Even foolish talking, and inconvenient jesting, and idle words, are sinful, being forbidden by God. If we profess wisdom, we must govern our tongues, and think before we speak. Time and place must be regarded by us, and we must sometimes refrain our lips even from speaking good. Men often sin by a multitude of words in praying, in preaching, and giving advice ;—

—But he that refraineth his lips is wise.

He discovers his modesty and self-command. He keeps himself innocent from much sin, and prevents many dangers to which perpetual talkers expose themselves.

Let us not carry this maxim to excess. There is a time to speak, and if our words are well ordered, they may be very useful ; for,

Ver. 20. *The tongue of the just is as choice silver—*

His conversation is useful, and very precious, not only like silver, but choice silver, which has been well purified in the fire. Our tongues deserve not this praise, unless they are refined from vanity, malignity, and falsehood, in all its diversity of forms.

How eagerly would we court the conversation of a man possessed of endless treasures and unwearied liberality, freely imparting to every petitioner! The conversation of a wise and righteous man, is still more valuable, for he distributes treasures of knowledge, more precious than gold and rubies.

If his tongue is like choice silver, his heart is still richer in value, for that is the good treasure out of which he brings good things.

—*But the heart of the wicked is little worth.*

It is worth less than nothing, for folly and malignity have possession of it, and his tongue is furnished from that bad treasure with froth and wickedness. If he speaks any thing good, it is but silver dross, covering a useless potsherd. Let us therefore avoid the company of the wicked, which can do no good; but let us endeavour to derive pleasure from that of the righteous; for,

Ver. 21. *The lips of the righteous feed many; but fools die for want of wisdom* (Heb. *heart.*)

Food is better than silver, which is useful as a medium of commerce, but which cannot satisfy hunger nor preserve life. Useful discourse is precious like the finest silver, and nourishing to the soul as food to the body. Knowledge, faith, charity, and every holy disposition, is increased by it. The righteous man feeds many with knowledge, for he finds it sweet to himself, and wishes not to eat his morsel alone. His heart is a storehouse of provision for the soul, and like a hospitable landlord, he delights in distributing it to others. But the wicked die for want of heart. Knowledge is no less necessary to the soul than the heart to the body, or food for the preservation of life. Fools therefore are in a bad condition, for they neither have knowledge nor hunger after it, otherwise they might be supplied from the lips of the wise. Therefore go from the presence of a foolish man, when thou perceivest not in him the lips of knowledge. But abide by the righteous, for the words of their mouth, when they speak like themselves, are better than necessary food.

Ver. 22. *The blessing of the Lord it maketh rich, and he addeth no sorrow with it.*

Men generally wish to be rich. But what is the surest way of having such a wish gratified? Diligence is necessary, but not to be depended on; for without the blessing of the Lord on our labours, we may rise early and sit late, and oppress our bodies with toil, and our minds with anxious care, and after all continue in want; but the blessing of the Lord is that which alone makes a man rich. If it should not enrich him that enjoys it with gold, it will enrich him with what is far more precious—wisdom and grace. This blessing confers riches and preserves them, without exposing to harassing cares, their natural and common attendants. When riches bring with them vexations and fears, we would be better without them. Who would chuse to lie on a golden bed with thorns spread under him, and thorns for his covering? But the blessing of the Lord is a hedge about all that a righteous man hath. His labours are pleasant, his gains are safe. His portion is beyond the reach of danger, and his heart is preserved from vexation, in getting, or keeping, or using, or loving the world, because the Lord is his confidence.

The belief of this proverb would sweeten our toils, and make us spiritually-minded about earthly things, and eradicate every dishonest disposition. No man can look for the divine blessing on the work of fraud.

Ver. 23. *It is a sport to a fool to do mischief—*

That man has arrived at an advanced stage of folly, who takes as much pleasure in it as if it were an agreeable amusement. This, however, is to be expected in its natural course. Sinners at first feel much uneasiness from the operation of fear and shame, but they are hardened by the deceitfulness of sin, till at length they not only cast off all restraints, but become impudent in sin, and think it a manly action to cast away the cords of God, and to pour insult and abuse on their fellowmen. But it were far safer to sport with fire than with sin, which kindles a fire that will burn to the lowest hell. It may now be a sport to do mischief, but in the lake of fire and brimstone it will be no sport to have done it.

———*But a man of understanding hath wisdom.*

And therefore it is impossible that he should be so awfully infatuated. He is deeply sensible of the misery and ruin that is in sin, but his delight is in holiness; and in the exercises of it he experiences that heartfelt pleasure, which the sweetest sins could never afford.

Ver. 24. *The fear of the wicked, it shall come upon him: but the desire of the righteous shall be granted.*

It is scarcely supposable that a wicked man can wholly rid himself of fear. His terrors may be suspended, but they are like a sleeping adder, which will awake and pierce his heart with a venomous sting; and his fears are not fancies. Ten thousand times greater misery than he can apprehend is appointed to him for the portion of his cup, by the irreversible sentence of his Almighty Judge. His guilty conscience does sometimes torment him with fear where no fear is, but if he escapes the hand of man, he shall fall into the hands of the living God; and if he is not struck down by the storm of lightning, his day will come to drop into hell. But let not the righteous be afraid; his desires are pure, being regulated by the will of God revealed in his word, and the God that hears prayers will grant them, if not at present, yet at the time most suitable in the judgment of Infinite Wisdom. If what he wishes is not allowed, his desire is yet granted, for whatever he desires is with this reservation, " If it is agreeable to the will of God, and conducive, all things considered, to his best interest."

We read of righteous men desiring things which they did not immediately obtain; but they obtained all that was good for them at that time, and in another world were satisfied to the utmost desire of their hearts.

Ver. 25. *As the whirlwind passeth, so is the wicked no more : but the righteous is an everlasting foundation.*

We have no reason to envy the wicked the figure they sometimes make in this world. It is but like the bluster and noise of the whirlwind, which is soon over. His happiness and his fame are transitory. He shall indeed survive the grave, but annihilation would be a blessing to him, for he shall continue to live only to be miserable. The righteous man, on the contrary, is like mount Zion, which can never be moved. He is a living stone built upon the Rock of ages, for he is kept by the power of God, and neither principalities nor powers, nor life, nor death, nor any other creature, shall be able to separate him from the love of God, which is in Christ Jesus. When the blast of the terrible one is as a storm against the wall, Almighty grace is his strength and refuge. As the rock remains the same when the whirlwind has spent its force, so God's people, having his protection, shall enjoy unimpaired happiness, when the destructions of the enemy are come to a perpetual end.

Ver. 26. *As vinegar to the teeth, and as smoke to the eyes, so is the sluggard to them that send him,*

On any errand. It is a great point of prudence to chuse proper persons to transact our business, especially

if it be an affair of consequence. A man must feel
great vexation when he finds his affairs deranged or
ruined, and his wisdom called in question, through the
stupidity and negligence of those whom he trusts.
Solomon shewed his good sense by chusing for his service men of activity, as we learn from the history of
Jeroboam.

This proverb is of use to direct us in the choice of
magistrates, ministers, or wives; and to excite us to
shake off slothfulness in the service of our Master who
is in heaven, and who will cast into hell the unprofitable servant.

Ver. 27. *The fear of the Lord prolongeth days; but
the years of the wicked shall be shortened.*

Some sins have a natural tendency to shorten men's
days; others bring men to the gibbet. All provoke the
wrath of him in whose hand is our life and breath.
The contrary virtues have an effect directly the reverse.
But did not the wicked Jeroboam live to be old, whilst
the only righteous person in his family died in youth?
True, but the saint that dies in youth has lived as long
upon earth as infinite wisdom saw it good for him,
and his spirit is still life because of righteousness.
Whereas, if the wicked man should live to be an hundred years old, he is accursed. Even in this case, his
life is a shadow, and a thing of nought.

Could your physician give you a prescription for
lengthening out your days to any term you please, you
would think no price too high for it. Here is a tried
receipt for making you live as long as it can be good
for you to live. Shall we trust physicians more than
the Sovereign of life and death?

Ver. 28. *The hope of the righteous shall be gladness:
but the expectation of the wicked shall perish.*

The hope of the righteous is in the Lord. From
him they hope for every earthly blessing that appears

to infinite wisdom really good for them, and they shall not be disappointed *. But the great object of their hope is everlasting life †, and how can they fail of obtaining it ? Their hopes are founded upon the word of a God that cannot lie, upon the inviolable oath of Jehovah, upon an all-sufficient Saviour, and upon a covenant that is everlasting, ordered in all things and sure. This hope shall be gladness inexpressible and inconceivable.

Great things are said of the joys and glories of the heavenly world, but they are spoken in the language of men. The tongue of angels could speak greater things, but angels themselves cannot conceive that fulness of joy which ages hence the blessed shall possess.

The hopes of wicked men are contracted within narrow bounds. The objects of their hope are things which the unerring word calls vanity and vexation of spirit. They may obtain the body of their wishes, but alas ! without the soul. Happiness is the object of hope to all of us. With a view to this, we seek the riches and honours, the pleasures and friendships of this life, but should we possess the richest abundance of these things, and not find happiness in them, what doth it profit ? But if the wicked man should have his belly filled with worldly treasures, and should rejoice in them, his expectation shall nevertheless perish. Misfortune or death shall rob him of all that he placed in the room of God, and the remembrance of former pleasures shall greatly embitter his miseries. There is one dreadful ingredient of torture which the poor man that goes to hell will not experience,—the remembrance of prosperity enjoyed and abused.

Does the wicked man expect heaven ? How terrible will be the punishment of his presumptuous hopes,

---

*Ps. 34:9,10   †Titus 1:2

when he shall be hurled down headlong into the depths
of despair * !

Ver. 29. *The way of the Lord is strength to the upright : but destruction shall be to the workers of iniquity.*

Christ is the way, into which the upright man enters
by faith, and he walks in it by holiness of conversation.
He hates all guile, and hypocrisy is an abomination to
his soul. Whilst other men strengthen themselves in
their own imaginations by fraud and cunning, he derives all needful supplies of grace from him in whom
all fulness dwells. The testimony of his conscience em-
boldens and invigorates his soul, and he waxes stronger
and stronger. He is weak in himself, but his dependance is not on himself, but on God ; out of weakness
he thus waxes strong, surmounts every difficulty, and
turns to flight armies of aliens. How weak was Peter
when he denied his Lord ! but the way of the Lord was
strength to him, and when near the end of his pilgrimage, he looked forward to the death of the cross with
as much composure as a man does to putting off his
clothes when retiring to rest †. Upright men, when
feeling the weakness of their own strength, are sometimes filled with anxious thoughts, lest they should become weary and faint, and fall before their enemies ; but
through the grace of Christ their strength shall increase, and shall be suited to their needs. They shall
reach in safety the end of their journey, and be more
than conquerors ‡.

But what shall be the end of those that walk in crooked ways, and endeavour to secure their wishes by hypocrisy and iniquity ? Destruction shall be their portion. Destruction and misery are in their ways. If

---

*Matt. 7:22,23   †2 Peter 1:12   ‡Ps. 27:13,14, Isa. 40:29

they cannot now see this, they shall feel it at the
end of their journey.

Ver. 30. *The righteous shall never be removed ; but the
wicked shall not inhabit the earth.*

The righteous man is founded upon the Rock of ages,
for his dependance is placed upon a better righteousness than his own. He is guarded by Omnipotence.
Death and hell may rage, and seem to prevail, but he
is safe from every real evil. He may be removed to
another land, or to another world ; but heaven is his
country, and the mightiest of his enemies are unable
to prevent his entrance into it, or to banish him from
it *.

Even in this world the enemies of the righteous have
not the power of which they fancy themselves possessed. Neither Chaldeans, nor Sabeans, nor devils, could
deprive Job of a camel or a sheep, without the permission of him that would suffer no evil to befal that
righteous man, without making it work for good †.

" But the wicked shall not inhabit the earth." Is
Job then mistaken when he says, " The earth is given
into the hand of the wicked?" No. It is given into
their hand for a little moment, but they are not unfrequently driven out of it by visible judgments. At
the best, when a few years are gone, the king of terrors shall chase them away to hell, and they that made
shipwreck of faith or a good conscience for the treasures of earth, shall make shipwreck of these treasures
also.

Ver. 31. *The mouth of the just bringeth forth wisdom : but the froward tongue shall be cut out.*

Our first care must be, to keep our hearts with all
diligence ; and our next to govern our tongue, which
will otherwise be an unruly evil, full of deadly poison ;

*Rom. 8:38,39   †Matt 10:29-31

and the tongue will best be governed, when the heart is well furnished with wisdom, for the mouth of the just bringeth forth wisdom as naturally as a good tree bringeth forth good fruit. Wisdom is said to be a tree of life, and this tree of life bringeth forth the fruits of holiness in speech and behaviour, not once a year, but every day. How valuable would a tree be thought, that should bring forth the most delicious fruits in such abundance, and such frequency!

When our speech is with grace, and seasoned with salt, it ministers grace to the hearers, and keeps ourselves from mischief; whereas the froward tongue shall be cut out. It provokes God, and it oftentimes provokes men. Froward speeches may escape punishment from man, but they shall not escape God's righteous judgment, who will cut out their tongues, and make them fall upon themselves.

Ver. 32. *The lips of the righteous know what is acceptable; but the mouth of the wicked speaketh frowardness.*

How is knowledge ascribed to the lips of the righteous? Because their lips are directed by their hearts. They speak not thoughtlessly, but intelligently. Their lips are not devoted to flattery, nor do they slavishly comply with the sentiments and humours of men. But they know when it is fit to speak, and what is fit to be spoken. They know how to address persons of different dispositions, in a different manner, so as to please them, or what is of more importance in their estimation, so as to serve their best interests.

It is said of a certain General, that he had such a grace in his manner of behaviour, that a suppliant who had met with the refusal of a petition from him, returned better satisfied than he would from another who had granted the solicited favour. A prudent Christian has so much grace in his speech, that his reproofs and rebukes often gain him more favour and esteem, than others gain from their insinuating address. But the wicked man speaketh the words of deceit and folly, for what can be expected from a bad tree but corrupt fruit? and what shall be the end of a corrupt tree, but to be cut down, and cast into the fire?

Proverbs 11

Ver. 1. *A false balance is abomination to the Lord : but a just weight is his delight * .*

COMMERCE is a blessing of great value to men. In the same light are we to consider the invention of weights and balances, by which it is facilitated. These are instances of the divine goodness, for God has taught discretion to the merchant as well as to the husband-man. But by corrupt men, these, as well as every other instance of the goodness of God, have been abused. Whilst God furnishes them with the means of practising justice, the devil teaches them to turn the instruments of righteousness, into the means of defrauding one another.

False balances are not only hated, but abhorred by God. They are abomination itself in his eyes. But what is the meaning of this? Is the Lord's indignation excited against pieces of wood or of stone? No; this manner of expression points out the greatness of

---

*Chap. 16:11, 20:10

his displeasure against such as use them, and shews that such instruments of iniquity should be dashed in pieces.

As money was weighed in ancient times, bad money comes within the compass of this proverb. But not to limit its operations, we must observe, that villainy of every kind, and that especially which is committed under colour of justice, is condemned by it. As no iniquity is so odious to God as that which is cloaked by religion, so that injustice is the most detestable in his sight which is masked by hypocritical pretences of fair dealing. How deep in the pit must that man sink who is borne down by this double load of guilt in one sin! or if this be not heavy enough, oppression of the poor, whose cause God hath promised to avenge, will fill up the measure of the sin.

" But a just weight is his delight." For the righteous Lord loveth righteousness, and beholdeth the upright with a pleasant countenance. Honesty in dealing, though not an infallible mark of true piety, must always form a part of it.

Ver. 2. *When pride cometh, then cometh shame : but with the lowly is wisdom.*

The contrast between the two branches of this verse gives us this meaning.—Pride is joined with folly, and ends in shame. The humble man is wise, and shall be exalted to honour.

Pride consists in an immoderate self-esteem, and places its happiness in esteem and honour from others. No sin is more foolish than this ; it springs from ignorance of God, of ourselves and other men, and by the very means which it uses for the accomplishment of its ends, ensures disappointment. In seeking glory, it finds disgrace. Pride made Nebuchadnezzar a brute. It destroyed Herod with worms. It turned Lucifer into Beelzebub. By other sins, man rebels against God;

by pride he usurps his crown and dignity. No wonder, then, that God looks upon all those that are proud,
and abaseth them.

"But with the lowly is wisdom." Humble men
think of themselves as they ought to think. They
desire that God may be honoured, even at the expense
of their own honour ; but they shall be exalted by him
to the highest glory *. Christ humbled himself, and
was highly exalted, and became the brightest example
of what he so often declared, "He that humbleth
himself shall be exalted."

Ver. 3. *The integrity of the upright shall guide them ;
but the perverseness of transgressors shall destroy them.*

"I will teach thee," says David †. And what are
the great lessons that he introduces by this preface ?
They are truths which the generality of mankind suppose they have already learned : it shall be ill with
the wicked, and well with the righteous ‡. Solomon
knew that but few had learned these instructions sufficiently, and therefore we find that on them he insists
at considerable length.

Sincerity is one eminent branch of the good man's
character, and is of great use to him, for it guides
him in a safe way. The upright man earnestly desires
to stand perfect and complete in all the will of God.
Whilst others regulate their behaviour by then interests and passions, and the course of this world, he
endeavours to know the will of God, and to comply
with it in every instance. Nor does he deviate from
this rule, even when it leads in direct opposition to his
dearest interests and friendships. Conscious that he
cannot direct his own steps, he humbly commits himself to Jesus, who is given to be a Leader to the people,

---

*Matt. 5:5   †Ps. 32:8,9   ‡Verse 10

194 / *Exposition of Proverbs*

that he may be led by his good Spirit to the land of uprightness. Thus the upright man is kept from every dangerous mistake *.

"But the perverseness of transgressors shall destroy them." Their deceitful conduct shall be, not only the cause, but not unfrequently the means also, of their destruction.

Nathanael was a man without guile. We accordingly find, that though prejudiced against Jesus of Nazareth, his sincerity appeared in the means which he employed to arrive at the knowledge of the truth, and he was led by it in the right way. Christ's enemies were men of perverse spirits. They crucified him with a view to maintain their honour, and preserve their nation ; but by their perverse conduct both were destroyed.

Ver. 4. *Riches profit not in the day of wrath : but righteousness delivereth from death.*

" Treasures of wickedness profit nothing," said the wise man, in a preceding part of this book †. But mistake him not ; he did not say that well-gotten treasures profit much. Though we should allow that they are of some little use in the time of prosperity, they are altogether useless in the time of calamity. When God punishes a land, riches only make their owners a fairer mark, and a richer booty to the spoilers. When conscience stings, its wounds are poisoned by reflections on the abuse of riches. They make death more terrible. To the wicked who possessed wealth, it shall be said at the last judgment, " I was an hungered, and ye gave me no meat." Nothing of the world shall follow them to hell, but the bitter remembrance of the good things they possessed, and the guilt contracted by the influence of such a possession.

---

*Ps. 25:4,5,8,9,12,13   †Chap. 10:2

" But righteousness delivereth from death." In Jerusalem's day, the poor and the righteous alone escaped. The righteous shall not be subdued by the first, nor touched by the second death.

Ver. 5. *The righteousness of the perfect shall direct his way*—(and so he shall be delivered from death)—*but the wicked shall fall by his own wickedness.*

If the righteous man should turn aside from the right way, he shall not wander to destruction. His righteousness will rectify his way. He cannot enjoy pleasure in the way of sin, for it is contrary to the tastes that have been excited, and are still preserved, by the Holy Spirit *. When Christ's sheep wander into the paths of sin and error, the eye of the Shepherd is upon them, and his grace shall reclaim them †. But the wicked wander from mountain to hill, till they fall irrecoverably into the pit of destruction.

Ver. 6. *The righteousness of the upright shall deliver them; but transgressors shall be taken in their own naughtiness.*

" Who is he that will harm you, if ye be followers of that which is good ?" Righteousness disposes men to walk unblameably and inoffensively, so that none but savages will hurt them. There are such savages among the sons of Adam, but their mischief shall come down on their own head, whilst the righteous are delivered from their malice ; for they wait on the Lord, and keep his way, which is the way of life and peace. They cry unto God, and God delivers them, not only from their troubles, but from all their fears. Christ is the Captain of their salvation, and he will lose none of his soldiers. Though they should lose their lives in his cause, they are still overcomers ‡.

---

*1 John 3:9   †Ps. 23:3   ‡Rom. 8:37

Were it possible to obtain a medicine of universal efficacy, who would not endeavour to gain possession of it? or who would drink a poison always mortal, except when a remedy were speedily applied? There is no trouble from which righteousness does not deliver; nor did any one ever meddle with wickedness, but to his own sorrow.

Ver. 7. *When a wicked man dieth, his expectation shall perish; and the hope of unjust men perisheth.*

Men derive almost the whole of their happiness from hope. The wicke man laughs at the righteous, because he lives by hope; but the wicked man himself does the same, with this difference, that whilst the hopes of the one are coeval with eternity, those of the other are bounded by time. The expectation of the one has for its object things heavenly and durable, whilst that of the other is fixed on objects circumscribed by the present life. The present situation of the wicked man never yields him the pleasure which he wishes and expects, but there is ever something in view, in which, could he but obtain it, he would find rest. If his hopes are deferred, his heart is sick; if they are accomplished, he is still unsatisfied; but he comforts himself with some other hope, like a child, who thinks he sees a rainbow on the top of a neighbouring hill, and runs to take hold of it, but sees it as far removed from him as before. Thus the life of a wicked man is spent in vain wishes, and toils, and hopes, till death kills at once his body, his hope, and his happiness.

Wicked men may indulge themselves in hopes of eternal happiness too. They cannot deny themselves to be sinners, but they hope that they are not sinners of the worst sort, or at least that they will amend, and fly to Christ, and be as happy through eternity as those who are so foolish, or so timorous, as to come

into the Lord's vineyard in the morning, and bear the
burden and heat of the day, and have no better recompence in the evening, than those who began to work
at the eleventh hour.   Such hopes are highly pleasing
to the devil, who keeps his slaves quiet by means of
them, till they are brought into the same hopeless condition with himself.

Were the sun literally turned into darkness, and all
the worlds now enlightened by his beams, into dreary
dungeons, it would not be so shocking, as for one immortal soul that looks for happiness, to be drowned in
eternal despair.

Ver. 8. *The righteous is delivered out of trouble, and
the wicked cometh in his stead.*

Though Solomon celebrates so frequently the happiness of the righteous, he by no means insinuates that
righteousness will exempt men from adversity. Christ
himself suffered, and shall we claim uninterrupted
prosperity? The wicked often possess wealth and
ease, when the saints of God are beaten with the storm
of adversity; but it shall not be always so. The saints
are delivered, and misery comes upon those that despised and hated them.   But there is this difference
between the troubles of the righteous and those of the
wicked.   The righteous have first their evil things,
and when they receive their good things, the remembrance of former distress fills them with additional satisfaction.   They rejoice, like the weather-beaten mari-
ner who has escaped from the waves and tempests.
The wicked have first their good things, and the remembrance of them envenoms their misery, and is oil
to the fire where they are tormented.   The wicked
comes not again out of trouble, nor does the righteous
come in his stead.

This proverb is often true in a more literal sense,
for the wicked frequently comes into that very trouble

from which the righteous man is delivered. The Phi-listines came into David's place, when Saul was pur-suing him in the wilderness of Maon. Haman and his sons were hanged on the gallows designed for Mordecai; and the enemies of the Jews perished on that day which was expected to be fatal to the Jews. Herod thought to have destroyed Peter, but God put Peter's keepers and Herod himself in his place. The Jews, in the days of the apostles, persecuted the Chris-tians; but the unbelieving Jews were put into their place, when the Roman eagle was brought into their land and sanctuary. These things are done by God, as often as he sees it proper for his own glory, and for the advantage of his people *.

Ver. 9. *An hypocrite with his mouth destroyeth his neighbour : but through knowledge shall the just be de-livered.*

There are so many mischiefs in the tongue of a wicked man, that it is called a world of iniquity. None of them, however, is so bad as the deceit that is in the mouth of the hypocrite, whose tongue is like a sharp razor, working deceitfully. Abner's hands were not bound when he was engaged in fair battle, and we find, that over Asahel, though a mighty and a swift enemy, he gained an easy victory. But how different was the fate of this victorious champion, when attacked by Joab! Then he died as a fool dieth, and for this reason; he was deceived by the ensnaring professions of friendship made by his treacherous assailant. Such is the difference between an open enemy and a false friend. Many souls have been ruined by the mouth of the hypocrite, whilst the servants of Satan have art-fully disguised themselves in the dress of the ministers

---

*Isa. 43:34, Prov. 21:18

of righteousness, and by fair words, and saint-like speeches, deceived the hearts of the simple.

It was an ordinary prayer of King Antigonus, " Deliver me from the hands of my friends." When asked why he did not rather pray for preservation from his enemies, he answered, " That he guarded against his enemies, but could not guard against false friends." Have we then no defence against them ? Yes, knowledge is a defence against this worst of dangers. Joseph and David were guarded by this armour, and were safe *. The knowledge of the truth will preserve our inward man, and as it is attended with prudence and integrity, it will in like manner greatly contribute to our present safety †.

Ver. 10. *When it goeth well with the righteous, the city rejoiceth ; and when the wicked perish, there is shouting.*

The righteous fear God, and live in the practice of justice and charity towards men. These virtues procure the esteem, even of those who have no experience of the power of religion ; and therefore, when it goes well with them, their neighbours rejoice ; but when the wicked fall, there is shouting, because they were living plagues, and employed their prosperity and power for the gratification of their own selfish and unrighteous passions. There was great joy in Judah when righteous princes were raised to the throne ‡, or good ministers entrusted with the management of affairs ||. When bad kings perished, their memories were infamous, neither were they honoured with burnings, or with a place in the sepulchres of the kings.

Righteous men are actuated by nobler motives than the applause of men, and yet they must regard the good-will of others, as a means of being useful §.

---

*Gen. 39, Ps. 17:4   †Prov. 2:11,12   ‡1 Chron. 30:26

||Isa. 22:23   §Eccles. 7:1

Wicked men, on the contrary, are like swine, of no use till they die ; and their fall is not a misfortune to others, but a relief.

Ver. 11. *By the blessing of the upright the city is exalted ; but is overthrown by the mouth of the wicked.*

No wonder that the advancement of the righteous is a cause of public joy. Their prayers, their holy conversation, their counsels, and their example, is a public blessing, by which the city is exalted, for some of the sinners in it are reformed. The young are allured by the beauty of goodness, virtue is encouraged, vice is discountenanced, and the city becomes, as far as their influence extends, a habitation of justice ; and righteousness exalteth a nation. But though inveterate corruptions should, in a great measure, obstruct their patriotic exertions, yet a city is preserved from ruin, or at least its ruin is deferred, on their account. A cloud of wrath hung over Judah in the days of good Josiah, and the corruptions of the land were too obstinate to be thoroughly removed by him, yet the threatened wrath was suspended till he was laid in the grave. God, as we are told, then sought for one to stand in the gap, to turn away his anger from the guilty land, but found none, and so his anger was poured out upon it to the uttermost.

" But the city is overthrown by the mouth of the wicked." Their mouth is a pestilence, which infects their neighbours, till the fatal venom of iniquity corrupt the body of the community, and ruin become inevitable ; or else their counsels prove destructive to its welfare or existence.

Have we any generosity of spirit ? Then it will inspire us with heartfelt joy to be instruments of happiness to all around us. Though we should be little better than savages, it must fill us with horror to think of ruining others as well as ourselves. Let us, then, depart from evil, and do good.

As far as our connections are within the compass of our choice, let us form them upon this maxim. It is good to have the heirs of blessing, and the instruments of blessing to others, for husbands or wives, masters or servants, friends or neighbours.

Ver. 12. *He that is void of wisdom despiseth his neighbour ; but a man of understanding holdeth his peace.*

No human creature is to be despised, for he is our neighbour. He is our own flesh, our brother, sprung from our common father, Adam. Honour all men. Men were made in the image of God ; and though that image is now lost, it is still a sufficient evidence of the sinfulness of despising, ·as well as of murdering, our neighbour, that in the image of God man was made *, and that we cannot say whether the persons whom we are tempted to despise, are not in that happy number of the chosen of God, for whose sakes the Son of God hath dignified our nature by assuming it, and whom he will again beautify with that glorious image which was effaced by the fall.

Do you allege that ·your neighbour is worthy of contempt, on account of his poverty, or meanness, or some remarkable weakness, by which he is rendered ridiculous? I ask you whether he is a fool. You say, No. Then confess that your contempt ought to rest on yourself; for Solomon says you are one, and want of wisdom is far worse than the want of riches, or beauty, or polite accomplishments.

Although it is a sin to despise any man, yet bad men are to be comparatively despised †. The vile person, though clothed with purple, and adorned with shining

---

*Gen. 9:5   †Ps. 15:4

202 / Exposition of Proverbs

talents, is to be despised, in comparison with the man
that fears the Lord, though poor and mean as Lazarus.

None are so contemptible as the contemptuous.
They are so void of sense, that they make themselves
the objects of scorn or indignation, by publishing their
insolence in the disparaging of their neighbours; but
" a man of understanding holdeth his peace." He
will not expose himself to the hatred of men, or to the
condemnation of hell, by saying to his brother, Raca;
and if he is insulted with the contempt of others, he
returns not abuse, but pity. Should some mud stick
to his clothes, he will not defile his hands by throwing
it at his adversary, but rather leaves it till time makes
it easy to be brushed off.

Ver. 13. *A tale-bearer revealeth secrets; but he that is
of a faithful spirit concealeth the matter.*

Much of our wisdom lies in the prudent choice of
friends. A well-chosen friend sweetens the present
life, and assists us in our progress to a better. An unworthy friend will bring on us disappointment, vexation, and remorse. But what sort of persons are we
to avoid or to chuse for our friends? We must not
chuse one that takes pleasure in telling every thing he
knows. You may be sure that such a one will betray
your secrets; for though he should have no malignity
of disposition, his anxiety to rehearse every private
story that he has picked up, will prove to him an irresistible temptation to expose you.

The scripture, however, does not condemn all re-
vealing of secrets. There are some secrets which the
laws of justice and charity bind us to reveal *. But it
is a proof that a man has no command of his tongue,
when he can risk the uneasiness and displeasure of his

---

*Lev. 5:5, 1 Sam. 20

neighbours, by publishing matters which can be of no benefit to him to whom they are communicated.

But that man is to be chosen as your friend, who is of an honest and faithful spirit. Your heart will be relieved of its sorrows, by pouring them into his bosom ; and you may rest assured that he will cause you no uneasiness by blabbing what you would not have the world to know.

Here we see that a well-governed spirit will govern the tongue. An unrestrained tongue is an evidence of levity, or of some worse quality in the heart. And if the spirit be faithful, the tongue will be cautious and friendly. The communication between the spirit and the tongue is so easy, that the one will certainly discover the quality of the other, for out of the abundance of the heart the mouth speaketh.

Ver. 14. *Where no counsel is, the people fall ; but in the multitude of counsellors there is safety.*

In our private concerns it is dangerous to trust our own wisdom, and it is our interest to advise with wise and faithful friends, in every important business of life. But in the affairs of countries, public calamity must be the inevitable consequence of the sovereign's being not wise enough to know his need of asking and following the advice of wise men. If he asks the advice of wise men, and yet follows that of fools, he is no better than Rehoboam, who by such conduct rent his kingdom, and but for the kindness and faithfulness of God to David, in reserving two tribes to his grandson, would have lost it all.

Solomon had wisdom not only to teach, but to practise this maxim. He had wise counsellors under whom his kingdom flourished, and their counsels might have preserved the kingdom in the hands of his son. But God infatuates those whom he intends to punish ; and there is not a plainer evidence of infatuation than when men presume on their own sense, or prefer the counsel of the vain and foolish to that of the sober and the wise.

Great is the judgment with which God visits a land, when he removes wise and faithful counsellors from the management of its concerns *. In our intercession for kings, then, let us pray that God may furnish them with good counsellors, and with wisdom to make a proper use of them.

Ver. 15. *He that is surety for a stranger shall smart for it ; and he that hateth suretiship is sure.*

Friendship or charity may, on some rare occasion, make it our duty to become surety for one that is not a stranger † ; but still our friendship must be guided by discretion, that our own peace, the welfare of our family, and our ability to pay our just debts, may not be brought into danger.

" He that is surety for a stranger shall smart for it," for he will lose his money, and involve himself in difficulties, or at least feel many anxious thoughts till relieved from the rash obligation. Or should he escape all these misfortunes, the same levity of mind that induced him to become bound for another man's debts, will entangle him in new engagements, so that he must have extraordinary good fortune if he never smart for it. " He that hateth suretiship," on the other hand, is comparatively sure, for perfect certainty is not in earthly things. He is at least secure against those self-reflections which sting the mind of the thoughtless squanderer, who signed away his peace and property, the talent of beneficence entrusted to him, and the bread of a family dependent on him, because, forsooth, he could not utter the word *no*, to one that seemed to trust his generosity.

---

*Isa. 3   †Philemon

He that conscientiously observes this and other
rules of Scripture about his worldly substance, keeps
the way of the Lord ; and the man who, while he does
so, trusts in the Lord, has promises respecting earthly
things, that impart a security to which other men have
no parallel.

If the Scripture condemns those who risk their substance by a species of prodigality that has in it a tinc-
ture of generosity, how worthy of condemnation are
those unfaithful stewards of providence who spend their
Master's substance on cards, or on riotous living and
harlots ; thus using the bounties of God for the service
of the devil, and for ruining their own souls and the
souls of others !

How infinite was the grace of him who became surety for enemies ! He was sure to smart under agonies
unknown in our world, and to be impoverished, though
possessed of unsearchable riches. How small, when
compared with this, was the generosity of Paul in becoming surety for a poor slave, or of Dion in risking
his life for his friend at the court of Syracuse !

Ver. 16. *A gracious woman retaineth honour, and
strong men retain riches.*

It is not a set of fine features, or a blooming complexion, that makes a woman gracious, but faith in
Christ, and the fear of God ; prudence and modesty,
humility and attention to the duties which she owes to
her parents, her husband, and her children.

A woman beautified with these lovely graces, is possessed of true honour, for such ornaments are in the
sight of God himself of great price. If she is in the
married state, her possession of such virtues will be
the means of conferring upon her husband more happiness than a crown could bestow.

But the children of the serpent would rob the daughters of Eve of their honour. Partaking of the subtilty

and malice of their father, they would, for the sake of a little contemptible gratification, turn the paradise of the gracious woman into a dreary desart.

As strong men will not suffer their riches to become a prey to depredators, so a gracious woman will hold fast her virtue against those villainous spoilers, who would rob her of the ornaments, with which, when compared, oriental pearls are like the mud in the mire, the diamonds of Golconda like the stones of the street.

That she may be successful in holding fast her virtue, she must commit herself to the keeping of the Seed of the woman, who was manifested to bruise the head of the old serpent, and to destroy the works of the devil. If Eve in her perfect state could not protect herself from the serpent when yet young, how shall the fallen daughters of Eve protect themselves against that old serpent, who, by the diligent practice of nearly 6000 years, has now become a proficient in the art of tempting!

She must read the Bible, guard against idleness, and shun the society of the bad, as she would a house infected by the pestilence. If in a single state, she must shew all deference to her parents, and care for the things of the Lord; if married, she must care for her husband how to please him, and by her dress and behaviour prove herself a daughter of Sarah *.

Let her, in a word, treasure up the instructions of Lemuel's mother. On them let her form her character, and by them regulate her general deportment. Then shall her husband and her children, her neighbours and acquaintances, yea, and her own good works also, praise her in the gates. Nor shall her honour be

---

*1 Tim. 2:9, 1 Peter 3:1-6, Prov. 31:11-31

confined to herself, but her husband shall be honoured with her.

Ver. 17. *The merciful man doeth good to his own soul; but he that is cruel troubleth his own flesh.*

It is the mercy of our Lord Jesus Christ to which we must look for eternal life *. He that has this hope in him will compassionate the distressed, and endeavour to imitate that mercy on which all his hope depends. And God is so full of mercy, that men shall be no losers, but great gainers, by that mercy which they shew to others. Though it should be considered in no other light than a debt which they already owed to God and to their fellow-creatures, yet the gracious rewards of the merciful man are rich in this world †, and at the last day they shall be so transcendantly great as to fill with amazement the happy receiver ‡.

That they may be losers by the exercise of mercy, and that they know not what they may need for themselves, are the only objections which men can urge against it. But if they really believed the Bible, they would shew mercy, because they know not what they may need, and would regard such loss better far than gain ‖.

" But he that is cruel troubleth his own flesh." Why did not the wise man say, " his own soul?" He knew that a cruel man cares nothing for his soul. If you would obtain a hearing from the merciless man, say nothing about his soul. He values it less than his dog. But if you could convince him that his want of mercy will be hurtful to his flesh, he would think a little about his ways. And it is evident from Scripture, that his flesh, no less than his soul, is under a fearful curse. He shall have judgment without mercy.

---

*Jude 21   †Ps. 41   ‡Matt. 25:37   ‖Eccl. 11:1,2

How awful is this sentence, when even merciful men need infinite mercy to save them * !

But who is the cruel man ? Scarcely any person will take with this detestable character. Julius Cæsar, who had been the death of many hundred thousands, did not think himself a cruel man. Hazael, a few hours before he murdered his master, could not believe himself to be such a dog as to be cruel. But the contrast in this verse teaches us, that to want mercy, is a sign of cruelty. He is not the only great transgressor who strips the naked, but that man also who gives not bread to the hungry, nor water to the thirsty.

Ver. 18. *The wicked worketh a deceitful work ; but to him that soweth righteousness shall be a sure reward.*

Solomon's heart was large as the sand on the seashore. He could have amused and surprised us with new discoveries in every proverb, but he was directed by the Holy Spirit to seek our profit rather than his own fame, and to inculcate again and again the same interesting and necessary truths, that we may learn and practise them.

That sin is attended with extreme misery, and righteousness with great happiness, he has already informed us at considerable length † ; and we here find him resuming the subject, dilating upon it, and exhibiting it in a variety of lights. If we consider our ways, we shall find that there is no vain repetition in his words, for none of us have been sufficiently attentive to them. If we had, no motives, however alluring or terrifying, would have reconciled us to any neglect or violation of the divine law. The ground that is particularly bad, must be ploughed over and over, to prepare it for a crop.

---

*The expression, "his own flesh", may perhaps rather mean those who are related to him by blood.   †Ver. 3-11

" The wicked worketh a deceitful work." None would be so rich and happy as the servants of Satan, were his promises all performed; but the misery is, that he will promise kingdoms, though he cannot, like Chaldean robbers, have a single sheep without the divine permission ; and what is worst of all, those that trust his promises are paid with fire and brimstone.

The devil was a liar from the beginning, and yet so infatuated are men, that they will trust him more than the God that cannot lie. The devil places pleasure and profit before them ; God, by the threatenings of his word, sets an everlasting hell before them. But they will venture through it, in order to enjoy the vanities with which the great tempter allures them. They have the presumption to think, that by their plausible pretences they shall not only be able to cheat their fellow-men, but to elude the all-seeing eye of God, while, alas ! the devil is cheating them to everlasting misery.

" But to him that soweth righteousness shall be a sure reward." All men are sowing seed in the course of their lives. Wicked men sow the wind, and shall reap the whirlwind. Righteous thoughts, and words, and actions, are seed that shall shoot up in happiness inexpressible. The sower must wait and exercise long patience, but the harvest shall abundantly recompence his patience and his toil. He may sow in tears, but he shall reap in joy. He may be at much expense, and so was Isaac, when he sowed much corn in a time of famine. The good patriarch might be a little straitened whilst his corn was growing in the fields, but the Lord gave him an hundred-fold, and will give much more than an hundred-fold to the sowers of righteousness,—an hundred-fold in this life, and in the world to come, life everlasting. Who would not expend more seed than he could well spare on so fruitful a field !

Husbandmen may be disappointed of their hopes,

and through adverse providences, the harvest may become a heap in the day of desperate sorrow; but if there be truth and righteousness with God, or certainty in the word of the faithful Witness, the reward of the sowers of righteousness shall be sure *.

Ver. 19. *As righteousness tendeth to life, so he that pursueth evil, pursueth it to his own death.*

Our best life is the gift of God, through Jesus Christ, on whose righteousness our title to it stands. Our personal righteousness is the proof of our title, and our preparation for the possession of it. He, therefore, that lives in the practice of sin, that only evil, "does it to his own death." It is natural to all men to hate the devil, and death, and hell; yet so infatuated are wicked men, that they willingly serve the devil, and love death, and push on towards hell, though God thunders in their ears this awful sentence, "He that pursueth evil, doth it to his own death." And there must be truth in it, if God be the Sovereign of life and death; for,

Ver. 20. *They that are of a froward heart are abomination to the Lord; but such as are upright in their way are his delight.*

There is inexpressible malignity in sin, for the most merciful God threatens, and detests, and curses, and will destroy them that live in it. Uprightness is a noble quality, for the Lord greatly delights in it.

He boasted, if we may speak so, to the devil of Job's invincible integrity. Christ speaks of an upright Nathanael, as a wonder in the world. How wonderful is the grace of God, that takes such kind notice of grace so imperfect as that which may be found on earth! It is but a faint and sullied beam from himself, who is the Sun of righteousness.

---

*Matt. 6:20, Heb. 6:10

How forcible motives are these to deter men from sin, and allure them to holiness ! Are we men, or are we stones rather ? We shew ourselves to be so, if we are impressed, neither by the tremendous denunciations of his displeasure, nor by the displays of his loving-kindness. Sinners flatter themselves with the blasphemous hope that the word of threatening shall be wind, and that by some means they shall escape the vengeance of the Lord. But hear, O sinners ! believe and tremble;

Ver. 21. *Though hand join in hand, the wicked shall not be unpunished ; but the seed of the righteous shall be delivered.*

If all the wicked on earth should combine with all the devils of hell, to prevent the execution of judgment, it would only be a combination of thorns fully dry against the devouring flame. Do sinners imagine that they shall be safe, though so many dreadful threatenings stand pointed against them ? Let them read with horror that portion of Scripture contained in Deuteronomy, chap. xxix. from the 18th to the 25th verse. The man that hardens his spirit against these words, is an infidel.

But upon mount Zion, and upon Jerusalem, shall be deliverance, and the righteous shall enjoy it, and their offspring with them. No believer in Christ can secure his unbelieving children ; but present deliverances are often granted to the ungodly seed of the godly. That blemish in David's line, king Ahaz, was not utterly destroyed, because God would still give a lamp in Jerusalem to his servant David.

When some of Sir Thomas More's children complained to him that they could make nothing of their posts under him, because of his strict administration, he answered, " I will do justice to all men for your sake, and will leave you a blessing."

Ver. 22. *As a jewel of gold in a swine's snout, so is a fair woman which is without discretion.*

Solomon does not deny that beauty is an amiable quality, for he compares it to a jewel of gold. But he denies that beauty without discretion can render a woman lovely. The nature of a swine is not altered by its being adorned with nose jewels, such as those which some of the ladies of Zion used to wear. It is still, with all its decorations, a swine; it loves the mire, and its ornaments, instead of concealing its ugli_ ness, only render it so much the more an object of scorn and of ridicule. Every eye will be attracted by it, and every beholder astonished by so unnatural a conjunction of vileness and adorning. A beautiful woman may be admired for a time, but when her vanity and folly are detected, admiration is turned into loathing.

If beautiful women would gain and preserve the honour that belongs to the gracious woman, let them beware of those who are disposed to flatter. When their flatterers compare them to angels, and speak of their lilies and their roses, let them remember, that a wiser and more honest man compares beauty, without discretion, to a jewel of gold in a swine's snout.

Look to thy face in a glass, (said one of the wise men of Greece), and if thou hast beauty, disgrace it not by an unseemly behaviour; but if thou art ugly, make amends for it by the beauty of thy conversation.

Ver. 23. *The desire of the righteous is only good; the expectation of the wicked is wrath.*

A righteous man will not indulge the natural desires of the flesh and of the mind, but will endeavour to limit his wishes by the rules of the Bible. In consequence, indeed, of the remaining darkness of his mind, and distempers of his heart, he may desire things not good for him ; still, however, it is his wish that nothing may be granted him, inconsistent with the will of that God, who knows infinitely better than his people do what is good for them, and who will give them what is good though they ask not for it, and who will keep back nothing needful for them, however averse to receive it they may be.

For this reason it is that the desire of the righteous shall always end in what is good for them, for their desires are presented to that God who hath assured them, that if they ask any thing according to his will, he heareth them. No righteous man would for a world consent that these words, " according to his will," should be dropped from this promise of Scripture.

The righteous man is happy when his desires are either granted or refused, but " the expectations of the wicked," gratified or disappointed, " are wrath." The Israelites had flesh to satisfy their lusts, but leanness was sent into their souls, and the wrath of God soon squeezed out all the sweetness of their quails. They, at another time, desired a king, and God gave them a king in his anger, but took him away in his wrath. " The expectation of the wicked shall perish." Here is misery, but it is not all their misery. The perfection of it is, that their " expectation is wrath."

Ver. 24. *There is that scattereth, and yet increaseth ; and there is that withholdeth more than is meet, but it tendeth to poverty.*

Liberality is one eminent branch of the character of the righteous, but because there are many objections in the heart of man against the practice of it, urgent motives are here addressed to us. The instructions delivered in this and the four following verses, will, if they are but believed, be a sufficient answer to every objection.

There is that scattereth his substance by profusion and luxury. That man diminishes his substance till it comes to nothing. But he that disperses by giving to the poor, by liberal distributions for the support of the commonwealth in times of danger, or for the service of religion, shall increase his substance. He is like the husbandman, who sows with good will and unsparing hand, that precious seed which is to produce a joyful harvest. It is God who gives all that we enjoy, and by his secret blessing, or by remarkable interpositions of providence, the liberal man is often made to abound in riches, and enabled more and more abundantly to serve his fellow-men *. Abraham sat at his tent-door to watch for passengers, and those who came, he urged to partake of his bounty, with more earnestness than other men beg an alms. Job never ate his morsel alone; and the latter end of both these men did greatly increase.

Of all the rich men that have come to poverty, I never heard of any that was ruined by a discreet liberality, but " there is that withholdeth more than is meet, and it tendeth to poverty." Men may give something to the poor, and yet be impoverished, without being exceptions to the truth of this proverb ; for though they give some small matter off their superfluities, yet they withhold more than is meet. They are like a husbandman sowing an acre with half a bushel of grain, who will soon reduce his substance to nothing †.

What will become of him who is so far from being generous, that he is not just ? He withholdeth of *that which is right*, as the word may be rendered, and brings the roll of God's curses into his house, to consume the timber and stones thereof.

---

*2 Cor. 9:7-11   †2 Cor. 9:6

Ver. 25. *The liberal soul* (Heb. *soul of blessings*) *shall be made fat; and he that watereth shall be watered also himself.*

He is not the truly charitable man who has an open purse, but not a charitable heart. The thoughtless prodigal, when he is scattering his money, may bestow his share upon the indigent; but though he should give them all he has, it will not prove him possessed of the grace of charity.

The good man not only gives his bread, but draws out his soul to the hungry. He knows the grace of our Lord Jesus Christ, who was rich, and yet became poor for our sakes; and his charity, produced by this knowledge, is suitable to the design of the gospel, for it is out of a pure heart, and a good conscience, and faith unfeigned.

The man of liberal soul shall *be made fat.* He prospers in his soul, and if God think it good for him, he shall prosper in his body and in his circumstances also. He waters others with the blessings of his bounty, and he shall be watered himself with the blessing of Divine mercy, till he become like a watered garden, or like a spring of waters, whose waters fail not *.

Say not, then, you would be liberal if you could. Every man who has a liberal soul, however little his purse be, shares in the blessedness of the liberal. Two mites from a poor widow, will be as acceptable in the temple-treasury, as two pounds from one who abounds in wealth; and the poor who pour forth prayers for those distressed persons whom they have not money to relieve, are liberal in the sight of God; for if there be first a willing mind, it is accepted according to what a man hath, and not according to what he hath not.

Did not charity forbid, a Christian would be glad

---

*Isa. 58

on his own account that there are very poor persons in the world, for in relieving their necessities, he does a thousand times more good to himself than to them. That saying of Christ is certainly true, " It is more blessed to give than to receive."

Persons may exercise charity in selling as well as in giving, for,

Ver. 26. *He that withholdeth corn, the people shall curse him ; but blessing shall be upon the head of him that selleth it.*

Bread is the staff of life. The king himself is served by the field. But the husbandman, or trader in corn, must not withhold or sell merely as it serves his own interests, but must consider himself as a steward in God's great family, and use that talent with which he is entrusted, for the benefit of others, as well as for his own advantage. He must not withhold his corn from the market in order to increase the price, and enrich himself at the expense of the poor, and the risk of their life and health. If he does so, he counteracts the kind design of Providence in making the corn spring out of the earth, and discovers a mean, selfish, and unfeeling heart. He grinds the faces of the poor, and tempts people to murmur at the allotments of Providence, and to utter imprecations against himself. Thus he at once shares in the guilt of their curses, and exposes himself to the effect of them ; for though such curses are very sinful, the sin lies chiefly on the inhuman object who was the tempter to them, and they are not to be ranked among the causeless curses which shall not come. When defrauded labourers, or the oppressed poor, cry against the author of their distresses, the cry enters into the ears of the Lord of Sabaoth : much more will he hear the cries of a whole province or people, against him who is the instrument of withholding from them the necessaries of life. " But blessings shall be upon the head of him that generously sells it," when it was in his power to enrich himself by withholding. Although he takes a reasonable price for this useful commodity, he yet exercises more useful and extensive liberality, than he who bestows his superfluities to feed a few of the indigent.

It is not said the people shall bless him. Men are more ready to curse their oppressors than to bless their benefactors. Besides, they may think it superfluous to give both a price and a blessing for their food. But we are not to serve men chiefly from a regard to their thanks, but to look above them, to that God who delights in goodness, and who will not fail to recompense it in its different expressions of giving, or lending, or selling.

Though no blessings should reach the ear of the man who generously sells, they shall descend from heaven upon his head. God looketh down upon the children of men, and considereth all their ways; whatever, therefore, our business is, it is our duty to perform the offices of it with a view to the glory of God. And God is glorified when we do all our works in charity, endeavouring faithfully, in our respective stations, to serve our generation according to the will of God. When we look, not only on our own things, but also on the things of others, we are serving ourselves most effectually; for,

Ver. 27. *He that diligently seeketh good, procureth favour; but he that seeketh mischief, it shall come unto him.*

God is infinitely good, and is still doing good from heaven. He gives us rain and fruitful seasons; yea, he has bestowed upon us the inestimable gift of Christ, and salvation through his blood. Surely the consideration of this goodness might dispose us to labour diligently in promoting the good of other men, though in doing so we should be obliged to forego much happiness of our own. But God in his goodness hath provided a sufficient answer to all those objections against serving others, which are taken from our own interest. He that diligently pursueth good, may put himself to much toil and expense ; but he obtains favour, and that is an abundant recompense for all the labours and sufferings of love. He will likely have the favour of men, for when a man's ways please the Lord, he maketh even his enemies to be at peace with him ; but he is sure of the favour and blessing of God *.

But when a man seeks mischief, it is questionable indeed whether he shall effect his malicious purpose, but it is certain that the mischief he does to himself is greater than that intended against his neighbour. The just Lord is known by the judgment which he executes, in causing the contrivers of evil to fall into their own snares.

Ver. 28. *He that trusteth in his riches shall fall ; but the righteous shall flourish like a branch.*

After all that Solomon can say, many will still trust to their chests and to their bonds, more than to the promises of God. Their money is their strong castle in which they hope to be safe, and the fountain whence, they expect supplies of comfort. A text in the Proverbs is not so good as a full purse, and therefore they will not part with their money to others, but will keep it for their own use. Confidence in money is a sin that has produced much sin, prevented many acts of goodness, and will, at the day of judgment, be found a general article in the charge against the wicked. The Scripture frequently warns men against this instance of idolatry †, and calls on ministers to preach against it.

---

*Luke 6:38   †Ps. 49 & 52, Eph. 5:5

They that trust in riches shall fall like the flower of the grass, or like the leaves of a tree. Their riches shall leave them ; or if they should die in the midst of their wealth, they can carry nothing of their glory along with them. Their wealth cannot keep them from falling into hell, or mitigate the horrors of the infernal lake ; but the righteous shall flourish as a branch.

The righteous man trusts not in the unfaithful mammon, but in the name of the Lord *. He thinks the promise of God better security than the earth can afford, and trusts his money in the hands of him who says, " He that giveth to the poor lendeth to the Lord, and he will recompense again what he hath given unto him." This man shall not fade like the leaves, but shall flourish like the branch of a tree †. A branch may during winter appear withered, but it drops not from the stock, and in the spring it revives and grows. So the righteous man, though he meets with seasons of affliction, shall revive and flourish. He is ingrafted into the true Vine, and partaking of his vital influence, shall abound in the fruits of comfort and righteousness. At death he shall be transplanted into the celestial paradise, where all the trees of righteousness shall flourish in immortal beauty.

Ver. 29. *He that troubleth his own house shall inherit the wind ; and the fool shall be servant to the wise of heart.*

The eye of God is still upon us, and he observes how we behave in our different relations. He punishes with disappointment, poverty, and disgrace, the man who is a scourge instead of a blessing to his own family.

A man is a plague to his family, when he is of a domineering and quarrelsome temper, bursting into

---

*Job 1:5, 31:13-15

passion at every trifling omission of his will and pleasure ; when by covetousness he oppresses his servants and children with bondage and hard labour, scarcely allowing them to enjoy life ; when by prodigality he wastes the bread and portion of his children ; when, by his disregard to mercy and justice, he brings the curse of God on himself and his house ; when, by irreligion, he neglects the spiritual welfare of his family, and encourages them in evil by a bad example.

The troubler of his house shall possess vanity, disappointment, and misery. The evils that he brings to his dependants are doubled to himself. Those who might be his best friends, he makes his enemies ; and his vices, so troublesome to others, produce in the end torment and ruin to himself. He has all the marks of a fool, and through the natural consequences of his folly, and the merited judgment of God, is likely to be reduced to a slavish dependance on the wise of heart, who shew their wisdom by such a government of their families, as promotes the holiness and happiness of those whom Providence has entrusted to their care *.

Providence does not always bring these punishments upon men, lest we should forget that there is a judgment-day coming ; but they are often inflicted as an earnest of what all persons of like behaviour are to expect at the great day of accounts.

Ver. 30. *The fruit of the righteous is a tree of life : and he that winneth souls is wise.*

The righteous shall flourish as a branch, and they bear the fruits of the tree of life, for they are ingrafted in Christ, and derive supplies of spiritual influence from him. No fruit-bearing tree that is seen in our cursed earth, is a sufficient emblem to represent the excellency of the righteous man. He is like that noblest tree of

---

*Prov. 18:10,11   †Jer. 17:7,8

paradise, which was planted by the hand of God himself, and was distinguished above all the trees in the
paradise of God.   His fruits are such as tend to produce and nourish a nobler life than any of the trees of
the garden of Eden.   Christ is indeed the life of souls,
and those who are not united to him continue in death ;
but he is pleased to honour faithful ministers and edifying professors, by making them instruments of imparting his best blessings unto men.   It is for this
reason that diligent ministers are said to save themselves
and their hearers.   How excellent is the righteous man
above his neighbours ! His gracious words, his holy conversation, his prayers, his admonitions and instructions,
are means of rendering service to others, more valuable
than silver, or gold, or life itself.   Let Christians therefore endeavour to be fruitful in the knowledge of our
Lord Jesus Christ, and labour to win souls to their Redeemer.   Even women, who are not allowed to speak
in the church, may by this means share the reward of
those who turn many to righteousness.   What know
they but that they may save their husbands or neighbours, and allure to the faith of Christ those that did
not obey his word * ? They are wise who are wise unto
salvation ; how truly wise, then, are they who are instruments in converting and saving the souls of others
from death † ! They are by the world counted wise,
who, by means of their skill in business, leave their
friends rich.   But they shall at the great day be declared by the Judge of all wise, who can say, " Behold
I, and the children which thou hast given me." These
are my joy and crown of rejoicing.   Happy are all they
who shall be able thus to speak on that eventful day,
which seals the characters of men.

Let us also learn from this passage, to value the

---

*1 Peter 3:2, 1 Cor. 7:16   †James 5:20

friendship and conversation of the righteous. If we knew of any tree that bore fruit which could prolong the life of man to an hundred years, it would be esteemed more valuable than the treasures of kings, and we would spare no trouble or expense to have it transplanted into our gardens. What value, then, should we put on those whose fruit is the fruit of the tree of life, and whose conversation is instrumental in saving souls from death!

Ver. 31. *Behold, the righteous shall be recompensed in the earth; much more the wicked and the sinner.*

This verse is introduced by a word that calls for our attention, and contains an observation which explains all the proverbs which express the happiness of the righteous and the misery of the wicked, and answers an objection against them which naturally springs up in our minds.

It is evident from experience, and Solomon himself observes it, that there is a righteous man to whom it happens according to the work of the wicked, and a wicked man to whom it happens according to the work of the righteous. How, then, can it be said of the righteous, it shall be well with them; and of the wicked, it shall be ill with them?

We are to remember that the righteous need trials, and deserve chastisements. David suffered many afflictions, but he acknowledges that his sin and folly were the causes of them; and it was necessary, in order to keep the enemies of the Lord from blaspheming, that he should suffer in his person and family, when in the matter of Uriah he had turned aside from following the Lord. But the recompense of the errors of the righteous is confined to this life. They may suffer much severe correction, but there is no condemnation to them; for Jesus delivers them from the wrath to come, and in his blood they have a complete pardon of their iniquities ; so that their calamities are not the effect of divine wrath, but trials of their faith, or the corrections of a father.

Now, if the righteous are chastened so severely, how dreadful is the condemnation of the world ! if fatherly corrections break the bones and drink up the spirits of God's people, what imagination can conceive the horrors of that inflamed wrath which is the portion of the wicked ! Believers smart for sins committed through infirmity, fully forgiven through the blood of Christ, and sincerely lamented by themselves. But who knoweth the power of God's anger in crushing the wicked, when the day of grace is past, and the time is come to make the praise of God known in the vessels of wrath fitted to destruction ! " If the righteous scarcely be saved, where shall the wicked and ungodly appear ?"

Proverbs 12

Ver. 1. *Whoso loveth instruction loveth knowledge ; but he that hateth reproof is brutish.*

PYTHAGORAS took to himself the name of Philosopher, or lover of wisdom, rather than the name of wise man, which had been assumed by the sages before him, because he thought that the greatest men might, with more propriety, be called seekers, than finders of wisdom. If a man be a lover of knowledge, though much ignorance still remains with him, he is in the sure way of finding it *. But is there any man so foolish, and so like a beast, as not to love knowledge? Solomon tells us, that those who love instruction, love knowledge; but those who hate reproof are brutish. Let us, therefore, examine ourselves by this mark. The lover of knowledge will take pleasure in the Bible, and in sermons, and in conversation with the wise. He will be glad of reproofs, which serve to convey the most seasonable and necessary instructions, though in a manner so mortifying to human pride, that they are not relished but by those who prefer their real good to the applause of men. The lover of knowledge will count that man his real friend, who honestly tells him his faults, and would chuse to be a member of that family and church which is governed by the rules of Christ; for though he values liberty, he does not place it in being allowed to do evil when he pleases, without check.

But he who hates instruction, and cannot endure the reproof of charity, is brutish. He is like the horse or the mule, which bites and kicks at the man who performs a painful operation upon it, though absolutely necessary for removing a dangerous distemper; or like a dog, or sow, which will shew as much rage at the man that casts a pearl before it, as if he were killing it with a stone †. He is surely a brute, and not a rational creature, who has swallowed poison, and will rather suffer it to take its course, than admit the necessary relief of medicine, lest he should be obliged to confess his folly, in exposing himself to the need of it.

*Phil. 3:13　†Ps. 32:9, Matt. 7:6

There is ordinarily in offenders a strong aversion to
the administration of Christian discipline. They think,
that by it their honour is wounded ; but they ought
to consider, that by their sin the wound is already
given to their honour, and that a cheerful submission
to this ordinance of Christ, is the only way by which
it can be repaired.

There is an equal indisposedness among professors
of religion, to receive Christian reproof. Drunkards
and swearers often discover less displeasure against a
reprover, than some that consider themselves first-rate
Christians. The man, therefore, that ventures on the
friendly office of admonition, must exercise much prudence, and shew, by his manner of dispensing it, that
he is constrained by charity, lest he irritate instead of
reforming.

Asa was a good man, and yet he was angry at a
prophet of God for reproving him. He certainly
ought to have made Asaph's confession, " Thus foolish was I, and ignorant ; I was as a beast before
thee.

Ver. 2. *A good man obtaineth favour of the Lord ; but
a man of wicked devices will he condemn.*

We are to shew forth the virtues of him that called
us out of darkness into his marvellous light, by endeavouring to shine in the exercise of such Christian
graces, as correspond to those attributes of God that
shine with resplendent lustre in the work of our salvation. The exercise, therefore, of charity and goodness,
is highly becoming those on whose account such miracles of goodness and love have been displayed.

A good man forms no devices for serving himself,
to the prejudice of his fellow-creatures. Could a window be opened in his breast, you would see charity
ruling in his heart, and disposing him earnestly to

wish for the spiritual and temporal advantages of his neighbours, and to imitate our gracious Saviour, who went about doing good; for the Spirit of Christ is in him, and the fruit of this Spirit is in all goodness. He does not value himself on this account, as if there were any merit in paying a debt which he owes to men on God's account *. All his hopes are founded upon that infinite goodness, which provided salvation for self-ruined sinners; yet his goodness is well-pleasing unto the Lord, who blesses him with the smiles of his countenance, and will remember him concerning all his works, and all his thoughts and designs of love, according to the multitude of his mercies †.

We must not do as others do to us, nor be discouraged in the practice of goodness, by the unthankful returns which we meet with from ungrateful men, but perform our duties to our fellow-creatures, from a regard to God, and with a view to his acceptance through Christ ‡. Is the praise or gratitude of men worthy to be the subject of a thought, when we read that a good man shall obtain favour from the Lord? If our goodness is produced by a regard to men, it is not goodness, but selfishness in disguise, and verily its whole reward is from men ||.

"But the man of wicked devices will he condemn." Such a man may be artful enough to disguise his selfish plans, under the mask of religion and benevolence, like the old Pharisees; but the eyes of the Judge of the world are like a flame of fire, they pierce into the secrets of every soul, and there is no dark design harboured, which shall not be completely disclosed in the day of Christ. When our Lord was upon earth, he discovered and condemned the corrupt hearts of many

---

*Rom. 13:8   †Eph. 6:8, Neh. 13:14,22,31   ‡Heb. 13:15,16
||Matt. 6:2

hypocritical rogues; and at the day of the revelation of the righteous judgment of God, no vain pretender to goodness shall stand in the congregation of the righteous. Even those that refused to minister to the necessities of others, shall be commanded to hell; and how shall they escape, whose hearts were pre-occupied with wicked devices, to the ruin or damage of those who were made of the same blood with themselves!

Ver. 3. *A man shall not be established by wickedness; but the root of the righteous shall not be moved.*

A man sometimes appears to be established, and often hopes to be so by wickedness; but it is all a delusion. Had Zimri peace who founded his throne on treason? A man may with more reason hope to build himself a sure house upon pillars of ice, than to establish his fortunes upon an accursed ground.

" But the root of the righteous shall not be moved." The leaves of the trees of righteousness may wither, their branches may be tossed hither and thither by the tempests of tribulation and affliction; but they are rooted in Christ *, and kept night and day by the Almighty †, and therefore their root is safe from the rage of earth and hell.

Ver. 4. *A virtuous woman is a crown to her husband; but she that maketh ashamed is as rottenness in his bones.*

A virtuous woman fears the Lord, reverences her husband, manages her house with prudence and care, behaves charitably to the poor, and kindly to all. To what should we compare such a woman? Should we resemble her to a bracelet, or say that she is a necklace of gold to her husband? Such comparisons would be quite below her worth. She makes him as happy as a king, and procures him such respect and honour, that she deserves to be compared to that royal orna-

---

*Col. 2:7   †Isa. 27:3

ment that encircles the head of Majesty. She is to her husband a crown enriched with those lovely virtues, which shine with more radiant lustre than the diamonds of the East.

She is health to her husband's bones, for the sight of her amiable behaviour, and the pleasure of her society, inspires him with that habitual cheerfulness which doth good like a medicine. But the woman that wants virtue makes her husband ashamed, and is as rottenness in his bones. Her peevish temper or passionate behaviour, her extravagant expences or her sordid avarice, the levity of her speech or the scandal of her vices, make him the object of pity or scorn when he is abroad, and fill him with anguish at home. She is not a help, but a torment to him that hath made her bone of his bone, and flesh of his flesh. A man may get out of a fever in a few weeks; but the misery of this living disease is, that unless the Almighty grace of God work an uncommon cure, it will prey upon a man's bones and spirits, till the death of one of the married parties brings relief.

Let such, then, as have wives to chuse, consider that the man should be the glory of Christ, as the woman of the man; that a good wife is from the Lord; and that it is therefore their interest to live to the praise of Christ, to resolve to marry only in the Lord, and to seek this precious gift from him, by humble prayer.

Let wives consider seriously, whether they wish for happiness and honour to their husbands, or disgrace and misery; and whether it be better for themselves to prove helpers to the joy, and crowns to the head of their husbands, or living plagues to them, and fires to consume their vitals *.

---

*1 Cor. 11:5-10

Let husbands give honour to their wives, and encourage them in virtue, by their kindness and approbation. What tender love does Christ shew to those, whom he is pleased to betrothe to himself in lovingkindness! So ought husbands to love their wives *.

Ver. 5. *The thoughts of the righteous are right ; but the counsels of the wicked are deceit.*

As far as we are warranted or concerned to judge of the character of our neighbours, we must draw our opinion of them from their words and behaviour ; but we are to form our judgment of ourselves, chiefly by our thoughts, which are the immediate product of our hearts; for as a man thinketh in his heart, so is he. The thoughts of the righteous are right. Evil and foolish thoughts often rise up in their minds, but they hate vain thoughts, and will not allow them a lodgingplace. Their love to God produces many delightful meditations concerning his excellency and grace, and constant desires to shew forth his glory. Their charity to men excludes ungrounded suspicion and evil surmises, and in their deliberations about their conduct, disposes them to consider not only how they may serve their own interests, but how they may contribute to the happiness of their neighbours. Should any plan be suggested to them that appears greatly conducive to their own advantage, it will be rejected with abhorrence, unless it consist with the happiness of those whom they are constrained, by the command of God and the love of Christ, to love as themselves.

But a wicked man's pleasure lies in those thoughts, that feed upon the earthly objects where his fancied happiness lies, and the schemes which he forms in his mind are crooked and artful. He must if possible be gratified in his pursuits, though others should be

---

*Eph. 5

rendered unhappy ; and because the persons at whose expense he means to serve himself, will naturally stand in his way, he contrives to cover his real designs with the false appearances of honesty and charity, that he may not be obstructed in their accomplishment.

Ver. 6. *The words of the wicked are to lie in wait for blood : but the mouth of the upright shall deliver them.*

There is a ready communication between the tongue and the heart ; when men's counsels are deceit, it may therefore be expected, that their words will be to lie in wait for blood.

There are passions in the hearts of wicked men, that are murder in the sight of God, and have a natural tendency to mischief and blood ; but through the good providence of the universal Ruler, they are checked by the terrors of conscience, or the fear of punishment from men, or some other means, and the world is prevented from becoming a scene of universal outrage.

But some wicked men are so unprincipled, that the life of their neighbours is of small account with them, if they can accomplish their own cursed designs. Their tongues have the subtilty and poison of the serpent in them, and by their devilish arts, they draw men into dangers fatal to their reputation, their souls, and their bodies. " But the mouth of the upright shall deliver them." Their wise answers preserve themselves, and their wise counsels preserve others from ruin. Thus Mephibosheth preserved himself from the snares of Ziba ; and our Lord Jesus Christ often preserved himself from the well-laid devices of his deceitful enemies *.

God will severely punish the wicked for their deceitful counsels and their deceitful tongues ; for,

---

*Isa. 33:16

Ver. 7. *The wicked are overthrown, and are not : but the house of the righteous shall stand.*

There is a mighty difference between the evils that befall the righteous, and those that come upon the wicked. Evil shall slay the wicked, so that they shall have no more existence in that world where their hopes and happiness lay, and their existence in another world shall be an everlasting curse ; but the righteous shall be established, and their seed with them *.

Ver. 8. *A man shall be commended according to his wisdom ; but he that is of a perverse heart shall be despised.*

It is not here said, that a man is commended according to his wisdom. There are some commended for their wit, and others for their cunning ; some for their genius, and others for their learning ; nay, some are foolishly commended for what in Solomon's estimation is nothing but folly. But praise built on a false foundation shall not continue, and wisdom will be found the only solid basis of a name. God approves of it, and men shall sooner or later join in its commendation.

John the Baptist did not affect the praise of men, and yet we find that by the people he was commended greatly, and even held in respect by the king. The Pharisees and the Priests procured the esteem of the people, and yet we find that Pilate saw through their false pretences, when they delivered up Christ to him ; and through the prevalence of truth, that veneration which they had engrossed, was in a great measure transferred to the apostles.

It is a great temptation to men to see wisdom despised, and qualities which have no necessary connexion with it applauded. The desire of respect is natural to men, and this prejudises them against that profession

---

*Verse 3, Chap. 10:25,30

232 / *Exposition of Proverbs*

or practice, which makes them forfeit the good opinion of men. This hindered many from professing the name of our Saviour *, and others from believing in him †. But the apostles shewed their wisdom, by glorying in shame for the name of Christ. They knew that this shame would end in royal honours ‡.

We should frequently think on the day of judgment, that day which will set the seal on all human characters. Then will the Lord himself commend the wise in the face of the world, and the perverse in heart shall be a universal abhorring.

Ver. 9. *He that is despised, and hath a servant ‖, is better than he that honoureth himself, and lacketh bread.*

Some people are such bond slaves to the applause and respect of men, that in order to make others think them happy, they render themselves miserable. For the sake of making a figure in the eye of the world, they live in constant straits and anxieties.

By the inspired moralist, this piece of folly is here censured; yet it is still very common, and very mischievous.

When men, through the pride of birth or station, or some unaccountable vanity of mind, are determined to live in such splendour as their income cannot support, the ordinary consequence is, that they run into debt, defraud their creditors, lose all trust from men, and expose themselves to the devil, who is too cunning to let slip the opportunity that thus presents itself, of tempting them to have recourse to the gaming-table, that decent substitute for the highway, or should this resource fail, to the highway itself, as a relief to their necessities. Starvation, or a jail, or a gibbet, or some-

---

*John 12:43   †John 5:44   ‡Matt. 5:11,12

‖Or, is servant to himself.

thing incomparably worse than all these, closes the scene.

Oh! how much better and wiser were it to reverence the providence of God, which fixes the lot of men, and to accommodate our minds to our circumstances, however narrow! In this way may we hope to enjoy the comforts, or at least the necessaries of life with composed minds, and be able to serve the Lord without distraction. If men should despise us because we cannot live as men of our rank do; it is not difficult to determine whether their opinion or our own peace of mind is to be preferred. Whatever men may say at present, yet afterwards shall a man be commended according to his wisdom.

To live above our income, that we may figure in the world, is to rebel against divine providence, and to forget him who used to feed on barley bread and fishes, while employed in accomplishing the work of human salvation. Paul travelling on foot, and living on the wages of a tent-maker, was more respectable than the pretended successor of his brother apostle with a triple crown on his head.

Ver. 10. *A righteous man regardeth the life of his beast: but the tender mercies of the wicked are cruel.*

How presumptuous are those men who despise their inferiors, and look on their happiness and comfort as matters unworthy of their regard! Though kings and beggars share in the same common nature, they have less goodness towards their fellow-men, than the righteous have for their beasts. A righteous man's mercy diffuses itself not only over the most abject of his neighbours, but even to creatures without reason. He will not deprive his beast of its food and rest, nor oppress it with unreasonable toil, nor sport himself with the misery and pain of those creatures which God hath subjected to his power. He considers them as servants to be employed for his advantage, but not to be tyrannized over. Are they animals good for food? Even in depriving them of life, he shews his humanity, by inflicting upon them no unnecessary degree of pain. But why should such a regard be paid to the lives and to the comforts of brutes? Because they are susceptible of pleasure and pain, and not so much our inferiors as we are inferior to him that made both them and us.

Heathens themselves were sensible of the mercy due to the animal creation. The Athenians excluded a man from a place in their government, because he killed a bird that fled to him for shelter; justly reasoning, that a man who could exercise cruelty to brutes, could not be safely trusted with the life or comfort of his fellow-men.

That God, whose goodness the righteous imitates, is good to all. In goodness he made and preserves the beasts. He would not suffer them to be all drowned in Noah's flood, and he considered them in sparing Nineveh. There are many laws in the books of Moses guarding us against wanton oppression; and these laws, inconsiderable as they may appear to us, are fenced with promises and threatenings. And what is equally worthy of our regard on this head, God on one occasion opened the mouth of one of the most contemptible beasts, to plead the cause of the dumb creation, and an angel took its part.

But wicked men are so far from exercising their compassion to brutes, that they are unfeeling to men; and when they appear to themselves or to others the most merciful, their kindness is often cruelty in disguise. When persons give to the poor, and join their gifts with insult and abuse, this is cruel mercy. When Pilate ordered Christ to be scourged, with a design to procure his release, was this mercy? and not rather injustice and oppression. Such was the mercy of the

Jewish council to the apostles *, and of the Philippian magistrates to Paul †.

Ahab's mercy to Benhadad was cruelty in another sense. He was cruel to himself and to his people, that he might preserve the reputation of the kings of the house of Israel. Of the like nature are those foolish compassions which are sometimes exercised by parents, and magistrates, and ministers, to the great damage of those under their inspection, who are encouraged in vice by the connivance, or the too gentle reproofs and punishments administered to them. But this kind of cruel mercy has been too often practised by the righteous themselves, of which Eli and David are striking instances.

Let us look to our virtues, and examine them attentively, that vice may not lurk under them undiscovered. We too often applaud ourselves for that which should rather cause us to mourn.

Ver. 11. *He that tilleth his land shall be satisfied with bread : but he that followeth vain persons is void of understanding.*

The business of the husbandman is so honourable, that it is here used by Solomon to signify every useful profession. Kings themselves are served by the field, and the only two universal monarchs practised husbandry.

The Spirit of God here teaches us, that we ought to have a useful profession, and to follow it with diligence, minding our own business, and not intermeddling with affairs in which we have no concern. That we shall be satisfied with bread, is the encouragement held out to pursue such a course as this. Some people think that they cannot have enough, unless they have more than the necessaries and decent comforts of life ;

---

*Acts 5:41   †Acts 16:37

but we are here instructed that bread should satisfy our desires, unless God is pleased to bestow more upon us. Having food and raiment, let us be therewith content. There are few that want these, and yet few are content.

There are others who think that they will not be able to live by their business, without over-reaching their neighbours, by means of those underhand practices which custom has interwoven with many professions; but says the wise man, " He that tilleth his land shall have enough ;" and Paul tells us, that he may have something more to give to him that needeth.

To be satisfied with bread, is a happy temper of mind, and is commonly the portion of the man of industry, which not only procures bread, but gives it a relish unknown to men that are above labour. A dinner of green herbs is commonly a sweeter meal to the labourer, and followed by more refreshing sleep, than all the luxuries of high life to a man of fortune.

" But he that followeth vain or idle persons, is void of understanding." The idle man deserves the name of a fool ; nor can he clear himself of it by alleging, that the love of company, or the example of others, allures him to this course of life. It must be both sin and folly for a man, whatever reasons he pretends for it, to indulge himself in a vice by which he endeavours to elude the sentence passed upon fallen man, and breaks so many commandments of God ; weakens the powers of his mind, and destroys the vigour of his constitution ; exposes his mind as a prey to chagrin, and his soul to the temptations of the devil; wastes his precious time, and lays himself open to all the miseries of a self-procured poverty. In short, all the creatures in heaven, earth, and hell, proclaim the folly of the idle man. Let us, therefore, avoid it, as a nursery of vice and misery, and fill up our days with the useful labours of our calling, and the more important concerns of our souls.

Ver. 12. *The wicked desireth the net of evil men ; but the root of the righteous yieldeth fruit.*

The original word, which in the 24th verse of this chapter is rendered *slothful,* signifies also *deceitfulness,* for slothfulness and deceit often accompany each other. Wicked men have more enlarged desires after earthly things than the righteous, and their hands often refuse to labour for necessary things. What, then, shall they do ? Their lusts must be gratified at the expence of conscience and honesty, and so they *desire the net of evil men,* to ensnare others, and drag their property to themselves, that their portion may be fat, and their meat plenteous. But a righteous man is above the temptations that lead men to over-reach their neighbours, for he has an inward principle of integrity and contentment, which tends to moderate his desires, and directs to praise-worthy means for the enjoyment of them. Thus, by the blessing of God, he obtains what is needful for himself, and something also to give to him that needeth.

The life of a slothful man is full of the worst kind of toils, and is often a scene of guilt and wretchedness ; whilst a good man, besides his happy prospects, enjoys much pleasure in those earthly things, which to others are vanity and vexation of spirit.

Ver. 13. *The wicked is snared by the transgression of his lips ; but the just shall come out of trouble.*

As birds are suddenly seized by the gin, and cannot work their way out of it, so wicked men are often ruined unexpectedly and irretrievably, by means of their ungoverned tongues. Adonijah was spared for his rebellion, but by one presumptuous petition, he shewed himself a dangerous man, and brought vengeance upon his own head. Nabal, by his insolent language, almost destroyed his whole family ; and as the corrupt tongue is set on fire of hell, so burning coals are its reward *.

A just man may be endangered by his own tongue, but through the mercy of God he shall be delivered, as David was, when he had engaged himself too far with the king of Gath ; and Isaac and Abraham, when they had exposed the chastity of their wives, by their dissimulation at the court of the Philistines.

Nor will God ordinarily suffer the just to perish by the tongues of the wicked. Sometimes he has done it, as in the case of Abimelech the priest; but just men are not ruined by death itself.

Ver. 14. *A man shall be satisfied with good by the fruit of his mouth ; and the recompence of a man's hands shall be rendered unto him.*

As a bad tongue is one of the worst, so a good tongue is one of the best things in the world. By a well-ordered tongue, we may be useful in winning souls to Christ ; in teaching the ignorant, strengthening the weak, and making the mourners to rejoice. By our tongues we may glorify God, even the Father of our Lord Jesus Christ, and spread the savour of that name which is so dear to every Christian.

When men use their tongues in this manner, they shall be satisfied with good by the fruit of them ; for they obtain the friendship and respect of men, they enjoy acceptance with God through Christ Jesus, and the testimony of their conscience, that they have in some measure answered the end of their being. They are assured, that every word which proceeds from a pure heart, is marked down in God's book of remembrance.

---

*Ps. 120

David often reflected with pleasure on the restraints he had imposed on his tongue, or the charitable use he had made of it as circumstances required * ; and at the last day, our Judge tells us, that by our words we shall be justified or condemned.

But our words will only prove us to be hypocrites, if they proceed not from sincere hearts, or are unattended with a suitable behaviour. Those trees will be cut down that produce no good fruit, though they should abound with the most beauteous blossoms; and therefore it is added, that the recompence of a man's hands shall be rendered unto him.

Let our words, then, be ordered in the fear of God, and with a view to the account that will be taken of them, first by our own consciences, and then by our Judge, who now hearkens and hears every thing that proceeds from our lips ; and our actions must be under the same influence, that we may not condemn ourselves, and be judged out of our own mouths as dissembling hypocrites.

Ver. 15. *The way of a fool is right in his own eyes; but he that hearkeneth unto counsel is wise.*

The greater fools are those that have the highest opinion of their own wisdom. Their self-esteem disposes them to neglect the advice of others, and to prosecute their own schemes, however foolish and dangerous, till they meet with fatal disappointments, which, after all, can hardly open their eyes, clean shut with pride and vanity.

The wisest men are they who are most sensible of their need to avail themselves of the wisdom of others, and most qualified to make a proper use of counsel.

This rule is to be observed, especially in the affairs of religion, for in none do men discover more folly,

*Ps. 38:13, 142:6, 120:7

and a greater degree of self-confidence. Multitudes walk under the influence of delusion and error, who, instead of suffering themselves to be set right, despise those that are able to give them good advice. Multitudes that make a sound profession of religion, are strangers to the narrow way that leads to life, and would yet exclaim against such as would give them, from scripture, the clearest proofs of the danger of the mistakes under which they labour, and the insufficiency of the evidences which they think they can produce, of their being in the right way.

We are not, however, to hearken to counsel without examination, because other men are liable to error as well as ourselves. Absalom was ruined by giving ear to treacherous counsel; and Rehoboam lost the greater part of his kingdom, by preferring the counsel of fools to that of wise men. In our spiritual concerns, the only infallible counsellor is he who is made of God unto us wisdom, to whose word we are carefully to attend, and on whose Spirit and grace we must exercise a daily and humble dependence *.

It is our wisdom to value the instructions and counsels of ministers, of parents and Christian friends, particularly of experienced and aged saints. But they must be able to prove the goodness of their advices by the Scriptures, which are the great and only rule to direct us to our chief end.

Ver. 16. *A fool's wrath is presently known ; but a prudent man covereth shame.*

The wise man here uses a very observable word, to express wrath. He calls it shame, for it is a shame for a man to suffer his reason to be tyrannized over by an unruly passion, which spreads deformity over his countenance, and hurries him on to expressions and actions

---

*Ps. 25, Isa 9:6

more like those of one confined in bedlam, than of one who is supposed to have the use of his reason. A man would reckon himself debased, if the form of his body were changed into that of a wild beast; and is a man in a condition one whit more respectable, when reason is trampled under foot, and the government of his body and his tongue subjected to the spirit of a tiger?

A fool disgraces himself by giving way to the impetuous sallies of passion. He discovers his temporary madness, by his pale countenance, his quivering lips, and his flashing eyes. His tongue, having thrown up the reins of reason, pours forth torrents of rage, and perhaps of oaths and imprecations; thus announcing to every one that he meets, that he is a fool. It is with difficulty that his hands are restrained from doing that which in a short time would become the source of bitter and unceasing remorse.

"But a prudent man covereth shame." When he finds his passions beginning to ferment, he does not give them full scope, but considers whether he does well to be angry, and how far it is lawful and safe for him to give way to this turbulent passion. He does not cover his wrath, that it may have time to work, and draw the powers of reason into its service, that it may break forth with more effect on some other occasion,—but covers it, that he may have time to suppress and destroy it, by considering its folly and wickedness, by meditating on the example and grace of Christ, and by fervent supplications for the support and assistance of the Spirit of meekness.

By such means as these the prudent man preserves his own honour, and covers the shame of his neighbour, who is likely to be gained by gentleness and meekness. Thus the noblest of all victories is gained, whilst the Christian subdues, not only his own spirit, but the stubborn soul of his adversary, and covers, by his charity, a multitude of sins.

Ver. 17. *He that speaketh truth sheweth forth righteousness ; but a false witness deceit.*

Men, destitute of a principle of integrity, may be guilty of much iniquity in witness-bearing, whilst they flatter themselves that they are speaking nothing but the truth.

A true and faithful witness will deliver his testimony fully, clearly, and impartially. He will not only tell the truth, but all the truth that he knows about the point in question, as far as it will open up the merits of the cause. He will use no language that may be misunderstood by the judges, nor dissemble matters so as to favour even that cause which he supposes to be the right one. He will give no unfair representation of matters, to gratify or serve a good man, or one who is his best friend ; nor will pity constrain him so to disguise facts as to serve the cause of the poor man, or him who is in danger of being condemned. If one should offer him a bribe, he will shake his hands from holding it, and shut his ears against every attempt made to bias his mind.

" But a false witness sheweth forth deceit." He utters falsehood, or turns truth into a lie, by his manner of telling it. Doeg, by a real fact misrepresented, was the death of eighty-five priests of the Lord ; and they who bore testimony against our Lord, are called false witnesses, though they repeated our Lord's words with but little if any variation, because the little difference in words made a complete change in the sense.

It is necessary for us to consider exactly what we say, when the character or happiness of others is at stake, and to be cautious whom we trust, lest by artful misrepresentations we be persuaded to do injuries to our neighbours, which we cannot repair.

Ver. 18. *There is that speaketh like the piercings of a sword ; but the tongue of the wise is health.*

The slanderer and backbiter, the railer, the flatterer, the unrighteous witness, and the unreasonable murmurer, have tongues which may justly be compared to sharp swords, by which they wound or destroy the peace and comfort, the reputation and prosperity, or the very lives of their neighbours. The seducer to sin or error, has a sword in his mouth to destroy the souls of men. But the tongue of the wise has a healing virtue to cure the wounds inflicted by the wicked tongue, and other diseases that affect the comfort or safety of men.

It is not enough to refrain our tongues from evil. By them we should endeavour to defend the character of the injured, to pacify those that are offended by the slanders and revilings of others, to comfort the dejected, to instruct the ignorant, to reclaim those that err, and warn those that are in danger.

For these purposes, we must not only consider what is fit to be spoken, but when also, and to whom it may be proper to speak.

Job is an instance of the healing power of the tongue ; his friends, of the bad consequences of misapplying the most certain and important truths. They were good men, and their words discovered much zeal for God, and concern for the welfare of Job, and yet to that good man they were drawn swords *.

Ver. 19. *The lip of truth shall be established for ever ; but a lying tongue is but for a moment.*

Let us always remember to speak truth one to another, for if we lose any thing by it, our gain shall counterbalance the damage. Our credit will be established, and we shall enjoy that confidence from men,

*Job 4:3, etc.

on which our success and usefulness depend. Truth is the ornament of the great, and to poor men it is their stock and livelihood. Some small matter may be gained by lying, in the meantime, but a great deal more is lost when men lose their character by it. Our Lord tells those that had left all for him, that they should have an hundred-fold more in this world, and in the world to come life everlasting. It may, on the other hand, be said of liars, that besides death everlasting, they shall lose an hundred-fold more in this life, than they can gain by such unhallowed means. The liar begins by making falsehood to be taken for truth, and ends in making truth to be taken for falsehood. Truth from his mouth is ever suspected, and will not in time of need serve that man who formerly made lies his refuge.

Hypocrisy is lying to God, but the fancied advantages of it soon come to an end. The hypocrite's profession soon withers, or by his behaviour is discredited. His character is lost, and his hopes perish; but that profession of the mouth which proceeds from faith and soundness in the heart, shall always flourish and bear fruit. Its honours and advantages shall endure for ever, and if it exposes men to present inconveniences, they shall be abundantly compensated at the judgment of the last day *.

Ver. 20. *Deceit is in the heart of them that imagine evil ; but to the counsellors of peace is joy.*

The more of art and contrivance there is in any sin, it is so much the more sinful, and exposes men to the more severe judgment. God has given us the endowments of our minds, as talents with which we are to occupy till our Master come ; but if men hide them in a napkin, they shall be punished as unprofitable ser-

---

*Matt. 10

vants ; and if they use them for doing mischief, their punishment shall be still more severe. If the servant is punished who is careless about his work, he shall be punished with much greater severity, who employs his thoughts in contriving, and his hands in executing, mischief against his fellow-servants.

Such persons have hearts full of deceitfulness, but their crafty devices shall recoil upon themselves, and they shall have no solid joy, but disappointment and disgrace, as the reward of their work. What did their father the devil gain, by employing his servants to bring our Saviour to the dust of death ? Ruin to his kingdom. What was the consequence of his shutting up Paul in a dungeon ? The furtherance of the gospel. Haman was rewarded with a gibbet, for erecting one for Mordecai ; for it is the glory of God to force a tribute of praise to himself, out of the wrath and cunning devices of men.

" But to the counsellors of peace is joy." Let us give praise to God for his everlasting purpose to save men by Christ Jesus, and for the counsel of peace between the Father and the Son ; and follow the pattern of the Prince of Peace, by promoting the peace and happiness of our fellow-creatures. When the wicked are so busy in sowing discord and mischief, we must not be careless in seeking peace and pursuing it, for to the counsellors and promoters of peace is joy. Their minds are serene, their consciences are full of peace ; they are respected by men, and receive a blessing from Christ, who says, " Blessed are the peace-makers, for they shall be called the children of God."

Ver. 21. *There shall no evil happen to the just ; but the wicked shall be filled with mischief.*

Are not sickness, and persecution, and death, incident to the just ? or must we become Stoic philosophers, and imagine that there is no evil in pain ? Solomon did not mean this. But the evils that befal the just are so inconsiderable, compared with their happiness, and have their nature so much changed by the grace of God, that it may well be said, No evil shall happen to them. These are not the unmeaning flights of a philosopher who sits in his closet, and when he feels no inconveniency of any kind, can declaim with great fluency on the inability of outward accidents to disturb the repose of a wise man. The primitive Christians were exposed to every thing that men would call evil, and yet they would scarcely admit that they merited the name of evil things to them; because they could not separate them from the love of God which is in Christ Jesus, and because they bore no proportion, in weight or duration, to the glory to be revealed, and for which they were the means of preparing their souls.

But whatever may be the present situation of a wicked man, he shall be filled with misery and mischief. The calamities of the wicked, even in this world, are very different from those of God's people, for they are envenomed by the consciousness of guilt, unallayed by the comforts of faith and hope. Those things are killing to the wicked, which are trials to the righteous; and the time is speedily approaching, when the ungodly shall be for ever stripped of those objects which they looked upon as their portion, and filled with misery and horror, to the utmost extent of their capacity *.

How foolish is it to be terrified from righteousness, by evils not worthy to be named, or allured to sin by those slight and momentary pleasures, which are not to be compared with the exceeding and eternal weight of misery!

---

*2 Thess. 1:9

Ver. 22. *Lying lips are abomination to the Lord ; but they that deal truly are his delight.*

How terrible a thing is it to be abhorred by the Lord, whose loving-kindness is better than life, and his frowns worse than the most miserable death? What would it avail us to gain the highest advantages, or to insinuate ourselves into the favour of the mightiest prince, by a method that must provoke the indignation of Him from whom every man's judgment must come?

Lying lips are the objects of the Lord's abhorrence, though man design no evil to others by them ; nor will he excuse a person for lying, even when he intends to serve the best and most friendly purposes by it. If God's own favourites should be so unwise as to adopt this crooked method of serving the gracious providence of God to them, the Lord will often make them to feel how abominable their lies are to him, even when he shews his favour to their souls. Jacob would have got the blessing without cheating his father, but it may be questioned whether he should have been cheated by his second father, had he not by his sin deserved it at the hand of God.

God's abhorrence of liars appears in the common course of providence, which generally deprives them of greater advantages than their lies could ever produce ; but it shall be manifested with awful severity in the other world, when none that loveth and maketh a lie shall enter into the celestial city, but all liars shall have their part with their great pattern the father of lies, in the lake that burneth with fire and brimstone.

" But they that deal truly are his delight." Why did not the inspired writer say, they that *speak* truly ? Because truth in our words is not enough, without truth in our conversation. There must be in the Christian, a uniformity of the heart, the tongue, and the life. This is that integrity which God requires, and which he beholds with a pleasant countenance.

How presumptuous are they who think it no great evil to tell a lie, unless some farther degree of evil is intended? Is it all one whether we provoke God or please him? Do liars imagine that God is a liar like themselves? and will suffer his faithfulness to be dishonoured, by exempting them from the punishment found written in his word?

Ver. 23. *A prudent man concealeth knowledge; but the heart of fools proclaimeth foolishness.*

A prudent man will certainly publish his knowledge, when he finds a proper opportunity of making it useful to his fellow-creatures *. But he will conceal it, when to publish it would only display his own vanity and folly.

There is a time to be silent, and at that time it is a piece of prudence to keep our knowledge to ourselves. Elihu was a better speaker than any of the other friends of Job, and yet had the good sense to observe a profound silence, till they who had a better title to speak had finished all that they had to say. Our Lord had in him all the treasures of knowledge, and yet refused to speak before his enemies and judges, when speaking could be of no use; and did not even open up all the treasures of his wisdom to his disciples, when they were not duly prepared for the discovery of them; and he gives us a very necessary caution against casting our pearls before swine, or giving our holy things to dogs †.

But a prudent man will not conceal his knowledge, as the discoverers of some useful secret in the arts often do, to feed their pride, or to gratify a malignant disposition. He lays it up as a good householder lays

---

*Chap. 11:30   †Matt. 7:6

up provisions in his storehouse, to be produced for use as occasion requires. " But the heart of fools proclaimeth foolishness." The fool's mouth, under the direction of a foolish heart, is the herald of his own disgrace. He presumes to speak of those things of which he has a very imperfect knowledge, and to dictate to those that are much wiser than himself. He is confident where wise men speak with caution, and publishes what he actually knows, without a due regard to times, and persons, and places ; and whilst he flatters himself that he has gained a character for wisdom and downright honesty, he is generally looked upon as an impertinent fool. A word spoken in season, how good is it! but out of season, it is a sign of folly, and a cause of mischief.

Ver. 24. *The hand of the diligent shall bear rule ; but the slothful shall be under tribute.*

We must not try to thrust ourselves into places of power, for an aspiring spirit is more likely to be humbled than exalted. But in the calling wherewith we are called, let us abide and walk with God ; so shall we obtain that measure of wealth which is the fruit of industry, and if it so please God, we shall be advanced to stations of more eminent usefulness and dignity. The advancement of Joseph and of Mordecai, of Moses and of David, and of the apostles, are eminent illustrations of this truth.

They that have the power of advancing others into public stations, should make choice of men approved for their industry, as well as other good qualities, for it is industry that gives life and motion to all the rest. Solomon advanced Jeroboam because he was an active man, and Pharaoh would have none but men of activity set over his cattle, although they had been the brethren of his favourite.

250 / Exposition of Proverbs

"But the slothful shall be under tribute." Like Issachar, who saw that rest was good, and bowed down his shoulder to bear, and became a servant to tribute; by their laziness they expose themselves to want, and reduce themselves to a slavish dependence on those who, through the blessing of God on their own diligence or that of their fathers, are in better circumstances.

Spiritual sloth weakens men, and exposes them to the power of their spiritual enemies. We must be strong, resolute, and active, if we would stand in the evil day, and escape the tyranny of the rulers of the darkness of this world *.

Ver. 25. *Heaviness in the heart of man maketh it stoop; but a good word maketh it glad.*

There is a necessity that we should be in heaviness through manifold temptations; but we must be aware, lest by giving free scope to anxious and melancholy thoughts, our hearts should sink in us like a stone, and our souls become altogether unfit to relish the comforts, or perform the services of life. Sadness of the countenance makes the heart better, but despondency of heart disqualifies men for thanking and praising God, for serving their generation, and for bearing the burdens of life. Life itself becomes burdensome, and is often shortened by excessive grief. There is nothing that claims our grief so much as sin, and yet there may be an excess of sorrow for sin, which exposes men to the devil, and drives them into his arms †.

"But a good word maketh it glad." Expressions of sympathy and friendship have a powerful virtue to soothe and allay the sorrows of the mind, and to prevent their dangerous effect ‡. Job's complaints would have been fewer, had his friends shewed him that pity

---

*Eph. 6:10-18   †2 Cor. 2   ‡Job 16:5

which he expected from them. But no words have such efficacy for this purpose, as the words of God. David had perished in the day of his affliction, unless the law of God had been his delight. His afflictions were many, his griefs often great ; but they never overwhelmed him, for the statutes of God were his song in the house of his pilgrimage.

Would you comfort them that are cast down ? Study the doctrines and promises of the Bible ; make yourselves acquainted with the records of the experience of afflicted saints ; and pray for the tongue of the learned, that you may be enabled to make seasonable applications from this spiritual dispensary, to the broken in heart.

Are you grieved in your minds? Remember that it is sinful and dangerous to brood perpetually over your sorrows. In order that you may have comfort restored, retire and read your Bibles, and see that ye resist not, by the indulgence of unbelief, that Spirit who is promised as a comforter. In the 14th, 15th, and 16th chapters of John's Gospel, are contained those words of Christ, by which he conveyed strong consolation to his disciples, when sorrow had filled their hearts, because he was about to leave them. Can there be greater sorrows on any earthly account, or are there any griefs too desperate to be relieved by such consolations?

Ver. 26. *The righteous is more excellent than his neighbour ; but the way of the wicked seduceth them.*

The wise man does not say that the righteous is more excellent than the wicked, but gives the unrighteous man the best designation of which truth will admit, for after all possible allowances are made on the side of the unrighteous, the superior excellency of the righteous man is still unquestionable.

The righteous man is possessed with the faith of Christ, and this faith works by love to God and man. He is not selfish in his disposition, but makes it his settled principle of conduct, to glorify God and to do good to man. He is under the government of inward principles, that render him steady in his good purposes, and dispose him, not only to seek for glory, honour, and immortality, but to perform conscientiously the duties of his station, and of every relation in which Providence shall be pleased to place him.

His neighbour may exceed him in many of those possessions and qualifications which are valued in the world, but the righteous man is still more excellent in every thing that is truly valuable. His neighbour may be able to perform more splendid acts of generosity, but he wants that charity without which it profits a man nothing to part with all his goods. He may possess wit, and the wisdom of the world; but that is foolishness with God, and can bear no comparison with that wisdom which is unto salvation. He may be very rich, but he has no interest in the unsearchable riches of Christ. He may be a duke, or a prince of the blood; but he is not a child of God, nor an heir of heaven. He may be clothed with purple, and fare sumptuously every day; but he is not clothed with the robe of righteousness, nor does he feed on the hidden manna. He may live in a magnificent palace, but he has no title to the house not made with hands, and to the mansions which Christ hath gone to prepare for his followers. He may be admired by men, but the righteous man is an eternal excellency in the eyes of God, and the Lord of hosts is to him a crown of glory, and a diadem of beauty.

Why then do men despise the righteous, and toil themselves in the chase of those things that are not to be compared with the objects that make the righ-

teous so excellent? Because their way seduceth them.
They are seduced by the devil and the world, otherwise they would not walk in such dangerous paths, and
in their wicked progress their seduction grows upon
them. They are more and more infatuated with the
deceitful charms of the world, and despising the
genuine worth of righteousness, are bewildered and
lost in the pursuit of vanities and lies.

Let us pray for the Spirit of wisdom, that our understandings may be enlightened to discern the true nature and the incomparable excellency of righteousness ;
for the light of the body is the eye, and the understanding is the light of the soul, and the whole course of our
lives will be directed by it *.

Ver. 27. *The slothful man roasteth not that which he
took in hunting ; but the substance of a diligent man is
precious.*

It is a great happiness for a man to eat of the labour
of his hands, and a great misery for a man to be deprived of the fruits of his industry. Disappointment
of hope is a grievous thing, especially when that hope
is the fruit of a man's own labour ; and the disappointment is mingled with bitter reflections on the toils sustained, with a view to the expected advantage. But
no disappointment of this kind is more grievous than
that of the sluggard, to whom labour is a burden which
nothing but necessity can render supportable.

If the slothful man took nothing in hunting, it would
vex him ; but to take, and not to roast,—this is altogether intolerable, and must make his heart sick ; for
his labour is vain, his hope makes him ashamed, and
Providence fights against him, depriving him of what
he had got, at the very time that he thought himself
sure of enjoying it.

---

*Matt. 6:20,21

" But the substance of a diligent man is precious." His toils sweeten his gains, and he enjoys them with pleasure and thankfulness. The blessing of the Lord infuses a sweetness into his substance, so that, (though little), it affords him more pleasure than the wicked and indolent can derive from great riches.

The substance of a diligent Christian, though small, is very precious to him, because it is not the fruit of his labours only, but of his prayers also, and he discerns in it the love of his heavenly Father, who, while he gives him the pardon of his sins, gives him also daily bread.

Ver. 28. *In the way of righteousness is life ; and in the path-way thereof there is no death.*

Solomon knew very well that Zion's travellers must die, but it is a kind of happy impropriety to call the death of the righteous by its own name. Christ's death was truly death, but the death of them that die in the Lord is only a sleep *, for Christ hath abolished death, and secured an uninterrupted life to them that believe in him †.

There is nothing that can subject the righteous man to the curse of the first, or to the power of the second death. Nothing can deprive him of that life which is hid with Christ in God.

What man is he that desireth immortal life? Let him enter into the new and living way. There let him walk, and in it he shall find no death ‡.

---

*1 Thess. 4:14   †Job 11:25, 26:15   ‡Isa. 35:8,9

Proverbs 13

Ver. 1. *A wise son heareth his father's instruction : but a scorner heareth not rebuke.*

THE reason why so many will not regard instruction, and listen to rebuke with meekness, is, that they think it a disparagement to their good sense. But in what does man's wisdom lie? Not in being infallible, or in needing no reproof, but in being sensible that he is liable to error and sin, and in a humble disposition to reverence instruction even when administered in the form of reproof, and enforced by needful correction. He is an unkind father who never checks the froward inclinations and behaviour of his children ; and he is a proud and haughty scorner who receives the rebukes of a father, or of any other wise person, with contempt and aversion. Eli's sons disregarded the mild admonitions of their father. Their father was punished in them for his excessive lenity, and they were destroyed for their stubborn contempt of advice.

If a wise son will regard the instructions and reproofs of a father, how much more should we be in subjection to the Father of spirits ! and how fatal is the stubbornness of those who cry not when he bindeth them * !

Ver. 2. *A man shall eat good by the fruit of his mouth . but the soul of the transgressors shall eat violence.*

Trees are often planted by one man and dressed by

---

*Zeph. 3:2

another, whilst the fruit of them is eaten by a third. But the tongue of the righteous is a tree of life, that yields its most precious fruits to themselves. They enjoy the comfort, and credit, and gracious acceptance of their own holy and useful discourse; and these fruits are produced, not once a year, but every day. But the tongue of transgressors is like a poisonous tree, that bears fruit often hurtful to others, but mortal to themselves *.

Ver. 3. *He that keepeth his mouth keepeth his life; but he that openeth wide his lips shall have destruction.*

We must not only avoid speaking evil, but prudently beware of speaking good when it would be unseasonable. A certain philosopher being silent in company, and asked the reason of it, answered, " I have often repented of speaking, but never of keeping silence." Destruction from God, and sometimes from men, is the punishment of an ungoverned tongue, which in this respect resembles an untameable monster, that often destroys its owner. Nabal had almost ruined his whole family by his intemperate railing at David. The mischief was indeed prevented by the prudent tongue of Abigail, and yet the remorse of his own mind was one means of bringing him to his latter end.

Why does the wise man insist so much on this subject? Because the tongue is a most unruly member, and yet it is absolutely necessary to bridle it. Who is the man that desires ruin and misery? Let him give a loose rein to his tongue. Who is the man that desires peace and happiness? Let him say nothing that he will repent of having said, ten or a hundred years hence.

Ver. 4. *The soul of the sluggard desireth, and hath nothing; but the soul of the diligent shall be made fat.*

---

*Chap. 12:14

Laziness has a double tendency to make men miserable, for it at the same time affords to the mind abundant opportunity to form boundless desires, and refuses the means of gratifying them. When men indulge an idle disposition, the desires of the mind are not idle, but enlarge themselves as hell, and grow into exorbitant wishes, which even the most successful industry could not satisfy. " But the soul of the diligent shall be made fat." He enjoys inward happiness, for his wishes are confined within the bounds of reason, and the success of his labours is sufficient to satisfy them.

Spiritual sloth is in like manner attended with poverty. There is no man that would not choose to be eternally happy, but the slothful man will not strive to enter in at the strait gate, or to walk in the narrow way. He has one mighty objection against heaven, that he cannot make sure of it in a morning dream. But the soul of the diligent Christian prospers, for he adds one grace to another, and is neither barren nor unfruitful. His corruptions are subdued, his graces are lively, his comforts pleasant, his usefulness great, and he has an abundant entrance into the everlasting kingdom.

Ver. 5. *A righteous man hateth lying ; but a wicked man is loathsome, and cometh to shame.*

It is not said that a righteous man never lies. David lied more than once, and yet he could say with truth that he abhorred lying. Though he lied to Abimelech the priest, and to the king of the Philistines, yet his fixed hatred of sin was an evidence of piety, to which those can lay no claim who never spoke a lie in their lives, if their abstinence from this sin was caused by some other motive than hatred.

A righteous man hates lying in all its forms, because it is contrary to the nature of God, and an abomination

to him.   God hates all liars, and therefore a good man
will not suffer such as tell lies to tarry in his sight * ;
and if temptation has hurried him into this sin, he
loathes himself, endeavours to repair every injury that
his lie has occasioned, and prays to God to remove far
from him the wicked way of lies.

They that hate lying are valuable members of society, and are blessed with that good name which is
better than precious ointment.   But wicked men are
loathsome to God, and come to shame.   Whatever respectable qualities they may possess, they are destitute
of a principle of truth and honesty.   That falsehood
which they sometimes use to serve a turn, is the same
thing in their characters as a dead fly in a box of precious ointment, which causeth it to send forth a stink-
ing savour.   God and men agree in almost nothing
but this, that a liar is detestable to both, and therefore
he must sooner or later come to disgrace.

Ver. 6.   *Righteousness keepeth him that is upright in the*
way ; but wickedness overthroweth the sinner.

No wonder that this truth is so often repeated.   The
righteous themselves retain not so lively an impression
of it as they ought.   In this case Abraham had not
dissembled about his wife, nor had the upright Jacob
had recourse to lying in order to obtain the blessing.

Let us never, to avoid danger, shun the path of duty,
or suffer ourselves to be allured into that of sin, as
though it were the way of rest and safety.   What God
hath joined together, let no man put asunder; what God
hath put asunder, let no man attempt to join †.

Ver. 7.   *There is that maketh himself rich, yet hath*
nothing ; there is that maketh himself poor, yet hath great
riches.

Some who have nothing affect a splendid way of liv-

---

*Ps. 101:7   †Chap. 11:5,6

ing, in order that others may believe them to be very rich. This is to love a lie, and to impose upon society, by exacting that respect which is commonly given to the rich, without any just pretensions to it. Such persons naturally run themselves into debts which they cannot pay, and thus ruin themselves and defraud their neighbours. They walk contrary to God's providence, and discover a worldly, proud, and unsatisfied disposition. They have spiritual riches, sufficient to satisfy the most enlarged desires, freely offered to them in the gospel. If they will be rich, why do they not seek after these true riches, which would fill all their treasures, and make silver and gold to appear as dross?

There are others who are rich, and conceal their riches under an appearance of poverty. These are ungrateful to divine providence, which hath bestowed on them this talent, not to be hid in a napkin, but to be laid out in serving God, in the exercises of liberality. They defraud themselves, and the poor, and God also, while they sacrilegiously retain in their chests what should be employed in his service.

Divine providence makes us either rich or poor, and it is our duty cheerfully to acquiesce in its disposal, and to suit our appearance and way of life to our circumstances, which are appointed for us by infinite wisdom. If we can make but a poor appearance, let us remember him that became poor for our sakes, and had not where to lay his head, while employed in procuring for us the true riches. If we are rich, let us be rich in good works, and remember that we are stewards, and must give an account.

These opposite faults, which are in this proverb censured by the wise man, originate in the same cause,— an excessive esteem of worldly riches. It is this that makes poor men pretend to have them, and rich men conceal them for the purpose of preserving them more

safely. All men are sensible of the conveniences that
wait upon riches, and the inconveniences that attend
poverty. But we should remember that there are inconveniences also that cleave to riches, and that poverty, as the wise man teaches, possesses advantages
peculiar to itself.

Ver. 8. *The ransom of a man's life are his riches :
but the poor heareth not rebuke.*

Our Lord tells us that a rich man shall hardly enter
into the kingdom of God. This saying, if it met with
implicit credit from us, would have a mighty influence
in checking our immoderate desires after riches. Do
we really desire to walk in that way which leads to
life? And would we not rather choose to walk where
there are fewest dangers, than to travel in places infested with robbers and murderers?

But even in regard to the present life, there are great
inconveniences that frequently attend riches. Rich
men are the persons whose houses are broken into by
thieves, who are attacked by highwaymen, and whose
lives are sometimes brought into danger by false accusations. They are often meeting with losses of their
property, and sometimes they would be glad to lose it,
if it might ransom their lives, like the ten men that
willingly parted with their treasures to Ishmael the
son of Nethaniah, that he might spare their lives *.

" But the poor heareth not rebuke." Money is
sometimes a defence ; but the want of it is a shadow
under which poor men live unnoticed by the plunderers.
A poor man can travel pleasantly in a road beset by
robbers, when he that carries a full purse trembles in
every joint. In public calamities, the poor are often
suffered to escape without a blow or a threatening,
when the riches of others cannot ransom them. When

*Jer. 41:8

Jerusalem was destroyed by the Chaldeans, the poor were put into more comfortable circumstances than they had before experienced since the days of the good Josiah.

Whatever be the disadvantages of our condition, let us bear them like Christians, still thankfully observing its advantages. Neither riches nor poverty have the power of rendering us either happy or miserable ; but, as we are taught, the righteous are truly happy, whilst misery is the sure portion of the wicked.

Ver. 9. *The light of the righteous rejoiceth ; but the lamp of the wicked shall be put out.*

The righteous have the light of comfort within their souls, the light of God's countenance shining upon them, and sometimes the light of prosperity in their outward affairs. Their light waxes clearer and brighter, and fills them with increasing joy. Clouds may sometimes obscure their light, but it cannot be extinguished ; for the Lord shall be their everlasting light, and therefore their sun shall go no more down.

The wicked have something that may be called light, but it is not the light of the star which shineth more and more unto the perfect day, but the light of a lamp, which would soon expire if it were left to itself, but is more frequently extinguished before it has time to consume away *.

In the other world, the righteous shall have no need of the sun or the moon, because the Lord God and the Lamb are their light ; whilst the wicked shall not have the benefit of a candle to mitigate the horrors of their darkness, or a drop of water to cool their scorched tongues.

Ver. 10. *Only by pride cometh contention ; but with the well-advised is wisdom.*

---

*Job 18:5,6

Contention is the fruit of anger and injuries, of drunkenness and covetousness, but it is oftener the fruit of pride than of any of them. Quarrels seldom, if ever, happen without pride as one part of their cause, and they very often proceed from pride alone. Pride and ambition made the disciples to dispute among themselves which should be the greatest. Pride raised the war in Jephtha's days, between the tribes of Ephraim and Manasseh, in which so much Israelitish blood was spilt, that might have been more usefully shed in taking vengeance upon Israel's enemies. Pride darkens the mind to one's own faults and the virtues of others, and on the contrary, represents one's own virtues and the faults of others in a very false and aggravated light. It produces contempt of others, and provoking speeches and insolent behaviour, and by these means is an endless spring of contentions and mischiefs. We can never live in peace unless we subdue our own pride, and keep ourselves as free as we can from all connection with proud men.

" But with the well-advised is wisdom." The proud and contentious are neither well-advised nor wise, for they despise the advice of others, and are enemies to their own peace. The humble will not easily suffer themselves to be drawn into contention. If they are insolently treated by others, they consider whether and how far it is lawful and expedient for them to give place to anger. Injuries done to them are like sparks falling upon a rock ; and they shew themselves to be truly wise when they will abate of their pretensions in point of honour or interest, to preserve peace, and to keep themselves and others from sin and trouble.

How wise was Abraham in consenting that Lot should have his choice of the pasture, though, for a variety of reasons, Abraham might have claimed the right of choosing to himself! But Lot was soon obliged to flee the pleasant fields he had chosen, and Abraham had the promise of all the land.

Ver. 11. *Wealth gotten by vanity shall be diminished; but he that gathereth by labour shall increase.*

The blessing of God is not in that money which is gotten by stealing and cheating, or by their polite substitutes, cards and dice, or by the exercise of professions prejudicial to the interests and morals of society; and where the blessing of God does not accompany riches, they will consume like snow before the sun. But he that gathereth by useful labour shall increase in substance, and therefore we must not only be industrious, but show a regard for the public interest in that calling in which we labour *. It is not enough to let alone stealing and to work, but we must work that which is good; so shall we have enough for ourselves, and something for others.

Ver. 12. *Hope deferred maketh the heart sick; but when the desire cometh, it is a tree of life.*

If we would enjoy happiness, we must labour diligently to keep our passions and desires under restraint; for they produce, when not duly regulated, disappointment and misery. If we indulge ardent desires, and confident hopes of obtaining a thing, the hope produces a borrowed pleasure, for which, if our hopes are disappointed, we repay a high interest. What stings did the hopes of Absalom and Adonijah leave in their minds, when they failed in their attempts to obtain the kingdom of their father! When the object of hope is deferred, the heart languishes and pines. When hope is destroyed, the heart dies outright.

It is cruel to disappoint the just hopes of others. If we make the eyes of the widow to fail, or keep the

---

*Eph. 4:28

poor from their moderate desires, we break that commandment which forbids murder. We must not withhold the wages of the hireling, for this reason, among others, because his heart is set upon it, and he will be filled with uneasiness if he does not receive it.

But when the desire cometh, the heart is revived and gladdened as with the fruits of a tree of life. But this is not the case if the desire was irregular and unlawful. Amnon enjoyed no pleasure by the gratification of his desire after Tamar, which was succeeded by remorse and vexation. Desires of lawful things, when they are crowned by enjoyment, impart pleasure to the mind, but that pleasure is for the most part soon followed by weariness ; and this proverb is verified chiefly in the righteous, whose desire is only good, and whose enjoyments far exceed their most sanguine hopes. Blessed are they that hunger and thirst after righteousness, for they shall be filled with the fruits of the tree of life, which grows in the midst of the paradise of God ; and they shall hunger and thirst no more, neither shall the sun light upon them, nor any heat.

Ver. 13. *Whoso despiseth the word shall be destroyed ; but he that feareth the commandment shall be rewarded.*

In many things we offend all, but we are not all despisers of the word of God. Good men have reason to lament their manifold breaches of the commandment, and yet they have a sincere love and esteem for it, earnestly desiring that their ways might be directed to keep God's statutes.

It was an evidence that Esau despised his birthright, when he sold it for a morsel of meat ; and men discover a contempt for the word, when they disregard its precepts, to gain some advantage, and some indulgence for the flesh. A tree may be sound at the heart, and yet have its branches broken by a strong blast ;

but a tree must be rotten which is broken with a gale of wind. In like manner, a strong temptation may prevail against a sound and lively Christian; but he is not sound in God's statutes, who falls before every temptation.

He that pours contempt upon a single word of God, however inconsiderable it may appear to him, shall be destroyed by the vengeance of God; for every jot and tittle of the law is enforced by the awful authority of the Lawgiver *. He that despises his authority despises not man but God, and shall have his place among those to whom it will be said, " Behold, ye despisers, and wonder, and perish." On the contrary, he who reverences the authority of the Lord, and earnestly endeavours, by the grace of God, to govern his steps, not by the fashion of the world, or with a view to serve himself, but according to the will of God, shall be rewarded with the gracious acceptance of God, and shall experience all that favour which God through Christ vouchsafes to such as fear his name †.

Ver. 14. *The law of the wise is a fountain of life, to depart from the snares of death.*

Fountains of living waters are highly esteemed in a desert land; and the holy instructions of a wise man are equally to be valued in this world, which is a wilderness full of pits and snares. These instructions are agreeable to the word of life, because they are fetched from it, and may therefore be called a law to us, and a fountain of life, whereby the soul is refreshed and quickened. There is living virtue in the word of truth, even when earthen pipes are the channel of its conveyance ‡.

In this desert land through which we travel, there

---

*Matt. 5:19 †Isa. 66:2 ‡Chap. 10:11

are innumerable snares spread for us by the great enemy of souls, who wishes to entrap us for our destruction, like a bird in the snare of the fowler. It is by
the word of God that we must keep ourselves from the
snares of this destroyer * ; and the word of God is
seasonably applied to particular circumstances, by a
wise counsellor, by which we are enabled to perceive
these snares, and animated to keep the straight way,
and to guard with resolution against the temptations
that beset us. By the advice of the prudent wife of
Nabal, David was preserved from bloodshed ; and by
the instructions of Nathan, he was delivered from a
dangerous snare in which he was already entangled.

We should value the friendship and counsels of a
wise man, as a happy means of promoting our spiritual
life and comfort, and of preserving us from the snares
of death ; and endeavour to have our minds furnished,
from the scripture, with that wisdom which will enable
us to perform such important services to others. The
tongue of a righteous man talketh of judgment, because the law of his God is in his heart †.

Ver. 15. *Good understanding giveth favour : but the*
way of transgressors is hard.

A good understanding lies not in dry apprehensions
of spiritual things, but appears in that good way wherein it directs men to walk ; for a good understanding
have all they, and they only, who do God's commandments. This good understanding giveth favour in the
sight of God and men ‡. It is the grace of God that
gives a good understanding to men, and grace is multiplied to them through the knowledge of God, and of
Jesus our Lord ||. God has the hearts of all men in
his hand, and shews his favour to men of good under-

---

*Ps. 17:4   †Ps. 37:30,31   ‡Prov. 3:4 ||2 Peter 1:2

standing, by disposing others to favour them, as far as it seems proper to his infinite wisdom. He turned the hearts of the Egyptians to hate his people; but when the set time was come, he gave them favour in the sight of these enemies, so that they enriched them at their own expense. God made Joseph and Daniel to be favoured in the season of their captivity; and the primitive Christians, at a time when they were mortally hated by the rulers of the nation. Let us keep ourselves in the love of God, and the respect of men will attend us, should it be necessary for us.

" But the way of transgressors is hard." Their practice is not only offensive to God and grievous to men, but unhappy to themselves. There are many present inconveniences that attend sin, so that sinners have a hell here as well as hereafter. They have restless minds, and unsatisfied cravings, and uneasy consciences, to torment them. They draw upon themselves the frowns of providence and the hatred of men, and through manifold tribulations they make their way to everlasting fire.

Let sinners be persuaded to enter into the way of life. It is a narrow but a pleasant way, and rest is found in it for the soul *.

Ver. 16. *Every prudent man dealeth with knowledge; but a fool layeth open his folly.*

The wise man does not hide his talents in a napkin, but makes use of his knowledge to direct his choice and pursuits, and every part of his behaviour in life.

Knowledge buried in the head is like the miser's money, which he locks up in a chest, and which is of no use either to himself or others; but the knowledge that is joined with prudence, beautifies every discourse and every action. Those, on the contrary, who live at

---

*Matt. 7:13,14, Isa. 55:7, Matt. 11:29

random, are constantly rushing into dangers and mischiefs, and are like an ignorant physician, who cannot distinguish between poisonous and medicinal herbs, and may therefore administer a poison instead of a cure.

Fools might be esteemed half wise, if they had sense enough to keep their folly to themselves; but they presume that they are wise, and talk of things of which they know as little as brute beasts, and meddle with things quite above their capacity. Thus they discover their pride and ignorance, whilst they imagine that every one must think them as wise as they think themselves.

Ver. 17. *A wicked messenger falleth into mischief: but a faithful ambassador is health.*

Persons under authority, often think that they do no wrong whilst they execute the commands of their employer, however unlawful these commands are; but the doers of evil shall fall into mischief, whoever they are that excite them to it. Those servants of Nebuchadnezzar, that cast the three children into the fire by their master's command, were consumed to death, and none pities them *.

Unfaithful servants of princes, are to be reckoned among wicked messengers. Such was Hazael, who indeed obtained his master's throne by his treachery; but his new dignity led him into crimes, which will cause his name to be abhorred for ever. Such also was Haman, whose mischievous designs so signally recoiled upon himself.

Corrupt ministers are wicked messengers, who fall into the ditch, and draw others along with them, to add to their eternal disgrace and torment.

Even common servants who are unfaithful in a little,

---

*2 Kings 1

shall fall into mischief, as Paul assures them: He that doth wrong, shall receive for the wrong done.

But a faithful ambassador is an instrument of procuring advantage and comfort to his master and to himself. Such was Mordecai in the king's court; Paul in the gospel ministry; and Joseph in the house of Potiphar and Pharaoh.

Let us undertake no business, but what may be warrantably executed; and having undertaken it, let us perform it faithfully as to the Lord.

Ver. 18. *Poverty and shame shall be to him that refuseth instruction; but he that regardeth reproof shall be honoured.*

A man that follows vicious courses, and will not be persuaded to abandon them, must be left to himself. Disgrace and ruin will soon make him feel that which he would not believe; and then every admonition formerly given him, will be like an envenomed dart in his soul, inflaming his conscience with tormenting remorse.

Persons think it incompatible with their honour to receive reproof, but the dishonour lies in needing, and not receiving it. He, on the contrary, who regards it, and profits by it, shall be honoured as a man adorned with humility and meekness, and shall be turned from that course which disgraced him, into that way of life which is attended with true and solid honour *.

Ver. 19. *The desire accomplished is sweet to the soul; but* (or *and*) *it is abomination to fools to depart from evil.*

The deceitful pleasures which fools think they enjoy, or the gratification of their desires, is a means of hardening them in their sinful courses. They find the life of their hands, and therefore their eyes are shut to the wretchedness of their state. Their minds are under

---

*2 Sam. 12

an infatuation, from the influence of the pleasures of sin, and the god of this world. In consequence of this, their hearts cleave with obstinacy to those sins that effectually exclude true happiness.

No satisfaction of desire can give solid and durable happiness to a vicious man. The pleasures of sense lie in fancy, rather than enjoyment, which rather extinguishes than bestows real pleasure, because it destroys the pleasing imaginations that were produced by hope. For this reason, a bad man cannot possess real felicity, which cannot be separated from true holiness. His heart is filled with aversion to goodness, and he abhors the thought of forsaking his beloved lusts. His desires are so perverse, that the fulfilment of them cannot satisfy him, but must add to his misery. Sin poisons every enjoyment, and provokes divine justice to blast all his hopes, and what he desires shall utterly decay.

Ver. 20. *He that walketh with wise men shall be wise: but a companion of fools shall be destroyed.*

Wisdom is so valuable, that those who know the worth of it, will take advantage of every opportunity of improving in it. And the society of wise men is a valuable means for attaining this. He who converses with the wise will learn wisdom from their words and example, which will have a powerful tendency to produce in him a resemblance to their goodness.

For this reason we ought to make the wise our companions and friends. David would not have a wicked servant in his house ; and though he had learned much wisdom from God's testimonies, he was yet sensible, that, in order to preserve and increase his wisdom, it was necessary to avoid the fellowship of evil-doers, and to make those men his companions that feared the Lord.

For the same reason, we ought to attend the worshipping assemblies of God's people. Thomas would have been sooner cured of his unbelief, and recovered from his despondency, had he been present with the rest of the apostles when our Lord first appeared to them. David thought with deeper concern 'upon his exclusion from the place where the multitude kept the holy days, than his banishment from the royal palace.

But a companion of fools shall be corrupted, or destroyed. Bad company has a still stronger influence than that which is good, because the corruption of human nature readily complies with it. A healthy man cannot communicate health to the sick, but a person infected with the pestilence may communicate the contagion to a thousand. Our Lord safely conversed with sinners, because he was free from all danger of being corrupted ; and it may on some occasions be our duty also to mingle with the wicked, that we may use means for reclaiming them : but in ordinary cases, guilt or grief is all that a godly man gets by the company of sinners. Lot chose the neighbourhood of Sodom for his dwelling, because it afforded pleasant pasture. He forgot that the Sodomites were impudent sinners, but he soon found that daily griefs were the best things he could expect from such wicked neighbours. The grace of God kept him unstained by their profligacy ; but he was obliged to flee for his life, and to leave his pleasant possessions and his plenteous flocks behind him, that he might escape their punishment.

A church that is become obstinate and incurable in apostacy must be left, for this reason, that we may avoid her sins and plagues *.

Ver. 21. *Evil pursueth sinners : but to the righteous good shall be repaid.*

Mischief is allotted to such as obstinately persevere

---

*Rev. 18:4

in sin. **They** perhaps do not feel their misery and danger, but enjoy the transient pleasures of sin and the world, and think themselves secure of a long continued term of prosperity; but Solomon here assures them, that misery is pursuing them, as the hound pursues his prey, and will not desist from the chace till it is destroyed. Sinners may flee away as on eagles' wings; but vengeance follows them on the wings of the wind. They may look for safety and deliverance; but their eyes shall fail, and escape shall perish from them, and their hope shall be as the giving up of the ghost *.

If sinners desire to escape, let them flee to the Saviour of sinners, and cast away their transgressions †. Let them depart from evil, and do good, while their day of grace continues; for, if they resist the calls of wisdom, their desolation will come like a whirlwind ‡.

"But to the righteous good shall be repaid." Imperfect as their goodness is, not a single instance of it shall lose its reward. What can be less than giving a cup of water to a thirsty disciple of Christ? yet that shall be mentioned at the great day, to the praise of the followers of the Redeemer.

God is so abundant in goodness, that he gave a reward to Nebuchadnezzar and to Jehu, for services done to him from a principle purely selfish. Much more will he reward those services that are done from love to his name ||. Even the children, and the more remote descendants of the godly, have often experienced the overflowing kindness of God to their pious progenitors; for,

Ver. 22. *A good man leaveth an inheritance to his*

---

*Job 11:20   †Ps. 68:20.21   ‡Prov. 1:21-32 ||Heb. 6:10

children's children, and the wealth of the sinner is laid up for the just.

A good man is ever righteous and merciful. He is blessed, and his children and grand-children are blessed after him. He leaves to them the good-will of men, and many precious promises ; the influence of his example and instructions descends to his posterity, and they are enriched with substance for his sake. David left an inheritance to his children for seventeen generations, and they were not dispossessed of it, till by intolerable provocations they had extorted punishment from God.

But is this always true ? It is to be remembered that the proverbs are often to be understood of what generally happens, though not always. But when this sentence is not verified, we may conclude that good men, by the defects of their goodness, have forfeited this blessing to their children, which was the case with Eli ; or that divine wisdom sees some better method, in these instances, of testifying that kindness which God has for them.

It is better to be the son of a poor saint, than of a great lord, for every believer will acknowledge, that a single promise in the Bible is far better than a large estate ; and parents that are anxious about the state of their families after their own death, if they believe the scriptures, will be more desirous of leaving them an estate in promises, than in land and money.

But many believe not this truth. They fill their brains with projects, and their souls are vexed with anxious cares about obtaining portions to leave to their children. In these labours they may be successful ; but in the mean time the thoughts of eternity are banished from their own minds ; and when they are inheriting the fruits of their earthly-mindedness, what pleasure can it give them, to think that their children are

rioting in the enjoyment of wealth, and probably laying up to themselves treasures of vengeance!

But their success in worldly pursuits is very doubtful. Their posterity may fail, or be reduced to poverty;
for the wealth of the sinner is laid up, not for his posterity, but for the just. Riches are still changing
masters, according to the direction of God, who made
the wealth of the Egyptians and Canaanites to come
into the possession of the Israelites, and who still distributes the gifts of his bounty to them that are good
in his sight *.

Ver. 23. *Much food is in the tillage of the poor; but
there is that is destroyed for lack of judgment.*

Better is the industrious poor man, than the rich
man who wants discretion and integrity; for though
a man be poor, yet when he improves his little stock
by honest labour, he shall not want, nor in the greater
part of cases shall he need to beg, or to be put into
the poors-roll. There is plenty of food in his tillage
for himself and his family; and having food and raiment, he should be therewith content.

But some are ruined by want of integrity. They
endeavour to increase their wealth by those dishonest
and unhallowed means that bring the curse of God
into their substance, and it melts like the Israelitish
manna before the rising sun.

Others are brought to poverty by indiscretion.
Frugality and economy must be joined with industry.
Our Lord could feed men by miracle, and yet he would
not suffer the fragments to be lost. The seven years
of extraordinary plenty, could not have preserved
Egypt from ruin, had not Joseph laid up the corn
against the years of scarcity.

---

*Job 27:15,16

Ver. 24. *He that spareth his rod hateth his son; but he that loveth him chasteneth him betimes.*

Parents feel those lashes with which they are obliged sometimes to chastise their children; but they love them with no true affection, if they are not willing to endure the smart of them for the good of their children. There is not a groan of the believer, but is felt at the heart of Christ; but Christ does not for that reason spare his correcting rod: " Whom I love, (says he) I rebuke and chasten."

The foolish fondness of too indulgent parents is accounted by them parental love; but the Spirit of God calls it hatred. That affection which is prejudicial to the spiritual interests of its objects is love in the language of men, but hatred in the language of the Holy Ghost. A parent would be accounted a hater of his child, were he to suffer him to keep a knife in his hands till he gave himself a mortal stab; and he deserves the same character, who by fond indulgence suffers his son to bring himself to a gibbet, or to expose himself to the damnation of hell.

But he who loves his son, chastens him as soon as he begins to discover that folly which is bound up in his heart. He will not, indeed, chastise him with blows, when words are sufficient to answer the end; but he will administer the rod, when words have small influence; and imitate the skilful physician, who prescribes medicines, neither too weak, lest the disease should remain uncured, nor too strong, lest the constitution should prove two weak to bear them.

The early days of childhood are a proper season for correction, because vice has not then obtained deep and firm root in the heart. A young bullock may be tamed, but if you suffer it to grow old in idleness, you will sooner break its neck, than break it to the yoke.

Ver. 25. *The righteous eateth to the satisfying of his soul; but the belly of the wicked shall want.*

God's blessing gives to a righteous man food and contentment, but the wicked man wants one or both of them. The family of Jacob were well fed, when the Egyptians were almost starved; and Elijah had food to his satisfaction, when Ahab and his courtiers were obliged, with anxious hearts, to traverse the country for a supply of pasture to their cattle.

The righteous man must sometimes live on coarse fare, when the wicked riot in plenty. But Daniel was happier in his pulse, than the other servants of the king of Babylon in the luxuries of the royal table. The family of Christ, too, enjoyed more pleasure in their barley-loaves and fishes, than the rulers who despised them in their sumptuous entertainments.

If a righteous man has little, that little is better than the riches of many wicked. The wicked is often reduced to want by his own vices, and the judgment of God upon him; but if he has much, he still wants the blessing of God, which alone can sweeten it, and therefore in the midst of sufficiency he is in straits.

Proverbs 14

Ver. 1. *Every wise woman buildeth her house; but the foolish plucketh it down with her hands.*

Diligence in business is often recommended by So‑lomon, as a means of obtaining riches, or at least a competency; but he here informs us, that the care of the wife is necessary, as well as the industry of the husband.

A wise woman is frugal, and saves. She is industrious, and gains. She is religious and charitable, and brings down a blessing from heaven upon her family; for if the houses of Laban and Potiphar were blessed for the sake of religious servants, a house must be still more favoured by Providence, for the sake of a religious mistress.

"But a foolish woman plucketh it down with her hands." As if it were a small thing in her eyes to suffer it to go to ruin, she uses her own hands to demolish it. The idle and careless woman uses one of her hands, but the extravagant makes use of both, in this ruinous work. How soon, in such a case, must a house become a heap of rubbish!

This verse directs men in the choice of wives. A woman may be rich and beautiful, and yet prove a plague to her husband and his family, for nothing is more necessary to ruin a house than a bad wife. But a wise and virtuous woman is a rich portion to her husband, though she brings nothing with her. Her father would give her a portion if he were able; but let it be remembered, that she is a daughter of the Lord Almighty, who gives a better portion of graces and blessings with her, than the wealthiest of earthly parents can bestow.

Ver. 2. *He that walketh in his uprightness feareth the Lord; but he that is perverse in his ways despiseth him.*

Most men pretend to the fear of God, but pretensions go for nothing when they are confuted by facts. The scripture lays down plain marks, by which we may know whether we are really possessed of that truth of religion, which lies in an affectionate reverence to the Most High.

The truly religious man, is he that walks in his uprightness; and the faith that is not attended with godly sincerity in the heart, and endeavours after universal obedience in the life, is a dead faith, which gives no evidence of spiritual life.

The good man not only receives Christ, but walks in him. He not only enters in at the strait gate, but continues travelling in the narrow way, till he comes to the end of his faith and holiness in the heavenly world.

He walketh in his uprightness, shewing a constant regard, not only to the common duties of a man and a Christian, but to those also that are incumbent on him on account of the particular relations and circumstances in which he is placed.

Upright walking is a sure and true evidence of the fear of the Lord; for that fear consists in a deep impression of the divine excellency and authority, by which men are disposed to abstain from whatever God forbids, however pleasing to the flesh it may be, and to walk before him unto all well pleasing.

Men of corrupt minds and a perverse behaviour, may speak much to the praise of God, and profess a high veneration for him, but they are so far from fearing the Lord, that they despise him. Every wilful sin is a plain proof that they disregard his authority, and defy his vengeance; insult his patience, and turn the grace of our Lord Jesus Christ into lasciviousness.

Let stubborn sinners learn from this observation, the exceeding sinfulness of their perverse conduct. It contains in it a downright contempt for God, which is a crime that can scarcely be charged upon devils. What punishment is sufficient for such as despise the authority of their Maker, and pour contempt on the grace of a Saviour? To them it shall be said, " Behold, ye despisers ! and wonder, and perish."

Ver. 3. *In the mouth of the foolish is a rod of pride; but the lips of the wise shall preserve them.*

Pride is a root of bitterness, producing a rod of insolence and rudeness in the mouth of the foolish. By this rod they strike and wound their neighbours, who are better than they, but it proves also a rod of correction to themselves.

The wise man does not call the instrument of their punishment a sword, but a rod; meaning probably in this manner to intimate, that their pride shall be abased by punishment of an ignominious kind. They shall not die like heroes, but their punishment shall be that of slaves and fools, and shall yet prove destructive to them, for God can arm with vengeance the meanest instruments. Pharaoh was tormented by flies and frogs, and Herod was eaten up with despicable worms.

But the lips of the wise will preserve them from the rod which is in the mouth of fools, and from that vengeance which overtakes the proud. The humility of their hearts instructs their mouths in the language of meekness and kindness, and their piety and prudence preserve their lips from speaking evil *.

Ver. 4. *Where no oxen are, the crib is clean; but much increase is by the strength of the ox.*

As the wise man teaches us to be diligent in business, so the providence of God encourages us to practise this virtue. As he hath done so in giving us other animals to assist us in our labours, so we ought thankfully to employ them. Where no oxen or other beasts of husbandry are, there is no food for man or beast; but there is much increase by their labour. Oxen and asses testify, as Isaiah speaks, against the ingratitude of God's people; and here Solomon insinu-

---

*Ps. 34:12,13

ates that they bear witness against the laziness of the sluggard also. If oxen do not employ their strength for our benefit, the fault is not theirs, but ours.

If oxen serve us so well, we should not grudge them that food which they earn by their labour, and which is necessary for the preservation of their strength. God would not have the mouth of the ox to be muzzled when he was treading out the corn. That law was in part, though not chiefly designed for the benefit of oxen; for the God who made all things, shews his regard and bounty to them in his laws, as well as in his providence.

We should praise God for his bounty to the irrational creatures, since they not only discover the riches of the Lord, but perform useful services to us. What is man, that God should give us the dominion over so many useful animals, and keep them in subjection to us, even in our fallen state?

Ver. 5. *A faithful witness will not lie : but a false witness will utter lies.*

In the mouth of two or three witnesses shall every word be established ; but the witnesses ought to be men of veracity, otherwise twenty witnesses are no better than so many ciphers. A faithful witness is one that will not lie ; but a man who has no principle of honesty, will, on the smallest temptation, utter lies without scruple.

Judges, and juries, and elders of the church, must be cautious what testimonies they receive. Justice requires that no man should suffer in his person or character, upon exceptionable grounds. What man can enjoy security, if liars are to receive credit?

How mean a character is that of a liar! His testimony cannot serve his neighbour, and ought not to hurt him. In his mouth, even truth is suspected for a lie.

It is unjust and uncharitable to indulge suspicions against our neighbours, on the report of a liar, or even of common fame, which is generally a common lie.

Ver. 6. *A scorner seeketh wisdom, and findeth it not ; but knowledge is easy unto him that understandeth.*

A scorner may seek wisdom, but he never seeks it with right views, nor does he seek after that wisdom which best deserves the name. The wisdom of the prudent is to understand his way, but the scorner seeks wisdom to gratify a curious fancy, to feed his pride, and to enable him, by the display of his wit, to make a figure. But he cannot find it, and the reason is plain : He has not a due value for the wisdom that comes from God, and he seeks it not with that earnestness and humility without which it cannot be found. He does not resign his understanding to the instructions of God, nor can his pride suffer him to receive with meekness the instructions and reproofs that give wisdom. The Greeks sought after wisdom, but Christ crucified was foolishness to them. They were already too wise to admit of the preaching of the cross, and scorned a tent-maker who would inform them of new doctrines, which had never entered into their own minds, and who would prove them by other methods than their own favourite ones,—eloquence and reasoning.

" But knowledge is easy unto him that understandeth." For he knows the inestimable worth of knowledge, and seeks for it as for silver. Conscious of his own ignorance, he thankfully improves the means of knowledge, and daily depends upon Jesus, the great Teacher, to open his heart for receiving it. Reproof, as a means of wisdom, is precious to him, and the knowledge which he already possesses fits him for making progress in it, for to him that hath shall be given.

Ver. 7. *Go from the presence of a foolish man, when thou perceivest not in him the lips of knowledge.*

We must not willingly enter into the company of fools, but if, through ignorance of their character, we happen to do so, we must not stay in it, lest we be corrupted by their foolish conversation. We are either like them whose company we frequent, or shall soon be like them. Evil communications will efface our impressions of the evil of sin, and corrupt our own manners. Lukewarm persons, who are perhaps the least dangerous of bad companions, will, if we take pleasure in their company, transfuse their lukewarmness into us. Ephraim mixed with the people, and he soon became a cake not turned.

But when are we to leave the company of a foolish man? As soon as we perceive that he has not the lips of knowledge. As trees are known by their fruit, so men are known by their words and works; but they are soonest known by their words, which are the most plentiful and the easiest products of the heart. We are not to suppose men to be fools without evidence, but profane or foolish words come from folly in the heart; for a good man out of the good treasure of his heart bringeth forth good things, and an evil man out of his evil treasure, evil things.

Men may think themselves so steady in goodness, that they are in no danger of being corrupted by evil communications: but none are so ready to fall as those that think they stand. Let Peter be a witness, who on this ground ventured into temptation, and fell before it. But though we were secure against all danger to ourselves, our rashness might embolden weaker Christians to mingle with dangerous society, and so our practice prove a temptation to those for whom Christ died.

This commandment of God should strike terror

into the wicked. God will not allow us to keep company with them, and is it to be supposed that he will
admit them to his own eternal fellowship? Either
God or they must change, before they can be received
into heaven *.

Ver. 8. *The wisdom of the prudent is to understand
his way ; but the folly of fools is deceit.*

When men are acquainted with every thing but
what they ought to know, they are only notable fools.
If we had hearts large as the sand on the sea-shore,
and filled with a world of things, whilst we remained
ignorant of the way of attaining true happiness, we
should resemble that philosopher who was busied
gazing at the moon, till he fell into the ditch.

We are travellers to another world, and our wisdom
lies in knowing the way that leads to the world of
happiness. There is no way that will bring us to
heaven but Christ ; nor is any man wise to salvation
who does not value the knowledge of a crucified Saviour above all other knowledge. We must endeavour
to know the good, and acceptable, and perfect will of
God; to be acquainted with the difficulties of our way,
and how to surmount them; to know the enemies
that may be expected to oppose our progress, and in
what manner to conquer them, and what refreshments
may be met with in the way to animate our spirits in
pursuing our journey.

It is a piece of necessary wisdom also, to acquaint
ourselves with the business and duties of our own particular callings, that we may discharge them with honour and success. They are fools who know other
people's business better than their own. Some people,
if you will take their own word for it, could reign
better than the king, and preach better than the minis-

---

*2 Cor. 6:14

ter. They know, in short, how to manage in every
condition but their own. These are the busy-bodies
and meddlers in other men's matters, who in scripture
are condemned, and by their neighbours held in derision.

"But the folly of fools is deceit." That which they
call wit, the scripture calls folly. They mean to deceive others, but they deceive themselves worst by it.
They may trick their neighbours out of their money,
but they cheat themselves out of their souls.

All that wisdom of the serpent that is not recon-
cileable with the harmlessness of the dove, is folly; and
every piece of deceit practised on our fellow-men, is a
dangerous imposition on our own souls.

Ver. 9. *Fools make a mock at sin ; but among the righteous there is favour.*

Foolish men make a sport of their own sins, when
they ought to be humbled to the dust on account of
them. Because they are not presently punished, they
think that punishment shall never come, or, like brute
beasts, they consider not what shall be hereafter. But
if eternal burnings are a serious matter, sin that
kindles them can be no just matter of indifference or
sport.

Fools sport at the sins of others, which is far less
human than to laugh at the fits of a man convulsed
with agony, or the pains of one giving up the ghost.
Sin is the sport of devils only, and those who make it
a jest are devils clothed with flesh. Some of them are
so like their father, that they will tempt men to sin
that they may laugh at them. Such laughter will end
in weeping and howling.

"But among the righteous there is favour." They
have too much good-will to one another, and to all men,
to make a sport at sin. They are affected with the sins
of others, as a man would be if he were brought into

a lazar-house. A man of spiritual discernment perceives sin to be the most loathsome and dangerous of all distempers, and his eye affects his heart with tender compassion for their misery.

The righteous have a principle of charity, that disposes them to rejoice in the goodness and happiness of others as their own. Paul scarcely begins an epistle, without strong expressions of his joy in the prosperity of his fellow-Christians. This charity completed will multiply the blessedness of the heavenly state.

Ver. 10. *The heart knoweth his own bitterness; and a stranger doth not intermeddle with his joy.*

The things of a man knoweth no man, but the spirit of a man that is in him. And a man's own tongue cannot express the bitterness of the griefs that he often feels, or the sweetness of the joy he experiences.

We must not be censorious of the griefs of others. There are some who do not express that grief which we think they ought to feel for their miscarriages, or the adversities with which they have met; but they perhaps grieve more than they appear to do. Sorrow may fill their hearts when they are alone, though company spreads cheerfulness over their countenances. God is the true judge of the measure of our repentance for sin, or our humiliation of spirit under his afflicting hand.

This observation should lead us to compassionate the sorrows of the afflicted. They have inward uneasiness that we cannot feel. Their griefs are frequently too strong for them to subdue, and when they would comfort themselves against sorrow, their hearts are faint within them. Job's friends would not have vexed him so much with their severe censures on his complaints, had they thoroughly weighed his griefs and calamities *.

---

*Job 6:1,2

It is a great comfort to Christians, that our Redeemer bore our griefs, and knows our sorrows, and is touched with the feeling of them. For this reason should the broken in spirit pour forth all their sorrows at the throne of grace, and firmly expect from it all needful succours.

There are joys that equally exceed the knowledge of a stranger, especially the joys of religion, which an unrenewed man cannot relish or understand. These are sometimes unspeakable, and full of glory. Christians do not now enter into the joy of their Lord, but streams of joy enter into their souls from the overflowing fountain of pleasures, and refresh their hearts amidst the sorrows of this wilderness to such a degree, that they can rejoice greatly in the God of their salvation, at the very seasons when they are pitied by the world, as of all men the most miserable.

Sinners cannot understand how all the ways of wisdom should be pleasantness and peace, but they should consider that they want those purified understandings and affections, without which spiritual joys cannot be relished. Let them believe the Scripture, and the experience of all good men. Let them taste and see that the Lord is good, and that there is no want to them that fear him. Christians do indeed feel sorrows peculiar to themselves, but these are the seeds of inexpressible gladness.

Ver. 11. *The house of the wicked shall be overthrown, but the tabernacle of the upright shall flourish.*

The upright man is far happier in the meanest circumstances, than a transgressor in his greatest prosperity. Though a wicked man overtop his neighbour as far as the cedars of the mountain do the creeping shrubs of the valley, he shall be filled with the strokes of divine vengeance. Though he dwell in a magnificent palace, the tempest of indignation shall beat it down ;

but the righteous man, though at present he appear, like the incarnate Saviour, a tender plant, shall grow like the cedar in Lebanon ; and though his dwelling-place is a tabernacle, it shall flourish, and prosper, and grow into a palace. It is far better to dwell in a cottage where the blessing of God rests, and in which is heard the melody of joy and praise, than in a palace which lies under the curse of the Lord *.

Ver. 12. *There is a way which seemeth right unto a man, but the end thereof are the ways of death.*

The wisdom of the prudent is to understand his way ; and happy is the man who understands it indeed, for many whose end shall be destruction, think that they are travelling in the ways of life.

The Jews in Isaiah's time thought their way right, when they endeavoured to please God by multitudes of costly services, whilst they were mocking and insulting the Most High, by attempting to bribe him into a connivance at their injustice and inhumanity. The Jews in our Lord's time walked in the like paths of self-deceit, in setting the traditions of the elders on a level with the commands of God, and seeking righteousness, not by faith, but as it were by the works of the law.

Some professing Christians would join their own works to the righteousness of Christ, as the ground of their acceptance with God. They stand with one foot upon a rock, and the other in a quagmire, and must sink in the mire †. Others, on pretence of seeking justification by the faith of Christ, are careless about holiness, and consider not, that the faith which does not lead men to holiness will never bring them to heaven ‡.

There are many who expect to please God by serving him, not according to the rule of his word, but according to the inventions and commandments of men,

*Prov. 3:33, Job 5:18   †Gal. 5:4   ‡James 2:14

and suppose that they are serving him when they are breaking the second commandment, and provoking the Lord to jealousy.

Some are so perverse that they think they are doing God service, whilst they are doing mischief to other men, and indulging those uncharitable tempers which God abhors *.

We should always keep our eyes on the end of things, and learn with certainty what end we are to expect to our course of life. How terrible will it be for men to hear themselves condemned by the Judge of the world, for those actions for which they expected to hear these pleasant words, " Well done, good and faithful servant !"

Let us give earnest heed unto the word of God, and compare our expectations and practice with it. Let us daily pray that God may lead us in that way of holiness, in which the wayfaring man, though a fool, shall not err.

Ver. 13. *Even in laughter the heart is sorrowful; and the end of that mirth is heaviness.*

The joys of this world cannot make a man happy. They are often false, and they commonly end in heaviness.

It is very common for men to put on a face of joy, whilst the heart pines away with grief. Some put on the appearance of joy to prevent or remove suspicions about their behaviour, and endeavour to cover a guilty conscience with smiles. It would surely be far better to own their sins, and to seek after the pleasures of pardon, and then they may rejoice in God through the atonement. Others, from a pride of appearing happy, conceal their uncomfortable circumstances and dejected spirits under the appearances of mirth, when they

---

*John 16:2

ought to acquiesce in the providence of God, and to seek those pleasures which the world cannot give nor take away.

There are others still, who laugh when their hearts are sorrowful, from an ambition of appearing heroes, who cannot be subdued by misfortunes. They are like the Stoic philosopher, who, under a severe fit of the gravel, discovered at once his weakness and h's desire of concealing it by these words : " Pain, thou mayest rack me, but thou shalt not make me confess that thou art an evil thing." An affected joy under tribulation, is as despicable as the triumphant joy of a believer is glorious.

The end of this, and of all worldly mirth, is for the most part heaviness. In this valley of tears our joys are few and weak, and pains tread upon their heels. Our greatest comforts are avenues to our bitterest calamities. Heaven is the land of joys, and the only joys on earth worth the naming, are derived from the hope of possessing them *.

Ver. 14. *The backslider in heart shall be filled with his own ways ; and a good man shall be satisfied from himself.*

A true saint may slip with his feet, but his heart is ordinarily perfect with the Lord his God. The backslider in heart is the lover of sin, who departs, in the course of his life, from God and his laws with purpose of heart.

Such a man is never filled with sin, but takes so much pleasure in it, that he revolts more and more, adding drunkenness to thirst. He shall, however, be filled with sin, either in this world or the next, when he feels its painful consequences, and finds that God

---

*Rom. 8:18. 5:2

has marked all his steps, and will not acquit him from any of his iniquities.

This will be the end of all impenitent sinners, but chiefly of such as have not only forsaken the law of God, but also violated their own solemn vows, and after professing holiness, turned like the dog to his vomit, and like the sow that was washed to her wallowing in the mire.

Apostacy is a horrible affront to the ways of righteousness, and is commonly, though not always, the forerunner of final impenitence and despair *.

" But a good man shall be satisfied from himself. The springs of his satisfaction are in God, and he abhors the thought of glorying, save in the Lord, and in his cross ; and yet it is true that he shall be satisfied from himself. His pleasure does not lie in comparing himself with those that are worse than he, but he proves his own work, and has rejoicing in himself and not in another. His soul is fitted for relishing true satisfaction, and filled with that holiness which is the same thing to the inner man, that health is to the body. His good works are not the grounds of his confidence, but through Christ they are accepted of God, and graciously rewarded. " Say ye to the righteous, It shall be well with him ; for they shall eat the fruit of their doings †."

Ver. 15. *The simple believeth every word, but the prudent man looketh well to his going.*

Readiness to believe what people say, being supposed to proceed from a good temper, is commonly regarded a small fault. But none has ever proved more mischievous to the world.

Daily experience shews that many have their fortunes ruined by giving too easy credit to those knaves

---

*James 3:14   †Isa. 5:10

who will say or swear any thing that serves their own interests.

History is full of examples of men who have lost their lives by means of their credulity, amongst whom were those great men Abner and Amasa. Others have by this means been robbed of their comfort, as was Jacob for the space of twenty years, though he may well be excused for believing the mournful tidings of his son's death, especially when confirmed by so many plausible circumstances.

Some have been betrayed into the worst of sins, by believing groundless reports of others, as Saul in the case of David, and we might almost add, David himself in the case of Mephibosheth. The nation of the Jews was threatened with desolation by the easy temper of Ahasuerus, who believed without examination the malicious suggestions of the wicked Haman.

Multitudes have been seduced into the most dangerous errors and damning sins, by seducers whom they believed, either from an implicit faith, or from want of care in searching the oracles of truth.

The whole world was ruined by the simplicity of Eve, and the easy credit she gave to the serpent.

A prudent man will therefore look well to his goings. He will not risk his fortune and happiness, his life and soul, by believing groundless reports, or receiving doctrines that are destitute of sufficient proof.

He will not withdraw his love from men, or do them hurt, because they have the misfortune to become the butt of slander.

There is nothing in which we are so ready to be deceived as in points of religion, and no errors are so dangerous as these. A prudent man will therefore call no man on earth master, but will look upon Christ as his only Master. The Scriptures he considers as his only rule, and the Spirit that dictated them as their

292 / *Exposition of Proverbs*

great interpreter. He searches the Scripture, and seeks wisdom from God by daily prayer.

As Christ is the only way to the Father, the man that is spiritually wise enters into his religious course, and walks in it, depending on this Saviour alone for acceptance. As there is great danger in stepping aside from the path of God's commandments, he pays a strict regard to the least of them *.

Many deceivers are gone out into the world, and the old deceiver is still walking about, seeking whom he may mislead and destroy. The prudent man is therefore sober and vigilant. He informs himself of the devices of these enemies of his salvation, and whilst he guards against them by taking heed to God's word, he commits himself to the guidance of him who led Joseph like a flock through the desert, and arrives safely at that paradise where there is no subtile serpent to betray.

Ver. 16. *A wise man feareth and departeth from evil; but the fool rageth and is confident.*

A wise man will foresee apparent or probable dangers, and will guard against them. Nehemiah foresaw the danger he was in from the enemies of the Jews, and used every proper means to prevent their incursions, and this fear was very consistent with courage, for he scorned to use any mean shift for his own safety.

A wise man trusts in God's mercy; but this trust is consistent with fear, not with that tormenting fear which is cast out by faith and love, but with that reverence of God, and that necessary caution, which makes persons depart from sin, and to flee from it as they would from the devil and hell. Noah is an instance of this fear †. Paul himself, that noble believer, who was always triumphing in Christ, lived under the

---

*Matt. 5:19   †Heb. 11:17

influence of this holy temper, and kept his body in subjection, lest when he had preached the gospel to others,
he himself should be a cast-away.

A wise man indulges not anxious fears about the
evils that may come at some future period, for he trusts
in the gracious providence of God *.   But he trembles
at the word of God, reverencing its precepts, considering its threatenings with awe, and fearing lest he
should seem to come short of the promised blessings.
This fear is a bridle to the soul, to curb the workings
of the passions, and to restrain it from every appearance of evil.

" But the fool rageth and is confident."   Some are so
foolish as to think it a sign of a brave spirit to live superior to all fear, as if it were men's glory to be like
the leviathan, who is made without fear.   Fools despise
the threatenings of the Bible.   They are filled with
rage at those providences and reprovers which would
check them in their course of sin; but their confidence
is daring presumption, which hurries them on to those
courses that end in despair.   They will rush on in sin,
if you should set everlasting burnings before them ;
but their haughty spirits will be tamed when they shall
cry to the rocks and mountains to fall on them, and
hide them from the face of the Lamb.   The Assyrian
monarch raged against God and his people, and was
confident that God himself could not stop· him in his
victorious course ; but he soon found a hook in his nose,
and a bridle in his jaws.

Ver. 17. *He that is soon angry dealeth foolishly, and
a man of wicked devices is hated.*

Rash anger is a fruit and evidence of folly.   Because another man has done me an injury, am I to do
myself a greater, by suffering my passions to domineer

---

*Matt. 6:25-34

294 / *Exposition of Proverbs*

over my reason, and expose me to the vengeance of God *? He that is soon angry speaks and does many foolish things, which may cost him many bitter thoughts through his whole life †. But a man of wicked devices is far worse than a passionate man, for he harbours malice in his breast, and his soul is the habitation of him whom malice makes a devil, though he was once a glorious angel. Wo unto the man of wicked devices, for he walks in the way of Cain, and is hated by God and men. Providence may keep him, by the restraints of fear, from embruing his hands in his brother's blood; but in his heart he daily commits murder, and cannot have eternal life abiding in him. Simeon and Levi procured reproaches from their father for this evil disposition, when the other tribes were receiving blessings ‡.

Ver. 18. *The simple inherit folly, but the prudent are crowned with knowledge.*

Folly is hereditary to men that spring from Adam, who lost to himself and to his posterity that excellent wisdom which beautified his soul in the state of innocency.

Folly is like a field that produces nothing but weeds and poisons, and brings forth in great plenty the grapes of bitterness. This is the inheritance of the simple who love simplicity, and will not hearken to the counsels of wisdom; with these fruits they shall be filled abundantly, but they shall never see the floods and the brooks of honey and butter.

The prudent have a royal heritage. They shall inherit glory, and their knowledge is not only a chain to their necks, but a diadem of beauty to their heads. It makes them honourable as kings, and prepares them for the possession of those celestial glories, compared

*Matt. 5:22   †Chap. 12:26   ‡Gen. 49, Chap. 12:2

with which crowns and sceptres are but yellow dust for the wise shall shine as the brightness of the firmament.

The most prosperous sinners are objects of compassion to the wise, because they are fools, and the fruit of folly are their inheritance. But the saint in rags is to them one of the excellent of the earth, for he is possessed of those glories that confer inconceivable dignity on a beggar, whilst an emperor without them is mean and despicable *

Ver. 19. *The evil bow before the good, and the wicked at the gates of the righteous.*

Bad men follow courses which have a tendency in their own nature, and by the appointment of God, to bring them to a state of slavery and dependance. Good men, through the blessing of God on their virtue and industry, are often placed in circumstances that enable them to relieve the wretched and unhappy, so that their favour is humbly courted by those that once despised them.

There have been instances in which this proverb was verified in a very remarkable manner. The Egyptians bowed down before Joseph, and Moses, and the Israelites. The proud king of Babylon almost worshipped the captive Daniel, and Elisha's favour was solicited by three kings, one or two of whom were bad men. But it is certain, from experience, that the reverse sometimes takes place, and good men are made to bow done before the wicked. It is, however, certain, that goodness infallibly conducts to honour, and wickedness to disgrace in the end †.

It is because men believe not the scripture that they shun religion in those branches of it that are under disrepute, or that they make any compliances with the

---

*Ps. 15:4   †Mal. 4:1, Ps. 49:14, Rev. 2:26,27

wicked of the world with a view to honour from men. God is the King of nations, and the great fountain of honour; and those that honour him he will honour, but those that despise him shall be lightly esteemed. If at any time God's people are under a cloud of disgrace, they have full assurance that it will be soon blown away. Christ himself was once a servant of rulers, but all things are now put under his feet; and it is a faithful saying, If we suffer, we shall also reign with him.

Ver. 20. *The poor is hated even of his own neighbour; but the rich hath many friends.*

The poor man's neighbour, in this place, must signify one that lives in his neighbourhood, or one that is obliged by the ties of relation to love him. All our neighbours of the human race have a title to our love, but those whom Providence has connected with us by the bonds of vicinity or relation, have a double title to our regard; and to despise or hate them, or to be indifferent to their happiness, is a very great sin.

Our love to our neighbour deserves not the name, if it is founded only upon his riches; poverty, or distress, instead of diminishing, ought to draw it forth into action. It is base to profess love to persons in the time of their prosperity, and to be cold to them in the day of their distress. All men censure Job's friends for behaving harshly to him at a time when they could not shew too much tenderness and compassion *.

The rich hath many friends, but little reason to place much confidence in many of them. They are generally not friends to himself, but to his coat and his table. Let him wear rags, and live on bread and water, and he will find who are his friends.

Let us try our love to our neighbours, for there is much hypocrisy in men's regard to their fellow-crea-

---

*Job 6:14

tures, as well as in that respect which they shew to their Maker. Unfeigned love to Christ cleaves to him, whether religion be well or ill spoken of; and true love to our neighbours is the same, whether they are in adverse or prosperous circumstances, excepting that it appears most when there is most need to discover it.

The poor need not be discouraged because their friends have forsaken them. It is not true that their friends have forsaken them, if they have given them no other reason for it than becoming poor. They were not friends but dissemblers, and it is no loss to know their insincerity. They have reason to rejoice that Christ is the poor man's friend, and that he shews his friendship most in the season of greatest need *.

The rich man needs not boast of the multitude of his friends, for many of them are very probably dissemblers, who want to serve themselves at his expence. A man need not call himself rich, although he has many guineas in his pocket, if he has reason to think that most of them are counterfeits. The friendship of Christ is necessary for him as well as the poor man, and in that he may rejoice and triumph at all times. David was driven from his throne, and multitudes of his friends became his enemies ; but his rejoicing was this, that he had one sure and all-sufficient Friend †.

Ver. 21. *He that despiseth his neighbour sinneth : but he that hath mercy on the poor, happy is he.*

However common it is for men to hate or despise the poor, it is a great sin, and exposes men to misery. A man's poverty divests him not of that relation to ourselves, and to our Maker and our Saviour, which gives him a title to our love; nor does it weaken the obligation of that great commandment, which requires us to love our neighbours as ourselves.

---

*Ps. 72:4,12-14   †Ps. 3:3

We shew our contempt of the poor, not only by trampling upon them, but by overlooking them, or by withholding that help for which their distress loudly calls. The Levite and the Priest that declined the giving of assistance to the wounded traveller on the way to Jericho, were notorious breakers of the law of love, in the judgment of our Lord. The good Samaritan was the only man that performed the duty of a neighbour.

He is an unhappy man, who is chargeable with this sin *. " But he that hath mercy on the poor, happy is he." He needs, and he shall have, that mercy which he cannot merit †.

If those that do not shew mercy are punished, an heavy vengeance will fall upon the cruel and mischievous.

Ver. 22. *Do they not err that devise evil? but mercy and truth shall be to them that devise good.*

The doers of evil are abhorred by the Lord, and the more of deliberation and industry that is found with sinners, the more severely will they be punished. The plotters of mischief promise to themselves success in their plans, and expect great advantage from them ‡. But are they not grossly mistaken? undoubtedly they are. They shall be baffled by the wisdom and power of the God whose kingdom ruleth over all. They may bring their devices to pass, but they shall not be able by the accomplishment of them to gain their ends. Instead of doing hurt to the people of God, and disappointing the purposes of the Most High, concerning his own glory, and the happiness of his chosen, the wrath of man shall praise God, and promote the salvation of his people; and what remains of the wrath of God's enemies, beyond what would serve these

---

*Matt. 25:42 †Matt 5:7, 25:35 ‡Ps. 12:4

glorious purposes, shall be restrained. Whatever profit wicked men propose to themselves, they shall find to be loss ; and if they should triumph in the accomplishment of their devices, a moment will put an end to their boasting. The builders of Babel expected to make themselves a glorious name ; but they made themselves a by-word to every generation. The proud king of Babylon expected to set his throne above the stars, and to be like the Most High, and with that view he ravaged the nations, and turned their countries into deserts : But how is he fallen from heaven! and great Babylon which he built for the honour of his majesty, become the dwelling of every loathsome creature !

If wicked men employ their thoughts to contrive mischief, aud shew so much diligence in the service of sin, although they have such a miserable reward ; let God's people exercise the same diligence in the service of righteousness, by seeking out and seizing opportunities for doing good, and their labour shall not be in vain in the Lord.

God's servants are oftentimes tempted to weary in well-doing, because they find they can do little good to others by their labours, which are frequently attended with much toil, and many disquieting and anxious thoughts to themselves. But to him that soweth righteousness shall be a sure reward at last, for his reward is not in the hands of men, but with the Lord, and his work is with his God. He cannot, indeed, pretend to merit any thing from the Lord, for he stands in need of mercy. But mercy shall not be denied to him ; for he is interested in the promises that are derived from the grace, and secured by the faithfulness of God. If God so exactly fulfil his threatenings against the devisers of evil, the Father of mercies will not be slack to fulfil his words of grace to those whom he has beautified with his own likeness, and disposed to be faithful in his service*.

Ver. 23. *In all labour there is profit ; but the talk of the lips tendeth only to penury.*

Some men, if they cannot obtain employment of an easy or genteel kind, would rather be idle than descend below their fancied rank, or expose themselves to the drudgeries of a vulgar profession ; and whilst they are busied in contriving plans for business more suitable to their taste and spirit, and talking of them, they waste their time in idleness.

But no useful business is to be despised, for in all labour there is profit, and the lowest professions in life may be a mean of procuring subsistence to him that is diligent in it, and to his family.

Men must not, however, expect success in their labour without the blessing of God ; and therefore, to industry must be added a dependance on God's providence, a due regard to the service of God, and a disposition to contribute a proper proportion of the fruit of their labours to pious and charitable uses ; otherwise God may blast their labours in righteous judgment, and then no diligence in business can be a security against want †.

As in religion it is not the man who speaks, but the man who does, that gives proof of his sincerity † ; so in earthly business, it is not the man who talks fluently, and lays down plausible schemes of business, but the man who labours, and does all his work, that has reason to expect the blessing of Providence. Those that wear their working instruments in their tongues, are always the most useless, and sometimes the most hurtful members of society. They work not at all,

---

*Eph. 6:8   †Hag. 1:9, 2:17, Ps. 127:1   ‡Matt. 7:22-28

but are busy-bodies in other men's matters ; and whilst they pretend to manage those affairs with which they have nothing to do, they bring themselves to poverty by neglecting their own. Like the sons of Jacob, when their father refused to send Joseph with them, they spend more time in deliberating about a thing, than they might have taken to perform it. If they are professors of religion, their slothfulness causes an offence against the good ways of the Lord ; but with what justice, is plain from this text.

Ver. 24. *The crown of the wise is their riches ; but the foolishness of fools is folly.*

Riches are far from being useless in the hands of a wise man. They place him in an eminent situation, so that he is like a city set on an hill, and his wisdom shines and gives light to multitudes around him. Abraham and Lot could not have afforded us so illus- trious proofs of their hospitality, had they been poor men. Solomon was wise enough to chuse wisdom, rather than mines of gold and silver ; but without riches his wisdom could not have executed plans of such advantage to the church of God, nor built a temple so celebrated in every age. When men have riches, it will soon be known whether they have wisdom or not ; for wisdom will avail itself of riches, to make itself evident by the noblest acts.

But poor saints have no reason to be dissatisfied with their condition ; it requires a greater degree of wisdom than perhaps they have, to overcome the temptations of wealth, and to make it a crown to them. And if their wisdom is despised among foolish men, yet God is well acquainted and well pleased with every good disposition of their heart, although they have not the means of displaying it in acts of goodness. Many that could never give any thing but a tear and a prayer to the distressed, shall be classed with Abraham and Lot in the kingdom of God, whilst others that exercised splendid acts of beneficence, shall be thrust down to the pit with the uncharitable.

If good men are spoiled of their wealth, they need not lament, as if they had lost their crown. For riches are an ornament of grace to the head of wise men, even when they are lost. Job's patience in the loss of every thing, did as much honour to him, as his extraordinary beneficence whilst he was the richest man in the East. We honour his memory still more, when he sewed sackcloth upon his skin, and defiled his horn in the dust, than at the time when judgment was his robe and his diadem. Riches are transitory possessions ; but the crown of the wise is incorruptible, for the honours of charity and patience are eternal.

But the foolishness of fools is still folly, when they are in their best and highest condition. Riches give a man fair opportunities to serve God and man by his wisdom ; but instead of making a fool wise, they make him seven times more a fool, and render his folly visible to the world. If Rehoboam had been in a lower situation, his folly would have done less mis- chief in his own time, and might have been forgotten when his eyes were closed. Men are generally eager in the pursuit of riches for themselves and their chil- dren ; but if Solomon may be trusted, it is far better to want them, unless wisdom is first got to manage them ; for they are instruments of good or evil, as men have, or want wisdom. An Athenian philosopher used to cry out to his fellow-citizens, O ye Athenians ! why do ye toil yourselves to procure estates for your children, and yet take no pains to give them that edu- cation which will teach them to make a right use of their estates ?—When you see drunkards, and debau- chees, and oppressors, you have reason to pity them that they ever had the command of a single shilling.

Pray earnestly for wisdom, and leave it to Providence to determine your outward condition. Wisdom will make every condition good and pleasant.

Ver. 25. *A true witness delivereth souls; but a deceitful witness speaketh lies* *.

Some have an aversion to appear as witnesses in a court of justice, as if swearing were never lawful; but it is men's duty to bear witness when they have a call to it; and by bearing witness, God may be glorified, and the lives and properties of the innocent preserved †.

But we must never lie on any pretence. Neither the preservation of our own life, nor a regard to the life of our neighbours, is a sufficient motive to induce us to dishonour God, by violating the law of truth. Rahab was approved, not for her dissimulation, but for her faith and her good works. We may redeem the life of our brother, in some cases, with our own life, but a lie is too dear a price for it.

But a deceitful witness speaketh lies, and these lies are often swords to destroy the innocent. The liar breaks not the ninth commandment alone, but frequently the sixth and the eighth also.

Ministers and professors of religion are God's witnesses, and it is of infinite importance to give faithful testimony for God. Whilst they hold forth the word of life, souls may be edified and saved; but the profession and preaching of false doctrine, is pernicious to the everlasting interests of men ‡.

Ver. 26. *In the fear of the Lord is strong confidence; and his children shall have a place of refuge.*

Riches are a crown to the wise, but the fear of the Lord is incomparably better. The grace of fear is so

---

*Prov. 12:17, 14:5   †Prov. 24:11,12   ‡Isa. 43:12, 2 Tim. 2:16,17

great a point in religion, and so inseparably connected with every holy disposition, that it is ordinarily used to denote piety in all its branches. In piety there is strong confidence, for godly men are safe from every danger, and know, or may know, that they are safe. Neither earth nor hell shall be able to destroy them, for the place of their defence is the munition of rocks. They are the children of Jehovah, and their almighty Father is their sun and shield. Death itself shall not destroy them, but convey them to those mansions that are made ready by Christ for their reception in their Father's house.

By his children, we may understand the children of them that fear God. Our goodness can merit nothing from God for ourselves, far less for our children. But God is so abundant in goodness and truth, that he has spoken good, and has often brought it to pass, not only concerning his people, but also concerning their seed for many generations *. All men wish to do every thing that lies in their power for their children ; but death will soon remove us out of the world, and what will we then do for them or ourselves ? The estates that are left them, often vanish like snow in the month of March. The best thing we can do for our children, is to fear God, and whether we live or die, the word of God liveth, and his promise abideth for ever.

They that do not chuse the fear of the Lord, chuse death and ruin, but,

Ver. 27. *The fear of the Lord is a fountain of life, to depart from the snares of death.*

The fear of the Lord includes in it the faith of Christ, and they that believe on the Redeemer, have in them a well of water springing up unto life everlasting. They enjoy true life, and every thing that

---

*Rom. 11

can render life happy, and are preserved from those temptations and sins that are snares and nets to entangle and destroy those that have not the fear of God before their eyes. The fear of God is attended with every blessing, and a preservative against all misery. Happy is the man that feareth the Lord *. We may say to him as Abigail to David, " Thy soul shall be bound up in the bundle of life with the Lord thy God ; but thine enemies shall be like stones bound in a sling." But of those that reject the fear of the Lord, we may speak in truth what Bildad says, in a very unjust allusion to Job, " He is cast into a net by his own feet, and he walketh upon a snare †.

Ver. 28. *In the multitude of people is the king's honour; but in the want of people is the destruction of the prince.*

The wise king gives many good instructions to his brethren in office, and is thereby doing good to us all ; for kings without wisdom are public calamities, but well-instructed kings, with their long arms, are the ministers of God for good to millions. In this passage he directs kings to govern in such a manner as to make their subjects happy, that they may not be tempted to leave their country, and retire to a land of greater liberty, but encouraged to rear up an offspring for the service of their king and country.

This instruction is conveyed in a powerful motive to enforce it, which is, that the glory and safety of a prince lies in the multitude of his loyal subjects, and his disgrace and ruin in the want of men attached to his government, and prepared to venture their lives in his defence. In the happy days of Solomon, the people enjoyed peace and plenty, and the children of

*Ps. 128:1, 34:8-10   †Job 18:8-10

Israel and Judah were like the sand of the sea in multitude, eating and drinking, and making merry. In the miserable reign of Jehoahaz, the people of Israel were made like the dust by threshing, so that he and his kingdom were on the brink of destruction, when the God of mercy raised up saviours to prevent their extirpation.

It is the glory of the great King of Israel, that his subjects cannot be numbered for multitude ; and the lovers of his name will contribute their zealous endeavours, by their holy conversation and their prayers, to increase the number of his subjects.

Ver. 29. *He that is slow to wrath is of great understanding ; but he that is hasty of spirit exalteth folly.*

Anger is a more ungovernable monster than the leviathan, and needs much more than a double bridle for curbing it ; and more is provided by Solomon, who is constantly repeating his admonitions to us, to be on our guard against the incursions and ravages of this fury. Many people are in a gross mistake on this point, and imagine that meekness is a sign of stupidity, and an high and outrageous sense of honour an evidence of great spirit ; but the inspired philosopher makes it his business to correct our false apprehensions of things, and assures us, that he is the truly wise man who keeps his passions in subjection to sanctified reason ; and that the man who gives way to anger, upon every provocation, is not only a fool, but so far gone in folly, that he lifts it up to public view, and proclaims by his behaviour, that he has given to folly the throne of his heart.

Moses was the meekest, and he was for that, as well as other reasons, the wisest man of his age. Solomon was in the zenith of his wisdom when he spared those rebels Abiathar and Adonijah; but he was in his decline when he sought to destroy the man to whom God had promised a part of his kingdom.

A philosopher advised Augustus Cæsar, when he felt himself angry, to say nothing till he had taken time to repeat all the letters of the Greek alphabet. When we find ourselves provoked, let us check our passions, till we are able, with greater coolness than Jonah, to answer that question, " Dost thou well to be angry ?"

Ver. 30. *A sound heart is the life of the flesh ; but envy the rottenness of the bones.*

Most men will allow that religion is the best thing for the soul. But the body is generally regarded more than the soul, and they are prejudised against religion, because it is considered as unfavourable to the interest and comfort of the outward man. This false apprehension, Solomon endeavours in many places of this book to remove. According to his doctrine, holiness is the health of the soul, and diffuses its influence over the body ; but sin, which is the disease and death of the soul, is a slow poison also to the body in its present state.

A heart purified by the grace of God, and set at liberty from corroding and turbulent passions, enjoys the pleasures of a peaceful conscience, and a sweet joy, which gives a grace to the countenance, and communicates health and vigour to the bones. That cheerful heart which doth good like a medicine, is chiefly the gift of sacred wisdom ; and that benevolence which inclines us to do good to others, is sure to do good to ourselves, so that the fruits of charity always begin at home *.

" But envy is the rottenness of the bones." It is a torment and punishment as well as a sin, so that uncha-

---

*Chap. 3:8

ritableness, as well as the virtue opposed to it, begins at home. The envious man is impoverished by another's riches, and tormented by another man's happiness ; and every person that seeks his own happiness, is endeavouring to make the envious wretch miserable. A certain author speaks of a woman who was dissected after her death, and a serpent found in her heart. But the envious man has a serpent in his heart whilst he lives, that is constantly tormenting him. He is not only disfigured by his evil eye, but pines away under a distemper that consumes his bones, and is a greater enemy to himself than to any other man. He has a hell within himself, and is on the road to that hell which is prepared for the devil and his angels,— where a place is allotted to him amongst adulterers and murderers *.

Envy in the devil was the occasion of our ruin ; envy in the Pharisees brought our Lord to the cross ; envy in ourselves is rottenness to our bones, and damnation to our souls. May the God of love free us from this baneful passion !

Ver. 31. *He that oppresseth the poor reproacheth his Maker ; but he that honoureth him hath mercy on the poor.*

To oppress the poor by taking advantage to ourselves from their poverty, is a monstrous iniquity : To oppress them by the refusal of that mercy which they need, is a less degree of wickedness, but sufficient to procure condemnation †.

He that oppresseth the poor, either by insults and injuries, or by neglect, reproacheth his Maker, who made man after his image, and by his providence allots to men their several stations in life, requiring the rich and the poor to be useful to one another ; the for-

---

*Gal. 5:20   †Matt. 25:42

mer by kindness, the latter either by their labour, or if they are disabled from work, by their prayers for their benefactors. Oppression and uncharitableness make it evident that men revere not the works of creation and providence, but are atheists either in opinion, or at least in practice; and that the commandments, and promises, and threatenings of God, are despised by them as idle fancies. What would have hindered the oppressor of the poor from joining with the enemies of Christ, had he lived in Jerusalem near 1800 years ago?

Every man that places more confidence in the promises of God than in the bonds of men, and trusts more to the living God than to a piece of shining dust; every man that regards the authority of God in his precepts, and the providence of God in its administrations, will exercise mercy to the poor, and contribute to their relief; and if we say that we love God and hate our brethren, or if we say that we love them, and yet act as if we hated them, then we are liars, and the truth is not in us *.

Ver. 32. *The wicked is driven away in his wickedness ; but the righteous hath hope in his death.*

All must die ;—but there is an immense difference between the death of the righteous and that of the wicked. This difference is not always discernible to observers, but it is real and wide, as the distance between heaven and hell. The wicked man is chased out of the world in which his portion lies and all his hopes are circumscribed, into a world of unmingled misery and unchanging despair. He lived in sin and dies in sin, and his sins lie down with him in the dust, and afford everlasting nourishment to the worm that shall never die, and fuel to the fire that shall never

---

*Verse 21

be quenched. If he should die as quietly as a lamb, that does not lessen his misery, but only suspends it a few moments; if he should feed his vain mind with the hopes of heaven to the last, yet he dies into hopeless anguish.

" But the righteous hath hope in his death." He believes in Christ, and dies not in his sins *. His death is the destruction of sin, that gave him so much trouble in his life. He departs from this world, and from his own body, but it is to a better country, where he is absent from the body, and present with the Lord. His death is full of hope, for he expects to be with Christ, which is far better for him than the best things he could hope or wish for on earth. His hopes may be weak and languishing, but still he has so much hope in Christ, as to venture his soul in his hands; and if his faith is mingled with fears, these fears shall vanish as a thin cloud, and these anxieties, when he is leaving his body, will add to the triumphant joy which he will feel, when angels appear to convey his soul to the regions from whence fear and sorrow are for ever banished. Death is a grim serjeant to the wicked, sent to arrest them for their crimes; to believers it is like Joseph's waggons sent to convey his father to his best-loved son.

The wicked are unhappy in their lives, for there is but a step between them and the king of terrors. The righteous are blessed in their lives, for their salvation is drawing nearer every day. They are most blessed in their deaths, for to them to die is Christ. Now they are saved by hope, then they die in hope, and through eternity they shall enjoy what they waited for in hope.

Ver. 33. *Wisdom resteth in the heart of him that hath*

---

*John 8:24

understanding; but that which is in the midst of fools is made known.

Wisdom does not lie buried in the heart of the wise man, for his tongue bringeth it forth for the advantage of others on every proper occasion *. But it is hid in his heart, like a precious treasure that he wishes to preserve from those robbers that would deprive him of what he values above gold and silver. He does not make a vain and useless show of his wisdom to draw the applause of men, for he is not like those philosophers, falsely so called, who valued the reputation of wisdom above wisdom itself. He does not pretend to give instruction to those that are fitted to instruct himself, for he is readier to learn than to teach, except when he sees a proper call to instruct others; and he will not make his wisdom cheap, by casting his pearls before swine, and prostituting his holy things to dogs. Nevertheless he is willing and ready to produce some of his precious stores, when he sees a probability of doing good by them to others. He is like a rich and generous man, that takes no pleasure in boasting of his wealth, but still keeps something in readiness to serve his friends.

But that little sense which fools may have is soon known, and found to be what it really is, and not what they fancy it to be. If they know any thing, they think it useless till others know that they know it. This folly is wisdom in their own eyes, and therefore they publish it abroad, till all men know by their own testimony that they are fools. Some people are so weak as to think that much speaking is a sign of much sense, and silence a proof of ignorance. But a wise man is often known by his silence, and a fool by

---

*Chap. 15:3

his multitude of words; whereas, if he could have held his peace, he might have been taken for a wise man.

Ver. 34. *Righteousness exalteth a nation, but sin is a reproach to any people.*

This proverb is verified in the whole history of the nation of Israel, and in those promises and threatenings that received their fulfilment in the events which befel them.

Some allege, that God dispenses no rewards and punishments to the nations, but such as are the native consequences of their behaviour, without any particular direction of providence, from a regard to their good or bad conduct; and that the history of the things that befel Israel as a nation, affords no ensample unto nations that are not under the Mosaic covenant. But, besides that Providence has affixed prosperity or misery to virtue or vice, as their natural consequences, we find God punishing many nations on account of their sins, by calamities that were not the native results of their sins. The histories of Genesis, and Exodus, and Joshua, and the predictions of all the prophets concerning the heathen nations, might be quoted in proof of this point: and even under the New Testament, we find prophecies of the miseries that would come upon public bodies for their sins *.

Great is the regard which a righteous God has for righteousness. The virtue even of heathen nations has been rewarded with prosperity, and their vices have brought reproach and ruin on them. Righteousness, such as heathens could practice, made Greece and Rome to flourish, and exalted them to glory. But the last of these nations, after it was advanced to the highest pitch of worldly grandeur, was soon brought to extreme misery, and debased to the most wretched

---

*Matt. 22:1-7, Rev. 8:21

servitude, when corruption and wickedness, in opposition to the dictates of natural light, was become common in it.   Let us all, therefore, if we love our country, oppose wickedness to the utmost of our power, for
a remnant of righteous persons may sometimes prove
for a time the pillars of a land *.

It is the interest of kings to promote righteousness, and to discourage iniquity among their subjects; and this they will do, if they deserve that noble
title.

Ver. 35. *The king's favour is toward a wise servant,
but his wrath is against him that causeth shame.*

Many kings have indeed erred in this point, but
they have frequently been made to see their error, like
Ahasuerus, who nourished in his bosom that serpent
Haman, and overlooked the faithful services of Mordecai; but afterwards destroyed him to whom he had
so shamefully given his confidence, and exalted the
preserver of his life.

Solomon had told us that riches are a crown to the
wise †, but here he tells us that poverty and mean circumstances will not hinder men from being crowned
by wisdom.   A servant that fears the Lord, and manages the affairs entrusted to him with prudence and
faithfulness, obtains the favour of his master, although
he be a king.   A foolish servant is a shame to himself
and to his master; and although for a while his folly
and vices may be concealed, yet in the end they
bring down that displeasure upon him which is often
attended with vengeance.

Some masters may be so ungrateful, as to despise
the best servants, or through prejudice they may be
led to treat them with great injustice; but time will

*Isa. 1:9   †Verse 24

convince them of their mistake, and cause them to alter their conduct, as we find in the case of David and Mephibosheth ; but if they prove so inhuman and wicked as to continue enemies to their best friends, let such servants remember how David was used by Saul, and consider whether he was a gainer or a loser by the persecutions he underwent.

The great King who reigns over heaven and earth, will reward faithful servants, who do honour to his gospel by the proper discharge of the duties of their stations ; for he despises not the lowest services of the meanest men, but he is a severe Avenger of the wrongs done by men, to those with whom his providence has connected them *.

Proverbs 15

Ver. 1. *A soft answer turneth away wrath ; but grievous words stir up anger.*

WRATH is a fire that burns unto destruction, and it is our duty to bring water to quench this fire. A soft answer to provoking words is like water to a fire. By gentle language, joined to liberal presents, Jacob pacified the fierce resentments of his brother Esau. He prayed to God, and trusted in him for the preservation of his family, but he did not neglect the proper

---

*Col. 3:22-25

means of calming his brother's angry spirit. There are some tempers so untractable that they cannot be pacified, but these are rare, and seem to be under some powerful influence of the devil, like that of Judas Iscariot, who was not reclaimed by the kind words of our Lord from executing his bloody purpose; or those miscreants that seized on our Saviour, although to his ordinary gentleness he added his miraculous power in healing the ear of Malchus.

But there are some who cast oil upon the flame of anger, and make it to burn more fiercely by their grievous and provoking words. What can such persons expect, but to be consumed by their own rashness? Anger is a short madness, and when two mad persons are engaged in combat, they both are in danger of receiving deadly wounds. Let us, therefore, endeavour to bridle our passions, and guard ourselves by the meekness of wisdom from the fierce passions of other men, lest, by biting and devouring one another, we be consumed one of another. The fierce words of the men of Judah and Israel, when they were bringing back David to his throne, kindled a new war, which, without active and prudent management in David and his generals, might have produced fatal consequences *.

Ver. 2. *The tongue of the wise useth knowledge aright, but the mouth of fools poureth out foolishness.*

The wise man knows when he ought to be silent, and when he should speak; and will not cast his pearls before swine, and give his holy things to dogs. His words are good, for they are spoken in due season, and he knows how to address himself in a proper manner to different persons, according to their tempers and circumstances. Gideon used very different language

---

*Chap. 12:18

to the angry Ephraimites, from that which he used to the men of Succoth and Penuel, otherwise the end of the Midianitish war had been the beginning of a more dangerous civil war. But our Lord is the most glorious instance of the right use of knowledge. The different answers he made to his friends and enemies, whether open or disguised, whilst they give proof of his admirable wisdom, afford us a pattern of prudence, joined with inflexible integrity. But fools turn the little wisdom and knowledge they have into folly, by their way of using it ; for the very instruction of fools is folly.

Their mouths pour out foolishness, as a fountain casteth out her streams. They are not masters of their tongues, but their tongues are masters of them. Whilst wise men have the fear of God set for a sentinel upon the door of their lips, their lips have neither a door nor a watch, but every thing that is within comes out ; and as their hearts are little worth, their conversation is empty and vain *.

Ver. 3. *The eyes of the Lord are in every place, beholding the evil and the good.*

The eyes of men can be but in one place, because themselves are circumscribed in one place. But the eyes of that God who fills heaven and earth are every where. Angels are full of eyes before and behind, but God is all eye, and darkness and the shadow of death hideth not from him. He is in heaven by his glorious presence ; and that high and holy place is like a watch-tower, from whence he espies the evil and the good. Evil men flatter themselves that none sees or knows their wickedness, as if God could not see through the dark clouds ; but he is a witness of what they speak and do in their bed-chambers, nor does a single thought

---

*Chap. 12:23, 13:16

of their heart escape his notice. " Beware, Cato looks on," was a proverb among the Romans ; but a greater than any man on earth is still looking on us, and shall we do that before the eye of God, which we durst not be guilty of in the presence of a child ? Alas ! how is the God who sees all things despised and insulted by the sons of men ! But he will not be mocked ; he beholds and judges, and will punish the evil-doer *.

His eyes behold the good also ; and this is their great consolation, when they are overlooked or ungratefully used by men. God knows their integrity, and beholds with a pleasant countenance their humble and sincere endeavours to please him, and to do good to men. Every thought of his name, and every good word that they speak, is written before him in a book of remembrance †. He beholds with an eye of pity all their secret sorrows, and puts their tears in his bottle ; and not a moment does he withdraw his eyes from the righteous ‡.

Good men need not fear that God will forget any of his gracious promises. They will be all accomplished to them in due season ; for his eyes run to and fro through the whole earth, to shew himself strong in their behalf; and his providence is constantly employed to glorify his faithfulness, in fulfilling that word which he hath magnified above or upon all his name.

Ver. 4. *A wholesome tongue is a tree of life, but perverseness therein is a breach in the spirit.*

The tongue that administers proper and seasonable counsels, comforts, and reproofs, is a wholesome tongue. Unmerited rebukes, reproaches, unkind words, and cruel mockings, are perverseness in that

---

*Ps. 11:4,7   †Mal. 3:16   ‡Job 36:7

little member, which boasteth and can really effect great things. The advantages derived from a healing tongue are like the fruits of the tree of life,—the erring are reclaimed, the dejected are comforted, the weak are animated and invigorated by it. When Job was in deep distress, he was very sensible how pleasant these fruits were which he had no opportunity to taste, and tells his friends, that if they had been in his situation, he would have strengthened them by his words, and assuaged their grief by the moving of his lips. The words of God have a divine virtue for healing the diseases and the wounds of the spirit. This is the dispensary from which we are to derive healing words for the broken in spirit *.

But perverseness in the tongue is a breach in the spirit. It wounds and pierces, it breaks and bruises, the heart of him that is reproached by it. Job would not have exposed himself so much to the censures of Elihu, if his more aged friends had behaved more kindly to him. His patient spirit felt most sensibly the piercing edge of their unjust reproofs. David felt none of his afflictions more bitterly, than the keen reproaches and insults of his enemies. And our Lord Jesus Christ exemplified his unconquerable patience in bearing the contradictions of sinners, and enduring with all meekness, though not without afflicting sensibility, the indignities that were poured upon him †. When we are exposed to the scourge of the tongue, let us remember that He was tempted like as we are, and imitate his patience, and trust in him for the supplies of needful grace.

Ver. 5. *A fool despiseth his father's instruction, but he that regardeth reproof is prudent.*

---

*Prov. 12:25   †Ps. 22:6,7, Isa. 1:7,8

A father's instruction proceeds from love, and it is folly and ingratitude to despise it ; and yet some children are such enemies to themselves, and so unnatural to their best friends, that they break the spirits of their affectionate parents, by spurning at those admonitions that are needful for their own welfare. They are like froward patients, who are angry at the physician for giving them medicines which are salutary, but unpalatable. In a father's instructions there is authority. The authority of parents over their children has been acknowledged by the wildest nations, and is ratified in that law which was spoken by the mouth, and written by the finger of God. When they reprove their children, the authority of God is joined to the authority of parents, to enforce their admonitions ; for they are expressly required to attempt the reformation of their children by rebukes and corrections. He that despises his father's reproofs, despises not only man, but God. This is folly in the extreme, and he that was a fool before he received instruction, becomes mad when he resists it.

If a fool despises his father's instruction, it is not to be supposed that he will pay much regard to the admonitions of other men ; but a prudent man will receive correction, and be thankful for it, not only from a father, but from any person, though inferior to himself in station or wisdom. David suffered himself to be reclaimed by the wife of Nabal, and Sarah received with meekness the reproofs of a heathen king.

Persons may receive instruction, when it does not touch their pride, and yet have no solid wisdom ; but he that receives reproof with calmness, and makes use of it for the correction of his life, gives a sure proof of his prudence. There are many persons who come to church, and sit as God's people sit, and appear very attentive to the preaching of the word ; but if there is any occasion to administer the censures of the church to them, they are like a horse or mule when their sores are touched ; and the bit and bridle will scarcely hold them in from coming nigh unto their reprovers.

Ver. 6. *In the house of the righteous is much treasure ; but in the revenues of the wicked is trouble.*

That there is much treasure in the house of some righteous persons, is certain ; but it is equally certain that some of those who are rich in faith, have no silver and gold, and can scarcely find daily bread. Solomon was not ignorant of this, and explains this proverb, ver. 16, 17. There is incomparably more of solid treasure in the little that a righteous man hath, than in the substance of many wicked. Another explication of this maxim may be drawn from chap. xiv. 11. iii. 34. The blessing of the Lord is in the house of the righteous, and that is a more precious treasure than the gold and diamonds in a thousand mines. The riches of the wicked, in which they pride themselves, often consist of paper ; and if bonds and charters make a man rich, the righteous cannot be poor, when they have bonds upon God himself for every thing they need, and the charter which shews their sure title to the everlasting inheritance. The devil robbed Job, but he could not make him poor, for his chief treasure lay quite out of the reach of that enemy. Had he served God, as the devil said, for hire, he had been poor indeed ; but a good conscience, and faith in the living Redeemer, could not be torn from him as long as he lived.

" But in the revenues of the wicked is trouble." When good men have nothing, they possess all things ; when bad men have much, they are in straits, for their craving desires are still larger than their possessions, and whatever they have, they want satisfaction, and are still crying, Give, give. They have, besides, a bad conscience, and a drop of that bitter ingredient is sufficient to swallow up an ocean of earthly delights. Do we wish to be rich? let us learn from the Bible what it is to be rich, that we may not spend our time and labour in the pursuit of feathers and vanities.

Ver. 7. *The lips of the wise disperse knowledge : but the heart of the foolish doeth not so,* (or *is not right.)*

The wise man does not boast of his wisdom, or make a vain parade of his knowledge, but he is far from grudging the benefit of it to others. He does not behave like that foolish man who grudges to the fields the precious grain, and keeps it shut up in his storehouses, till it is destroyed by vermin. He scatters the good seed of knowledge, where there is any probability that it will do good; and as the husbandman, although he will not sow upon the rock, will nevertheless commit his seed to that ground where he is not certain of a good increase, and is not deterred by every cloud from his work ; so the wise man will endeavour to do good, even to those that may possibly disappoint his kind intentions, and prove ungrateful for his offices of love. He that disperses knowledge wisely, shall not be disappointed of a harvest of gracious recompences to himself*.

But the wicked man cannot disperse knowledge, for he has not a right heart. There is no good treasure in his soul to furnish useful instructions to others, but an evil treasure within, from which he brings forth evil things. He sows the seed of tares and hemlock, and shall reap destruction to himself.

Our tongues are our glory, and should be used for the glory of God, and for the good of men ; and therefore we ought diligently to store our hearts with that

---

*Prov. 10:31

knowledge and wisdom which will be of infinite advantage to ourselves, and make us useful to others.

Ver. 8. *The sacrifice of the wicked is an abomination to the Lord; but the prayer of the upright is his delight.*

Wicked men may abound in the external acts of religion, as if they intended to compensate the defects of the inward man, by a double measure of bodily exercise. By this means they flatter themselves into dangerous and presumptuous hopes of the favour of God, and sometimes gain a name among the godly, who are neither qualified nor authorized to search the secrets of the heart. But God, who cannot be deceived, sees the insincerity of their hearts, and loathes their most splendid and costly services, as so many presumptuous attempts to bribe the great Judge into a connivance at their wickedness.

No man would chuse to put himself to a great deal of trouble to no purpose. But hypocrites not only lose the benefit of their services, but provoke God's indignation by them. The wicked and their sacrifices are detestable to him; he counts them a trouble, and will not long bear with them. How miserable are unrenewed sinners! Their righteousnesses are abominable and provoking iniquities; what need have they to disclaim their own goodness, and seek to win Christ and be found in him, clothed with his righteousness, and purified by his Spirit!

But let not God's people be afraid of this text, although they are often obliged to confess that they are carnal, sold under sin. They walk in the light, and have fellowship with God; and the blood of Jesus Christ, the Son of God, cleanseth them from all sin. Their prayers are unworthy of divine acceptance, but through the Beloved they are well pleasing to him. Whilst the costly services of the wicked are detested by him, he delights in the meanest services of the up-

right. This was a truth to be believed, whilst the Old
Testament ordinances were yet in force ; how much
more are we encouraged to believe this truth, who
have so clear revelations of that great High Priest who
is passed into the heavens, and appears in the presence
of God, making intercession for us, and recommending
our weak and imperfect services to his Father ! Prayer
is God's delight, and should it not be ours also, who
stand in so much need of the benefit of it ? When
God requires from us the severest instances of self-
denial, it is our duty and interest to please God rather
than ourselves ; but when he delights in prayer, and
takes pleasure to have his richest favours asked by
needy creatures, shall we not come often to his throne
of grace ? He that commands us to pray, and delights
in the voice of prayer, and hath appointed his Son to
be our advocate, will not turn a deaf ear to the petitions of his suppliants.

Ver. 9. *The way of the wicked is an abomination
unto the Lord ; but he loveth him that followeth after
righteousness.*

Wherefore do we offer sacrifices, and God sees not ?
Why do we perform the most splendid services, and
meet with contempt, instead of thanks ? will the hypocrites say. What does the Lord mean by requiring
duties, and yet refusing to accept of them when they
are performed ? The fault is in the sinner himself ;
his hands are full of blood, or, at least, his heart is polluted with iniquity, and therefore he cannot reasonably
expect acceptance to his most costly oblations *.

The whole course of the wicked man's life is detested by God, who is of purer eyes than to behold sin, or
to look upon iniquity. The sinner's principles are
corrupt ; his thoughts are evil continually ; his words
are all vain, or vile, or hypocritical ; his holy things

*Isa. 1

are deeply stained with his pollutions, and he is a mocker of God when he thinks he is praying or praising. Not one of his innumerable iniquities are forgiven, for he is without Christ, and has no interest in the blood of atonement.

If the very heavens are not clean in God's sight, how abominable and filthy is the man that drinketh iniquity like water ! and how detestable is the course of his life to him whose glorious holiness makes the angels to cover their faces ! Yet, detestable as sinners are to God, their situation is not hopeless, unless they make it so by stubbornness in sin and unbelief *.

Though God hates all sin, even in his own people, yet so rich is his grace, and so prevalent is the intercession of Christ, that he loves his people even in this world, where their righteousness is imperfect, and their course of life stained with many sins. At the best, they are but followers of righteousness. Paul himself could not say that he had attained, or was already perfect ; but their hungerings and thirstings after righteousness are sure evidences of the love of God to them, and presages of that perfection which they shall attain in due time. Like as a father pitieth his son, and takes pleasure to see his feeble efforts to please and serve him ; so the Lord delights in every breathing of desire, and every aim to obey his will which he sees in his people. Their righteousness towards men, and faithful discharge of the duty of their stations, is accepted in his sight, as well as their praises addressed to himself †.

Ver. 10. *Correction is grievous unto him that forsaketh the way; and he that hateth reproof shall die.*

When a traveller loses the right way, he is glad of one that can set him right. When a man is on the

---

* Ezek. 33:11, Isa. 55:7   †Ps. 37:23

edge of a concealed pit, he will thank the person that pulls him back with violence, and tells him of his danger. But many men are such enemies to their own souls, that they cannot endure necessary reproofs and corrections, and would rather be suffered to go to the place of torment at their ease, than terrified with apprehensions of their danger, whilst there is time to make a retreat.

Let such persons consider, that however grievous correction is, yet hell is much more grievous ; and that however they may get free of the former, there is no possibility of getting out of the latter. Who pities Ahab for his fall at Ramoth-Gilead ? He was forewarned of his danger by Micaiah, but he hated the holy prophet for telling him the truth. Equally unpitied shall they be who perish for refusing reproof, and all the words of instruction which they heard in the day of grace, shall be like flaming thunderbolts in their consciences through endless ages.

Ver. 11. *Hell and destruction are before the Lord ; how much more, then, the hearts of the children of men !*

Hast thou seen through the gates of death, or have the doors of the shadow of death been opened unto thee ? No. The world of spirits is hidden from the eyes of all living. Many vain disputes have been carried on by men about the place and state of the departed. But this concealed region is open to the eyes of him with whom we have to do. The outer darkness of the place of the damned is light before him. He knows perfectly every thought of his grand adversary, and is entirely acquainted with every design and every feeling of all the fiends of darkness. Why then do wicked men flatter themselves with the hopes of secrecy in their wicked actions ? The most secret principles of their conduct, the most retired thoughts of their hearts, are bright as the day to his eyes. At the day of judgment there will be a revelation of the secrets of all hearts, and then it will appear, that not a single imagination of the thoughts of the heart was a secret to him whose eyes are like a flame of fire.

Wo to them who seek deep to hide their counsel from the Lord, and whose work is in the dark *. But happy are they who labour, that whether present or absent, they may be accepted of him. He knows their hearts, he knows all the purposes that their enemies form against them, and will disappoint the most crafty devices of those that hate them †. God has saved to every creature that loathsome spectacle, the heart of man; but his eye beholds all the deceitfulness and desperate wickedness of it. How astonishing is the patience that bears with such vile creatures! How wonderful that love which gave his Son to die for them, and gives his Spirit to sanctify them, and accepts of their services, though defiled with stains infinitely offensive to the eyes of his glory!

Ver. 12. *A scorner loveth not one that reproveth him; neither will he go unto the wise.*

Wisdom is necessary in a reprover, lest his reproofs meet with that cutting reply, Physician, heal thyself; and much skill is required in dispensing reproofs, that they may not irritate instead of reforming.

However wise the reprover is, a scorner will hate him, at least he will not love him; and as an evidence of his aversion, he will not go to him, but avoid his company as if he were an enemy, because he mortifies his pride; for the scorner is as impatient of rebuke, as if, like the Pope, he laid claim to infallibility.

Here is a trial of true wisdom. The seed that sprung up pleasantly for a time, but withered when the sun rose in its strength, was an emblem of those hearers,

---

*Isa. 29:5   †Job 5:12-16

that cannot endure persecution for the gospel; and how could we endure persecution, if we cannot bear a friendly admonition, or a needful censure from the pastors of the church ! The Apostle Peter received with meekness a sharp reproof from Paul, and we find him afterwards speaking of him in very friendly language *. David was a king and a prophet, yet he could receive with thankfulness a reproof from those that were by many degrees his inferiors †. Some think that he called one of his sons Nathan, in token of respect to the prophet of the same name, who reproved him for the blackest crimes.

The rebukes of Christ in his word and providence are fruits of the tenderest love, and the wise will love him the more on their account, and thank him for the necessary discipline of the covenant.

Ver. 13. *A merry heart maketh a cheerful countenance; but by sorrow of the heart the spirit is broken.*

There is so close a connection between the soul and body, that when the latter is pained, the former feels its pains; and when the mind is oppressed with grief, the body cannot enjoy its health and vigour. On the other side, a healthy body is of great advantage to the operations of the mind, and the joy of the heart spreads itself over the countenance, It makes the eyes brisk and sparkling, and gives a pleasant grace to the aspect in the eyes of every beholder. If one could paint as well as Jezebel, he could not make his face so lovely as it is rendered by the cheerfulness of the spirit.

Every thing that tends to promote a well-regulated joy in the mind is valuable, for it serves both soul and body at once. Meekness and contentment with our lot, peace and love, afford a continual feast to the mind, and make us agreeable to others. These virtues are not

---

*2 Peter 3   †Ps. 141

to be acquired, in their true excellency, but from God, for they are fruits of his Spirit, and are the property of the believer in Christ *. Christians should remember, that to rejoice is their duty, their privilege, and an ornament to their profession. The world has been too much tempted by Christians themselves, to think that there is little pleasure in religion. Why should we not constantly verify that saying of the wise preacher, " A man's wisdom maketh his face to shine."

The effect of sorrow is often dangerous, and sometimes destructive. It blunts the edge of the understanding, impairs the memory, destroys the vigour of the soul, and if too much indulged, may utterly destroy reason, and sink a man into despair. There are indeed sorrows required by religion, but these have no danger in them, for they are mingled and attended with the sweetest pleasures. It is sin and not religion that makes sorrow needful, and religion forbids sorrow, even for sin, to be carried to a dangerous height, lest Satan should thereby gain an advantage ; for we are not ignorant of his devices, and know that some of his most dreadful temptations are founded on that constitution of body or mind that disposes men to the entertainment of melancholy thoughts.

The kingdom of God is not a kingdom of darkness, but of righteousness, and peace, and joy in the Holy Ghost.

Ver. 14. *The heart of him that hath understanding seeketh knowledge; bat the mouth of fools feedeth on foolishness.*

Here the most intelligent men know but in part, and they are the wisest men that are most sensible of the imperfection of their wisdom, " I know nothing," said the wisest of the Greeks, " but that I know nothing ;" and

---

*Gal. 5:19

the wisest of Christians compares his present attainments to those of a child. Desires of wisdom, discovered in the ardent pursuit of it, are the best evidences we can give of our wisdom.

There are many that use the ordinary means of knowledge, and yet have no true wisdom; but their fault lies more in the heart than in the head. They are formal and careless in their endeavours to obtain knowledge, because they have not a cordial love to the truth. They read and hear, but they do not meditate and pray. If knowledge would drop into their minds as the dew upon the earth, they would be very glad of it; but they will not incline their ear unto wisdom, nor apply their heart to understanding. The truly wise have a higher esteem of knowledge than of gold and rubies, and their hearts are deeply engaged in the search of it. They use the means of knowledge, but will not be satisfied with the use of them without obtaining the end, and therefore they depend upon Christ as the great teacher, and earnestly plead for the illuminations of his Spirit, to brighten their understandings with discoveries of the truth, and to furnish them with that practical wisdom, without which they cannot be happy. Such seekers of wisdom shall not be disappointed; they shall know God to their joy in this world, and in heaven they shall know even as they are known.

But the mouth of fools feedeth on foolishness, for they have no relish for wisdom; they can drink in vain and frothy discourse from morning till night, as if it were sweet wine; and when good men meditate by day and night on the law of God, the vain imagination of fools supplies them with thoughts suited to their corrupt minds, in which they delight as much as in their necessary food. God has provided marrow and fatness for the entertainment of our minds, but these foolish creatures rather choose to feed on wind and chaff. Their mouth poureth out foolishness, and they cannot do better, because they neither have, nor desire to have, any thing better within their hearts, and out of the abundance of the heart the mouth speaketh.

Ver. 15. *All the days of the afflicted are evil; but he that is of a merry (or good) heart, hath a continual feast.*

To him that is afflicted, pity should be shewed from his friend, for none but those that have experience can tell what a gloom affliction uses to spread over the mind, and what unceasing sorrows it produces, when it is not soothed by the consolations of friendship, or alleviated by the vigour of the mind. The patientest of men tells us that his thoughts, disquieted by pain, and embittered by the unkindness of his friends, turned night into day, and made the light short because of darkness *. In distress the night cannot put an end to the fatigue of the day by the refreshments of sleep, and the pleasant light of morning can convey no cheering influence to the anxious mind.

But a good and cheerful heart is a continual feast. The pleasures of a peaceful conscience and a healthful soul, are sweeter than those which sensualists enjoy when they are revelling in all the pleasures that riches can give. The longest feast that we read of, lasted only six months †; but it was impossible that the nobles of Ahasuerus could be merry all that time. Feasting continued too long, becomes an insupportable burden; but the feast of a soul that enjoys well-grounded mirth never ends, and needs not suffer interruption. The mirth of fools, Solomon tells us, is like the crackling of thorns under a pot, and therefore it cannot be the mirth that is meant by him in this place. The joy

---

*Job 17:12   †Esther 1

of the Lord is the strength and life of the heart. When affliction makes a man to abhor dainty meat, the joys of God's salvation feed the soul as with marrow and with fatness. Paul was exposed to constant sufferings, and could safely protest that he died daily ; yet every day he enjoyed those pleasures that were better than wine. The days of affliction could not suspend his happiness, for he was exceeding joyful in all his tribulations, and gloried in his infirmities, and sung praises in dungeons, and gave thanks to God, who always made him to triumph in Christ. This continual feast, which lost not its relish in the days of evil, was not peculiar to apostles. The first believers in Christ were so lively in the exercise of faith and hope, that the days of affliction were in general good and happy days to them *. How valuable is religion ! what fools are they that seek or expect happiness without it ! and how much are religious persons to be blamed, when they are sad from day to day, as if they were not the King's children, or their Father were unkind to them ! The question that Eliphaz puts to Job without sufficient reason, may pierce into their consciences, " Are the consolations of God small with thee † ?"

Religion is the soul of joy, it can cheer the afflicted, and will not suffer the poor to be unhappy.

Ver. 16. *Better is little with the fear of the Lord, than great treasure, and trouble therewith.*

It is the blessing of God that makes any thing pleasant and satisfying. It is sufficient alone to make the beggar rich, and without it the man is poor who calls whole counties his own. And his blessing is upon his own people, and upon their basket and store, whilst the wicked and all they have are under his curse. It is God that gives both food and gladness, and without

*Heb. 10:34, 1 Peter 1:5,6   †Job 15:11

gladness, what good can our food do to us? and this gladness is ordinarily given to him that is good in his sight; but to the sinner he giveth travel, to gather and to heap up, that he may give to him that is good before God *.

If a Christian has but little, it is pleasant to him; because he considers it as the gift of his heavenly Father †, and tastes in it the love of his Saviour, through whose grace every thing is pure and sanctified to him. The wicked have their food from the providence of God which ruleth over all, the righteous have their bread by covenant and promise ‡. If they have little in possession, they know that they shall have every thing necessary and good for them, from the possessor of heaven and earth; and when they are pinched with straits, it is not for want of good will in their heavenly Father, but because his goodness to them is directed by wisdom. If they have scarcely any food at all, they have promises on which they can feed, with a pleasure never tasted by the men of the world when their corn and wine do most abound ||.

Trouble is the inseparable companion of great treasures, when they are not sanctified by prayer, and sweetened by the fear of the Lord. They are like water to a man in a dropsy, which doth not quench, but inflame his thirst. Anxiety and care, an ill conscience, and the uncertainty of present things, embitter the portion of the men of the world. Nothing can be really pleasant that wants the blessing of God. A little that a righteous man hath is better than the riches, not of one, but of many wicked §.

The love that religion promotes, tends greatly to sweeten their outward enjoyments.

---

*Eccl. 2:26 †Matt. 6:11 ‡Hos. 2:19, Matt. 6:33
||Ps. 37:19 §Ps. 37:16

Ver. 17. *Better is a dinner of herbs where love is, than a stalled ox, and hatred therewith.*

Love is a pleasing affection of the soul, and diffuses cheerfulness all around it. It gives a relish to the scantiest and coarsest meal. Water is sweeter than wine, and dry bread more pleasant than fat things full of marrow, when this delightful affection gives a relish to them. Ruth and Naomi were happy when they lived on the gleanings of the fields of Boaz, and in the fulness of their satisfaction poured their blessings on the head of him that allowed them the scanty pittance. But selfishness, and hatred, and variance, makes every pleasant dish insipid or bitter.

The conversation of friends is far pleasanter than any dish at the table. Where hatred is, there is silence or sullenness, or at least hollow mirth, and tasteless ceremony ; but where love and the fear of God is, the table conversation is delightful and useful. We find even an heathen poet reflecting with rapture on the pleasures of such entertainment *. How blessed were the disciples of our Lord, when they sat at meat with him ! Barley loaves and fishes were probably ordinary fare with them, but they were entertained with divine discourse.

Such pleasure as they enjoyed in their Master's company we cannot now expect ; but his religion is admirably fitted to promote our present happiness, for love is his great commandment. He enforces love between husbands and wives, as well as among friends, by motives which no Christian can withstand.

If love is necessary to sweeten our ordinary meals, we must never come to the Lord's table without exercising supreme love to Christ, and fervent love to our fellow Christians. We must consider ourselves as one

---

*O noctes cœnæque deum! — HOR.

body and one bread, when we are all partaking of one bread. Love is a pleasant passion, but let us beware of anger, which makes a man a torment to himself, and a plague to his neighbours.

Ver. 18. *A wrathful man stirreth up strife; but he that is slow to anger appeaseth strife.*

It will be our wisdom, if possible, to avoid the company of a passionate man, for it is almost impossible to live in peace with him. He is almost' perpetually giving offence, and yet he cannot bear the least shadow of offence to be given to himself. You cannot act or speak so cautiously, but he will find or make some occasion for a quarrel, for tow is not more inflammable than a mind in which passion rules over reason.

But if you cannot avoid his company, be sure to keep a strict guard over your spirit, and by this means strife may be prevented or appeased. It is one of the amiable glories of God, that he is slow to anger ; and considering how much we are indebted to his patience, we are strongly obliged to copy after him, as dear children.

A passionate disposition makes a man the firebrand of society ; but meekness makes him a blessing to his neighbours. He that appeaseth strife, does us as much service, as he that quenches the fire that is burning down a house.

We must learn of Christ, who was meek and lowly of heart ; so shall we find rest to ourselves, and pacify contentions, and enjoy a double blessing from the great Author of blessings. " Blessed are the meek,— blessed are the peace-makers."

Ver. 19. *The way of the slothful man is as an hedge of thorns ; but the way of the righteous is made plain.*

It is but little that a slothful man can be prevailed on to do ; but that little gives him great trouble and fatigue. A diligent man finds himself easy and cheerful in the exercise of his profession; but the slothful man cannot be content, but when he is permitted to doze or sleep. When he is on the way of his duty he cannot proceed far, for he sees a hedge of thorns before him, and no opening to give him passage. Whatever business he is employed about, he finds unconquerable difficulties, and inextricable perplexities in it, so that he either leaves it undone, or slubbers it over, and does nothing to purpose. Such a man is fit neither for heaven nor earth. His dispositions do not at all suit the present state of mankind, to whom God has appointed labour and sweat; nor do they suit the law of Christ, which requires men to rejoice and work righteousness *.

" But the way of the righteous is made plain." The wise man mentions righteousness in this place rather than diligence, because the latter is included in the former, and is not sufficient without it, to make a man's way plain. The man that joins to industry the practice of justice towards men and piety towards God, may find difficulties in his way; but he is not diverted by them from his duty, nor discouraged from making progress. In worldly affairs, hard labour, with the blessing of God, conquers every thing. In the course of the spiritual life, difficulties and discouragements vanish away before faith, and mountains are threshed down to vallies, by that power on which faith relies †.

Ver. 20. *A wise son maketh a glad father; but a foolish man despiseth his mother.*

Nothing can make a dutiful child happier, than to contribute to the happiness of his parents; and this filial disposition must not be confined to childhood, but dwell in us whilst either father or mother dwell

---

*Matt. 7:23-27   †Job 17:8,9, Isa. 41:13-15

upon the earth. If our parents should require us to do some great and hard thing for them, nature and gratitude would enforce our compliance; but all that they require is, that we should be wise and happy, for their felicity is bound up in our welfare. Surely he is an unnatural fool that will not gratify them in such kind desires.

Epaminondas, one of the best of the Greeks, having gained a glorious victory over the enemies of his country, said to them that complimented him on it, that his chief pleasure in it was the pleasure that the news would give to his father and mother.

Nature and Scripture condemn the folly of those that despise either father or mother. If our dependance is chiefly on our father, yet we have experienced more tenderness from our mother, and have cost her greater sorrows *.

Religion, if it had free course, would turn this earth into a kind of paradise, by making all men a blessing to one another. The duties we owe to human society, and to our respective relations, are enforced in the Bible by motives, which nothing but folly and impiety can resist.

Ver. 21. *Folly is joy to him that is destitute of wisdom: but a man of understanding walketh uprightly* (or, *makes his way straight.*)

It is a sign of prodigious folly for a man to take pleasure in sin, which gives mortal wounds to the soul, provokes the displeasure of the Almighty, and could not be expiated, but in the groans and blood of a Redeemer ; and yet all wicked men take pleasure in it. It is with the utmost propriety that the wise man gives the name of fool to the sinner, and allows the character of wisdom to none but the godly.

---

*Chap. 10:1, 31:17

We have in this verse a mark whereby we may know with certainty whether we are wise men or fools ; and this mark is explained at great length by Paul, and illustrated by his own example *.

Wise men are not wise in every instance of their conduct, for weakness and temptation too often betray them into sin, yet they hate sin, and account their indwelling corruption a body of death ; but sin is not only practised by the wicked, but it is loved by them. Folly is their joy, and therefore they sin even without a temptation. It is their meat and drink to sin, and they roll iniquity as if it were a sweet morsel under their tongue. They often feel stings of conscience from the word of God ; but they hate not those sins that are condemned by it, but the word that condemns them. They dislike salvation itself, because it is a deliverance from sin.

But the wise man's employment is to cleanse his way, and make it straight. He hates sin that dwells in him, and loathes himself for his impurities. He takes pleasure in holiness, and loves the law of God, because it testifies against his iniquities. He joins earnestly with the Psalmist in that prayer, " O that my ways were directed to keep thy statutes !" and instead of being satisfied with such a degree of holiness as may amount to the lowest evidence of true grace, he will not count himself completely happy, till his grace is completed in the glory of the heavenly state †.

Ver. 22. *Without counsel purposes are disappointed, but in the multitude of counsellors they are established.*

Wisdom is profitable to direct, and all our affairs must be conducted by it, and nothing done rashly and

---

*Rom. 7:14-25   †Prov. 10:23

precipitately ; for what is done too hastily, is generally repented of at leisure.

As we should endeavour to make our knowledge and wisdom useful to other men, so we should take the benefit of other men's wisdom, for we were designed by our common Creator to give and to receive, and by a commerce of wisdom to enrich one another.

The proud and selfish man, that thinks himself above advice, meets with disappointment and shame. But by a multitude of counsellors, (that is, of wise counsellors, for none else deserve the name), purposes are established, and their success is generally ensured. This is so important a truth, that Solomon takes care we should not forget it, and therefore repeats it in this place, out of a former passage of this book *.

Solomon often speaks of the destruction of the proud, and the exaltation of the humble. This is chiefly owing to God's hatred of pride and love of humility ; but the natural tendencies of virtue and vice serve Providence in this, as in other cases. The proud man takes the course that leads to disgrace and ruin, whilst he trusts so much to his own wisdom, that he consults with neither God nor man. The humble man acknowledges God in all his ways, and employs the wisdom of other men with his own, and his way is prosperous, because it is wise.

Ver. 23. *A man hath joy by the answer of his mouth ; and a word spoken in due season, how good is it !*

It is not a good objection against endeavouring to do good by our words, that we are often unsuccessful in our endeavours to serve our fellow-creatures in this way ; for although, by the perverseness of men, our kindness may be rendered unprofitable to them, yet a man

---

*Chap. 11:14

hath joy by the answer of his mouth. It will be a pleasure to us to reflect, that we have discharged our duty, and used our tongues for the ends for which they were made. It can give us no true satisfaction, that we have gained the applause or good-will of men by sinful silence, or by flattering men's humours and prejudices ; but if we have lost the favour of men by faithfulness to their best interests, the testimony of an approving conscience will abundantly counterbalance our damage. The joy that arises to a man from the answer of his tongue, will not be confined to this world ; but at the day of judgment, those that have been converted by our words from the error of their ways, and edified in righteousness, will be a crown of rejoicing to us ; and Christ himself will take a gracious notice of every word that has been spoken in his cause. Our Judge assures us, that by our words we shall be justified or condemned ; and when the works of charity are mentioned with honour, the words which proceeded from that noble principle shall not be forgotten.

To make words really good, it is necessary that they be spoken in due season ; for as the showers of rain in their proper season fertilize the ground, but at a wrong time drown the hopes of the year, so words have good or bad effects, as the time of speaking them is well or ill chosen. Abigail would not tell Nabal of his danger till he was sober ; and Job's friends wounded his spirit in a cruel manner, by speaking things excellent in themselves, and very suitable to Job, if he had been the man they believed him to be. It is one of the properties of a wise man, that his heart knoweth both time and judgment.

A single word spoken in due season, is inexpressibly good. It may revive the desponding soul, preserve from death or save a soul, for death and life are in the power of the tongue *.

Ver, 34. *The way of life is above to the wise, that he may depart from hell beneath.*

All men are travellers either to heaven above, or hell beneath. The writers of Scripture knew nothing of the middle place, which perverters of Christianity have found out since their days, by the assistance of the ancient heathens.

There is but one way of life, and Christ tells us that he is that way, and no man cometh unto the Father but by him. Those only are in the way of life, that have received him by faith, and walk in him by a holy and heavenly conversation, to which true faith in Christ always leads him that possesses it.

This way is above, and they are great deceivers of themselves, who imagine that Christ will save those from hell that will not accept of his salvation from sin, which leads to hell. Without holiness, no man shall see the Lord; and the faith which does not make a man heavenly in his affections and conversation, will never conduct a man to the regions of blessedness. The Son of God came from heaven to earth to purchase our salvation, and he is gone to heaven to plead for it, and the hearts of all that have the living hopes of heaven will follow him thither †.

Our everlasting abode must be either in heaven or hell. Salvation from hell is the half of heaven. The threatenings of hell are a fence about the way to heaven, and whilst we are travelling in it, they are of great use to make us serious and earnest in pursuing our course ; for how is it possible that we can flee

*Job 4:2,3, 1 Sam. 25:33, Acts 16:31. Compare 1 Tim. 4:16
†Col. 3:1,2

with too much speed from everlasting burnings, when our flight is directed, not, like that of the manslayer, to a place of banishment, but to the world of happiness and pleasure?

Let us try ourselves by this mark of true wisdom. Do we mind earthly or heavenly things? If earthly things be the chief object of our regard, our way is below, and our names are written in the earth, because we forsake the fountain of living waters. If our affections be set on things above, then, when Christ our life shall appear, he will receive us into the celestial mansions, that where he is we may be also.

David and Paul explain this character of the wise man, from their own example, compared with that of worldly men *.

Ver. 25. *The Lord will destroy the house of the proud, but he will establish the border of the widow.*

We have already heard how detestable pride is to the Lord, and how it provokes his vengeance. Here we are told that God destroys the dwellings and families of the proud, as well as their persons. Proud men value themselves upon their magnificent palaces, their great riches, and their prosperous families, and provoke the Lord to destroy those things which are turned by them into idols, and used as the pillars of that creature confidence which he abhors. Nebuchadnezzar prided himself in the splendour of his palace, and the magnificence of his royal city. But he was driven from it to dwell among the beasts; and some ages after his death, his family, which he had exalted by his ravages, was rooted out of the world, and great Babylon, which he had built for the honour of his majesty, became a monument of the triumphs of God's power over the haughtiness of worms. Haman boasted of his riches

---

*Ps. 17:13-15, Phil. 3:18-20

and the number of his children; but Haman and his ten children were soon hanged, and his riches given to his hated enemy.

Let us never be vain of any thing, unless we wish to have it destroyed. God abhors pride even in them whom he dearly loves, and shews his resentment of it by humbling providences, that remove man from his purpose, and hide pride from man. David was proud of the vast numbers of his subjects, but God soon shewed him that great hosts save not a king, and that three days may greatly lessen the numbers of a people. Hezekiah's heart was lifted up, but he was soon obliged to humble himself, being assured that the treasures which he had so ostentatiously shewed to the Babylonish ambassadors, should be carried with his posterity to their own land.

God is terrible to the proud, but he is gracious to the helpless and desolate. Proud men often attempt to aggrandize their houses, by removing the landmark of the widow and fatherless; but the Lord establisheth the border of the widow. Let dying husbands leave their fatherless children and widows in the hand of God *, and let widows trust in him. If they are desolate and weak, and liable to oppression, that should not be a discouragement, but a strong motive to them to commit themselves unto the Father of mercies, and the God of all comfort †.

There is often more meant than expressed in the words of God. Widows in this place are to be understood of those that are in desolate circumstances, and exposed to injuries of any kind. Their distressed situations make them proper objects of compassion, and infinite compassions are with God. He hath erected a throne of mercy, and the Redeemer sits upon it, and

---

*Jer. 47:1   †Ps. 10:14   1 Tim. 5:5

is exalted, that he may have mercy upon the poor and destitute *.

From the acts of terror and of grace here represented to us, we may take occasion to join in the song of the mother of our Lord: " He hath scattered the proud in the imagination of their hearts; he hath put down the mighty from their seats, and exalted them of low degree †."

Ver. 26. *The thoughts of the wicked are an abomination to the Lord; but the words of the pure are pleasant words.*

Solomon already told us that the way of the wicked is detestable to God; and here he tells us that his thoughts, no less than his words and actions, are abominable to him. Men see not the hearts of one another, and are too ready to imagine that they shall never be called to an account of what passes in their minds; but we must remember that the difference between God and man is infinite. Man looketh only on the outward appearance, and his rewards and punishments can reach no farther than his knowledge of the facts that deserve them. But it is the prerogative of the Father of spirits to search the hearts and to try the reins of the children of men, to render unto them according to their ways. The thoughts of the wicked are full of selfishness, impiety, pride, and impurity, and must be infinitely offensive unto the pure eyes of Jehovah; and whenever wicked men are, by the convincing operation of the Spirit, made to discern the secrets of their own hearts, they become loathsome to themselves.

Wicked men must forsake their thoughts, as well as their outward practices of wickedness; for what is the profit of making clean the outside of the cup and plat-

---

*Ps. 72:4,12-13.   †Luke 1:51-53

ter, whilst the inner part is full of impurity? God requires us to give him our hearts for his residence. A heart which should be God's habitation, if full of abominable thoughts, is like the royal chambers of Pharaoh filled with frogs.

If the thoughts of the wicked are abominable to God, their words cannot be pleasant to him, for how can those that are evil speak good things? If the words should be good when the thoughts are vile, they are like potsherds covered over with silver dross. God desireth truth in the outward parts, and abhors those that flatter him with their tongues, or seek the applause of men by making their tongues the instruments of hypocrisy.

But the thoughts of the pure are well pleasing to the Lord, and their words are pleasant in his ears. God is of pure eyes, and delights in those that are made pure by the blood and Spirit of his Son. Their hearts are cleansed from iniquity, and produce those holy thoughts and words which are acceptable in the sight of the Lord their God and Redeemer *. Their prayers and praises are a sweet odour in his nostrils. Their confessions are music to his ears †. Their common discourse, when it is seasoned with salt, and ministers grace to the hearers, is heard by him with delight. It is a solemn consideration, that God hears every thing that we say, and is pleased or displeased with it. He hearkens and hears what the wicked say, and his judgment of them is, that they speak not aright ‡. When those that fear him speak one to another, he hearkens and hears, and a book of remembrance is written before him for them that fear the Lord, and think upon his name ||. What have we to

---

*Ps. 19:14   †Jer. 31:18   ‡Jer. 8:6 ||Mal. 3:16

do on earth, but to labour that in our thoughts, and words, and ways, we may be accepted of him * ?

Ver. 27. *He that is greedy of gain troubleth his own house ; but he that hateth gifts shall live.*

The counsel of the wicked shall cast him down, for he is cast into a net by his own feet, and he walketh upon a snare. Instead of gaining what he expects by his iniquity, he exposes himself to those miseries which he most dreads, and that which he thought would be a shield to defend him, proves a killing sword. The covetous man is an instance of this truth. His heart is set upon gain, and he expects that it will render his life comfortable and happy. But he finds, by bitter experience, the truth of what he would not believe from the mouth of Christ, that a man's life consisteth not in the abundance of the things which he possesseth. He that is greedy of gain shall not live ; so the wise man insinuates in the last part of the verse. He either shortens his days by his anxieties about the world, and those sinful methods which he takes to obtain the things on which he has placed his heart, or he embitters his life by his distracting cares. He designs to secure his family against want and contempt, and to raise it to eminence and honour ; but he covets an evil covetousness to his house, and consults shame to it, whilst he sins against his own soul †. He kindles a fire in his dwelling, which shall consume the tabernacles of bribery.

If men could obtain what they seek by sin, it would be a pitiful compensation for eternal misery ; but the same Almighty God that punishes the wicked in hell, reigns by his providence upon earth ; his face is ever against the wicked, and if they prosper and flourish for a while, like the grass, it is that they shall be destroyed

---

*2 Cor. 5:9   †Hab. 2:9,10

for ever * ; and they are the wretched instruments of mischief, not only to themselves, but to those whom they most love, and whom they mean to serve by their sins.

Money is a good thing when it is possessed by the wise, but the love of money is the root of every evil, and therefore covetousness is not to be named among the saints. If we love ourselves and our children, if we wish for quietness and peace on earth, if we cannot think without horror of dwelling in everlasting fire, we must take heed and beware of covetousness.

" But he that hateth gifts shall live," and his house shall stand. It is not enough for us to refrain from dishonest gain, but we must shake our hands from holding of bribes. This is the difference between the disposition of good and bad men, with relation to sin. Bad men may for many reasons abstain from the outward commission of it ; but good men hate sin, and every thing that leads to it. He that hateth bribes is not a loser by his justice, unless a little money be more valuable than life, and the blessing of God to sweeten it. His family are great gainers, for the just man walketh in his integrity, and his children are blessed after him.

Jeremiah gives us several striking illustrations of this proverb †.

Ver. 28. *The heart of the righteous studieth to answer ; but the mouth of the wicked poureth out evil things.*

The righteous man has a good treasure in his heart, out of which he bringeth good things ; but he does not depend upon this good treasure, so as to speak any thing upon a subject that occurs most readily and easily to him. He wishes to speak nothing that may do hurt to others, or lead them into mistakes, but on every occasion, and especially in affairs of importance, to say

*Ps. 92:7,8   †Jer. 17:11, 22:13-19

what is best and most seasonable. He therefore considers what is fit to be answered to any man with whom he converses, and his words as well as his affairs are ordered with discretion. Without thought the righteous would speak like fools, as David did when he was provoked by the churlish words of Nabal, and in his fury vowed to destroy the house of Nabal, and cut off the innocent with the guilty.

In matters of great consequence that require delicate management, it is needful, in answering men, to lift up our souls to God in secret prayer for the direction of our tongues. Nehemiah prayed to the Lord in the presence of the king of Persia, before he answered his question ; and it is remarkable with what insinuating eloquence he was taught of God to address the king, in such a manner as to obtain great favour for himself and for Israel.

But a wicked man has little sense of the importance of the government of the tongue, and wants the bridle of the fear of God to manage this unruly member, and therefore he pours forth evil things. But for all his vain and wicked words he must one day account.

Ver. 29. *The Lord is far from the wicked; but he heareth the prayer of the righteous.*

The Lord is not far from any man, for in him we all live, and move, and have our being. But as wicked men are far from God, through the alienation of their hearts, and the wickedness of their works, so the Lord is far from them, he will have no fellowship with them. The righteous cry, and the Lord hears them ; but he does not hear the cry of the wicked, and beholds them afar off. Wicked men think they may safely go on in sin, and if trouble come upon them they will cry to the Lord, and all shall be well. Many have been ruined by such presumptuous expectations, and sad experience has at last convinced them that the

Almighty was under no obligation to attend to their voice in adversity, when they would not hear his voice in the day of his forbearance.

The prayers of the righteous are graciously heard. God does not always give a present answer to them, but they need not wonder at that, for he did not give a present answer to his own Son crying to him in the days of his flesh. He will hear at the time, and in the manner, that appears best to himself. And wise heathens could see, that it is proper to leave it to the wisdom of God to determine what is best for us. If we do not obtain a speedy answer to our mind, we must wait on God, for he is a God of judgment; blessed are all they that wait for him. Our Advocate who presents our petitions is always heard, and the worthy name in which we pray is ever prevalent with God.

The blind man whom Christ healed *, made a noble use of the truth contained in the beginning of this verse. He drew from it an irrefragable proof of the divine mission of Christ. But there are too many that draw a very bad conclusion from it. If our prayers cannot be heard, say they, we may give over praying. The prophet Isaiah draws a very apposite instruction from this truth, teaching sinners to leave their sins, and not their prayers †. " When ye make many prayers," says God, " I will not hear; your hands are full of blood." What then must they do? are they for ever excluded from the favour of God? No; the Lord is far from the wicked, and yet brings near his salvation to them. He shows them a fountain of blood in which they must be washed and purged from their blood and filth, and then their prayers will come with acceptance before him ‡.

---

*John 9   †Isa. 55:6,7, 1:15-18   ‡Acts 8:22

Ver. 30. *The light of the eyes rejoiceth the heart; and a good report maketh the bones fat.*

Truly the light is sweet, and we ought to give thanks every day to God, who makes the sun to shine, and formed that amazing piece of mechanism, the eye of man, and contrived it so as to fetch in a thousand pleasures, not only from the objects that surround us, but from those glorious luminaries that are millions of leagues distant from the place of our abode. If Bartimeus was transported with gratitude to Christ when he restored to him his sight, why should we be less grateful to our Maker, who gave us this noble organ of sense, and has constantly preserved it, and made it the instrument of so many pleasures and advantages? It is very ungrateful to make our eyes the instrument of rebelling against our Maker, which is every day done by the adulterer and drunkard. On the contrary, when our eyes give joy to our hearts, it is highly proper to improve this pleasure into adoration and praise, by magnifying the work of God which we behold.

"And a good report maketh the bones fat," for the ear as well as the eye ministers delight and advantage to us. Pleasant views are cheering to the spirit, but glad tidings are no less reviving to the heart, and the pleasures received from them is marrow to the bones, and health to the whole man.

No reports have this effect so much as the glad tidings of salvation to lost sinners. We must thank God that we receive so many curious discoveries by means of the sense of hearing, but above all, that the gospel of his grace has reached our ears. Gratitude teaches us to turn away our ears from the instruction that causeth to err from the words of knowledge, and from all corrupt and uncharitable conversation, and to attend with earnestness unto the voice of the Lord, addressing us from day to day. Faith cometh by hearing, and hearing by the word of God.

Have any of us lost the sight of our eyes ? That is a sore affliction, yet let us be thankful if the use of our ears remains to us, by which we enjoy the agreeable converse of our friends, and the opportunities of serving God, and waiting on him in his sanctuary.

Ver. 31. *The ear that heareth the reproof of life, abideth among the wise.*

There are great differences among reprovers. Some reproofs are not the reproofs of life, and these deserve little regard from us. There are not wanting persons that will rebuke others for doing their duty, and curse them because they will not see with the eyes of their unjust reprovers. But in opposition to these gainsayers, and perverters of the right ways of the Lord, we must hold on our way, and never be ashamed of the testimony of the Lord.

But the reproofs of life are valuable. Our Lord teaches us to account them pearls, and Solomon in this expression gives them an equal commendation, and frequently lays it down as a mark of wisdom, to pay a proper regard to just and needful reproofs.

But how shall we know whether we have this character of wisdom ? It is not by saying to that friend who reproves us, that we are obliged to him. Good manners will make almost any man to say that. But here is the trial of our submission to rebukes, " The ear that hears them abides among the wise."

If we have a just sense of the value of reproofs, we will count that faithful friend that reproves rather than flatters, a treasure, and frequent his company on that account. We will not passionately leave that Christian society with which we are connected, because the word of God is faithfully applied in it to the correction of vice, and discipline impartially administered, although we ourselves should become the objects of it. The servant that loves a faithful reprover, and truly regards his own soul, will chuse to live in a house where God is feared, and family religion enforced ; and every man possessed of this humble disposition, will chuse that company in which he is most likely to be told of his faults.

Those that reprove others, ought to dispense their salutary admonitions with meekness and prudence, that they may not render this ordinance of God disgusting and offensive by their manner of dispensing it, and render themselves accountable for the mischief done by this means to precious souls.

Ver. 32. *He that refuseth instruction despiseth his own soul; but he that heareth reproof gaineth understanding.*

We are born like the wild ass's colt, and need not only instruction, but reproof, to make us wise ; but some are such enemies to themselves, that they will not suffer themselves to be taught wisdom. The scorner hates his reprover, but he is the greatest enemy to himself, whilst he spurns at the physician for giving him those prescriptions that are absolutely necessary for his health, though disagreeable to his vitiated palate. He is more brutish than the horse or mule, for these animals, although they want the benefit of reason, and are stubborn at first, will rather be tamed than destroyed.

But the man is happy who suffers the word of exhortation and reproof, for though he is at present chargeable with many faults and follies, yet he is in the way of reformation, and takes the sure method of getting understanding. He is meek and teachable, and God will bless to his soul that word which he receives with meekness.

Solomon gives us frequent advices on this point, but

they are all needful, for no duty is harder to our proud spirits, than receiving reproofs with calmness, and applying them to the correction of our lives.

Ver. 33. *The fear of the Lord is the instruction of wisdom ; and before honour is humility* *.

The fear of the Lord is the beginning of wisdom, and it instructs men in every other branch of wisdom; for a right impression of the excellencies of God upon our spirits, will dispose us with due reverence to search the scriptures, and to acquiesce in the wise instructions which they contain ; it will powerfully influence us to make a thankful use of Christ, as he is made of God wisdom to us, and to follow the conduct of the Holy Spirit. The fear of the Lord will be a preservative to us from sin and folly, and an incentive to all holy conversation and godliness ; and a good understanding have all they that do the commandments of God.

" And before honour is humility." For whilst we humbly renounce our own righteousness, and place all our dependence on the grace of God, we are exalted in imputed righteousness ; and when we are pure in spirit, we are prepared for the kingdom of heaven. He to whom all judgment is committed, hath declared, and will make it good, " He that humbleth himself shall be exalted."

The honours of this world are so short-lived, that they are scarcely worth the naming. Sometimes the proud push themselves into high stations, and yet they cannot attain the summit of their ambitious aims, without the permission of that Providence from which promotion comes ; and it is certain, that God hates the proud, and will not suffer them to rise into eminence for their real advantage, but rather to signalize his

---

*See Proverbs 9:10, 11:2

vengeance, by spurning them, in due time, into disgrace and misery.

Alexander and Julius Cæsar blazed for a time ; but how much more illustrious and durable were the honours of David, who thought himself quite unworthy to be the king's son-in-law, and compared himself to a partridge and a flea, but was exalted by God to the throne of his kingdom over Israel, and to the greater honour of being a prophet in the church, and the sweet singer of Israel !

Proverbs 16

Ver. 1. *The preparations of the heart in man, and the answer of the tongue, is from the Lord.*

A MAN cannot put his heart into a proper order, nor manage his thoughts so as to be ready for any good word or work, by his own abilities. We cannot expel sin from our hearts, nor furnish them with holy dispositions ; and when our hearts are purified by the grace of God, we cannot, without new supplies of grace, prepare them for praying, or speaking to the edification of our fellow Christians. One of the best of men tells us, that he was not sufficient of himself to think any thing as he ought. It is our duty to prepare our hearts, and fix our thoughts for every religious service to which we are called ; and it is our sin when we are

careless about it : but we must not attempt this work
in our own strength. In every thing we must direct
our eyes to God, the fountain of all goodness, praying
to him, as David did for his people, that he may prepare our hearts unto himself *. To encourage us to
apply to God for his needful assistance, we are here
told, that the preparation of the heart belongs to him ;
and in other passages of scripture we are encouraged
by his promises, to expect this favour at his hands †.

We must depend on God for every thing. The answer of the tongue is from the Lord, as well as the
preparation of the heart. He fashions the hearts of
men, and makes their tongues to speak what he pleases.
He pressed Balaam's tongue, against his heart, into the
service of Israel, and would not suffer Laban to speak
to Jacob either good or bad, when he came to him
with a full resolution to do him some mischief. Caiaphas was made to speak a noble truth, when he designed only to suggest a politic counsel ; and Pilate had
not power to pronounce the condemning sentence
against our Lord, till it was given him from above.

However well our thoughts are ranged in our minds,
yet we cannot utter them to the advantage of men,
and the glory of God, unless the Lord enlarge our
hearts and loose our tongues ; and therefore David
prays that his lips, which were closed, might be opened, and Paul begs the prayers of the Ephesians, that
utterance might be given.

We must beg from God the gifts of the Spirit for
ministers, and the gift of prayer and Christian confer-
ence for ourselves, under a firm persuasion that we are
altogether unable of ourselves to think or speak, or perform any good thing, and that every good and perfect
gift is from above, even from the Father of lights, who

*1 Chron. 29:18   †Ps. 10:17, Phil. 2:13

bestows his gifts freely, but requires the praise of them to be rendered back to himself.

The truth contained in this text must not slacken, but encourage our Christian diligence *.

Ver. 2. *All the ways of a man are clean in his own eyes ; but the Lord weigheth the spirits.*

How different is the judgment which men form of themselves, from that which God makes of them ! He looks down from heaven to see how men behave, and behold, he sees all men walking in ways that are not good. They are filthy and abominable, and yet so blind, that they generally think their way clean and pure. They will acknowledge that they are not free from sin, but they have no impressions of the evil of sin. Their great transgressions they account venial trespasses. Their lesser iniquities, which they daily commit, are accounted mere motes, not worth the minding ; and every slight appearance of goodness, their vain imagination exalts into a shining virtue.

The reason of men's good opinion of their ways is, that they are unacquainted with their own spirits, and take no pains to be acquainted with the secret principles and aims that animate and direct the course of their life. No kind of knowledge is more necessary, nor seldomer sought after and obtained, than the knowledge of a man's self.

But it will profit us nothing to be pure in our own eyes, if we are abominable in the eyes of Him with whom we have to do, for not he that commendeth himself is approved, but whom the Lord commendeth. The better that a bad man thinks of himself, he is the more abhorred of the Lord, who is the irreconcileable enemy of pride and self-conceit, and calls those men

---

*Ezek 36:27, Phil. 2:12,13

who boast of their goodness, a smoke in his nose, a fire that burneth all the day.

The Lord is our Judge, and our sentence must come from him. He weigheth our spirits in a just and unerring balance ; and if they are destitute of faith in Christ, and love to God and holiness, he will condemn our way. The most splendid actions, and shining appearances of virtue, without purity of heart, will make us, in his sight, only like whitened sepulchres, beautiful without, but inwardly full of rottenness and dead men's bones.

Let us examine our own hearts and ways, under a deep impression of this truth, that God is greater than our hearts, and knoweth all things. The word of God is the rule by which we must search and try ourselves, for God will judge us by it at last ; and we learn from it, that none shall be able to stand in judgment with God, who have not been made to discern the impurity of their heart and conversation, and compelled to build their confidence upon him that saves the lost.

It is not impossible for men to attain a comfortable knowledge of their own sanctification. Although a ragged beggar, when he dreams of crowns and sceptres, thinks himself as sure of his fancied dignity, as if it were a reality ; yet a king will not doubt of his royalty, nor imagine that it may be only a dream. But those who have obtained this precious blessing, of knowing assuredly that they are purified in heart and life, have, at the same time, an humbling sense of remaining impurities. Their dependence is not upon themselves, but upon Christ ; and they would dread the thoughts of being brought into judgment with God on the ground of their own righteousness, knowing that no flesh can be justified before him *.

---

*Ps. 143

Ver. *3. Commit thy works unto the Lord, and thy thoughts shall be established.*

The just God has appointed much toil to the sons of Adam, to be exercised therewith; and it often becomes a burden that makes us to groan and cry out for ease. And here God in his mercy directs us to a method of finding ease and comfort under the heaviest burdens. Roll (Heb.) thy works upon the Lord. But how shall we cast them upon him? Shall we ascend into the heavens to find him for this purpose? No; David explains this point of instruction at great length in the thirty-seventh Psalm, and tells us that we are to commit our work unto the Lord, by trusting and resting in him, and waiting patiently for the event. Paul directs us * to do it by prayer and supplication, with thanksgiving. And as Hannah, when she had prayed about her sorrows, went away, and was no more sorrowful; so when our burden is cast upon the Lord by fervent supplications, we ought to banish every anxious thought, believing that God is mighty and faithful, and will give a good account of that which is entrusted to him by his own direction. We must not, however, neglect the use of proper and warrantable means for accomplishing our designs, for it is presumption, and not faith, to believe God's promise, and disregard his command. Joshua was to depend upon God alone for victory over the Canaanites, and yet he was required to be strong and courageous, to fight with them, and observe all God's commandments; and he seems to have erred when he sent only 3000 men against Ai, to save toil to the people.

Our worldly affairs are to be committed to God, as well as our spiritual concerns †. In every thing we must depend upon God's help, ask his direc-

---

*Phil. 4:6   †Prov. 3:6

tion, and refer ourselves to his will.   In the meantime,
we must undertake nothing inconsistent with our
duty to God and men, for it would be gross impiety to interest the most holy God in things opposite to his own will.   Had David been employed in
acknowledging God when he prepared his men for
marching with the Philistines against Israel, the Amale-
kites would never have found an opportunity to destroy
Ziklag.   And yet David's encouraging himself in the
Lord his God *, after he had felt the bad consequences
of his rashness, teaches us this comfortable lesson,—
that although we have been turned by our own rashness out of God's way, we are not excluded from the
benefit of this gracious direction.   David still committed his work to the Lord, and the mischiefs occasioned
by his unadvised conduct were soon retrieved.

What a pleasure is it for a weary man to be allowed
to cast his burden upon one that is well able to bear
it !   But it is our mercy, that we are allowed to cast
our works and burdens upon the Almighty †.   And
we are assured that he will then establish our thoughts,
and bring what concerns us to a comfortable end.
Perhaps the event will not suit our present views ; but
in that case it will appear that our views were not a-
greeable to the gracious intentions of God, and in that
case it will be our happiness to have them disappointed.   The will of the Lord be done, and let our own
will be done as far as it consists with his.   It was a
prayer of a famous divine,   ' Let my will be done, O
Lord,—my will, because it is thine.'

Ver. 4. *The Lord hath made all things for himself ;
yea, even the wicked for the day of evil.*

Every rational agent has some end of his work in
view.   And God, in all his works of creation and pro-

---

*1 Sam. 30:6   †Ps. 55:19

vidence, has the noblest of possible ends in view,—the glory of his name, and the manifestation of his divine excellencies. He is infinitely blessed, and needs no glory from us ; but he is infinitely wise and holy, and he will be glorified by us, or upon us.

Every creature should be used by us as a mean of raising our thoughts to its Creator, for what being is there that wants a tongue, to declare his glory to the rational mind ? The dumb fishes will declare unto us that the hand of the Lord hath made them *.

But does not God lose his glory in some of his creatures ? are not wicked men and devils dishonouring him every day to his face ? Yet God shall never be disappointed of his great end. He will distrain a revenue of praise from those that will not give him the glory due unto his name, and will force the wrath and wickedness of his enemies to praise him. Pharaoh was an insolent rebel against the Sovereign of the world, and yet in very deed God raised him up, to shew in him his power, and that his name might be declared throughout all the earth.

Tremble, ye stubborn sinners! God must be glorified in you, and if you will not be persuaded to give him glory before he cause darkness, by accepting of his gracious salvation, and turning from your sins, there remains nothing for you but a fearful looking for of judgment, and of fiery indignation. The Lord of hosts will be exalted in judgment, and God that is holy will be sanctified in righteousness. The day of evil is the day of the display of the glorious holiness of God. You cannot expect to escape, unless God could be persuaded to renounce his glory for you ; and you may with much more reason hope, that the earth should be forsaken for you, and the rock removed out of its place. Aaron was a highly-favoured saint, and yet when his two

---

*Job 12:9

sons affronted God by offering strange fire, they were immediately consumed ; and the reason was, because God would be glorified in all that came nigh unto him. The flames of hell will shine for ever to the glory of God, and afford a subject for the songs of heaven *.

How admirable are the glories of the Lord ! Every creature in every world, and every thing that falls out in any part of his dominions, concurs to shew forth his praise. Of him, and through him, and to him are all things ; and to him be glory for ever and ever. Amen.

The proud amongst those that do wickedly, shall be dreadful monuments of the vengeance of the Almighty, and not one of them shall escape.

Ver. 5. *Every one that is proud in heart is an abomination to the Lord : though hand join in hand, he shall not be unpunished.*

We have heard already, that a proud look is greatly offensive to God * ; but although there be no appearances of pride in the countenance or behaviour to provoke the displeasure of the Almighty, yet he is the searcher of the heart, and if he finds it governed by pride, he will execute the vengeance written in his word upon the haughty sinner. Man looks on the outward appearance, and frequently makes false judgments. The demure Pharisees were counted humble and self-denied men, when they were hunting after the praise of the people ; but their inward pride was well known to our Lord, who tells them, that what was highly valued by men was abhorred by God.

The proud abound in the world. This abominable sin is natural to the posterity of him that fell by attempting to be like God. The forms of it are very various, and the grounds of it cannot be reckoned up,

---

*2 Thess. 1:9, Rev. 19   †Chap. 6:17

for it is an insatiable monster that will find nourishment to itself in any thing.   Some are proud of their
dignity, and power, and high birth ; others boast themselves because of their great riches.   Some are proud,
like Goliath, of their stature and the vigour of their
limbs ; others boast of their beauty, and that pleasing
form which shall soon be turned into corruption.   Some
are proud of their righteousness, and others (O the infatuation of the human race !) glory in their shame.
But whatever shape pride may assume, and whatever
is its ground, it is seen by the all-seeing eye of God,
and makes the man in whom it dwells and reigns, an
object of his abhorrence and avenging arm.

None can imagine the terrors of that punishment
which is inflicted by the hand of the Lord, on those
whom his heart abhors.   But is there no possibility of
avoiding it ?   None, unless the haughty spirit be
humbled into a submission to the righteousness of
faith.   Though hand join in hand, those that walk on
in pride shall be abased, and spurned into hell.   Unknown myriads of angels fell by pride into the bottomless pit, and are groaning, and shall for ever groan,
under the power of God's wrath.   Although all the
proud on earth should enter into a confederacy with
all the legions of devils and damned spirits in hell,
and exert their utmost combined force to oppose the
execution of Almighty vengeance, they will only be
like mountains of tow and rotten wood, reared up to
oppose the progress of a raging flame *.

Ver. 6. *By mercy and truth iniquity is purged ; and
by the fear of the Lord men depart from evil.*

It is plain from scripture, that Christ hath by himself purged our sins, and by one offering for ever per-

---

*Mal. 4:1, James 4:6-10

fected all them that are sanctified. To pretend to
substitute any thing of our own in place of his perfect atonement, or to join our own works to his blood
to procure our pardon, would be as foolish as an attempt to extinguish the sun, and supply its place with
a candle ; or to improve the brightness of that luminary, by lighting a torch at mid-day. We must not
therefore imagine, that Solomon meant in this place to
recommend mercy and truth to us, as means of procuring the favour of God and the pardon of our sins,
for the scripture cannot contradict itself.

Some, by mercy and truth, understand the mercy
and truth of God, two attributes which shine with illustrious brightness in our salvation, and are frequently
mentioned together by the sacred writers, when they
celebrate the glories of it *. Christ, our atonement,
was the mercy promised unto the fathers, and when
God bestows pardon through Christ, he discovers the
riches of his mercy according to his word ; for he is
faithful and merciful when he fulfils that promise of
the covenant, " I will be merciful to their unrighteousnesses, and their sins and their iniquities will I remember no more."

None shall receive the benefit of pardoning mercy,
but in consistency with the truth of God in his word ;
and therefore hopes of safety, not grounded on the
scripture, shall end in shame and disappointment †.

The Hebrew word which we render *purged*, is
sometimes used to signify the cause or mean of deliverance from temporal mischiefs, or death. In this
sense I think it may be said, that by mercy and truth
in men, iniquity is removed; according to that exhortation of Daniel to the king of Babylon, " Break off

---

*Ps. 89:1,2, 117:2 †Isa. 28:17

thine iniquities by shewing mercy to the poor, if so be it may be a lengthening of thy tranquillity *."

It is a mighty recommendation of mercy and fidelity towards men, that we are so infinitely indebted to the mercy and faithfulness of God, to whom we are to shew our gratitude, by imitating those amiable attributes that appear with such lovely glories in our pardon and salvation ; and whilst we thus shew forth the virtues of our God and our Saviour, in doing good to men, we are consulting and pursuing our own best interest and comfort.

But mercy and truth to men, must have the fear of the Lord joined to them, to make them Christian graces. Morality is not solid without piety, and piety is not genuine without morality. The fear of the Lord is a soul-purifying grace, and we must cleanse ourselves from all filthiness of the flesh and spirit, perfecting holiness in the fear of God. When Joseph's brethren were terrified that he would do them some injustice, he assures them that they might banish every anxious thought, for, says he, " I fear God." The fear of God will not only dispose men to abstain from manifest acts of injustice, but it will keep them from every instance of harsh and ungenerous conduct. Nehemiah would not oppress the people by exacting the ordinary perquisites of his office, because he was under the constraining influence of this gracious principle †. You may safely trust a man that has the fear of God in him, for herein he will exercise himself to have a conscience void of offence, both towards God and towards man ‡.

---

*Prov. 3:3,4. See chap. 6:35, 13:8, 16:14, 21:18, where the word rendered *ransom,* or *pacify,* corresponds to the word in our text.
†Neh. 5:15   ‡Ps. 36;1, Gen. 20:11

Ver. 7. *When a man's ways please the Lord, he maketh even his enemies to be at peace with him.*

It is very natural for men to endeavour to please those whom they love, and on whom their interests depend ; and often they despise and provoke God, by preferring the favour of men to the approbation of their Judge*.

Every true Christian is disposed, by the grace of God, to endeavour to walk so as to please God ; and if there were no other happiness but what this world affords, it would still be our wisdom to prefer the pleasing of God to the favour of men, because the hearts of all men are in his hand, and he disposes our neighbours to love or hate us, according to his will.

When we have lost the favour of our friends or superiors, we are disposed to reflect on them for their unkindness or ingratitude ; but we should rather consider seriously, whether we have not provoked our great Benefactor to deprive us of the good-will of men, by our ingratitude to himself. Wolsey made this melancholy reflection, when he was turned out of his master's favour : " Had I served God as faithfully as I served my prince, he would not have forsaken me thus at last." But if he had served God more faithfully, it is probable that his prince had not forsaken him at last ; or if this calamity had in that case befallen him, it need not have produced such a bitter reflection.

When we have lost the favour of our friends, or stand in fear of enemies, it is our wisdom to use proper means for softening their resentments ; but that is not the first nor the chief thing we have to do ; our first work should be, to make our peace with God, if we have offended him, for he fashioneth the hearts of men

---

*Gal. 1:10

according to his pleasure; and whether they act as friends or enemies, they are ministers of his providence *. Jacob did well in giving so large presents to Esau, and addressing him in such submissive language ; but neither his complaisance nor his gifts turned his brother's alienated heart to him. These were, indeed, means which God blessed for that purpose ; but the principal mean which Jacob used for this purpose, was weeping and supplication, and by these he had power with God, and, by consequence, with men, and obtained the glorious name of Israel.

God has often given favour to his faithful people in the eyes of strangers and enemies, which appears in the instances of Joseph in Egypt, David at Gath, and Daniel in Babylon. These and the like examples of God's sovereignty over the hearts of men, and goodness to his people, may satisfy us that God will sooner or later reconcile the hearts of enemies to his servants, when he sees it for their real benefit. Job was long an object of indifference to some of his friends, and aversion to others of them, yet at last the hearts of all his acquaintances were disposed to love and serve him.

If one endeavours to prove what is the good, and acceptable, and perfect will of God, and yet misses the favour of men, he may rest satisfied in this, that he is at peace with God, and that his providence will make the wrath of men to promote his noblest interests. The martyrs, when they lost their lives, were overcomers, and obtained brighter crowns than the mightiest of their adversaries ever wore †.

Ver. 8. *Better is a little with righteousness, than great revenues without right.*

The fruits of unrighteousness may be pleasant in the mouth, but they are bitter in the belly ; and a man

---

*Prov. 21:1, Ps. 105:25   †Rev. 12:8

that consults his true interest, will rather live on bread and water, or starve, with a good conscience, than enjoy the revenue of kings, without the approbation of God and his own heart.

There are too many in the world who would rather be rich by unfair means, than enjoy the pleasures of a good conscience with poverty; and therefore the Spirit of God cries to us again and again, that a little with honesty and the fear of the Lord, is better than affluence without it *.

Ver. 9. *A man's heart deviseth his way; but the Lord directeth his steps.*

The first verse of this chapter is in many translations made to express the same truth. " The preparations of the heart belong to man, but the answer of the tongue to the Lord †.

The Lord has a sovereign influence over the hearts and thoughts of men, and they can devise nothing without the concurrence of his providence, for in him we live, and move, and have our being. When men are even taking unhallowed means to determine their conduct, the holy providence of God, by undiscerned influence, overrules their minds, and decides in their councils. When the king of Babylon used divination to direct him whether he should direct his march to Rabbah or Jerusalem, it was the Lord that determined him to come against his own people, to punish them for their iniquities. Yet Solomon affirms with truth, that a man's heart deviseth his way, because man exercises full freedom of will in forming his projects.

---

*Chap. 15:16   †To account for the variety of translation in this and many other places, it is necessary for the English reader to remember, that the meaning of the Hebrew particles is very indeterminate, and the verb often omitted.

The decree and providence of God do not interfere with the free-will of rational creatures, far less can
man's free-will preclude the absolute dominion of the
Most High, over the hearts, as well as the fortunes
of men *.

The sovereign dominion of God shines clearly
in the disposal of men's ways. They either execute their counsels or not, as his wisdom has determined. They sometimes accomplish their own
counsels, but whether they do or not, they never fail
to accomplish the purpose of God. Those that know
not God, those that will not acknowledge his decrees and providence, and those that set themselves in
the most avowed opposition to God, are all of them
employed as instruments in the execution of his decrees. The devil himself was deeply concerned in the
accomplishment of the glorious purpose of God about
our salvation.

God not only determines the event of a man's devices, but every step in his progress. He not only directs every step of his people †, but every step in the
walk of every man, and even of his greatest enemies,
is ordered by him ‡. And accordingly, we find
Isaiah and Micah, when they speak of the Assyrian
invasion of Judea, naming the particulars of their
march, as if they had been writing an history, rather
than a prophecy ; for they were inspired by Him who
worketh all things after the counsel of his own will,
and makes use of all creatures as the ministers of his
providence ||.

What comfort to God's people may be derived from
this point ! Our heavenly Father has all hearts, and
tongues, and hands under his management. A dog

---

*Ps. 33:15   †Prov. 3:5   ‡Jer. 10:25
||Isa. 10, Mic. 1.

cannot move its tongue against any one of us, unless he give it commission *.

Whatever befals us by the spite of men, should lead our thoughts to God ; and when we consider it as a piece of his providence, we shall see that we have no reason to complain, but much reason to adore †.

Let us never lay down any plan of conduct, without acknowledging God. If we will not take notice of his providence in proposing our measures, we shall find in the prosecution of them, that there is a providence which will have its course, in spite of all the wisdom and strength of men.

Ver. 10. *A divine sentence is in the lips of the king ; his mouth transgresseth not in judgment.*

It is too evident that this sentence contains not the character of all kings, but only of those who deserve this noble title by their wisdom and goodness. It would not be a perversion of the original text, in this and other passages which speak of the excellent qualities of kings, to translate them as advices, rather than descriptions of their behaviour,——*Let a divine sentence be in the lips of the king, and let not his mouth transgress in judgment.*

Great sagacity and penetration is necessary, for those that govern whole nations. The higher men are exalted, they need the more wisdom, because ignorance and folly are attended, in men of station and power, with very destructive consequences. Kings are not born wiser than other men, but they are under stronger obligations than their subjects, to use with unceasing diligence the means of attaining wisdom, and to pray for it to Him who is the Fountain of wisdom and royalty. When God calls men to any station for

---

*Isa. 54:17   †Lam. 3:37-39

which great degrees of wisdom are requisite, let
them ask it of God, who giveth liberally and upbraideth not *.

Justice is equally necessary in kings, for without
this, great talents only render them terrible scourges
to their subjects and neighbouring nations †.

This text directs our sentiments about kings. We
are not required to shut our eyes, and to believe manifest lies of the greatest men ; but it is sinful and
dangerous to entertain groundless prejudices against
kings, and to weaken their government by speaking
to their disadvantage ‡.

How worthy is our Lord Jesus Christ to wear upon
his head many crowns! He is the wisdom of God,
and all his administrations are judgment and righteousness ‖.

Ver. 11, *A just weight and balance are the Lord's ;
all the weights of the bag are his work.*

It was a custom among the nations who knew not
God, to ascribe divinity to the inventors of useful arts;
but the Scripture teaches us to ascribe all good inventions to the one living and true God. It was he who
taught the merchant, as well as the husbandman,
discretion ; and the appointment of weights and measures, as instruments of justice in trade, is to be ascribed to him.

A man that puts the royal stamp upon base metal,
is accounted a traitor to his prince ; and it is a daring
wickedness for men to use those weights and balances,
which are God's appointments for the benefit of society, as means of injustice to their fellow-men.

---

*2 Chron. 7:12, 1 Kings 3   †1 Kings 10:9
‡Job 34:18, Eccl. 10:20   ‖Ps. 97:2

But a just weight and a just measure are approved by him, for he loveth justice and establisheth equity.

Ver. 12. *It is an abomination to kings to commit wickedness, for the throne is established by righteousness.*

Should not wickedness be abhorred by the poor on the dunghill, as well as the king on the throne? No doubt. But sin is greatly aggravated by the place that a man holds in society, and what is pernicious to one individual in a private man, is mischievous to a kingdom in a sovereign. Jeroboam not only sinned, but made Israel to sin, and his iniquity spread itself from Dan to Beersheba, and continued to diffuse its poison many hundreds of years after he was laid in his grave.

Kings must not only abstain from wickedness, but abhor it and punish it ; and it is their interest to do so, for great hosts save not a king, nor is his throne secured by the largeness of his dominions, and the valour of his soldiers, but by righteousness, which brings down the blessing of God, and attaches to him the hearts of his subjects.

How greatly does God recommend righteousness to our love and practice ! He makes it the instrument of safety and happiness to families and nations, as well as private persons. The histories of nations shew us, that the number of years has been hidden to the oppressor, that long and happy reigns have seldom been enjoyed but by good princes, and that national convulsions and revolutions have been the ordinary consequences of public injustice.

Thy throne, O God, is for ever and ever. Why? The sceptre of thy kingdom is a right sceptre; thou lovest righteousness, and hatest iniquity *.

---

*Isa. 9:6,7, Jer. 23:5,6

Ver. 13. *Righteous lips are the delight of kings, and they love him that speaketh right.*

There have been too many kings that loved flattery much better than the lips of truth; but they have always found the smart of it. Jeroboam had almost lost an arm, and Ahab lost his life, because they could not bear plain dealing.

David was a wise prince, who would not suffer liars to abide in his sight, and loved Nathan for his sharp reproofs.

It is the duty of those who have the ear of kings, to give faithful and just counsels, and to tell them necessary though displeasing truths. By this they will at last gain favour, when flatterers are become the objects of their just abhorrence. Micaiah was honoured as an honest prophet, when Zedekiah the son of Chenaanah was obliged to flee into an inner chamber to hide himself; and even the proud kings of Babylon bestowed the highest honours upon Daniel the captive, for his sagacity and honesty in foretelling the most dreadful calamities.

If God requires his vicegerents upon earth to abhor liars and flatterers, how detestable must they be to himself! None of them are ranked by him among his own people, of whom he says, " Surely they are children that will not lie *."

Ver. 14, 15. *The wrath of a king is as messengers of death, but a wise man will pacify it. In the light of the king's countenance is life, and his favour is as a cloud of the latter rain.*

It is the duty of all men to govern their passions, but especially of kings, because their anger may prove deadly. On the other side, their favour misplaced is of such consequence, and attended with so much ho-

*Isa. 58:8, Ps. 5:5

nour and advantage, that it may give encouragement to wickedness. The good emperor Theodosius the Great, made the latter part of his life unhappy to himself, by the effects of his rash anger, in causing many of the Thessalonians to be murdered ; and many princes have been ruined by means of unworthy favourites.

A wise man will not rashly incur the hatred of his prince, or if he has provoked his anger, will endeavour by proper submissions to appease it. And it is a very justifiable piece of prudence in those who are admitted to the presence of monarchs, to make themselves agreeable, by every mean that consists with a good conscience *. We have reason, however, to be thankful, that we are not plagued with arbitrary monarchs, as many nations were in ancient times, and still are in our own age. Let us do that which is good, and we need not much fear the frowns of princes.

If the wrath of kings, which reaches only the body, and is circumscribed within the limits of the present life, be dreadful as messengers of death, who can stand before the wrath of Him that can kill both soul and body, and torment them in an everlasting lake of fire ! How infatuated are they that provoke his displeasure by wilful rebellion, and will not accept the benefit of that reconciliation which his grace has provided ! Is it all one to us whether we are crushed for ever under the avenging arm of God, or blessed with the smiles of the King of heaven, infinitely more refreshing than the dew upon the grass, or the clouds of the latter rain, which mature the precious fruits of the earth ? We are children of wrath ; but Christ is our peace, and through him we are called to the enjoyment

---

*Eccles. 8:2-5

of that favour which is the fountain of felicity; and shall the favour of God be less esteemed by us than the smiles of a great man by his fellow-worms !

Ver. 16. *How much better is it to get wisdom than gold ! and to get understanding rather to be chosen than silver.*

If you ask a rich man that wants wisdom, whether gold or wisdom is best? he will answer, gold. But he is a fool, and his word deserves no regard. If you ask the same question at a poor wise man, he will give the preference to wisdom; but you will say he is not a competent judge, because he wants experience and impartiality. Here we have a clear and full answer to the question, by a man celebrated equally for his wisdom and riches; and he tells us that it is impossible to declare or imagine, how much wisdom is better than silver or gold. Most men prefer gold to wisdom, and thereby discover their ignorance and folly; for as much as heaven is higher than the earth, and eternity exceeds a moment in duration, so far does wisdom exceed riches in value. It is uncertain whether riches will do us any service, but it is certain they can do little. It is uncertain how long they will continue with us, but it is well known, that they will in a few years at most be useless to us; whereas the least degree of saving wisdom is of immense value, and has the promise of the life that now is, and of that which is to come. Receive wisdom, therefore, rather than silver, and the instructions of wisdom rather than choice gold *.

Ver. 17. *The high way of the upright is to depart from evil; he that keepeth his way preserveth his soul.*

To live in any known sin is utterly inconsistent with wisdom and uprightness. It is the property of a sincerely religious man to depart from sin of every kind,

---

*Chap. 3:14,15

and in every degree. He will not allow himself in any sin, however profitable or pleasant, or however dangerous the opposite course of holiness may be. He will not indulge sin in his words, or in his most secret thoughts, more than in his actions ; but keeps at a distance from every appearance of evil. He knows that there are many temptations surrounding his path, and that he has a corrupt nature within him, which is a constant and indwelling temptation ; and therefore he walks circumspectly, not as a fool, but as a wise man, and daily prays that he may be led and kept in the way of uprightness by the good Spirit of the Lord.

Happy is the man that keepeth his way ; he walks in a safe path wherein he shall not stumble, for it is the highway of the King of heaven. He preserveth his soul, for he is preserved from the paths of the destroyer. He walks in Christ, and is led by the Spirit of Christ, and no lion nor ravenous beast shall be let loose to destroy him ; but he shall come at length to the Zion of blessedness with songs and everlasting joy upon his head.

By this mark we ought to try our uprightness, and by this rule to guide our steps *

Ver. 18. *Pride goeth before destruction, and an haughty spirit before a fall.*

Pride is a common and dangerous iniquity, and our kind instructor multiplies his cautions against it. The danger of pride is plain from every history of the great transactions that have come to pass in heaven and in earth. The prophets describe the destructive consequences of this sin with all the strength of their divine eloquence, and all the sublimity of the prophetic style †. The history of the evangelists shews us what amazing

---

*Ps. 18:23, Isa. 35:8-11, 49:10,11   †Isa. 14, Ezek. 29:31

humiliation was necessary to expiate the guilt contracted by the pride of man. And the tendency of the preaching and writings of the apostles, was to cast down every high imagination of men, that no flesh might glory, but in the Lord *.

Might not this loathsome disease become a cure for itself? Can any thing afford us greater cause of humiliation, than to find ourselves guilty of a sin so exceedingly unreasonable and presumptuous as pride? Shall a worm swell itself into an equality with the huge leviathan? What is man that he should be great in his own eyes? or what is the son of man, who is a worm, that he should magnify himself as if he were some being greater than an angel? Was the Son of God humbled for us, that we might not perish for ever, and shall pride ever be suffered to reign in our souls † ?

Ver. 19. *Better it is to be of a humble spirit with the lowly, than to divide the spoil with the proud.*

Although pride were not followed by destruction, and humility were attended by the most afflicting circumstances, yet humility is to be infinitely preferred to pride.

The word here rendered *humble* might by an inconsiderable variation signify *afflicted*. Humility and affliction are often in scripture expressed by the same word, and described as parts of the same character. Low and afflicted circumstances are often useful, by promoting humiliation of spirit. The reverse sometimes takes place, but it is an evidence of a very intractable spirit, if we cry not when God bindeth us, and continue unhumbled under humbling providences. The cottager that has his little Babylon of straw, is less excuseable than the mighty Nebuchadnezzar walking

---

*1 Cor. 1:29   †Chap. 11:2, 16:5

in his pride through the splendid chambers of his stupendous palace,

However mean the circumstances of the humble man may be, he is incomparably happier than the most prosperous of proud sinners. Alexander and Severus, after all their mighty conquests, are said to have lamented the emptiness of their acquisitions. I have been all things, said the last of these mighty men, and nothing is of any use. The joys and triumphs of the prosperous sinner are unsubstantial and fleeting as the wind. But the humble and afflicted Christian is a happy man, for his poverty of spirit makes him content and thankful. The God that knows the proud afar off, looks on him with complacency, and dwells with him, to revive his contrite spirit. He believes that he is in the circumstances which his heavenly Father knows to be best for him. Christ declares him blessed, and he shall be blessed through eternity.

Ver. 20. *He that handleth a matter wisely shall find good ; and whoso trusteth in the Lord, happy is he.*

We ought not only to avoid every thing sinful and foolish, and to exercise ourselves diligently in our necessary businesses and duties, but likewise to do every thing that we undertake wisely and discreetly.

The prudent management of affairs is attended with great comfort and advantage. It will give us reasonable hopes of success, command esteem from others, and prevent the evil consequences that usually result from indiscretion. David's name was much set by when he was in the house of Saul, because he behaved himself prudently on every occasion ; and Solomon's prudent administration filled the Queen of Sheba with amazement, and made her almost to envy the servants that had the pleasure of attending him, and seeing and hearing his wisdom.

In our religious course, we are required to do every

thing in a decent, orderly, and prudent manner. This will conduce to our own comfort and happiness, to the glory of the God of order, and to the edification of the body of Christ ; and it will prevent our good from being evil spoken of by those that desire to find occasion against us.

But whether we are employed in the business of the world, or in that of God, we must not trust to our own skill and prudence. To God we must look, and on him we must depend for direction, and help, and success ; for a man's heart may devise his way, but the Lord directs his steps *.

Happy is the man that trusts all his concerns in the hands of God. His heart is freed from anxious cares. He receives all needful supplies of wisdom and strength. He is led in the way of safety, and shall at last inherit God's holy mountain.

Ver. 21. *The wise in heart shall be called prudent ; and the sweetness of the lips increaseth learning.*

A good name is better than precious ointment, and this blessing is enjoyed by the wise in heart, and enables them to be serviceable to other men by the communication of their wisdom. Although the heart is the seat of wisdom, it must not be buried there, but discover itself in the speech and conversation, that many may be edified ; for we were not born for ourselves alone, but as we are made of one blood, and joined together by endearing relations, so we are bound to be useful to one another.

That our wisdom may be useful, we should endeavour to produce it to advantage, by a graceful and engaging manner of expression. It is not uncommon with bad men to set off their corrupt sentiments by dressing them in all the beauties of language, and by

---

*Verse 9

this means multitudes are seduced into error and folly.
Is not wisdom far better entitled to this recommendation than folly ? The expression of our thoughts in
proper language will increase our learning, by making
them more clear and distinct to ourselves, and thus enabling us to pursue them into their native consequences.
And learning will be diffused amongst others, whilst it
is conveyed to them in a clear and engaging manner.
What satisfaction must it give a man to improve his
neighbours in the most useful knowledge ? It makes
him a public good, as we are told in the next verse.

Ver. 22. *Understanding is a well-spring of life unto
him that hath it ; but the instruction of fools is folly.*

Our plenty of water makes us less sensible than the
inhabitants of Palestine, of the propriety of that meta-
phor, whereby every thing that is useful or pleasant
is in scripture compared to water. It was one of the
recommendations that God himself gave to his people
of the land of promise, that it was a land of fountains
of water, as well as a land of milk and honey ; and the
blessings of Christ are compared to water in many passages of the scriptures.

As waters in a thirsty land, so is a wise man to his
friends and neighbours. He has in him a well of living waters, and these issue forth in quickening and refreshing discourse. His wise and edifying converse is
not confined to those times when he is professedly instructing or counselling his family or friends, but when
he acts in character, his familiar converse ministers
grace to the hearers. But when fools are giving their
instructions and counsels, they cannot hide that folly
which cleaves to them continually. They must still be
themselves, and it is to be lamented that fools are for
the most part more consistent than wise men. Wise men
have folly still remaining in them, and therefore are
not wise in every thing ; but fools are entirely destitute

of wisdom, and discover their foolishness when they are most earnestly endeavouring to appear wise *.

Every man, when he builds a house, seeks a situation where he may be furnished with plenty of wholesome water ; and if we believe the wise man when he commends the wise, we shall be desirous of their society and friendship, and account their neighbourhood a blessing †.

Ver. 23. *The heart of the wise teacheth his mouth, and addeth learning to his lips.*

The wise man commended a graceful manner of expression to us ‡, but there is a false eloquence which he rather wishes to guard us against.   Pompous words, and turns of wit, and fine thoughts that want solidity, will not make a man truly eloquent.   The true excellency of language consists in expressing just and important thoughts with clearness and force, that they may be understood and felt by the hearer.   A man that understands a subject well, although he is but an ordinary speaker, will do more justice to it than the finest speaker in the world, that has not a clear view of it.   And we cannot expect to make others feel the importance of the things we speak, unless our own hearts are duly impressed with them.

This text is a good rule for preachers, and directs them to a proper taste for pulpit eloquence.   They ought to understand and feel the truths they explain and recommend, and this will greatly assist them to find out acceptable words, by which their hearers will be edified.——It likewise directs hearers in the choice of their pastors.   A voluble tongue may enable a preacher to entertain them for a time, but they cannot expect to be fed with knowledge and understanding by one whose heart is not furnished with the truths of the

*Job 11:12   †Chap. 13:14   ‡Verse 21

gospel, and impressed with a deep sense of their importance.

The tongue of every wise man is governed and taught by his heart. God is our great Teacher, and he has directed us to be teachers to ourselves. " My reins," says David, " instruct me in the night." The heart, by its wise deliberations, must instruct and guide the members of the body, the eyes, the hands, the feet, and particularly the tongue, which is hardest to be taught of them all. The tongue of the just is as choice silver, when that of the wicked is little worth ; and it is the heart that makes this mighty difference *.

Ver. 24. *Pleasant words are as an honey-comb, sweet to the soul, and health to the bones.*

Friendly converse is a very agreeable and useful thing. It relaxes and amuses the mind, dispels anxiety from the thoughts, furnishes us with useful information, promotes mutual kindness, and makes us to return with renewed vigour to the businesses of life.

Words that convey proper counsels and consolations to persons in perplexity and distress, are pleasant and medicinal like honey from the comb. They revive the drooping spirit, and strengthen the feeble knees.

" The words of the pure are pleasant words." The truths of God are unspeakably pleasant to every man that has not a most vitiated relish. They deserve to be expressed in the most pleasant language, but unless they are debased by a manner of expression quite below their dignity, they must be pleasant to the heart, and nourishment to the soul. The honey that drops of itself from the comb, is not so sweet to the mouth as the words of God to the spiritual relish. It is a feast to Christians to hear these truths delivered by the preachers of the gospel ; but they are not enter-

*Chap. 10:20

tainments merely for the Lord's day. Christians should accustom themselves to useful and religious communications. Our Lord, in the days of his humiliation, set us an example of entertaining one another with them at ordinary meals and social meetings. How greatly would our comfort and spiritual strength be increased by such useful converse ! Such discourse is pleasant in the ears of God himself, and why should it not be pleasant to those who profess to be followers of God as dear children * ?

Ver. 25. *There is a way that seemeth right unto a man ; but the end thereof are the ways of death.*

It is no evidence that a man is in the right way, that he thinks himself to be in it. There are some that toil themselves all their life in the practice of things which have not the stamp of divine institution, and yet are called by the name of religion. God, instead of saying to them as they expect, " Well done, good and faithful servant," will ask them that mortifying question, "Who hath required these things at your hands ?" Some are treasuring up to themselves the fiercest indignation, when they are feeding their pride with ungrounded imaginations of doing to God acceptable service. Let us therefore give earnest attention to the word of God, as a light shining in a dark place.

There are many of the human race who think they are in the high road to heaven, and yet know nothing experimentally of Christ, without whom no man shall see the Lord. How terrible will it be for those that imagine themselves in the way to heaven, to find themselves at last in the lake of fire and brimstone ! Alas ! why should men indulge themselves in their own deceivings ? Will it make a man well when he is dying, to think he is in a good way ? It will only keep him

---

*Chap. 15:26

from employing the physician till his case is beyond recovery. Examine yourselves impartially by the word of God, by which you must be judged at the last day. If you are then found in a state of condemnation, there is no relief. But, behold, now is the accepted time, and the day of salvation. Judge yourselves, and fly to the hope set before you, and you shall not be judged.

So common and dangerous is self-deceit, that the wise man, directed by the Spirit, did not judge a single warning against it sufficient. Again and again he cries to us, to see that we are in the right way that leadeth unto life *.

Ver. 26. *He that laboureth, laboureth for himself; for his mouth craveth it of him.*

A man's industry in his calling is no sure sign of virtue, for although it is a duty commanded by God, and necessary to be practised, yet profit and necessity may constrain a man to labour, who has no regard either to God or man.

But this proves that idleness is a most inexcuseable sin. It is not only condemned in the scripture, but it is a sign that a man wants common reason, as well as piety, when he can neither be drawn by interest, nor driven by necessity, to work. Self-love is a damning sin where it reigns as the chief principle of action; but the want of self-love where it is required is no less criminal. They should be left to starve who have strength, and want will to labour.

But may those be idle who are exempted by their circumstances from the necessity of labouring for bread ? By no means. Idleness wastes precious time, it enervates the body, and rusts the faculties of the mind. It is an endeavour to elude the sentence pro-

---

*Chap. 14:12, 16:2

nounced upon fallen man, and an introduction to every vice *.

Ver. 27. *An ungodly man diggeth up evil; and in his lips there is as a burning fire.*

If the bishops of England will not learn diligence, said the godly Latimer, from Christ and his apostles, they may learn it from the devil, who is still busy in his diocese. We may add, that slothful Christians, if they will not learn diligence from the example of those who through faith and patience inherit the promises, may be roused by considering the restless activity of ungodly men, who employ themselves in the service of sin, as busily as the slave who digs in a mine to supply the avarice of his unfeeling master. The service of sin is the worst of drudgeries, for that cruel master obliges the poor wretches who are enslaved by their own corrupt lusts, to fatigue their minds in contriving, and their members in executing their imperious commands.

Some of the ungodly dig up mischief, by reviving stories that ought to have been for ever buried in forgetfulness. Themistocles told one that proffered to teach him the art of memory, that he rather wished to learn the art of forgetfulness. There are too many that remember what ought to have been for ever forgotten, and thereby kindle up the flames of contention. In their lips there is as it were a burning fire; for their words are as dangerous as fire kindled in the thatch of a house, which threatens to burn it down, and set the neighbouring houses in a flame. When men have such a fire kindled in their tongues, it is easy to see by whose breath it is blown up. The devil was a liar and a destroyer from the beginning, and endeavours to make men as like to himself as possible. For this end

---

*Chap. 14:23

he fetches coals from the bottomless pit, and sets the tongues of wicked men on fire, that they may spread the infernal flame around them, destroying peace and charity to the utmost of their power from the earth. What shall be given to these wicked tongues ? Burning coals of juniper, and they shall not have a drop of water to quench them.

Ver. 28. *A froward man soweth strife, and a whisperer separateth chief friends.*

He is a wretch that spreads dissensions and enmities among men, who ought to live as brethren in unity. Such a person, Solomon has already told us, is abhorred of the Lord *.

One of the most dangerous of these classes of men that sow strife, is that of the whisperers. These men do not think fit to slander their neighbours openly, but secretly defame one man to another. They report their idle or false stories by way of secrets, and generally endeavour to procure credit by pretending to lament these faults which they tell with pleasure, and which they often forge, or at least make them a great deal worse by their spiteful manner of relating them. This kind of evil-speakers is like serpents in the way, or adders in the path, which hiss and sting men when they are dreading no evil. Men may oppose open enemies, and ward off blows which they see, but how can a man guard himself from the invisible arrows that are shot by the whisperer, whilst he keeps himself concealed from view ! By these agents of the wicked one, irreparable breaches are often made in families and neighbourhoods, and incurable jealousies excited amongst the dearest friends.

It is our duty never to lend an ear to the whisperer, nor to believe any thing bad of our friend and neigh-

---

*Chap. 6:4,19

bour, unless the cowardly backbiter will venture to become an open accuser. If our own characters are in any danger from these arrows that fly about in darkness, let us commit them to God: " Deliver my soul, O Lord, from lying lips, and from a deceitful tongue."

Ver. 29. *A violent man enticeth his neighbour, and leadeth him into the way that is not good.*

The devil never did any good to any of his servants, and yet some of them seem to have more zeal for their master's interest, than many of the servants of Christ. These are too careless about gaining others to the obedience of their Redeemer ; whilst violent men compass sea and land to make others as much the children of hell as themselves.

Such tempters to wickedness are to be abhorred as the greatest plagues of mankind. Thieves deprive us of our money, and murderers deprive us only of a short life ; but these factors of hell who would seduce us to sin, attempt to rob us of heavenly treasures, and to destroy our immortal souls. The Spirit of God warns us at great length, in the first chapter of this book, to avoid their snares.

Whenever any man would lead us into a way that is not good, let us remember what the end of that way is, and hear his words with the same indignation as if he were persuading us to cast ourselves into a burning fiery furnace.

The character of the seducer might be sufficient to set us on our guard—

Ver. 30. *He shutteth his eyes to devise froward things ; moving his lips, he bringeth evil to pass.*

He takes so much delight in wickedness that he shuts his eyes, to meditate mischief with an undisturbed mind, and vigorously employs the faculties which God has given him, in the service of his grand enemy.

His tongue is a fire, a whole world of iniquity ; but it has not enough of wickedness in the compass of its power to gratify his infernal thirst for sin, and therefore he speaks with his feet, and teaches with his fingers, and winks with his eye, to express the malignity of his heart, and give the signal to his companions in wickedness.

Strange ! that the sons of Adam should thus abandon themselves to wickedness, and serve sin with so much toil, when the wages of it is death. Men complain that the way to heaven is full of difficulty and danger. But broad as the way to hell is, there are many who undergo much more fatigue in it than the way to heaven requires, and they have not the comforts and joyful hopes to entertain them under their toil and sweat, that the travellers to Zion enjoy. They pass through a hell of labours and fears, to a hell of fire and brimstone.

Shall we join in a confederacy with these workers of iniquity ? Let us rather abhor their company, unless we wish our souls to be hereafter gathered with sinners.

Ver. 31. *The hoary head is a crown of glory, if it be found in the way of righteousness.*

Both Scripture and reason teach us to honour grey hairs. It is reported, that when an aged man went into a public assembly at Athens, and every seat was filled, none of the Athenians moved to give him place. Whereupon the Lacedemonians, who were in a seat by themselves, rose up to a man, to give him a place. All the Athenians applauded their polite behaviour ; whereupon the old man observed, that the Athenians knew what was right, and the Lacedemonians practised it.

But old men are not always wise, neither do the aged always understand judgment, and thus they forfeit that honour which they might otherwise expect.

Old age is an honour, and royalty is an honour; but
better is a poor and wise child, than an old and foolish
king who will no more be admonished. His self-conceit and intractable disposition, debase at once the
lustre of his crown, and the glory of his grey hairs;
but to be an old saint, is an honour that entitles a man
to the highest respect. None but fools will despise
him for those infirmities, which are the inseparable attendants of grey hairs. How provoking to God such
insolence is, may be learned from the story of the two
she-bears that tore forty and two children for saying
to Elijah, " Go up, thou bald head; go up, thou bald
head."

The honour bestowed by God upon old Christians
in lengthening their days, the experience they have
gained, and the usefulness of their former life, should
engage us to pay them great respect. We honour them
whose heads have been encircled with crowns by the
hands of men, and will we refuse honour to those
whom God himself hath crowned with silver hairs!

It is a comfort to aged Christians to find due respect
paid to them, and they should endeavour to secure this
respect, by avoiding peevishness and covetousness, which
are vices incident to this period of life, by bearing with
young persons, although they have not learned so much
wisdom as themselves, by submitting with cheerfulness to the unavoidable weaknesses of age, by trusting in God *, by shewing the faithfulness of God and
the advantages of religion to the rising generation, and
by bringing forth the various fruits proper to that time
of life.

Young persons should remember that old age is fast
hastening to them, and show that regard to the old,
which they will then expect to meet with from the

_____
*Isa. 46:4

388 / *Exposition of Proverbs*

young. They ought to enter into the way of righteousness, that they may be found in it by old age or death. If age should find them in the way of sin, their situation is very dangerous, though not altogether desperate.

Ver. 32. *He that is slow to anger is better than the mighty; and he that ruleth his spirit than he that taketh a city.*

The meek obtain the noblest victories, and enjoy the happiest kind of authority. They have power over their passions, which are brought under the dominion of reason, and are not suffered to make such insurrections as those which disquiet the spirits of the proud and haughty.

The conquerors of nations and cities have been celebrated by historians and poets, and their valour and success dazzle the eyes of the generality of men; and yet few of them deserve praise. Seneca observes, that such heroes as Alexander the Great deserve the same kind of honours with wild beasts, and earthquakes, and pestilences, or any other instrument of desolation to mankind. Some conquerors are nevertheless truly honourable, who have exposed their lives in just and necessary wars, for the service of their country and the suppression of tyranny. Gallant exploits of such true heroes, are celebrated in the inspired writings.

But he that is slow to anger and rules his passions deserves far higher praise, for he gains a nobler victory. Others conquer the bodies of men, but he conquers his own soul. The conquerors of nations fight with the arms of other men, but the meek have no soldiers to deprive them of any part of their praise. Most of the celebrated heroes conquered at the expence of their fellow-creatures, and spread horror and devastation around them like the tigers of the desart; but the meek of the earth are public blessings, and deserve the love of all men. Of earthly conquerors it may be said, that they have slain their thousands and ten thousands of men, by their swords and warlike artillery. But of the meek we may say, that they have put to flight armies of devils by the sword of the Spirit and the shield of faith; for these malignant spirits fight against our souls, to support the dominion of our passions over our reason. Other conquerors have their praise from men, and chiefly from men of foolish minds, for the wise look upon the generality of them as the plagues of the world; but those that are slow to anger have their praise from the unerring Judge, who exalts the meek to inherit the earth, whilst he looks upon the proud ravagers of nations with disdain, and spurns them into the dust. The conquerors of cities and nations are wretched slaves to their own imperious passions, which forced Alexander to kill some of his best friends, and made him so unhappy, that he almost killed himself. The meek enjoy the sweet and glorious liberty of the sons of God. The crowns of conquerors soon wither; but the honours of him that rules over his own spirit shall continue through every generation. Do we wish to enjoy honour and power? Let us fight against the corrupt affections of our own mind, with the armour of righteousness on our right hand and on our left. To be our own masters, will be more glorious for us than if we were masters of the world.

Ver. 33. *The lot is cast into the lap; but the whole disposing thereof is of the Lord.*

By lots men refer the determination of an event to that which in respect of men is purely casual, and comes not within the compass of men's knowledge or power; but it is wholly determined by the Lord, who does all things, great and small, according to the counsel of his own will. A remarkable instance of this truth we have in the division of the promised land amongst the tribes of Israel, which was done by casting the lot into the laps of men; but these lots were managed by divine providence in such a manner, that Jacob's predictions in blessing his children were exactly accomplished.

For this reason, lots are not to be used by way of amusement, but in matters of importance worthy to be referred to the arbitration of God, and incapable of being otherwise decided to advantage.

This proverb teaches us, that the things that fall out to our view by pure accident, are within the compass of Providence, which so entirely regulates every thing, however inconsiderable, that a sparrow falls not to the ground, nor a hair from our head, without our heavenly Father. Time and chance happen to all men, and the most important events of the life of men, and of kingdoms and nations, turn upon very small hinges, which do not come within the verge of our knowledge and care. The safety of the Jewish nation in the days of Esther, depended upon a very great number of accidents, that appear to us very unimportant, and very remote from the interests of God's people. But the Lord of hosts, who is wonderful in counsel and excellent in working, was their saviour and hope in the day of evil. Time and chance are his, and the feast of Ahasuerus, the disobedience of Vashti, the pride of the king and his ministers, the conspiracy of Bigthan and Teresh, with the discovery of it by Mordecai, the beauty of Esther, the departure of sleep on a certain night from the king's eyes, the fancy that struck him to have the Chronicles of the kingdom read for his amusement, the superstition of Haman, the event of his lots, and the good-humour which Ahasuerus happened to be in when Esther came into his presence to petition for the life of her countrymen,—all these things wrought together, under the direction of the Lord, for the salvation of his chosen people.

Think not that your mountain stands immoveably strong, for if God hide his face, you will be troubled. He can make the veriest trifle the instrument of destroying all the strength of your confidence, and the mighty are taken away by him without hand.

Trust in him at all times, and trouble not yourselves with anxious thoughts about the things that shall come to pass in the future parts of life. We never discover so much folly, as when we set up for prophets ; for the things that are to come to pass, depend upon a very complicated chain of causes, consisting of innumerable links, which are quite out of the reach of our view, but are every one of them under the eye and in the hand of God. Blessed are those that give up all their fortunes to the will of God, with a cheerful resignation. Nothing shall befal them, but according to the will of Him that loves them better than themselves, and knows infinitely better what is good for them.

Proverbs 17

Ver. 1. *Better is a dry morsel, and quietness therewith, than an house full of sacrifices with strife.*

Solomon expresses the most delicious entertainments by the word *sacrifices,* intimating his hope, that none would presume to offer unto God a sacrifice, but of the best of their cattle, for the best of beings is to be honoured with the best we can give him *.

The flesh of the peace-offerings was a feast for the family and friends of the offerer, and there could not be a more delightful feast, when piety and friendship gave a relish to the entertainment. But the most delicate provisions are turned into gall and wormwood by variance, whilst the bitterest things are made sweet by love and friendship.

Solomon has already given us the instruction contained in this verse †. But it is useful to have it still before our eyes, for peace and friendship are not only the balm of life, but of great importance in our religious course. Strife is productive of innumerable sins, and renders us unfit for the duties we owe to God, as well as those of our various relations. Love and peace make every service to our families and friends pleasant, and prepare us to lift up holy hands to God, without wrath and doubting.

Ver. 2. *A wise servant shall have rule over a son that causeth shame, and shall have part of the inheritance among the brethren.*

A low situation does not disqualify men from obtaining and using wisdom, nor from enjoying the honours and benefits of it; nor will an elevated rank support men in folly, or hinder them from feeling its mischievous effects.

A poor wise man is too often despised, but it is only by the unwise; for those that have wisdom set an high value upon it, wherever it is found, and honour the meanest person that appears to possess it. It is perhaps owing to the partiality, and not the wisdom of parents, that this proverb has not been more frequently verified in the letter. Children that are a shame to

---

*Mal. 1:14   †Chap. 15:17

their parents, have sometimes brought disgrace upon themselves, from those that once loved them with a tender affection, and still love them. Reuben was the beginning of Jacob's strength, and yet he lost his dignity to a younger brother, who, according to the fashions of those times, was to be in some degree under his government. But even when partiality prevails over reason in the behaviour of parents, folly, by its native consequences, and the just providence of God, does often reduce men from honour and wealth to poverty and disgrace, and place them below those over whom they once tyrannized ; and wisdom exalts servants from poverty to wealth, or even to power. Joseph was a slave in Potiphar's house, and then a prisoner, but he was made lord over Potiphar himself.

Servants have often for their wisdom shared in the inheritance. Solomon himself married his daughters to two of his own subjects. Jarha, an Egyptian servant, was taken into the family of his master, and became the head of a family in Israel *.

This verse gives parents a proper hint about the distribution of their estates, and directs those who have the disposal of places of trust, to pay a greater regard to wisdom and integrity, than to high birth, or great estates, or the connections of friendship and kindred.

How excellent is wisdom, which raises the slave from grinding at the mill, and the beggar from the dunghill, to places of distinction, and to the truest honours, because they are the pure fruits of goodness ! How miserable a thing is folly, which degrades the high, and brings misery upon the latter days of those who flourished like green bay-trees in the prime of their life !

Ver. 3. *The fining-pot is for silver, and the furnace for gold ; but the Lord trieth the hearts.*

---

*1 Chron. 2:34,35

As the fire tries metals, and separates the dross from them, so the Lord tries the hearts of men; for his eyes are like a flame of fire, and he perfectly discerns all the secrets of the heart. Men are too often strangers to themselves, and mistake the principles by which they are governed; but God is greater than our hearts, and every thought is naked and open to his eyes. He knows our words before they are pronounced by the mouth, and our imaginations before they are framed in our minds.

This is God's prerogative. There is not a greater folly among those corrupters of Christianity, the Roman Catholics, than their practice of praying to saints and angels. Thou, Lord, even thou alone, knowest the hearts of all the children of men, and therefore oughtest to be feared, and to receive all religious homage.

It is vain for men to worship God with the lips, whilst the heart is removed from him; nor will our good deeds to our fellow-men be accepted of God, when they do not proceed from a principle of love *.

This proverb may likewise be understood of those awful providences by which the spirits of his people are tried, as gold and silver are tried by the fire. Afflictions and calamities are like a furnace which God has in Jerusalem, by which dross is discovered, and purged away †. But herein God discovers his kindness, that he does not keep his gold in the fire till it is entirely free from the dross, for if such a furious heat were applied to it as is requisite to make metals entirely pure, it would be altogether destroyed. " I have refined thee," says he, " but not with silver; I have chosen thee (or made thee a choice vessel) in the furnace of affliction ‡.

---

*1 Cor. 13:1,2, Rom. 2:28   †Mal. 3:2,3   ‡Vide Septuagint

Ver. 4. *A wicked doer giveth heed to false lips ; and a liar giveth ear to a naughty tongue.*

Solomon has often warned us against compliance with temptation ; and every man that is not wicked will surely follow his advice, for he is a wicked doer that giveth heed to false lips.

Wicked men have a great treasure of evil in their hearts, and yet have not enough to satisfy their own corrupt dispositions. They are like covetous men, in whom their large possessions only increase their lust of having, and therefore they carry on a trade with other wicked men, who are able to add to their store of iniquity, by flattering and counselling them in sin. Their heart gathers iniquity to itself, not merely by its own corrupt imaginations and contrivances, but by hearing the devilish lessons of those that have made a greater proficiency in that wisdom which cometh from below. They are blessed who hunger and thirst after righteousness, but cursed are they who add drunkenness to thirst in the service of sin, for they shall be filled with their own devices*. By hearkening to the wicked instructions of Jezebel, Ahab destroyed himself and his house ; and the politic advices of Jonadab proved no less fatal to the apparent heir of David.

A liar is a wicked doer, and giveth ear to a naughty tongue, for by the lies of other men he increases his own stock, and is enabled to retail his abominable stories with a better grace. He can say that he gives the story as he heard it, (although he has no scruple to make some additions), and thinks this a sufficient justification of himself, if the falsehood of what he has told is detected. But a man shews himself to be a liar and slanderer, when he gives too easy belief to bad stories, that he may have the barbarous satisfaction of

---

*Ps. 64:5-7

spreading them. An honest man will not wound his neighbour's character, by trusting the words of a tale-bearer, and divulging what may very possibly be false. And even when there is too much ground for believing the report, he will be backward to spread it any farther, without some good reason.

Ver. 5. *Whoso mocketh the poor reproacheth his Maker; and he that is glad at calamities shall not be unpunished.*

It is our indispensible duty to compassionate the poor, and if Providence puts it in our power, to relieve them; and yet some are so destitute of bowels, that they will trample them lower in the dust, by insult and oppression.

The reason why poor men are more exposed than the rich to reproach, is, because they are supposed incapable of taking revenge; but it ought to be remembered, that God is mocked through their sides. If God should appear in human shape, would we dare to insult him? Would not the fear of a just and dreadful vengeance deter us? And to mock the poor, amounts to the very same thing. God did actually appear in our nature, and he was then poor for our sakes; and those that despise the poor, despise them for a reason that reflects upon our Saviour himself when he dwelt among us; and poor Christians are members of his body, and every injury done to them he considers as done to himself *.

The reason of this proverb extends the meaning of it to all persons that are despised, or held up to ridicule, on account of any defect of body or mind, or misfortune in circumstances, that does not affect the moral or religious character of men. When we are what God made us, and meet with calamities from the

*Matt. 25:42

appointment of providence, every indignity or affront offered us reflects upon our Maker. Let no man, therefore, be ashamed of any circumstance in his condition that is not the fruit of sin, unless he is ashamed to own his Creator.

To rejoice in calamities, is a mark of a child of the devil. Christ wept for the miseries that were to befal his implacable enemies for their cruelty to himself. We find the people of God rejoicing and praising God at the destruction of their enemies, but their satisfaction was caused, not by any pleasure in the miseries of their enemies, but by the discoveries of God's mercy to themselves, and the vindication of his righteousness, by the infliction of deserved punishment on the irreconcileable enemies of God *. A savage delight in the misery of enemies, is often represented in scripture as the temper of the worst of men, who thereby expose themselves to signal vengeance †.

Ver. 6. *Children's children are the crown of old men; and the glory of children are their fathers.*

Children are the means of preserving the name of their parents when they are dead; and whilst they are alive, it is their delight and honour to be surrounded with descendants, except when they are so unnatural to the instruments of their being, as to disgrace them by their manners.

When persons are now on the verge of the grave, and every thing else becomes insipid to them, their children's children are a great comfort, and procure them much respect, when they are trained up in the way wherein they should go. Old men are therefore bound to give thanks to God for giving and sparing to them a posterity on the earth. "I had not thought," said Jacob to his beloved son, "to see thy face, and lo, God hath

---

*Exod. 15, Ps. 35:9,10   †Ps. 35:19-26, Ezek. 26:2, 25:2, 35:15, Obad. 12

shewed me thy seed also." Children are an heritage from the Lord, and ought to be instructed in his ways, that parents may have pleasure in them, and in their young families, when the days come wherein they would otherwise be obliged to say, We have no pleasure in them.

It was a custom among the Romans, for men that wanted sons, to adopt young men, and give them the title and privileges of sons, that their name might not die with themselves. Christians to whom God has denied, or from whom he has taken away the blessing of children, may find a better method of having some to be their crown and glory. If, by their holy example and religious converse, they win souls to Christ, these shall be their crown of rejoicing in the day of Christ *.

Some children are so destitute of natural affection, that they care not how soon their parents die, that they may enjoy their estates, and become masters of their own actions. These are profane persons like Esau, who thought he would have it in his power to kill Jacob, when Isaac, who was now an old man, was dead. Dutiful children will think it an ornament to them to have their aged parents still alive, even when their poverty and weakness make it the duty of their children to labour for their support.

But are parents of every kind a glory to their children? The hoary head is not always a crown of glory to the man that wears it, or to his family, but only when it is found in the way of righteousness. The seed of the righteous are respected for the sake of their parents by good men, and even God himself has a regard to them. Perhaps no history but that of David's family gives us an example of a crown transmitted from father to son for seventeen generations. Why

---

*2 Cor. 1

did not God make the house of Ahaz like the house of Jeroboam the son of Nebat, or the house of Baasha the son of Ahijah? Because he would give a light to his servant David in Jerusalem.

Verily there is a reward to the righteous, which extends to their families and posterity. By righteousness children are a crown to their parents, and parents are a glory to their children ; and therefore we ought not only to practise, but to promote and maintain it amongst our connections *.

Ver. 7. *Excellent speech becometh not a fool : much less do lying lips a prince.*

Fools make themselves ridiculous, by affecting to speak of things beyond their reach, or to use language too high for their abilities. For a wicked man to talk like a Christian, is equally unseemly. When a covetous man talks in praise of liberality, or a hypocrite commends the integrity of David, they condemn themselves.

For a beggar who wears rags to put upon his breast the coronet of a Duke, is ridiculous, because the agreement of things to one another is requisite to the beauty and propriety of any thing. Professions of religion joined to wicked practices, are equally absurd. In nothing is consistency to be more studied than in ordering our words and conversation.

When a bad man has the tongue of a saint, he discredits religion, and brings suspicion upon truly religious men. The profane world will say, Do you hear how finely that man talks ? and yet he can take the advantage of his neighbour in a bargain : they are all alike, and their professions are but nets to catch the unthinking. Good words will do no good to a bad man, but aggravate his condemnation ; out of his own mouth

*Gen. 18:19

400 / *Exposition of Proverbs*

shall he be judged. They are not acceptable to God. As Christ would not suffer devils to make confessions of faith, even when their doctrine was sound ; so God will not suffer the hypocrite to take his covenant into his lips, because such a holy thing is polluted when it comes into the mouth of dogs *.

Lying lips are no less unbecoming in the mouth of a prince, who ought to honour the dignity of his station by the dignity of his manners. A prince of our own is said to have frequently used this proverbial saying, " He that knows not how to dissemble, knows not how to reign." You may judge from the text before us, whether he deserved to be called the Solomon of his age. It was certainly a nobler saying of one of the kings of France,—that if truth were banished from all the rest of the world, it ought to be found in the breasts of princes.

A man's dignity obliges him to a behaviour worthy of it, and of him whose favour has conferred it. All Christians are advanced to spiritual honours of the most exalted kind. They are the children of God, and heirs of the eternal kingdom, and ought to resemble their heavenly Father, who is the God of truth. When a young prince desired a certain philosopher to give him a directory for his conduct, all his instructions were comprised in one sentence, " Remember that thou art a king's son." Let Christians remember who they are, and how they came to be what they are, and act in character †.

Ver. 8. *A gift is as a precious stone in the eyes of him that hath it ; whithersoever it turneth it prospereth.*

Gifts have a very strong influence in gaining love. They are like precious stones in the eyes of those

---

*Ps. 51:16   †Rev. 1:5,6, 1 Peter 2:9

that receive them, charming their eyes, and power-fully turning their affections to the giver ; and their influence is almost universal, for they work upon the heart of the wise and the self-denied, as well as of the foolish and selfish.

It was a sign of Abigail's prudence to meet David with generous presents, as well as a persuasive speech, when he was coming in fierce resentment to extirpate her husband's family ; and when Jacob met his incens-ed brother, he not only endeavoured to pacify him by submissive words, but also loaded him with noble gifts, which were perhaps the most effectual means, (next to Jacob's prayers), to regain his lost friendship.

Such is the efficacy of gifts, that God expressly for-bids them to be received by judges from parties that have a cause to be decided by them, because they blind the eyes of the wise, and pervert the words of the righteous.

What influence should the gifts of God have upon our hearts ! They are more numerous than the hairs upon our head, and far more precious than pearls and diamonds. Surely they must have a constraining in-fluence upon every heart that is not harder than the nether milstone.

Ver. 9. *He that covereth a transgression seeketh love ; but he that repeateth a matter separateth very friends.*

As we are required to love our neighbours as our-selves, so we ought to promote love in the world, and to seek the love of other men to ourselves. It is no piece of the self-denial that becometh the followers of Christ, to be unconcerned whether we are loved by our neighbours or not; for then we should be careless whether they obeyed God and performed their duty, or lived in the neglect of it. Whatso-ever things are lovely, are to be minded and prac-tised by us ; and nothing is more lovely than to cover transgressions, as nothing is more hateful than the repeating of them.

To cover our own transgressions, like Adam, would be very dangerous, but we have the noblest examples to recommend to us the covering of other men's faults. How lovely was the behaviour of our Redeemer, when he excused the unfriendly behaviour of his three disciples in the garden of Gethsemane, and when he bestowed such high commendations on their fidelity in his discourse with them, and his prayers to his Father, although he knew that they would soon forsake him in his sufferings, and make the best shift they could for themselves ! Nor was his goodness confined to his Apostles ; he excused even his murderers, when he prayed to his Father for their forgiveness. Who is like unto the Lord our God, who covers our iniquities by his pardoning mercy, and removes them as far from us as the east is from the west ! Surely the faith of his pardoning mercy must mightily persuade us to cover by the mantle of charity the offences of our fellow-sinners.

Love covereth all sins *. Paul teacheth us how this is done †, and our self-love may give us much light and direction on this point. Had we a love to our neighbours like that which we bear to ourselves, we would not be ready to observe their faults, unless they were very glaring ; we would make much allowance for the temptations that seduced them, and consider how liable we ourselves are to fall before temptation; we would not keep our eyes fixed upon their faults, but consider likewise what there is in them to provoke us to love ; we would not be harsh in reproving, nor backward in forgiving them, nor would any consideration provoke us to cast in their teeth those old faults that seemed to

*Chap. 10:12   †1 Cor. 13

be forgotten: By such a behaviour as this, love is sought and gained. Was it possible that Joseph's brethren, cruel as they had been, could refuse their love to him, after the apologies that he so kindly made for their faults * ?

But he that follows the contrary method of behaviour seeks hatred, and alienates the affections of the most cordial friends from one another. The censorious man, the tale-bearer, the person that revives old quarrels, is a mortal enemy to charity, a faithful servant of the accuser of the brethren, an enemy to him who is our peace with God and with one another. If such dreadful punishments are threatened to those who are destitute of love, what shall be the portion of those who scatter the seed of enmity and variance through a whole country, by the stories they tell, and by the lies and misrepresentations which they mingle with their idle tales!

The meaning of this proverb must not be stretched into a prohibition of punishments or censures necessary to be inflicted on offenders, or of friendly reproofs, all which are recommended in other places of this book.

Ver. 10. *A reproof entereth more into a wise man, than an hundred stripes into a fool.*

The wise man gives us many marks, by which fools may be distinguished from wise men ; and does not insist more on any of them, than the different uses they make of rebukes and corrections. He not only tells us that the wise man hears rebuke, and the fool scorns it ; but that one rebuke will have a better effect on a wise man, than an hundred stripes on a fool.

Fools have sometimes received correction, and made a good use of it ; but they were fools no longer, for the rod and reproof gave them wisdom : but it is a sign

---

*Gen. 45:8

that folly is deeply ingrained, when an hundred rods leave men as great fools as they found them.

Wicked men have uncircumcised ears, and they cannot hear the word of the Lord; they have hard hearts, and the works of God, in which he speaks louder than in words, leave no impression. On the contrary, we often find them walking contrary unto God, and making their faces harder by those means that should have wrought the very opposite effect. Ahaz, in the time of his distress, trespassed yet more and more against the Lord. This was that king Ahaz. David was of a very opposite spirit; and when Nathan said unto him, "Thou art the man," he replied, "I have sinned against the Lord," and immediately composed the fifty-first psalm, to testify his deep repentance to the church, and to every generation of mankind.

We must not be so strict in trying other men by this mark of wisdom, as ourselves, for wise men are not wise in every piece of their behaviour. Asa's heart was perfect with the Lord his God all his days, and yet he was very angry with a prophet for giving him a just reproof in the name of the Lord. But such is not the ordinary temper of God's people, for God takes away from them the heart of stone, and gives them hearts of flesh, and they have the Spirit of God dwelling within them, who opens their ears to discipline, and seals their instruction.

It is good to have tender hearts, susceptible of impressions from reproof, and from the providence of God. As a lively faith will enable the Christian to bear the greatest trials, so a tender conscience will enable him to derive spiritual improvement from the gentlest afflictions, which are not to be despised, because they come to us on a message from God *.

---

*Prov. 3:10

This text likewise teaches us to make a difference, according to the dispositions of men, in the reproofs or chastisements that we are called to dispense unto men. Eli reproved his children with words, when they deserved an hundred stripes, if the law had allowed it ; and some parents provoke their children to wrath, instead of reforming them, by their severities.

Ver. 11. *An evil man seeketh only rebellion ; therefore a cruel messenger shall be sent against him.*

Some of the wicked are very pestilent members of society, who, casting off all fear of God and the king, employ themselves in those wicked courses which expose them to the vengeance of the laws, so that the messengers of justice must be employed in their disagreeable task of punishment for the benefit and peace of society.

But others of the wicked have some fear of the king, although they have no fear of God before their eyes ; and their corrupt dispositions take another course, which exposes them to equal danger, though from a different quarter. Their employment is to carry weapons against the King of the world, and they pursue their rebellious courses without intermission. There is much iniquity in their actions, there is a world of iniquity in their tongues, and the imaginations of the thoughts of their hearts are only evil continually. They are blind, and know not what they are doing ; for whilst they think they are only gratifying their own dispositions, and making use of their liberty, they are provoking God, by a continued course of disobedience to his will.

A cruel messenger shall be sent against these rebels ; for rebellion is as the sin of witchcraft, and stubbornness is as iniquity and idolatry. God has innumerable messengers of justice, for every instrument of vengeance is at his command, and employed at his pleasure, to avenge his quarrel upon the breakers of his laws. Beasts and men, diseases and death, angels and devils, are in arms at his call, to seize upon the criminals whom he means to punish.

The weakest creature, considered as a messenger of the Almighty, is irresistible by transgressors. The proud spirit of Pharaoh was humbled to the dust by flies and frogs, as well as by the evil angels, which were sent among the Egyptians. The hornets fought with success against the accursed Canaanites in the days of Joshua, as well as the destroying angel who fought for Hezekiah against the Assyrians.

God sometimes employs terrible messengers to chastise his own people. When David numbered his subjects, 70,000 of them were destroyed in three days by a visible messenger of severity, under the direction of an invisible minister of providence. If God takes such vengeance of the rebellions of some whom he pardons, what will the end be of them that seek only rebellion!

Let the wicked cast down their weapons of iniquity, and acquaint themselves with God, and be at peace with him through Jesus Christ, otherwise they may expect that dreadful messenger of God, the king of terrors, to be sent against them, to plunge them into everlasting burnings *.

Ver. 12. *Let a bear robbed of her whelps meet a man, rather than a fool in his folly.*

What a mercy is it that a fool is not always in his folly, under the irresistible impulse of domineering passions, driving on in his career of mischief, without fearing God or regarding men! If a gracious providence did not rein the wicked of the world by a strong bridle, the world would become more uninhabitable than those desarts, where lions and bears are constantly prowling and destroying.

---

*Job 16:14, Isa. 27:4,5

No creature is fiercer than a bear bereaved of her whelps. Hushai thought he could not use a better argument to affright Absalom from following the dangerous counsels of Ahitophel, than by comparing the fierce valour of David and his mighty men to the rage of a bear bereaved of her whelps. And yet this animal in its greatest fury is not so dangerous as a fool in the heat of passion. A bear in its rage makes no distinction between those that have robbed her and others, but falls upon any one she sees, and tears him in pieces; and yet you may by proper means escape from her, or secure yourself from her violence. But a fool in his folly will neither be reduced to reason by just reproofs, nor soothed by the mildest language, but behaves like the venomous adder, that will not be charmed by the wisest charmer. The most furious of beasts are men whose passions rule their reason, and make use of the understandings they have, to enable them to behave more brutishly than natural brute beasts can do.

Alas! that rational creatures, made after the image of God, should debase themselves to such a degree, that the savage animals should not furnish sufficient emblems to represent their folly! Why should any human creature chuse to be a beast, or a devil, rather than a man!

Let those that give up themselves to the government of passion, consider this text, and be ashamed, and shew themselves at length rational creatures; and let us all beware of rousing the sleeping passions of such madmen, if we value our own safety and innocence.

God's people ought to be on their guard lest they should, under provocation, be seduced into an imitation of such folly. David behaved too like a bear in her rage, when he was inflamed by a provocation from Nabal, and swore that he would destroy all the males in his house, although he afterwards found that some of them had pleaded his cause. However, let us not debase that noble character by applying to his behaviour the comparison in our text, for before he had time to execute his cruel purpose, he was again himself, the persuasions of Abigail having made him meek as a lamb.

Ver. 13. *Whoso rewardeth evil for good, evil shall not depart from his house.*

Ingratitude is one of the vilest sins, and gives a clear discovery of a disposition base beyond expression ; and the punishment of it shall be proportioned to the degree of its guilt. The ungrateful man brings evil, not only on himself, but likewise on his house ; and this misery, which so great a sin procures, does not come like a stranger to the house, to tarry for a night, but takes up its residence, and abides in it for ever.

Ingratitude to Gideon kindled a fire in Shechem, which consumed the inhabitants of that place and its environs, together with Abimelech their tempter *. But the most striking illustration of this sentence, is the history of the Jewish nation. Never was such ingratitude shewed to any benefactor, as they shewed to the Son of God, and never was the punishment of any people so dreadful, and of so long continuance. That scattered people proclaim to every nation under heaven how dangerous the sin of ingratitude is, especially when God our Saviour is the object of it.

Although we are grateful to men for their favours, yet if we take no notice of God as the supreme Benefactor, we are as justly chargeable with this sin, as those who have a present sent them by a friend, and return all their thanks to the carrier that brings it.

---

*Judges 9

The worst ingratitude in the world is a continuance in unbelief or disobedience, in opposition to the gracious declarations of the gospel. Those that despise the riches of gospel-grace, must burn for ever in fiercer flames than those to whom the grace of God that bringeth salvation never appeared, although they lived in constant disobedience to the will of God, as far as nature discovered it.

Ver. 14. *The beginning of strife is as when one letteth out water ; therefore leave off contention before it be meddled with.*

No creatures are more dangerous than fire or water, when they become masters instead of servants to us ; and the mischiefs that arise from contention are illustrated from the rage of both these elements *.

When a breach is made in the bank that confines water, the water seizes the opportunity, widens the breach more and more, pours itself forth in mighty currents, and gathering new force continually, it soon becomes altogether irresistible, breaks through every obstacle in its way, and sweeps along every thing that meets it, with a violence which cannot be controuled.

Such are the dismal effects of contention, which might have been checked at the beginning, but gathers fury in its progress, and will soon lay desolate a man's peace, and credit, and comfort, and conscience, and hurry him on to speak and to act in such a manner as if he were altogether bereaved of his reason, and transformed into a raging bear.

The effects of debate do not always stop at the persons with whom it begun. This deluge often sweeps away houses, and countries, and nations, and leaves a

---

*Chap. 26

scene of confusion and ruin in those places which formerly were the seat of prosperity and peace *.

We must therefore endeavour to get out of contention, whenever we find ourselves engaged in it, with as much haste as a man that endeavours to make his escape from a deluge of waters, by which he is in danger of being overwhelmed †.

But it is still better to leave off contention before it be meddled with. The banks of rivers are more easily preserved, than repaired after a breach is made. To keep ourselves out of this snare of the devil, it is our duty to mortify every selfish disposition, to keep every passion under the government of sanctified reason, to avoid every thing that may give offence, to be backward in conceiving offences against others ; and in our dispositions, words, and actions, to observe that great rule of doing to others as we wish that others should do to us ‡.

There are some cases in which contending is a duty. The apostles write unto us, and exhort us to contend earnestly for the faith which was once delivered to the saints ; and a zeal for truth and holiness is a necessary branch of Christian temper. But in striving for the faith of the gospel, we must avoid the wrath of man, which worketh not the righteousness of God, and carefully preserve the holy fire of religious zeal, from all mixture with that unhallowed fire of selfish passions which has so often usurped its name, and brought it into discredit with superficial observers.

Ver. 15. *He that justifieth the wicked, and he that condemneth the just, even they both are an abomination to the Lord.*

That condemning the just is a grievous crime, there is no doubt. But some will be startled at the wise

---

*Judges 12   †Gen. 13   ‡Ps. 34:11,12

man's assertion, that justifying the wicked is a crime of the like nature and malignity.

But we rebel against God by turning to the right hand, as well as by turning to the left, from that way in which we are commanded to walk. Justifying the wicked has an appearance of mercy in it, but there is cruelty to millions in unreasonable acts of mercy to individuals. It was not altogether without ground observed by a senator to the emperor Cocceius Nerva, when his detestation of his predecessor's cruelty seduced him into extremes of clemency,—That it was bad to live in a state where every thing was forbidden, but worse to live in a state where every thing was allowed. Historians tell us, that the provinces of the empire suffered more oppression under the administration of this mild prince, than in the bloody reign of Domitian.

Judges are guilty of this detestable sin, not only when they pronounce unrighteous sentences, but when they obstruct unnecessarily the judging of causes, whereby the righteous have their righteousness in part or for a time taken from them. Lawyers, and witnesses, and jurymen, are guilty in various degrees of these crimes, when they wilfully contribute their influence to the perversion of justice, or withhold their influence in their respective situations from the support of a righteous cause, where they are called to its defence.

Private persons in common life are not frequently chargeable with justifying the wicked, because they are not called in most cases to condemn them; and yet they may incur this guilt on some occasions, by pleading the cause of the wicked in opposition to truth, or to that justice which they owe to the innocent and oppressed, or by taking the part of transgressors in such a manner as to countenance their sins.

But the sin of condemning the righteous, or pronouncing too severe sentences upon those that have been overtaken in a fault, is very common in ordinary conversation, and the scripture often warns us against it *.

Ministers are guilty of this sin when they preach doctrines unscripturally rigid, making those things to be sinful which are not condemned in the word of God, or carrying the marks necessary to discover grace to a pitch too high to suit the generality of true Christians, or applying to particular persons those terrors that do not justly belong to them.   Such was the fault of Job's friends.

It is a more dangerous error in preachers, to explain away the commandments of God like the old Pharisees, to accommodate the characters of real Christians to many hypocrites by unsound representations of them, or to flatter the sinner into a false belief that he is a righteous man †.   By all these methods righteousness is discouraged, and wickedness favoured, in contradiction to the mind of God.

God never condemns the righteous, but it is his peculiar glory to justify the ungodly, through the execution of the curse upon his righteous Son.   In each of these divine transactions, the injustice condemned in our text is discovered to be detestable to God, for righteousness shines with more awful splendour in the infliction of punishment upon our Surety, and in our absolution from guilt, than in the flames of the lake of fire and brimstone.   God would not justify his own elect to the disparagement of his inflexible justice, but condemned all their sins, and punished them in Christ ;

---

*Matt. 7:1-5, Rom 14, 1 Cor. 4, James 4:14   †Ezek. 13:10

and so he is just, and the justifier of him that believeth in Jesus,

Ver. 16. *Wherefore is there a price in the hand of a fool to get wisdom, seeing he hath no heart to it ?*

If fools had no means of obtaining wisdom put into their hand, their folly would be excusable ; but when they have a price allowed them for procuring wisdom, and yet have no heart to it, what apology can be made for them ?

Every thing that gives us an opportunity of becoming wise, is a talent for which we must account to our great Lord. Bibles, and divine ordinances, and time, and leisure, and wealth, which enables us to furnish in greater abundance the means of knowledge, are a price put into our hands to get wisdom, and if we use them not to this valuable end, we despise the riches of God's goodness, and act like unreasonable creatures. Nay, the meanest animals reprove us, for the stork and the crane observe their seasons for flying to warmer climates; and the ants, though a feeble people, never neglect the gainful business of the summer and harvest.

How is the fool so stupid as to neglect such important business as the gaining of wisdom, and trifle away his time and talents in vanity? Surely if he were informed of a rich inheritance to be got on easy terms, he would shew a proper regard to his own interest. Does he not know that wisdom is infinitely more precious than land or gold ? No ; this is the reason of his carelessness. He has no heart to wisdom, he knows not its value, and has no relish of its pleasures. That which is more precious than rubies, is to him more worthless than a pebble. That which is more sweet than honey, is tasteless as the white of an egg.

Is this price, then, put into his hand in vain ? To himself it is worse than in vain. Every mean of wis-

dom shall prove galling to his remembrance, when his
eyes are opened, for opened they shall be at last, to
discern the glory of that which he despised. The
worm that is to prey upon him for ever, will be continually fed by the recollection of sermons despised,
and days of the Son of man wasted in idleness. But
this price will not be lost to those who put it into the
hands of the fool ; for their generous endeavours to turn
the foolish to the wisdom of the just, will be as graciously rewarded as the more successful attempts of
others to serve their generation *. Nor will God be a
loser of glory by the self-ruining folly of sinners, but
his justice will for ever triumph in the revenges executed upon the despisers of his long-suffering and
grace.

Ver. 17. *A friend loveth at all times, and a brother
is born for adversity.*

There are many false friends that profess love for
their own advantage, and discover their insincerity
when they have no more ground to hope that their interest will be served by it. There are fickle friends
that love for a time, and grow indifferent to our interests, without any reason but their own inconstancy.
But a true friend is steady in his love, and prosperity
and adversity, honour and dishonour, evil report and
good report, make no more difference to him, than
the changes of the air to a man of a healthy constitution.

Some false friends become cool in the day of prosperity, for they grudge to see their equals exalted
above them; but a true friend rejoices in the prosperity
of those whom he loves, although he possesses a share
in it only at second hand. Jonathan was one of the
noblest instances of this truth, who loved David, and

---

*Isa. 49:4

rejoiced in his prospects of advancement at his own expence *.

Adversity is commonly reputed the touchstone of friendship. That is the season when our hollow friends forsake us, but a real friend then acts the part of a brother, and discovers his friendship more than ever. Jonathan encountered the fury of a tyrant in a father, and risked his life for David, for whom he had formerly given up with cheerfulness his prospects of a crown.

We must not, however, be too rigorous in trying our friends by this mark, for perfection is not to be found any where among men, and the strength of prejudices or fears, may sometimes make real and worthy friends to act in a manner unworthy of themselves. The love of the disciples to Christ was approved by himself, " Ye are they which have continued with me in my temptations ;" and yet through fear they forsook him, and fled in the day of his strongest temptation. Job's friends, through an unhappy mistake, added greatly to his afflictions, and behaved like enemies ; yet that patient sufferer still calls them his friends, and solicits their sympathy †.

We ought to shew proper attention to our friends in their distresses, thatwe mayapprove the sincerity of our former professions, and in the day of our own distress to make due allowances for the weakness of human nature ‡. But no friend but Christ deserves our unlimited confidence. In him the text received, and still receives, its most glorious accomplishment. He remembered us in our low estate, and forgets us not in his own exaltation. Afflictions are the seasons when his kindness is most richly experienced, and our pro⸗

---

*1 Sam. 20   †Job 19:21   ‡Job 6:14, Matt. 26:4

vocations do not alienate his affection from us. This is our beloved, and this is our friend. In him we will trust, and to him we will devote our hearts.

Ver. 18. *A man void of understanding striketh hands, and becometh surety in the presence of his friend.*

Solomon warns us often against rash suretiship, and yet many professors of religion have opened the mouths of enemies by the temptations into which they have run themselves by forgetting this exhortation. Why should religion bear the blame of what it testifies so often against, that every man who reads this book must observe it, and have it in his mind, unless he wilfully despises the instructions of the wise man? If we would hearken to Solomon, he would teach us to be richer and happier, as well as better Christians *.

Ver. 19. *He loveth transgression that loveth strife; and he that exalteth his gate seeketh destruction.*

Pride is a destructive sin, in whatever form it discovers itself; and the Spirit of God, by Solomon, gives us many warnings of the danger of it, and of those sins that are produced by it.

Only by pride cometh contention, and from the love of contention spring an innumerable multitude of iniquities; for as charity is productive of every virtue, so that he who loveth another hath fulfilled the law, and will do no hurt to his neighbour; so he that takes pleasure in strife hath broken the whole law, and is ready to do every bad thing, for where there is envying and strife, there is confusion and every evil work.

But who is the man that loveth contention? Those who are engaged in it, allege that they love peace as much as any man, but they are forced into it by the perverseness of other men. However, when men are almost always engaged in strife, they afford too strong

---

*Chap. 6:1 etc.

presumption that they love it. If a man is always engaged in law-suits, or in angry contentions with his
neighbours either about religion or politics, or those
things that concern his private interest, he is surely a
lover of strife. It is an evidence no less clear of love
to contention, when persons seize every opportunity
for beginning a quarrel, and cannot make the least
sacrifice of self-will, or interest, or humour, for the sake
of peace. Now, if strife be productive of so many sins,
it must be attended with a proportionable train of miseries, and therefore our interest as well as duty requires us to avoid every thing that may lead us into
angry disputes. If we love God, we will love our
brother also ; and if we live in the faith of reconciliation with God, we will follow peace with all men.

The love of expensive vanities, is another sign or
pride, and is likewise censured by the wise man. He
that exalts his gate, and builds to himself a house
magnificent beyond what his station requires, or his
circumstances allow, seeketh destruction. The slothful man exposes himself to misery ; but he waits for it
till it comes upon him like a traveller. The aspiring
man, that cannot be happy without a stately dwelling,
and a splendid manner of living beyond what his estate
will bear, seeks for destruction, and sends a coach and
six to bring it to him. Let us hate pride, for it makes
a man miserable in this world as well as the next. It
makes men unsatisfied with the condition allotted them
by God, and tempts them to waste their substance,
and to cheat and oppress their neighbours, in order to
gratify their own ambitious disposition, and leads on the
person in whom it reigns, to the practice of many sins
which bring down destruction from the Almighty *.

---

*Jer. 22:13,14, Amos 6:3,4

Ver. 20. *He that hath a froward heart findeth no good ; and he that hath a perverse tongue falleth into mischief.*

A man of a froward and perverse spirit, makes use of art and dissimulation to gain his ends, and thinks himself so wise, that he has no reason to fear a disap_pointment ; but he indulges himself in an error which the whole scripture condemns, and which no man of real honesty can fall into, that some profit may be gained by sin.

The froward in heart is an abomination to the Lord *. And the Lord is the universal Ruler, and will never suffer a man to enjoy any solid satisfaction in that which he detests. He will most certainly frustrate those expectations which are founded upon a contempt of his majesty, and a presumptuous notion that the power and wisdom of a creature can successfully oppose the Creator †.

The froward in heart and in tongue will not only meet with a total disappointment of his hopes, but fall into extreme misery. And this is the most deplorable condition that we can imagine, when one is not only divested of every thing comfortable and good, but loaded with the opposite miseries. This severe punishment is begun in this world, as experience teaches every day, and it is consummated in that punishment of loss and of sense, which the wicked suffer in the everlasting world.

How foolish are the men whose wisdom lies in a skill to do evil ! Their own feet cast them into a snare, and their own tongues, by which they hope to execute their wicked contrivances, fall upon themselves, and grind them to powder. Honesty and integrity is our best wisdom ; and upright men walk on firm ground,

---

*Chap. 11:20   †Ps. 12:4,5, Job 5:12,13

when the men that boast of their crooked arts fall into their own snares.

Ver. 21. *He that begetteth a fool doeth it to his sorrow; and the father of a fool hath no joy.*

How little are earthly objects to be trusted! Men's families are the sources of their expected joys, and the birth of children is generally accounted a joyful occasion; but many children are the causes of grief, and not of joy, to their parents. By their folly they are a disgrace to those that might have expected better returns of their fondness, and fill those evil days of old age with additional pains, when it was expected that the sight of them would have relieved every pang. He that has the unhappiness to be father to a fool, hath no joy, either in his son or in any thing else, for every pleasure is deadened, and every distress embittered and poisoned, by the sight of a child despising the very instrument of his existence, and treasuring up endless miseries for himself.

Unnatural are those children who make their parents miserable, by means of that fond affection to their unworthy children, of which they cannot divest themselves. Unwise are those parents who look for comfort to their children, and do not look above them to the Father of lights, who alone makes any thing a blessing to us. It must greatly increase the affliction of those who meet with this sore calamity, to have occasion of reflecting, that they have been careless in using those means that might have driven away foolishness from their children, or in praying for that blessing on which the success of all means depends.

Ver. 22. *A merry heart doeth good like a medicine; but a broken spirit drieth the bones.*

The intemperate mirth of sensualists is a slow poison to the body, and therefore cannot be here meant. Innocent amusement is here allowed, as a mean of promoting or preserving health; only it must not be turned into a business, to consume our days in vanity, and make our health useless to us; but the mirth principally recommended by the inspired writer, is that cheerfulness which religion bestows; for he tells us, that the ways of wisdom are all pleasantness and peace, and that sorrow and wretchedness are inseparable attendants of sin.

The things of this world are so incapable of affording permanent satisfaction, that Solomon wrote almost a whole book to shew that they are vanity and vexation of spirit; but wisdom, he tells us, makes the face to shine, and inspires the heart with pleasure.

A merry heart diffuses its influence through the body, and preserves its vigour and health, or tends to restore it where it is lost; but a broken spirit crushes the frame of the body, enfeebles its powers, makes the flesh to wither and decay, and burns the bones like an hearth. Christ himself, in his agony, felt the effect of strong sorrows in his flesh.

Every thing that tends to spread a gloom over the mind, is to be avoided. There are cases, indeed, where we are called to mourn and weep, but that grief which religion requires and infuses, is not dangerous to the animal frame, because it brings the sweetest joys in its train. It is sin that brings the most dangerous sorrows along with it, and not repentance, which is a medicine to remove the cause of the worst distempers. When David was stubborn, and did not confess his sins, his bones waxed old, because of his roaring all the day long. But when he confessed his sin, the joys of pardon healed his bones, and renewed his vigour, so that he praised God, not only for pardoning all his iniquities, but likewise for renewing his age like the eagle's.

The joys of God's salvation will be a mighty antidote against every grief, and strengthen the body and
soul against those bad impressions which the multiplied calamities of life too often make *.

Ver. 23. *A wicked man taketh a gift out of the bosom,
to pervert the ways of judgment.*

It is said of Sir Matthew Hale, that glory of the
English Bench of Justice, that when a cause was
brought before him by a gentleman who had sent the
present of a buck, he called for the gentleman, and desired him either to withdraw his plea, or name the
price of his present; and although the judge was told
that it was no more than he used annually to send to
the circuit judges, yet he absolutely refused to admit
the cause, unless he was allowed to pay down the full
price of the present; whereupon the gentleman chose
to lose his cause, that he might not suffer the affront of
taking money for a gift. He is a wicked judge that
accepts of bribes, and an honest man would rather
lose his cause, however just, than gain it by such a
base thing as a bribe. It must have been a great bondage for Paul to be confined to a prison, when he
loved the pulpit so well, had not his will been sunk in
the will of God; yet he would not offer the least
bribe to his covetous judge, who detained him in
prison, expecting that money would be offered for his
freedom.

Wicked men take their gifts out of the bosom, that
they may do it without public observation; but why
should men thus affront the omniscient God? Can
any man do a thing so secretly, that God shall not see
it? Or will it be any profit to us to have our sins
hidden frem the eyes of men, when they are all before
the great Avenger? That which is done in secret,

*Hab. 3:17,18, Ps. 46:4

shall one day be revealed to the view of an assembled world, and then the omniscience of God will be vindicated from all the insults put upon it in this world, by those foolish men who were not ashamed to do those things before the face of God himself, in which they would not have wished the meanest of their fellow-creatures to detect them.

Ver. 24. *Wisdom is before him that hath understanding ; but the eyes of a fool are in the ends of the earth.*

Knowledge is often useless to the possessor of it, either because he is ignorant of those things which he ought to know, or because he wants wisdom to make the proper use of his knowledge ; but true wisdom is of constant use to him that possesses it, for he does not suffer it to be buried in his mind, but applies it for the direction of his life. It guides him in the choice of his great end, and makes him steady in the pursuit of it. He keeps it still before his eyes to guide all his steps, and walks in his way safely, for wisdom preserves him, and discretion keeps him *. Thus we find David regulating his life. He hid the word of God in his heart, and kept it before his eyes, and so he did not wickedly depart from his God †.

We must not only learn wisdom, but keep it in our eyes, that it may be a light to our feet ; for a man that has wisdom in his mind, and forgets to use it, is like one that has money in his chest, but forgets to carry some of it with him when he is going a long journey, to bear his necessary expences. He will be at a great loss, on many occasions, that has money in his house, but none in his pocket.

But a fool wants wisdom in his heart, and there is no wisdom before his eyes ; for instead of employing his understanding to fix upon the great end of life, as the mark

---

*Chap. 2:13   †Ps. 119:11, 18:21,22

at which he aims, his eyes are at the ends of the earth, roving up and down to look at every thing that comes in his way, except that on which his view should be constantly and steadily fixed. He has a roving fancy that is perpetually misleading his mind, and never minds what he ought to mind in the first place. He is either doing nothing, or nothing to purpose, or nothing of what he should do, but lives at random, and tosses to and fro like a ship in the sea, without a pilot and a helm. Such a man is perpetually in chase of shadows, and when he has overtaken one of them, and finds no substance in it as he expected, he begins to pursue another ; and so his days are spent in vanity, and he enters into the eternal world without any serious thought of making provision for his long home.

Our duty is, to fix our eyes upon the things that are not seen, and to live under the powerful influence of an eternal world ; and whatever lesser objects we may be called to regard in our journey through life, to tread that path which leads to eternal life, without turning out of it to the right hand or left, on any consideration whatever.

Ver. 25. *A foolish son is a grief to his father, and bitterness to her that bare him.*

This instruction would not be repeated so often, if it were not useful for many excellent purposes.

It teaches parents to avoid that common fault of too fond indulgence to the faults of their children, for a child left to himself is for the most part a grief to his father, and bitterness (which is the greatest degree of grief,) to his mother, whose maternal tenderness was more likely to spoil him by its excess, than the fondness of a father.

It is a lesson to children, to beware of converting the kindness of their parents to themselves into a torment, by bad behaviour.

It instructs those that have not the pleasure of a rising family, to acquiesce in the providence of God, when they recollect that children are but an uncertain comfort.

It instructs those that have not yet entered into family-connections, to chuse their partners in life with prudence, and to marry none that are likely to set a bad example before their children, or to neglect their religious education.

If parents have the misfortune to be plagued with foolish and wicked children, let them remember David, and the afflictions he suffered from his family, and the comforts that refreshed his soul under this distress *. Let those that can look upon their children with pleasure, bless God, and ascribe the praise to his name.

Ver. 26. *Also to punish the just is not good, nor to strike princes for equity.*

It is a bad thing when children, that ought to be a joy to the hearts of their parents, under every misfortune, prove their heaviest cross. But here is a worse evil censured; when magistrates, that are the ministers of God for good by their office, prove the ministers of Satan in the administration of it, by punishing the just, and perverting an institution of our gracious Creator, into an instrument of unrighteousness.

To punish the meanest of men without ground, is a very bad thing, for it is a discouragement to virtue, and a strong incentive to wickedness; but it is doubly wicked to strike princes for equity, by punishing inferior rulers for acting according to the eternal rules of righteousness, and refusing to truckle to the humour and caprice of their sovereigns. It was the fear of this that determined Pilate to condemn the holy One and the just.

---

*2 Sam. 23:5

Subjects may be guilty of striking princes for equity, by smiting them with their tongues, or seditious practices against their authority, whilst they endeavour, in the administration of their office, to serve the true interests, rather than gratify the unreasonable wishes, of those whom they govern. Moses had a large experience of this rebellious disposition, in the people whom he led through the desert; and it is probable, that Solomon himself saw reason to complain of it in his reign.

Parents and masters of families may be charged with the crime of punishing the just, by groundless severities to those who are under their charge *.

Rulers in the church are in like manner worthy of censure, when they administer the ordinance of discipline to the injury of those whom they rule, by rebuking them for things that are not criminal, or for real crimes which cannot be proved.

Ver. 27. *He that hath knowledge spareth his words; and a man of understanding is of an excellent spirit,* (or, *He who is cool in spirit is a man of understanding.*)

As we must not be hasty with our mouths to utter any thing before God, so it is foolish to be swift to speak even before men. The empty vessel makes the greatest sound, and the man that has nothing to say that deserves hearing, is commonly most prodigal of his words. When Xenocrates the philosopher was quarrelled for silence in a meeting of friends, he answered, That he had often repented of speaking, but never of silence.

Persons should not be fond of hearing themselves speak at any time, but double caution is necessary when we meet with provocations that put our minds into a ferment. The wise man's knowledge teacheth his mouth to speak the words of truth and soberness,

*Eph. 6:4,8

but angry passions are the worst instructors to the tongue in the world. Floods of venom are poured from them when they have mastered reason, and obtained the command of the lips *.

A man of understanding having the government of his tongue, shews the excellency and coolness of his spirit, either by silence, or by the meekness of his words, as the occasion directs him. David had such a command of his passions through the power of faith, that he said nothing amiss when he was tried with the most provoking usage in the time of distress, a season when the spirits of other men are discomposed by mere trifles. He was like a man that heareth not, and in whose mouth are no reproofs, " for in thee, O Lord," says he, " do I hope. Thou wilt hear, O Lord my God †."

But if a man spare his words, may he not lay himself open to the suspicion of being an ignorant man or a fool ? No.

Ver. 28. *Even a fool when he holdeth his peace is counted wise ; and he that shutteth his lips is esteemed a man of understanding.*

The silence of a fool is almost always a covering to folly, and a sign of some degree of wisdom, yet it is not always a sign that his folly is in any degree cured. Absalom held his peace when his sister was ravished by Amnon ; but his silence proceeded from sullenness and cunning, and prepared the way for the execution of his furious revenge.

It is a good sign that a fool is not incurable, when he has learned to hold his peace from a sense of his own ignorance, and a desire to learn from others. It is as difficult a thing to learn to be silent, as to learn

---

*James 1:19,20   †Ps. 38:12-15

to speak, and although unseasonable silence is not a good thing, yet unseasonable speaking is far worse.

It is often a point of real wisdom to be silent, for there is a time to be silent, and a time to speak, and the wise man's heart knoweth both time and judgment. When men have no call to speak on a subject, or when they have not duly considered it; when they are discomposed by passion, or in the company of those whose passions render them incapable of hearing reason; and finally, when they are more likely to expose themselves to damage than to do good to others by speaking,—then to hold their peace altogether, will be their best method of behaviour.

It is sometimes our duty to hold our peace even from good, but we must not run into one extreme to avoid another. Silence which is occasioned by cowardice, when we are manifestly called to bear testimony for truth, is a dangerous sin*. Nor must we desert the defence of oppressed innocency, to prevent inconveniency to ourselves †.

Proverbs 18

Ver. 1. *Through desire a man, having separated himself, seeketh and intermeddleth with all wisdom.*

MEN'S wisdom in this world is imperfect, and appears much more in desires than attainments ‡. But

---

*Matt. 10:32, Rev. 21:3   †Prov. 31:8, 24:12

‡Phil. 3:13,14

these desires are not feeble and ineffectual wishes, like those of Balaam, when he desired to die the death of the righteous, and yet had a prevailing love to the wages of unrighteousness. Genuine desires of wisdom and holiness will dispose a man to separate himself from every thing that would obstruct the attainment of it, and to use every proper mean for obtaining it.

We are not called to give up every connection with the world, but in the calling wherewith we are called, we are directed to abide with God. But we must lay aside every unnecessary incumbrance, and avoid that load of worldly cares which would press us down to the earth, and keep us from travelling in that way of life which is above to the wise. Worldly cares, and the lusts of other things, are the thorns that choak the good seed of the word, and hinder it from bringing forth good fruit. David was called to the government of a kingdom, but he did not suffer the weighty cares of government to alienate his soul from the word of God, which was still his meditation day and night. How far it is a man's duty to separate himself from other things to learn wisdom, depends upon his particular circumstances ; for the same person, in different situations, is required to employ a greater or lesser part of his time for this purpose. The labourer, that must attend upon his own business with diligence in its proper season, should employ himself in beholding God's work, when his hand is sealed up by stormy weather *.

The person that desires wisdom with earnestness will seek and intermeddle with it : although he depends on God for this precious gift, yet he will not make the freeness of divine grace a pretence for laziness ; but by reading and hearing, meditating and conversing, praying, and practising what he knows already, he will

---

*Job 36:6,7

follow on to know the Lord, and on such means the blessing of God may be expected *.

It is not one branch of wisdom only that the lover of wisdom will seek after. It is his earnest wish and endeavour, that the word of Christ may dwell in him richly in all wisdom. He regards both knowledge and practice as necessary parts of wisdom, that his eye may be clear, and his whole body full of light. He wishes and endeavours to be sound in the faith, and to attain a large measure of acquaintance with the law and the gospel. He is careful to understand his own way exactly, and to have every one of his steps ordered in the word of God. Every branch of religion is valuable in his eyes, and the Spirit shall lead him into all truth.

Ver. 2. *A fool hath no delight in understanding, but that his heart may discover itself.*

The disposition of fools is entirely opposite to that of the lovers of wisdom, for they have no pleasure in understanding. Novelty, or curiosity, or a desire to make a figure by their knowledge, may sometimes induce them to bestow some pains to procure knowledge; but their eyes were never opened to discern the divine beauty of truth and holiness, and they have no spiritual sensation, to relish the sweetness of that which every Christian declares from experience to be sweeter than honey from the comb. Herod heard John gladly, and did many things because of him; but his obstinate continuance in the sin of incest was an evidence that he had no true delight in wisdom, for that would have disposed him to abhor every false way. In the 58th chapter of Isaiah, we read of wicked men that delighted to know God's way ; but we learn from the follow-

*Prov. 2:1-6

ing part of that discourse, that their delight in wisdom was an empty pretence. They hoped to make satisfaction to God for their sins by their observation of ordinances, without seeking any experience of their sanctifying influence. Their delight was not placed on God or his ways, but on those advantages to themselves which they fondly hoped to obtain by bodily exercise. The hearers resembled by the stony ground received the word with joy, and for a time seemed to profit by it ; but they had no cordial relish of the gospel. Their delight was only a transient flash of affection, and it soon appeared that they loved their bodies more than their souls, and preferred their ease and safety to the gospel of salvation.

The delight of a fool is, that his heart may discover itself. Some of the wicked are decent in their outward conduct, and their pleasure lies in the inward indulgence of their corrupt disposition ; but others of them are not ashamed of their folly, and take delight in making it visible to all men by its fruits. They discover their pride and vanity, their sensual and irreligious dispositions, by their tongues and practices ; so that you may easily see that they are corrupt trees, because they bear nothing but corrupt fruit.

This proverb instructs us to distinguish between fools and wise men. A wise man seeks and intermeddles with all wisdom, because he delights in it after the inward man. If we love not wisdom, but take pleasure in the thoughts of foolishness or in the outward expressions of folly, we must be ranked in that black catalogue of which so many bad things are said in this book, for as a man thinketh in his heart, so is he.

Foolish thoughts too often come into the minds of the wise, but we must suppress them as soon as they enter, lest by giving them licence to pollute our hearts,

and stain our conversation, we should incur the reputation of folly *.

Ver. 3. *When the wicked cometh, then cometh also
contempt, and with ignominy reproach.*

Pride is one ingredient of the wicked man's character, and this disposes him to treat those with contempt
who are better men than himself. When he makes
his appearance, you need not wonder if you find contempt, and ignominy, and reproach in his company,
for he wishes to exalt himself upon the ruins of the
honour and good name of his neighbours.

The proud man has sagacity to find materials in
great abundance to furnish him with those titles of
scorn and reproach which he heaps on other men.
Poverty and calamity, natural infirmities, or ungrace-
fulness in behaviour, foibles and failings, are all employed by him for exposing his neighbours to contempt
and laughter. But good men are the chief objects of
his spleen, and if he can find nothing else to afford
him a handle for holding them up to scorn or reproach, he can make a dextrous use of their very virtues to serve his pride and malice.

To expose our innocent neighbours as the objects of
contempt or ignominy, is a very wicked thing, especially when they are saints who are treated in this dis-
respectful manner. He that mocketh the poor, reproacheth his Maker ; he that casts dirt in those faces
that shine with the beauties of holiness, is an enemy to
Christ, and to his beauteous image. What a pity is it,
that even the saints themselves should reproach or insult one another ! And yet it cannot be denied, that
party disputes have sometimes afforded instances of
this melancholy fact.

---

*Prov. 30:32

When we meet with contempt and reproach, let us remember that our Lord Jesus Christ met with it in a much larger degree for our sake, and hath left us an example of bearing it with patience. He hid not his face from shame and spitting; but gave his back to the smiters, and his cheeks to them that plucked off the hair.

But wicked men shall be paid in their own contempt. Michal despised David for his piety, and lived all her days under the reproach of barrenness. The text may admit of another meaning besides that we have given, that dishonour and disgrace follows wickedness at the heels. The wickedness and pride of men shall be re-compensed with shame and everlasting contempt *.

Ver. 4. *The words of a man's mouth are as deep waters, and the well-spring of wisdom as a flowing brook.*

The words of a crafty man may be compared to deep waters, because it is impossible to turn his thoughts from them; but this is not owing so much to his wit as his want of conscience, for he scruples not to speak in direct contradiction to his real sentiments; but God knows, and will reveal and punish his iniquity †.

The wise man seems here to speak of the words of a man that is furnished with a rich treasure of true wisdom. His words are like deep waters, not because he delights to express himself in riddles, and to conceal his treasures of wisdom from the eyes of others. He uses great plainness of speech; but there is more of solid sense and useful instruction in his words, than another man can apprehend at hearing them. Whilst men of shallow understandings pour forth a flood of words, in which there is scarcely a drop of matter, the truly wise man spares his words; but what he says

*Chap. 11:2   †Ps. 64:6,7

contains much in its narrow compass. Such were the words of Solomon himself, which filled the queen of Sheba with amazement, for the sagacity of that wise princess could not penetrate the depths of that wisdom which he conveyed in his discourses.

How valuable is the conversation of the wise! Their words are like oracles that deserve to be remembered, and to be the subject of our thoughts; and they supply us with refreshment and pleasure, like a flowing brook which never runs dry, but is ever ready to afford drink to the thirsty traveller *.

It is the word of God which furnishes the heart of a wise man with all those treasures of knowledge which are so justly compared to a spring of living waters. And the faithful sayings of God deserve this high character above all the words of the wisest men, that they are like deep waters. Our ears can receive but a little of them †, and therefore they ought to be our study day and night. We cannot expect much benefit by a cursory view of the scriptures; but when we search into any part of them, with a dependance on the Father of lights, we shall find not only treasures, but rich mines of what is more valuable than the purest gold.

Ver. 5. *It is not good to accept the person of the wicked, to overthrow the righteous in judgment.*

It is a very bad thing to justify the wicked, and a worse thing to condemn the righteous; but both these iniquities meet in the sin condemned in the text.

Although God loves the righteous, he will not accept their persons, so as to give wrong judgment for them against the wicked; and therefore, when David prays against his enemies, we usually find him plead-

---

*See Chap. 16:22   †Job 4:12

434 / *Exposition of Proverbs*

ing the goodness of his cause *. And Peter exhorts oppressed Christians to commit their souls in well-doing to God as to a faithful Creator.

If it were possible to accept the person of God himself, yet God hates partial dealings so much, that he would certainly reprove it †. Job's friends condemned that good man out of zeal for the glory of God, for they could not conceive how God could be righteous unless Job were wicked; and yet God did not approve of their conduct, but sharply censured them for endeavouring to vindicate his glory at Job's expence.

This sin of partiality in judging is no less detestable in ecclesiastical than in civil administrations. When men of riches and power are allowed to trample upon the liberties of the poor and mean, and when those that ought not to have a place and a name in the church, are permitted to usurp those powers that evidently belong, by Christ's appointment, to the body of the faithful, is it not plain that church-rulers are become partial in themselves, and judges of evil thoughts? Whatever property men may have in manses and stipends, they cannot from thence infer a right to constitute spiritual relations, which ought to be founded in mutual choice ‡.

There are other instances of partiality in church managements equally condemned in this place ||. When we take it on us to judge other men, without any call, against the command of Christ §, we too often run into this iniquity of partial judgment, by censuring the same faults in different persons, with different degrees of severity, as our affections lead us.

Ver. 6. *A fool's lips enter into contention, and his mouth calleth for strokes.*

*Ps. 17   †Job 13:8,10   ‡James 2 ||1 Tim. 5:21
§Matt. 7:1

Solomon has already represented very clearly the folly and danger of contention, and observation abundantly verifies his words ; and yet there are many people so foolish that nothing will warn them. Their lips enter into contention, and their mouth calls for strokes. Whilst they pour forth the venom of ill-nature in a torrent of spiteful reflections against their neighbours, they do not consider that they are calling for a stroke to themselves, by kindling up those passions which may provoke their antagonists to return their rage with good measure. That profane apostate, the emperor Julian, used to banter the Christians with that precept of our Lord, " When thine adversary smites thee on the one cheek, turn to him the other also :" but Christians consult their ease as well as their consciences when they obey this precept in the spirit of it ; whereas proud and passionate fools, when they give vent to their rancorous spirits, because they cannot bear the shadow of an indignity, not only turn the other cheek to their adversary, but smite, and urge, and almost force him to strike and destroy them. It may be justly said, that—

Ver. 7. *A fool's mouth is his destruction, and his lips are the snare of his soul.*

For men to be destroyed on account of the transgression of their lips, is a grievous though just punishment ; but the text represents the calamity which they bring upon themselves, in a still stronger light. They are not only the causes, but the agents of their own destruction ; by their lips they are caught in a snare, and by their lips they are ruined. It was a severe, though unjust censure, which Eliphaz passed on Job, when he said, " Thine own mouth condemneth thee, and not I, and thine own lips testify against thee." But here Solomon tells us that fools, who have not the command of their tongues, are not only condemned, but punished by their own mouths. Their own tongues, as David expresses it, shall fall upon them; and when men's tongues fall upon themselves, they are crushed under the weight. The tongues of other men may pierce into our vitals, but the sharpest and most envenomed words of other men can never wound a man so incurably as his own.

It was a more mortifying punishment for Haman to be hanged on a gibbet erected by himself, than if he had been hanged in the most disgraceful manner on any other gallows. The contentious fool is like Haman; he erects a gallows for himself, and twists those cords by which he is strangled. But Haman could not well know that he was working for himself; whereas the lover of strife has fair warning of his danger from the word of God, and therefore must fall unpitied if he will not be reformed.

Ver. 8. *The words of a tale-bearer are as wounds, and they go down into the innermost parts of the belly.*

It is just that a fool's mouth should become the instrument of his own destruction, for his words are arrows that make deep, and sometimes fatal wounds in other men.

Men may in some cases report the faults of others, without exposing themselves to the censure of this text. Joseph reported the faults of his brethren to his father, that his authority might reclaim them; and we are authorised by our Lord to complain to the church of an offending brother, when he will not suffer himself to be gained by a private admonition. But when men publish bad things of their neighbours through spite or levity, or to have the pleasure of hearing themselves talk, then they deserve the name of tale-bearers, and incur the reproofs given to such pestilent members of society in this book.

The tales which this kind of men tell are sometimes entirely false, and at other times have some truth in them, although they seldom want some dash of slander, to heighten their relish to those who love to feed on the faults and misfortunes of their fellow-creatures.

The words of tale-bearers are as wounds, and these wounds are of a very dangerous kind, for they pierce into the inmost parts of the belly. They wound the character, and often destroy the usefulness of those who have the misfortune to be the mark of these arrows of the tongue. Those who give these deadly wounds do not always mean all the mischief they effect, being instigated, not by downright spite, but by a pleasure they have in speaking, whilst they are destitute of good materials for conversation. But why can they not hold their peace? If you kill your neighbour in sport, or for want of better employment, will it be a sufficient excuse for you to allege that you had no intention to do it, or that you did it for want of better employment? Know you not that a man's name is as dear to him as his life, and his usefulness perhaps dearer to him than either of them? By wanton cruelty to others, men often bring serious misery upon themselves.

Ver. 9. *He also that is slothful in his work, is brother to him that is a great waster.*

Slothfulness in business is commonly a companion of tale-bearing; and both of them are more dangerous iniquities than men generally apprehend, and need to be seriously and frequently remonstrated against.

A man with half an eye may see that the prodigal will soon reduce himself to husks; and with a little attention, we may know that a slothful man is only a younger brother to him, and will come to poverty as certainly, though not with so much speed. The man that runs will speedily arrive at the end of his journey, but he that follows him with a slower pace, will arrive at it in good time. He that spends his days in riot, takes his estate and casts it into a devouring gulph; but he that neglects his business, suffers a moth to devour his substance. Both these sins are breaches of the eighth commandment, though in different degrees.

There is the like difference between the careless Christian and the profane sinner. Sloth in religion is a consumption which preys upon the vitals, but open profaneness is a burning fever, which will more rapidly destroy the constitution. Let us not be slothful, otherwise we are followers, though at a distance, of those who have already plunged themselves into perdition by their wickedness. But let us follow them, who by faith and patience inherit the promises.

Ver. 10. *The name of the Lord is a strong tower; the righteous runneth into it, and is safe.*

Nations use to provide fortifications and arms for their defence, even in time of peace; and if they are so imprudent as to neglect these precautions, they are in imminent danger of destruction when an enemy makes an attack. In like manner, when we know that life is exposed to the incursions of calamity, and that we are surrounded with legions of invisible enemies, it is our wisdom to be provided with a sure defence, that we may be safe in the day of battle and war.

No creature in heaven or earth can defend us against the assaults of misfortune, or the more dangerous attacks of invisible adversaries, nor have we any power or wisdom of our own to afford us security. Our safety is only in the name of the Lord, that God with whom is everlasting strength and sufficiency, and who reveals himself through his blessed Son our Saviour, as the refuge of fallen men. In this great name protection is to be found from the distresses of the present life, from the tyranny of sin, from everlasting wrath, from the temptations of the devil, from the terrors of death, from every evil, and from every fear.

David in the day of his distress haunted the caves of

Engedi, and the mountains of the wild goats ; but we find in his history, and in many of his psalms, that these were insufficient for his protection, and that his confidence was ever placed on God himself as his tower of salvation. In him he trusted, and was helped ; and therefore his heart greatly rejoiced, and with his tongue did he praise him.

But he was not the confidence of David alone ; he has ever been the dwelling-place of the generation of the righteous. They run by faith and prayer into this high tower in the day of their calamity and danger, and they are not at a loss when unexpected dangers are ready to overwhelm them, for no enemy can be so near to distress as God is to preserve. He is ever a present, a very present help in the time of trouble *.

But are poor sinners excluded from this refuge ? Will they be expelled from it, if they come to shelter themselves under the protection of the merciful God ? No, in no wise. The righteous runneth into it, and none that run into it continue unrighteous. But it is accessible to sinners also, for the name of the Lord is " the Lord, the Lord God merciful and gracious, long-suffering, and abundant in goodness and truth, keeping mercy for thousands, forgiving iniquity †," &c. And sinners are invited into this tower of salvation by God himself ‡.

Eternal safety is enjoyed by all that run into this tower, for it can never be undermined, or scaled, or destroyed, by all the devils in hell ; and no enemy can break into it by force, or find a way by fraud to enter. None can so much as climb up to this refuge, to endanger the safety of those happy persons who have made it their habitation ; nor is there any want of ne-

---

*Ps. 46   †Exod. 34:6,7   ‡Isa. 55:7,8, Job 6:37

cessaries ever felt in it, for he that is the defence of his people is their all-sufficient portion, and heavenly Father. The place of their defence is the munition of rocks ; bread shall be given them, and their water shall be sure.

Surely if we have any wisdom, we will endeavour diligently to learn the way of running into this tower; and we cannot learn it better than by taking David for our pattern, whom we see, in many of his psalms, fleeing unto God to hide him. Let us read these divine compositions, and pray for the same spirit of faith which animated that holy man, and endeavour to follow the steps of his faith *.

Ver. 11. *The rich man's wealth is his strong city, and as an high wall in his own conceit.*

Few of the rich are righteous. God is the hope and strength of his people ; but the rich are generally dazzled with the lustre of their gold and jewels, and mistake those precious metals for gods ; and so they say unto the gold, Thou art our hope, and to the fine gold, Thou art our confidence. They trust not to the Rock of ages, but lean upon a broken reed which will soon break, and pierce their arms, and leave them to fall into perdition, after they have been pierced through with many sorrows.

Riches are good things when they are well used, but confidence in riches is a grievous sin, because it is an alienation of the spirit from God, who requires the homage of the heart still more than the worship of the knee. It is a source of many iniquities, because it prompts men to injustice and oppression, to despise God, and to forget death and judgment. It shuts up men's bowels of compassion from the indigent, and makes it as difficult for men to get into the kingdom of

---

*Deut. 33:26-29

God, as for a camel to pass through the eye of a needle.

This second warning the wise man here gives against this vain confidence. Examine yourselves, ye rich men, and see whether you have not the symptoms of this vain confidence. Trust not in uncertain riches, but in the living God, and shew that your confidence is in God by a readiness to lend unto the Lord *.

Murmur not, ye that are poor, because you are not under the same temptation with some others, to make to yourselves gods of gold. Trust in the Lord, and you shall want no good thing.

Ver. 12. *Before destruction the heart of man is haughty; and before honour is humility.*

The ruin of all mankind, and of millions of angels, is a tremendous proof of the first part of this text. The abasement and exaltation of our Redeemer, is a glorious illustration of the other clause.

Solomon gives us repeated warnings of the danger of pride, and the necessity of a humble spirit; but we need them all, for vile and worthless as we are, humility is a very great stranger in our world, and pride is a sin so insinuating, that most men's hearts, and even their religion, is quite corrupted by it.

Proud men stand on the edge of a fearful precipice, from whence they will soon tumble into destruction. But blessed are the poor in spirit; they may be at present in the valley of abasement, but they shall dwell for ever with God in his holy hill, for theirs is the kingdom of heaven.

Ver. 13. *He that answereth a matter before he heareth it, it is folly and shame unto him.*

Men pique themselves upon their penetration and

---

*1 Tim. 6:17, Ps. 62:10

quickness of discernment, and to display this talent, are often too hasty to give their judgment upon a point, before they are well informed of it ; but this rash manner of judging, especially in matters of consequence, is their folly and shame ; they discover their ignorance and pride, when they expect to have their sagacity applauded. Instead of pronouncing peremptorily upon a half hearing of a thing, it is often needful to hear it once and again, and to hear different persons concerning it, that we may not be drawn into false conclusions by the prejudices and partiality of those whom we first heard on the subject.

This is a necessary instruction to magistrates, who may be guilty of crying injustice, by pronouncing a hasty sentence in a cause that comes before them. Philip king of Macedonia, having given sentence against a widow in a cause she had before him, was so sensible of his injustice upon second thoughts, that he condemned himself to pay her damages. But kings are seldom so honest as to acknowledge their mistakes, and therefore they ought to be very careful that they do not fall into them. The pride of sovereigns established that law in Persia, that the royal decrees should not be reversed ; and other princes, although they do not make such pretences to royal infallibility, have nevertheless too high a sense of dignity to be easily brought to an acknowledgment of errors.

Ministers of the word of God are instructed by this rule, not to be rash with their mouths to utter any thing as the word of God in the pulpit, but to consider well what they are to say in the name of the Lord ; and to use due deliberation and enquiry before they give their judgment in cases of conscience, lest they should make sins and duties which God never made, by a wrong application of the word of God to particular cases, or distress the minds of God's people, and encourage sinners, by giving a rash opinion on the state of their souls.

This rule is to be observed by all men in giving advice, or in judging of men's characters or actions, when they have any call to judge on them.

The Jews condemned our Lord as a Sabbath-breaker, because he made a man whole on it; but he tells them that they sinned by judging too rashly : " Ye judge according to outward appearance, but judge righteous judgment."

We ought to be the more cautious in forming and pronouncing opinions, because we are so little disposed to admit conviction if we fall into mistakes, or to retract them upon conviction. It is commonly supposed that ministers cannot repent, although they do not claim, like the Pope, the gift of infallibility ; and there is too much reason for the supposition, provided it be not restricted to that order of men ; for the same pride that makes one set of men stubborn in their wrong opinions is to be found in other men, although it is not perhaps so much strengthened by particular circumstances, nor so visible in their conduct, because they meet not with the same temptations to discover it. How many do we find who will not change their sentiments about religion, or about persons and things, upon the clearest evidence, and give way to anger upon the least contradiction to their favourite notions, as if their dearest interests were attacked ! Saints themselves are not entirely delivered from this selfish disposition, as we see in the behaviour of David to Mephibosheth, after he had pronounced a rash sentence in his case.

Ver. 14. *The spirit of a man will sustain his infirmity ; but a wounded spirit who can bear ?*

When the spirit of a man is free of wounds, it will enable a man to bear an incredible load of distress. That courage which is derived from natural constitution, or moral principles, enabled some of the pagan heroes to behave with astonishing firmness under the greatest pressure of calamity. Cæsar subdued all the world except the invincible soul of Cato, and Epictetus suffered his barbarous master to break his leg, without the least expression of resentment. But the true Christian is the true hero. Thousands, through the faith of Christ, have encountered with resignation and joy the rage of beasts, and flames, and tyrants. Cato and Brutus were cowards compared with the apostle Paul. They killed themselves, and deserted their country, that they might escape from the miseries of life. But Paul was content to die every day for the service of the church, and yet still live absent from the Lord, the life of all his joys.

But a wounded spirit is absolutely intolerable. It is a very hell upon earth, and has often made the most courageous of men, and the best of saints, to roar through the disquiet of their hearts. When the conscience is pierced with a deep sense of guilt, and the heart alarmed with the dreadful apprehensions of eternal misery, then the affrighted eye seems to behold upon the walls the hand-writing that amazed the mighty king of Babylon, and unsinewed all his joints. Every earthly comfort is to a man in this situation like the white of an egg; mirth appears to be madness, and nothing has any relish, but what gives some prospect of deliverance from this intolerable anguish.

Blessed be Jesus, whose soul was amazed, and environed with sorrows not his own. He never knew sin, and yet he felt the tremendous impressions of wrath upon his blessed soul, for he bare our sins in his own body on the tree, that by his stripes we might be healed.

If the presages of hell are so astonishingly dreadful,

what must hell itself be ? May we have grace to flee to Jesus, who hath delivered us from the wrath to come.

It is sin that causes this terrible anguish which none can endure, and sin unpardoned will cause it sooner or later in every transgressor. Why then should we thus wound and mangle our own souls, by fighting against God ? If we shoot these arrows against the Almighty, they cannot wound his honour ; but he can soon dip them in the venom of his wrath and curse, and shoot them back into our own souls *.

Ver. 15. *The heart of the prudent getteth knowledge ; and the ear of the wise seeketh knowledge.*

The prudent man has a due apprehension of the value of knowledge, and seeks it with all his heart, and finds it. The Spirit of God writes the word of truth upon his heart, and inscribes it in his inward part ; and whilst others have it only in their memories or tongues, he has it in his heart, which is filled with the love of knowledge, and enriched with this precious treasure.

But he is not satisfied with that measure of knowledge he has already got. He would not part with it for mines of gold, or mountains of prey, but he wishes still to add to his stock, and therefore his ear is employed in seeking knowledge.

The ear is the learning sense, and the wise man will hearken attentively to any man that can give him useful information ; but he attends chiefly upon the ministry of the word, because that is the appointed mean of increasing his knowledge and animating his soul. Although he meditates daily on the testimonies of God, yet he does not satisfy himself with the suggestions of his own mind, but feeds his meditating faculty with the word read and heard †.

Those that wish for no more knowledge or grace

---

*Ps. 1, 21, 22   †Rom. 10:17

than they think absolutely necessary for getting to heaven, all that think their stock of knowledge sufficient, and all those that neglect the means of grace, are excluded from the class of prudent men by this sentence of Solomon.

Ver. 16. *A man's gift maketh room for him, and bringeth him before great men.*

It is a shame for great men to love, Give ye. They should remember what our Lord says, " It is more blessed to give than to receive." Great men have received their great power, to do good to others ; and poor men should not find the way so strait to their presence, as to have occasion for gifts to widen it. The King of glory admits the meanest of men freely into his presence, and will do justice to the poor and needy, and send them every needful supply *.

It appears from this proverb, that riches cannot satisfy the heart of man ; the great and rich of the world are as eager to receive, and as much under the influence of money, as the poor. Silver and gold may dazzle the eyes, but they cannot fill, even whilst they encumber the heart.

Yet it is not in every case unlawful for great men to receive gifts, nor for men of inferior station to bestow them. Great men may cheerfully receive them as expressions of gratitude, for favours of a higher kind conferred, or to be conferred on their inferiors. And poor men may lawfully give them to procure favours, though not to obtain justice in a court of law †.

Blessed be the Lord, who makes us welcome to come to his throne without money and without price, to receive the richest gifts. May his gifts make room for him in our souls !

---

*Ps. 72:12-14   †Gen. 33, Rom. 2:3

Ver. 17. *He that is first in his own cause seemeth just; but his neighbour cometh and searcheth him out.*

When God came down to take vengeance on the men of Sodom and Gomorrah for their wickedness, he said, " I will see whether the wickedness is as great as the cry that is come unto me; and if not, I will know." God is not ignorant of any thing that men do, but he speaks in our language, and intends, by this manner of expression, not only to represent his own justice, but to teach righteousness to earthly judges. By judging in a cause without searching it out, David injured the son of his generous friend; and Ahasuerus, by the like conduct, exposed the people of his queen to destruction, and signed a warrant for her own death, and was forced to see that the Persian laws could not make their kings infallible.

An eloquent speaker will make his own cause appear a great deal better, and that of his adversary a great deal worse than it really is; and therefore a just judge will not decide, nor even form a judgment within his own mind, till the parties are both heard. Claudius the emperor, who had no malignity but what was put into him by others, has rendered his name for ever infamous by judging causes after hearing only one of the parties, and sometimes neither of them.

Rome, in its pagan state, would never have allowed of a court so manifestly contrived by the father of wickedness, as that of the Inquisition; but made it a rule that no man should be reputed guilty till he had seen his accuser face to face, and enjoyed the liberty of answering for himself.

In private life, it is proper that we should know what a man can say for himself and his behaviour, before we punish him in his character. If we will judge our neighbours, we should certainly act the part of impartial judges, and not believe bad things of men, upon the report of tale-bearers, or those who are too plainly under the influence of prejudice against the persons whom they accuse.

In religious disputes, it is a great injustice to depend for the character of a sect, or an impartial representation of their doctrines, upon one whom partiality has blinded, and rendered unfit, however honest he may be, to do them justice. Party-spirit has as much influence as gifts, to blind the eyes of the wise, and to pervert the words of the righteous.

It may, however, be a great satisfaction to us, that we may judge, as far as we have any occasion to do so, for ourselves, in the most important religious contentions, without hearing either of the parties. A man may easily know from the Bible, whether Christ is the supreme God, without the help of either Clark or Waterland. The Bereans could readily judge whether Paul's doctrine was true or not, by searching the scriptures, without putting themselves to the trouble of hearing what the Jewish doctors could say against it.

Causes between private persons are thus to be decided by an impartial judgment, founded upon good evidence ; but how shall those contentions be decided, that arise between princes, who are too high to have any magistrate above them, and too proud to refer their differences to an arbitrator ?

Ver. 18. *The lot causeth contentions to cease, and parteth between the mighty.*

The contentions of princes are very dangerous, because pride will not suffer either party to yield, and their power enables them to interest millions in their cause. How often have oceans of blood been spilt, and nations been loaded with the most oppressive taxes, and great kingdoms utterly subverted and laid desolate, in the prosecution of their quarrels ! The good agreement of kings, is like ointment on Aaron's head, which descended to the skirts of his garments. Their animosities are like dangerous wounds in the head, which are felt to the sole of the foot.

Why may not the lot determine their quarrels ? They are too great to refer their causes to an earthly judge, but the whole disposing of the lot is of the Lord.

It is a mercy to men that God has provided a method so safe and easy for determining controversies, that must otherwise be decided by the sword ; but it is the sin of men, that they will rather have matters settled their own way, whatever it may cost, than by means of an ordinance of God.

As the whole disposing of the lot is of the Lord, those who agree to have their businesses determined by it, must reverence the providence of God in it, and rest cheerfully satisfied with the determination, and thus it will make contentions to cease.

Let us never prostitute to trifling uses, an ordinance designed for such great and merciful ends.

Ver. 19. *A brother offended is harder to be won than a strong city ; and their contentions are like the bars of a castle.*

That law which binds us to love our relations, obliges us, if we have unhappily differed with them, to be easily pacified, and even to seek peace with them, although we have been the wronged party. Abraham would not live in a state of contention with Lot, because they were brethren ; and to put an end to the strife of their servants, he yielded to him, though only his nephew, the power of chusing what part of the land he would take to himself.

But such is the perverseness of human nature, that contentions between brethren are generally more irremediable than any others. When we meet with provocation where we thought we had all the reason in the world to expect a contrary behaviour, we can scarcely find in our hearts to bestow forgiveness ; and thus it is easier to win a strong city, or to break in pieces the bars of a castle, than to heal breaches in families and amongst near friends.

It is therefore our duty to guard against those mischiefs which are so much easier prevented than removed; and with this view, we must not wantonly provoke our friends, nor be ready to take offence at their conduct. But if we are involved in contention with them, the authority of God should constrain us to mortify that unforgiving disposition which would prevent a cordial reconciliation. The love of Christ has broken in pieces for us the gates of brass, and cut in sunder the iron bars of our infernal prison ; and why should not our most stubborn enmities be dissolved by the apprehensions of it ?

Jacob used all possible means to obtain the good graces of his brother Esau after their unhappy difference, and yet it is a question whether their reconciliation was cordial and lasting. Their posterity kept up the strife, and Edom did tear perpetually, and kept his wrath for ever, as Obadiah tells us. This example teaches us what means we should use for healing such breaches, but at the same time admonishes us to prevent, if possible, the need of using them.

Ver. 20. *A man's belly shall be satisfied with the fruit of his mouth ; and with the increase of his lips shall he be filled.*

Bad men are never satisfied with their vain or wicked discourse, and a good man never thinks he has served God or his generation sufficiently by the good use of his tongue, which is his glory. But both good and bad men shall be filled with the product of their tongues, in happiness or misery.

If a man were possessed of a field exceedingly pro-

ductive, either of good fruits, or of noisome and poisonous herbs, according to the cultivation bestowed on it,
what pains would he use to clear it of every weed,
and to have it sown with good grain ! and yet when
the harvest is come, he may take his choice whether
he will eat of the product or not.   Such a field is the
tongue of man, with this difference, that a man is
obliged to eat the fruit of it, although it should be
worse than hemlock.   What care, then, should we use
to pluck from our hearts every root of bitterness, and
to have them furnished with knowledge and prudence,
that our discourse may be good, to the use of edifying !

The fruits of the tongue are either very bitter, or
very pleasant.

Ver. 21. *Death and life are in the power of the tongue ;
and they that love it shall eat the fruit thereof.*

Our tongues, as we have been frequently told in this
book, are often the instruments of life or death to
others.   But it is the fruit of our own tongues with
which we must chiefly be filled.   A fool's mouth is
his destruction *, and a wise man's mouth is oftentimes his safety.   He that would live a long and a
happy life, let him take care how he uses his tongue †.
And at the last day, when evil-speakers are cast into a
fiery furnace ‡, the fruits of the sanctified tongue will
be produced as evidences of a man's title to everlasting
life.

It is not the use of the tongue on some particular
occasion that will determine a man's happiness or
misery, but the love of a good or bad tongue.   Saints
may, through the influence of provocation and passion,
speak unadvisedly with their lips ; and sinners may
speak many good words, when their hearts are not
right with God.   But he that loves to speak as be-

*Verse 7   †Ps. 34:11,12   ‡Ps. 141, Rev. 21:8

cometh a saint, shall eat good by the fruit of his mouth ;
and he that takes pleasure in vain or ungodly discourse,
shall meet with a just and dreadful recompence.

If, after all that the wise man has said, we bridle
not our tongue, with what eyes will we look to Solomon at the last day ! or rather, how shall we look our
Judge in the face, who speaks to us in this book, and
who taught the same lessons by his own blessed mouth
in the days of his flesh * !

Ver. 22. *Whoso findeth a wife findeth a good thing,
and obtaineth favour of the Lord.*

It was not good for man in the days of innocence to
be alone, and an help meet for us is still more needful,
amidst those calamities that embitter the life of fallen
men ; for two are better than one, because when one
of them meets with a misfortune, the other is ready to
afford some relief.

A wife that is rottenness in her husband's bones, is
no doubt a bad thing, for sin and folly will turn the
choicest blessings of life into oppressive burdens. Such
a woman deserves not this endearing title.

A good wife is an excellent thing, and is to be
sought from the Lord. When Abraham wanted to
have a wife for his son, he prayed to God. His servant prayed, and Isaac went out into the fields to meditate, and probably to pray likewise.

The man that has found a wife, has obtained favour
from the Lord, and ought to acknowledge him with
thanksgiving. It is God who made the woman for
the man, and has preserved an equality between the
sexes by his providence, and appointed marriage, and
directs every man to his own wife, and disposes her
heart to this tender union. If we are to thank God
for the pleasures of friendship, what thanks are due to

*Matt. 5:22, 12:36,37

him for the pleasures of the most delightful union, whereby of twain are made one flesh !

Ver. 23. *The poor useth entreaties; but the rich answereth roughly.*

It cannot be denied that the rich have many particular advantages ; but the poor have no reason to repine, for poverty has also its gains, one of which is, that it teaches us one of the best lessons,—that of humility. The poor have a daily experience of their dependent condition, which instructs them in the language of submission and lowliness ; and when the Spirit of God sanctifies this condition of life to a man, it leads him to great improvements in that grace on which Christ pronounces the first of his blessings—poverty of spirit. A little of this holy and humble temper is worth all the gold and silver in the world.

Some, indeed, are poor and proud, and they are the most inexcusable of all the proud persons that can be found on the earth, for they not only sin without a temptation, but in opposition to a providential remedy. However, their poverty still preserves them from many bad fruits of pride that are to be found with the rich.

The rich answer roughly, for their riches produce self-confidence, and that makes them insolent towards God himself *. And it need not surprise poor men, that those who can say, Who is the Lord ? can give rough and uncivil words to them.

We should all consider the advantages of our different situations, that we may be thankful, and make a good use of them, and the temptations that are incident to our respective situations, that we may be on our guard. Let poor men take heed that the necessity they lie under of using intreaties, may not degene-

---

*Prov. 30:9

454 / *Exposition of Proverbs*

rate into a slavish meanness of spirit, disposing them to sell their consciences for bread ; and let the rich remember, that they are infinitely more dependent on the great Patron of the poor and needy, than the poor on them. Those that give nothing but good words to the poor in their distress, are declared to be destitute of charity. In what class, then, must they be placed, who cannot afford even this poor favour ?

The poor and the rich are alike poor before God, and without his rich bounty must be eternally wretched. If poor men supplicate the rich for their favours, with what words shall we express our meanness and absolute dependence, before Him who regardeth not the rich more than the poor ! But he never gives a rough answer to his suppliants. Let us therefore come boldly to his throne of grace, that we may obtain every needful supply *.

Ver. 24. *A man that hath friends must shew himself friendly ; and there is a friend that sticketh closer than a brother.*

A man that hath found a wife must shew himself affectionate and tender; a father must discover kindness; every person must endeavour to fill up the offices of the various relations in which he stands. A neighbour must shew himself a social man ; and he that has a bosom friend, must discover in his behaviour all that union of souls that is the very essence of friendship. Religion requires us to perform all those kind services to one another, which, if they were duly discharged and returned, would still make our world in some measure a picture of paradise.

We must not suffer unreasonable disgusts to alienate our affections from our friends, but cleave to them

---

*Job 23:3-7

while we live ; we must often gladden their hearts by our company, and share in all their joys and sorrows. We must not renounce their friendship for their imperfections, nor even for those temporary coldnesses which they may discover in the day of our distress, unless their behaviour is such as to shew that their professions of regard were not sincere. Above all, we must shew our tender sympathy in the time of their calamity, otherwise our alienation will greatly embitter their distress *.

To excite us to this duty, we are told that friends sometimes stick closer than the nearest relations. The greatest acts of generous heroism have perhaps been performed by those who were not connected by the bonds of relation or affinity. None of David's brothers ever gave him such proofs of their attachment as Jonathan ; and even his wife Michal, though she loved him, did not love him so well as that gallant friend did. She lied to his prejudice, to screen herself from the resentment of her father ; but Jonathan bravely incurred the resentments of his father, and cheerfully gave up his prospects of a crown, for David. When our Lord was crucified, his disciples forsook him and fled, and James and Jude, who had the honour of being our Lord's brethren, among the rest ; but the beloved disciple looked on his sorrows with the eye of a friend, and received his charge about his mother with thankfulness and obedience.

If this is a reason for our friendly behaviour to our friends, what regard ought we to shew to our Lord Jesus Christ, who sticks to us infinitely closer than any friend ! Having loved his own which were in the world, he loved them unto the end. Neither death,

---

*Job 6:14-19

nor sin itself, can separate us from his love. What shall we render to him for his marvellous loving-kindness? Love and obedience; for we are his friends, if we do whatsoever he commands us.

Proverbs 19

Ver. 1. *Better is the poor that walketh in his integrity,*
than he that is perverse in his lips, and is a fool.

So depraved are the understandings of men, that the
rich are generally honoured for their wealth, although
their conversation shews them to be destitute of any
valuable quality ; whilst the poor are despised, though
they are adorned with the beauties of religion. To
give an outward respect to the rich, according to the
innocent fashions of the place where we live, is not a
sin ; for if providence make a distinction, we may do
it likewise, between the rich and the poor ; but it is a
sign of great corruption in our minds, to value the rich
as if they were worthier men, and more deserving of
our esteem and affection than the poor, when grace
hath made a plain difference in favour of the poor, of a
kind infinitely more important than the outward gifts
of providence ever made. The bad effects of this unjust preference are severely censured by James, in the
first half of the second chapter of his epistle.

We ought undoubtedly to follow God, in the judgment which he gives of things and persons, as far as that judgment is revealed ; and we find that he sets no value upon riches. He bestows them oftentimes on those whom he abhors, and denies them to his favourites. But the upright, however poor, are his delight. He glories in Job as a perfect and upright man, and he still bestows higher commendations on him, after he was stripped of all his substance, because he had given additional proof of his stedfast integrity *.

When Christ was on earth, he was a poor man that walked in his integrity, and surely the lovers of Christ will never value a man the less, because he is as Christ also was in the world. In short, the upright man, however poor and mean, is not only a man of better dispositions and behaviour than the rich sinner, but he is also incomparably happier and richer, and shall be rich as long as God himself is rich.

Be satisfied and thankful, ye that are taught by the Spirit of God, to walk in your integrity. You are rich in faith, and heirs of the kingdom ; and in this world you have and shall have every thing that infinite wisdom and love sees fit for you †.

Here the poor may see a certain method of being rich, or of obtaining what is far better than riches. Labour not to be rich in gold and silver, but seek after that which Christ calls the true riches, and which he will dispense unto those that seek them in his appointed way ‡.

Let not the rich man glory in his wealth : if he is perverse in his lips, he is poor and miserable, and blind, and naked ; and the esteem of men will not counterbalance the abhorrence of God ||. Go to Christ under deep impressions of your poverty, and buy of him gold tried in the fire, and you shall be truly rich.

---

*Job 1,2   †1 Cor 3:21,22   ‡John 6:27, Matt. 6:33
||Ps. 10:4

Ver. 2. *Also that the soul be without knowledge, it is not good; and he that hasteth with his feet, sinneth.*

The want of that knowledge which we need for our direction through life, is very pernicious; for we are in a dangerous world, full of pits and snares; and the man that has not eyes in his head, must fall, sooner or later, into destruction. When the blind are led by the blind, they cannot well avoid falling into the ditch. But blind sinners are led by a quick-sighted and crafty devil, who will certainly land them in perdition *.

Although we have knowledge in our heads, it will not profit us, unless we have it also in our hearts. Knowledge, when it is not loved and reduced into practice, will serve only to bear testimony for God against the abuser of light, and to heighten his condemnation. A man of much knowledge, and a bad practice, carries about him, like Uriah, that which will prove his own death.

To want knowledge, is not good: to have knowledge, and not to use it as the directory of our life, cannot be one jot better; and he that hasteth with his feet, and takes no heed to his way, sinneth.

It is no sin, but a duty, to run in the way of God's commandments; and it was an evidence of David's wisdom, that he made haste, and delayed not to run out of the paths of sin, when he considered whither they would lead him; but to run on, without consideration, whithersoever our fancy or our passions lead us, exposes us to much sin and danger; and therefore we are commanded to walk circumspectly, keeping our eye upon the ground we tread, that it may not be slippery, and observing the rule of duty, that we may not transgress it. Even in those businesses that are lawful, we will be drawn into sin, without circumspection; for the devil has snares spread for us everywhere in this evil

---

*Eph. 2:3

world, and he that makes haste to be rich, shall not be innocent.

Although we ought to run in the ways of the Lord, and not faint, yet rashness in our religious course will be attended with much sin. We must carry the lamp of truth with us, otherwise, by running in the dark, we will certainly stumble *.

As rashness and inconsideration are sinful, so they are the causes of a great deal of the sin that is in the world. Men would not choose, or at least they would not so resolutely keep the ways of iniquity, were it not that they want knowledge and thought, as Isaiah clearly shews in the case of idolaters †.

Ver. 3. *The foolishness of man perverteth his way, and his heart fretteth against the Lord.*

Let no man say when he is tempted, I am tempted by God: God tempts no man, but every man is tempted when he is seduced into evil by the blindness of his own mind, and the perverseness of his own heart. The world and the devil may indeed persuade us to sin, but none of them can force us. When a man sins, he does more mischief to himself than all the legions of hell can do to him; and therefore, whenever our way is perverted, we must chiefly blame ourselves. It would be blasphemy to charge the most holy God with our sins, and it is folly to transfer the fault unto our seducers; for if our enemy should persuade us to stab ourselves to the heart, it is our own madness to comply.

When our way is perverted, we soon feel the miserable consequences of our folly; for wretchedness, in one form or other, follows sin, as the shadow follows the body: but we are so loath to blame ourselves for the consequences of our own folly, that our hearts will rather fret against the Lord, as if he were the cause of our ruin. Adam laid the blame of his fall upon the woman, whom God gave to be with him, indirectly

---

*Chap. 4:12   †Isa. 44:19,20

transferring his own folly to his Maker; and it is natural and common for men to follow the example of their common parent. This corrupt disposition is not entirely rooted out of the saints themselves. It was David's fault that he did not cause the ark to be carried in the proper manner from the house of Obededom; and yet when God made a breach upon the people on that account, David was displeased.

Men are oftener guilty of this sin than they imagine. Our hearts fret against the Lord, by fretting at the ministers and instruments of his providence; and therefore, when the people murmured against Moses in the wilderness, he tells them that their murmuring was not against him and his brother Aaron, but against the Lord. David would not fret against Shimei, because he looked upon him as an instrument employed by God for his correction.

Instead of fretting, it is our duty to accept of the punishment of our iniquity, and to bless God that matters are not so bad with us as we deserve; for wherefore should a living man complain, when the damned have no just reason to do it? If our troubles come upon us without any particular reason from our own conduct, yet reflections upon God would be very unjust. Job's troubles were extremely grievous, and they came upon him without cause in himself, as God testifies, Job ii. yet he was made humbly to acknowledge his great folly in reflecting upon God for his distresses, before his captivity was turned back.

Ver. 4. *Wealth maketh many friends, but the poor is separated from his neighbour.*

God commands us to love our neighbours as ourselves, whether rich or poor, and to shew a peculiar tenderness to the poor on account of their destitute circumstances; but such is the depraved disposition of

men, that the rich have many friends, but the poor man
is not known by him that lives at the next door.

The rich have many temptations to high-mindedness,
and this is one of them: that they meet with a great
deal of respect, and every person professes friendship
to them, and they naturally think that they are possessed of many good qualities, which draw to them the
esteem of mankind; but they ought to consider, that
money answers all things, and is one of the chief attractives of esteem in the world. Let them throw away
their money, and those that once made their court to
them will leave them, as quickly as the eagles leave a
field of battle when the carcases are all devoured. Job
was the most respected man in the east, when he was
the richest; but when he was spoiled of his wealth,
he that had been as the tabret of the people, became
their byeword. Jerusalem, in her prosperity, was the
princess among the provinces, but in the day of her
calamity all her friends dealt treacherously with her,
and became her enemies. A very ordinary virtue in an
ordinary man, is a shining virtue in a man of fortune;
but if he should become poor, all the lustre of his great
qualities is entirely gone.

When the poor man is separated from his neighbour,
let him remember and imitate the apostle of the Gentiles, who was often reduced to poverty and hunger.
Paul laid very little stress on good report or bad report,
for he knew that none of these things, nor any thing
else, could separate him from the love of Christ *.

Ver. 5. *A false witness shall not be unpunished, and
he that speaketh lies shall not escape.*

A false witness does one of the greatest injuries to
his neighbour, and one of the greatest possible dishonours to God. He breaks at once the two great commandments, of loving God, and loving his brother, and

---

*See chap. 14:20

therefore deserves severe punishment *. But if he escape punishment from the magistrate, he shall be punished by God with the loss of credit, and other miseries, in this life, or at least, with an eternal punishment hereafter; for those that bear false witness against their neighbours are an abomination to the Lord, and how is it possible for them to escape †?

Liars are here classed with them that bear false witness, for they are so much alike, that the ninth commandment, which directly forbids the bearing of false witness, does also, by good interpretation, forbid whatsoever is prejudicial to truth; and those that can allow themselves to tell lies in common conversation, will, in all probability, bear false witness, and confirm it by an appeal to heaven, when they have a sufficient temptation. Some liars may expect to be safe, because their lies are not of a mischievous kind, but when they do evil that good may come, they expose themselves to just condemnation. All liars, says our great judge, shall have their part in the infernal lake ‡.

Ver. 6. *Many will entreat the favour of the prince, and every man is a friend to him that giveth gifts.*

It is, no doubt, a right thing to honour princes, and to seek their favour when we need it, if God is not neglected, from whom every man's judgment comes. The Lord is the king of kings, and it is a plain evidence that we forget God, when we are less anxious about his favour, than men are about the favour of our fellow worms.

Princes need not pride themselves in the homage that is paid to them, for their favour is sought by men, not so much out of regard to their persons, as from a regard to their power. Kindness and liberality have a greater influence for gaining the hearts of men, than dignity of station. There are many that seek the ruler's

---

*Deut. 19:16-21   †Chap. 6:10   ‡Rev. 21:8

favour, but every man loves him that is generous. When power and generosity meet in the same person, he becomes an object of universal esteem, like Marcus Antoninus, who was lamented by every man when he was dead, as if the glory of the Roman empire had died with him.

How inexcusable are we, if we do not love God with all our hearts. His gifts to us are past number, and all the gifts of men to us are the fruits of his bounty, conveyed by the ministry of those whose hearts are disposed by his providence to kindness. " I have seen thy face," said Jacob to Esau, " as the face of God." His brother's favour he knew to be a fruit of the mercy of him with whom he spake and prevailed at Bethel.

In our love to the rich and liberal, we exceed the bounds of duty, if we reserve not a proper share of our regard for the poor, who cannot give us any thing, but have a title to receive from us. But the greatest part of men are of a different mind from Christ Jesus, and think it more blessed to receive than to give.

Ver. 7. *All the brethren of the poor do hate him, how much more do his friends go far from him? he pursueth them with words, yet they are wanting to him.*

The brethren of the poor hate him: This is very hard: He might have expected that though all men had forsaken him, yet his brethren would have shewed compassion in the time of distress. A brother is born for adversity, and he ought chiefly at such a season to shew that he is a brother, and if he does not, he greatly aggravates the distress of such a near friend by his unkindness *, and gives a fair pretence to those that are not connected with the poor by such endearing ties, to forsake them. We make ourselves guilty of other men's sins, when we tempt them to sin by our example, especially when our obligations to the opposite duty are much stronger.

*Job 6:15

This sin is very general, and almost universal among men, although nature, as well as scripture, testifies against it. The best of men have often complained in the time of their afflictions, that they were forsaken and abhorred by those whom they most loved, and those from whom they had reason to expect the greatest kindness *.

But how do they discover their hatred? by behaving like aliens, and turning a deaf ear to their entreaties. This is a sufficient evidence of hatred in the wise man's view, and therefore we may justly conclude, that there is more of this abominable sin in the world than those that are chargeable with it will be willing to acknowledge. The want of love is hatred, though in a lesser degree than malice or spite, and therefore the apostle John distinguishes the righteous from the wicked, by this mark of loving or hating their brethren †. By extending this observation into its native consequences, we might convict all wicked men of enmity against God himself ‡, for they do not love him, but despise his laws, and have a reigning aversion to every mean of fellowship with him.

When poor men are real Christians, it is a double iniquity to despise them for their poverty, for they have a double claim to our regard, and their Redeemer is a severe avenger of their wrongs ‖.

To disregard the importunity of the poor when we are able to help them, is a sign of a very hard heart, and provokes God to disregard the prayers of such unmerciful creatures, in the day of their own distress, and to punish them without mercy §.

When the poor are overlooked, let them remember his text to their comfort. When God testifies against this conduct of their friends, it is a clear evidence that his ways are not as men's ways, nor his thoughts as

---

*Job 19, Ps. 31 & 88   †1 John 2:10 etc.   ‡Rom. 8:7

‖Job 19:28,29   §James 2:13, Ezek. 16:50

their thoughts. When Job's friends scorned him, his eyes poured out tears unto God. Christ was left in his distress by all his disciples, but he was not alone, for the Father was with him. But it is an encouragement to our faith, that he had, in the days of his flesh, so large experience of the sorrows of poverty, for in that he himself hath suffered, being tempted, he is able also to succour them that are tempted *.

Ver. 8. *He that getteth wisdom loveth his own soul: he that keepeth understanding shall find good.*

Spiritual wisdom is not natural to men, and the best scholars, and greatest philosophers, live and die fools, unless they get into their possession that wisdom which cometh from above, and is taught in the holy Scriptures.

The way of getting this wisdom is to be sensible of our need of it, to trust in him to whom all the treasures of wisdom and knowledge belong, for the communication of it, and to be diligent in the use of the means which he hath appointed, and will bless, for conveying it to us.

We must not only get, but keep this precious treasure, retaining it in our hearts, shewing it forth in all our behaviour, and refusing to part with it on any account †.

Many think that those men who are so careful to seek and retain wisdom, are great losers, buying it at too high a price, and refusing to part with it at the risk of every thing that is valuable in the eyes of men. But the Spirit of God assures us in this place, that they are great gainers, and never can be losers. They may hate their wealth and ease, their friends and life, for the sake of wisdom, but when they do so, they are lovers of their souls, and millions of lives are not to be put in competition with an immortal soul. They may meet with loss and disgrace, with persecution and death, but still

*Heb. 2:18   †Chap. 23:23

they find good, for they not only find those eternal advantages which infinitely outweigh every temporal loss *, but even these losses themselves are good to them that find wisdom, which, like the pretended philosopher's stone, turns every thing into gold. That is truly good to us, which does us good, and that does us good which makes us good, or brings us nearer to the possession of the chief good. The keeper of wisdom does not always find that which appears good to a carnal eye, but he always finds that which appears good in the eyes of God, and consequently in his own eyes. Paul found much good in the things that appear the most frightful objects in nature to the greatest part of men.

Ver. 9. *A false witness shall not be unpunished, and he that speaketh lies shall perish.*

These sins are very pernicious, and yet Solomon knew and found them so common, that he publishes a double warning against them, almost in the same breath, verse 5.

Ver. 10. *Delight is not seemly for a fool, much less for servants to have rule over princes.*

Wisdom turns every thing to a man's advantage and honour, but folly turns gain into loss, and makes a man ridiculous and contemptible, when he is surrounded with every thing that might make him happy, and procure him respect. Delight is a thing that all men wish to enjoy, but when a fool is furnished with every mean of pleasure, his folly is heightened into madness, and he is found to be seventimes more a fool than he appeared to be when he was in other circumstances. A whip is proper for an ass, and a rod for the fool's back, but delight and the means of procuring it are the same thing to a fool, as a golden bridle to that lazy animal †.

---

*Rom. 8:13   †Chap. 14:24

It is still more unseemly for servants to have rule over princes, for although servants have as good blood in their veins as princes, and are born with the same rational powers, yet their education and habits of life, make them quite unfit for the arts of government. And pride, that universal vice, has never a greater opportunity of gaining full dominion in a man, than when he is unexpectedly raised from the lowest to the highest stations. But this proverb, like many others, is true only in general, and not in every particular instance; for Joseph was very justly raised, from slavery and imprisonment, to reign over princes, and Solomon himself assures us, that a wise and poor child is worthy of much more respect than an old and foolish king.

Besides the instruction contained in this sentence, to those that have the disposal of high offices in their hands, it teaches us all to value wisdom above pleasure, and all the means of pleasure. Wisdom can make a man happy without them, and wisdom alone can make them means of happiness to us, and enable us to use them without abusing them into means of our own dishonour.

It teaches us also to be pleased with our own condition. How ridiculous would an illiterate rustic appear, were he to be placed in a pulpit, or a man of low birth if he were seated on a throne! It is God's office to choose our stations, and ours to discharge with cheerfulness the duties of them.

When God raised Joseph, and Saul, and David, to power, and when he called fishermen to be apostles, this proverb could not be applied to them, because God gave them a spirit suited to their offices, and in like manner, when he raises the meanest of the sons of men to spiritual honours, he bestows upon them a suitable disposition of soul. Those that are made kings and priests unto God and the father of Christ, have the spirit of sons, working in them those heavenly tempers which become those who are exalted so highly by the grace of God.

Ver. 11. *The discretion of a man deferreth his anger, and it is his glory to pass over a transgression.*

Are you affronted by any person? Now is the time for knowing whether you are a wise man or a fool. If you are a fool, you will follow that maxim of fools, that a man behaves honourably when he will not suffer any man to give him the least shadow of affront, without forcing him to repent it, if possible, or at least shewing that it is rather the want of power than will, that hinders him from taking revenge. If you are wise, then you will not suffer passion to domineer in your breasts, but when you find it raising insurrections, will force it to yield to the dominion of reason and religion; and before you display it in your words and behaviour, you will consider calmly whether you have reason to be angry, or so much reason as passion would make you believe; and if you have reason, yet another question still remains, Dost thou well to be angry? or dost thou well to be angry to such a degree?

A wise man will not only defer his anger, but pass over offences. Joab could suppress his anger at Abner for killing Asahel, but he was not a wise man, for his resentment broke forth at a fit opportunity, and instigated him to shed the blood of war in the time of peace. David was a man of a very different spirit. He not only restrained Abishai from killing Shimei, when he was fleeing from Jerusalem, but he pardoned that offender when he was returning in triumph to his palace. It was not revenge, but the love of peace, and a desire of the public welfare, that made David charge Solomon, on his death-bed, to keep his eye on that dangerous traitor.

It is our duty and wisdom to pass by, not only slight

offences, but injuries of a deeper dye, such as may be called transgressions ; for we need sometimes the forgiveness of such from men, and every day we are obliged to supplicate the forgiveness of transgressions from God, and we are bound to forgive men, even as God, for Christ's sake, hath forgiven us.

It is the discretion of a man to be slow to anger and ready to forgive; for as it is not the water that surrounds a ship, but the water which soaks into it, that sinks it, so it is not the injury done by another man that endangers us so much as the impression it makes upon ourselves. Our fretful and revengeful thoughts are the torment of our hearts, and deprive us of the government of our own souls, and it is a piece of folly, when our neighbour does us an injury, to do a much greater to ourselves, when we mean to be revenged on him.

It is a greater glory for a man to govern himself, than to take strong cities, and rule over mighty nations. It is the wisdom and honour of sinning creatures, to behave to offenders as men that need pardon for themselves. It is the glory of Christians to learn meekness and lowliness from Christ. It is the glory of pardoned sinners to shew forth the virtues of him that called them, to which they owe so much, not only in their praises but in all their conversation.

Ver. 12. *The king's wrath is as the roaring of a lion, but his favour is as dew upon the grass.*

We must be loyal to the king for wrath, if we will not be loyal for conscience sake ; for here the Bible requires it, and represents the great danger of disobedience, to affright those that will not be governed by a sense of duty. As the lion among the beasts of the forest, so is a king among men, and as the roaring of the lion is terrible to the beasts, so is the displeasure of the king to those that offend him. But his favour is pleasant and refreshing like the dew upon the grass.

We must not wantonly provoke the displeasure, and forfeit the favour, of one that can do us so much good or evil ; yet if conscience interfere with the king's commands, we must obey God rather than man, for what is the roaring of a lion, or the rage of a tyrant, to the torments of a mind enraged with a sense of guilt ; or what is the dew on the grass, or the smiles of a monarch, to that peace of God which passeth all understanding, and made the martyrs happier in their dungeons, and at stakes, than their tyrants were upon their thrones *.

Ver. 13. *A foolish son is the calamity of his father, and the contentions of a wife are a continual dropping.*

When children behave ill, they are a great cross to their parents, but a peevish and contentious wife is a much greater cross, for children may be turned out of doors when they cannot be reclaimed, but death only, in ordinary cases, can separate those that are joined in marriage. As the rain that drops through an old house rots the timber, and will, in time, wear away the very stones, so the everlasting reflections and complaints of a peevish woman prey upon the vitals of a man, and consume his heart with unceasing anguish.

Women were made to assist and comfort their husbands, and therefore they ought to behave with a meek and quiet spirit, for it will never be of advantage to a woman to cross the end of her creation. Those who make such a near friend unhappy, must bring a double share of unhappiness on themselves.

But husbands must not impute peevishness to their wives, without good ground. We are all the sons of Adam, and all women are the daughters of Eve, and it would be very unjust to call a woman contentious, for

---

*Daniel 3

every instance of bad humour to which vexations may provoke her.

If a man has a froward wife, let him consider his own behaviour. Few women have so little of the heart of a woman, or a human creature, as to make those men unhappy that treat them with discretion and tenderness, or if women really deserve this character, gentle admonitions, and kind usage are the best means of reclaiming them.

If a wife has so much of the spirit of a tiger, as still to vex a good husband, his duty is to acknowledge God in this providence, and to consider it as a just correction, or a necessary trial. This will dispose him to perform his duty to a wife that does not perform her duty to him, and to become better by her means, if he cannot make her better by all his endeavours and prayers.

When men that have good wives consider this text, and the too frequent illustrations of it which the observation of the world gives us, it will teach them what reason they have of thankfulness to God, for appointing them a happier lot. It is not chance, nor our own discretion, but the providence of God that gives any of us a prudent wife.

Ver. 14. *Houses and riches are the inheritance of fathers, and a prudent wife is from the Lord.*

Houses and lands are given us by God, but he gives them to us by means of our parents or progenitors, whose industry acquired them. The providence of God shines more remarkably in bestowing good wives on men, for they cannot come by inheritance ; and no man can guess beforehand what wife shall fall to any man's lot.

Prudence in a wife, includes not only skill in the management of domestic affairs, but likewise that good sense that makes her an agreeable partner, and directs her to that kind of behaviour which makes her husband happy in this connexion. To these qualities, if piety be added, it renders her a far greater blessing than any possessions that parents can transmit.

We are to thank God for every outward enjoyment, but chiefly for those in which his favourable providence appears most plainly. Houses and lands may tend, in a great degree, to render life comfortable, but a virtuous woman is an uncommon blessing, for her price is far above rubies.

He that findeth a wife has reason to thank God *. He that findeth a good wife has many reasons to be thankful. It was God that gave her prudence, that brought him into acquaintance with her, that disposed him to choose her for a wife, and determined her mind to comply with his desires.

When we receive a rich present from a friend, gratitude obliges us to use it according to his wishes. If a wife is a rich present from God, her husband is bound to shew her all that respect and kindness which God requires. Whatever character a wife deserves, God commands her husband to love her, but when a wife is prudent, the husband would be inexcusable that did not love her with the tenderest affection.

If a man desires to have a wife, he must acknowledge God by earnest supplications ; for he alone knows the hearts of men and women, and exercises a sovereign influence over their affections; but let him not presume to affront God by pretending to seek a wife from him, without seeking prudence in her, preferably to houses or land ; for God declares, that a prudent wife is a far richer gift than those things which are so much valued by the generality of men. When children wish to enter into marriage, they cannot expect the countenance of their parents, if they make a choice directly opposite to the judgment of their parents ; and how can we expect that our heavenly Father should

---

*Chap. 18:22

give us his countenance in pursuits opposite to his declared will?

Ver. 15. *Slothfulness casteth into a deep sleep, and an idle soul shall suffer hunger.*

A man would make himself universally despised, if he kept his bed all the time that other people are at work ; and yet a slothful man might as well be in his bed, for whilst he is awake, he is sleeping, and when he is at work, he is idle. Slothfulness is to the body like rust to iron ; it is a consumption to all the powers of the mind, and by its stealing influence and stupifying nature, it casts a man into a sleep, not of an ordinary kind, but a deep sleep like that of death. When a man does nothing as it ought to be done, he is like one buried alive, and may be numbered with the inhabitants of the land of silence and rest.

Would you avoid hunger and poverty, things so much dreaded by mankind? Then avoid idleness, which brings these miseries upon men, and deprives them of that pity which waits upon virtue in distress. Idleness brings hunger, and along with it temptations to fraud and theft, by which means it has led many to a gibbet.

Ver. 16. *He that keepeth the commandment, keepeth his own soul ; but he that despiseth his ways, shall die.*

As the word of God is called the Scripture, (or the writing,) as if there were no other writings in the world, because there are none that can bear a comparison with it, so the precepts of the Bible may be called the commandment, because, although there are men that have a right to command, yet the precepts of God lay an obligation upon us, of force infinitely superior to any thing else in the world. The authority of parents and kings is derived from God, and we are bound to obey them, because God requires it, and when their com-

mandments interfere with the will of God, we are bound
to obey God, and not man.

The commandment of God is to be observed and
obeyed by us in all things, and through the whole
course of our lives. We must keep it, not only as the
apple of our eye, but as our life and soul.

He that keeps the commandment keeps his own soul
from those sins that would bring death and ruin upon
him, and from the temptations of the adversary, that
watches our halting, and seizes every opportunity he
can find to do us a mischief. But how can a man keep
his own soul? Is not the Lord our keeper? Certainly; but in converting and keeping men, he deals with
them as rational creatures. We greatly abuse the doctrine of free grace, if we imagine that it supersedes the
necessity and advantage of obedience. Although the
glory of salvation belongs entirely to Jesus, yet
he condescends to give to faithful ministers the honour of being workers under him *. And although
the glory of the strength of Christians stands in him,
yet when he communicates the influences of his grace,
he makes themselves instrumental, under his agency,
in their own preservation from the snares of the destroyer. He that is born of God keepeth himself, and
the wicked one toucheth him not.

Care and thought are absolutely necessary in those
that resolve to keep the commandment; for he that
despiseth his ways, shall die. The saint must not only
endeavour to understand and remember the rule of the
law, but likewise to observe his own way, that he may
direct his steps, and form his course of behaviour in an
agreeableness to it. The travellers that have their
faces towards the better country, must have their eyes
in their head, for there is no going to heaven by guess,
and those that live at random must die. This truth is
clearly taught by the apostle Paul in language suffi-

---

*1 Tim. 4:16

cient to alarm the stoutest sinner, if any thing could alarm him. " If ye live after the flesh, ye shall die," &c. *

Ver. 17. *He that hath pity upon the poor, lendeth unto the Lord, and that which he hath given, will he repay him again.*

Without the pity of the heart, the bounty of the hand is unacceptable to the Searcher of hearts; and professions of pity are mere hypocrisy, without the fruit of bounty, if it is in the power of our hands to shew it†,

How great is the mercy of the Lord to the poor! He hath appointed them to be the receivers of a part of his revenue, and what is given to them he accounts to be lent to himself. This mercy is not confined to the poor of his own people; although he interests those especially in our bounty ‡, yet he would not have us to restrict the fruits of our compassion to them. Our Lord dispensed his cures to the ungrateful, although he knew what was in man, and God causes his sun to rise, and his rain to descend, upon the evil and the good, and requires us to give a portion to seven, and also to eight, dispersing the fruits of our liberality, as the husbandman scatters his grain, although he does not certainly know whether shall prosper, either this or that ‖.

" He that giveth to the poor, lendeth to the Lord." This is an argument for charity of wonderful force. No Pagan moralist could ever produce a motive for any social duty, equal to this. It is sufficient to open the closest fist, and to enlarge the most selfish heart. Does God shew so much regard to the poor, and shall we be indifferent to their happiness? Can we lose any thing by lending it to the Lord? Men refuse to give when they do not expect to receive, and they expect

---

*Rom. 8:13   †John 3:17   ‡Gal. 6:10   ‖Eccl. 11:4.6

no return from the poor. If the rich were desirous to borrow from us, we would think our money safe in their hands, and esteem their bonds as good as money in our purses. But all the earth belongs unto the Lord, and shall we not trust our money in his hands, by giving to the poor? Here is his bond, and it must be a good one, if the Scripture is the word of God. The richest man in the world may, for ought we know, be poor to-morrow, or he may prove unfaithful to his word. But the Lord is the everlasting possessor of heaven and earth, and he cannot lie, nor deceive any one that trusts in him. Had we lived in the days of Christ's humiliation, when he had the goodness to live on the contributions of pious women, it is natural for us to think that we would cheerfully have given to him all our living, and thought ourselves greatly indebted to him for accepting it. We have not now Jesus with us, but the poor we have always with us; and when we have them to receive the fruits of our bounty, it is the same thing as if we had Christ himself.

God will be sure to repay what is given to the poor at his command, with great increase. The greatest usurer on earth cannot make so much of his money, as the man that gives to the poor. " Thou shalt be recompensed," says Christ, " at the resurrection of the just." Is that a long time to wait for it? Then you are assured, by the same faithful witness, that you shall have an hundred fold, even in this life, for every thing you part with on his account, Luke xiv. Matt. xix. Men that may be safely trusted with our money, are not always ready with their payments. A poor man cannot have his money from them when he needs it, but God repays what is given to the poor at the best time ; and if he does not return it in money, he pays it in what is incomparably better *.

*Ps. 40:1,2

Ver. 18. *Chasten thy son whilst there is hope, and let not thy soul spare for his crying.*

If you mean to do good to your children by correction, begin in due time. For if he be left to grow up under the government of self-will, it is to be feared that he will become like a horse or mule that were never taught to obey the rider; and when these animals come to a full age, without being forced to obey the rein, you may sooner break their necks than break them to obedience.

But your heart melts, and your bowels yearn to hear the cries of your poor child, and you cannot give him another harsh word. Let him alone then, and leave him to the government of his own passions, unless you think that it would be still more grievous to have your grey hairs brought with sorrow to the grave, and to hear him curse you at the left hand of your Judge, for suffering him to destroy himself, than to hear his groans for a few moments.

After all, parents ought neither to inflict unnecessary chastisement on their children, nor suffer their angry passions to mingle themselves with the duty here recommended. Those parents that make an angry use of the rod, need a rod to their own backs. ("Chasten thy son, so shall he be hopeful; but be not raised in thy wrath to insult him.")

An offending child must not be spared for his crying, and far less must he be spared for his anger. If his wrath procures his deliverance, he will soon learn the way of escaping all chastisement; and if thou deliverest him once, thou must deliver him again and again, till he is past all hope of amendment. This seems to be at least a part of the meaning of the next verse.

Ver. 19. *A man of great wrath shall suffer punishment; for if thou deliver him, yet thou must do it again.*

When Peter asked our Lord how often he should

forgive his offending brother, he received a very surprizing answer : Not until seven times, but until seventy times seven. But will not this give great encouragement to men to offend their brethren, and to give every indulgence to their angry passions? No, for it does not imply that an outrageous person shall escape from punishment. It was once said to a man that was killing his adversary, let him alone, and he will die of his own accord. So may it be said to a man that thirsts for revenge upon his passionate antagonist, let him alone, and he will take revenge upon himself. Although you spare him at this time, he will soon expose himself again to punishment, and it cannot be supposed that he will always escape. You ought rather to pity him, than rage like him, for he is his own irreconcileable enemy, and will be sure to plunge himself into mischief.

Anger is said to be a short madness, but the passionate man is always mad till he gains the victory over the tyrants that domineer in his soul. He has sober fits, but he so frequently relapses, that you cannot say he ever possesses the use of reason. Any man that wishes evil to him may deprive him of the use of his understanding, by a single word, or even by a look.

Are your souls subject to those storms of passion ? Turn your anger upon itself. You are displeased with other men, because you take them for enemies ; but your worst enemies are the passions of your own heart. Do you not hate that monster, Vitellius, who said that the carcase of a slain enemy was a pleasant sight, but the carcase of a slain citizen more pleasant? Why then don't you hate the violent tyrants of your own breast, that would wreak their fury upon the names and bodies of your neighbours, but discover it most of all in tearing your own souls ? You are every day torturing yourselves, and exposing yourselves to a severe retalia-

tion from those whom you insult, and to a more severe
vengeance still, from your Judge, who will call you to
account for every angry thought and every passionate
word.

Ver. 20. *Hear counsel, and receive instruction, that
thou mayest be wise in thy latter end.*

A friend that can give us good counsel is a precious
treasure, and nothing but folly and self-conceit can
keep us from valuing his good advice as more than
fine gold.

If the counsels of our friends deserve respect, the
counsels of the word of God are infinitely more useful.
The testimonies of the Lord were David's counsellors
in all his difficulties, and they made him wiser than the
ancients.

Every name of our Redeemer is dear to the true
Christian, and one of them is Wonderful Counsellor.
He gives us counsel by his word and Spirit. Our
ears and souls are his, and shall we not employ them
in hearing and treasuring up his counsels, that we may
direct all our actions by their light?

Instruction is very much needed by us, for we are
naturally ignorant and foolish. When God gives us
instruction, either by his word and ordinances, or by
the rebukes of his providence, we must receive it with
submission and meekness. Instruction, either by words
or blows, would be welcome to us, if we had a due
sense of our own stupidity, and of the value of our souls.

But what will we gain by hearing counsel, and receiving instruction? It will make us wise; " for the
entrance of God's word giveth light, it giveth understanding unto the simple." The rod and reproof give
wisdom, and wisdom is far more precious than gold
and rubies. Without counsel and instruction, we must
be fools for ever, and if we refuse wisdom, when it is
presented to us in those means of God's appointment,

our folly is desperate and stubborn, and admits of no excuse.

But we have used these means, you will say, and have acquired but very little wisdom from them. But a little wisdom is a very great attainment, and if you think that you have got none at all, yet you must still continue to use the means, and so you shall be wise at your latter end. A man will spend several years in learning a business that will enable him to live comfortably through the remainder of life, and we have no reason to grudge a whole lifetime employed in receiving instruction, if it make us wise at our latter end.

At our latter end it will be seen whether we have been fools or wise men. If our days are spent in the pursuit of perishing things, to the neglect of our eternal interests, we shall be forced to leave these vanities to which we sacrificed our souls, and at our end we shall be fools*. When the men that choose the world for their portion come to the close of life, and their former conduct presents itself to their eyes, how will they curse and tear themselves in their rage, at their own blindness and madness! Even whilst they are eager in the pursuit of vanity, and flattering themselves with the delusive hopes of many days of pleasure before them, they cannot forbear from wishing, like the covetous soothsayer, that they may die the death of the righteous, and that their last end may be like his.

But mark the follower of wisdom, and behold him that hearkens to the counsels of the Almighty. His latter end is peace and happiness. Those who hated his holiness, and despised his condition, are now obliged to acknowledge that his life was spent in wisdom, and that his last hour is blessed.

Do you think that you have already gained enough

---

*Jer. 17

of wisdom? You are quite mistaken. You are yet a child, and speak as a child, that thinks himself a scholar if he can repeat the letters of the alphabet. A Christian must live and die learning*.

Ver. 21. *There are many devices in a man's heart; nevertheless, the counsel of the Lord that shall stand.*

Men's hearts are perpetually filled with projects, and they seldom consider whether these projects are agreeable to the mind of God or not. But the counsel of the Lord revealed in his word, shall stand good after all the plans they can form. It is the way of happiness to hear his counsel and receive his instruction; for the world passeth away, and the lusts thereof, but he that doth the will of God abideth for ever, and must prosper whilst he acts by the direction of these unerring counsellors, the testimonies of the Lord†.

But the counsel of God is generally used in Scripture to signify the purpose of God concerning the events that shall come to pass; and this counsel comprehends every thing that has come or shall come to pass in the world, either by the immediate agency of God, or by means of any creature; for the worst of men, and devils themselves, are employed by the providence of God in executing his decrees. Men and devils act in an agreeableness to their own wills as far as their power reaches, but they are still under the absolute dominion of the Lord; and whether they are able or not able to execute their own devices, they are executing his decrees. How strange is the wisdom of divine Providence! Millions of creatures know nothing of the true God, millions of them are his constant enemies, and are incessantly employed in devising and executing those purposes which have for their objects the gratification of selfish and corrupt affections, that are filled with enmity against God,

---

*Phil. 3:14   †Verse 20. Ps. 1:4

and yet they all concur in fulfilling his secret will. His counsels leave them to their own free will; and their free will, however corrupt, is managed by his holy providence to serve his own glorious designs, and where it would lead men beyond the line of his decrees, he powerfully and invisibly controuls it.

It is vain for men to form any purpose, and to think of carrying it into execution, without acknowledging the providence of God. The Apostle James warns us in strong language against this piece of practical atheism*.

When we meet with hardships from the cruelty of men, let us consider this truth, and behave meekly and humbly. They do nothing without the observation and permission of God. Christ submitted quietly to those sufferings which he underwent from the hands of barbarous men, because it was necessary that the Scriptures should be fulfilled, and the determinations of God's hand and counsel performed. What David did pleased all the people, and shall not we be pleased with what the King of Heaven does?

Let the people of God rejoice. The counsels of God concerning them are glorious in wisdom and grace, and though hand join in hand, they shall not be unaccomplished. The counsels of their enemies are dangerous, but no weapon formed against Zion shall prosper. All the counsels of the wicked shall be executed or frustrated according to the good pleasure of God, whose eyes run to and fro through the whole earth, to shew himself strong in the behalf of them whose heart is perfect towards him†.

Let sinners tremble, for their counsels and works are in the hand of God. He may suffer them to prosper for a time in mischief, and to bring some of their wick‐

---

*James 4:13-17   †Mic. 4:10-13

ed devices to pass, but their mischiefs shall rebound upon themselves, and their nets shall entangle their own feet. God may use them for a time to accomplish his gracious though awful designs upon his people, but he will in a short time call them to account, and punish them for all the evils they have done, and for the greater evils they have imagined *.

Ver. 22. *The desire of a man is his kindness, and a poor man is better than a liar.*

A man's benevolence is not in proportion to the good deeds he performs, but to the real desires he has to do good, if it were in his power.

A man may perform many acts of kindness, and yet not perform all that he ought. When a rich man bestows a few of his superfluities, they may amount to a considerable sum, and yet in the balance of the sanctuary they will not equal in weight the little pittance that a poor man gives, when he stretches himself to the utmost of his ability, or even beyond it†. A rich man may even give more than a man could reasonably desire him to give, for the purposes of charity or public service, and yet be entirely destitute of charity and public spirit, seeking only the praise of men, whilst he professes, like the old Pharisees, much better things.

On the other side, a man may give only two mites, or nothing at all, and yet possess a generous soul, like that of Job, who never ate his morsel without sharing it with the poor. As God only knows the heart, the day of judgment will be the grand discoverer of the real characters of men. In the meantime, we must not love those only who bestow much kindness on us, nor confine our esteem to those who signalise themselves by their extensive liberalities; for the virtues, as well as the vices of men, are often concealed under rags, and

*Ps. 21:11, Isa. 10:12   †2 Cor. 6:3

pinched by poverty, so that they cannot display their blossoms, or produce their proper fruits.

The poor man that cannot give, and is obliged to receive, is a much better man than the liar who professes kindness, and yet does nothing to verify his professions by works. Good words are good things in their proper place, and do well become the mouth of the Christian, but good words instead of good deeds are mere hypocrisy ; of so gross a kind, that even men often discern it, and despise the pitiful wretch who endeavours to shelter the baseness and selfishness of his spirit under empty professions. Do you say to your poor brother, be thou warmed and clothed, whilst thou givest him nothing to shelter him from the pinching cold, or to fill his craving appetite, although thou art well able to do it ? Thou joinest hypocrisy and lies to the want of charity, and a poor man that lives upon the bounty of the parish is a more respectable man than thou.

Let us learn to value men by their hearts, as far as they lie open to the judgment of candour and charity, rather than their professions and appearances, which are so frequently delusive. Thus shall we be enabled to choose our friends, and to put a proper value on their kindness ; and by this means we shall be preserved from that injustice so frequently condemned by the wise man, of despising the poor, and paying an undue respect to the rich.

This proverb also teaches us to examine our own hearts, that we may know how far we are under the influence of a kind and charitable spirit. God will not accept of all the substance of our houses, instead of the charity of the heart. At the same time, desires are not real, nor are they genuine marks of goodness, if they are not followed by suitable performances, when the providence of God puts it in our power*.

---

*Philemon 6

Ver. 23. *The fear of the Lord tendeth to life, and he that hath it shall abide satisfied; he shall not be visited with evil.*

Religion is the soul of happiness, it makes the present life long and happy, as far as a long and happy life is really for our advantage, and it is the beginning of eternal life in the soul. He that is governed by the fear of the Lord enjoys heart-felt satisfaction, and the joys that spring from it are not like the short-lived joys of the world, that die away into sadness and misery; they last through life, they are vigorous in old age, when the pleasures of sense have lost their relish, and they triumph over death and all its terrors. Christians are indeed exposed to heaviness through manifold temptations, but the fear of the Lord, and the faith of Christ, has often produced joy unspeakable and full of glory in such seasons; and the disquiets which the people of God often feel, are owing for the most part to the imperfections of their religious dispositions, and are blessed by God as means of improving their grace, and introducing sweeter joys into their souls. Christians have unfailing grounds of satisfaction, for they have health in their souls, they know that all their affairs are managed by a wise and gracious Providence, and they have the sure promises of the life to come. If God himself can give satisfaction to the souls which he has made, they have it, or shall have it in due time, for he manages all things for their good, and his eternal excellencies are their portion.

The saint of God is entirely delivered from the miseries of man's fallen state, as far as it can consist with the plan of his recovery which divine wisdom has contrived. The calamities which he suffers are unstinged to him through the Redeemer's cross, which, like the tree that Moses cast into the waters of Marah, makes bitter things sweet. He is not visited with any unnecessary evil, and those evils that visit him are made good on the whole by the tendency which they have to do him good, and make him good. Reproaches and tribulations, sicknesses and deaths, are the common lot of men, and they are very evil things to those who are strangers to God, but they are good to them that love God, for they are appointed and useful means to make them partakers of God's holiness, and prepare them for that blessed world where sins and sorrows are no more*.

Ver. 24. *A slothful man hideth his hand in his bosom, and will not so much as bring it to his mouth again†.*

Solomon was a mortal enemy to sloth, as every wise man will be. He has often told us of the mischievous effects of this vice, and here he holds up the sluggard as an object of contempt and laughter, to make him ashamed, if possible, of his laziness, and to awaken us to diligence in the duties of our calling and religion.

It is a mark of a sluggard to make a great business of a little affair, and to make much ado about nothing at all. It is a business to the sluggard to take his hand out of his bosom, and it is a grievous affair for him to put it to his mouth to feed himself. Were it not for shame, he would desire to be fed like an infant, and he will at length be tempted to grudge that men cannot live like trees, on which their proper nourishment falls down from the clouds.

A man that employs his hands with diligence, is able not only to support himself and his family, but to give something likewise to him that needs‡; and he finds less trouble in his work, and enjoys more contentment than a sluggard would do, if you should bring every thing to him that is needful for his support, with-

---

*Chap. 4:26,27, 3:7,8, John 8:52

†The word *bosom* ought to have been *dish*. ‡Eph. 4:28

out any labour of his own hands, because the things that no man can do for him are oppressions to his sluggish soul. It is a greater burden to a sleepy man to strip himself and go to bed, than for another man to perform some laborious service.

Awake, thou sluggard, out of thy deep sleep, unless thou desirest to be miserable through life; for life itself is an intolerable slavery when every piece of work is a burden.

Beware of spiritual sloth, which makes every duty of religion a toil. God loves a cheerful servant, that rejoices and works righteousness, but he will accept of no drowsy and spiritless services, which are a dishonour to him and to his ways. To the slothful Christian it seems a burden to pray, and to believe in Christ, although by these duties we only ask, and receive, and eat our spiritual food. The lively Christian admires the grace of God, which hath made these holy exercises our duty; but the sluggard grudges that he cannot have heaven in a morning dream.

Ver. 25. *Smite a scorner, and the simple will beware; and reprove one that hath understanding, and he will understand knowledge.*

The wise man has already told us that it is needless to reprove a scorner, because his pride will make reproofs useless to him. What, then, is to be done with him? Shall he be suffered to proceed in his wicked courses, and to corrupt others by his example? No; he ought to be smitten, at least when he lays himself open to the vengeance of the laws; and although there is little hope of reclaiming one that is so much hardened in wickedness, yet his punishment will be useful to other men, who will hear, and fear, and do no more so wickedly. The simple and thoughtless will be made to see how dangerous it is to follow the example of one that has suffered unto imprisonment, or whipping, or death, for his vices, and those who would not be restrained from evil by the fear of God, and the thoughts of an eternal world, will be checked by the fear of men, and the terror of present punishment. It is a necessary thing in a land to punish gross offences; for without the execution of justice on the wicked, iniquity would overflow all its banks, and men would not live with safety among their fellow-creatures. We have, therefore, reason to bless God for the institution of magistracy *, and should concur in our stations to assist in the execution of the just laws against vice.

But a wise man needs not be smitten for his faults, which are generally of a much less atrocious nature than those of the scorner. He is not, however, to be connived at, or left to his own wisdom, to inform him of his miscarriages. Men are commonly too dim-sighted to discern their own miscarriages in a proper light, and reproofs are means appointed and blessed by God for bringing wise men themselves to the exercise of a lively sorrow and repentance.

Are you afraid to reprove a wise man, lest he should take it amiss? You need not fear this, if he is really a wise man. He will love thee for reproving him, and will understand knowledge. A fool is displeased when he is supposed capable of falling into a fault; but a wise man is meek and lowly, sensible of his imperfection and frailty, and when he goes out of the road of duty, is glad and thankful to be set right.

This proverb teaches us, how vain it is for men, through the pride of character, to cavil at admonitions, and endeavour to justify themselves in opposition to plain fact. Instead of serving our character by this behaviour, we greatly hurt it. When we receive reproof with gratitude, we shew ourselves wise men.

---

*Rom. 13

When we are displeased with it, we shew that we are fools, or at least that our wisdom is mingled with much folly. To affect the character of perfect men, is a plain evidence that we know not ourselves, and do not remember the present state of human nature.

Ver. 26. *He that wasteth his father, and chaseth away his mother, is a son that causeth shame, and bringeth reproach.*

Some children are so graceless, as to think it no sin to steal from their parents, and to take at their own hands that portion of the goods which they think belongs to them. Others abuse the fondness of their parents, and ungratefully make use of it as a mean of robbing them by their own consent. Both these kinds of wicked children may be said to waste their parents. There is another kind of children who have some reverence for their father, because their interest depends on his will; but they have so little regard for their mothers, that they chase them away from their houses, by rendering their life uncomfortable, or by wasting that portion of goods which pertains to them. Esau, profane as he was, had some regard for his father, and sought his blessing with many tears; but he valued not his mother, and resolved to kill her dearest son, as soon as her husband's head was laid in the dust. On the other side, dutiful children will at all times endeavour to make their mothers happy, especially when they are reduced to the affliction of a widowed condition.

Those sons that behave so undutifully to their parents bring a reproach on themselves, which spreads to the whole family. They are monsters of mankind, who are entirely destitute of natural affection, and feel no gratitude for the highest obligations which one human person can receive from another. They barbarously disappoint and counteract the most reasonable hopes that can be formed by men, and prove the torment and disgrace of those who had the best reason to expect comfort at their hand. They violate the strongest obligations to duty, and make themselves unworthy of the least confidence from men. They greatly provoke the author of their being, by their base conduct towards the instruments of it. God hath placed in his law the duties we owe to our parents next to those we owe to himself, and will severely avenge the neglect of them. How, then, can they escape punishment, who do not only neglect, but scandalously counteract these duties! If the injuries done to strangers, or inferiors, expose men to the displeasure of the Most High, what punishments hang over those that wound, in the tenderest part, the persons to whom under God they owe themselves?

Is God so careful to enforce the rights of parents upon their children, how careful should parents be to inculcate on their children their duty to God, the sense of which, in the minds of their children, is their own best security for that regard which is due to themselves.

If God be the father of the human race, and of Christians in particular, what fear is due to him? What monsters of undutifulness are they that provoke him to anger continually?

Ver. 27. *Cease, my son, to hear the instruction that causeth to err from the words of knowledge.*

There are many deceivers in the world, who make it their business to clothe error with the appearance of truth, and to weaken the motives to holiness which are set before us in the word of God. And the exhortation in this verse speaks to us as children, warning us to beware of their artifices and insinuations.

Error may be rendered very plausible, for the Devil himself came to men with Scripture in his mouth *; and

---

*Matt. 4

no wonder if his ministers can presume to plead both
Scripture and reason in behalf of their pernicious doctrines : but a quagmire is not the less dangerous, because it is covered with beautiful verdure, and has the
appearance of solid ground ; nor is poison the less pernicious, because it is covered with honey. Error is
error after all that can be said for it, and all the shapes
which it can be made to assume.

It is, no doubt, our duty to prove all things, and to
take nothing upon the mere testimony of men that
concerns our precious souls, and it is the property of
a sincere soul, like Nathaniel's, to be open to conviction, where there is danger of a mistake. But this does
not imply that we are to be ever learning, without
coming to the knowledge and assurance of the truth.
The truth may be known, because it is plainly revealed in the Bible ; and when we have found that which
is good, we ought to hold it fast, that no man take our
crown—to contend earnestly for it against all opposition, and to shut our ears against those instructions
that would shake our regard to those things which are
most surely believed amongst us.

It is dangerous for men to lend a ready ear to those
that would exalt the dignity of human nature, to the
dishonour of the righteousness and grace of Christ, or
loosen the obligations of men to obey every law of God,
because the corruption of our natures gives countenance
to every thing that favours pride or carelessness ; so
that, when we think we are well fortified against the
delusions of seducing spirits and false teachers, and
rashly venture to hear what they can say for themselves, we are in great danger of being perverted, and
falling from our fancied stedfastness.

The apostle John tells us, that it is a great and dangerous sin, when a man comes to teach false doctrine,
to receive him into our houses, or to bid him God

speed; and Christ tells us, that his true sheep hear and
know his voice, and follow him, but will not follow a
stranger.

Perhaps you have already given too much ear to the
teachers of corrupt doctrine. The exhortation is chiefly addressed to you, by him that knows your danger.
Cease to hear such instruction. The time past is sufficient to have listened to it. Examine carefully how
far your judgment or practice have been perverted, by
comparing them with the Scriptures. Adjust your
profession and practice to that unerring standard. Endeavour to know the present truth, and to be established in it. Learn by the word of God, and prayer, to
distinguish between truth and error. Hear those teachers that are of God, and preach sound doctrine; and
beware of itching ears, which would tempt you to
drink poison into your ears and hearts, instead of the
sincere milk of the word *.

Ver. 28. *An ungodly witness scorneth judgment, and
the mouth of the wicked devoureth iniquity.*

This is not the first nor second time that Solomon
has informed us about the wickedness of false witnesses. It would be a great injustice to admit the testimony of a profligate wretch, against the life or fortune of his neighbour; for he neither regards man, nor
fears God. He scorneth judgment, and has no reverence for the most sacred and venerable objects. He
bids defiance to eternal justice, and swallows down the
most enormous iniquities as if they were sweet wine;
for his conscience is become hardened in iniquity, till a
trifle will be a sufficient temptation to him to swear
against innocent blood.

It is greatly the interest of a nation to take order that
a sense of religion be preserved amongst the members

*1 John 4:1-6, Matt. 7:15, 2 John 9

of it. When men generally lose their reverence for an oath, the bonds of society are broken, honesty becomes a prey, and ruin advances with hasty steps.

Let all men beware of those sins that are counted little, for they are like little thieves that get in at the window, and then open the door for bigger villains to get in. When men learn to lie without scruple, because they hurt none but themselves, they will next learn to bear false witness, when they are tempted by love or fear, and from thence they will proceed to greater degrees of wickedness, till at length they will scarce put the devil to the trouble of tempting them to any sin, but drink iniquity like water. Every sin tends to harden the conscience, and a conscience long hardened in sin, will in time be seared as with a hot iron.

However stupid the consciences of ungodly men are, and whatever flatteries they use for deceiving themselves, their iniquity will in the end be found hateful.

Ver. 29. *Judgments are prepared for scorners, and stripes for the back of fools.*

Scorners, in the pride of their hearts, think themselves secure from the vengeance of the law, and are sometimes so profane as to laugh at the threatenings of the Almighty. But the day is coming when their laughter shall be turned into heaviness. The God whom they despise, is the judge of all the earth, and it is his glory to exercise his high office in righteousness. He takes no pleasure in the death of the wicked, but if they will not turn and live, they must die, and their blood shall be on their own head, and the Lord shall be known by the judgment which he executeth. The judgments that shall be inflicted on scorners, are already prepared, and determined for them. It is the triumph of lively Christians that they can look back to the days of eternity, and rejoice in the contemplation of a kingdom prepared for them before the foundation of the world. But sinners have great reason to tremble with astonishment, when they reflect upon the immutable decrees of God, for an everlasting hell was designed in them for every unrepenting transgressor *. As kings have their officers of justice, and instruments of vengeance ready to terrify profligate subjects into obedience to the laws, so the Everlasting King has every instrument of vengeance reserved among his treasures, to terrify men from sin, or to destroy them if they go on in their trespasses. Their punishment shall be disgraceful to the last degree, for stripes are prepared for the backs of fools. They shall suffer ignominious wounds as the basest of criminals, and their reproach shall never be wiped away.

Because sinners feel not the strokes of judgment, they foolishly think that they shall for ever escape. But did the old world of the ungodly escape, although they were spared an hundred and twenty years? Christ himself, the beloved Son of God, when he was bearing iniquity not his own, was not spared. Justice and judgment took hold of our blessed Surety, and he gave his back to the smiters, and his cheeks to them that plucked off the hair. If God spared not his own Son, will he spare stubborn transgressors?

Perhaps you imagine, sinners, that vengeance will be long delayed, and that your sufferings are reserved to another world. Perhaps it may, and for ought you know, it may not be so. But, allowing that you should enjoy all the prosperity that your hearts can wish till you die, are you sure that you shall live another year, or another day? Your life depends absolutely on him whom you treat as an enemy; and when his much abused patience is at an end, where, O where are you!

---

*Matt. 25:41

Proverbs 20

Ver. 1. *Wine is a mocker, strong drink is raging, and whosoever is deceived thereby is not wise.*

W<small>INE</small> and strong drink are creatures of God, which are very useful to men when they are seasonably and moderately used, but by abusing them we sin against the goodness and law of God, and against our own souls and bodies.

Wine deceives and mocks those that use it to excess, and punishes those that abuse it as an instrument of dishonour to him that gave it to men to cheer their hearts. It promises refreshment, but it steals away men's senses, till it makes them the objects of scorn to the sober. It made the venerable patriarch Noah a laughing-stock to his own son. It deprives men of their reason, and gives the government of the mind to the passions ; and then those that were men of good behaviour in their sober moments, become insolent and outrageous. When the king of Israel was made drunk with bottles of wine, he forgot his dignity, and stretched out his hand with scorners *.

Wine has been the beginning of many quarrels that have ended in wounds and blood; for it rouses the passions, it turns suspicions into certainties in the eye of the drunkard, and thus inflames resentments into irreconcileable animosities. It gives full range to all the hidden vices of the soul, and produces new vices of a dangerous kind. It destroys the power of reason, and infuses into the soul all the fury of a wild beast.

---

*Hos. 7:5

He that suffers himself to be deceived by it is not wise, for he wastes his memory and understanding, as well as his money ; he wounds his conscience, he enslaves himself to a tyrant, and enters upon a course which, when it becomes habitual, will render him useless and miserable upon earth, and exclude him from the kingdom of heaven. When wine and strong drink are greedily swallowed down, they swallow the drunkard, and turn him into an unclean beast *.

Wine had the honour of being used in the service of God under the law, and is still used in it under the gospel, and why should we use it in the service of Satan ? It is not allowed by God but with moderation, to the greatest men on the greatest occasions. Neither birth days of kings, nor happy meetings of friends, nor the transacting of the most important businesses, will justify men in excess of wine †.

We should remember, that the day of Christ is approaching, and take care that our hearts be not overcharged with surfeiting and drunkenness; we must remember from whom we receive the refreshments of life, and endeavour to glorify him in the use of them. We are called to the hope of drinking of the rivers of God's pleasures, and shall we fill ourselves with wine, wherein there is excess ‡.?

Ver. 2. *The fear of a king is as the roaring of a lion ; whoso provoketh him to anger sinneth against his own soul.*

Solomon had probably seen too much evidence of a seditious disposition in that people over which he reigned, and therefore warns them again and again of the sin and danger of provoking kings to anger. Men have such a degree of self-will and pride, that they can scarcely be prevailed upon to submit to the necessary

*Isaiah 28:7,8   †Hos. 7:5   ‡1 Cor. 10:31, Eph. 5:8, Ps. 36:8

restraints of their liberty. Liberty is a valuable thing, but licentiousness is the ruin of nations.

If the fear occasioned by the displeasure of a king is so intolerable, what must it be to encounter the wrath of Him whose voice is not only like the roaring of a lion, but like the sound of many thunders. His voice shakes the heaven and the earth, and neither men nor devils shall be able to endure the terrors of it. To sin against Christ is to sin not only against our lives, but against our immortal souls *.

Ver. 3. *It is an honour for a man to cease from strife, but every fool will be meddling.*

It is an honour for a man to leave off strife before it be meddled with, and to overlook these things that might stir up anger †. But when a man is engaged in contention, is it an honour for him to give it up ? Will not the world say that we have a bad cause, or weak arguments, or a mean spirit, if we have not the last word ?

No matter what the world says, if the Spirit of God says other things. It is here declared to be honourable for a man to give up a debate for the sake of peace and quietness. By so doing we testify our humility and meekness, our obedience to God, and our aversion to sin. Christ did not strive, nor cry, nor cause his voice to be heard in the street, and surely it is a man's honour to imitate, as far as our weakness will allow, the meekness and gentleness of Christ. It was wise in Paul to make an acknowledgment of his error in speaking disrespectfully of the high priest, although that partial judge well deserved the sharpest reproof for his partiality and tyranny; and it would have been wise in Job's friends to have yielded to the force of his convincing arguments, rather than, by endeavouring to

---

*Rev. 1:10-20   †Chap. 17:14, 19:11

maintain their errors, to expose themselves to the displeasure of God, and to the just mortification of being obliged to have recourse to the intercessions of that good man whom they had so deeply injured.

But every fool will be meddling; for a fool is so self-conceited, that he can bear no contradiction; so impertinent, that he will have a hand in every other man's business; so proud, that he cannot bear to be found in the wrong; and so stubborn, that he will have the last word, although his lips should prove his destruction. Amaziah was fairly warned of the danger of meddling with the king of Israel, but he would not hear reason, nor cease from strife, till he was brought with his kingdom to the verge of ruin. Zedekiah, the son of Chenaanah, entered into contention with the good prophet Micaiah, and had the insolence to strike that faithful servant of the Lord, but was soon after compelled to flee to an inner chamber to hide himself.

This is one difference between wise men and fools: The former are for peace, the latter are ordinarily keen for battle *. This may be illustrated from the difference between the behaviour of Nabal and David; Nabal had a very bad tongue, for as Nabal was his name, so folly was with him. He gave a very provoking answer to a very civil message from David, and thereby exposed himself and his family to ruin; David had human nature, and his passions were too fierce, but it was his honour that he was easily pacified, and although he did not leave off contention, as he should have done, before it was meddled with, yet he left it off before it came to a fatal extremity.

Ver. 4. *The sluggard will not plow by reason of the cold, therefore shall he beg in harvest, and have nothing.*

It is one plain evidence of sloth for a man to be dex-

*Ps. 120:7

trous in finding excuses to shift off necessary work. If a small inconveniency be allowed as an apology for idleness, excuses will never be wanting.

The sluggard will not plow by reason of the cold, and he will not sow because the ground is not in good order, and he will not weed his field because of the heat of summer, and he will not reap in harvest because he cannot endure to bend his back, and is afraid of an headache. But is there any other useful business that can suit him, since husbandry is so disagreeable? No, one business would oblige him to a sedentary life, another is attended with too much fatigue, a third is too mean for a gentleman, a fourth requires a man to rise early in the morning. He will sleep or lean on his elbow, or he will divert himself with any kind of sport, or he will talk till you are tired with him, or he will play at cards, for although he abhors business, he loves busy idleness. He will either do nothing, or what is worse than nothing.

But he that will not work must beg, and this is surely a mean employment for a man that is able to work; but although he can conquer shame sufficiently to betake himself to it, his misery is, that nobody will give him any thing, for why should drones eat the labour of the bees? Even in harvest, when plenty smiles all around, and when the hearts of men are enlarged with joy, and bestow liberal quantities of food upon their beasts, the wretched sluggard finds that every man's bowels are shut against him. The industrious and disabled poor have then a good time, for the law of God requires the gleanings and leavings of the fields to be allowed them; but the same law requires that he who will not work should not eat.

Spiritual sloth is discovered by this mark, and attended with the like misery. The careless Christian will not attend the house of God, by reason of the cold of winter, or the heat of summer; he will not keep up the worship of God in his family because he is encumbered with worldly business ; or if shame and love of character oblige him to perform those services which the eyes of men behold, there is so much attention of spirit necessary for the duties of the closet, that he cannot find in his heart to perform them at all, or to perform them to any good purpose. What will become of such sluggards at the end of the world ? Our Lord tells us, they will beg and have nothing*.

Ver. 5. *Counsel in the heart of man is like deep water, but a man of understanding will draw it out.*

The heart of man is a great deep, and there are thoughts and devices in it as much past numbering as the creeping things and fishes in the sea. God alone searches the heart, and tries the reins of the children of men. By one glance of his eye he pierces into the bottom of our souls, and knows our thoughts infinitely better than we ourselves.

But although a man cannot go to the bottom of a deep well, he may draw out some of its water for use by means of a bucket, and although a man cannot penetrate into the bottom of another man's heart, he may find out some of his thoughts and contrivances, his purposes and designs, or form such conjectures about them as are necessary to regulate his own motions. A man of understanding, without the gift of prophecy may know many things that are useful to be known about the counsels of those that are most desirous to conceal them. David discovered, and represented before his God the secret projects of his enemies against him, when both the inward thought and the heart of every one of them was deep ; and Job saw clearly what his friends aimed at by all their flaming discourses about the misery of the wicked, before they named himself as the object of that vengeance which they described†.

---

*Matt. 25:1-11   †Job 21:27,28

A man of sagacity has a knowledge of human nature, which assists him in finding out the contrivances and designs of particular men. He can avail himself of their gestures, their general course of behaviour, their behaviour in particular instances, and on sudden emergencies, their silence, their words, even when they are disguising their thoughts, their connections and company, their interests and humours, to form our judgment of their thoughts and designs, and by this means he is often enabled to guard himself and his good name from the snares of the wicked. Wisdom is profitable, you see, not only for the life to come, but likewise for the present life; but hypocrisy and dissimulation profiteth little. It is often detected by men, it is always known to God; and the day is coming in which he will make manifest the secrets of all hearts.

Ver. 6. *Most men will proclaim every one his own goodness, but a faithful man who can find.*

It is very natural for men to have an high opinion of themselves, and there are few men who have not a better opinion of their own worth than any other man has, but a man of consideration will discern the folly of self conceit, and will be cautious of publishing his own imagined virtues to the world.

There are few who have the good sense to consider these facts, and therefore it is very common in conversation to hear men proclaiming their own praises either directly, or by plain insinuations. If they are ashamed to talk of their own generosity and charity in an avowed manner, they catch at the good opinion, and applause of other men, by a variety of methods, sometimes commending virtue and goodness with a design of shewing their own love to it, at other times running down their neighbours, for the want of these virtues, imagining that the depression of other men will be their own exaltation. Sometimes they insist upon particular instances of goodness, which they think, from some known pieces of their behaviour, will be a mean of leading persons to think of themselves, and on other occasions, they will take occasion, from what others in the company are saying, to hale into the conversation some of their own good deeds, as if they had been led to mention them without any previous design.

But a faithful man can rarely be found. A man is not a proper witness in his own cause, for he is ready to form, from the influence of self love, too good an opinion of himself. If the love of our wives or children covers their faults, and magnifies their virtues, self love must have a still greater influence in bribing our judgments, so that an honest man's testimony of his own goodness can scarcely be taken. But among boasters, you will scarcely find a man so honest as not to exceed, in his own praise, the bounds of what he himself knows to be fact.

The Scripture declares, that a truly good man is rarely to be found, and yet if men's own word could be taken, there is scarcely a bad man to be found. We have therefore great need to be cautious in forming our judgment of ourselves, lest we deceive our own souls, and pass a sentence upon ourselves, opposite to that which our great judge will pass upon us at the last day.

Nor must we be rash in trusting men, and choosing friends. He is one among a thousand, who possesses such kindness and integrity, as will entitle him to the character of a faithful friend.

We learn, in the last place, from this proverb, to let strangers praise us, rather than our own lips, except when evident necessity obliges us ; for self praise will make an hundred to conceive a bad opinion, sooner than one wise man to entertain a good opinion of us.

Ver. 7. *The just man walketh in his integrity, his children are blessed after him.*

The just man lives by the faith of the Son of God,

for, like his father Abraham, he believes in the Redeemer, and his faith is counted to him for righteousness ; but although he is pronounced by God a righteous person, for the sake of a righteousness not wrought by himself, yet he is not the less earnest in endeavouring to be holy in all manner of conversation, for he knows that those men deceive themselves who turn the grace of God into lasciviousness, and that he who doth righteousness is righteous, even as God is righteous.

The just man is a man of integrity, for he follows after perfection, although he knows that he cannot reach it and live. He does not think that a good and kind behaviour towards men, will compensate for the neglect of his duty to God, any more than a social behaviour will atone for disloyalty to his prince, and therefore he makes it his daily practice to walk in all good conscience before God, and to testify the utmost gratitude to him that loved us and died for us. At the same time, he feels the force of that saying of Scripture, which is sufficient to strike an alarm into the most hardened consciences of those that neglect morality whilst they profess religion, "If a man say I love God, and hateth his brother, he is a liar *. The integrity of the just man, is not like the pretended integrity of the moralist, for it includes piety, justice, sobriety, and a conscientious regard, to every precept of God, without excluding those that appear to vain men to be of small importance, or those that most directly oppose the prevailing disposition of the mind.

The just man walketh in his integrity, for his righteousness is not like the morning cloud, but like the light of the sun, which shineth more and more unto the perfect day. God tries him, the devil and the world, and the flesh, solicit him to sin, but he will not turn

---

*1 John 4:20

aside into the ways of iniquity, or if he should, he will not continue to walk in them, but returns with bitter regret to that 'good and straight way, which leadeth unto life, and continues in that path till the end of his life, for his heart is set upon it, and upon that heavenly city to which it leads. As for such as turn aside unto their crooked ways, it is plain from Scripture that they never really knew the way of life *.

Blessed is the man that fears the Lord. He is blessed in the day of prosperity, and in the day of adversity; he is blessed in life and death; he is blessed after death, for he rests in his bed, and enters into peace. His soul is blessed in heaven, and he leaves blessings to his children upon earth. If the children of Jehu, who never took heed to walk in the law of the Lord, were blessed with outward prosperity, to the fourth generation, how much more may the truly godly expect a blessing to their seed? It is said of the wicked man, that God layeth up iniquity for his children, he rewardeth him, and he shall know it; and will the God who delights in mercy, exercise less kindness to his own people, than severity to the wicked? Far from it †. Whilst the rich man rejoices that he has much treasure laid up in his house, to be enjoyed by his family after him, the godly man has much more reason to believe that God has a treasure of blessings laid up for his children.

Are you children of the godly? know ye the God of your fathers, and plead this promise at his throne of mercy ‡.

Ver. 8. *A king that sitteth in the throne of judgment scattereth away all evil with his eyes.*

Kings have majesty in their countenances, and when

*1 John 2:19   †Exod. 20:5,6   ‡1 Chron. 28:9, 2 Chron. 6:42

they preserve their dignity of character, their eyes are terrible to the breakers of the law. This awe of royalty is impressed by God upon the minds of men, for the peace and benefit of human society, and kings are obliged to use that authority with which the Most High has dignified them as his ministers, for the encouragement of virtue and the suppression of vice. Kings in our days don't sit on the throne of judgment in their own persons, but by delegates, but both they and those who are employed by them as judges, are bound to observe this rule. Kings are accountable for the choice they make of persons to be employed under them for the administration of justice, and those that serve them must account also to the King of all the earth.

How tremendous is that Eternal King, whose eyes are like a flame of fire, and how shall sinners be able to stand before him, at whose presence the heaven and the earth flee away, and no place is found for them! How can men presume that the Judge of all the earth will suffer sin to go unpunished, when he will not permit his vicegerents on earth, to leave open wickedness to go unpunished. But earthly kings can punish only the outward enormities of men's lives. The universal Judge brings every work into judgment, with every secret thing. Earthly kings reach only the body, but the King of heaven can destroy both soul and body in hell fire.

Ver. 9. *Who can say, I have made my heart clean, I am pure from my sin?*

If we say that we have no sin, we deceive ourselves, for we were conceived and shapen in iniquity, and unless our hearts are made clean, we must remain for ever abominable in the sight of the most holy God. The depravity of the human race is not here expressly asserted, but it is taken for granted, as an incontestable truth.

The call of God to sinners is, Wash ye, make you clean : Cleanse your hands, ye sinners, purify your hearts, ye double minded. But neither our righteousness nor our strength lies in ourselves. Except Christ wash us, we have no part in him, and remain under the reigning power of sin. But even those that are washed by his blood and spirit, cannot say that they have made their hearts so clean, that they are entirely pure from their sin. They are daily employed in cleansing themselves from all pollutions, and yet the leprosy of sin will cleave to their earthly tabernacles, till they are pulled down by death.

If sin dwells in the best of us, our dependence must be on the grace of the Redeemer, by whose blood our sins are expiated, and by whose powerful agency we crucify the flesh with its affections and lusts. Purity of heart ought to be our constant sudy, for so far as our hearts are cleansed, we are pure from our sin ; and under all the imperfections of our holiness, we have reason to join thanksgiving with our sorrows, for although no man on earth can lay claim to perfect purity, yet every believer in Jesus has abundant encouragement to hope that he shall be presented in due time, without spot or blemish, before the throne of God.

Ver. 10. *Divers weights and divers measures, both of them are alike abomination to the Lord.*

Once hath God spoken, yea twice have we heard this, that unjust weights are detested by God *; and it is plain that unfair measures come under the same condemnation. But here they are expressly mentioned, so that no man can pretend to observe the letter of the law, whilst he transgresses the spirit of it. If a man keeps one measure or weight for selling, and another for buying, or if he keeps one for selling to people

---

*Chap. 11:1, 16:11

that have too much skill to be cheated, and another for selling to the ignorant and unwary, he exposes himself to the hot anger and severe vengeance of God, who hates all unrighteousness, especially that which lies in perverting the means of justice *.

If the perversion of the instruments of just trade is detestable to God, how much does he abhor the perversion of law and justice, and every kind of partiality in those whom he entrusts with the adminstration of government, in church or state. Injustice in merchants is very bad, but unrighteousness in those that bear the sword for God, or rule in the name of Christ, is a great deal more dishonourable to God, and offensive to the eyes of his glory.

Ver. 11. *Even a child is known by his doings, whether his work be pure and whether it be right.*

Except ye be converted, says our Lord, and become as little children, ye cannot enter into the kingdom of God. Sincerity is one of those qualities wherein we ought to resemble children, for they cannot disguise their inclinations, but a little attention to their childish talk and behaviour will enable a person to discover their present dispositions, and to form a probable conjecture concerning their future behaviour.

One thing appears in the behaviour of children with too much evidence, that they are the descendants of Adam. The selfishness, vanity, and revengeful spirit, that appears in all of them, are lineaments of the image of the first transgressor. But there is a very great difference among them in their temper, which may be justly considered as an indication of a greater difference in the manner of their conduct, when they arrive at manly years. Some are kind and obliging, and easily managed, others are intractable, sullen, and spiteful ;

*Micah 6

and it is the duty of parents to improve and cherish the good dispositions which they discover, and to check every appearance of vice, before it is matured by time into settled habits. Parents generally consider the genius and inclinations of their children, to direct them in the choice of a profession, but they ought to be no less careful to consider their turn of mind in their earliest years, to direct themselves in their religious education. Herein several parents discover their partial fondness for their children, regarding with applause every appearance of goodness as a happy presage, but considering every instance of perverse behaviour as an instance of childish ignorance, which time will reform of course; but Solomon tells us, that their bad, as well as their good behaviour, when they shall become men, may be conjectured from their childish doings.

Children of a pleasant disposition may disappoint the expectations that have been formed of them, but in that case parents may generally thank themselves for neglecting to avail themselves of their good dispositions, to graft on them religious instructions, or for permitting them to fall into the dangerous society of those that not only live in sin, but, like Jeroboam, make Israel to sin.

When bad dispositions appear in children, it is necessary for parents to use betimes those means which God has appointed for reclaiming them. The rod and reproof give wisdom; and when these, and the like means, are neglected, or not accompanied with fervent prayer, parents have great reason to reflect on themselves with shame, if their children prove thorns in their eyes, when their vices have attained the vigour of riper years, and confirmed custom.

There is an old proverb that says, a young saint makes an old devil, but Solomon was not the author of it.

Ver. 12. *The hearing ear, and the seeing eye, the Lord hath made even both of them.*

And did he not make every other part of our bodies, as well as the eye and the ear? No doubt, but we ought not to rest in general truths, when we contemplate the wonderful works of God. It is highly proper for us, to survey with attention the particulars of what the Lord hath done for us, and we shall find abundant materials for gratitude and praise, in every member of our body, in every faculty of our soul, and in every event of our life.

It is said that the famous physician Galen learned the absurdity of atheism from the consideration of the human eye. The structure of it clearly displays the amazing wisdom of God, and his goodness shines with no less brightness in the pleasures and advantages derived from the ministry of this admirable organ. The ear is that sense by which we enjoy the pleasures of society and friendship, by which we learn the most interesting and entertaining truths, and by which we receive the instructions of life.

It is by the kind agency of our Maker that our eyes see, and our ears hear, for in him we live and move. When he pleases to withhold his influence, we see, and do not perceive, like Hagar at Beer-lahai-roi. We hear a voice, and know not what it says, like the companions of Saul in his journey to Damascus.

To use these instruments of sense as inlets to temptation and sin, is as unnatural as for infants to rend that breast which gives them suck. How shocking is it to deserve the reproof that the prophet gave to Belshazzar! "The God in whose hand thy breath is, and all thy ways, hast thou not glorified." We are God's creatures. Our senses are his; our souls are his; all our enjoyments are from his bounty, and our activity depends upon his all-governing providence. Whether, therefore, we see, or hear, or think on those objects which we are acquainted with, by means of our bodily senses, or the exercise of our rational powers, let us mind above every thing, the glory of God.

Ver. 13. *Love not sleep, lest thou come to poverty, open thine eyes, and thou shalt be satisfied with bread.*

Sleep, must be taken, but not loved. Sleep, as well as food, is necessary for refreshing our frail bodies, but neither food nor sleep must be used for their own sakes, nor must we be intemperate in either of them. Sleep taken in a moderate degree, is the nurse of nature, it recruits our animal powers, and prepares us for the labours of life; but excess of sleep enervates the body, and stupifies our souls, and is loved only by sluggards. We have received time and talents from God, to be used according to his direction, and to waste the one, and bury the other, is a very great sin; and yet by immoderate sleep, we do both in some degree, for all the time that we sleep beyond what is needful for us, our talents are unemployed, and the time of our life is running on in vain. Long life is universally desired, and death set at as great a distance as possible, but the lover of sleep voluntarily gives up a considerable part of his life, and during all the time that he wastes in needless sleep, he might as well be in the state of death, for any thing he does, or enjoys. I remember Dr. Doddridge gives this reason for his being able to write so many books, notwithstanding all the weighty employments that were constantly lying on him, that he found a great difference between rising at five, and rising at eight in the morning, the one making several years more in the course of a life than the other.

Poverty and hunger, in the course of things, according to the righteous appointment of providence, are the ordinary consequences of too much sleep; plenty and satisfaction, the consequences of early rising. Open thine eyes, rise and go to work, for he that gets out of bed, and sits idle at the fire-side, is still sleeping, even when he is awake. But he that rises to his employment, shall have bread for himself and his family. It is not said, he shall have every thing that an unbridled appetite might crave, but he shall have, by the blessing of God, bread to eat, and raiment to put on. These things would have satisfied Jacob, although he was brought up in a very rich family, and these things will generally satisfy a man diligent in his business, for his work makes both sleep and food pleasant to him.

If persons that love their work, should prove unsuccessful in business, or be disabled from working, they will meet with pity and relief, whilst starving sluggards, are hated and despised.

Ver. 14. *It is naught, it is naught, saith the buyer, but when he is gone his way, then he boasteth.*

Solomon was a teacher to men of all ranks, for he was acquainted with the life and manners of men in every profession, and writes instructive proverbs for merchants as well as kings. There is one piece of fraud censured in this verse, which is very common with the lower sort of dealers, and is scarcely reckoned a piece of unrighteousness. It is the art of buyers to get a good bargain, by depreciating the commodity which they mean to purchase. The inspired moralist, that he might come home to men's bosoms, gives us their very words, " it is naught, it is naught." What is the ill of saying this ? Why, if it be not true, it must certainly be a lie, and no lie is of the truth, nor any lying habit consistent with the character of an honest man. Men may, if they please, form to themselves rules of morality from the general practice of the world, but these are not the rules by which they must be judged at the last day. If we were heathens, we could not be excused in using little tricks that come not within the compass of the criminal law, but we are Christians, and our bibles testify against them, and threaten punishment to those that go beyond and defraud their brother. Indeed, very little is to be made by such poor artifices but guilt, for they are so common that almost every man sees through them.

The people that use these pitiful tricks in making a bargain, don't think there is much evil in them, for they boast of their art and good fortune. But men's shutting their eyes will not alter the nature of things. Ephraim became a merchant, the balances of deceit were in his hand, he loved to oppress, and yet he would not have it said, that any iniquity was to be found in him that were sin; there was either no sin in his conduct, or if there was any, it was very venial *. Men bless and applaud themselves in their dexterity to impose upon their neighbours, but what says the spirit of God about them ? " Woe to them that call evil good, and good evil." Whilst they boast of the goodness of the commodities which they formerly called naught, they denounce this woe against themselves.

The spirit of this proverb includes in it, a condemnation of the like methods that sellers use to get bad commodities disposed of. When a man commends his wares above their value, or gives a false account of the price which they cost him, or of the price that he was offered for them, or when he uses deceitful means to conceal their bad properties, he is dealing unrighteously, and seeking the gain of extortion, by which he is not so likely to fill his purse as to wound his character, and bring the curse of God upon his substance.

Ver. 15. *There is gold, and a multitude of rubies, but the lips of knowledge are a precious jewel.*

It is a great deal easier to spread riches than wisdom

---

*Hos. 12

through a nation. In the days of the wisest of kings, silver was plenteous as the stones, but wisdom was still a rare commodity*. Yet Solomon never ceased to inculcate the superior value of wisdom, but such is the depravity of man's understanding, that the gifts of fortune are generally preferred to those of the mind, and you will find many that learn the art of being rich, for one that acquires the lips of knowledge.

The wisest and richest of kings, inspired by the Author of wisdom and riches, frequently reminds us, that the lips directed by true knowledge, are a more precious jewel than any that can be found in the mines of the east; and a deep impression of this truth would be of very great advantage to our souls. When a man values gold and rubies above wisdom, he lies exposed to a thousand temptations of a very dangerous kind, for he is like a blind man that knows not whither he goes, and will leap into a pit, if he imagines that money is at the bottom of it, because he sees not how deep it is, and how impossible it will be to get out. But he that prefers the lips of knowledge to riches, has his eyes in his head, and steadily observes the ways of religion and happiness.

Did we really believe this truth we would not grudge time, and expense, and labour, in obtaining wisdom for our own benefit and the use of others, and would account a wise and faithful friend, one of the most precious treasures. The word of God would be valued as it deserves, and the world would lose its tempting influence.

Ver. 16. *Take his garment that is surely for a stranger, and take a pledge of him for a strange woman.*

We lately heard that the love of sleep will soon reduce a man to poverty and hunger. It is not, however,

---

*Eccl. 7:28

the speediest method of becoming poor, for nothing will so soon ruin a man's estate and credit, as rash surety-ship. If you see a man that engages in cautionry for one that is a stranger to him, and especially for a strange woman, trust him not if he should swear, and offer you the surest bonds for payment; he will in a very short time become a bankrupt, and therefore lend him no-thing, and if you sell him any thing without ready mo-ney, be sure to have a sufficient pledge. You may even take his garment without any breach of charity, for the law about restoring the garment taken by way of pledge, was made for the benefit of the poor and unfortunate, and not for those that are running to ruin by their own wil-ful folly. If a man, by an excess of generosity, hurts himself by engaging in suretyship for his friends, he plays the fool, and yet he may be pitied; but how can that man expect pity, who squanders away his substance for the sake of people with whom he has no connexion, or of bad women, with whom it is infamous to have any dealings?

Ver. 17. *Bread of deceit is sweet to a man, but af-terwards his mouth shall be filled with gravel.*

There is some kind of pleasure in sin, by which the devil draws men into his snares, and keeps them entang-led. There are indeed some sins in which we cannot discover any pleasure, but those who practise them appear to love the devil's service so well, that they will do his work without any wages; such are profane swear-ers, and the agents for infidelity; but sinners in general must have some present enjoyment from their sins, to compensate for the guilt and danger of them.

A man would not do a piece of injustice without the prospect of some gain and satisfaction from it, and when he has gained what he expected, he feels some pleasure from it, and applauds himself for his wit and success; for his present advantage drowns for a time the thoughts of what shall come to pass hereafter.

But men should always remember, that the time now present, was some years ago far distant, and yet is now come, and our feelings of pain and anguish are as lively as ever, and the time to come will one day be present, and bring its sensations of happiness and misery along with it. He is rather a brute than a rational creature, who would rather be happy for a day, and miserable for the rest of his life, than deny himself the present pleasures which are sure to bring lasting misery in their train. Such are the gains of dishonesty; they are like pleasant bread in the mouth of the covetous man, but his teeth are afterwards tormented with gravel, and his belly is racked with pains more grievous than those of the fiercest diseases that ever preyed on the human constitution. Providence usually crosses and disappoints unrighteous men, and makes them to vomit up the riches which they have swallowed down, and they produce a worm in the conscience, that gnaws the soul with teeth more poisonous than those of the viper.

Zophar uses every terrible image to illustrate the miseries of the unjust man, and yet all are insufficient to describe the terrors of that vengeance, which the wrath of God inflicts on those who have the presumption to think, that any advantage can be gained by sinning against God, and wronging their fellow creatures.

Ver. 18. *Every purpose is established by counsel, and with good advice make war.*

Wisdom lies, in the first place, in forming right purposes, and secondly, in devising, and executing proper plans for bringing these good purposes to pass. However good our designs are, yet rashness and inconsideration will be sure to render them abortive; and, besides our own wisdom, it is necessary for us, in all matters of importance, to take the advice of the wise and upright. If we have such a high opinion of our own wisdom, that we think we have no need of counsel from other men, we prove ourselves fools of the worst kind, for there is more hope of any other kind of fools, than of those that are wise in their own conceit. Do we restrain wisdom to ourselves? are we wiser than Solomon, who had too much sense to think himself above the need of a privy council of the wisest men in the nation*?

Above all things, war is to be made with good advice, for the want of which, many nations have been brought to desolation. It is one of the greatest judgments to a land, when the wise counsellors of it are removed, or infatuated, or when the sovereigns of it are so unwise as not to make use of their counsels. Rehoboam, foolish as he was, had the sense to make use of his father's instruction in this point, although he had neglected it a little before, in another affair of no less consequence. By his neglect of it, he lost ten tribes, but his observing it afterwards, was the mean of preserving his authority in the other two.

We have need of good advice in our spiritual warfare, for our enemies are incomparably superior to us in strength and skill. We may receive great benefit from the counsels of some of our fellow soldiers, but the word and Spirit of God are infinitely the best counsellors in this, and in every other point. They only shall overcome, who are strong in the Lord, and use those divine weapons that God has prepared for our defence, and cry for God's help against the enemy. These are the counsels given us by the Spirit of God, and as our success entirely depends upon his help, we must comply with his instructions.

---

*1 Kings 12

Ver. 19. *He that goeth about as a tale-bearer revealeth secrets, therefore meddle not with him that flattereth with his lips.*

Flatterers are generally tale-bearers. They sooth and caress a man to fish his secrets out of him, and they tell the secrets which they have got by these base means, to the next companion they meet, and perhaps make very considerable additions to them, for they take the liberty to add conjectures of their own to what they have heard. By spreading their stories, they sow the seeds of contention among neighbours, and their words are as wounds which go down into the innermost parts of the belly.

Beware, then, of those flatterers, that cajole you with good words, and fair speeches. Self love makes us flatterers of ourselves, and disposes us to be well pleased with those that comply with all our humours, assent to all our opinions, and approve of all our actions. But those who speak us fair are not our friends, but for the most part the most dangerous enemies we have. If we give them our company, we are very likely to hear stories about ourselves that will vex us ; if we tell them any of our secrets, we may be sure of having them divulged, and represented to our disadvantage. When they tell us stories about other people, we may judge how they will behave to us, for when they were in the company of these persons, they flattered them as much as they now flatter us, and by their pretences of friendship, they made a shift to pick up these tales with which we are now entertained.

It is an excess of self love, that makes the company of a flatterer tolerable. It is the want of love to our neighbours that makes us bear with tale bearers, but if we will not discountenance them for the sake of our neighbours, let us do it for our own, for they will mete out the same measure to us, that they have already meted out to other men *.

Ver. 20. *Whoso curseth his father or his mother, his lamp shall be put out in obscure darkness.*

For a man not to honour his father and his mother, is a violation of one of the ten commandments in the letter of it. A curse was pronounced from mount Ebal upon him that setteth light by his father or his mother : The miserable condition of the Africans, and the negroes in America, is a monument to this day of God's judgments upon a man, who lived 4000 years ago, for discovering his father's shame. But is it possible that any man can rise to such a pitch of impiety, as to curse his father or his mother ? It seems it is. But wo to them who are chargeable with it. Had they lived under the Mosaic law, they must have died without mercy †. But if they live in our times, their sin is not the less, and although they should escape punishment from men, they shall not escape the vengeance of the Father and King of the universe.

When those crimes that deserve death are unpunished by men, the perpetrators of them are not always so safe as they expect ; God often permits them to fall into other crimes, that bring them to the gallows, as we may learn from the confessions and last speeches of many malefactors who have lamented their disobedience to their parents, as the first step to their ruin, or acknowledged other crimes worthy of death, besides these for which they suffer. But if those who treat the instruments of their being with insult and outrage, should escape every visible testimony of vengeance in this life, their lamp shall be extinguished in the blackness of darkness. The punishment prepared for all impenitent sinners, is described in Scripture by this gloomy

---

*Prov. 13:11   †Lev. 20:9

image; but surely there are regions of thicker darkness than the rest in hell itself, for those who are guilty of crimes that would shock the ordinary run of sinners.

Ver. 21. *An inheritance may be gotten hastily at the beginning, but the end thereof shall not be blessed.*

We have been often told, that no profit can be made by the wages of unrighteousness; but experience seems to contradict this truth, for we have seen or heard of several that have amassed great treasures by fraud and extortion.

This does not, however, militate against any thing which the inspired moralist has said, for he never meant to deny that treasures may be obtained by wickedness. They that will be rich may get riches by cheating and lying, by fraud and oppression, by grinding the faces of the poor, and by toiling their poor servants till they groan under their hard bondage. These and a thousand other ways of getting, and saving unjustly, may put money in their pockets, but the fact is that it is of no use to them, when they have got it.

Treasures of wickedness profit nothing, for a very plain reason, because they are not attended with the blessing of God, and it is only this blessing that preserves riches and makes them a comfort to men. It is far better to have nothing, than to have the riches of kingdoms without the blessing of God, for those that want it, will find every thing they have a curse.

But you will say, how do they succeed in getting an estate without the blessing of God? wait a little, and it will be seen that there is no blessing in what they have got. If they have been heaping up mountains of gold, they will be found only mountains of snow, which the curse of God will soon melt. He shall not be rich, neither shall his substance continue, neither shall he prolong the perfection thereof upon the earth; what he gets unjustly shall not only be blasted, but it shall blast every thing that he had got by fair means. Ahab lost not only the garden of Naboth, but his life, and kingdom, and family, by his wickedness.

Beware of anxiety about wealth, for covetousness disappoints itself. It leads men to poverty, by pushing them on to unfair methods of gaining money. Stronger arguments might be advanced, and will be found in this book, against this sin, but this argument will have a deeper impression upon the minds of some persons, than any other. It is addressed to the only ear by which the covetous man can hear, for he is deaf to every thing but what concerns the mammon of un-righteousness. If he believes any thing that God says, he must see that he is taking a very foolish course, when he endeavours to enrich himself by those very means that are declared in Scripture to be the surest methods of bringing poverty and ruin.

Ver. 22. *Say not thou, I will recompense evil, but wait on the Lord, and he shall save thee.*

If private revenge were allowed, it would soon fill the land with confusion and blood ; for whilst men's passions are kindled by the smart of a fresh injury, they cloud the judgment, and hurry on those who are under their power, to the most dangerous irregulari-ties. By indulging them, we would be driven on to make very disproportionable returns for the wrongs done to us ; we might wreck our vengeance on the blameless, as David would have done, if Abigail had not disarmed his fury ; we might bring upon ourselves the guilt of the bloodiest crimes, and make ourselves miserable through all the remainder of our days. Most wisely, therefore, and graciously we are forbidden to avenge ourselves, or so much as to say that we will do it. It is a bad thing to have any thought of revenge, but if we say, or swear, that we will take satisfaction at our own hand from him that has offended us, we are entangled in a dangerous snare by the devil, who will endeavour to persuade us that our honour is doubly engaged by the provocation received, and by our word to take revenge.

To say that we will recompense evil, is the same thing with saying, that we will step into the throne of God, and wrest his thunderbolts out of his hand, to hurl them against all that we judge to be our enemies ; for vengeance is mine, saith the Lord, and I will repay it.

But our corrupt hearts are dexterous in mustering up objections against our duty, and the inspired writers are equally dexterous in answering them. If I suffer the wrongs done to my credit and estate to pass unrevenged, says one, I expose myself to every shaft of malice, and may expect still greater injuries than those I have already received. There is no fear of that, says Solomon, wait on the Lord, and he shall save thee. Art thou defrauded in thy interests ? wait on the Lord who gives and takes away at his pleasure, and he will make up, if he sees it good for thee, all thy loss. Amaziah, king of Judah, was none of the best of men, and yet at the persuasion of a prophet of the Lord, he could part with an army that cost him an hundred talents, because the Lord could easily give him much more than that. Art thou wronged in thy credit ? Trust in the Lord, and he shall bring forth thy righteousness to the light, as you find he did in the cases of Job, and David, and Mephibosheth. Whatever injury you have felt, or fear, commit thyself to God with a calm and forgiving spirit, and he will either prevent your fears, or make a rich amends for the malice of your enemies ; only you must give him his own time for doing it, for he that believeth does not make haste, but waits God's leisure, as it well becomes us to do when it is God whom we trust.

We must not wait on the Lord for destruction to our enemies. David was blessed with divine inspiration, and had directions for praying against some of his spiteful enemies, but herein we are not to consider him as a pattern for us. We have the noble example of our Lord Jesus Christ, who rendered not railing for railing, but prayed for his persecutors, leaving us an example that we should follow his steps. Wait on the Lord, and whatever way he deals with thine enemies, he shall save thee, and that is all thou canst reasonably desire.

Will you still insist that it is better to secure yourself against new injuries, by revenging the old? The question is clearly this: Is your safety and protection best lodged in God's hand or your own? By indulging your revengeful spirit, you do yourself a greater hurt than your greatest enemy can do you, for you gratify his ill-nature, when you suffer it to make a deep impression on your spirit, without which it could do you little or no hurt; but by committing your cause to God, you turn his ill will to your great advantage, making it an occasion for the exercise of the noblest graces, which are attended with the sweetest fruits, and with the rich blessing of God.

Ver. 23. *Divers weights are an abomination to the Lord, and a false balance is not good.*

Injustice is a poisonous weed, that springs up very plenteously in the heart of men, and it needs great pains to pluck it up, and the inspired writer does not grudge his pains for this purpose. When he might have been dazzling us with new discoveries of surprising truths in every sentence, he repeats the same warnings over and over, to reclaim men from every instance of dishonesty. How inexcusable will the unjust trader be, if he continues unreformed, after all that the Spirit of God has inculcated so frequently for his conviction and amendment *.

Ver. 24. *Man's goings are of the Lord, how can a man then understand his own way?*

The steps of all men are ordered by the Lord. Bad men are under the dominion of his providence, as well as good men who rejoice in his sovereignty, and he has a righteous hand in the most unrighteous actions of men. They sit deliberating and contriving, but they are under the eye of God, who laughs at their impious imaginations, and without suspending the freedom of their wills, determines them to concur in the execution of his holy and immutable purposes. They know not, when they are consulting, how they will determine; and when they have determined, whether they shall be steady in their purpose; and when they are fixed in their minds, whether they shall be able to perform what they intend; and if they perform it, whether it shall answer their intention, or some purpose entirely opposite to what they designed. But known unto God are all the thoughts that come or shall come into the minds of men, and how far their measures shall prosper, and what shall be the event and consequences of them. All the affairs of particular persons, and all the weighty businesses of states and kingdoms are in his hand like the potter's clay, to be moulded into any shape he pleases. And he will manage every thing wisely for his own glory, justly towards men, and graciously towards his own people.

Go to now, ye that say we will do this or the other thing, without any impression of God's sovereignty, or dependence on his providence. It is presumption in you to dream that your motions are under your own sovereign direction. Are you sure that you will be in the

---

*Verse 10

same mind an hour hence, that you are in at present? Alexander the Great went to Jerusalem with an inten- tion to wreak the fury of his revenge upon the people of God, and when he arrived, he shewed them greater favour than he ever did to another conquered nation. But if your resolutions should continue the same, do you live and move in yourselves, that you can be sure of the continuance of your life, and ability for doing what you propose? The kings and princes of the world sought to destroy our holy religion in its infancy, but the emperors who ruled the world were driven from their thrones, or chased out of the world, and of the kingdom of our Redeemer there shall be no end; for he that sits in heaven, saw from his dwelling place all their foolish contrivances, and baffled all their efforts, and said, "Yet have I set my king upon my holy hill of Zion." If you should be able to accomplish your de- signs, are you sure that they will have the effects you propose. The rulers of the Jews crucified Christ to gratify their spite, and to secure their place and nation from the Romans, but Christ conquered every enemy by his cross, and the Almighty executed the most tre- mendous vengeance by the hands of the Romans on the murderers of his beloved Son.

A conviction of this truth would make us to acknow- ledge the Lord in all our ways, and to endeavour to walk before him unto all pleasing. It would raise us above those strong temptations which have all their force from the fear of men's displeasure, or the hope of their favour. It would make the believer in Christ cheerful under every cross, whilst he could say, my heavenly Father rules all, and mine enemies can do nothing without his providence. It would raise us above all earthly confidences, being persuaded that the kindest and most powerful friends can do nothing for us, but as God pleases to incline and enable them. This

truth has also a mighty influence to destroy our confidence in our own strength and wisdom. The children
of Israel made great promises to God at mount Sinai,
but they soon broke them, for the Lord had not given
them eyes to see, nor ears to hear, nor hearts to understand *. Peter was very sincere in promising to cleave
to Christ, although all men should forsake him, but by
his self-confidence, provoked God to withhold the succours of his grace, and was left to behave, not like a
rock, but like the slender twig which bends before the
gentlest blast.

Ver, 25. *It is a snare to the man who devoureth that
which is holy, and after vows to make inquiry.*

Stealing and robbery are crimes so detestable and
pernicious to men, that they are every where severely
punished. But God is greater than men, and to rob
God is a greater and more dangerous crime than those
by which our fellow men are wronged in their substance. But will a man rob God? Can any man be so
bold as to try it, or so mighty as to accomplish it?
Malachi complains that this crime was very common
in his time, and there are too many instances of it, even
in these latter days. He that gives to the poor lends unto the Lord, and that which is appropriated to the service of the Gospel and the support of the ministry, belongs unto God, and should be given to his servants
as the receivers of his revenues, and therefore, when
the poor are cheated of their dues, or those that labour
in the gospel are deprived of their hire, or any thing
alienated that was justly devoted to the service of God,
a robbery is attempted, and, in some sense, executed,
upon God himself, who cannot be pleased with so base
and ungrateful conduct towards him, from whom we receive every thing that we possess.

*Deut. 29

The man who applies to his own use, and devours that which is holy, is greatly mistaken if he thinks himself a gainer. He is just in the same degree a gainer by his dishonest conduct, as the silly bird, when it snatches at the bait which the fowler has placed for it to draw it into his snare. The people of Judah in Haggai's time, were crossed and disappointed in all the labours of their hands, because they bestowed their money upon building houses to themselves, rather than in building the temple of the Lord; and in Malachi's time, the whole nation was cursed with a curse for robbing God in tithes and in offerings.

It is no less a snare for a man, after vows, to make inquiry, in order to evade the obligation of his solemn engagements. Some men are much more forward in making, than in paying vows. Their religion lies in transient flows of affection, not in solid piety. When their affections are roused by some remarkable providence, or allured by some pleasant, or roused by some alarming sermon, they are ready with their promises to the Most High, like Israel in the wilderness, but when their affections return to their usual temper, they endeavour to find out some shift, to free their consciences from their obligations, which they voluntarily took upon themselves. Their conduct draws them into the snares of the devil, who will suggest an hundred pretences to excuse the breach of them. We must therefore be leisurely and considerate in making vows, and speedy in performing them.

If we are Christians, we have engaged ourselves to be the Lord's. Justice and truth and gratitude require us to pay our vows, and every transgression against Christ, derives the great aggravation of treachery from our sacred promises. If our promises to men must be kept inviolate, how much more our promises to God. If it is sinful to make inquiry after vows, who can express the guilt that arises out of downright violations of them!

Ver. 26. *A wise king scattereth the wicked, and bring-eth the wheel over them.*

Such a king was David * and his son Solomon, and above all others the king that sits upon the throne of David for ever, who breaks in pieces the wicked like a potter's vessel.

The wicked in the nation are like the chaff among the wheat, and in those ancient times, the husbandman used to bring the wheel over the grain to separate from it the chaff. In like manner, the king who does not loll in his palace to indulge his pride and leisure, but sits upon the throne of judgment, will treat the wicked of the nation, breaking and dispersing them, that they may not prove a nuisance to society, an infectious plague to the country, and provocations of the wrath of God, against the whole nation.

Kings have but a limited power for this purpose, and must confine their punishments within the bounds of law. But the king of Zion, will thoroughly purge his floor by the fan in his hand, and will scatter all the impenitent sinners in his dominions, like the chaff before the wind †.

Ver. 27. *The spirit of man is the candle of the Lord, searching all the inward parts of the belly.*

The Father of our spirits, has bestowed on us a glorious distinction from the fowls of the air, and the beasts of the field. Our bodies were framed by his powerful agency, but our spirits were created by him within us ‡. In our animal bodies we have some resemblance of the brutes, but our intellectual faculty raises us to some degrees of likeness to the angels of God, for

---

*Ps. 101:1   †Matt. 3:11   ‡Zech. 12:1

they are candles lighted within us, by him that breathed into man's nostrils the breath of life, and made him a living soul.

By the light of reason, especially when it is brightened by divine revelation, we are enabled to survey many of the wonderful works of God, and to discern the evidences of his eternal power and Godhead. By this candle we can take a view of the wonderful structure of our own bodies, which are fearfully and wonderfully made. But the most necessary kind of knowledge which it gives us, next to the knowledge of God, is that of our own spirits. Deep as the hearts of men are, yet this candle of the Lord searches all the inward parts of the belly.

A king that was perfectly acquainted with the constitution, laws, and history of every country but his own, would be only an intelligent fool ; and the man is equally void of true judgment, who is thoroughly versed in every art and science, in all histories, and every branch of commerce and law, and yet is unacquainted with his own heart, where his main business lies. Heathens themselves were so deeply impressed with the importance of self knowledge, that it was a general opinion among some wise nations that the celebrated maxim "Know thyself" came down from heaven.

Reason rightly employed, will make us acquainted with the excellent nature and uses of our faculties, with our personal dispositions and talents, with our defects and constitutional faults, with our prejudices, and the temptations by which we are most ready to be overcome, with our state and frame in relation to God. The mention of these different branches of self knowledge, is enough to show the value and necessity of it. We are commanded to keep our own hearts with all diligence, and how can we keep them without some knowledge of their most important concerns ?

But we do not know ourselves unto perfection ; and therefore we ought to search deeper and deeper into our own hearts, to keep an eye upon the movements of our own minds, and the frame of our hearts under prosperous and adverse providences, and under injuries from men, or whilst we are employed in the performance of our duty to God, that we may improve in self-acquaintance. Above all, we ought to compare our hearts with the word of God, and to pray earnestly that God may discover us to ourselves, and preserve us from those self flatteries by which multitudes are deceived into eternal ruin. It is God alone that searches and knows infallibly the heart of man, and without the help of his Spirit, the candle within us will mislead us like wild fire, till we fall into the ditch of perdition.

Ver. 28. *Mercy and truth preserve the king, and his throne is upholden by mercy.*

A king must scatter and crush the wicked, but he will prove a tyrant unless he temper his severity with clemency and goodness. Severity to criminals is exercised by a wise king, from a principle of mercy to the community at large, and he will spare where he can spare without betraying his trust. Such behaviour secures the affections of his subjects ; and is attended with the blessing of providence, by which thrones are established. But unmerciful severity has often overturned the mighty from their seat. The Emperor Aurelian was called an excellent physician to the state, except in taking too much blood. His rigour drew upon him the hatred and fear of some of his own servants, who deprived him of his life after he had performed many signal services to the empire.

Truth must be joined with mercy in the administration of a good prince. Dissimulation may serve a single turn, but faithfulness and uprightness, in conjunction with clemency, are the sure and lasting pillars of the throne. If truth were banished from all the world beside, said Lewis IX. of France, it should be found in the breasts of kings.

How glorious is the Prince of the kings of the earth! Mercy and truth go before his face, his throne is a throne of grace, and faithfulness is the girdle of his reins.

Ver. 29. *The glory of young men is their strength, and the beauty of old men is the grey head.*

Equality of age and dispositions naturally produces affection and friendship, but difference of age and talents tends too much to produce mutual alienation. To remedy this, the wise man puts the old and the young in mind that each of them have their different endowments, which should endear them to one another.

Old men should not despise the young for their want of experience and gravity, for God has honoured them with vigour of body, which qualifies them for active service to God and their generation. How could old men defend their lives and properties, or how could they subsist, if they were not assisted by the strength of the young?

Far less should the young despise the old for their infirmities, or for that fretfulness of temper which old age too often produces. For God hath favoured them with length of days, and crowned them with grey hairs, the badge of their experience, and, it is to be hoped, of their wisdom. If the hoary head is the beauty of old men, it should draw respect from the young, who are commanded by God to rise up before the hoary head, and to honour the face of the old man.

It was a saying of Lewis XI. of France, when he was old, that if he had possessed in his youth that wisdom he had now acquired, or if he were still in possession of the vigour of youth, he could conquer all the world. It was better, it seems, for mankind that he did not possess both these qualities at once. God is wise and good in distributing his gifts amongst men of all ranks and ages, that none, by having every good quality, might become an idol to himself and others, and none, by wanting every thing valuable, might become an object of contempt.

Let young men beware of debasing their glory, by abusing their strength to the service of sin. Let old men endeavour to make their grey hairs venerable by wisdom and piety, by cheerfulness, and the command of their temper. Finally, let old men remember that they were once young, and young men remember that they would be glad to be one day old.

Ver. 30. *The blueness of a wound cleanseth away evil, so do stripes the inward parts of the belly.*

We are naturally very averse to chastisement and pain, and Solomon often represents a due regard to chastisement as a sign of wisdom, and here he tells us the great advantage of it to overcome our aversion. Correction and affliction for the present, seem to be not joyous, but grievous; but there is a far worse evil from which they are a means of reclaiming us. Sin is infinitely worse than affliction, and affliction is really turned into a blessing to those that rightly improve it, for those wounds that leave a blue mark behind them cleanse away evil, and stripes are instrumental, not only in reforming the life but in cleansing the heart.

Parents ought not, therefore, to spare the rod through foolish pity; at the same time they ought to join instruction and prayer with it, for still it must be remembered that the blessing of God alone can make it useful for cleansing the inward parts of the belly. Children ought to welcome the rod of chastisement, as a necessary means for their spiritual advantage.

The chastisements inflicted by magistrates upon malefactors that deserve not death, may have the same happy effect, and therefore mercy ought to mingle itself with the punishments inflicted upon them. According to the law, when a man deserved stripes he was not to receive more than forty, and the reason given was, "lest thy brother should seem vile unto thee." He was to be considered as a brother that might be reclaimed, and was not to be treated contemptuously, lest, by despair of recovering his character, he should be hardened in sin. The like tenderness is to be used in the administration of church discipline, that offending brethren may be gained.

Corrections from God are gracious and merciful, even when they are most severe, for his design in them is to make us partakers of his holiness, and to purge away sin. They are a tried medicine which God has often blessed for curing that vanity and earthliness of mind, that lukewarmness in prayer, that pride and thoughtlessness about eternal things, which are so common and dangerous distempers among men. Many that once groaned and cried out bitterly because of their afflictions, are now praising God for them among the choirs of angels, and many have seen great cause to be thankful on their account, before they left the valley of tears. Thou hast dealt well with thy servant, said the much afflicted king when he reviewed the providences of God towards him *.

---

*Ps. 119:65, 71

Proverbs 21

Verse 1. *The king's heart is in the hand of the Lord, as the rivers of water : he turneth it whithersoever he will.*

It is men's ordinary way to court the favour of princes and great men, as if their happiness depended on the smiles of kings, whilst they make little scruple of forfeiting the favour of God, by bending their consciences into a compliance with the humours of those for whom they entertain such undue respect. The like compliances are too often made, to avoid the displeasure of those that have power to hurt or kill the body.

Solomon directs us not to forfeit the favour of princes, or incur their displeasure, by any needless or wanton instances of disrespect. At the same time, he instructs us in the first place, to seek the favour of God, which is infinitely more necessary for us, than the friendship of the greatest men, and to avoid every thing that may displease him, if we should offend the mightiest tyrant in the world ; for the favour of God is all in all to us, and his wrath is tremendous beyond all conception, whilst kings are entirely dependent on the King of kings, and have their hearts governed by him, in such a powerful, though invisible manner, that they must, whether they design it or not, execute his unchangeable counsels.

The currents of water may be directed into any channel that is cut out for them by the hands of men ; even the mighty river Euphrates had its course changed by Cyrus, at the siege of Babylon. The waters still retained their nature and properties, and yet the power of that great prince managed their natural tendency to descend, in such a manner as to gain his purpose, and to take that great city, whereof they were reckoned the sure defence. The like influence has God upon the hearts of kings. He destroys not their natural faculties, nor takes from them the freedom of their wills; and, what is still more wonderful, he leaves them for the most part under the power of those natural corruptions which dispose them to exalt themselves above God, and to oppose his will. Yet still he makes them the instruments of his pleasure, and the ministers of his providence. Nebuchadnezzar thought himself almost a god*, and laid waste the Lord's land, and burnt his temple, and yet God calls him his servant, and used him to accomplish his work upon his people, as really as that noble king of Persia, whom he called his shepherd and anointed, and employed in doing his pleasure upon Babylon, and delivering his captives.

Those that walk before God unto all pleasing, may behold the stern countenances of tyrants without trembling, for God can easily turn their hearts to favour those whom they hated. The history of the three heroes in Babylon is a noble encouragement to all that are called to the like encounter for conscience sake. The fury of the king was raised to madness, his countenance was like a flame, and his fiery furnace burnt with a fierce rage; but all on a sudden the king commanded them out of the furnace, and he almost adored those whom, a few moments before, he could have torn like a wild beast with his own teeth.

It is certain that God has often suffered kings to wade in the blood of his people. This is a strange providence, but we can understand the consistency of it, with the truth delivered in the text; Daniel and John account for it to our satisfaction †.

If the heart of kings is in the hand of the Lord, why does he suffer them to use their power so frequently in

---

*Isa. 14   †Dan. 11:33-35, Rev. 6:9-17

536 / *Exposition of Proverbs*

opposition to the interests of his kingdom ? This is a
piece of the mystery of providence, which will be cleared up in due time, but appears dark to us at present.
Meanwhile, we must believe that God is righteous and
holy in all that he does, and suffers men to do ; he has
brought a rich revenue of praise to himself, out of the
dark administrations of providence in former ages, and
will in the end pour such light upon his ways, that he
shall appear in all things to be wonderful in counsel,
and excellent in working *.

Ver. 2. *Every way of man is right in his own eyes,
but the Lord pondereth the hearts.*

This is the same useful instruction which the wise
man already gave us †, and no admonition is more necessary to be inculcated than this : that men are too
often flatterers of themselves, and ought to remember
that they have a judge who will not be mocked nor imposed on, but searches the spirits, to give to every man
according to his ways, and the inward disposition of his
spirit. The inspired writers of both testaments insist
greatly on this point, and our Lord in his sermons frequently warned men against the dangerous influence
of self-deceit ‡.

Ver. 3. *To do justice and judgment is more acceptable to the Lord than sacrifice.*

It was a very common fault among the people of the
Jews, to lay too great a stress upon the performance of
sacrifice, as if that could atone for their sins, and give
them a title to transgress the moral law ; and the wise
man warns them against that piece of self-deceit, in
this verse. Solomon was far from undervaluing sacrifice as an institution of God, and a means of faith. No
man ever offered a greater number of beasts to God, or

---

*Rom. 11:33, Rev. 10:7, 19:1,2   †Chap. 16:2   ‡Deut. 5:28,
Ps. 36:2, Isa. 1:11, Jer. 2:35, Matt. 3:9, Gal. 6:7, Matt. 7:22, 13:25

did so much to encourage men in the observation of the ceremonial law, unless we may except the lawgiver himself; and perhaps the glory of the temple which he built, and the splendour of the temple service, might dazzle the eyes of men in his days, and occasion them to entertain too high an esteem of the ordinances that belonged to it. If any man had reason to say, the temple of the Lord, the temple of the Lord, Solomon had much more, but he learned otherwise from the Spirit who instructed him.

Sacrifices were appointed by God, they typified Christ, they were acceptable to God, as expressions of faith and obedience; but they were detestable to him when they were valued on their own account, as if they had been instituted for their own sake, or to give men opportunity of pleasing God so much, as to procure an allowance for the neglect of more important service. Sacrifices were appointed for a single nation; judgment and justice are required from every nation, and from every man under heaven. Sacrifices were required by a positive law, that depended on the pure will, not on the nature of God, and the observation of them was dispensed with on many occasions; but the love of justice is founded in the nature of God, obliges all men at all times, and can never be dispensed with. The law of sacrifices is long ago abolished, but the law of righteousness is an eternal statute. Sacrifices had no goodness in their own nature; and when men rested on them, they were abominable to God. Judgment and justice are a part of the image of God in man, and have an everlasting excellency in their nature. Sacrifices typified Christ, and were set aside in consequence of his great oblation; but is the law of justice abolished by the faith of Christ? nay, it is established, and shall continue when heaven and earth are no more.

If we would shew ourselves to be Abraham's seed,

we must keep the way of the Lord, to do judgment
and justice. It is a gross hypocrisy, it is a grievous dishonour to Christianity, and a ruin to the souls of men,
to pretend religion, and observe the forms of divine
service, and yet live in the neglect of those duties which
we owe to our fellow men *.

Ver. 4. *An high look, and a proud heart, and the
plowing of the wicked, is sin.*

The state of wicked men is miserable beyond expression, for they are every day and every hour adding to
those treasures of guilt which are already more than sufficient to sink them into the bottomless pit. They are
unclean before God in all the labours of their hand, and
those works which are accepted at the hands of others,
as instances of obedience to God, are reckoned to the
wicked in the number of their sins.

That an high look is abominable to God, is no surprise to us, for it is abominable even to men, and must
be infinitely more abhorred by God. We do not wonder to hear that the pride of the heart is hateful to him,
for he is the Searcher of hearts, and is jealous of his
own honour, and cannot bear that men should exalt
themselves into a rivalship with him ; but how the plowing of the wicked should be sin is not so plain, because
they are commanded to plow, and severely reproved
for the neglect of that work by which they ought to
support themselves and their families. If they are
plowing when they should be praying, or on Sabbath
days, every man will see that they are sinning ; but how
can their ordinary plowing be sin, when we are told
that plowing is a duty ?

Whether we eat or drink, or whatsoever we do, we are
required to do all to the glory of God. But the wicked man neither eats nor drinks, nor plows, nor sows, to

*Isa. 1:11

the glory of God, and therefore he lives in a course of sin, even when he is employed in those actions that are most innocent or necessary. His soul is infected deeply with the venom of sin, which spreads itself over all his conversation; for to the unbelieving and impure there is nothing clean. They are corrupt trees, and no fruit that grows upon them can be good. Their hands are defiled with sin, and their fingers with iniquity, and, therefore, every thing they touch must be defiled by their impurity *.

What then must the wicked do? Must they let alone all work lest they should sin in doing it? By no means. Idleness would bring upon them far more guilt than the labour of their callings, for that is sinful in itself; whereas plowing is sinful only by means of their own impurity communicated to it. Their business is to get free of that plague of sin that spreads infection to every thing they meddle with. Let them have recourse, like the leper, to Christ, that he may make them clean, and then being pure, every thing will become pure to them.

Some render these words thus: " The lamp or prosperity of the wicked is sin." Their prosperity is turned into a snare, and an occasion of sin to them by their wicked dispositions, which use it as an incentive to pride and impiety. Because their candle shines with brightness, they think it will never be put out, and think they stand in no need of the Sun of Righteousness to illuminate their souls. Wickedness is a most unhappy thing, for it perverts the objects that are most desirable in themselves to means of sin and ruin.

Ver. 5. *The thoughts of the diligent tend only to plenteousness, but of every one that is hasty only to want.*

Is not the hasty man a diligent man? He is often bu-

*Hag. 2:24, Tit. 1:15

sier than those who think before they act; and one would think that he must carry the prize of industry. Yet Solomon will not allow him a share of the praise that he bestows upon the diligent, because his activity is not under proper direction, and therefore cannot serve any good purpose. True diligence lies between laziness and too much speed, and is directed to its end by prudence and consideration. We must remember that we are rational creatures, and act as such both in our religious and civil affairs, and not suffer ourselves to be hurried hither and thither, by the impulse of humour and passion, or to be pushed on in any enterprise, however commendable, without thinking of the means proper for obtaining success.

Saul was in too great haste to make an end of the Philistines, and, therefore, he laid the people that were fighting with him under a curse, if they should eat any meat till the sun went down, by which step the victory was hindered from being complete. In common life, we see multitudes of persons that make too much haste to be rich, and so make themselves poor, by plunging into a multiplicity of business, and bringing confusion and embarrassment into their affairs. A man, by running himself out of breath, weakens his strength, and is later in arriving at the end of his journey, than another man, who walks at leisure, and puts himself under no necessity of stopping; and a man that minds his business, and carries it on with a prudent activity, is in a fair way of being rich, when another man, that drives on post haste to get an estate, becomes a bankrupt.

Although lukewarmness in religion is a very detestable disposition, yet rashness is no less dangerous. No business of life requires so much thought and prudence. Many, under the impulse of a rash zeal, have run briskly, and soon stopped and turned aside; and young converts, when their passions were more deeply tinctured with religion than their judgments, have too often hurt their own comfort, and the cause of religion itself, by their indiscreet forwardness in displaying their attachment to it. Christ would not have any person to embrace his cause without considering the cost of it*.

Ver. 6. *The getting of treasures by a lying tongue, is a vanity tossed to and fro of them that seek death.*

A lying tongue is an abomination to the Lord, and yet some will venture upon his displeasure, if they can make any profit by it; and it must be confessed that some present gain may be made by lying †, but then it answers no good purpose. Who would part with his sincerity, and the pleasure of a good conscience, for a little smoke, or for a handful of chaff? and all the treasures that can be made by a lying tongue, however great, are no better. They are vanities and lies that deceive the possessor, making him to believe that he is rich when he is miserably poor. They are a vanity tossed to and fro, like chaff or smoke in the wind, which will soon be out of sight; for riches gotten by vanity are soon consumed into nothing ‡.

But this is not the worst of the matter; for the persons that use such methods of obtaining riches seek death. Although they abhor the thoughts of death, yet in the judgment of God they love and seek it, for they take a sure method of bringing eternal death upon themselves, if not a miserable death in this world. Whilst others are walking towards the region of destruction, they are running to it post haste. They make haste to be rich, but greater haste to be damned, for neither their dishonesty nor their lies, will suffer them to be admitted into the kingdom of God.

Ver. 7. *The robbery of the wicked shall destroy them; because they refuse to do judgment.*

---

*Luke 14:25-33   †Chap. 12:19   ‡Chap. 13:11

It is impossible that the unrighteous should escape punishment, for they bring it upon themselves by the work of their own hands. Although there should be no magistrates to pass sentence upon them, or executioners to execute the sentence, yet their own robbery should destroy them. Their sin is the seed of misery, and it cannot fail of producing its proper fruit. They have none but themselves to blame for the vengeance to be poured out upon them. Their punishment cometh forth from the Lord of hosts, but the cause is in themselves.

Is their sin then unpardonable ? No. The blood of Jesus can cleanse from all sin. Zaccheus the publican was probably an extortioner, but salvation came to his house. His sin was pardoned, and he was made to abhor it as much as ever he had loved it ; and if he had taken any thing from any man by iniquitous means, he resolved to restore fourfold ; but this was a rare miracle of grace. When men have entered upon a course of injustice, they are seldom brought to repentance, for they are entangled in the snare of the devil, in such a manner that they seldom get out. Repentance brings with it restitution of what is gained by unrighteousness ; and when men restore, they are obliged to confess to their shame, their former acts of unrighteousness, and sometimes to impoverish themselves and their families.

These are terrible inconveniencies, to which men, in general, will not submit ; but the very thought of them is often sufficient to stifle all motions of their spirits towards any thing that is good. They will rather run the risk of God's wrath, than think of exposing themselves to disgrace and poverty in this world. Thus they go on in sin, and violently suppress the remonstrances of conscience whilst they live ; and when they die, they envy those grosser offenders who were condemned to the gallows, because the shame and punishment to which they were doomed, were effectual means of removing those peculiar obstacles which hinder the reformation of the unjust.

Beware of entering into this snare of the devil, if your hands are yet untainted by the pollution of filthy lucre, for there are mighty impediments to repentance for this sin. If you are entangled in these snares, remember that shame and poverty at present, are but painted misery in comparison of hell fire. Fly to the blood of atonement, which purged away the sins of the great transgressors at Corinth *. Repent, restore, shake your hands free of unrighteous gains ; for whilst you hold them fast, you are exposed to the destruction threatened in the word of God, because your hands refuse to do judgment.

Ver. 8. *The way of man is froward and strange : but as for the pure his work is right.*

The way of man is froward. Is the way of every man froward? or is it consistent with the dignity of human nature to contrast the way of man in general with the right work of the pure ? Are not men justly distinguished into the froward and the pure ; why then does Solomon speak as if all men were froward ? There is certainly truth in the division of men into the pure and impure ; but this distinction is the work of grace and not of nature, for men are all sprung from the first transgressor, and have derived a corrupt disposition from him, and till they are renewed by the grace of God, their way is froward and strange. They are all together become corrupt, and have done abominable things, if we may believe the testimony of the omniscient God himself †.

In our state of innocency our way was straight and even, whilst the glory of God was our great end, and

---

*1 Cor. 6:9,10   †Ps. 14, Rom. 3:10-18

the will of God the rule of our practice; but in our fallen state we walk in a crooked and perverse way, following the bent of our own evil inclinations, and seeking after happiness in creatures, which are like broken cisterns that can hold no water. Our course of life is directly the reverse of what it ought to be, for instead of making the will of our Creator the rule of our behaviour, we make it our business to provoke him to anger continually, by trampling upon his authority and despising his laws. Our way is a strange way, being a course of estrangement from the God that made us for his glory, and framed our natures to a capacity of enjoying him, and receiving happiness only in him. Till we are restored to communion with God through the mediation of Christ, we are aliens to the commonwealth of Israel, and our conversation is a continued proof of alienation from the life of God.

But as for the pure, he is raised above other men, and his work is very different. He is purified by the Spirit of Christ, and created in him unto good works. His work is regulated by an unerring rule, and directed to the noblest end, for his constant endeavour is to cleanse his way by taking heed thereto according to the word of God, and to walk in the world as Christ walked ; and he lives not to himself, but unto the Lord.

It is too natural for us to think that, if we are no worse than the generality of our neighbours, we are safe. But Solomon and Paul teach us, that, to walk as men, is not to walk like saints *. Whilst we are following the course of this world, we are walking in the broad road that leadeth to destruction, and not in the narrow way that leadeth unto life †.

Let every man prove his own work; but it must not be tried by the maxims or example of the world, but

---

*1 Cor. 3:3   †Eph. 2:1-3, Matt. 7:13,14

by the word of God, by which God will judge us at the last day *.

Ver. 9. *It is better to dwell in a corner of the house top, than with a brawling woman in a wide house.*

A man might dwell on a house top, if it were flat like the houses of the ancient Israelites ; but it would be a very uncomfortable place of dwelling, because it is exposed to rain and wind, to frost, and snow, and lightning ; but as the least of two evils is to be chosen, a wise man would rather choose to dwell on a house top, and be confined to a single corner of it, than to have his ears dunned, and his spirits crushed, with the endless brawls of a peevish and fretful wife. A man on a house top would have at least some intervals of comfortable weather, but a brawling woman will never want something to make her uneasy to herself, and a torment to those who have the misfortune to be connected with her. She is perpetually vexing her children and servants, but her husband is most to be pitied, because she is of one flesh with him. She may be a scourge in the side of others in the family, but she is rottenness in her husband's bones. She is the greatest plague to him to whom she is bound by every obligation to be the greatest pleasure. She is one flesh with him, and yet she is a constant grief to his spirit. She torments herself most of all, and, next to herself, all others in proportion to the obligation she lies under to behave in the very opposite manner.

God said, it is not good for man to be alone, and therefore made woman to be an help meet for him, and yet the contentious woman is such a perverse creature, that she perverts the design of our Creator, and proves a scourge instead of an help. She makes it better for a man to be in the most solitary circumstances imaginable than with her.

---

*Gal. 6:4, 2 Cor. 10:12

Those who choose a wife for the goodness of her portion, rather than the sweetness of her temper, are not Solomon's disciples. He declares that the married life is better than the single *. But he likewise tells us in this place, that it is much better to live alone in the deepest poverty, than to enjoy affluence with a clamorous and peevish woman.

Ver. 10. *The soul of the wicked desireth evil: his neighbour findeth no favour in his eyes.*

The difference between evil and good men does not lie in complete freedom from what is evil on the side of good men. Paul was one of the best men that ever lived, and yet he confesses that he had not obtained perfection in goodness, but found evil present with him, when he was most inclined to do good. But herein lies that goodness which the saints attain in this life, that they love what is good with an ardent affection, and hate that which is evil with their whole soul, although they cannot do all that good they wish to do, and too often do that evil which they hate †. On the contrary, bad men are not only doers of iniquity, but their souls are fully inclined to it. With their souls they desire evil; and although their consciences frequently remonstrate against sin, and are a strong bridle upon the lusts of most unregenerate persons, yet sin dwells as a king in their inner man, and is not resisted with hatred like a tyrant, but is suffered to possess the throne of the heart.

This is a miserable disposition, for sin is the worst of all evils. No man expressly and directly desires misery, and yet all that love sin desire the worst of misery in reality, for sin is the sickness, the death, the ruin of the soul.

The desire of all unrenewed men is towards evil, and

---

*Chap. 18:22   †Rom. 7:15-21

not one of them would think himself happy if he were
not suffered to enjoy the pleasures of some sin : yet
their relishes for these cursed pleasures are very different, and the desires of evil in some are stronger than
in others. There are many that have some regard to
the voice of conscience, and the great principles of morality, and many others that push on in their pursuit of the pleasures that suit their vitiated taste, in
spite of their own consciences, and their neighbours
and friends find no favour in their eyes. Saul persecuted David, although he had been the champion of
Israel, and was his son-in-law ; for his corruptions had
gained the victory over his conscience and feelings, and
he pursued the gratification of his malice with unre-
lenting fury.

This is the tendency of sin ; to sink a man deep in
the abominable gulf of self-love, and to harden his
spirit against those whom he ought to love most ten-
derly. Let us therefore choose our friends from the
number of those who love God ; for their hearts are
enlarged with charity, and in their eyes their neighbours find favour. Those are bad persons who are so
entirely swallowed up by a selfish spirit, that they will
scarcely perform an office of charity, or good neighbourhood, without the expectation of a return. If we
are good men, let us shew it by doing good. Our
neighbours and friends have a special title to expect
good at our hands.

Ver. 11. *When the scorner is punished, the simple is
made wise ; and when the wise is instructed, he receiveth
knowledge.*

It is a bad thing in a family, or church, or nation,
when scorners are not duly corrected or punished.
It was a sign that the inhabitants of Laish were a ready
prey for any invader, when there was no magistrate in
the land to put them to shame. Those that are too

unwise to see the evil of sin, have sense enough to see
the evil of shame and pain ; and when they behold these
disagreeable consequences following sin, their dispositions to wickedness receive a check, to their own great
advantage, as well as the good of the society to which
they belong.   If the fear of censure or punishment does
not make men holy, it will make them sober ; and this
is a good thing in itself, and puts men in a fair way to
become still better, by leading men to the means whereby holiness is ordinarily produced.

   The wise that do not expose themselves to punishment, are not beyond the need of instruction, and
sometimes of admonition and rebuke.   David was one
of the best of men, but he was not faultless in his behaviour, and we find what happy effect instruction and
rebuke had upon his soul.   He improved in knowledge
and grace by the ministrations of the sanctuary, and
the rebukes of the prophets *.   A rebuke entereth more
into a wise man, than an hundred stripes into a fool.

   Even the simple man receives knowledge from the
instructions and rebukes that are given to the wise.
He is so foolish that an attempt to instruct himself
awakens his jealousy and anger.   He thinks you know
him, or take him for a fool, when you begin to instruct
or admonish him ; but when he sees that the wise are
instructed, and are thankful for it, he is forced to see
his own stupidity, and his conscience tells him, If the
men that are so much wiser and better than I can pretend to be, are so thankful for instruction, surely I
have much greater need of it.   The rebukes that are
administered to them ought to enter ten times deeper
into my heart, who deserve them so much better. The
simple begins to learn wisdom, when he applies to his
own case that which is said or done to other men †.

---

*Ps. 27:4, 2 Sam. 12:24   †Chap. 19:25, 1:5

Ver. 12. *The righteous man wisely considereth the house of the wicked ; but God overthroweth the wicked for their wickedness.*

We have a clear illustration of this truth in the conversations between Job and his three friends, all of whom had considered the house of the wicked, and God's providence in overthrowing it, but with very different degrees of wisdom.

Eliphaz had considered the sudden overthrow of the wicked man, and the unhappy end of his prosperity, and from thence inferred the justice of God, the danger of sin, and the necessity of repentance to sinners. His two friends joined with him in opinion ; and we have no reason to doubt that they had received great benefit from the observations which they made upon the providence of God, to the wicked in their own days, as well as in ancient times ; for they had taken advantage of the wisdom of the ancients, and of the histories which had been handed down to them, to increase their own stock of knowledge *.

Job had considered the house of the wicked with more wisdom, and learned much instruction from the providence of God concerning it. He had observed so many instances of the downfal of prosperous trangressors, that he saw wickedness to be a very dangerous thing, however prosperous it might be for a time, and therefore he abhorred the counsel of the wicked †. At the same time he observed, and understood from the reports of travellers, that some wicked men lived and died in affluence, and were buried with great pomp, and had stately monuments erected for them ; from thence he justly inferred that the wicked were reserved to a future day of wrath, and defended his own character against

---

*Job 5:3,4, 8:8, 20:4,5, 22:16   †Job 21:16,17

his friends, with solid arguments drawn from the unequal distributions of providence in this world *.

It is a great point of wisdom to learn instruction from the calamities that befal the wicked, or have befallen them in former times. By this means we may render all the histories of past ages very beneficial to ourselves. We find that the destruction of the old world by the flood, and the burning of Sodom and Gomorrah, were means of impressing the mind of Eliphaz with an abhorrence of sin †, and the prophet Ezekiel severely censures the Jews in his time, because they had not taken warning by the fate of Sodom and Israel ‡.

It is not safe for us to pronounce men wicked merely because they are overthrown; but when God makes his judgments upon sinners manifest, it is our duty to observe it, and to glorify and fear God §. And although we have no reason to think that those who meet with signal calamities are worse than other men, unless we have good evidence of it, yet their calamities are loud warnings, and calls to repentance ‖.

Ver. 13. *Whoso stoppeth his ears at the cry of the poor, he also shall cry himself, and shall not be heard.*

There may be a very good excuse for not giving to the poor; but insensibility to their extreme distress is an unnatural and a crying iniquity. Our eyes and ears are organs fitted by nature for working upon the heart, and exciting bowels of compassion in us; and if we regard not the cry of the poor with sympathy, we put a force upon nature by stopping our ears. When Eliphaz meant to convince Job that his trangression was infinite, he charges this among other horrid crimes upon him,

---

*Job 21:27-34, 24   †Job 22:18   ‡Ezek. 16:56, 23:11
§Rev. 15:4, Ps. 64:10,11   ‖Luke 13:1-5

that he had not given water to the weary to drink, and had withholden bread from the hungry ; but Job was innocent, and could with a good conscience declare that he never withheld the poor from their desire, nor caused the eye of the widow to fail *.

Those that are hard-hearted to the distressed, should remember that they cannot make a covenant with death, nor hinder the scourge of distress from reaching themselves. They also shall cry, for the days of distress will come upon them ; and whilst they shew no pity to the poor, they harden the spirits of men against pity to themselves, and provoke God to leave them to fall without succour.

If we should never fall into distress that needs relief at the hands of our fellow creatures, it is certain that we need help from God to our souls, and although we feel not our need of his pity at present, the day is coming when we shall feel it at our hearts, and cry out for mercy. Our poor fellow creatures need a few pence from us, but we need talents at the hand of God ; and when we disobey his voice, and refuse to shew mercy unto men, we have just reason to fear that we shall have judgment without mercy to ourselves. God is a most gracious God. He delights in the voice of prayer, and continually answers those requests that believers present unto him in the name of his Son ; but he has not bound himself to hear those cries which necessity extorts from the wicked. This is a part of the extreme misery of those who refuse to hear the cries of wisdom, that they shall cry out in their time of calamity, and he will not hear them, and the same punishment is here threatened to those who will not hear the cries of the poor.

What extreme wretchedness is this, to cry and not

---

*Job 22:7, 31:6

be heard by a most merciful God! How provoking is
the sin which is so severely threatened! When David's
enemies cried unto the Lord, and were not heard, it
was plain that they were doomed to irremediable misery. Job could not imprecate severer vengeance upon
himself, on supposition he was guilty of the crimes
charged upon him, than this, Let my cry have no place.
This is the height of the misery of the damned, that
their cries are not regarded with pity by God. This
truth need not however discourage us from presenting
the prayers of faith to the throne of grace; for the prayers here spoken of, are only the cries of strong distress
extorted from men that have not the love of God, or
the love of Christ in them. It is rather an encouragement to pray; for it shews us that the refusing of prayer is God's strange work, and a piece of his severity to
great sinners who are destitute of compassion to their
fellow men.

When we have reason to complain that we cry and
shout, but God shutteth out our prayer, let us consider
our ways; perhaps we have shut our ears on some occasions against the cries of the poor. This was one
reason why God accepted not the prayers and fasts of
those people whom Isaiah speaks of in the 50th chapter of his book.

The poor may see in this threatening, great encouragement to themselves to apply to his throne of mercy.
He that condemns uncharitableness so much in others,
is full of love and pity, and listens with a gracious ear
to the sighs and groans of the poor and destitute *.

Ver. 14. *A gift in secret pacifieth anger, and a reward
in the bosom strong wrath.*

Anger is a very outrageous passion, and strong wrath
makes a man like a savage beast, which attacks in its

---

*Ps. 102:17

fury any creature that comes in its way. Yet such is the power of money and presents, that the fiercest rage is assuaged by them; and therefore when a good conscience allows, it is often a piece of prudence to disarm an enemy by gifts, rather than to fight with him. By such means did Jacob and Abigail secure themselves from those enemies that threatened them with destruction. But to give, or to receive bribes, is a very sinful thing, because it is a perversion of justice. For ministers to receive gifts to soften their severity in censuring offenders, (if such unfaithful ministers can be found,) is one of the worst instances of corruption.

Although men are generally fond of receiving, yet they are as generally unwilling to be reckoned fond of gifts, and therefore those who have the art of giving will do it in secret, and avoid every appearance of ostentation in themselves, and every thing that might cause a blush in the receivers of their gifts.

If the love of gifts is so universal and so powerful in the hearts of men, we ought to try our own hearts, how far we are influenced by it, or whether we believe our Saviour's words, that it is more blessed to give than to receive. Take heed, says our Lord, and beware of covetousness. We must keep a double guard against this sin, because it is so natural to us, and yet so dangerous. Those who receive gifts should take heed to themselves lest they receive a bribe under the colour of a gratuity. What is given in such a manner as to shun the light, deserves to be at least suspected *.

Have gifts such a powerful influence to disarm resentment? Then let no man plead, in apology for the fury of his passions, that he is not able to conquer them. If money can conquer them, shall reason, and the fear of God, and the command of Christ, be too

---

*Chap. 17:8, 18:16

554 / Exposition of Proverbs

weak to bridle them? Surely the commandments of
our God and Saviour have too little authority with us,
if they have less influence upon our spirits than gold
and jewels have upon the spirits of almost all men.

Ver. 15. *It is joy to the just to do judgment, but destruction shall be to the workers of iniquity.*

Men that are utterly unacquainted with the spirit of
religion, and view it only at a distance, form very false
notions to its prejudice, and are affrighted from it with
much the same reason that children are afraid to walk
in the dark. They fancy that religion is a dull and
melancholy thing, and that it affords and allows no
pleasure to saints, at least whilst their present life continues; but the wise man here tells us, that the very
doing of what is right is a part of its own reward,
bringing with it an heart-felt satisfaction. Love is the
soul of our obedience; and a well-regulated love is a
delightful passion, communicating pleasure to all the
toils and dangers that are endured for its sake. Jacob
endured the sultry heats, and chilling frosts, for seven
years, with great pleasure, for the love he had to Rachel, and the holy love of Christians will dispose them
with greater joy to encounter the assaults of the tempter, to mortify the deeds of the body, to strive against
sin, and to continue resolute in piety, notwithstanding
of all the discouragements which often attend it.

The joy of the saints in doing judgment is not complete in this world, because the flesh which remains in
them lusts against the spirit; yet it vastly exceeds in purity and vigour the highest joys of sinners. The Christian is unspeakably more happy in resisting and van-
quishing the lusts of the flesh, than the worldly man
is in gratifying them.

This sentence is a mark by which we ought to try
ourselves. Many do judgment without taking pleasure in it; their consciences will not suffer them to do

otherwise, but their hearts are on the side of sin ; or they will do many good things with pleasure, because their constitutional and beloved sins are not affected by them ; but there are other things at which, like King Herod, they stop short, because they will rather risk damnation than part unreservedly with the pleasures of sin.   But the just man takes pleasure in the way of God's testimonies, without any exception to particular steps of it, as far as it is known to him.   He lifts up his hands to the commandments of God which he loves, and in his measure he resembles Christ, whose meat and drink it was to do his Father's will : nor is his love of the commandments confined to the first table of the law : it is as much his joy to pay his debtor, as to re- ceive payment of what is owing to himself, and to be- stow charity on the poor, as to receive a present from some rich friend.

The wicked have an aversion to judgment.   Perhaps they are not immoral in their conduct, but it is no plea- sure to them to render unto God his due; and they say of his service, Oh ! what a weariness is it !   Their re- ligion is but a dull lifeless form ; but there is some ini- quity which is relished as honey by them, and drunk greedily as water.   But that sin which is sweet in their mouth is bitter in their belly, and shall be found more deadly than poison ; for destruction shall be to the workers of iniquity *.

Ver. 16. *The man that wandereth out of the way of understanding, shall remain in the congregation of the dead* †.

The way of holiness is the way of understanding ; for a good understanding have all they that do God's commandments, and all besides are fools.   Whilst men

---

*Chap. 10:29

†Shall remain in the congregation of the giants (who perished by the flood.)

wander in the forbidden paths of sin, they are dead whilst they live, and are sinking themselves deeper and deeper into the dungeon of misery.

But of all the wanderers in the ways of sin, those are in the most dangerous condition who were once to appearance walking in the ways of understanding, and have now turned aside into the ways of darkness. It had been better for them never to have known the ways of righteousness, for they bring great reproach upon the ways of God, and behave as if they had found iniquity in the Holy One. They sin against convictions and vows ; they prejudice multitudes against the way of truth ; and bring the blood of many souls upon their own heads. They harden their spirits against God, and if their consciences are ever again awakened, they are in danger of sinking into the hideous gulph of despair. Although apostacy is not in itself an unpardonable sin, yet it is sometimes an introduction to it, and never fails to render repentance extremely difficult, and almost impracticable *.

These unhappy wanderers once ranked themselves, and were ranked by their neighbours, among the living in Jerusalem, but they were no better than stalking ghosts ; they belong to the congregation of the dead, and, without astonishing exertions of omnipotent grace, must for ever remain amongst that wretched crew.

Those that walk in the light must die, but their death is an entrance into a better life ; for it cannot dissolve their blessed connexion with the Lord of life : but those that wander out of the way of understanding, are twice dead, they are like trees plucked up by the roots ; death will be the king of terrors to them, because it opens their passage into the lake of fire and brimstone, which is the second death.

---

*Heb. 6:4-6

Consider, ye revolting sinners, the greatness of your guilt and danger *; be thankful that your situation is not yet altogether desperate. There is hope even for you, in the all-sufficient Saviour, but fly to him without delay, before the decree bring forth, before the fierce anger of the Lord come upon you, till there be no remedy †.

Ver. 17. *He that loveth pleasure, shall be a poor man, he that loveth wine and oil, shall not be rich.*

Love not the world, nor the things of the world, for if any man love the world, or the lusts of the flesh, or other things in it, the love of the Father is not in him.

Must pleasure then be renounced, and every earthly satisfaction given up? Who will enter into the ways of wisdom, if she insists on this? Pleasure is not to be absolutely renounced. The truly religious man finds more pleasure, even in his earthly enjoyments, than the happiest sensualist; but pleasure must not be loved as our chief happiness. Our hearts must be given to God, and nothing earthly must be suffered to usurp his throne in our souls.

It is no hardship imposed on us, to be forbidden the love of pleasure, for the sensualist by his love to the delights of the flesh, undoes every thing that is dear to him. He not only wounds his soul, but prejudices his health, and wastes his estate: if he is rich, he makes himself poor; if he is poor, he reduces himself to beggary, and perhaps to a prison. Even in the land of Canaan, where vines and olives abounded, poverty was the ordinary consequence of dissipation and revelling: and how can a man escape poverty, who lives in a country, where the climate concurs with the scripture, to forbid extravagance, and to threaten poverty as its present recompense?

---

*Jer. 25   †Jer. 3:12,14

We see every day instances of the truth of this proverb, in men who have reduced themselves to hunger and want, by gratifying the love of pleasure. Gluttons, and drunkards, and revellers, are fools for this world, as well as the world to come; they exhaust, by their intemperance, the very source of their pleasures, and after contracting by habit an unconquerable desire after wine, and other objects of a sensual taste, they are reduced to a want, not only of the luxuries, but even of the necessaries of life.

Let us therefore, if we wish to be happy, follow the Apostle's rule: The time is short; let those that rejoice, be as if they rejoiced not, and they that use this world, as not abusing it. Feasting is not unlawful, but when men feast without fear, their joviality leads them to revelling, which is expressly condemned in Scripture. Let us make no provision for the lusts of the flesh, but put on the Lord Jesus Christ.

Ver. 18. *The wicked shall be a ransom for the right-eous, and the transgressor for the upright.*

"I gave Egypt for thy ransom," says God to his people, "Ethiopia and Seba for thee." When Jerusalem appeared to be on the point of ruin, God gave a diversion to the Assyrian forces, by means of Tirhakah king of Ethiopia. In like manner, Achan was a ransom for the people of Israel in the days of Joshua, and the seven men of Saul's sons in the days of David. In these, and in many other instances, the righteous were delivered out of trouble, and the wicked came in their stead *.

When the wicked flourish, and the righteous meet with humbling providences, we must not take offence at the providence of God, or the way of holiness. The proud are not happy, and those that tempt God are not delivered: God tries the faith and patience of his peo-

---

*Chap. 11:8

ple, and will in due time make it to appear, that they are gold and jewels in his eyes, and that he puts away the wicked of the earth like dross.

God's people need not despair when they are in trouble and see no likely way of getting out of it: God can see methods of relief, when they cannot see them, and he can perform wonders for their relief. Israel in Egypt was brought very low, and their oppressors were too mighty for them; it seemed impossible for them to escape out of the land of bondage, or if they could get out of it, to be safe from the pursuit of their enemies. But their Redeemer was wise and mighty, and gave Egypt for them. By the plagues of Egypt, their release was accomplished, and by the drowning of Pharaoh and his army, they were preserved from their pursuers.

But God's people must walk uprightly, if they wish to enjoy the benefit of this special favour. If they step out of the path of integrity, God may shew that he is no respecter of persons, to their cost. Jonah for his flight from the presence of the Lord, was made a ransom for the heathen sailors that were with him in the ship. Those that shall not be condemned with the world, may expect to be chastened, although others should escape.

Ver. 19. *It is better to dwell in the wilderness, than with a contentious and angry woman.*

Contention and anger commonly go together, and they kindle a flame that can scarcely be extinguished. The wise man has already told us, that it is better to dwell in an ill-thatched house, or even on a corner of the house top, without any covering from the storm, than with a contentious woman; but here he goes farther, and says that it is better to dwell in the wilderness, than with a contentious and angry woman. The wilderness would make a very bad habitation, because there are the lions' dens, and the habitation of dragons, so that a dweller in the desert would be not only destitute of every conveniency, but exposed to constant perils of his life. Yet it would be a more desirable habitation, than a wide house with the company of a woman that was tormenting her husband with everlasting brawls. The contentious woman is a greater monster than the tiger of the desert, and her tongue is more noisome than the tongue of the viper.

A contentious woman is not worse than a tyrannizing husband. A man may more easily make his escape from the presence of a scold, than a woman from the face of a brutal tyrant; and the delicacy of her mind makes her more susceptible of melancholy impressions from bad usage, than persons of the other sex ordinarily are.

When a husband and wife find the marriage yoke sweetened by love and peace, they should bless God for the happiness they find in each other's society. Their pleasures are the most delightful which this world can afford, and they are indebted for them to that kind providence which has made them one flesh and one soul.

Ver. 20. *There is a treasure to be desired, and oil in the dwellings of the wise, but a foolish man spendeth it up.*

Works of charity are requisite, but don't imagine that they will make you poor. Christ commands us not to lay up treasures on earth, but to lay up treasures that never decay, nor become a prey to thieves. But he does not require us to give every thing away to the poor; on the contrary, he insinuates that a prudent householder has in his treasure things new and old. We must give alms of all that we possess, but we are not called to give all that we possess in alms; that would be at once to drain up the fountain of beneficence, and preclude ourselves from doing good, as we see occasion, through the remaining part of our lives.

Solomon directs us to be liberal in charitable distributions, and yet he tells us in this place, that the wise have a desirable treasure, not only of the necessaries, but likewise of the comforts and conveniencies of life. Charity dispensed with wisdom, will not hurt but improve a man's estate. Was there ever a more liberal man than Job, and yet he was the richest of all the men in the east. Abraham abounded in hospitality, and he abounded no less in flocks and herds. It seems a riddle, and yet it is a certain truth, that expenses and losses on God's account are real gains.

Poverty is often the lot of the wise and religious, but it is not the native consequence of piety. Industry, and temperance, and frugality, are recommended by religion, and these are natural means of plenty. Above all, godliness has the promise of the life that now is, and therefore it must be a great error to imagine that worldly prosperity is inconsistent with the grace of God; for God delighteth in the prosperity of his servants; and if he does not smile upon their outward estate, it is because his love is directed by infinite knowledge, which sees a different condition to be, for the present, more conducive to their best interests.

But if the good man has not a treasure of the good things of this world in his house, he possesses a large treasure for himself and his family in the promises of God *. A man is not poor, although he wants ready money, if he has plenty of good bills. The Christian may want every thing that glitters in the eye of flesh, but he has rich treasures laid up in heaven, and the written word of God is his security.

But a foolish man spends and devours the substance

---

*Ps. 37

of his family. His wealth is consumed by idleness or extravagance, or by the blasting curse of God ; or if he is still rich in possession, he does not hold it by a sure tenure. Sin is often the destruction of men's estates, as well as their souls, and brings present misery as well as eternal ruin. But, however the wicked may flourish, or the righteous decline in the world, (for this world is not the place of full recompenses,) the righteous man when he is poorest is immensely rich, and the richest of sinners is miserably poor.

Ver. 21. *He that followeth after righteousness and mercy, findeth life, righteousness, and honour.*

This world is not the place of perfection. The best Christians must confess their daily failings, but their desires of holiness are sincere, and accompanied with vigorous endeavours. Slothful professors have some cold desires after it, and sometimes their desires are accompanied with endeavours, but these are weak and ineffectual, or however ardent they may appear to be, yet they soon spend their force, and all their goodness is like the morning cloud and the early dew. Christians that deserve the name, are, like Caleb and Joshua, of another spirit, for their endeavour is to follow the Lord fully. They are followers of the Lamb whithersoever he goes, and whatever it may cost them.

The grace of the gospel teaches us, not only to live godly, but to follow righteousness and mercy, and these two virtues cannot be separated in practice. To be righteous, is to render unto every man his due. Now love is a debt we owe to every man, and mercy is due to the unhappy. The great rule of righteousness is to do to others, as we would wish to be dealt with, if we were in their circumstances, and certainly we all wish to enjoy kindness and pity from our neighbours, as circumstances require. The righteous, says David, shew-

eth mercy, and giveth *. And in another place he says
that the righteousness of the merciful man endureth
for ever.

It is in the strength of Christ that we must follow
after righteousness and mercy. As his righteousness
is the ground of our hopes, his grace is the fountain of
our supplies. He is the vine, and unless we are branches ingrafted into this vine, our fruits will not be good.
Love and fidelity are mentioned among the fruits of his
Spirit †, and those that have not his Spirit are sensual
and selfish, and bring forth fruit only to themselves.

Men think they will be losers, by following righteousness and mercy with too much eagerness, but the
Scripture assures us that they shall be great gainers.
They may suffer present loss, but their gains will be
infinitely greater. They shall find life, and life is the
foundation of every enjoyment. What is sweeter than
life? and yet the life of most men is but a vain
shadow and an empty dream; but that life which comes
from the special favour of God, and is secured by promise, must be a pleasant and happy life. Some have
lost their life for the sake of righteousness, but Christ
assures us that their loss was unspeakable gain. They
shall find righteousness; for as those that love cursing,
shall have cursing poured into them like water, and
like oil into their bones, so those that love righteousness shall meet with righteous dealing from men ‡,
and the righteous God will take care of their interests,
and fulfil his faithful promises to them. The justice
of God is engaged on their side, through the mediation
of Christ, and he cannot be unrighteous, to forget their
works and labours of love §. They shall find honour,
for their upright and generous behaviour is very likely to procure to them honour from men. If fools should

*Ps. 27:21   †Gal. 5:22   Luke 6:38
||Ps. 36:10, Heb. 6:10

despise them, they will be respected by the wise and good. If all men should despise them and cast out their names as evil, they are precious and honourable in the eyes of the Lord. They shall at last be dignified with a place at Christ's right hand, with approbation from their judge, and with an eternal crown *.

Ver. 22. *A wise man scaleth the city of the mighty, and casteth down the strength of the confidence thereof.*

Men are generally so deeply sunk in flesh, that they value the endowments of the body, and the outward bounties of providence, above the noble qualities of the mind. This error is corrected by Solomon in this verse. He tells us that in every point of view, the qualities of the mind are preferable to those of the outward man. Counsel is better than strength for war, for one wise man will take a city defended by many strong men, although they have the advantage of high walls, and strong fortifications on their side. By the wisdom of Cyrus in turning the current of the Euphrates, was Babylon taken, notwithstanding of its stupendous walls and numerous defenders. By the discipline of the Romans were the brave and strong nations of Gaul and Germany subdued, and in almost every battle, it has been found that wisdom is better than weapons of war †.

If military wisdom is so much preferable to strength, how excellent is that religious wisdom so much commended in this book ! This divine wisdom even in war has a vast superiority over the wisdom of generals and ministers of state, for it leads men to victory, because it teaches them to trust in the Lord of hosts. By this wisdom Abraham conquered four kings when they were flushed with victory. By this David, the stripling, overcame lions, and bears, and giants. By this many of the old believers waxed valiant in fight, and turned to flight

*Job 36:7   † Eccles. 9:13-18

the armies of the aliens, for they knew their God, and were strong, and did exploits. By this wisdom the weakest believer is victorious through the blood of the Lamb, and the word of his testimony, over the dragon and his angels.

Ver. 23. *Whoso keepeth his mouth and his tongue, keepeth his soul from troubles.*

A furious horse needs a double bridle to restrain its fierceness, and it seems the tongue of man needs more than a double bridle to keep it in from doing hurt. The wise man never ceases to admonish us about this point, and in this place he mentions particularly two of the instruments of speech, and puts a bridle on each of them. As an high-spirited horse, if its fury is not curbed with a strong hand, will hurry its rider along, without regarding pits, or precipices, or deep waters, and expose him to extreme jeopardy of his life, so an unbridled tongue will make a man hateful to God and men; plunge him into contentions and debates, and expose his estate, and life, and credit, to extreme danger.

Who is the man that wishes to enjoy a quiet and peaceable life? Let him set a guard over his mouth, and refrain his tongue from profaneness and corrupt communication, from railing and reviling, and all evil speaking, from foolish talking, and from inconvenient jesting. Let prudence and the fear of God stand continually like centinels at the door of his lips. Let him follow the instructions of David, and Solomon, and James *. Let him pray to God to keep the door of his mouth, and remember that an ungoverned tongue is inconsistent with religion and happiness, and exposes a man to the same danger as a ship when it wants a pilot and an helm, and is ready to dash against every rock that comes in its way †.

---

*Ps. 34:11,12   James 3   †Chap. 18, 20, 21

Ver. 24. *Proud and haughty scorner is his name, who dealeth in proud wrath.*

The anger of a proud man is very fierce. When he meets with the smallest shadow of an affront or provocation, his passions are on fire, and his vengeance must be satiated, be the consequence what it will. He would have every man to do him homage, and when his opinion is contradicted, or his humour not complied with, he rageth like a tempest, which threatens to spread desolation and ruin. Such was the proud wrath of Haman, which could not be glutted with the blood of Mordecai alone, but thirsted after the blood of a whole nation.

What does the proud worm design by all this fury? It is his honour that set him in a flame. He thinks highly of himself, and cannot bear the thought that another man has not the same deference for him which he has for himself. To repair the fancied attacks upon his honour, he gives way to revenge, and seeks the reputation of a man of honour and spirit, but he disappoints his own views, and meets disgrace, when he is hunting for praise. He shall be called a proud man, and that is a character so base, that a proud man cannot bear it, for pride seeks to hide itself under any covert rather than be seen. He shall be called a haughty scorner, for he puffeth at his enemies, and pours contempt upon his reprovers. Now a haughty scorner is a very hateful character, for the scorner is an abomination among men.

Haman the Agagite, and Uzziah king of Judah, have brought great dishonour upon their memories by their proud wrath. Moses and Job, are men of glorious memory, for their humility and meekness. The godly man is not ambitious of praise, but he receives honour from God. The proud man cannot live without houour and applause, and his ambition and pride load his name and memory with contempt.

Ver. 25. *The desire of the slothful killeth him, for his hands refuse to labour.*

Ver. 26. *He coveteth greedily all the day long, but the righteous giveth and spareth not.*

Solomon has already said enough to banish sloth out of the world, if those who are under the power of this vice were not besotted with it; but here he tells us a worse thing about it than in any of his former proverbs, for he represents it as a degree of self-murder. The slothful man brings diseases upon himself, by reducing himself to want of the necessaries of life, and the refreshments of sleep, for he will not labour for his food, nor take that exercise which prepares the body for quiet rest; but besides this, his very desires are hurtful to his constitution, for his mind must be employed, when his hands are idle. His wants, and the time that lies heavy upon him, are strong incitements to those insatiable cravings of desire which rack the heart and have a sickening influence upon the body. If the desire accomplished is a tree of life, those desires that cannot be accomplished, must have the quite opposite effect. If hope deferred make the heart sick, how cruelly must it be tortured by those insatiable desires that are not sweetened by any mixture of hope.

What is the reason that the slothful man's desires have such a pernicious influence upon him? His hands refuse to labour. If you bid him go and work, he will perhaps promise to do it, like that son who said to his father, I go, sir, to work in the vineyard. He is sensible of the necessity of it, he wishes earnestly to enjoy the fruits of labour, he has even some faint wishes that his hands would submit to the toil of labour; but the loss is, that his hands will not comply, because they must be taken out of his bosom if they work. If he could work with his tongue or his feet, without his hands, he would be a very industrious man ; but he hates work because it does not consist in talking or sauntering about *.

Slothfulness is very prejudicial to the soul, as well as the body. As sleep is the nurse of our animal constitution, so the deep sleep into which slothfulness casts a man, is the nurse of the body of sin. The sluggard coveteth, he coveteth greedily ; greedy covetings are his constant employment ; although he will not work for necessaries, he could not be happy without the luxuries of life. Those greedy workings of covetous desire, are a strong temptation to him to pilfer and steal, and sometimes they push him on to those crimes that procure the gallows.

Wicked men disappoint themselves by their sins of that wished enjoyment, which they seek and hope to obtain by their iniquities. The sensualist deprives himself not only of pleasures, but of necessaries, by casting away that money that should procure them †. The vain and proud bring infamy upon their name, by the very means they take to support their honour ‡; and slothful men, whilst they seek rest and ease, endure much more fatigue than the diligent man, because they make themselves a prey to the restless workings of their own unbridled desires.

But the righteous giveth. He does not say the diligent man giveth ; for all bad and selfish men are not slothful. Some men toil hard, not from any regard to God's authority, but entirely for their own interest ; they do not glorify God in their labours, for they do not work with their hands, that they may have to give to him that needeth, a part of what they have earned. The righteous man is of a nobler spirit, for he is ever merciful, and his mercy is one motive to his industry. He

---

*Prov. 13:4   †Verse 17   ‡Verse 24

labours in his calling, and the blessing of God gives him success, and he shews his thankfulness to God, by giving with an unsparing hand. The slothful man covets the fruit of other people's labours, but the good man does not wish to eat that morsel alone, which is procured by his own sweat and toil. God is well pleased with his bounties, for he is a cheerful and liberal giver *.

Ver. 27. *The sacrifice of the wicked is abomination : how much more when he bringeth it with a wicked mind.*

We have already heard that the sacrifice of the wicked is an abomination to the Lord : we are here told, that it is an abomination, although it is presented with the very best dispositions that a wicked man is capable of. Some unregenerate men are anxious for eternal life, because they cannot always live on earth ; some of them have a great deal of seriousness in their devotions, and will even worship God in the exercise of tempers of mind that have some resemblance of love to God, and faith in Christ. Will not such service be accepted of God ? By no means. Our great teacher tells us to make first the tree good, and then the fruit ; for a corrupt tree, at the best, produces corrupt fruit. It must, therefore, be a very foolish thing, for men to dream of preparing themselves for Christ by a course of serious devotions, or of waiting till they are in a better disposition for believing in Christ, before they will venture to commit the salvation of their souls into his hands. Without his grace, we can have no good dispositions, nor do any thing that is acceptable to God, for it is only in the beloved, that we are accepted †.

What then must bad men do ? Must they be driven to despair ? or must they give up with duty ? No ‡. It is certain that without faith it is impossible to please God ; but it is equally certain, that they are fully war-

---

*2 Cor. 9:7   †Eph 1:6, John 15:5   ‡Acts 8:22

ranted to believe in Jesus. Let them make a thankful
use of this privilege, and from henceforth do all that
they do, in word or in deed, in the name of the Lord
Jesus Christ.

If the sacrifice of the wicked at the very best is an
abomination, how abominable must it be at the very
worst? It is more than abominable, if he brings it with
a wicked intention. Balaam presented many rich sacrifices; but they were designed to bribe the Holy One
of Israel to be unfaithful to his people, and changeable
in his purposes. It is a detestable thing for men to
think they can prevail on God by the multitude of their
holy services, to dispense with sin, and suffer them to
escape unpunished, although they still live in the practice of injustice towards men, and in the neglect of several necessary duties which they owe to God *.

It is no less presumptuous for men to be diligent in
the practice of religion, to obtain the applause of men.
This was the vice which our Lord so frequently reproved in the Pharisees, and this fault is still too common among the professors of religion. It will be a
comfortable evidence that we are not under the reigning power of it, if we are as conscientious in the secret
performances of religion, as in those that come under
the view of men.

Nothing can be more detestable, than to cover vice
with professions of religion. Some have the daring
presumption to walk on in the ways of sin, and to practise the forms of duty, that their character may be
shrouded under the mask of piety. These are followers of the Scribes and Pharisees, against whom our Lord
pronounced so many dreadful woes †. They walk in
the cursed way of Jezebel, who caused a feast to be proclaimed, that she might destroy an innocent man, and

*Isa. 1:11-16   †Matt. 23

yet keep up the forms of religion and law ; and they are likely to perish in the gain-saying of Korah *.

Ver. 28.   *A false witness shall perish : but the man that heareth, speaketh constantly.*

He is a false witness that speaks what he has not been assured of, by the testimony of his ears or eyes, or some other way that secures him from the danger of lying. He may possibly speak what is true, without having sufficient evidence of it ; but it is evident, that he is a man of a loose conscience, who speaks things with a greater air of certainty than his ground of belief will warrant. " We testify," says the faithful witness, " the things that we have seen and heard," and his followers must imitate his example.

The false witness was to be punished by the magistrate, according to the law of Moses ; but if he should escape the punishment which his crime deserves from men, God says he shall perish, and his threatenings are not wind and vanity †.

But he that hears the words spoken about which he bears witness, and will say nothing without sufficient grounds of assurance, betrays not himself by any self inconsistency, nor exposes himself to punishment from God or man.   He shall live when liars perish, his character shall continue good when liars loose all credit, and whilst he lives, he shall have the honour of being sustained as a good and credible witness ; for lying lips are but for a moment, but the lip of truth shall be established for ever.

Wherefore, putting away lying, let us speak truth every man to his neighbour, especially in witness-bearing.   If the commandment of God, and the mighty motives of his gospel, will not induce us to do so, let us regard our own honour and interest, which suffer irreparable injury by every deviation from truth.

---

*1 Kings 21:9,10, Num. 16   †Chap. 19:5,9

Ver. 29. *A wicked man hardeneth his face: but as for the upright he directeth his way.*

The wicked man walks in a crooked path, where peace and happiness never were, nor shall be found. God calls upon him to leave this cursed way, and to turn into the straight way of life. He thunders in the curses of his law, and orders his ministers to lift up their voices like trumpets, to proclaim in his ears the dangers of his course. He deals with him by his providence, and makes him to feel some of the first fruits of that vengeance which is the fruit of sin. He sets before him the peace and pleasure to be found in the way of holiness, that he may be encouraged to leave the way of destruction; but the perverse sinner disregards the voice and providence of the Lord. The ways of sin are so pleasant to him, that he will venture the consequences, rather than be turned out of them for the present.

The wicked man has many devices to harden his face in his sinful course. He walks in the same paths as other men do, and many are much worse than himself. He has time enough before him, to repent and serve God. He does many good things to overbalance his evil deeds, or he will make amends for all at once, by fleeing to the mercy of God at last. By such corrupt reasonings as these, he hardens himself in iniquity, and sets God at defiance, setting at nought the terrors of his wrath, and trampling upon the grace and blood of the Redeemer, who came to turn ungodliness from Jacob. By degrees he contracts so powerful habits of sin, that his conversion is almost impossible; he casts off shame and fear, and sins without restraint, till he finds that there is justice and vengeance, as well as forbearance with God *.

---

*Ps. 68:21

But the upright man directeth and establisheth his
way. He may slip with his feet, but he recovers himself by the aids of divine grace. If he turns aside, as
a good man may do, he will not persist in sin, but, like
Job, he confesses with self-abhorrence his vileness, and
will proceed no farther in it *. He endeavours, in the
general course of his life, to keep at a distance from sin
and temptation, and to order his conversation with such
prudence, that he may not by surprise be ensnared into sin, nor meet with any occasion of stumbling. Thus
did David direct his way, when he had the word of
God in his heart to keep him from sin, and fortified
himself with firm resolutions, and fervent prayers, when
he knew that he was to meet with snares in his path †.
Thus did Abraham direct his way, when he was commanded to sacrifice Isaac. He never told Sarah, nor
even his servants that attended him on his journey,
that he had received so strange a command from God,
for he was fully resolved to obey the voice of the Lord,
and wished to obviate every advice in opposition to his
duty. Let us follow the example of these holy men,
making straight paths for our feet, that what is lame may
not be turned out of the way; and to him that ordereth
his conversation aright, will God shew his salvation.

Ver. 30. *There is no wisdom, nor understanding, nor
counsel against the Lord.*

Wisdom excelleth folly, as much as light excelleth
darkness, and Solomon often directs us to manage all
our affairs with discretion and counsel, by means of
which purposes are established; but he warns us in this
place, not to trust to our own wisdom or prudence, nor
to dream that they can accomplish any thing without the
permission and pleasure of God. Wisdom and counsel
can do much with the blessing of God, but all the wisdom of men and angels could do nothing in opposition

*Job 40:4   †Ps. 119:11, 141:3,4

to his counsels, which are all executed by the arm of omnipotence.

There is, no doubt, wisdom and strength in many of the sons of men, but with God is wisdom and strength in an infinitely superior degree*. One wise man excels another wise man so much that he can manage him as if he were a child ; but the only wise God turns the wisdom of all the philosophers in the world into foolishness, and the foolishness of God is infinitely wiser than the best wisdom of creatures.

Herod formed a project deep as hell to destroy our infant Saviour ; but Jesus lives and reigns. Herod and his family were soon extinct. The like success has attended all the contrivances of men to destroy the church of our Redeemer, and God hath glorified himself upon the mightiest and wisest enemies of his people, by making their infernal devices the means of ruining themselves, and of advancing the interests of Zion†. Let Zion rejoice because of God's judgments, and let all the daughters of Judah be glad, for the Lord of hosts hath purposed good concerning her, and who shall disannul his purpose ? The enemies of Zion may associate and combine, and form their plans for her destruction, but they shall not stand, for the Lord hath founded Zion, and the poor of his people shall trust in her‡.

There are men who aspire to honour, and in their pride would exalt themselves in opposition to the will of God, who hath annexed honour to piety, and disgrace to pride and ambition§. But shall they succeed ? The Lord hath purposed to stain the pride of all glory, and they shall be scattered in the imagination of their hearts. There are some that try to carry on their plans for enriching themselves and their families, in spite of God. But poverty and ruin is the fruit of their pre-

---

*Job 12:12,13   †Ps. 12:19, Mic. 4:11-13

‡Is. 8:9, 14:25,32   §Prov. 18:12, 22:4

sumption*. In short, all that seek for profit or pleasure, in transgressing the law of God shall find loss and
misery.

Trust in God at all times, acknowledge him in all
your ways, and be not afraid that any of his gracious
counsels shall be frustrated. But those that harden
themselves against God shall be ruined without reme-
dy†.

Ver. 31. *The horse is prepared against the day of battle, but safety is of the Lord.*

Solomon here teaches better than he practised, for we
need from God not only light to guide us in the way,
but grace to walk in it ‡. He provided 40,000 horses
even though God had expressly forbidden the kings of
Israel to multiply horses, lest their hearts should be
drawn away from the hope of Israel. But this proverb
was abundantly verified by the consequences of the
change that Solomon introduced into the management
of public affairs, for from his days the people never
made such a figure in war, as they had done in former
days, when the judges of Israel went on foot against
those that fought from chariots of iron §.

Horses and warlike preparations of every kind are
nevertheless necessary to be used in war, when they
are not expressly forbidden by God. Yet if you trust
in horses, you will find that they are flesh and not spirit, and that they cannot afford safety to those whose
hearts are turned from the Lord‖. When the people
of Judah went down to Egypt for help, and trusted in
the Egyptian horses for safety against the king of As-
syria, the prophet Isaiah, with a loud voice, remonstrated against their conduct, and cried that their strength
was to sit still, and wrote it in a table, and noted it in

---

*Prov. 10:2,3   †Chap. 19:21   ‡Ezek. 36:27   §Judges 5
‖Ps. 33:17

a book, that it might continue for ever and ever as a testimony on record against those that trust in chariots and horses rather than the name of the Lord *.

Are we obliged to fight for our liberty and religion? let us set up our banners in the name of the Lord, believe in him as the Lord of armies, that mustereth the hosts of the battle, and decides the fate of war, and beware of every thing that might provoke him to sell us into the hands of our enemies†.

Prudence obliges a nation to avoid dangerous wars‡. Religion teaches us, if possible, as far as lieth in us, to live peaceably with all men. But necessity is sometimes laid upon Christians to expose themselves to jeopardy in the high places of the field, for their country and religion. In such cases the firm belief of this proverb will encourage us to venture into the field against a superior force, persuaded that every bullet has its direction from God, and that he is able to give us the victory, or to make defeats and deaths our advantage§.

Salvations of every kind belong to him. The means of safety must not be neglected, but God alone must be trusted, and when the means are attended with success, the glory is to be ascribed to him. Joshua employed the whole force of the armies of Israel against the nations of Canaan, and he praised those tribes that generously and faithfully assisted their brethren to subdue the country ; but he was fully sensible that it was not their sword and bow that had gotten the land, but God's right arm and favour, and the light of his countenance‖.

In our spiritual warfare, we must arm ourselves with the whole armour of God, but our strength must be in the Lord, and in the power of his might. If we must trust him for safety in fighting with flesh and blood,

---

*Isa. 30:7,8   †Judges 5:8, Deut. 23:9, Ps. 20:5   ‡Luke 14
§Judges 5:9, Ps. 44   ‖Josh. 23:3

how can we wrestle successfully against the powers of hell without his divine succour *?

Proverbs 22

Verse 1. *A good name is rather to be chosen than great riches, and loving favour rather than silver and gold.*

A great fame is none of the most desirable objects, but a good character and the love of men are frequently represented by Solomon as valuable blessings.

Riches are greatly esteemed in the world, and, under the management of wisdom, serve very valuable purposes ; but they don't contribute so much to the quiet and happiness of life, as the esteem and love of our neighbours, nor do they qualify us so much to honour God and do good to men. Paul does not require it as a qualification in church rulers to be rich, but he requires that, along with knowledge and good behaviour, they should have a good report among Christians, and even heathens. He was sensible that the most useful instructions from a suspected person would have no better relish than wholesome food presented in an unclean dish. Our Lord requires all Christians to do those good works that are esteemed by men, not indeed that they may receive praise from men, but that God may be glorified on their behalf. The like exhortations are frequently given us by the apostles of Christ†.

But we must still remember that a good name and the favour of men are not to be compared with the pleasures of a good conscience, and the favour of God ; for if the friendship of men is so pleasant and

*Eph. 6:11-13,18   †Rom. 12:17, 2 Cor. 8:21, Phil. 3:8, 2 Peter 2

useful, God is greater than men, and his favour is infinitely more valuable. And we have no reason to be vexed if we lose the esteem of men in our endeavours to please God. The esteem and good will of men are to be valued chiefly because they will enable us more effectually to serve the interests of God's kingdom, and to do good to the souls of men. When they are valued for their own sakes, they become a snare to us, as they were to some of the ancient Jews, who would not confess Christ, because they loved the praise of men more than the praise of God. When our names are cast out as evil, for a good cause, we have reason to rejoice and triumph, because we are made partakers of the sufferings of Christ, that when his glory shall be revealed we may be glad also with exceeding joy.

If we seek chiefly to please men, we are not the servants of Christ, but if we are the servants of Christ, we must endeavour for his sake, to please men, for their good to edification, and for the honour of his gospel. We must value our character above money, and avoid every thing that is mean, although it might promote our outward estate. We must not only attend to the secret duties of religion, but those also that recommend it to the world, and take all care that our good be not evil spoken of, and that religion meet with no reproach by our misconduct. We should be thankful to God, if we enjoy the benefit of a good name, and employ our influence for the advancement of his glory, but we must abhor the thoughts of making any sinful compliances with the course of the world for the sake of our credit, remembering that instructive saying of God, " Them that honour me, I will honour, but they that despise me shall be lightly esteemed."

Ver. 2. *The rich and poor meet together, the Lord is the maker of them all.*

What is a king to a man ? what is a crown and a

throne to a thinking substance, capable of enjoying God? Majesty is a high sounding title, but the name of a reasonable being would be accounted much more noble, were not kings reasonable beings like other men. The things wherein men of different circumstances agree, are infinitely more important than those wherein they differ; yet such is the vanity which generally attends riches and power, that great men often treat persons of mean station, as if they were some lower rank of animals.

The poor and rich are made of the same blood, and the same glorious power is displayed in the formation of their bodies, and the creation of their souls. They breath the same vital air, and enjoy the light of the same sun. They owe their support equally to the earth, and shall return to the same dust. Their souls are equally precious, and shall dwell in the same eternal habitations, unless there is a distinction between them of a very different kind, from that which makes the rich too often to trample upon the poor, and the poor to return their contempt with the no less criminal passion of envy. They are alike lost in Adam, and have the same right to salvation, through Christ revealed to them in the gospel.

They meet together in the same family, and church, and nation, and they are useful to each other, if they comply with the designs of providence. The rich man's wealth would be of little use to him without the labour of the poor; and the rich man ought to return protection and wages to the poor. Like members of the same body, they ought neither to despise nor to grudge at one another, but to contribute their joint endeavours to the good of the whole.

The Lord is their common creator and father, and by his providence he hath made this man rich and the other man poor, and can invert their conditions when he pleases, as the experience of every day declares.

Why should the rich man despise his poor fellow creature? Did not he that made you make him? Did not one God fashion you both in the womb *? Did God frame you of finer clay, or form you of better blood, than that of Adam? or do your riches make you better, or wiser, or even happier than the poor man? The horse is not so much worse than brutish, as to reckon itself a nobler animal than another of its own species, because it has got a finer saddle on its back.

Let not the poor grudge at their poverty, and repine at him that has given a larger portion of land and money to their fellow men, for he is the Lord. He hath given you more than you can claim by the rights of justice, and if he has given more to some others than to you, he has given them what was his own and not yours, and has commanded them to be kind and useful to such as you, in the spending of it †.

Ver. 3. *A prudent man foreseeth the evil and hideth himself: but the simple pass on and are punished.*

Common prudence will teach men to provide for their security against plain and evident dangers. Drunkards, and whoremongers, and rash sureties, are destitute of common sense as well as religion, otherwise they would not rush upon certain destruction for a momentary gratification.

This mark of prudence appears chiefly in those who partake of the wisdom that is from above. As Noah, when he foresaw the deluge, prepared an ark to the saving of his house, so the prospect of the deluge of wrath alarms them, and instigates their flight to that blessed refuge which God hath provided for our souls. When Moses foretold the tremendous storm that was

*Job 31:16   †Matt. 20:15

to destroy the fields and cattle of Egypt, it was seen who of Pharaoh's servants were fools, and who were wise. The foolish left their cattle in the fields to perish, the wise amongst them put their cattle under a shelter. Now God threatens punishment to sinners in his word, but he is pleased in his great mercy to shew us where we may find refuge. Christ is an hiding place from the storm, and a covert from the tempest; and those who are made truly wise, will give no rest to their eyes, nor slumber to their eye-lids, till they are hidden under the covert of his righteousness. Besides that terrible wrath which shall seize upon all sinners at last, God oftentimes gives commission to particular judgments, to avenge his quarrel upon a land or church. Now prudence will enable us in some measure, to discern the signs of the times, and to judge of effects from their causes. There are some men so stupid, that they will not see God's hand when it is lifted up, but the wise man, by the threatenings of the word and the appearances of providence, can see God's hand when it is about to be lifted up, and enters into those chambers of safety which are provided for his safety in the evil day.

It is only sensual and earthly wisdom that teaches men to shelter themselves from danger, by venturing on sin, or neglecting duty. This is just as wise, as it would be for a man to run upon a drawn sword to avoid the scratch of a pin *. But the simple walk in darkness. They see not the evil coming, or if they see it, they are so senseless that they pass on in their dangerous course, till they meet with deserved punishment, and they are more stupid than many of the brutal creation, who foresee the storms and run to their shelters †. Many of the feathered tribes, before the cold sets in, fly away to warmer climates. How then do ye say,

---

*Dan. 3   †Job 36:33

582 / Exposition of Proverbs

we are wise, and the law of the Lord is with us, if you are more senseless than the beasts of the earth, and less wise than the fowls of heaven? Will you call yourselves reasonable creatures, and Christians, when neither reason nor revelation can make you so prudent about your best interests, as instinct alone renders animals that cannot boast of these precious gifts *.

Ver. 4. *By humility and the fear of the Lord, are riches, and honour, and life.*

Many great things are said of humility in Scripture, and many precious promises are made to it. But the humility meant, is not that false humility that is often found among the proudest of men, nor that constitutional modesty, or that condescension of temper and behaviour, which is the mere effect of good sense, and is a very amiable quality, but not a Christian grace. Christian humility is that which has the promises belonging to it, and it is always joined with the fear of the Lord. It arises from an apprehension of the glorious excellencies of God; for when our eyes are open to his terrible majesty, we cannot but perceive our own meanness; when we behold his spotless purity, we must be ashamed of our own loathsomeness; when we contemplate his awful authority, we feel our obligations to deny our own perverse wills; when his sovereignty is felt, we cannot but yield the management of all our concerns into his hand; and when we have the knowledge of his righteousness, we are obliged to renounce our own works, and submit to the righteousness of God. Thus Job and Isaiah were humbled. They saw God with the seeing of the eye, and humbled themselves in the dust before him.

Humility, arising from an impression of the glories of God, is attended with other Christian graces, and an

---

*Jer. 8:7,8

holy conversation. The humble man will walk humbly with his God, and bend all his endeavours to please the Most High.

By this humility are riches, and honour, and lives, (marg.) These things are greatly valued by the sons of men, especially when they attend one another. Riches are universally coveted, and yet many that possess them are discontented, because they covet the addition of titles and dignities to their wealth; and some that have riches and honours in abundance are more unhappy than those who want them, because they must die, and leave their beloved dignities and riches to others. But here Solomon instructs us, in few words, in a short and sure way of attaining those blessings, which men so ardently covet, and in securing them against every contingency, and even against death itself. But if we follow his direction, we must renounce the wisdom of the world, which teaches the opposite doctrine. It is generally believed, that if men would obtain riches and greatness, they must push themselves forward, and make themselves men of importance, and that they must not too scrupulously adhere to their duty, but in some cases venture to displease God by venial sins, to secure the favour of men. But we are here taught that humility and the fear of the Lord are the straight road to every thing desirable; and if we believe that God is the fountain of life, and every blessing, the doctrine of Solomon will be clear as the light. For to whom do kings give their favours? to their friends or enemies; to those whom they love, or to those whom they hate? We know that the Lord delights in the humble, and takes pleasure in them that fear him; and as he waters the humble vallies with the fructifying showers, so he refreshes with his abundant blessing, those who are low in their own eyes, and willing to render the glory of all that they receive to the Giver. If the humble want any thing that is good in this world, they shall possess unfailing treasures and a crown of life in heaven *.

Ver. 5. *Thorns and snares are in the way of the froward, he that doth keep his soul shall be far from them.*

When the children of Israel spared the Canaanites, in opposition to the commandment of God, they found the consequences of their sin, though it might seem a little one, very troublesome, for the remnant of the accursed nations were thorns in their eyes, and snares and traps to them, and scourges in their sides. Such shall sin be to every froward transgressor. It is generally allowed that the end of transgressors is miserable, but we are assured by Solomon that their way is hard, and that it is all covered over with thorns and snares. The tyranny of lusts, the cravings of inordinate desires, the disappointment felt in the enjoyment of the pleasures of sin, which never answer expectation, the stings of conscience, the bitter fruits of many sins even in this world, and the sore rebukes of providence, are thorns and briers which pierce the souls of transgressors every day. And as Gideon taught the men of Succoth, with thorns and briers, so men, if they were not become brutish, would learn, from the pains that attend or follow the pleasures of sin, that it is an evil and a bitter thing to forsake the Lord +.

The wicked cannot get free of these miseries, for snares are in their way, by which they are held fast, as a bird in the snare of the fowler. They are compassed by God with a net, and all their efforts will be insufficient to disentangle them ‡

There are snares also in their way, by which the devil holds them fast in sin, so that they cannot get free from his tyranny. They resolve to repent at last,

*Matt. 5:3   †Matt. 8:22, Luke 8:14   ‡Job 22:10

but they find that Satan keeps them fast in the cords of their sins. They are like galley slaves chained to their work, and nothing but almighty grace can work out deliverance for them *. Such is the malignant nature of sin, that it turns every thing into a snare, and an occasion of sin. Adversity and prosperity, the comforts of the table, the ordinances of God, and Christ himself, are a snare to the froward †.

Who is the man that shall be preserved from these snares and thorns ? He that keepeth his soul by watchfulness against sin and temptation, by prayer, and, above all, by committing it to the care of him that is the keeper of Israel. He shall be preserved from every evil thing, he shall be far from those thorns and snares which the froward man is continually meeting in his path.

Are these things so ? Did not Job keep his soul with all diligence, and even the souls of his children, and yet he met with snares, and nets, and darkness, in his paths ‡. This cannot be denied, but Job was only tried for a moment, to improve his graces, to raise his name, and to brighten his crown. The people of God may expect manifold tribulations, but, amidst them all, they have peace in Christ : And what are the tribulations of the world to the peace that is in him ! They shall be preserved by the power of God, through faith unto salvation, and whilst they sow in tears they can rejoice in the hope of reaping in joy §.

Ver. 6. *Train up a child in the way wherein he should go, and (or also, or even) when he is old, he will not depart from it.*

Take this child, said Pharaoh's daughter to Jochebed, nurse him for me, and I will pay thee thy wages. Chil-

---

*2 Tim. 2:26   †Prov. 1:32, Ps. 69:22, Isa. 8:14
‡Job 19:6,8, 22:10   §Rom. 8:28, 2 Cor. 5:17

dren are an heritage of the Lord, and he lays claim, in a special manner, to the children of professing Christians, as his own *. And he commands them to be nursed and trained up for himself, and those that obey his orders shall be richly recompensed, in the good behaviour of their children, or at least, in the approbation of God, and the satisfaction of their own minds.

Satan will soon address himself to your children, to bespeak them for his service. Their reason will no sooner begin to operate than he will take advantage of that foolishness which is bound up in their hearts, to fix them in his service. Endeavour therefore to be beforehand with him. Instruct them in the knowledge of God, of their own fallen condition, of the way that God hath provided for their recovery, and the way of holiness wherein they should walk. Convince them, by methods suited to their tender years and weak minds, that religion is pleasant, and necessary for them. Check the first appearances of vice, by such means as will not give them a disgust at instruction. Accommodate yourselves in the methods of your instructions to their capacities and dispositions, that they may be drawn to religion with the cords of love, and with the bands of a man. Parents do not give the same food to all children, but attend to the difference in their constitutions and tastes, in their care of their bodies? and why should they not make the like difference in their management of their minds? Let all your instructions be sweetened by good nature, and enforced by good example, which has a greater influence than precepts upon all men, and especially on children. Correction must likewise have its place in training up your children; and God must be earnestly implored to crown the whole with his blessing.

When children are thus trained up, they will be led

---

*Ezek. 16:20

into the paths of life and peace, and even when they are old they will not turn aside out of them. Timothy from a child was trained up in the knowledge of the holy Scriptures, and the faith which dwelt in his grand-mother and mother, dwelt in him also, for the scrip-tures made him wise unto salvation. It is a great plea-sure to parents to see their children walking in the truth, and it is an unspeakable heightening of that plea-sure, when their own instructions and admonitions have been blessed by God, as means of conducting them into that good path. Parents love their children, be-cause they were the instruments of their existence, but they will look upon the fruit of their bodies to be doubly their children, when they are spiritual fathers to them, as well as the fathers of their flesh. But how painful must it be to the heart of a parent, to see the misbehaviour of a child, whose Christian education was neglected? Every wicked act in such a child, must be a wound in the heart of his cruel father, who by his cruel negligence, left his child to be a prey to the devil, and, carried captive by that cruel tyrant, to be employ-ed in his hellish drudgery. If the father lives to see him die in such a situation, what an hell must it be to his own soul. Even the agonies of a wounded consci-ence are unequal to the torment of reflecting that, in spite of all the obligations of nature, and interest, and religion, a poor child was suffered to be carried away by Satan to the lake of fire; where he is now justly cursing the instrument who brought him into the world in a sinful state, because he never used the proper means for preventing that horrible misery, to which he is now reduced.

Will children always walk in that way wherein they are trained up? For the most part this will be the case, God is a sovereign dispenser of grace, and he is not under any obligation to bestow it upon the children of his faithful people; but this proverb teaches us, that he uses to bless the attempts of parents, to train up their children in the nurture and admonition of the Lord. If parents are disappointed in their expectations from their children, they will be free at least of those terrible remorses which sting the hearts of careless parents, when their children prove wicked. They have the pleasing consciousness of having done their duty. They can pray, with humble boldness, that God may yet bless his own appointment for their children's advantage; for the seed of early instruction may be many years buried under ground, and at last spring up. They may even form some pleasing hopes, that although they have not the pleasure of seeing their houses such with God as they could wish, they may see at the great day, some at the right hand of Christ, who gave them too much reason to fear the contrary. The instructions of Hezekiah had no influence upon Manasseh, till he had been long in his grave; and yet Hezekiah will be able, we hope, to say at the last. Here am I, and the son whom God hath given me.

Ver. 7. *The rich ruleth over the poor, and the borrower is servant to the lender.*

When Job's three friends endeavoured to convince him that he was a great sinner, and could make no impression upon him, Eliphaz at last ventures roundly to tell him, what his transgressions were; but as he had only conjecture to go upon, he could only judge what those sins were that he was most likely to fall into, and fixes upon those that were most natural to a man in his circumstances. Job was the greatest of all the men in the east, and therefore Eliphaz tells him, that he had taken a pledge from his brother for nought, and had tyrannized over the poor; for he knew that the pride of riches often displays itself in such conduct, and that those whose circumstances enable them to lend to others, are too often betrayed, by their circumstances, into insolence and oppression. It is not for nothing that Paul directs Timothy to charge those who are rich in the world, not to trust in uncertain riches, nor to be high-minded. Rich persons ought narrowly to examine their own hearts and conduct, whether they are not puffed up with vanity, and disposed to behave imperiously towards their inferiors, especially those who are obliged to have some dependence upon them, and whose circumstances oblige them to be in their debt. Let them remember that they have received their riches from God, by whose providence things are so managed, that this man is poor and the other man rich; this man must borrow, and another man is able to lend. Let them attend to their own poverty and absolute dependance in respect of God, before whom the rich and the poor are equal, and by whose justice, those who take their brethren by the throat, because they owe them a few pence, will have the many talents exacted, in which they stand indebted to God.

This proverb is a warning to men to be industrious and frugal, that they may not lose their liberty. Men who labour diligently in their callings, need not cringe to the rich, nor live in any man's debt. Some persons care not how much they borrow, never remembering that the day of payment is coming, and that a man has as many masters as he has creditors. Paul did not choose to be burdensome to any man, nor to be meanly dependant upon the generosity even of those who were best affected to him, but he laboured, working with his hands, and helped by his labours to supply the wants of his friends.

Ver. 8. *He that soweth iniquity, shall reap vanity, and the rod of his anger shall fail.*

The husbandman does not expect to reap wheat if he has sown tares, and yet men are often so foolish as to expect, that, after sowing to the flesh, they shall reap the same thing with those that sow to the spirit; and, therefore, Paul warns men not to suffer themselves to be deceived in this momentous point *. Solomon gives a like warning in this place, and so does Hosea †.

He that lives in the practice of any sin, is sowing iniquity; for the thoughts of the mind, the words of the mouth, and the labours of the hand, are seed which shall spring up and produce a corresponding harvest. Men expect pleasure and profit from sin, but it will yield them nothing but disappointment and mischief. The wages of sin is death, and the truth of God stands engaged for the payment.

This harvest of disappointment and misery is sometimes begun in this world, as Eliphaz assures us from his own observation ‡. But the first fruits of it only are reaped at present: the full harvest is at the end of the world §; and then sinners will be horribly amazed at the immense crop of misery, produced from that seed which they thought had been for ever buried. In vain do sinners think that their works are forgotten, because they are not presently recompensed; the husbandman would be thought a fool, who mourned as if he had lost his seed, because he cannot reap in the beginning of summer, when all the world knows that there must be a long interval between seed time and harvest. Sinners shall reap in due time, if they give not over their sowing.

Wicked men will not think of these things in time,

---

*Gal. 6:7 †Hosea 10:13 ‡Job 4:8 §Matt. 13

but indulge their pride and folly, and many of them beat their fellow men with the rod of their anger, abusing their prosperity for the support of their insolence ; but their rod shall not always abide in its strength, God will wrest it out of their hands, and break it in pieces, and punish them with the more dreadful rod of his own wrath. Eliphaz was an eye witness of this truth also, and describes it with great force of language. The roaring of the lion, and the voice of the fierce lion, and the teeth of the young lions are broken : the old lion perisheth for lack of prey, and the stout lion's whelps are scattered abroad *.

Ver. 9. *He that hath a bountiful eye shall be blessed, for he giveth of his bread to the poor.*

" Mine eye affecteth mine heart," says the mourning and merciful prophet, " because of all the daughters of my people." There is a correspondence between the heart and the eye in the merciful man ; for the sight of misery produces compassion in his soul, and the tenderness of his heart beams forth in his eyes. The man whose eyes are the index of a bountiful heart, is a blessed man, for he enjoys the sweetest of earthly pleasures, that of kindness and beneficence, and pleasant reflections on his own conduct. He shall be blessed by all the wise and good, the blessings of widows and orphans shall come upon his head, the loins of the poor bless him, and he shall receive abundant blessings from God, who will not leave him unpitied in the day of his distress, but make all his bed in his sickness. He shall enjoy blessings in his body, and blessings in his outward estate, and blessings in his inner man ; he shall be blessed in his person, and blessed in his family ; he shall be blessed upon the earth, and blessed in the day of

*Job 4:10,11, Ps. 37, Isa. 9:4

judgment, for his bountiful works performed from a principle of faith and charity, will be produced as the evidences of his interest in the Redeemer *.

He shall surely be blessed, for he giveth of his bread to the poor, and thereby makes it to appear that his tears of sympathy are the expressions of genuine charity. He is not one of those hypocrites that say to their neighbours, " go away, be ye warmed and filled," whilst they give them nothing of what is necessary for the body. He gives, and he does it with an air of kindness which cheers the heart of him whom he relieves. He gives not of the bread of other people, but his own, for he would abhor the thoughts of robbery, for acts of charity. He does not give all his bread, for he does not think it his duty to rob himself and his family, that he may give to others ; but he gives liberally out of what he possesses, and that which is left to himself is sanctified to him.

Some that have a bountiful eye have no bread to give, but they will give what will turn to as good an account to the donor, and sometimes will be as pleasing to the receiver; tears and attention, and offices of tenderness and prayers to Him that is able to help.

Those that are unfeeling in their dispositions, and cannot open their hands but to receive, are already cursed with an hard and contracted heart. They are more savage than the wandering Arabs of the land of Tema †. They have not the faith of Christ, nor does the love of God dwell in them, and their ears shall hear, at the great day, those dreadful words, " Depart from me, ye cursed, into everlasting fire ‡."

---

*Ps. 41:1-3, Isa. 58:7-11, 2 Tim. 1:17,18, Heb. 6:9,10
†Isa. 21:14   ‡1 John 3:17,18, Matt. 25:41

Ver. 10. *Cast out the scorner, and contention shall go out, yea strife and reproach shall cease.*

Hagar, for her insolent behaviour, was obliged to flee from the house of Abraham. She humbled herself, and was again permitted for a time to dwell with that happy family, but her son Ishmael, by his contemptuous behaviour, procured his own expulsion, and that of his mother, at the appointment of God himself. It would be happy for all families, and churches, and societies of every kind, if scorners could be cast out of them, for they are the authors of strife and reproach, of debates, and revilings, and railings, whereby the sweets of society are poisoned, and turned into gall. But if this cannot be well accomplished, we ought at least to avoid all friendship and fellowship with them, and to exclude them from every voluntary society, formed for mutual improvement or entertainment. Peace is essential to the comfort of men, but peace cannot be maintained whilst scorners are allowed to sow the seeds of variance by their rude reflections and unmannerly reproaches. Their behaviour is such, that they will inflame the passions of the best natured men that do not keep out of their way ; and when they have once kindled the fire, none can tell when it will be quenched. We are commanded, as far as lies in us, to live peaceably with all men, and therefore it is necessary to set a mark on those who cause divisions and offences, and to avoid them. But will contention cease, if these firebrands of society are cast out ? Yes, unless we have too much of their disposition in our own breasts. We must expel from thence the principles of scorning, those proud and fiery passions from whence all divisions arise.

How long, O ye scorners, will you delight in your scorning ? Don't you observe what brands of infamy are set on your name ; what a plague you are to all around you, so that the wise exclude you from their company, because your dispositions are so wicked and perverse that there is no bearing with you? Why do you indulge that arrogance which makes you the serpents of human society? Go and learn of Him that is lowly and meek, and you shall find rest to your own souls, and become the delight of those amongst whom you were an abomination *.

Ver. 11. *He that loveth pureness of heart, for the grace of his lips, the king shall be his friend.*

No saint can say that he is perfectly pure from his sin; but every saint may safely say, that he is a lover of purity, and a hater of hypocrisy. The pharisees loved the reputation of purity, and they were very pure in their own eyes. They thought themselves as clean as those pots and vessels which they purified with such exactness, whilst they were in reality like cups and platters, whose outside was clean, but the inward part filled with every impurity. But real saints are more anxious to approve themselves unto God, than to enjoy reputation from men, and their outward holiness proceeds from a love of purity in the heart †.

The pureness of heart, here meant, consists chiefly in sincerity and uprightness, and stands opposed to all dissimulation. The love of it is necessary to grace in the lips, which must be directed by an honest heart, and admit no pollution of flattery and doubleness, which so much stains the communication of a great part of mankind ‡.

The lips may assume an appearance of purity and sincerity when there is none in the heart, but this empty appearance cannot be long supported. A very small degree of sagacity will enable a man soon to discover it, and the discovery is attended with abhorrence.

*Prov. 24:9   †Rom. 2:28-30   ‡Ps. 12

Grace in the lips is necessary to recommend pureness of heart. We ought always to speak the words of truth, but we ought to speak it in the most pleasing manner possible, that we may not render it unacceptable by our manner of representing it. Daniel shewed his integrity and politeness at once, by the manner of his address to Nebuchadnezzar, when he was called to give him very disagreeable information.

Every man ought to be a friend to the man of integrity, and the king himself, if he is not an absolute fool, will be a friend to him that joins purity of heart with gracefulness of tongue. Daniel, the captive, on this account, found favour with two haughty kings of Babylon. It is the general opinion, that flattery is necessary in our conversation with great men, if we wish to recommend ourselves to their favour; but the surest way of gaining and securing the favour of any man, is to seek above all things the favour of Him that has the hearts of all men in his hands. The favour gained by flattery and complaisance, soon decays. The favour, lost by truth, is in time recovered. Falsehood may support itself for a year or two, but truth stands on an immoveable foundation, for it is supported by the God of truth, as we are told in the next verse.

Ver. 12. *The eyes of the Lord preserve knowledge, but he overthroweth the words of the transgressor.*

When knowledge in the mind is attended by pureness in the heart and grace in the lips, they form an amiable and worthy character, which draws to it the eyes and hearts of wise men: but that is not the principal recommendation of it, for the eyes of the Lord himself preserve knowledge, and watch for good over the man whose lips and conversation are regulated by it. The king should be his friend, but there are Ahabs among kings who have not so much sense as poor Belshazzar, but love only those that speak pleasing things to them, whether true or false : but the King of kings will surely be his friend; his eyes are upon him for good, and every loss that he sustains for his adherence to truth shall be gain. But the words of the transgressor are overthrown by Him. He disappoints their hypocrisy, and brings evil upon them, instead of those advantages which they expected from their cunning and insincerity.

It is mostly safe to follow the counsels of a wise man, for they are likely to be attended with happy success, and if it is in his power he will contribute for his own honour to the success of them; but it is always safe to follow the counsels of God, who can insure and command success, and will not suffer any man to lose in the end, by obedience to his will. God did not indeed interpose in the same visible manner, for the support of John Baptist, as he had formerly done for the preservation of Shadrach and his companions. But John the Baptist had done his work, and was fit for a better world, and this world was not worthy of him ; we cannot suppose him a loser, because his integrity procured him the crown of martyrdom, and he now praises God as cheerfully for the administrations of providence towards him on earth, as the three children who escaped the violence of fire, or he that came unhurt out of the lion's den.

Ver. 13. *The sluggard saith, there is a lion without, I shall be slain in the streets.*

The sluggard will not plow by reason of the cold, and he will not move out of his house lest a lion should meet him, and kill him in the streets. This is a very odd excuse for his laziness. Lions are seldom found in the fields in the day time, and it is a very extraordinary thing, if they be found in the streets. Does the sluggard himself believe there is any truth in it ? If he does, why does he sleep in his house, since it is possible that it may be set on fire by some accident in the night? Why does he ever take a meal, for some have been choked by the bread which they put into their mouths?

When we are employed in the duties of our calling, we need not vex ourselves with the apprehension of lions. "I will give mine angels charge over thee," says God, "and they shall keep thee in all thy ways." Thou shalt tread upon the lion and adder, the young lion and the dragon shalt thou trample under thy feet. But let the sluggard remember that there is a lion in that bed where he dozes away his time, and in that chamber where he sits folding his arms together. The devil goes about like a roaring lion seeking whom he may devour, and he rejoices greatly when he lights upon a sluggard, for he looks upon him to be a sure prey. Poverty, like an armed man, is fast marching up to the sluggard, and will soon prevail against him, like a king prepared to the battle.

We are safe from the lions in the way of duty, and never safe when we avoid it. Lions, when they met David feeding his sheep, were torn in pieces by him like kids. A lion unexpectedly came upon that young man of the sons of prophets, who declined his duty when he was commanded to smite his neighbour, and rent him in pieces.

Ver. 14. *The mouth of strange women is a deep pit: he that is abhorred of the Lord shall fall therein.*

If you will believe the fond admirer of the strange woman, her cheeks and lips are like the roses and lilies, her eyes are like stars, and her mouth drops honey. But if you will believe Solomon, speaking from the mouth of God, her mouth, and every thing about her that charms the hearts of men, is like a deep ditch, made for catching the unwary passenger, and all her flatteries and blandishments are so many traps and snares, set by the devil to catch men, that he may take them captive and keep them fast till their doom becomes irreversible as his own. Solomon had discoursed at great length on this point, in the beginning of the book, but young men need to be frequently put in mind of it.

They are unhappy that fall into this ditch, for it is a proof of the Lord's heavy displeasure, when men are suffered to fall into it, and therefore, in order to be preserved from this danger, it is necessary for us, not only to observe the precepts of God, levelled against the sin of uncleanness, but to observe the whole system of divine precepts, because God may suffer us to fall into this sin, to punish us for others. The heathens were given up to it, as Paul tells us, for their idolatry. They had dishonoured God by their vain imaginations and their abominable worship, and God in justice suffered them to dishonour their own bodies, and to make themselves brutes, as they had represented God himself by the images of brutes.

Have we been left to fall into this sin? Our situation is very dangerous, for nothing less than divine power can raise us out of this ditch; and how can we expect miracles of divine power to be exerted in our behalf, when we have drawn upon ourselves the sore displeasure of the Lord? But our situation is not altogether desperate, for miracles of mercy have often been performed by the Lord. Let us acknowledge his justice, and humble ourselves under the tokens of his displeasure, and look to him with earnest expectation and ardent cries, till he raise us up out of the deep pit, and set our feet upon a rock.

Ver. 15. *Foolishness is bound in the heart of a child, but the rod of correction shall drive it far from him.*

Men generally use children like play-things, and divert themselves with their childish tricks and follies;

but there is another kind of foolishness in children, that is too serious and mournful to be the subject of sport. Sin is the very essence of folly, and sin dwells in young and old, and none of the children of Adam, except him that was, in a peculiar sense, the seed of the woman, could ever deny with truth, that he was shapen in iniquity and born in sin.

This foolishness dwells in the hearts of children, and makes their way froward and strange *, for the understanding is darkened, the will perverted, the affections sensualized, and the disposition rendered averse by it to every thing good, and turned to evil. It is bound in the heart by cords that no man can loose, and twines to it like ivy to the walls of a house. It is not more natural for a man to breathe, than for a child of Adam to violate the law of the Lord, and to covet forbidden fruit.

When parents rejoice with a fond heart over the fruit of their bodies, they should remember that they were the instruments of conveying a corrupt nature to their children, and be deeply concerned to have this mortal disease effectually cured. But how can this be effected? Who can bring a clean thing out of an unclean; or who can say that he has made either his own heart or any other person's clean? God only can loose the bonds of sin, and drive foolishness away from the heart, and therefore his grace must be sought for this end. But whilst his favour is earnestly supplicated, the methods appointed by his wisdom are to be used with a dependence on his blessing. Parents ought to join correction to instruction, and to use it as an appointment of God, on which his blessing may be expected. The rod of correction shall drive this foolish-

---

*Chap. 21:8

ness far from the child, and he is a cruel parent that loves the ease of his son more than his soul, and would rather see him grow up in folly, than endure those painful feelings which compassionate parents suffer, when they are scourging the son whom they love.

Ver. 16. *He that oppresseth the poor to increase his riches, and he that giveth to the rich, shall surely come to want.*

Sin pays its servants very bad wages, for it gives them the very reverse of what it promised. Whilst the sin of oppression or injustice promises mountains of gold, it brings them poverty and ruin. "Shalt thou reign because thou closest thyself in cedar?" said the prophet to Jehoiakim. It could not be, for he used his neighbour's service without wages, and gave him nought for his work. There is a flying roll of curses which enters into the house of the thief and the oppressor, which consumes it with the timber and stones of it. Injuries done to the poor are sorely resented by the God of mercy, who is the poor man's friend, and will break in pieces his oppressor. The threatenings of God against the robbers of the poor are sometimes laughed at by the rich and great, but they will find them in due time to be awful realities *.

But if the oppression of the poor is an impoverishing sin, will not liberality make a man rich? True liberality, exercised to proper objects, will. But not that which is exercised to the rich. Some give to the rich for the same reason as they oppress the poor. They propose to gain the favour of the great, and to receive tenfold for every present they make, and so they expect to be soon rich. But he that giveth to the rich with these views shall surely come to want. If he would give to the poor he might have an hundred-fold,

---

*Isa. 5:8,9, James 3:4

but he has only God's word for that, and rather chooses to trust the generosity of rich men; but when they see the trick, they are on their guard, and will pay with scorn the man that designed to impose on them with deceitful professions of regard.

It is plain from reason, as well as Scripture, that it is not always a sin to give to the rich, but it is very often a sin; and that, not only when men are in danger of hurting their families, or wronging their creditors by it, but likewise when they give those superfluities to the rich, which are due to the poor. We are not proprietors but stewards of the gifts of providence, and must distribute that which he has entrusted to our care according to his will. And it is his pleasure that we should make to ourselves friends, by the mammon of unrighteousness, not of the rich but the poor *.

Ver. 17. *Bow down thine ear, and hear the words of the wise, and apply thine heart unto my sayings.*

It signifies nothing to speak to a man that is sleeping or inattentive, and yet we are often inattentive when we hear the word of God, especially the precepts of it, which we are too ready to look upon as an heavy burden, and a grievous yoke. Solomon was well acquainted with the heart of man, and knowing how many would read or hear his excellent precepts without bestowing proper attention on them, he rouses us by frequent calls for our most earnest heed to the things that are spoken.

We must bow down our ears to hear him with attention, reverence, and humility. The words of the wise deserve this regard from us, for they are means of communicating their wisdom to us. And if the words of wise men merit so much respect, we can never attend too earnestly to the words of the only wise God. He made our ears and shall he not be heard by us?

Our hearts must be applied, as well as our ears, to

---

*Luke 16:9

the knowledge contained in this book. We should labour to understand it with our minds, to fix it in our judgments, to impress it on our consciences, to have it treasured up in our memories that it may be constantly ready for our use. God requires us to give him our hearts, and if we only lend an ear to him, we render him only a little bodily service. The word of God is very pleasant, and the sweetness of it is relished when it enters into the heart.

Ver. 18. *For it is a pleasant thing if thou keep them within thee; they shall withal be fitted in thy lips.*

Honey from the comb is sweet to the taste, but all the words of God are sweet to the soul. Wine gives a pleasant refreshment to the faint and thirsty, but the truths of Scripture are sweeter than wine, for they give refreshment to the inner man. Shall we value those things that are delightful to the organs of taste, and yet despise those pleasures that fill the soul with heart-felt satisfaction? Shall every joy be pursued with eagerness, and that only contemned which arises from the word of God? Do you say, you never received any pleasure from the word of God, and that an entertaining history gives you more entertainment than any thing that Solomon has said? The reason is too obvious. Solomon tells you that the words of instruction are pleasant to a man when they are kept within him. It was a severe reflection, which Christ made upon the Jews, my word hath no place in you. The same may be made, with too much reason, upon those that taste not the sacred joys of the Bible.

As the word of God is pleasant to the relish of a saint, so its dwelling in the heart is attended with happy consequences, for it shall be fitted in the lips. The knowledge of truth will supply the lips with wisdom, and enable them to talk with discretion and judgment. A talent of speaking with propriety, and wisdom on any subject, is a great ornament to him that has it, and enables him to be useful to others; but it must be founded on knowledge, for how can any man communicate that knowledge which he does not possess. But clear and distinct apprehensions of things, will always enable a man to speak of them with ease and plainness, to others.

The application of the heart to the words that have been spoken to us, will also tend to encourage our confidence in God.

Ver. 19. *That thy trust may be in the Lord, I have made known to thee this day, even to thee.*

Ver. 20. *Have not I written to thee excellent things, in counsels and knowledge.*

The chief design of this book, is to instruct us in every duty that we owe to God and man ; and confidence in God is a fundamental duty, without which we can perform nothing aright. Solomon calls sinners, in the beginning of the book, to return unto God, depending on his mercy, according to his promise. He directs us about believing in Christ, and in God his father who set him up from everlasting *. He expressly enjoins us to trust in the Lord with all our heart, and to renounce all self-confidence †. And the whole strain of his proverbs, wherein he constantly insists on the advantages of righteousness, and the misery that follows vice, encourages us to commit our souls in well-doing unto God. Confidence in God, is our shield against temptations, and the means of deriving from God through Christ all the supplies of grace needful for our assistance and support in the ways of holiness ; and every thing said in this book, when it is duly considered, will contribute to strengthen our trust, as well as to direct our practice.

That our trust in God may be encouraged, and our steps directed, we must read and hear this book with

---

*Chap. 8   †Chap. 3

application to ourselves. " I have made known to thee, even to thee," says the inspired penman. It is God that speaks, and he speaks to each of us in particular, and we ought to receive what is said into our hearts, believing that the word of exhortation speaketh to us in particular, as really as if it had been written for our own use, without a view to any other person in the world. Till we hear the word as the word of God, and as his word addressed unto us, we hear it not with due regard.

God hath not only spoken, but likewise written unto us by Solomon. " Receive I pray thee," said Eliphaz to Job, " the law at his mouth, and lay up his word in thine heart." Job did so, for he esteemed the words of God's mouth more than his necessary food. Did the holy men pay such reverence to the word of God, when there was no scripture, and shall we shew less regard to it, when God has been graciously pleased to write unto us the great things of his law and covenant.

The things that are written are not only words of truth, but excellent and princely things, worthy to be written by the wisest of men, by inspiration of the spirit of wisdom. God refers it to our own judgments, whether they are not excellent. If we discern not their excellency we are blind and stupid. They have an excellency that far surpasses the most valued objects upon earth. Their value lies not in a glittering appearance, like gold, and silver, and diamonds, nor in affording entertainment to a curious mind, like a well written history, but in affording counsel, to make us prudent in all manner of behaviour, and in giving us knowledge, to enrich the mind with the most precious truths. To be wise, to understand our way to heaven, to know God and his Son Jesus Christ, and the acceptable and perfect will of God, are excellent attainments; and the things written in this book are of excellent use to assist us in acquiring them.

To have the judgment settled about the great things

that are intimately connected with our best interests, is another benefit to be derived from a due attention to this book.

Ver. 21. *That I might make thee know the certainty of the words of truth ; that thou mightest answer the words of truth to them that send unto thee.*

If a man has a cause depending before a court of law, wherein his all is concerned, he will certainly be anxious to know what lawyers he may most safely trust, and what are the surest means of obtaining an happy event to the suit. Religion is our all, and it is a criminal sluggishness and stupidity in men, to be careless whether they are rightly instructed in it or not. Our teachers have instructed us in the principles which they themselves believe, and ministers teach us, every Sabbath, those doctrines which are professed in the church to which they belong. We believe that their instructions are sound and good, but on what ground do we believe this ? We do not believe in the infallibility of any particular church, and we must have better warrant for a right faith, than the testimony of men. This and other books in Scripture, were written to establish us in the truth, by shewing us whether that is the true doctrine of God wherein we stand. We have not a sure hold of the truths of God, unless we are sure that they are the truths of God, and we can be assured of this only by the Scripture. A scriptural knowledge, will preserve us from being like children tossed to and fro with every wind of doctrine, of which we are in constant danger whilst we are unacquainted with the Scripture, although we had the knowledge of every truth in our religion, by instruction from men.

But there is still another great advantage arising from a serious regard to this book. By establishing our minds in the truth, it will enable us to satisfy others that send to us for information about the principles of truth and duty. Men were not born for themselves only, we are members one of another, and ought to consult the good of the body, and of other members of it besides ourselves. As men, when they perform the duties of their callings, are useful members of civil society, so if we live as becometh saints, and seek after the knowledge of the truth, we will be useful members of the church of Christ, ready to give an answer to every one that asketh us a reason of our faith and hope, to instruct the ignorant, to satisfy the doubts of the scrupulous, and to fix those that waver.

Such are the pleasures and advantages to be found in the book of God, and in the Book of Proverbs in particular. He has gained every point, says an heathen poet, who has mingled the pleasant and the useful together. These attractives of the soul are nowhere joined together with such exquisite skill as in the word of God ; and if we read it with a superficial eye, and hear it with an inattentive mind, we despise not men but God. We despise him, when he is employing all the methods of divine condescension and wisdom to recommend his truths to our hearts. O let it not be said, that we give a patient hearing to all that speak to us, except only to him, to whom we are indebted for the faculty of hearing and understanding any thing. He that hath an ear, let him hear the great things which the Spirit of God speaks unto men.

Solomon now proceeds in his directions about the conduct of our life. His following proverbs, are generally expressed at greater length than the foregoing ones, for under the direction of infinite wisdom, he solicits our attention, by every method of address.

Ver. 22. *Rob not the poor because he is poor, neither oppress the afflicted in the gate.*

The gate was in ancient times, amongst the eastern

nations, the place of judgment, and therefore this instruction is to be understood to respect judges. They
are forbidden to take advantage of the friendless and
indigent circumstances of the poor and afflicted, to oppress them by perverting justice in favour to the rich.
The Scripture forbids us to countenance a poor man in
his cause, but it is far worse, and more ordinary, and
therefore more frequently forbidden, to oppress a poor
man in judgment.

This is a crying sin, which contains, together with
injustice, the most unmerciful cruelty, and is a plain
evidence of an inhuman and cowardly disposition. This
was one of the sins for which Eliphaz guessed that
Job's calamities had come upon him ; but that good
man was of a very opposite spirit. He did justice to
all men, but to the poor he was merciful as well as
just. " If I have lifted up mine hand against the fatherless," says he, " when I saw mine help in the gate, then
let mine arm fall from my shoulder blade, and mine
arm be broken from the bone."

Not to relieve the poor and afflicted, when we can do
it without injury to ourselves, is hard : to oppress them,
and add to their affliction, is brutal and monstrous. It
is to act not like men, but like the monsters of the desert, which prey upon the weaker animals. For magistrates to be guilty of this crime, is a perversion of an
institution of God into an engine of abominable wickedness.

If poor men had rich friends to plead their cause, or
avenge their injuries, men would not rob them because
they are poor. Well, they have a friend that will plead
their cause, and break in pieces their oppressors. If a
great man should take the part of a poor man, he would
reckon himself safe, but God is infinitely greater than
any man, and here it is declared that he will be the
advocate and avenger of the poor and oppressed.

Ver. 23. *For the Lord will plead their cause, and spoil the soul of those that spoiled them.*

He pleads their cause with admirable eloquence in his word. " What mean ye, that ye beat my people to pieces, and grind the faces of the poor ?" saith the Lord God of Hosts. Who can answer such pleadings as these? However, they are but words, and bad men look upon words to be but wind. But God will plead the cause of the poor, by furious rebukes of providence also. He will render unto their oppressors severe vengeance for their wickedness. Have they rifled the poor of their little all ? God will rifle the oppressor, not only of his substance, but of his life and soul. The robber of the poor is a poor unhappy creature. It is terrible to have the justice of God engaged against a man, but this is the unhappy case of the spoiler. He may obtain a temporary success in his extortions, but when he makes an end of spoiling, he must be spoiled. He has the mercy of God against him, as well as his justice. Mercy is that pleasant attribute of the divine nature, on which all the hopes of sinners must rest; but the mercy of God is engaged on the side of the poor and afflicted, against their persecutors. Mercy and justice meet together in this text, and make it both a promise and a threatening. What a terrible case is it, to have grace itself turned into a terror, and to be under the wrath of God because he is merciful. Yet such is the actual condition of those, whose conduct is a contradiction at once to the rules of justice and mercy. It shall come to pass, says God, that when the oppressed cries unto me, I will hear, for I am gracious *.

Let the mercy implied in this declaration, encourage the poor and afflicted to make God their refuge. Your tyrants may look upon these words as empty threaten-

---

*Exod. 22:27

ngs, which shall never have effect, but it would be a very ungrateful return in you for so much goodness, to consider them in the same light. The words of God whereby he encourages the needy, are pure words, they are like silver seven times purified *. Have you such a glorious advocate? commit your cause to him, with meekness, in imitation of our great example. Make no unconscientious compliances to avoid oppression, and take no unjustifiable steps to preserve yourselves, but trust to your great advocate, who stands at the right hand of the poor to deliver him †.

Ver. 24. *Make no friendship with an angry man, and with a furious man thou shalt not go.*

Friendship is the balm of life, when it is entered into with discretion, but it is a plague and a snare, when it is injudiciously contracted. Our divine teacher wishes us to be happy both in this world and the next, and extends his instructions to every thing that is connected with our happiness. He forbids us to enter into friendship with any bad man, and here he cautions us particularly against the friendship of the passionate. We must not so much as keep company with angry men, nor take a walk with them, if we can possibly avoid it. But what will be the great evil of making friendship with a man of this temper?

Ver. 25. *Lest thou learn his ways, and get a snare to thy soul* (or *life.*)

Is there any danger of learning that man's ways who makes himself so very disagreeable? No doubt there is, if we love him. We are either like our friends, or will soon be like them. Conversation has a mighty influence upon our manners, and evil communication corrupts good manners: When we see bad things practised by those we love, the horror of them abates, and we are insensibly drawn to the practice of them.

---

*Ps. 12   †Ps. 109:31

But if we make passionate men our friends and companions, we are in great danger of becoming like to them, on another account. Although we should be good-natured, yet their unreasonable behaviour will be apt, on many occasions, to set our temper on fire, and from occasional bursts of passion, we may be led by degrees to contract obstinate habits of falling into a passion, on every trifling occasion ; for custom is produced by frequent acts, and in time becomes a second nature.

Thus we are in danger of being ensnared into sins of fatal consequence to our souls, for although anger is not always a sin, yet to be under the government of imperious passions, is very sinful and very dangerous *.

Our lives may be exposed to danger, if we walk with furious men. When Cain walked with Abel in the field, his furious passions subdued his reason and his natural affection, and he slew his brother. There have been many Cains in the world, who have wounded or slain their friends by the impulse of fury. But if we should escape this danger, yet by contracting an habit of being angry, our tongues may in time become rebels to reason, and bring down mischief on our heads.

Consider this proverb, ye that give a loose to your passions. Perhaps you suppose that you have good qualities to atone for this bad one. But you are quite mistaken. The meaning of this instruction is plainly this, that no good qualites should induce us to enter into friendship with an angry man. It is taken for granted, that a passionate man may have some qualities that would engage esteem, if they were separated from this wretched temper, for otherwise no person would be in danger of contracting an intimacy with a furious man. But it is plainly asserted, that these qualities in conjunction with such a temper, forfeit their claim on

---

*Matt. 5:23

our friendship. Don't you see, then, that your miserable temper casts a shade over every thing that might otherwise adorn you, and that you are fit only for a desert, where you can disquiet none but yourselves. God himself is so much displeased with you, that he will suffer none that will take his advice to be intimate with you, or so much as to keep your company. Fly then to his mercy for pardon, and implore the exertions of his power, to subdue your ungovernable passions. Let your souls be impressed with the example of our meek Redeemer, and watch over your spirits, that you may not again disturb the peace of society, and deserve to be sent forth to dwell among the beasts of the desert.

Ver. 26. *Be not thou one of them that strike hands, or of them that are sureties for debts.*

Solomon has already said much against rash suretyship *; but bad examples have a greater influence upon many people, than good precepts, and because many others make little scruple of putting their name to a bond for another man, we are in danger of being seduced into the same dangerous practice ; but before we follow any man's example in any thing, we should observe what the event of it is likely to be. If other men do bad things, and smart for it, it will be no motive to a wise man to run into the same error. Let us at least consider one thing, in this case : Suppose the principal debtor should prove unable to pay the creditor, will we be cheerfully willing to take his place, or are we sure that we will be able, if called upon, to pay his debt ? We are rich at present, but we know not whether we will be rich or poor at the day of payment. And,

Ver. 27. *If thou hast nothing to pay, why should he take away thy bed from under thee ?*

You may say, it will never come to this. The law of Christ will not suffer the creditor, to exercise such ri-

---

*Chap. 6, 11:15

gour, if I should be unable to pay. How do you know that ? Are you sure that the creditor, and his heirs, and executors, will not depart, in any instance of conduct from the law of Christ, when their interest pushes them, and the laws of the land will bear them out.

Religion, you see, allows and requires us to pay a proper attention to our own interest and comfort. It requires no instances of self-denial, but such as are more for our own interest than self-gratification in those instances would be. It does not forbid us to love ourselves, when it requires us to love our neighbours as ourselves. Indeed, we cannot hurt ourselves, for the most part, without hurting some other men also. What can we do for the poor, for our families, for our friends, if our bed is taken away from beneath us ?

A philosopher, when he saw a generous young man spending his substance too liberally upon one that pretended great poverty, told him, that " perhaps the man he was serving was an honest man, but he was certain that he himself was honest; and therefore," added he, " you are doing an unjust thing, for you are ruining an honest man, for one that is, for aught you know, a rogue."

Ver. 28. *Remove not the ancient land mark which thy fathers have set.*

Naboth would not sell the inheritance which his father had left him, when he was offered a very good price ; but there are some who have so little respect for their fathers that they will remove, if possible, the land mark which their fathers have set, and so little regard for justice, at the same time, that they intend to give no price at all for what they add to their estate by such unjustifiable means.

It may be alleged by the covetous, that our fathers were under a mistake about the just bounds of their inheritance. Could that be proved to the satisfaction of the other party concerned, or to the conviction of the judge, it would be a good plea. But this can seldom be done. If ancient usage and prescription be not allowed as a good claim to property, nations might soon be convulsed and broken in pieces.

Land marks are means of preserving peace, as well as maintaining justice, and therefore the removing of them is a breach both of peace and honesty. It is so great a sin that a solemn curse was pronounced against it from Mount Ebal*.

It is above three thousand years since this curse was pronounced, and we learn from it that land marks were a very ancient mean of distinguishing property; that it is the will of God that men should know what is their own, and that every unrighteous invasion of another man's property, is an abomination to him.

Ver. 29. *Seest thou a man diligent in his business? He shall stand before kings, he shall not stand before mean men.*

To be a busy body in other men's matters is a scandal, but it is a pleasant sight to behold a man diligent in his own business †.

Some persons look upon the slothful, not to receive instruction, as Solomon did from the sight of his work, but to take encouragement to themselves, in following his example, or in being only a little better than he is. They would not choose to be the greatest sluggards in the world, but if they can name a man more slothful than themselves, they think that no man is entitled to censure them. Solomon directs us, on the contrary, to look upon the industrious man, that we may be excited by the advantages which he gains by his labour, to go and do likewise.

Such a man shall stand before kings. This does not

---

*Deut. 27:17   †1 Peter 3:15

imply, that every man who deserves this character can expect the honour of being appointed to the high offices of state, but it points out to us that great activity is necessary in the servants of kings, and that great activity in private stations is the way of obtaining honour and advancement. If other kings were as wise as Solomon, this proverb would be oftener verified in the letter of it, for he advanced Jeroboam to the charge of the house of Joseph, because he saw that he was an active man. That Pharaoh, who reigned in the days of Joseph, would have none to rule over his cattle that was not a man of activity.

If the diligent man does not obtain the honour of standing before kings, his industry, with God's blessing, will, for the most part, preserve him from the disgrace of standing before mean men.

Some women, by their industry, joined with other virtues, have obtained the honour of an alliance with the noblest families, of which Rebecca and Ruth are famous instances.

If we are diligent in our spiritual business, the advantage will be vastly greater *. Let us watch, then, and pray always, that we may be accounted worthy to escape those miseries which shall come upon the wicked, and to stand before the Son of Man †.

---

*Luke 12:35-38   †Luke 21:36

Proverbs 23

Verse 1. *When thou sittest to eat with a ruler, consider diligently what is before thee.*

WE must add to our faith virtue, and to virtue knowledge, and to knowledge temperance. Temperance is to be preserved at all times, and to be guarded in a special manner when we are called to eat with a ruler; for then is the trial of this virtue, and in a time of trial we are in great danger of falling, unless we consider the temptation, and watch against it.

We ought, therefore, to consider diligently the plenty, the variety, the delicacy of the dishes that are served at the great man's table, the danger of being drawn to intemperance, and the abominableness and danger of that vice.

Ver. 2. *And put a knife to thy throat, if thou be a man given to appetite.*

A man given to appetite is in great danger of running to excess on such an occasion; for his fleshly lust within, and the well-spread table before him, combine to betray him; and men's consciences are too often so lax, as to think that the laws of temperance are to be dispensed with, when there is a fair opportunity, and a strong temptation to break them.

A man of a sensual and gluttonous disposition ought to mortify his appetite. Gluttony is a great sin, as well as drunkenness. "Take heed," says our Lord, "lest your hearts be overcharged with gluttony and drunkenness, and the cares of this life." If the disciples of Christ were under obligation to guard against this sin, although they sat almost always at mean men's tables, what need have those to take heed, who are admitted to entertainments where every thing concurs to solicit their appetite, and to throw them off their guard.

" But it will be very painful," says the glutton, " to deny my craving appetite, when it is so strongly solicited. It will be as uneasy to abstain, as to have a knife stuck in my throat." Be it so, better to have a knife in your throat than to have your soul betrayed by it to sensual indulgence. Is not affliction rather to be chosen than sin ? Is it not better to pluck out a right eye, or to cut off a right hand, than to be betrayed by them to pleasant sins ?

This verse is rendered by some interpreters, " Thou hast put a knife to thy throat, if thou art a man given to appetite." Sensual gratifications are prejudicial to the body, as well as the soul, and are the frequent causes of sickness, and weakness, and death. It has been often said, that the throat has killed more people than the sword.

Ver. 3. *Be not desirous of his dainties, for they are deceitful meat.*

His dainties have a good appearance to the eye, and they are delicious to the taste, and powerfully tempt an ungoverned appetite ; but remember that the forbidden fruit did the same, and yet the eating of it " brought death into the world, and all our woe." When you see a number of dishes of very different kinds, think with yourself, " Here are fevers, and agues, and gouts, in disguise. Here are snares and traps spread along the table to catch my soul, and draw me into sin. Sense gives a good report of this plenty, but reason and religion tell me to take heed, for it is deceitful meat."

His meat is deceitful in another view. The ruler himself has no generous or friendly intention in treat-

ing you.   He makes great professions of kindness and
regard, and the civilities of a ruler open the heart, and
put a man off his guard.   His real design very probably is, to pump out some secret from you, or to gain
you by his flattering caresses to some mean or sinful
compliance with his pleasure.   Such are the ends designed, and too often effected, by means of those feasts
that are given at the elections of members of parliament,
and on some other public occasions of the like nature.
It is often difficult, if we attend them, to return as in-
dependent Britons, and as temperate Christians as we
went.

Ver. 4. *Labour not to be rich ; cease from thine own
wisdom.*

To be rich has been the lot of many saints ; and when
God bestows riches upon us, we are not required to
throw them into the sea, as a certain old philosopher
did ; but when God denies us riches, we must not
reckon ourselves unhappy on that account.   Solomon
often speaks of riches as a reward that wisdom frequently bestows on those who love her, but here he
cautions us against supposing that wisdom encourages
the love of riches—that universal passion which has
been so mischievous to the human race, since the beginning of the world.

In our fallen condition, we must labour and sweat
for our subsistence ; but that kind of labour is useful
to the body, and not prejudicial to the mind.   The labour after riches here forbidden, is exceedingly hurtful
to both.   It arises from an immoderate esteem of present things, and an aspiring mind.   It is joined with
a distrust of God's providence, and an hurry and distraction of men's thoughts, which renders them unfit
for the service of God.   It destroys all relish for the
comforts of life, that might be enjoyed at present, and
is a continual incentive to unmerciful and unjust be-

haviour. It is a pity that we do not more attentively
consider the alarming things that are said by our Lord,
and the apostle Paul, on this subject *.

But you will say, money is a necessary and an excellent thing. It keeps a man from want and dependence; it raises him to dignity and consequence; it
furnishes every thing that is desirable in life. But
cease from thine own wisdom, which is not the wisdom
from above, but that earthly, sensual, and devilish wisdom so greatly condemned in the Scripture. Money,
under the direction of wisdom, will indeed serve all
these purposes, and some others too, of far greater value. But the love of money is not merely a bad thing,
but the root of all evil, and a confidence in money is a
very foolish thing.

Ver. 5. *Wilt thou set thine eyes upon that which is not?
for riches certainly make themselves wings, and fly away
as an eagle towards heaven.*

Wilt thou let thine eyes fly upon money with eager
joy? Thou shalt soon see them fly away never to return.

To look at other men's money with covetous desires,
and an admiration of the happiness of the possessor—
to look upon our own money with rapturous delight,
because our hand has gotten much, is to make to ourselves gods of gold, as the ancient Israelites did, and to
give them the worship of the soul, and therefore covetousness is called idolatry; and to rejoice in money more
than in God, is to say to the gold, Thou art our hope,
and to the fine gold, Thou art our confidence.

It is foolish, as well as sinful, to set our eyes and our
hearts on riches. Will a man set his eyes upon a mere
nothing? But what does Solomon mean by calling
them so? Does not their splendour shew that they are

---

*Luke 12:15, 16:11-13, 1 Tim. 6:10

true substance ? It must be confessed that they are very glittering nothings, but so are bubbles upon the water, when they shine with the rays of the sun, which make them to glare for a moment, but don't hinder them from vanishing the next. Our Lord tells us that they are not the true riches, and that a man's life does not consist in the abundance of them. The wise preacher has written a book to prove, that they are the very vanity of vanities. Philosophers in every age have declaimed in proof of this point, and all men are sensible of its truth at the season when the eyes of men are forced open to the sight of truth.

But in this passage Solomon means the uncertainty of riches. They are not, for they fly away out of sight never to return. They are mine to-day, they were another man's yesterday, they will be yours to-morrow, and whither they shall have flown in a few weeks, we cannot tell.

But how do they get away ? They make to themselves wings. Whilst you sit brooding upon them, they are fledging ; and although you should try, by bills and bonds, and bars, and bolts, to clip their wings, you will not be able to hinder their elopement; and when you think to recover them, you are often making wings to what is left you. The eagle is the swiftest of birds, and with the swiftness of an eagle they mount up towards heaven, and receive their commission to whom they should next go. Doth the eagle fly by thy command, or canst thou bring him back, like the hawk, to thy lure ? As little can you recover those riches of which Divine Providence has bereaved you.

Those who place their happiness on worldly wealth, build their foundation on a flood poured out, as some render Job xxii. 16. Their joy is short, and dashed with a large infusion of fear and vexation. Their disappointment is certain ; their end is dreadful : for those who mind earthly things above heavenly things, are enemies of the cross of Christ, and their end is destruction; but true Christians seek for the true riches, their conversation is in heaven, and their treasure is in a place where there is no moth nor rust, nor any of those feathers which compose the eagle wings of riches, with which they flee away *.

Ver. 6. *Eat thou not the bread of him that hath an evil eye, neither desire thou his dainty meats.*

The Scripture directs us about the choice of occasional companions, as well as friends. There are some persons whom we must not receive into our houses, and there are some to whose houses we are forbidden to repair, or to sit at their tables. We are not, on every occasion, forbidden to eat with a ruler, although his dainties are generally deceitful meat; nor are we absolutely forbidden to feast with heathens and bad men †. But we are forbidden to eat at the table of him that has an evil eye, although it should be covered with dainty meat, and his words full of kindness.

A selfish and churlish disposition discovers itself in the eye, so that the miser declares his character against his will. Perhaps, through shame, he endeavours to hide his churlish disposition under the mask of a plentiful entertainment; but his malignity peeps through his eyes, which betray him in spite of all that he can say or do; for nature abhors dissimulation, and often detects it.

But why must we not eat his bread, nor partake of his dainties? Because it is not the quality of the food, that you are to consider, but the disposition of the company, and especially of the entertainer.

Ver. 7. *For as he thinketh in his heart, so is he : Eat and drink, saith he to thee, but his heart is not with thee.*

It is not a man's words and professions that must

---

*Phil. 3:18   †1 Cor. 10

determine his character, and direct our correspondence with him, but the disposition of his heart, which is often discovered by the general course of a man's behaviour, to be very different from what he would have men to believe it is. A man that rolls in his mind impious thoughts of God, is a wicked man, however good his words may be, and a man that indulges a selfish disposition is unfit to be a companion or a friend, although he invites you to his table, and never ceases, when you are there, to tell you how welcome you are, and how earnestly he wishes you to eat and drink.

You see how vain it is for men, to pretend that kindness which they do not feel. They are discovered more easily than they imagine, and the professions they make are means of rendering their dissimulation more evident ; for true kindness delights not in many words.

Let men then either be what they profess, loving not in word nor in tongue, but in deed and in truth, or else let them lay aside the profession of what they are not, for it is idle to add the guilt and shame of hypocrisy, to that of a sordid and selfish disposition.

But when that which is set on his table is full of fatness, may we not make a very delicious meal, and pay him for it, to his satisfaction, by agreeable conversation ? No.

Ver. 8. *The morsel which thou hast eaten, shalt thou vomit up, and lose thy sweet words.*

Men often think it a noble piece of diversion, to spunge upon a miser, and to take advantage of an invitation extorted from him by shame, to prey upon every thing that is in his house ; but Solomon teaches us that this diversion will end in vexation. Thou mayest eat the morsel with pleasure, but thou shalt repent of eating it, as much as if thou hadst vomited it up. All thy agreeable or useful conversation is lost upon him, and he is so far from thinking it a proper recompense for the expense he has bestowed upon thee, that he will endeavour to extort some thing in return, which it may be very inconvenient to grant, and yet when thou refusest, he will brand thee with the character of the ungrateful guest.

When we are called by God to a feast of fat things, and hear his blessed voice calling us to eat that which is good, and let our souls delight themselves in fatness, we may safely venture, at the gracious invitation, to make use of Christ, and the blessings of his salvation, as our own ; to suspect the sincerity of the gospel call, is to suspect the God who is abundant in goodness and truth of an evil eye.

Ver. 9. *Speak not in the ears of a fool, for he will despise the wisdom of thy words.*

A fool cannot utter wisdom, but there might be good hopes entertained of him, if he could hear it ; but there are many fools, who are equally unfit to speak and to hear. Concerning such, this direction is given, and not concerning fools of every kind, for there are some that want wisdom, and have some conviction of the want of it, and these are on the road that leads to wisdom, the first step of which is to become a fool in one's own eyes.

The fools to whom we are forbidden to speak the words of wisdom, are those that will despise the wisdom of our words, and even these are sometimes to be dealt with by those that have a call, by their office or church connexion, to do so, even after they have refused admonition ; for the souls of men are precious, and if there is some hope, though faint, of doing them good, we must not decline the disagreeable task of reprovers *.

Our Lord orders the gospel to be preached to every

---

*Matt. 18:15-17, Titus 3:10

one that will hear it, not excepting scorners *. But he will not have his gospel forced on those that obstinately reject it †. He himself left the Gadarenes, when they preferred their swine to him, and the Nazarenes, when they wanted to destroy him.

Although the worst of sinners are to be invited to repentance, in the public assembly, yet there are some to whom our Lord tells us, it is needless and unsafe to administer personal reproofs. These are the dogs and swine that would trample our pearls under their feet, and turn again and rend us. How pitiable is the case of such persons, when our Lord himself directs us to give them up to themselves.

Those that are reproved by ministers, and Christian friends, may learn from this verse, that they have no reason to take it amiss, or to think that they are treated with contempt. They are considered as offenders, but at the same time as offending brethren, who are not incurably perverse. They would be treated in a very different way, and might reckon themselves with more justice, to be considered in the light of scorners, and dogs, and swine, if there were no means used to recover them to repentance.

Ver. 10. *Remove not the old land mark, and enter not into the fields of the fatherless.*

May we then remove other people's land marks, and enter into their fields? By no means, but there is less danger of that. Wicked men are afraid to do any injury to those who have it in their power to retaliate, or powerful friends to espouse their quarrel. Pure religion and undefiled before God and the Father, is this, to visit the fatherless, and the widows in their affliction, and to keep himself unspotted from the world. And yet there are none so ready to be trampled upon,

---

*Prov. 1:22   †Matt. 10:14

in this evil world, as the fatherless and widows. But let the poor and fatherless commit themselves to God, and the widows trust in him, and he will make their adversaries to know, that the mightiest on earth are not more dangerous to be meddled with, than themselves.

Ver. 11. *For their Redeemer is mighty, he shall plead their cause with thee.*

He that meddles with the widow and fatherless, needs better armour than he that touches the sons of Belial, who must be fenced with iron and brass. God himself hath undertaken their defence, and dare we provoke the Lord to jealousy, are we stronger than he ? He graciously calls himself their kinsman or Redeemer. They have lost the best of earthly friends. But there is one in heaven who calls them to trust in him, as their husband and father, their Redeemer and advocate. He hath promised to supply their wants, and protect them from every enemy. Their enemies set themselves in opposition to God, and endeavour to make him a liar, by frustrating his promises, but they do it at their peril.

Perhaps those that oppress the widow and fatherless, may allege that God is the Redeemer only of his own people, and that the poor and fatherless, whom they oppress are none of them. To this it may be answered, that God executeth righteousness and judgment for all that are oppressed. He is the great lover of righteousness and mercy, and the avenger of all that are unrighteous and unmerciful. One part of the office of the kinsman redeemer under the law, was to avenge the mischiefs done to his poor friend ; and this part of it God will perform for all that are oppressed, without exception, so that the oppressor will feel the terrors of the threatening contained in this declaration, although the fatherless and the widows through their unbelief, should lose the comforts of that grace, which is

discovered in it. But how do you know, O ye presumptuous opposers of God's mercy to the poor, that
those whom you wrong are not God's people? Can you
know the hearts of men? If you can do this, can you
also look into the heart of God, and into the book of
life, to know who are the objects of his special favour?
How do you know but God may choose those whom
you afflict, in the furnace of affliction. The oppressors
of Judah, said, we offend not, for they have sinned
against the Lord, the habitation of justice, and the
hope of their fathers; yet for their sakes, he sent to Babylon, and brought down the Chaldeans and their nobles, whose cry was in their ships. He thoroughly
pleaded their cause, for he had chosen them in the furnace of affliction. And the vengeance of the Lord, and
of his temple, was upon Babylon and Edom, and Am-
mon, and all that had afflicted them*.

Here the widow and the fatherless, may find comfort under every injury, and instruction how to derive
the greatest advantages out of the greatest wrongs, by
making use of the injustice of the enemy, as a motive to
flee to God as their Redeemer, and a plea in their supplications for help †.

Ver. 12. *Apply thine heart unto instruction, and thine
ears to the words of knowledge.*

This direction is often repeated, but there is need for
it: too often we hear as if we heard not. An hour or
two passes after we have been reading a chapter, or
hearing a discourse on one of the most important subjects, and scarcely a trace of it is left upon our minds.
I have read of a minister, who was preaching a sermon
on the day of judgment, and the awful truths which he
delivered made such an impression on the audience,
that they all appeared to be alarmed, but the preacher

*Isa. 47:4, Jer. 50:33,34   †Ps. 10:14

told them that he had something yet to tell them more awful than any thing he had said, that in two hours they would be as little affected with these things, as if they had not heard them ; which accordingly proved to be the case.

Let us take heed that we be not found among those of whom it is said, that the word preached did not profit them, not being mixed with faith in them that heard it, for the word will not be a means of salvation to us, unless it is received with meekness, and ingrafted into our souls *.

Ver. 13. *Withhold not correction from thy child ; for if thou beatest him with the rod, he shall not die.*

Ver. 14. *Thou shalt beat him with the rod, and shalt deliver his soul from hell.*

Parents are here required, to give due correction to their children, with their own hands, and not to entrust that office entirely to others ; at the same time they are forbidden to withhold it from them, even when they are under the care of others. If teachers are employed to instruct them, they must have the power of correcting likewise, and no offence must be taken at them for using it. Parents would take it amiss, if any thing they thought necessary for their children, was withheld from them by those under whose care they are placed ; and what is more necessary than correction? The world will think that man cruel, who does not give food and raiment to his child, but Solomon looks upon him also to be a cruel man, who does not give needful correction.

But the fond hearts of parents will suggest several objections to this duty. They cannot bear the cries and sobs of their children ; they are afraid they will die under their hands. There is no fear of this, answers

*James 1:22

the wise man, they only wish to frighten you by their complaints. They shall not die but live. Beat them with the rod, for it is one of the means that God has appointed for delivering them from an untimely death in this world, and destruction in the next. What an idea does this give us, of the usefulness of the rod of correction ! What parent that loves his child, and has any sense of the terrors of eternal punishment, will spare his rod, after he has heard this saying of God? Would you not force your children to suffer bleeding by the surgeon, if you saw it necessary for the preservation of their lives, and are their souls less precious than their bodies? You think that gentle means are always the best, but does not God tell you that this does not hold in every case? No doubt Eli and David wished well to their children, and their parental fondness told them that gentle admonitions and time, would correct all the disorders in their families. But they mourned at last over these children, that had been so much hurt by their indulgence. Whether the disorders in David's family, were the occasion of Solomon's making so many proverbs on this subject, I shall not say, but after what he has said, and after what Eli and David suffered, those parents that perform not this duty, are more inexcusable than these good men were *.

Your children may perhaps complain of your severity, when there is no ground for it. But this is easier to be borne, than it would be to hear them curse you, at the last day, for suffering them to take their course in sin.

Ver. 15. *My son, if thine heart be wise, my heart shall rejoice, even mine.*

Ver. 16. *Yea, my reins shall rejoice, when thy lips speak right things.*

Solomon was a wise father, and had the same wishes

---

*Chap. 22:15

for his son as for himself. He did not greatly mind whether he was to be very rich or not, but his main concern was, that he might be wise; for he knew that if he was a fool, the riches he was to leave him would do him no good *.

Parents may form a judgment of their own dispositions, from their wishes about their children. Worldly men make it their great work to provide those things for their children, which they account their own best things. Saints desire above all things, that the hearts of their children may be richly furnished with wisdom, and that their lips may speak right things; for the heart is the throne of wisdom, and by the lips she discovers her possession of that throne. Those that are evil cannot ordinarily speak good things, and the lips will undoubtedly speak good things, when there is a good treasure in the heart.

Language cannot express the cordial joys that a wise parent feels, from the wise and good behaviour of a son; and when parents enjoy this blessing, let them consider, to heighten their joy and thankfulness, the smart that others have felt from the undutifulness and folly of their children. It seems probable that Solomon was taught by painful experience, to speak so feelingly of the joys of happy fathers. Rehoboam was far from being his father's son, yet his father did not give him up as desperate. He was a fool, but who knows, said his father, whether he shall be a wise man or a fool, when I am dead †. Let parents use every means recommended by God, for making their children wise. Then shall their souls be glad, and their reins rejoice, in the happy effect of their endeavours, or at least in the consciousness of having done their duty. It is likely that Rehoboam received at last some benefit from the

*Eccles. 2:18,19   †Eccles. 2:19

instructions of his father, for he behaved so well during a part of his reign, that in Judah things went well.

Ver. 17. *Let not thine heart envy sinners, but be thou in the fear of the Lord all the day long.*

When we see the wicked flourishing in prosperity, and the people of God languishing under oppression, we are sometimes tempted to doubt, whether there is a providence, and whether the promises and threatenings of God be true or not, and to grudge that there is not a present distribution of rewards and punishments, according to the works of men. Unfit as we are for managing our own affairs, we are too much disposed to usurp God's office of governing the world ; and if he does not shower down blessings into the lap of those whom we esteem, and fire and brimstone upon the head of the wicked, then we think that God cannot see things through the dark cloud, or is unfit to manage them. But we are here directed to banish envy from our hearts, and as an antidote to this mischievous passion, to be in the fear of the Lord continually.

Envy at sinners is a great enemy to the fear of the Lord. Asaph's feet had almost stumbled when he looked with a grudging eye at the prosperous circumstances of transgressors ; but by the fear of the Lord, he was preserved from falling, and was recovered from his dangerous situation ; for a deep and heart-affecting impression of the infinite excellencies of the divine nature will silence our murmurings, and subdue the insurrections of our spirits. If we are deeply impressed with a sense of the righteousness and holiness of God, and of his wisdom and goodness, we will believe that his ways are all judgment, and that there can be no unrighteousness in his administration, even when we cannot discern the reasons of it. " Clouds and darkness are round about him, but righteousness and judgment are still the habitation of his throne *."

*Ps. 97:2

We are required to live in the fear of the Lord all the day long. Whether we are in prosperous or in adverse circumstances, and whether the wicked around us rise into affluence and power, or sink into insignificance and misery, an impression of God's perfection, and of the happiness that attends religion, and the misery that follows sin, must dwell upon our hearts, and govern our conduct. This fear of God will banish from our minds impious reflections upon God, and dispose us to keep his way, even when wicked men are in power, and threaten to banish all religion out of the world ; for still we shall believe that it will be well with the righteous and ill with the wicked, perhaps in this world, but most certainly in the next *.

Ver. 18. *For surely there is an end, and thine expectation shall not be cut off.*

If things were to continue in their present state through eternity, or if there were no eternity before us, much might be said for the wisdom of impiety, and the folly of religion ; but reason and tradition give us probable arguments for a future state, and the Bible assures us of it. Job saw the prosperity of the wicked with astonishment, but the counsel of the wicked was far from him, for he knew that their day was coming ; and when he saw that some of them died amidst friends and prosperity, and were honourably buried, he inferred that there was a day of wrath to which they were reserved †. He was in like manner fully persuaded, that his living Redeemer would raise his own dust at the last day, and wipe off all his reproach, and give him the transporting sight of the divine glory, to his eternal happiness. His hope of this blessedness was so lively, even when there was no Scripture, that he expresses an ardent wish that his profession of hope might be in-

---

*Ps. 59:9   †Job 21:15,30

scribed for ever on the rock, with a pen of iron and lead. And it was written, not on a rock, to be read by the dwellers in the land of Uz, but in the book of God, to be seen and read of all men.

Did Job triumph in this blessed hope amidst afflictions that would have swallowed up all the courage of a philosopher and hero? Shall we faint, who are instructed by Moses and the prophets, by the Apostles, and the Lord himself, concerning the unspeakable felicities of a future state, and the right we have to look for the mercy of our Lord Jesus Christ unto eternal life? Besides, we have a great cloud of witnesses to assure us that it is not a vain thing to wait for the salvation of the Lord, and that the expectation of the poor, although it may seem to be cut off, shall not perish for ever? Abraham had a promise of a son, by whom his seed were to be like the stars for multitude, and yet he waited till Sarah's womb, which was formerly barren, was now dead, before he had the promised son. He waited sixty years longer, before he saw any children by Isaac, but still he was persuaded that the word of God was true, and that his promise was the same thing as performance. He had the promise of Canaan, and yet he travelled through it as a stranger and pilgrim, but he trusted God, and what he had promised, he performed, long after Abraham went to sleep with his fathers. And those that give credit to the testimony of God, and wait with patience in the hope of the promise, are blessed with faithful Abraham.

Soldiers, in the uncertain hope of spoil, endure all the severities of the campaign, and encounter all the dangers of the battle; and shall not the professed soldiers of the Redeemer meet every discouraging providence without terror and complaint, when the God of truth says their expectation shall not be cut off *?

---

*James 1:12, 2 Thess. 1:6,7

Ver. 19. *Hear, thou my son, and be wise, and guide thine heart in the way.*

It is not sufficient, although it be necessary, for us to hear the instructions of the inspired moralist. We are called to learn wisdom, which is to be acquired by hearing under the influence of that blessed Spirit by whom these truths were dictated. Hearing without being made wise, will aggravate our guilt, and make our condemnation more dreadful. But to expect wisdom without hearing, is to expect nourishment by miracle without food. Let us hear then, with all that meekness and affection which is due to a kind father instructing his beloved children ; and with hearing let us join prayer to that God, by whose direction and in whose name Solomon speaks to us as children ; for our heavenly father will give the Spirit of wisdom and revelation to them that ask him.

What is that wisdom that we are called to seek after? Wisdom to guide our heart in the way, for Zion's travellers must have the way that conducts to blessedness in their hearts. Our feet and our hearts must be in the same good paths, for no man is truly religious, whatever his outward conversation is, unless his heart be right with God. The word of God is then truly useful to us, when we rejoice in the way of God's testimonies more than in all riches.

If we would have our hearts guided in the way, then we must hear what the wise man is going to say to us against intemperance in eating and drinking ; for as those that run in the Grecian races, and strove for masteries in their games, were obliged to be temperate in all things, in the view of a corruptible crown ; so those that have the eternal crown in their eye, must exercise a proper care over themselves, that they may not be overcharged, or pressed down with the immoderate use of meat and drink, and thereby rendered unfit for the Christian course.

Ver. 20. *Be not amongst wine-bibbers, amongst riotous eaters of flesh.*

Although we do not dethrone reason by drinking, yet if we impair the vigour of it, and render ourselves less fit for the business of life, and the service of God, than we are at other times, by the free use of the bottle, we are wine-bibbers.

Flesh is fit provision for our bodies, and it is freely allowed us by God, who has enlarged our charter for bodily provision, under the new testament dispensation, but it is great ingratitude to God to abuse his goodness in order to serve the lusts of the flesh. The body ought to be the servant of the soul, and ever ready to execute its commands; but when, by the riotous eating of flesh, or any thing else, our bodies are disabled from doing their duty, or have their vigour impaired, and the seeds of weakness, and drowsiness, and disease, sown in them, we sin against our own souls and bodies.

We are forbidden, not only to be drunkards or gluttons, but to be found in the company of such persons; for bad company is the common temptation which the devil uses to draw men to these sins. By giving them our company, we are exposed to their solicitations, and many that were once sober, have been enticed by them to go to excess at a time, and, by a repetition of the same rash conduct have been led on, step by step, to the greatest excesses, and the most confirmed habits of intemperance, till they became senseless brutes, a burden to their friends, and fit only for being laid in the grave, and consigned to those regions which shall be the everlasting habitation of those who make their belly their god.

Those who have been long inured to a temperate

course of life, must not think that they are at liberty to infringe this precept, and to mingle themselves with the sons of riot, because they are strong enough in their own eye to overcome all the temptations of sensuality. Christ charges his own disciples, who had been practised in every virtue under his own eye, and who had less temptations to this vice than any other men, to take heed to themselves that their hearts might not be overcharged with surfeiting and drunkenness ; and we find the apostle Paul, who was so often in want, very anxious that he might not transgress this precept *.

But what harm is there in learning the ways of the drunkard and glutton ? Much harm even in this world, as any man may see, that will but open his eyes ;

Ver. 21. *For the drunkard and the glutton shall come to poverty, and drowsiness shall clothe a man with rags.*

Poverty may be born with patience and cheerfulness, when it is merely a misfortune ; but that poverty fills the mind with remorse and vexation, which is the fruit of a man's own bad conduct. And no self-contracted poverty is so disagreeable as that which a man brings upon himself by gluttony and drunkenness, which at the same time that they deprive a man of the necessaries of life, create in him a craving appetite after superfluities and luxuries.

Miserable as men must be, by being reduced to such unhappy circumstances, they are almost unpitied when they fall into them ; for who will pity one for misfortunes into which he rushes with his eyes open ? If a man will not pity himself, it is vain for him to expect pity from his neighbours.

The drunkard or glutton may flatter himself with vain hopes that he shall escape poverty, and that to

---

*1 Cor. 9:27

morrow shall be as this day, and much more abundant; but reason and experience, as well as Scripture, confirm the truth in our text: for if the slothful man bring himself to want, the waster must do it much sooner, especially as luxury and revelling bring drowsiness and sloth in their train: for by a course of sensual indulgence, a man is indisposed to labour and prudent care; so that, whilst he throws away with one hand, he gathers nothing with the other to supply his numerous wants. The slothful man is brother to him that is a great waster, but when the great waster is likewise a slothful man, as is generally the case, poverty is coming to him with hasty steps, and with resistless force.

Hell is at a great distance, the sensualist thinks, and lies quite out of the view of mortals, and wine has so besotted him, that he cannot think seriously about it; but here he is told of one part of his punishment, which he cannot put off to a distant day, and must feel, unless he is stupified to an extraordinary degree; for his vitious relishes might themselves excite a proper sense of the mischief of poverty; and how hardened must they be in sin who cannot be driven from it, either by the terrors of the world to come, or the miseries of this?

Christians have nobler motives to keep them on their guard against intemperance; for the grace of God teaches them to live soberly, and their character as children of the light is inconsistent with drunkenness and revelling, which are works of darkness and of the flesh *.

Ver. 22. *Hearken unto thy father that begat thee, and despise not thy mother when she is old.*

Solomon takes it for granted that our fathers and mothers will give us good counsel and instruction; for

*1 Thess. 5:5-8, Gal. 5, Rom. 13:13,14, 1 Peter 4:3

they are monsters, and not parents, that are unconcerned about the present and eternal welfare of their children, and quite negligent of those means that may contribute to such valuable ends.

Children should consider what they owe to their parents, and what affection they discover in their good counsels and instructions, and what monsters of ingratitude they are, if they do not shew respect to those who have conferred obligations upon them, for which they can never make a sufficient recompense, and to those instructions which can have no object but their own benefit.

Mothers are to be honoured as well as fathers; nor must we despise them, but reverence their good advices, and kindly sympathize with their infirmities when they are old. They may then prove peevish and fretful, and lose much of their understanding, and become children a second time. But they took care of us when we were helpless children, and our froward passions did not then provoke them to cast us away, but engaged their pity and help *.

It is only when the instructions of parents are good and sound, that we must receive and comply with them, for we are bound to cleave to the truth at all risks.

Ver. 23. *Buy the truth, and sell it not ; also wisdom, and instruction, and understanding.*

The truth revealed in the word of God is infinitely valuable and interesting, and therefore we are commanded to buy, and not to sell it. Men are enriched by buying and selling other commodities, but in our dealings about truth we are enriched by buying alone, whatever be the price, and impoverished by selling, whatever price we might receive.

---

*Chap. 1:8

But why are we commanded to buy? Does God receive a price from us for his truths? By no means. But we are commanded to buy, because we must grudge no expence or toil in seeking the truth. The wise merchant is he that is so impressed with its value that he is willing to go and sell all he hath, that he may obtain possession of this precious treasure. Merchants will venture their money and their lives for those commodities by which they expect to make profit, although they often meet with disappointments and losses. Why then should those who profess to value the truth above every thing, be so careless about obtaining the knowledge and experience of it, when the value of it will abundantly recompense all our pains and losses in the search of it, although we should lose our life on its account?

On no account must we sell the truth. Had Paul been offered all the kingdoms of the world, and all the glories of them, for one article of truth, he would have answered, "I have suffered the loss of all things already for Christ, yea, doubtless, I count all things but loss and dung for the excellency of the knowledge of Christ Jesus, my Lord." We must rather part with our lives than with the truth, and here we have the example of the noble army of martyrs who loved not their lives unto the death for its sake. He that loses his life for the sake of truth, and a good conscience, is a great gainer *.

If it is a great sin to sell the truth, even when our life is offered for it, what shall we say of those who part with it in profession or practice, without receiving any price at all for it? Surely they have a small regard for the truth, or for the great Author of it, who

---

*Matt. 10:39

wantonly cast away this precious pearl, and take a pebble in its room.

We must shew the same sacred regard to wisdom, and instruction, and understanding, which are inseparably connected with the truth. For we have no true hold of the truth, however clear our apprehensions of it are, or however zealously we profess it, if we are not made wise, and led in the way of duty by its influence. That wisdom and understanding which is not grounded in truth, is but cunning craftiness and splendid ignorance, and that instruction which is not according to truth, is poison to the soul *.

Truth is to be received into the mind and heart, and rule our conversation. Those only are wise unto salvation who receive the truth in the love of it, and hold it forth in their profession, and walk in it till they reach the end of their course †.

Ver. 24. *The father of the righteous shall greatly rejoice, and he that begetteth a wise child shall have joy of him.*

Ver. 25. *Thy father and thy mother shall be glad, and she that bare thee shall rejoice.*

And what son is there so unnatural as not to wish for the happiness of his father and his mother? Your father has spent many anxious thoughts, and endured many toils on your account. Your mother has born you with sorrow and danger, and reared you up with tender anxiety, and what requital do they ask or expect from you? They love you with a disinterested affection; they earnestly desire you to pursue those courses which will make you happy; and they will be satisfied, and glad, and bless God on your account, when you walk in the ways of wisdom, because all their

---

*Job 21:34, 2 John 9   †2 Thess. 2:10, Phil. 2:6, 2 John 8

labours and toils are richly recompensed. Can you resist the wishes of your parents, and blast their hopes of gladness, when the joy they expect from you is no selfish pleasure, but that pure and disinterested joy which arises from your own happiness? Can you bear the thoughts of embitterng their old age, when it is attended with so many unavoidable pains and griefs, which will be sweetened by your good behaviour? Will you be the wretched instruments of bringing down the grey hairs of your parents with sorrow to the grave?

What a blessed thing is righteousness! It gives great pleasure to him that practises it. It diffuses joy all around. Your parents and friends, and all that fear God, will be glad to see you walking in God's truth. Our Father who is in heaven takes pleasure in it, and all the angels of God are glad to see righteousness and wisdom among the sons of men.

Ver. 26. *My son, give me thine heart, and let thine eyes observe my ways.*

This divine teacher, in the name of God, requires our hearts to be applied to the word of exhortation. " Set your hearts to all the words which I testify among you this day," said the Jewish lawgiver, " which ye shall observe, to do all the words of this law." The same demand is made on us in this and in several other passages of this book. And the demand would not be so frequently made, if it were not necessary. We are naturally indisposed to give a due attention to the word of God, for our hearts are vain, and earthly, and carnal ; and yet, unless we give our hearts to God and to his truths, we can receive no benefit by them. Paul gives thanks to God for the saints at Rome, because, from the heart, they had obeyed that form of doctrine which was delivered unto them, or rather, into which they were delivered, as into a mould, that their whole temper and life might be formed into a correspondence with it. Our Lord, in his parable of the sower, speaks of four different sorts of hearers of the word, and there was only one sort that received real benefit from it, and that was the set of hearers who understood it, and received it into an honest and good heart.

Our hearts are naturally intractable and perverse, and we cannot work them into a proper disposition for receiving his truths, but we must give them up to him that fashions the hearts of men at his pleasure. Our hearts, vile and worthless as they are, are claimed by him. He is our former and Redeemer, and he calls us to give up our souls and bodies unto him *. He will form them anew, and take away the stony heart out of our flesh, and give us hearts of flesh, and put his Spirit within us, and cause us to walk in his statutes.

Our eyes must be fixed upon the ways in which God directs us by his inspired penmen. Thus David regulated his life; he laid the judgments of God before him, and kept his mind fixed upon the directions of God in his word, and his feet were kept from stumbling and falling. The ways in which Solomon walked during a part of his life, are a warning to us that we may not involve ourselves in those snares that brought him into so much danger and distress; but the ways that he instructs us to walk in are those good paths wherein rest is to be found. He smarted greatly with the wounds made in his conscience by his correspondence with worthless women, and none of the Old Testament writers sound so loud alarms of the danger that we are in from the arts of such seducers.

He fell into the deep and narrow ditch, but by the grace of God he escaped with life, and warns us all not to risk our souls in the manner he had done.

---

*2 Chron. 30:8

Ver. 27. *For an whore is a deep ditch, and a strange woman is a deep pit.*

And when it is both deep and narrow, the danger is extreme. Who would choose to be in the situation of Jeremiah when he was cast into the dungeon, out of which Ebedmelech and his companions, delivered him with so much difficulty? but it is far more dangerous to fall into that narrow pit of which the wise man is now speaking, for none that go unto her return again, neither take they hold of the paths of life. Righteous men, such as Sampson and Solomon, were scarcely saved when they fell into this ditch? and where shall the abhorred children of the devil appear *?

Ver. 28. *She also lieth in wait as for a prey, and increaseth the transgressors among men.*

The profligate woman is not only a deep pit, but a robber; for a single comparison is insufficient to show the numberless mischiefs occasioned by her seductions. She lies in wait, not to rob men of a few pounds, but to rob them of all their substance and credit, of their health and comfort, of their bodies and souls. And those who voluntarily comply with her alluring insinuations, are confederates with her and the devil, against God and themselves. She increaseth the transgressors among men; for she spreads her nets and entangles those unwary men, of whom better things might have been reasonably expected, if they had escaped her, and when she has them fast, she blindfolds them, and leads them on through the ways of sin and folly, till she plunge them into the gulph of perdition. She is not only a servant but a factor of the wicked one, drawing as many as she can into his snares, and therefore if we love our own souls, we must avoid the doors of her house.

Would we be preserved from this mischievous enchan-

*Chap. 22:14

tress, who has been the instrument of drowning such multitudes in destruction and perdition, let us turn our hearts to the divine instructions of this book, and call wisdom our sister, and understanding our kinswoman. Let us put on the Lord Jesus Christ, and make no provision for the flesh, to fulfil the lusts thereof.

Ver. 29. *Who hath woe? who hath sorrow? who hath contentions? who hath babblings? who hath wounds without cause? who hath redness of eyes?*

He is no doubt a miserable man on whom all these misfortunes meet at once, and yet he scarcely deserves pity, for he brings them upon himself. If any man were attacked with a disease that had so many dismal symptoms, he would certainly draw pity from every beholder; but those of whom Solomon speaks, are persons that chuse both sin and misery at once.

Ver. 30. *They that tarry long at the wine, they that go to seek much wine.*

Wine is very useful to men when used to serve them, but when it is suffered to become their master, it is a raging tyrant, like fire or water, when they are not kept in their proper bounds. But who are they that suffer wine to rule over them? Those who are so fond of it, that they cannot rise when they have sat down to the bottle, but continue from noon-day till evening, till wine inflame them; and those who cannot want it, but go in search of it, feeling themselves quite unhappy when they are not pouring it down their throats, and who are such sensualists that they cannot be satisfied, unless a variety of ingredients are mingled with it, to make it higher flavoured, and more grateful to their nice palates. These are not the only persons that sin by abusing this good creature of God; for when men render themselves heavy, and languid, and unfit to think and act with composure, or to draw near to God in spiritual exercises, they are guilty of excess, although they

do not make themselves brutes, and bring upon themselves all the present mischiefs that are here mentioned.
But those who give themselves up to sensuality, to such
a degree as to tarry long at the wine, and go to seek
mixt wine, bring upon themselves, in part, the present
recompence of their error, for they do not only render
themselves obnoxious to an everlasting hell, but they
pull down sorrows upon themselves with their own
hands. They have some present pleasure to suit their
vitiated taste, but woe to that pleasure that brings so
much pain and vexation along with it. Wine is raging,
and pushes on the persons that swill it down, like madmen, to debates and contention. It takes from them, in a
great measure, the use of their tongues, and makes them
to stammer, and yet it fills their minds with so much
vanity and wickedness that they must speak, and pour
forth floods of profaneness and ribaldry, of nonsense
and ill nature. By this means drunkenness stirs up
squabbles and fightings, which end in wounds without
cause; for the drunkards themselves, when they are sober, confess that their quarrels had no object earthly, but
were produced by their own self-contracted madness.
Redness of eyes is another effect of immoderate drinking,
which ends in a weakness of the sight, in violent pain,
and sometimes in total blindness. If drunkenness is attended with so wretched consequences,

Ver. 31. *Look not thou upon the wine when it is red,
when it giveth his colour in the cup, when it moveth itself
aright.*

And what harm is there in looking upon the pleasant
liquor sparkling and mantling in the cup? What harm,
you may as well ask, was there in Eve's looking at the
fruit of the forbidden tree, or in Achan's looking at the
golden wedge, or Babylonian garment? Or what harm
is there in looking at a beauteous face, till lust is excited in the heart? To look with pleasure at a tempting

object, is very unsafe, for the imagination catches fire, and the passions are inflamed, and reason is gradually deposed from its throne. Such are the natural consequences of looking at the delicious liquor. Cæsar came, and saw, and conquered ; but the drunkard comes to the tavern, he sees the flowing blood of the grape, and is conquered. He drinks and tastes a little pleasure, whilst the liquor is passing down his throat, but,

Ver. 32. *At the last it biteth like a serpent, and stingeth like an adder.*

If drunkards saw an adder at the bottom of the glass, although it were dead, they would rather pour all the liquor into the street than drink it. But the wine itself is worse than any serpent. It infuses a deadly though slow poison into the drunkard, and his body becomes the seat of disease ; nor are the miserable effects of it confined to himself, but they are frequently entailed upon his posterity, who suffer by their father's fault, and are often obliged to drag out a wretched life in weakness and disease, and pills and potions.

But it stings the soul worst of all, for it breeds that worm of conscience in comparison of which the bite of an adder (or rather cockatrice,) is pleasure and health. It exposes the drunkard to the lake of fire and brimstone, which is the second death, where the wine of the fierceness of the wrath of Almighty God must be drunk, without intermission or end, and where the drunkard shall be punished, not only for drunkenness, but for a countless multitude of sins, to which this vice led the way. Other vices work their own way into the soul, but this mischievous vice makes way for every other vice, and especially for the damnable sin of uncleanness and filthy communication.

Ver. 33. *Thine eyes shall behold strange women, and thine heart shall utter perverse things.*

Drunkenness produces new vices, and discloses the old.

It removes every fence of reason and religion, and makes the person overpowered by it to resemble a city without walls, into which the besiegers find an open passage that they may enter, and commit what ravages they please. Lot kept himself pure in Sodom, and yet his daughters, by making him drunk, knew that they could easily draw him to incest, for they had seen the men of Sodom tempted, by their fulness of bread and intemperate drinking, to every excess of wickedness. A Roman author tells us, that, in the good days of Rome, drinking of wine was absolutely prohibited to women, lest drinking should tempt them to unchastity; for, as the same author observes, it shuts the door against every virtue, and opens it to every vice.

Drunkenness besots the heart, and makes it to utter perverse and abominable things by the tongue; unless that instrument of the soul is made quite dumb by the power of the liquor; for blasphemy is wit, and ribaldry is eloquence to a man that is turned into a brute. How loathsome would the heart of a wicked man be, were it laid bare to the world; but drink lays it bare as far as the powers of language can go.

Ver. 34. *Yea, thou shalt be as he that lieth down in the midst of the sea, or as he that lieth upon the top of a mast.*

Thy brain shall be giddy, thy reason disordered, thy mind altogether unhinged, and thy danger shall be extreme, like his who lies down in the heart of the sea, or on the top of a mast, the most dangerous of situations imaginable.

Can a man that is a slave to strong drink find no possible mean of escape from his bondage? He will not make his escape, for his heart is infatuated *, and he cannot prevail upon himself to forego a momentary in-

---

*Hos. 4:11

dulgence, although it should cost him the torments of a whole life, and of an awful eternity. He feels the inconveniences that result from his indulgence to his appetite. But his appetite has a sovereign dominion over his reason, and forces it to find out some pitiful shifts and pretences to excuse his continuance in his abominable habits.

Ver. 35. *They have stricken me, shalt thou say, and I was not sick; they have beaten me, and I felt it not: when shall I awake? I will seek it yet again.*

"Drink," says one, "steals away a man from himself, and leaves a brute in his stead." This is saying much, but not all. A drunkard is a self-made brute, and is far more senseless than a natural brute beast. It has been found upon trial, that a brute, after being once deceived by wine, would not venture upon it a second time; but the self-made brute, after he has felt an hundred times the mischiefs of drinking, becomes still fonder of his misery, and makes his understanding to serve only for palliating his folly. It is true, he says, I have felt some trifling disadvantages from the free use of the creature. My companions abused and insulted me, but what of that? Shall I deny myself the chief pleasure of life, because they struck me, and beat me? I was nothing the worse of it. I wish I could get free of that drink which now clogs my senses, and inclines me to sleep. I will return to the tavern after all that is come and gone. Why did not nature manage things so that a man might be always drinking? Life is not life in the intervals of it.

If wicked men can patiently bear such mischiefs for the sake of a beloved lust, which will at length bite like a serpent, and sting like an adder, why should we grudge at the little hardships that we sometimes undergo for the sake of religion, which will be so richly recompensed? If the servants of Satan are willing to bear innumerable crosses and curses for the love they have to his service, why should we bear with reluctance, in the service of God, those crosses which are blessings in disguise ?

Let those drunkards, that have any remainders of understanding, compare the inconveniencies that might attend the mortification of their appetite with the miseries that God hath inseparably joined to a continuance in their criminal indulgences. And if they can say that it is not a thousand times better to put a knife to their throat, than to be tyrannized over by such a pernicious lust, let them swallow down gallons every day of their life.

The Lacedemonians used to make their slaves drunk in the presence of their children, that when they saw what monsters men were turned into by sensuality, they might contract an irreconcileable aversion to this vice. Solomon gives us such a lively picture of this vice in the paragraph before our eyes, that we need not the sight of a drunken man to excite our detestation of drunkenness. Isaiah gives us a description of it equally shocking *. What excuse is left for a drunkard that has ever read the Bible ? How will his mouth be stopped at the last day ! How will he curse himself through eternity, for making himself first a beast, and then a devil !

An inferior master in the art of moral painting, gives us a just picture of drunkenness in these words, " Drunkenness is a distemper of the head, a subversion of the senses, a tempest of the tongue, a storm in the body—the shipwreck of virtue, the loss of time, a wilful madness, a pleasant devil, a sugared poison, a sweet sin, which he that has, has not himself, and he that com-

---

*Isa. 28:7,8

mits it, doth not only commit sin, but is himself altogether sin."

Let us therefore follow the counsel of the wise man. Be not amongst wine-bibbers; for he that goes to the tavern for the love of company, will soon go thither for the love of drink. Let us follow the like counsel of another inspired writer, "Be not filled with wine wherein is excess, but be ye filled with the Spirit. Let us walk in the spirit, and we shall not fulfil the lusts of the flesh." If, after all, we rather choose to follow the council of the wicked one, there is no help for it; but those that walk according to the prince of the power of the air, and fulfil the lusts of the flesh, must have their portion and dwelling with him whose galling yoke and crushing burden they prefer to the sweet yoke and light burden of the Redeemer.

Christ would heal you, but if ye will not be healed, howl, O ye drinkers of wine, for the fruit of the vine shall be cut off from your mouths. Joy shall wither away from your eyes, and a cup must be put into your hands, of which the wine is red. It is poured out full of mixture, and the dregs thereof you must wring out, and drink.

Proverbs 24

Verse 1. *Be not thou envious against evil men, neither desire to be with them.*

WE must be careful of our hearts as well as our lives, for out of the heart are the issues of life. Our hearts are well known to God, and he warns us, in the precepts of his word, against indulging an evil disposition, or corrupt passion, which might pollute our souls and conversation. He warns us particularly in this passage, against all envious thoughts at the sight of wicked men's prosperity, which are so natural to us, that the best saints have not been altogether free of this root of bitterness *. When we see waters of a full cup poured out to the wicked, and behold these gains and pleasures which are the present fruits of sin, we are too ready to say in our hearts, " O that God would relax in some degree his laws, that we might without incurring his displeasure, revel in those pleasures which the sons of Belial enjoy. Those men have a happier life at least than we have, whose consciences will not suffer us to imitate their lawless conduct." Such wicked imaginations are strictly prohibited in this place of Scripture. We must not account the proud happy, although they triumph over every enemy, and enjoy the world at their will. We must not entertain a thought of imitating their cursed manners: Why? Their hearts and their lips are black as hell ;

Ver. 2. *For their heart studieth destruction, and their lips talk of mischief.*

And which of the two is best for us, to have our hearts beautified with the lustre of holiness, and purified into unfeigned love of our brethren, or turned into a den of every malicious fiend: to have our tongues sweetened with honey and milk, or set on fire of hell ? The punishments of sin are very dreadful ; but sin itself is such a deformed ugly monster, that we are lost to understanding if we do not abhor it for its own sake.

But you will say, that sinners enjoy great advantage from their way of life. They acquire fine houses and elegant furniture, and every thing delightful in the service of sin. Is sin then attended with better fruits

---

*Ps. 73, Jer. 12

650 / *Exposition of Proverbs*

even in this world, than wisdom and holiness? By no means.

Ver. 3. *Through wisdom is an house builded, and by understanding it is established.*

Houses have been sometimes built through wickedness, but never established. By wisdom and knowledge they are built as it were on a rock, to stand firm against every blast *.

Convenient furniture is desirable, as well as a sure house; and this also is a fruit of that wisdom and industry which belongs to religion.

Ver. 4. *And by knowledge shall the chambers be filled with all precious and pleasant riches.*

Wicked men are represented by Solomon †, entertaining their fancies with high expectations of the precious substance, with which robbery and fraud will fill their houses, but what wicked men vainly expect, good men find, if God sees it to be good for them. Should the wicked prosper in their pursuits, their joy is mingled with the racks of a tormenting consciousness of guilt, and the apprehensions of a speedy period to the pleasures of sin. If good men are disappointed in their expectations and wishes as to this world, they have the consolation of knowing that they have mansions of blessedness prepared for them in Christ's father's house, and that their substance is the better and enduring substance, laid up for them in heaven. Although the Old Testament dispensation of grace abounded in promises of earthly blessings, yet many of the ancient saints met with innumerable crosses and afflictions. They were obliged to dwell in dens and caves of the earth; they were destitute, afflicted, tormented, and still they believed that God was faithful to his word, although outward events contradicted it; or if at any

---

*Job 20:19,20, Jer. 22:13,14, Job 5:24   †Chap. 1

time, doubts of God's faithfulness and goodness arose in their minds, they resisted the abominable thoughts so derogatory to the Most High, and called themselves brutes and idiots before God *. How inexcusable then must it be for us, who live in the sunshine of the Gospel, to give place to blasphemous doubts of the providence of God, and the truth of his word, when God does not think fit to give splendid palaces and fine furniture to his people? The promises respecting this life, belong to godliness under the new testament as well as the old; but they are to be understood in a consistency with the nobler promises that respect spiritual blessings, and the happy influence which crosses of different kinds have in the accomplishment of these promises. When God appoints poverty and losses to the wise, and bereaves them of the native fruits of their honest labours and temperate course of life, he is not breaking but fulfilling his word. And the most afflicted saints will find reason to say in the end of their course, " we know that all thy judgments are righteous, and that thou in faithfulness hast afflicted us."

Strength is reckoned an useful and necessary quality, for acquiring or maintaining any valuable property. Now,

Ver. 5. *A wise man is strong, yea, a man of knowledge increaseth strength.*

Health and vigour of body are not inseparable from that temperance and labour which religion requires; but they ordinarily accompany these virtues †. Religion is at any rate fitted to give us strength, and animate us with courage, because it directs us to depend on the arm of the Almighty, and to be strong in the Lord, and in the power of his might. If political and military wisdom supply the place of strength, the wis-

---

*Ps. 73   †Chap. 3

dom which is from above, has incomparably greater
efficacy. Many have been animated and emboldened
by it, to encounter giants, and mighty armies, and have
turned to flight, and utterly destroyed the most dreadful adversaries, combined in countless multitudes against
them *.

Wisdom teaches us not only to trust in God, but to
take advantage of that wisdom which God has granted
to other men, not merely for their own benefit, but to
render them useful to others who have the meekness
and humility of wisdom to consult with them.

Ver. 6. *For by wise counsel thou shalt make thy war,
and in multitude of counsellors there is safety.*

Wars are too often necessary by the covetousness
and ambition of men ; and those that have most of the
meekness of wisdom, are sometimes dragged into them,
and then wisdom is found to be of far greater value
than strength, or weapons of war. A multitude of wise
counsellors are far more useful to a nation engaged in
it, than a great number of valiant soldiers.

The wisdom of statesmen and generals is of great use
in its proper sphere, but the wisdom of saints is of incomparably greater use in fighting for the cause of liberty
and religion. In the wars of Israel, piety was commonly
attended with success, for those that knew their God
were strong and did exploits ; and if the wisdom of one
poor man could deliver a city besieged by a powerful
king, what may not be expected from the combined
wisdom of many ? But useful as wisdom is, there are
some men so egregiously foolish that they cannot attain this quality.

Ver. 7. *Wisdom is too high for a fool, he openeth not
his mouth in the gate.*

---

*Ps. 118, Josh. 1

A fool sees not the excellency of wisdom. Although
he may value the reputation of it, yet he wants eyes
to behold the real glory of wisdom ; or if he has any
sense of its value, yet he cannot bring his mind to that
degree of care, and diligence, and self-denial, which is
necessary to obtain the knowledge of it, far less can he
resist the imperious tyranny of his passions, to put his
soul under the government of wisdom ; and therefore
he continues a fool under all the means of wisdom that
are used with him. A price to get wisdom is of no use
but to render his folly more inexcusable ; for he has no
heart to it, but is deeply in love with his folly, and
must bear the shame and misery to which it exposes
him.

But if wisdom be too high for a fool, how can he be
blamed for not getting wisdom ? Because the fault is
not in wisdom, nor in the means of it, which God has
given us, but in the fool himself. Wisdom speaks to
men in plain language ; and we have no occasion to say,
" who shall ascend into heaven to bring her down from
above ?" But fools have corrupt minds, and perverse
hearts, and refuse to hear the voice of wisdom, or to receive the instructions of wisdom into their hearts,

A fool, through his incapacity of getting wisdom, is
unfit for speaking in the gate, the place of concourse
and of judgment. He is either made dumb by his consciousness of having nothing to say that deserves to be
heard, or if his self conceit open his lips, he betrays his
folly by speaking more effectually than others do by
their silence.

That the wisdom which is the gift of nature and
learning is necessary to qualify men for public offices
is universally allowed ; and that wisdom which is the
gift of the Spirit, is likewise highly requisite, if not
absolutely necessary. Jethro would have none to be

rulers in Israel that did not fear God and hate covetousness; for the fear of God is the most effectual preservative against all those temptations that attend power and high offices.

Ver. 8. *He that deviseth to do evil, shall be called a mischievous person.*

That tree is rotten which is broken by a gentle gale of wind, and the man has a rotten heart, who sins upon a slight temptation; but words are insufficient to express the malignity of that man's heart, who needs no temptation from the devil at all, but contrives and plots sin in his own mind, spending his thoughts about iniquity when he is lying on his bed, or sitting in his house, and searching out the most dextrous and effectual methods of gratifying his own depraved mind, and doing mischief to others. To be driven or drawn to sin is a bad thing, but to draw iniquity with cords of vanity, and to sin, as it were, with a cart rope, is hellish.

The person who does so shall be loaded with infamy. He may think himself a man of genius and wisdom. He may acquire to himself an honourable name among fools; but the God from whose sentence, promotion or infamy comes, calls him a master of mischief, and by this vile title he shall be known amongst all that are wise. He may be really a man of genius and learning, but all his talents, natural and acquired, concur to sink him so much the deeper in the gulph of disgrace. All his honour shall consist in his being not a private soldier, but a leader in the bands of hell. And in this dignity he shall share with Balaam, the son of Beor, who taught Balak to seduce the Israelites; with Jeroboam the son of Nebat, who made Israel to sin; with Jezebel, the wife and tutor of the most infamous of the kings of Israel; and with Beelzebub, the prince of devils.

Ver. 9. *The thought of foolishness is sin, and the scorner is an abomination to men.*

It is too general a notion that thoughts are of little consequence, and that words and actions only expose men to danger of punishment from God; but we are to remember, that there is an infinite distance between the judges of this world and the Judge of all. Earthly judges cannot penetrate into the hearts of men, and have no business with their secret thoughts; but it is the glory of the universal Judge, that He is the sovereign and searcher of spirits. He requires from us truth in our inward parts'; and when he comes to judge the world, all the churches shall know that he searches the hearts, and tries the reins of the children of men. If we study to shew ourselves approved unto him, we must not only cleanse our hands, but likewise purify our hearts; for foolish and sinful thoughts are contrary to his law, and abominable in his sight. He beholds with detestation all the impure workings of the mind, in wicked contrivances, in impious reasonings, in vain and foolish musings; and when he bestows the grace of his Spirit upon any man, he makes him to hate vain thoughts, as well as wicked actions *.

If the thoughts of foolishness are sinful, how sinful are scornful words. There is much more sin in the thoughts of bad men, than in their lips or lives, but when the lips are employed to express a sovereign contempt of all good admonitions, it is an evidence that the heart is desperately corrupt, and that thoughts of foolishness abound and overflow. The thoughts of foolishness are abominable only to Him that sees the heart, but the scorner is an abomination to men also. And if he is abominable even to those that have so much impurity of their own, how detestable must he

---

*Ps. 119:113, Gen. 6:5, Eccles. 12:14

be to Him that sees more evil in the least sin than we can discern in the greatest?

How long, ye scorners, will ye delight in your scorning? You are so miserably polluted with the defilements of sin, that your fellow sinners cannot bear with you; and how then will the Most Holy God suffer you to escape unpunished? Sit no longer in the seat of the scorner, but humble yourselves in the sight of the Lord, lest your bands be made strong.

Ver. 10. *If thou faint in the day of adversity, thy strength is small.*

If we sink into despondency, and think that our happiness is for ever lost, because God has been pleased to afflict us with some grievous calamity, it is plain that our strength and courage is but small. Where is the vigour of our faith, if we cannot believe that there is help for us in God? A lively faith in the God of Jacob as our refuge and our strength, would make us to stand firm and unshaken, although the mountains were removed, and the earth shaken, and overwhelmed by the swelling waves of the sea. It would make us to rejoice in the Lord, when every thing looks dreary around us *.

If we faint in our Christian course, and use unlawful means of escape when dangers surround us, it is a sign that our strength is almost nothing. The church of Philadelphia had a little strength, and she held fast the name of Christ, and did not deny his faith. Peter's strength was so far lost, when he denied his master's name, that he needed in some sense a new conversion.

As gold is tried in the fire, so our strength is tried in the furnace of affliction; and surely when men are tried, it is their interest and honour to see that they

*Ps. 46, Hab. 3:17,18, Rom. 8:18, 2 Cor. 4:14-18

come forth as gold, and not as reprobate silver. Trials are necessary for us, and appointed to us, and the times of trial are critical seasons; and therefore we ought to be prepared for them, that the trial of our faith may be found unto praise, and honour, and glory.

But how shall we be furnished with strength to stand in the evil day? Paul gives us necessary directions for this purpose*. Christ is the author of all grace. Faith and hope, and patience, are fruits of his Spirit; and we must not only receive those militant graces out of fulness, but depend on his power to maintain them in our souls; and then neither persecution, nor distress, nor any thing else shall be able to overthrow our souls, or destroy our comfort †.

Ver. 11. *If thou forbear to deliver them that are drawn unto death, and those that are ready to be slain ;*

Ver. 12. *If thou sayest, behold we knew it not : Doth not he that pondereth the heart consider it ? And he that keepeth thy soul, doth not he know it ? and shall not he render to every man according to his works ?*

We are required by God to love not in word or profession, but in truth and in deed, taking every proper opportunity to shew our love in its proper fruits. One of these is recommended in this text, which enjoins us to appear in the defence of those who are unjustly doomed to destruction. Christ laid down his life for us, and we ought also to lay down our lives for the brethren, and to risk every thing dear to us, in the cause of righteousness. By the same law of charity, we are required to interest ourselves in the cause of those who suffer any injurious treatment, and to do it without hesitation or delay. We must not be slack to

---

*Eph. 6:10-18   †2 Cor. 12:7

afford relief to our enemy's oxen or asses, if they are fallen into a pit, far less may we defer the giving of needful relief to our distressed brethren.

The wise man represents this piece of charity as a duty which we owe to our neighbours without exception ; and with him agrees our Lord in the parable of the good Samaritan. We are not the disciples of Solomon or of Christ, if we shew love to those only who are nearly related to us, or who are of the same religious profession with ourselves.

The wise man knew that this is a duty against which we are too ready to muster up exceptions, because the performance of it may expose us to trouble or danger ; but he answers every exception that can be made to it in few words, but with strong and convincing arguments. We cannot pretend that it is not our duty to relieve the oppressed, as far as our power extends ; but, as the priest that passed by the wounded man, kept at a distance, that he might not behold that object of compassion, so we are too ready to allege that we knew not the peril in which our neighbour was involved, or did not know that he was an innocent man, that did not deserve such treatment. If this be strictly true, and if our ignorance was not voluntary and affected, the excuse is good; but it is to be remembered, that no excuses for the neglect of duty ought to be sustained by our own minds that will not be sustained by God our judge. Excuses may serve to blind the eyes of men who are short-sighted, and who are obliged to judge on the charitable side in a doubtful case ; but God is greater than men, and knoweth all things, and will not be imposed upon by any false pretence.

God pondereth our hearts, and knows with certainty how far we act from a careless and selfish spirit, when we neglect the offices of charity to the distressed. In weighing the spirits of men, the want of charity alone serves to turn the balance; and the omissions of charity, which are known by God to spring from the want of that necessary virtue, exclude men from the kingdom of heaven *.

God is the keeper of our souls, and therefore we need not be afraid to risk our lives in obedience to his will. We cannot subsist one moment without his kind providence, and why should we scruple to risk every thing dear to us in the service of Him in whom we live, move, and have our being? We are always safe in the way of duty, we are never safe in neglect of it. For safety cometh from the Lord our judge and lawgiver; and if our lives are exposed in his service, he can easily preserve them, or compensate the loss, if he suffers them to be taken from us. But if we preserve them by declining our duty, we expose them to more dreadful dangers than death.

God renders unto every man according to his works. He will not forget the works of faith and the labours of love, and he will never suffer any man to be a loser by them. The greatest gains in the world, are the losses suffered for the sake of a good conscience; and the greatest losses are the gains of sin. If we neglect duty from the prospect of safety or advantage, the honour of God is engaged, to convince us by experience, that no profit is to be found in disobeying his will. Queen Esther could not have reasonably expected to secure herself, even in the house of her imperial husband, from the vengeance of God, if she had neglected to exert all her influence at the peril of her life, for the deliverance of the Jews, when Haman was pursuing them with deadly hatred †.

These truths are so plain, and so decisive in the present case, that the wise man propounds them in the

*1 Cor. 13   †Esther 4:14,15

form of questions, and leaves it to the consciences of men to return answers to themselves. A lively impression of our absolute dependance upon God, and our accountableness to him, would answer millions of objections against the hardest duties.

If we must not forbear to succour those whose lives are exposed to danger, it must be the extreme of wickedness to suffer immortal souls to perish, when our persuasions and instructions may be a mean of preventing it. It is indeed still worse by bad example or corrupt doctrine, to destroy the souls that must be happy or miserable through endless ages.

Ver. 13. *My son eat thou honey, because it is good, and the honey comb, which is sweet to thy taste.*

Ver. 14. *So shall the knowledge of wisdom be unto thy soul; when thou hast found it, then there shall be a reward, and thy expectation shall not be cut off.*

God, in his great goodness, has provided for our delight as well as our subsistence, and has given us leave to use honey, because it is sweet to the taste, as well as bread to strengthen our bodies. How great is his goodness, and how great is his beauty! But how great is our ingratitude, if we serve him not with gladness, amidst the abundance of our enjoyments?

All men relish those things that are sweet to the palate, but there are many that have no spiritual taste to relish those things that are sweet to the purified soul. Had we senses spiritually exercised, we would readily confess, that honey, and milk, and wine, are tasteless, when they are compared with that knowledge of God, and of his Son Jesus Christ, which makes us wise unto salvation. Honey is sweet to the mouth, but the knowledge of wisdom is sweet to the soul. The sweetness of honey lasts for a moment, but the sweetness of wisdom is everlasting. Honey soon satiates, and when it is taken in too large a quantity it is bitter in the belly, and hurtful to the constitution; but wisdom is the joy and happiness, the health and vigour of the soul.

There is pleasure in the knowledge, and pleasure in the practice of wisdom. As soon as we become wise, we taste exquisite satisfactions, of which we could not formerly frame an idea to ourselves, any more than a man that wants the sense of taste, could form a conception of the sweetness of honey. The sweetness of it is experienced more fully in our religious progress, and most of all at the end of our course. There shall be a gracious and abundant reward unto the wise man, for God has promised it; and the hopes that are founded upon the word of God can never make us ashamed. The wise shall shine like the brightness of the firmament, and shall enjoy celestial delights in the presence of him with whom is the fountain of life.

Let Christians hope to the end, for the grace that shall be brought to them at the revelation of Jesus Christ. Perhaps they may be brought into very trying situations, and the tempter will persuade them to say, our hope is lost, and we are cut off for our part. But the devil is not to be believed at any time, especially when his suggestions are so manifestly contrary to the word of the living God, who says, there shall be a reward, and thine expectation shall not be cut off. The living hope of the glory that is to be revealed to us, will sweeten every bitter thing that we meet with in the pursuit and practice of wisdom; for when the Christian soldier is sure of victory and white robes, and of admission to the new Jerusalem, and the tree of life, the toils and dangers of the field of battle are turned into gladness.

Ver. 15. *Lay not wait, O wicked man, against the dwelling of the righteous; spoil not his resting place.*

Ver. 16. *For a just man falleth seven times, and riseth up again; but the wicked shall fall into mischief.*

The people of God have many enemies : The principalities and powers of hell lay wait for their souls; and
there are men so desperately wicked, that they will not
scruple to lay wait for their lives or properties. Christians may entertain assured hopes of the eternal rest; but
if they expect an uninterrupted rest in this world, they
will find themselves mistaken. They have, nevertheless, a ground for strong consolation under every attack, and every instance of success in their enemies. They
must not expect exemption, but they may firmly hope
for deliverance from the cross. They may fall, but they
shall not be utterly cast down ; for strong is the Lord
God that helpeth them.

It is vain for sinners to hope that they shall be able
to do any real mischief to the righteous. They may
flatter themselves with the hopes of success in their unrighteous designs : they see the righteous fall before
them, and pursuade themselves that they shall not be able
to arise ; but the God who maintains their cause, suffers
them to fall into trouble to try and refine them, and
when he has accomplished his work upon them, will
raise them up with renewed vigour, and take a severe
vengeance upon their enemies. When they fight against
God's people, they fight against God himself ; and are
they stronger than he, from whom they receive the little
strength they have ? He is a wall of fire round about
his people, and their enemies are like stubble, fully dry,
or like thorns folded together.

Be not afraid, ye righteous, of the strength or cunning of your adversaries ; and believe not those tempters, who tell you that there is no help for you in God.
Be not dismayed at their success, nor let your falls into
calamity damp your hopes. You are taught by Solomon and Micah, to triumph even when you are defeat-
ed, because your losses will end in victory, and the victories of your enemies in ruin. " Rejoice not against

me, O mine enemy, though I fall, I shall arise, though
I sit in darkness, the Lord shall be a light unto
me, etc. *"

Perhaps you will say, had I fallen only once, I would
not be much afraid; but I have often fallen before the
enemy, and one day I must perish. But hear what God
says :—The righteous man falls not once or twice, but
many times, and still he rises. Your experience of former deliverances should encourage your hopes of new
deliverances, for the salvations of the Lord are never
exhausted. In six troubles he will deliver, and in seven there shall no evil touch you.

Woe to the wicked, and to the enemies of the righteous, they shall fall never to arise. They shall fall into misery. They shall fall into the grave. They shall
fall into the lake of fire, from whence there is no returning. They have a load of sins and curses upon them
heavier than mountains of lead ; and when they begin
to fall, they shall, like Haman, utterly perish. Babylon intended to destroy Zion, but Zion was purified and
redeemed, whilst the vengeance of Zion and of Zion's
Redeemer, sunk Babylon into irrecoverable perdition,
as a millstone is sunk in the mighty waters.

Ver. 17. *Rejoice not when thine enemy falleth, and let
not thine heart be glad when he stumbleth ;*

Ver. 18. *Lest the Lord see it, and it displease him, and
he turn away his wrath from him.*

He that is glad at calamities, shall not be unpunished, says Solomon in another place. But may we not be
glad at the calamities of our enemies ? By no means.
It would be unlawful and inhuman. We must not be
glad at the calamity of our enemy's ass, but help it out
of a ditch if it has fallen into one. It is very opposite
to the spirit of Christianity to rejoice at the misfortunes

---

*Micah 7:8-10

of our enemies. Our blessed Saviour prayed for his enemies, and commands us to pray for our enemies. If we
neglect prayer for them, we neglect a plain and positive duty, enforced by the noblest example. If we pray
for them, and yet rejoice when they fall, or even when
they stumble, and are in danger of falling, we are gross
hypocrites. If we have the hearts of monsters, and not
of men, why do we pretend to be Christians?

But does not Solomon say, elsewhere, when the wicked perish there is shouting? And are we not frequently told, that the righteous are glad at the vengeance executed upon the wicked? This is true; but
they do not rejoice, on such occasions, from a vindictive or selfish spirit. They rejoice that God is glorified, that wickedness is suppressed, and the people of
God delivered from oppression. Such was the joy of
Moses and the children of Israel, when Pharaoh was
drowned in the Red Sea. Of this kind shall be the joy
of the church of Christ in the day of Antichrist's destruction*. But to rejoice because mischief has befallen
our fellow men, or because we expect some advantage
from the misery of our enemies, is to behave like heathens or devils, and not like Christ, or his saints. We
must still remember that the eye of God is upon us, he
observes all the movements of our spirits, and the workings of our passions. He is well pleased when we look
with a pitying and generous eye upon the sins and miseries of our worst enemies; but looks with displeasure
on those selfish souls that rejoice at the calamities of
those that hate them. An unforgiving and revengeful spirit, in those that need so much forgiveness from
God, must be very provoking to him.

Our joy at the fall of our enemies cannot procure
their reconciliation to God, but it may kindle God's

---

*Exod. 15, Rev. 13

displeasure against us. He may suspend the present execution of judgment against them, and transfer it to ourselves; for if they wronged us, and exposed themselves to punishment, we have wronged God and them, and have exposed ourselves, in no less a degree, to punishment. If we rejoice at the fall or danger of our enemies, we ourselves have fallen into a greater evil, for sin has more evil in it than affliction, and brings affliction along with it. The whole book of Obadiah seems to be written to show the miseries which men bring upon themselves, by triumphing in the ruin of their enemies; and many chapters of the Bible insist on the same necessary subject*.

If this sin was so dangerous under the dispensation of Moses, how is it possible that those should escape punishment who are guilty of it under the Christian dispensation, when the law of love to all men (enemies not excepted) is so wonderfully enforced, that it is called, by Christ, his new commandment, although it is the old commandment, which we had from the beginning?

Ver. 19. *Fret not thyself because of evil men, neither be thou envious at the wicked.*

It seems that wicked men were often prosperous, even under the law, and that there is a strong disposition in men to make a bad use of the wise and good Providence of God, in sometimes allotting prosperity to the wicked, otherwise Solomon would not have so frequently cautioned us against indulging this propensity. He had guarded us against this sin by telling us of the future happiness of the righteous, and of the cursed disposition of the wicked. He now gives us another motive to quietness and composure under this strange providence of the universal sovereign†

---

*Ezek. 25:35   †Chap. 23: 17,18, 24:1,2

Ver. 20. *For there shall be no reward to the evil man, the candle of the wicked shall be put out.*

What avails a happiness (if it can be called by that name,) which continues only threescore and ten years, when the person that enjoyed it must continue for millions of ages ? Will it be any comfort to the wicked in another world, to reflect that they enjoyed their good things in this world ? Heaven is despised by the wicked at present, for they are stupified by their earthly enjoyments ; but it is not despised by the damned in hell. They know, to their sorrow, the immense value of the heavenly inheritance, and weep, and gnash their teeth, and melt away with envy, at that celestial happiness, from which they find themselves for ever excluded, and separated by a gulph that cannot be passed. There is no merciful reward, but there is a reward of justice and vengeance to evil men. They are shut out from the celestial city, and have their everlasting abode in those regions where rest and peace and hope never come. A perpetuity of bliss is bliss ; and those immortal souls that have no title to it, are the objects not of envy but of pity. When a prosperous transgressor is pining away under a loathsome and mortal distemper, we don't reckon him worthy of our envy, although he drags out his days in a magnificent palace, surrounded with pleasures which he cannot taste, and to which he must soon bid farewell ; and if we viewed things in the light of the word of God, we should not grudge at his prosperity, when he enjoys the most perfect health, for even then his soul is pining away to death, and his prosperity is precarious and transient. The joys of the just are permanent and increasing, like the light of the sun, which shineth more and more unto the perfect day ; but the prosperity of the wicked, is like the light of a candle : if you leave it to itself it will soon consume away ; but it may very probably be extinguished before it has time to burn to the socket. Shall those who rejoice in the light of day, grudge the happiness of those who dwell in a dungeon, enjoying only the light of one taper which must soon expire, and leave them buried in perpetual night.

Ver. 21. *My son, fear thou the Lord and the king, and meddle not with them that are given to change.*

Ver. 22. *For their calamity shall rise suddenly; and who knoweth the ruin of them both?*

To fear God is a duty so necessary, that there can be no religion without it. The excellencies and works of God, the favours we have received from him, the relations we stand in to him, the account we must give to him, and our absolute dependence upon him, loudly call upon us to fear him. He is so much to be feared, that the Fear of Isaac is one of the names given to him by Jacob; and the wise preacher tells us, that to fear God and keep his commandments is the whole of man,

To the fear of God, must be joined reverence to the king, for God's sake; for by him kings reign, and they are his ministers for our protection from enemies and wicked men, and for promoting virtue and suppressing wickedness. God has conferred dignity and power upon them, and they are entitled to honour for the sake of their office and work.

Yet we must not carry this reverence of royal dignity to a degree of adoration. We must be subject to every ordinance of man for the Lord's sake, but to the Lord for his own sake, because absolute dominion belongs to him. Although kings are called gods, yet they shall die like men; and when their commandments clash with the authority of God, they are worthy of no regard; and our safety lies in fearing him that has power to kill both soul and body, and to cast both into hellfire. If the wrath of a king is like the roaring of a lion, the wrath of God is infinitely more to be dreaded.

If we would preserve our religion and loyalty, we must not meddle with those who are fond of changes either in religion or government, for " evil communications corrupt good manners." The people of Israel, when they mingled with the nations, learned of them their ways, and changed their glory for that which did not profit ; and they were so fond of being like their neighbours, that they rejected the Lord from being king over them, and desired rather to have a royal tyrant like the other nations. When Absalom rebelled against his father, many followed him in the simplicity of their hearts.

The scripture does not require us to be subject to tyrants ; but single acts of maladministration will not justify men in casting off the yoke of government. In most cases, it is our duty and wisdom to be quiet and peaceable subjects, to those who have the possession of the throne granted them by divine providence, and to say with more sincerity than Hushai the Archite, " whom the Lord and this people choose, his will I be, and with him will I abide."

Impiety and disloyalty are great and dangerous sins. Kings are terrible enemies ; and God is infinitely more dreadful, and he is the avenger, not only of insults against himself, but of indignities and injuries to those powers that are ordained by him. How many were destroyed in the gainsaying of Korah, and in the rebellion of Absalom ? Who knows what ruin awaits those who are guilty of rebellion, which is as the sin of witchcraft ; or how suddenly, the tempest of vengeance may hurl those men into perdition, who fear not God, or do not reverence those who are authorized by him to administer justice among men. The apostle Paul spends a large part of a chapter in shewing the sin and danger of those who do not submit to the higher powers.

How miserable shall they be, who refuse subjection

to that great king whom God has placed on the throne of grace, and to whom he hath given a rod of iron, to crush those rebels that attempt to break his bands, and cast away his cords? The princes and judges of the earth must serve him, as well as the meanest of their subjects, and his enemies shall lick the dust. " Blessed are all they that put their trust in him, and obey him *.

Ver. 23. *These things also belong to the wise. It is not good to have respect to persons of judgment.*

Princes usually have a sufficient sense of those duties which their subjects owe them ; and they would generally find these duties better performed, if they had a proper sense of their own duties. The precepts of wisdom are binding on them, as well as on poor men, and the dominion of God extends alike to the prince and to the peasant.

All the precepts already delivered are precepts of wisdom, and those which follow were likewise dictated by the father of lights to the wisest of men ; and the best proof we can give of our wisdom, is to observe them. They are fools that will not hear the voice of wisdom, or look upon any of her precepts as superfluous. We may more reasonably complain of too much money in our purses, or too many clothes in our closets, than of too many precepts of wisdom in the book of God.

We have no reason to complain that God is strict in requiring our obedience to rulers. He is no less strict in requiring rulers to govern justly, and to make their subjects happy. In this verse, he commands them to do justice and judgment, like David, to all their people. Whatever favours they may confer on particular persons, they must be impartial in judgment. They must not accept the rich and great, nor their own favourites,

---

*Ps. 2

nor even a poor or a righteous man in his cause. To accept the person of any man is not good, but very wicked. Elihu durst not accept the person of Job, although he was the best man on the face of the earth, when he gave his judgment about the cause which he had debated with his friends. Although absolute dominion belongs to God, and he dispenses his favours according to his sovereign pleasure; yet in judgment he respects not his own favourites. When he determined by his providence the cause between his beloved servant David, and Saul whom he had rejected, he examined David, and proved him by night, and found nothing, judging him according to his righteousness, and not according to the special favour he had to him. And when the same good man had dealt injuriously with Uriah, he was punished before all Israel, and before the sun. In like manner, when the Gibeonites were treated with abuse and cruelty by the king of Israel, in zeal to God's favoured people, God gave full satisfaction to the Gibeonites. Kings and judges are honoured with the name of gods on earth, and they ought to imitate the justice of God in all their administrations.

But may not criminals be suffered to escape by a merciful perversion of the law, although the righteous must not be wronged? No:

Ver. 24. *He that saith to the wicked, thou art righteous, him shall the people curse, nations shall abhor him.*

Ver. 25. *But to them that rebuke him shall be delight, and a good blessing shall come upon them.*

He that justifieth the wicked is an abomination to the Lord; and his iniquity is attended with such mischievous consequences, that he is an abomination to men also, and provokes against himself the execrations of whole nations. If robbers and murderers escape unpunished, how can any man think himself sure of his life or property, when public encouragement is so evidently given to the pests of human society? Mercy is to be shewed to bad men, as far as it consists with equity, and the public good, but when it is carried farther it becomes cruelty to millions.

The curse causeless need not be dreaded, but the curse deserved is dreadful. It is sinful to curse men from the impulse of ungoverned passions; but those curses that are sinfully uttered, or wished by men, are often righteously executed by God; and therefore it is dangerous for us by our bad conduct, to tempt men to curse us in the bitterness of their spirits.

But those magistrates who faithfully execute their trust, shall have much pleasure from the testimony of their own hearts, and from the happy effects of their faithful and impartial administrations. They shall have the blessings of those who live under their government, and the blessings of men, when they are well earned, are ratified by God *. Job looked upon it as one part of his happiness, that he enjoyed the blessings of those that were ready to perish, and of every eye that saw him.

We may safely risk the abhorrence of all mankind, and despise their favour, when our duty requires us; for if we seek to please men at the expence of sinful compliances, we are not the servants of Christ. But as far as we are allowed by the law of God, it is our duty to practise those things that are of good report, living unblameably and usefully in our respective stations, that we may adorn the doctrine of God our Saviour in all things.

How important is the behaviour of men in elevated stations. Thousands or millions of men are losers or gainers by it, and applaud or abhor those who rule over

*Deut. 24:13

them. Kings and magistrates have much need of our
prayers, that they may receive wisdom from God. We
who are in inferior stations, have likewise our contracted
sphere of influence, and ought to consider how much
others are affected by our behaviour. Let us endeavour to
deserve at least their blessings, and to avoid every thing
that may justly incur their displeasure, or hurt their
interests.

If it is of so much consequence to the public, that
magistrates should punish the wicked; and if they would
incur universal hatred by the neglect of this part of
their duty, shall we deny to the sovereign Ruler of the
world, that praise to which he is entitled for his acts of
just vengeance? He is glorious in his administrations
of justice as well as mercy. Who would not fear him
and glorify his name, for he only is holy, for his judgments are made manifest? If he did not punish the
wicked, we would have reason to say, every one that
doth evil is good in the sight of the Lord, and he delighteth in them, and where is the God of judgment?

Those magistrates who give a right judgment in any
cause that comes before them, procure universal respect
and good will, as the wise man instructs us in the following verse:

Ver. 26. *Every man shall kiss his lips that giveth a
right answer.*

No doubt prejudices may take place, and obtain
ground among people, by which rulers may for a time
lose that approbation which is due to their conduct;
but the history of all ages proves the truth of this proverb. Good princes have in general possessed the cordial esteem of their subjects; and the tyrants of the
world are the men whose lives have been embittered,
and their deaths accelerated, by the hatred and insurrections of those whom they ruled.

This proverb contains an useful rule for private persons, as well as rulers. When we are asked an important question, or consulted on an affair of consequence, every man will esteem and love us, if we give a right answer; and that our answer may be right, it is necessary that it should be sincere, prudent, and meek. We must not give an answer calculated merely to please the person that advises with us; for that would not be consistent with integrity. We must consider all the circumstances of the affair, that we may give a proper and pertinent answer; and we must speak with that meekness, which renders wisdom lovely. If our answers to those that advise with us have these qualifications, although they may be sometimes distasteful, because truth compels us to speak things disagreeable, yet they will tend, on the whole, to the advancement of our character; and our character is no contemptible object, because the goodness of it is necessary for us in accomplishing the great business of life, glorifying God, and doing good to men. The instances of Joseph in his first conversation with Pharaoh, and of Daniel's plain dealing with Nebuchadnezzar and Belshazzar, are illustrations of this truth.

Let us never give a wrong answer to any man, if kings should kiss our lips for it. Zedekiah the son of Chenaanah, will tell us how little the royal favour which he obtained by his court flattery availed him, and how short its continuance was *.

Ver. 27. *Prepare thy work without, and make it fit for thyself in the field, and afterwards build thine house.*

Things absolutely necessary, are to be sought after in the first place, and, in the next place, those things that may minister delight and satisfaction. For this reason we are commanded by our Lord, in the first place, to seek the kingdom of God, and his righteous-

---

*1 Kings 22

ness, because the salvation of our souls is infinitely more interesting than our welfare in this world. But as there is a lawful care about the things of this world also, we are directed in this place, to mind the things most needful to our present subsistence and comfort, before we proceed to those things that have an inferior influence upon the comfort of our lives. Solomon takes it for granted, that we have already a house in which we can live, and enjoy shelter from the inclemencies of the weather : but perhaps we wish to have a more elegant and commodious house. A wish of this kind is not unreasonable, only it must be kept in due subordination to our most important concerns. The work of the field, on which our subsistence depends, is of more importance than the building of a better house, and ought therefore to be first attended to, and then we are at liberty to build our house, if we can afford time and money for it. This rule of the wise man is of great use for the wise management of our secular concerns, and by neglecting it, many have been reduced to poverty and contempt ; nor is it so remote from religion, as some inconsiderate persons may apprehend, for religion requires us to act prudently in the common business of life, and to do nothing that may reduce ourselves, or our families to want, or deprive our creditors of their just claims upon us.

In our religious concerns, the same rule ought to be observed. There are first principles which ought in the first place to be well studied, and then we must go on to perfection *· To think of going on to perfection without learning the first principles, is as foolish as to think of raising the superstructure of a house, without laying the foundation ; and to rest in the first principles, is as foolish as to lay the foundation of a house, and then to think that all our work is over.

---

*Heb. 6

God is a God of order ; and he requires us to do all things in their proper order, both in our civil and religious business.

Ver. 28. *Be not a witness against thy neighbour without cause, and deceive not with thy lips.*

It is in many cases a man's duty to bear witness against his neighbour, and then the glory of God and the welfare of society, call loudly upon him to perform this necessary, that disagreeable service ; but it is a great sin for a man to bear false witness against his neighbour, or to bear testimony against him from a principle of malice and revenge, when there is no call to declare even the truth against him. The real faults of other men must not be published by us, when there is no good to be done, nor any danger to be obviated by it. We would not wish our own faults to be wantonly blazed abroad to the world ; and why should we behave in one way to others, and expect another way of behaviour to ourselves ? This would be as unreasonable as keeping one kind of weights and measures for buying and another for selling.

We must not deceive with our lips, either before a judge or in private conversation. The gift of speech was given us, for glorifying God, and doing good to men ; and it is a wicked perversion of it to make use of it for dishonouring God and deceiving men, by flattery or falsehood, or by speaking truth in such a manner as to deceive ; for the history of the false testimony that was borne against our Lord, shows us that truth falsely and deceitfully represented, may become an instrument of deceit and mischief.

That truth is generally to be spoken, you will allow, but perhaps you will allege that you have some wicked neighbour, that has no right to truth from you, because he has borne testimony against you without cause, or by some other injury deserved a mischief at your hand. But,

Ver. 29. *Say not, I will do so to him as he hath done to me, I will render to the man according to his work.*

To speak in this manner would be the same thing as if you said, " Vengeance belongeth unto me, I will repay it." I will step into the throne of God, and hurl the thunderbolts of vengeance upon mine adversary.

What would become of us, if God should render to us according to our evil works. We need great mercy at the hand of God, and shall we render nothing but rigid justice to our fellow men, in direct opposition to the royal law of love ? When our neighbours do us an injury, shall we borrow weapons from hell to retaliate ? When we revenge injuries at our own discretion, we may do hurt to our enemies, but we do much greater hurt to ourselves ; for the punishment of malice and revenge to which we expose ourselves, is far worse than any vengeance which our feeble arm can inflict. Let us therefore show ourselves to be the disciples of Christ by loving our enemies and recompensing evil with good. Thus we shall heap coals of fire upon the head of our enemies, to melt them ; but by following an opposite course, we heap them on our own, to our destruction.

Ver. 30. *I went by the field of the slothful, and by the vineyard of the man void of understanding.*

The sluggard is wise in his own conceit ; but in Solomon's judgment, sluggard is another name for a man void of understanding ; for what understanding can that man have who buries himself alive, and neither performs the duties of life, nor takes the proper method of being able to enjoy and relish its comforts.

The slothful man hopes to escape poverty, because he is born an heir to fields and vineyards ; but Solomon, that great observer of the manners and conditions of men, passed by these fields and vineyards, and saw what was sufficient to convince any man, of the folly of such hopes.

Ver. 31. *And lo it was all grown over with thorns, and nettles had covered the face thereof, and the stone wall thereof was broken down.*

How could it be otherwise? Thorns and thistles, since the fall of man, spring up every where, to remind us of our rebellion against God, and the greatest industry can scarcely keep them down; but where slothfulness leaves them to spring up at will, the field must be covered with them, and every useful plant choked; or, if any thing useful for man springs up amongst them, it becomes a prey to every spoiler, because the stone wall is broken down and left in ruins.

Such is the situation of the sluggard's field and vineyard; and spiritual sloth is productive of the like effects in the soul of man. If we are careless about our spiritual interests, our souls will soon be overrun with noisome and pernicious vice; and left without guard against those destructive enemies, "that go about seeking whom they may devour." A neglected garden is disagreeable to the eye, but a neglected soul is a spectacle of horror. The stinging nettles of envy, the thorns of anger, and ungovernable passion, spring up abundantly in that scene of desolation. Every lust and every temptation have an uncontrolled influence; and the lion out of the bottomless pit wastes it at his pleasure.

But what pleasure could Solomon have in looking at the sluggard's vineyard? He saw nothing that did not afford instruction to his enlightened mind; for wisdom teaches us to improve every object, however unpleasant, to useful purposes, and finds nourishment for itself even in the folly of other men.

Ver. 32. *Then I saw and considered it well: I looked upon it, and received instruction.*

He did not take a cursory and superficial view of

this field, but spent many thoughts upon it. How useful is meditation? It is the nurse of knowledge and prudence. It furnishes our minds with truths, and applies them to the heart, and teaches us to live in a manner suitable to them. Solomon was already wise, but he wished to be wiser, and learned wisdom every day. Another man would have learned self conceit or self indulgence, from the field of the sluggard. Some persons, when they see the faults of others, applaud themselves for their superiority in virtue. No man, they think, can say they are bad men, because they know that some other men are worse. There are other persons that think it safe for them to do like other people, and to let alone what other people omit ; but to compare ourselves among ourselves is not wise. Our wisdom lies in learning from the example of other men, compared with the law of God, what we are to do, and what we are to avoid. We see the sluggard, the drunkard, the lukewarm professor ; but we see no good arising out of their vices, but much harm to themselves. They are condemned by the providence as well as the word of God. Their souls are unprosperous, and the outward circumstances of some of those kinds of sinners, have the marks of divine displeasure mingled with them. Is it not better to learn wisdom at the cost of other people than at our own expense ?

Solomon learned instruction from this dismal spectacle, the field and vineyard of the sluggard; and the instruction which he received he communicates to us in a proverb, which, for its importance, is repeated from a former chapter.

Ver. 33. *Yet a little sleep, a little slumber, a little folding of the hands to sleep.*

Ver. 34. *So shall thy poverty come as one that travelleth, and thy want as an armed man.*

The sluggard had no intention of suffering his field to be all covered with weeds, he only wished to indulge himself a little while in ease and sleep, and then he designed to rouse himself and root up all the weeds. His ruin was, that, when he had got a little sleep, he wished for a little more, and when he had taken the little more, he felt himself as little disposed to work as before; and so he loitered and wasted away the time, day after day, doing nothing at all, or nothing to purpose, till his field was all overrun with noisome weeds, and every good herb destroyed, and his vineyard lay in ruins. Thus poverty came upon him swiftly and unexpectedly, and with irresistible fury, and plunged him into the gulph of misery and remorse.

Would you avoid sloth? Beware of every temptation to it, and allow not place to any thought of delaying a necessary business. It was a maxim of a certain prince, who was celebrated for his success in every undertaking, never to defer that till to-morrow which could be done to day. Putting off things till to-morrow is the thief of time. It is unsafe in any business. It is infinitely dangerous in our spiritual concerns. Boast not therefore of to-morrow, for thou knowest not what a day may bring forth, but whatsoever thine hand findeth to do, do it with all thy might *.

---

*See Chap. 6:11,12

Proverbs 25

Verse 1. *These are also proverbs of Solomon, which the men of Hezekiah, king of Judah, copied out.*

A BOOK written by Solomon, and published by the order of Hezekiah, would deserve very high regard. But the proverbs of Solomon need no human recommendation. Their intrinsic worth, and their divine original, place them far above the compositions of the greatest philosophers and kings that were not favoured with divine inspiration.

Those servants of Hezekiah that copied out the following part of Solomon's proverbs, and joined them to the rest, are here mentioned to their honour. They were the publishers, and not the composers of the following chapters; but they performed a piece of service to the church for which their names shall live. If we cannot do so much for God and his people as some others have done, let us do what we can, and we shall in no wise lose our reward. The contributors of goat's hair to the tabernacle are mentioned to their honour, as well as those who gave silver, and gold, and precious stones; for if there be first a willing mind, it is accepted according to what a man hath, and not according to what he hath not.

Many of the following precepts respect the duties of kings. Hezekiah walked in the good ways of David and Solomon, and he desired instruction in his duty as a king. Every one of us ought to study the duties that belong to our respective stations, that we may be thoroughly furnished for every good work.

Ver. 2. *It is the glory of God to conceal a thing: but the honour of kings is to search out a matter.*

How arrogant are those men who must know the reasons of all God's works; or, if that exceeds their capacity, call them in question, or find fault with them, as if they knew better what God ought to do than God himself! There are unsearchable mysteries in the excellencies and ways of God. His way is in the sea, and his path in the mighty waters, and his footsteps are not known, and it is his glory that they are not known. His wisdom would not be divine, if we could understand him to perfection, nor his sovereignty absolute, if he were obliged to do nothing but what his creatures would approve.

The meanest of the creatures of God have qualities that we cannot fully understand; how strange then is it, that we will not allow his providence to transcend our comprehension, or that a doubt should be entertained about the mysteries of his grace, because they are incomprehensible to our feeble understandings? It was a good saying of a pious divine, " Lord preserve us from a comprehensible God." It is our duty to venerate and wonder, and not to pry with curious eyes into the secrets of God. The history of the fall is an everlasting warning to the sons of Adam to prefer the tree of life to the tree of knowledge.

But the kings of this earth are infinitely inferior to the God of heaven, and their honours are of an humbler kind. It is their honour to search out a matter. When God is said to search the hearts of men, he is spoken of in the language of men, for he beholds all things past, present, and to come, by one glance of his infinite mind; but kings, who need a great deal of knowledge and wisdom, must obtain it, like other men, by labour and diligence. It is their honour to be diligent in searching out every thing that princes ought to know;

They must employ much care, and make use of the wisdom of other men to inform themselves about all the interests of their kingdoms, and their various connexions with foreign states. They must endeavour to acquaint themselves with the dispositions and humours of their subjects, with the best means of suppressing vice, and encouraging goodness, and making their people happy, and the proper methods of preserving peace, or of defending their crowns and kingdoms from foreign enemies. When kings act the part of judges in their own persons, as they did in ancient times, their sphere of labour is greatly increased; for every intricate cause they must search out. They must neither refuse to judge in it because it is difficult, nor must they pass sentence without good ground, to save their own labour, but they must search things to the bottom, and judge wisely and righteously, as Solomon did in the case of the two harlots.

On these accounts kings cannot conceal their important affairs within their own minds. They must have assistants to bear the burden of government, and make use of the counsels and abilities of other men, to whom they must communicate their secrets. It is the glory of God to need no counsellor. It is the honour of kings to choose right counsellors and to follow their salutary advices. Yet it is not to be expected that their subjects in general should be their privy counsellors.

Ver. 3. *The heaven for height, and the earth for depth, and the heart of kings is unsearchable.*

No man can measure the height of heaven, or the depth of the earth, as little can the hearts of kings be searched out. But is every king a Solomon, with an heart large as the sand on the sea shore? Every king needs a very enlarged heart. The throne is not a bed of repose, but the seat of care and labour. What knowledge and prudence is requisite to understand the intri-

cate science of government, and to manage the complicated affairs of kingdoms ? and as kings are not born
wiser than other men, they certainly ought to improve
the many advantages they have, for acquiring that
knowledge which is suited to their station, and to pray
earnestly for wisdom to him by whom kings reign, and
whose servants they ought to be. Without a large
measure of wisdom they are fit only to be the tools of
their own ministers, who are often lovers of themselves,
and of their own families, more than of their king and
country.

But the heart of kings is oftener unsearchable in
another sense. Their designs cannot be known by
their subjects, or by foreign princes, because they in-
dustriously conceal them from the knowledge of all but
their privy counsellors; and this is often necessary, because a discovery of their counsels would obstruct the
execution of them. Besides, the affairs of government
are so various and complicated, they have so many designs to carry on, so many mischiefs to obviate, so
many opposite tempers of men to consider, and so many
unknown difficulties to encounter, that persons in a
lower station cannot possibly understand the reasons
of a great part of their conduct, or the ends which they
have in view. It is therefore presumptuous in subjects
to pry too narrowly into their behaviour, or to be rash
with their censures on the public management. Those
who take a liberty to despise dominions, and speak evil
of dignities, should be sure that they do not speak evil
of those things which they do not understand.

If the heart of kings, who are infinitely inferior to
God*, is so unsearchable, how foolish is it to think that
we can search out God unto perfection† !

---

*Verse 2   †Job 11:7-9, Rom.11:33

Ver. 4. *Take away the dross from the silver, and there shall come forth a vessel for the finer.*

Ver. 5. *Take away the wicked from before the king, and the throne shall be established in righteousness.*

The interests of prince and people are so evidently the same, and a bad king is so evidently his own enemy, that it may well be wondered at that so many kings have proved tyrants, and exposed themselves to the danger and infamy that are the inseparable attendants of oppression and injustice in men of high place. To account for this fact, we must consider that kings cannot govern their people without the assistance of ministers and counsellors, and these servants of government have private interests of their own, different from those of the prince and people, which they too often prosecute with a selfish and wicked spirit. To serve their own covetous and ambitious views, they too often corrupt the mind of their prince with the sweet poison of flattery, and lead him, by their misrepresentations, into false notions of the state of things in his kingdom, and of the character and behaviour of many of his subjects, and draw him on to compliance with their own interested or malicious views, to the prejudice of his kingdom, and the ruin of many of his faithful subjects. If we read the histories of nations with attention, we shall find that unjust wars, oppressive taxes, iniquitous laws, unjust executions, seditious and civil commotions, and the overturning of thrones, and the confusions of kingdoms, have originated in the wicked counsels of bad ministers. The histories of Rehoboam, and Joash, and Ahasuerus, are scriptural instances of this truth.

Wicked men are often compared in Scripture to dross; and as the dross must be separated from the silver before a beautiful vase can be framed, so the wicked must be removed from before the throne, that it may be established in righteousness; and kings need our prayers, that they may be furnished with wisdom to choose their counsellors and ministers from their best deserving subjects, and to turn all flatterers and self-seekers out of public employment. If Rehoboam had possessed so much wisdom, the kingdom might have remained entire in his hand; but Solomon his father could not infuse this wisdom into his mind by all his instructions, and God left him to his folly, that his awful purpose of dividing his people, and diminishing the kingdom of the house of David, might be fulfilled*.

Ver. 6. *Put not forth thyself in the presence of the king, and stand not in the place of great men.*

Ver. 7. *For better it is that it be said unto thee, come up hither, than thou shouldst be put lower in the presence of the prince whom thine eyes have seen.*

Impudence is a very disagreeable vice to any man, and it is especially odious to kings, who are jealous of their honour and dignity, and cannot bear those who would intrude into their presence, or push themselves without their own choice, into places of trust or power under them. It is ambition that prompts persons to seek high station, and royal favour; but ambition often disappoints its own designs, by an eager pursuit of them, and by those methods which it uses to accomplish them, and where it expected honour it meets with shame and disgrace. How mortifying must it be to a man who places his chief happiness in the smiles of a king, and those honours which are derived from earthly majesty, to find himself disgraced in the eyes, and by the order of that prince whom his eyes have beheld, and of whose favour he supposed himself secure! Kings, if they are wise, will look with a suspicious eye on those

---

*Isa. 22

who court them for high posts, and will seek out the modest and unassuming to fill every station of importance.

If we consult our interest and duty, we shall be contented with the stations in which the all-wise God is pleased to set us, and rather avoid than covet the place of great men. David was anointed with holy oil, and yet he could appeal to God for the falsehood of the charges that were laid against him, of an aspiring mind, and ambitious attempts to obtain a superior station to that which he occupied *. It is our business to mind the duties of our present station; and, if providence thinks fit to raise us higher, to follow its calls with humility and gratitude.

If it be a sin for us to put forth ourselves in the presence of a prince, what lowliness of mind becomes us in the presence of him, who regards not the prince more than the peasant! A due impression of divine majesty would humble us in the dust, and fill us with wonder at the least smile of God's countenance †.

Our Lord spoke a parable like this proverb of Solomon, and gives a wider extent to the instruction contained in it ‡. It is our duty to entertain such a low opinion of ourselves, as willingly to take a place even below our inferiors, as far as the duties and decencies of our station will permit. None are so likely to meet with disgrace as those that are too fond of honour, like the Pharisees, whom our Lord severely censures for loving the best seats in the synagogues, and the chief rooms at feasts. None have so much honour from God or man, as the meek and humble, whose temper it is, in honour to prefer their neighbours, and to serve them in love, and condescend to men of low degree.

*Ps. 131   †Job 42   ‡Luke 14:7-11

Ver. 8. *Go not forth hastily to strive, lest thou know not what to do in the end thereof, when thy neighbour hath put thee to shame.*

That is a good maxim,—"Do nothing till thou hast well considered the end of it." Many might have prevented shame, and poverty, and destruction, had they duly considered the possible and probable consequences of their words and conduct. Beasts have not the gift of reason and foresight, and therefore mind only present ease and comfort; but rational beings should act with reason, and not incur lasting misery, to gratify a fit of humour, or a transient passion.

If men considered the consequences of every important action before they entered upon it, it would cut off ninety-nine out of an hundred of the law-suits with which the world is pestered. If it be the desire of saving or gaining money that pushes men to go forth to strive with their neighbours at the bar, they should consider, that going to law is little better than fishing with a golden hook. A few fishes may possibly be caught, but something may be lost of more value than many fishes. If men are instigated by their pride to go to law, (and pride is the real cause of many more pleas than covetousness,) they should consider well, whether they are most likely to gain or lose the cause, or, if they gain it, whether the gain will compensate the loss of time, and money, and temper, which are inseparable from law-suits. That sense of honour which leads so many into contention, would keep them out of it, if it were under the regulation of prudence. That pride which plunges men into the gulph of the law, must end in the most galling remorse, when the cause is lost, and shame, instead of honour, is gained by it.

Contention of every kind ought to be avoided by us. Before we venture to gratify our rage by strife and debate, it is necessary for our peace and comfort, to consider with coolness, whether we have reason on our side. Self-love will tell us that we have met with wrong, although no real injury was done, or intended to us; and we cannot expect that the other party, or the judge, (if the matter be referred to a judge,) should have the same bias in our favour with ourselves.

Ver. 9. *Debate thy cause with thy neighbour himself; and discover not a secret to another,*

Ver. 10. *Lest he that heareth it put thee to shame, and thine infamy turn not away.*

If we are forced into debate, the more privately it is managed the better; and therefore, if we think ourselves ill used, our best course is to reason the matter with the offender in the spirit of meekness, to convince him of the wrong he has done to us, and to show him a forgiving spirit, which will be the most effectual means of bringing him to repentance, and to put an end to the difference, if possible, without exposing ourselves or our neighbours to the censure of the world, which will conclude that there are faults on both sides.

If we cannot bring our neighbour to a sense of his fault by this method, our great teacher allows and prescribes other methods of convincing him, which we ought to put in practice only when we are sure that we have met with an offence which will justify our conduct *. In other cases we must keep the matter to ourselves, as the wise man here directs us. When we make complaints of the injustice done us in another manner than our Lord directs us, we will not be believed, and ought not to be believed, till the other party has given in his defence; for he is an unjust judge that passes sentence till both parties are heard. Those who are ever complaining of the injustice of others, may or may not be believed, to the prejudice of those con-

---

*Matt. 18:15-17

cerning whom they may complain; but strong suspicions will most certainly be entertained to their own prejudice, and by their own tongues they bring an indelible reproach upon themselves, as men of a quarrelsome and unforgiving temper.

It is not uncommon for persons, when they are at variance with those that had once been their friends, to take every opportunity, and to use every means, however unfair, to blacken their characters; and if they have been entrusted by them, in the days of intimacy, with any secret, they will divulge it, to gratify their present spleen. This is base conduct, and must fix an everlasting stain on those that make use of such abominable methods to support their own credit and interests. A man that has the least degree of generosity in his nature, would rather suffer blame, or lose a cause, than defend himself by such dirty and dishonourable means; but when a man is reduced to such pitiful shifts, it is a strong presumption that his cause is not good. On the whole, if we would preserve ourselves from lasting disgrace, we must either leave off contention before it be meddled with, or, if that cannot be done, manage it with the weapons proper for a man and a Christian.

Ver. 11. *A word fitly spoken, is like apples of gold in pictures of silver.*

That words may deserve this character, they must be the words of truth; for falsehood and error are on no occasion fit to be spoken. And therefore Job reproves his friends for endeavouring, by false doctrine, to comfort him, and direct his exercise in the time of his distress*.

But words may be true and yet unfitly spoken, for although nothing is to be spoken but truth, yet truth is not always to be spoken. Doeg the Edomite was

---

*Job 21:34, 27:12

guilty of murder before he killed the priests of the Lord, by telling the enraged tyrant that David had received bread and a sword from Ahimelech. Jonathan was a man of a very opposite spirit, and discovered it by the seasonable mention he made to his father of David's exploit in slaying Goliath. By putting Saul in mind of this noble action, he disarmed for a time his angry resentments.

It is necessary to consider, not only what we speak, but likewise the persons to whom we speak, and the time and the place of speaking. Job complains with justice concerning Bildad, that he spoke things to him, which, though certain and important truths, were not at all fit to be spoken to him in his distressed situation. " To whom hast thou uttered words ?" says he. Nabal deserved a severe reproof from Abigail ; but she did not think it proper to speak to him about his foolish conduct towards David, till he awoke from his drunkenness. Paul preached in a very different manner at Jerusalem and Athens, when he was before Agrippa, who believed the prophets, and when he was before Felix, who acknowledged no other rule but the light of nature.

" A word fitly spoken, is like apples of gold, in pictures" (or network) " of silver." The words themselves are like apples of a golden hue. The manner of speaking them is like network of silver, whose elegant apertures give an additional grace to the pleasant fruit that is served up in the salvers of exquisite workmanship and precious metal. By words fitly spoken, the fiercest passions have been allayed, and the strongest enmities dissolved. By such words, wicked men have been checked in their career, fainting souls have been revived, the perplexed have been relieved from their difficulties, and Christians have been often invigorated in their work and warfare. Words fitly spoken unite the pleasant and the profitable, and thereby gain every point that words can gain.

In a time of persecution, some ministers met together to consult what was proper to be done in their situation. All of them wore a dejected countenance, and appeared almost at an equal loss to determine what their duty was in their distressed condition, till one of them observed, that they were all immortal till their work was done. This seasonable hint cleared up every countenance, and they parted with spirits ready to encounter every difficulty.

Ver. 12. *As an ear-ring of gold and an ornament of fine gold, is a wise reprover upon an obedient ear.*

No words have greater need to be fitly spoken, than words of reproof. Few are capable of reproving wisely, and fewer still are able to receive a reproof in a right manner.

Wisdom is necessary in a reprover, to direct him about the time and manner of giving the reproof. Elihu shewed great wisdom and great faithfulness, in performing this difficult office; and when Job had been irritated by the unjust reproofs of his friends, he was silent under the smart reproofs of Elihu; for he charged nothing upon Job, but what had some truth in it, and discovered his friendship for Job, and his good opinion of him, with regard to the general course of his behaviour, at the time that he rebuked him with great severity, for the unjustifiable expressions which came from him, when his mind was fretted with the weight of his troubles, and the injurious reflections of the former speakers.

An ear obedient to reproof, is a very rare thing. It is observed by an eminent divine of the last age, that the professors of religion are generally more stubborn against reproof than fornicators, or common swearers, and that they are ready to fly at the faces of men who reprove them, for those very faults which they daily confess to God. If there was more of the meekness of wisdom discovered in giving reproof, it is probable, that greater meekness and submission might be shewed in receiving it, and yet a due sense of the evil of our faults, and of the necessity of amendment, would make us to value just rebukes even from the mouth of an enemy.

It is a false sense of honour that makes us to fret at reproof; but if we had the same sense of honour with the wise man, we would not judge ourselves on a supposition that we are unblameable, and irreproveable, but reckon it our honour to receive reproof with gratitude, and improve it for the correction of our vices.

Ornaments of gold were worn in ancient days in the ears of people of distinction ; but nothing adorns the ear so much, in the judgment of the inspired philosopher, as the obedient hearing of wise reproof.

It would be a great honour to us to need no reproof, but this is scarcely to be expected in our degenerate race. We ought, therefore, if we have forfeited our credit by falling into sin, to recover it by welcoming needful rebukes, and if others have been overtaken in a fault, to hold them in the same esteem as formerly, when they have given proper evidence of their repentance, by submitting to reproof. By their sin, they have shewed themselves to be men of like frailty with ourselves ; by their obedient hearing of reproof, they have discovered a degree of meekness too rarely to be met with among Christians.

Ver. 13. *As the cold of snow in the time of harvest, so is a faithful messenger to them that send him, for he refresheth the soul of his masters.*

Nothing is more refreshing in the sultry heat of harvest, in those southern climes where the harvest is very early and hot, than the liquors which are mingled with snow, kept from the winter, to cool their drink in the hot season of the year. Equally refreshing to the soul, is the faithful execution of an important message by those that are entrusted with it. It is required of all servants that they be found faithful, and it is required in a special manner of messengers who are employed in distant and important commissions ; and fidelity is the more praiseworthy in them, because they are not under the immediate eye of their masters. Such a messenger was Eliezer to Abraham and Isaac, for he valued the service and interest of his master more than his necessary food, and God blessed him with success, to the great satisfaction of his venerable master, and his son Isaac.

If we are employed in any business for another person, we should make a point of managing it with the same activity as if it were a business of our own ; and whether we are successful or not, we shall give satisfaction to our employer, and receive his thanks, if he is not wholly destitute of the feelings of gratitude. If we are obliged to perform any affairs of consequence by the hands of other men, it will be our wisdom to entrust men of honour and tried fidelity with our affairs ; for he that is faithful in one thing, is likely to be faithful in another thing also, though of much greater consequence *.

Ministers of the gospel are messengers of Christ, for the benefit of the churches. If they are faithful, they are accepted of Christ and useful to men †.

Ver. 14. *Whoso boasteth himself of a false gift, is like clouds and wind without rain.*

Covetousness is so much detested in the world, that the persons who are guilty of this vice are ashamed of it, and desire to be esteemed liberal ; and therefore, if

---

*Luke 16:10   †Rev. 2:3, 1 Tim. 4:16

they have ever been able to master their disposition so far as to perform one generous action in the course of their life, they will boast of it as long as they live, and think themselves ill used if they are not honoured by other men with the character of being generous persons. But it is moreover very usual for them, to talk of charities which they never bestowed, and thus they add vice to vice. Their arrogance and dissimulation, added to their stinginess, makes them doubly detestable. They are like clouds carried about with the wind, that seem to be full of rain when there is not a drop for the refreshment of the weary earth.

Those that are large and ready in promising, but are never ready to perform, are likewise like clouds without water. When you ask any favour from them, they give you great reason, by their frankness and professions, to believe that they will serve you, but when they are called on for performance, some unlucky accident has come in their way, and they can do nothing for you at present. They will only give you new promises, which you may believe if you can, and they will be sure to perform them as well as the former ones. It is shameful to behave in this manner, raising expectations and then disappointing them, and perhaps reducing to great straits and perplexities the very men that were trusting to their friendship.

The apostles Peter and Jude speak of a set of men that may be compared to clouds without rain, because of their religious professions and promises. These are false teachers, who make large boasts of their knowledge in the mystery of the gospel, and promise liberty to men that will receive their doctrines, whilst they themselves are ignorant of all sound principles, and in bondage to corruption. No kind of corrupt teachers in our times answer this description so much as those of the church of Rome, who pretend to make a mono-

poly of heaven for those of their own church, and who
sell, for small pieces of money, the most wonderful promises, all which will be found by their deluded votaries to vanish into smoke when the performance is expected.

Ver. 15. *By long forbearing is a prince persuaded,
and a soft tongue breaketh the bone.*

A prince is not easily pacified when he reckons his
dignity despised, and his authority trampled under
foot. He is little used to contradiction, and therefore
has small experience of those situations in which forbearance is to be exercised. Yet strong as the passions
of princes generally are, such is the power of patience
and meekness, that those virtues allay their stormy passions, and a soft answer softens their hearts, although
they were as hard as their bones. Saul was so fierce
in his rage against David, that in spite to him, he slew
eighty-five priests of the Lord, and yet David melted
his heart unto softness by his generous behaviour, and
his calm defence of his own innocency. The tyrant
felt a temporary change in his temper, and said, " Is this
thy voice, my son David, return, for I will no more do
thee hurt."

If meekness and gentleness have such a powerful influence upon princes; if they can break hearts of stone,
how great must be their influence upon private men,
and persons of moderate passions?

It is certainly a piece of great folly if we will
not make use of these harmless weapons to end debates, when they are the most effectual means for that
en d.

But are there not some men that will not be wrought
upon by such means? Yes: But they are savage brutes,
and not rational creatures. Their hearts are made of
something harder than adamant; and they are objects
of our pity, because they are cursed with such unre-

lenting hearts that they cannot possibly taste any of those social pleasures that sweeten the life of man. Nothing can subdue the fierceness of their spirits but that grace which turns the flint into a pool of water *.

Ver. 16. *Hast thou found honey ? eat so much as is sufficient for thee, lest thou be filled therewith and vomit it.*

The God who has replenished the earth with his goodness, has not required us to lead a niggardly and uncomfortable life. He allows us to eat as much honey, and to enjoy as much of every earthly comfort as is sufficient for us, to strengthen our bodies, and to refresh our spirits ; all that he forbids is that excess in eating and drinking, and other animal enjoyments, which would enfeeble our frame, clog our souls, and end in bitterness.

Although we are allowed to eat as much honey as is sufficient, we must not eat what would suffice to satiate a ravenous appetite. Reason, and not appetite, must direct us when we have enough, otherwise there would be no such sin as intemperance in the world. Nature itself makes us to feel the bad effects of immoderate indulgence, which overloads the stomach, and turns the sweetest things into bitterness, so that no ease can be obtained till they are thrown off.

It is represented in the book of Jude as a great sin to eat without fear. When we are at a well covered table, there are more guests present than such as are invited, for the devil comes to graft some temptation upon the dishes which are served up, and very often he finds an opportunity of getting some iniquity to pass down the throat along with the meat or drink that is used. We are to remember at all times our chief end ; and it is explained by the Apostle in these words, " Whether, therefore, ye eat or drink, or whatsoever ye do, do all to the glory of God." From God we re-

---

*Chap. 15:1

ceived our food, and it is a very wicked thing in men to use it as a weapon of rebellion against him, by making a god of our bellies.

Nothing earthly must be suffered to engross our affections, so as to sensualize our souls, and alienate our minds from spiritual objects. The time of our connexion with the world is short, let us therefore rejoice as though we rejoiced not, and use this world as not abusing it, for the fashion of this world passeth away.

Ver. 17. *Withdraw thy foot from thy neighbour's house; lest he be weary of thee, and so hate thee.*

We must not indulge ourselves without restraint in any of the pleasures of life, however delightful. Honey is not so sweet to the taste, as the intercourses of friendship, amongst those that have a cordial love to one another, are to the heart. But as we must eat only so much honey as is sufficient for us, so we must use a prudent caution in our familiarities with our most affectionate friends. Although their houses are a home to us, yet we must not be frequenting them at every hour, nor continue in them till our company become wearisome. It is highly proper for us to visit our friends, and preserve by that means our mutual friendship, and enjoy the sweets of it; but it is very improper to teaze a friend by too frequent visits, which may have the unhappy effect of dissolving the closest intimacy, by creating disgust where love in former times took place. Our friends have their business to mind, and their time is valuable to them; and friendship is bought too dear by him that ceases to be master of his own time, and may be called off the most necessary employment to receive a visitant. Besides, we ought to consider the circumstances of our friends, and take care not to load them by our visits with expence which they may be unable or unwilling to bear. The freedom of friendship does not consist in a liberty to teaze one another, but in a liberty to contribute to one another's happiness and comfort, beyond what strangers can presume to use.

How different are the pleasures of earthly friendships from those which are vouchsafed to Christians in their admission to fellowship with God ! The oftener we visit the best of all friends, we are the more welcome, and the more we frequent his house to partake of the provisions of it, he is the better pleased with our conduct *.

Ver. 18. *A man that beareth false witness against his neighbour is a maul, and a sword, and a sharp arrow.*

This proverb is sufficient to strike an alarm into all evil speakers, that spread scandal against their neighbours, merely because they have nothing else to do, or because they have some little quarrel with them. Consider, ye that deal in such conversation, whether you could think of treating the objects of your defamatory discourse as Jael did Sisera, or as Joab treated Abner. Would you shrink with horror at the thought of beating out your neighbour's brains with a hammer, or of piercing his bowels with a sword, or a sharp arrow? Why then do you indulge yourselves in a piece of the like barbarity, destroying, as far as you can, that reputation which is dear to men as their life, and wounding all their best interests by mangling their character † ?

It is a happy thing to be free from this terrible mischief of a virulent tongue. We should therefore live unblameably, that we may take away all occasion from those that would reproach us. And yet the purest innocency will not be a sure protection to us from the tongue that speaketh evil. We must commit the care of our good name, as well as all our other interests, to the Lord, and he will preserve us from the scourge of the tongue, or from all the evil effects of it ‡.

---

*Song 5:1   †Chap. 19:5,9   ‡Job 5:23

Ver. 19. *Confidence in an unfaithful man in time of trouble is like a broken tooth, and a foot out of joint.*

A broken tooth, and a foot out of joint, are not only useless for their respective offices, but the causes of great pain and uneasiness. In like manner, a friend that does not shew kindness in the day of distress, is not only an useless friend, but likewise causes many painful feelings in those who trusted to his kindness. The supposed infidelity of Job's friends produced great bitterness of spirit in that venerable sufferer, and added greatly to that load of distress which lay upon his body and spirit; and he compares them to the brooks of Tema, which abounded with snow in the winter, but had no water in them for the thirsty traveller in the sultry heat of summer.

Let us be faithful in our friendships, as well as in the duties of every other relation. Insincerity and inconstancy in friendship is immoral and impious; as the forementioned sufferer observes, " To him that is afflicted pity should be shewed by his friend, but he forsaketh the fear of the Almighty *."

In the times of our distress, we have reason to expect sympathy from our friends, but we must not be too sanguine in our hopes; they may prove unable to help us, or unfaithful, or some temporary alienation may estrange them from us, or God for our chastisement or trial may bereave us of the comforts of their friendship, or trouble may fret our spirits, and make us to think that they are become cold to us, when they shew us all that friendship which ought to be expected from frail creatures like ourselves.

When we lament the treachery or insincerity of our friends, we should remember that David, and Christ himself, felt all the bitterness of this calamity. One of

---

*Job 6:14

our Lord's disciples betrayed him, and his most affectionate, and highly favoured friend forsook him. In many cases of this kind we have greater reason to complain of ourselves than of our false friends; for had we chosen our friends more wisely, and fixed our regard to them upon the ground of piety, we would not have found so much reason to complain of violated professions.

Ver. 20. *As he that taketh away a garment in cold weather, and as vinegar upon nitre; so is he that singeth songs to an heavy heart.*

He that takes away a garment in cold weather, leaves the person whom he robs of it to starve, and perhaps to perish. Vinegar poured upon nitre deprives it of all its virtue and usefulness; so he that tries to charm away deep-rooted sorrows by the help of music, does only sink the person whom he designs to cheer into a deeper melancholy. It is to be confessed that sorrows of a slight kind may be diverted and soothed by the charms of music, as the spirit of Elisha was composed for prophesying by a minstrel. But when the heart is laden with grief, it is exasperated and not revived by unseasonable and ill-directed endeavours to dispel the sorrow which feeds upon it. Mirth and gaiety, and the sprightly airs of vocal and instrumental music deaden the spirit, as vinegar does nitre, and are just as ineffectual to restore gladness, as the taking away of clothes in cold weather is to restore heat.

Is any man afflicted? let him pray. Does any man wish to administer comfort to the afflicted soul? let him weep, and not laugh, with those that weep. Is the heart oppressed with anguish, or the conscience laden with guilt? let the Scripture, and not instruments of music, be applied for relief. The music of David's harp may indeed be still used for driving away the evil spirit. His psalms are full of strong consolations, and we shall never sink into despondency whilst we muse on the precious and reviving truths which he presents to our consideration, and endeavour to walk in the steps of his faith.

It is doubtless our duty to administer comfort to the mourners, but we must take heed to use those means which are proper to the end, that we may not deserve that reproof which Job, with great justice, gave his friends, "Miserable comforters are ye all."

Ver. 21. *If thine enemy be hungry, give him bread to eat ; and if he be thirsty, give him water to drink.*

This precept is grievous to flesh and blood. We are disposed by our pride and rage to inflict a severe revenge, not only on our enemies, but even on our offending friends. To do to them as they have done to us is not reckoned sufficient, but sevenfold vengeance must be rendered into their bosom. A stab at the heart has been often returned by the modern men of honour for a rude expression.

But we that are Christians have not so learned Christ. Enmity against God is infinitely worse than enmity against us, and yet God spares his enemies, and does them good from heaven, giving them rain and fruitful seasons. We ourselves were sometimes alienated from God, and enemies in our mind by wicked works, and if we had been recompensed according to our works, we had now been in the lake of fire and brimstone ; but God who is rich in mercy, sent his Son to accomplish our redemption from ruin. By Christ, we that were guilty of horrid enmity against God have received the atonement. We are reconciled to God, and blessed with every spiritual blessing in Christ; and shall we now think that God lays an unreasonable command upon us, when he requires us to be charitable and kind to our enemies, and not to return railing for railing, but courtesies for injuries ?

It is easy for us to say that we forgive our enemies; but do we make it evident in our works that we forgive them in love? We may bring our minds without very great difficulty to overlook their injuries, and to bury them in silence; but a sullen disdain of injuries is no Christian grace. Our duty is to wish real happiness to our enemies in this world and the next, and to shew the truth of our love in praying for them, and in doing them good as opportunity presents, and their needs require. It was so habitual to the good Archbishop Cranmer to shew kindness to those that had wronged him, that it became a proverb: "If any man would have a good turn from the archbishop, let him do him an injury." But will not behaviour of this kind lay a man open to injuries? No.

Ver. 22. *For thou shalt heap coals of fire upon his head, and the Lord shall reward thee.*

It is said to be a custom to this day among the Arabians, to cure some diseases, by the application of burning coals to the head. The disease of rancour and spite will certainly be healed, for the most part, by those coals of love that Solomon here directs us to heap upon the heads of our enemies. As the hard metals are softened and melted by the fire, so the hard and stubborn spirit is softened and melted by the solid expressions of charity and meekness. He is a wild beast of the most untameable kind, that feels no shame for his own conduct, nor any warm emotions of gratitude to him whom he has offended, when he sees him returning good for evil. No enmity is stronger than the enmity of man's heart to God, and God makes use of his own kindness to subdue it; and we are to be followers of God as dear children, and try the like experiment upon our own enemies, as far as the infinite difference of persons and circumstances will admit the resemblance; and if our enemies are warmed into friends, have we not gained a nobler victory, by gaining our brother, than if we had humbled them to the dust? The pleasantest and noblest of victories is to overcome evil with good *.

But perhaps we shall be losers by kindness to our enemies? Who knows but their hearts may be untameably savage, and then our bread and water is thrown away upon them? Let them be what they will, it is not thrown away. If they persist to return evil for good, the Lord shall graciously reward thee. The Lord loves mercy and goodness, and there are no instances of it that he loves better, and rewards more bountifully, than those by which we most resemble himself, and cross our selfish and haughty spirits. David preserved the life of a railing Shimei from the rage of Abishai, as he had formerly done the life of a persecuting tyrant. The good man hoped that God would return him good for the evil that his enemies did to him, when he shewed kindness to them, and his hopes were not disappointed.

Ver. 23. *The north wind driveth away rain, so doth an angry countenance a backbiting tongue.*

Fair weather cometh out of the north, says Elihu †. This text probably induced our translators to render the verse before us in the manner they have done; for the original word, which stands for driveth away, more properly signifies, to produce, but the north wind may have different effects in different countries, and even in the same country at different times. But whether we follow the translation in the text, or that in the margin, it will give us very useful instruction.

It is a great encouragement to tale-bearers, to observe that their wicked stories are heard with attention. If a man looks upon them with a cheerful countenance, and listens to their tales, and makes them welcome to

---

*Rom. 12:21   †Job 37

704 / *Exposition of Proverbs*

his table, they naturally conclude that the person to whom they speak has as bad a heart as themselves, and they will not fail to bring him new stories of the like kind, as soon as they have got an opportunity to learn or to make them.   But if the receiver of stolen goods is a sharer with the thief in his guilt, and if any man that encourages another in evil partakes in his sin, then he that hears the backbiter with complacency is little better than himself, and would probably follow the same trade if he had the same talents for it. We cannot, therefore, clear ourselves from the sin of backbiting, unless we refuse to receive a bad report of our neighbour, and testify our displeasure, by all proper methods, at the base conduct of the assassins that would murder in the dark the good-name of their fellow-creatures.   When the murderers of Isbosheth brought their master's head to David, judging from their own disposition that it would be an acceptable present to him, he treated them in such a manner that no man ever sent another present of the like kind to him.   And if we gave proper evidence to those who expect to entertain us by ill-natured stories, that we have no relish for them, they would not trouble us a second time.   Anger is a bad passion, as it is commonly exerted, but we may be angry and not sin, and in this case, we sin if we do not put on an angry countenance.

But as the north wind, not only drives away rain in some places, but likewise brings it in other places, or at other times in the same place, so an angry countenance brings a backbiting tongue.   He that meets with insolent and surly treatment, may conceal his sense of the injury, from the person that uses him in this manner, because he thinks it more prudent to stifle his displeasure ; but he will be tempted to take revenge by speaking evil of him in his absence, for nothing is commonly more irritating, or sticks more deeply in the heart, than angry and imperious treatment, and no injury is harder to be borne with patience.

If other men speak evil of us, we should examine our own conduct impartially, that we may know whether we have not given them some provocation. If we have, we should look upon ourselves to be the more criminal persons ; as Judah acknowledged that Tamar was more righteous than himself, becasue his own behaviour had tempted her to the sin, for which he thought she deserved to be burnt. Other people have at least as good a right to talk against our ill conduct, as we have to give them occasion for it.

Let us neither speak evil of men, nor countenance evil speakers, nor give any man occasion to speak evil of us, nor burst into rage, when they have treated us in this manner, but in all things follow meekness, righteousness, charity, and the example of Christ.

Ver. 24. *It is better to dwell in a corner of the house top, than with a brawling woman, and in a wide house.*

Solomon put this proverb into his own edition of the proverbs, but the men of Hezekiah finding it likewise in those papers from which they extracted this appendix, inserted it here likewise. They justly considered it as an useful admonition to women, and to men that have wives to choose, and wished it not to be forgotten.

Ver. 25. *As cold waters to a thirsty soul, so is good news from a far country.*

Nothing is more the object of desire in a hot country, than cold water when men are thirsty ; and nothing is more agreeable than to hear glad tidings from a distant country. Good news are always agreeable, but good news from a far country are most agreeable of any good news, because they have been the subject of tedious and anxious thoughts, and because they generally respect some object of importance. Solomon had experience of this fact, when he sent his ships on voyages that lasted three years, and when he had affairs of importance to be transacted in other kingdoms.

We that move in the lower sphere of life have little concern with foreign countries, but if we have the generous spirit of Christians, it must give us great pleasure to hear of any thing that tends to the happiness of other nations, or the advancement of the Redeemer's kingdom among men. We daily pray that the kingdom of Christ may come, and it would certainly give us much joy to hear of any event whereby our prayers are fulfilled. Let us in the mean time rejoice at the good tidings brought to us from far countries by the prophets of God, who tell us of things that they have heard from the uttermost parts of the earth, even glory to the righteous.

Heaven is the better country from whence we have heard tidings that will for ever gladden our hearts, and fill our mouths with praise. Messengers from that blessed region have been sent to our earth with glad tidings of great joy to all the people of God, and to every Gentile nation, that to us is born a Saviour, and that he is now gone to his native heaven; and will appear again on earth to our complete salvation *.

Ver 26. *A righteous man falling down before the wicked is as a troubled fountain, and a corrupt spring.*

A righteous man falls down before the wicked when he is oppressed and cannot obtain justice, but is obliged to submit to injury and violence. When such injustice prevails in a country, every thing is in a state of disorder. The fountain of justice is poisoned; the public administration, instead of being a public blessing, is a general curse; and those who should be the

---

*Luke 2, Acts 1

fathers and guardians of the poor, are worse than
street robbers, for they not only pillage them of their
property, but grind their faces, and pull of their skins
and pick their bones *.

He that poisons a public fountain, deserves a thousand deaths; and those by whose mismanagement the
fountains of justice are corrupted, must be equally criminal in the sight of God. He is an enemy not to
men only, but to God, by giving encouragement to
wickedness, and suppressing goodness, and perverting
an ordinance of God into an engine for serving the
designs of Satan.

Those righteous men that fall before the wicked,
must take care that they fall not into sin, for they are
strongly tempted to it by their unhappy circumstances.
When wicked men drive the righteous into sin, the
fountains become corrupt, in another and worse sense
than that now mentioned; for those who are like
springs of water for the refreshment of their neighbours becoming polluted and loathsome, are a means
of perverting and poisoning those that are too much
disposed to judge of religion and duty from the behaviour of religious persons.

When the righteous persist under temptation in
duty, they have rich sources of comfort in the promises
of God, and the doctrine of a future judgment †.

Ver. 27. *It is not good to eat much honey; so for men
to search their own glory, is not glory;* (but a piece
of base conduct.)

Men may eat some honey, so likewise men are warranted to pay due regard to their own honour. If there
be any praise, Paul recommends it to us to think on it,
and our Lord enjoins us to make our light to shine before men, that they may glorify our Father who is in
heaven.

---

*Micah 2   †Ps. 12, Ezek. 34:17-23

708 / *Exposition of Proverbs*

But it is a loathsome thing to the stomach to eat much honey, and it is a loathsome thing for a man to be anxious about his honour, and to fish for praise, as too many do, who use a variety of methods to obtain the applause of men; sometimes putting on all the external appearances of humility with that view, and saying things of themselves which would inspire them with fury if they were said by another person, or believed by that very person to whom they are spoken.

We must value our own reputation because it enables us to be useful to men, and to glorify God; but when we indulge an unbridled desire after glory from men, we forget our chief end, we disqualify ourselves for the most important duties, we expose ourselves to the worst temptations; and if our fortune were equal to that of Cæsar, our ambition might draw us to equal in crimes that enemy of Cato, and cut-throat of mankind.

The humble are sensible that they deserve shame rather than glory, and would be content that all their glory were taken from them, that it might be ascribed unto God to whom it truly belongs. The vain and proud would rob God Almighty of his crown, that they might set it upon their own heads. But God will not suffer them to escape without a punishment suited to their crime. When Herod was affecting the honours of a god, he perished by a viler death than if he had died in a ditch *.

Ver. 28. *He that hath no rule over his own spirit is like a city that is broken down, and without walls.*

It is necessary for our happiness and peace, that we should have the government of our own spirits. He that possesses not himself possesses nothing, although he should possess all other things. As a city that is broken

---

*1 Cor. 15:11, Acts 12:24

down, and without walls, is exposed to the invasion of every enemy ; so the man who has not a mastery over his own desires and affections, is a ready prey to every devil, and his imagination is tainted, his corrupt desires are inflamed, and his active powers hurried into the most criminal excesses by every slight temptation. A city in flames, or a ship seized by a drunken and mutinous crew, are not so terrible spectacles as a soul where the judgment and reason are laid desolate by intemperate passions and appetites. What mischiefs have been wrought, and what oceans of blood have been poured out by the passion of anger alone, when it was unrestrained by the principle of conscience ? When Simeon and Levi heard the dying blessings of their father upon the rest of his sons, and the severe censures that he passed upon themselves, what remorse must have torn their hearts at the thought of that fatal day when in their cruel fury they slew so many men, and destroyed the city of Shechem.

Let us hold in with a strong and steady hand our disorderly passions, otherwise they will make us wild beasts, of a more furious kind than wolves and leopards ; because our rational powers will be forced into their service, and tend to no other purpose, but to make us more fell and destructive enemies of mankind. No leopards or lions ever destroyed men or beasts in such multitudes as those tyrants have done, who were slaves to their own love of glory and vindictive spirits.

It is a happy thing when the body is subject to the mind, and the mind deeply penetrated with an habitual sense of the authority of God. That we may be placed in this delightful state, we must give up ourselves to the Lord, and pray for the accomplishment of these promises, " I will put my spirit within you, and I will cause you to walk in my statutes :" " The wolf shall dwell with the lamb, and the leopard shall lie down with the kid."

Proverbs 26

Ver. 1. *As snow in summer, and as rain in harvest, so honour is not seemly for a fool.*

Snow in summer and rain in harvest are unseasonable, disagreeable, and sometimes very hurtful. In like manner, honours bestowed on foolish and wicked persons sit very ungracefully on them, and enable them often to prove hurtful to their inferiors. When Haman was raised to high station, he soon became hurtful to all men by his pride; and if providence had not baffled his designs, he would have ruined a whole nation of innocent men, and banished true religion out of the world.

This proverb contains a very important instruction to those who have the disposal of offices and honours in their hand. By advancing unworthy persons to stations of influence in church or state; they may render themselves deeply accountable for the follies and crimes of other men. One of the Caliphs of Babylon, was so sensible of this, that he voluntarily resigned his authority, and refused to choose his successor, that he might not be accountable for his conduct.

Most men are fond of honour and preferment, as if happiness were inseparably connected with it; but few are sensible how difficult it is to wear honours with a becoming dignity, and how much better the providence of God has chosen their situation than they could have chosen it for themselves. Great numbers of those princes who make a despicable or hateful figure in history, might have become a private station very well, and left the world lamented by all their acquaintances.

It belongs to God to determine our station in life, and to us to believe that he has determined it in his wisdom and goodness, and to fulfil the duties of it without aspiring to those honours that God has not been pleased to bestow upon us.

Those that are in stations of honour ought not to trust for honour to their stations, but to seek it by wisdom, without which, their exalted situation will only render their disgrace more visible. The infamous names of Pilate and Tiberius, and Caiaphas, might have been buried with those of the meanest instruments of their iniquities, if they had not, to their great unhappiness, filled high stations whilst they lived.

Ver. 2. *As the bird by wandering, as the swallow by flying, so the curse causeless shall not come.*

When you see a bird wandering about, or a swallow flying hither and thither, you are not afraid of any hurt from them. They will not touch you, but fly back to their nests. You have no more reason to be afraid of hurt from unmerited curses, whoever the persons are that pronounce them. They are but harmless lightenings, that will not blast you; they will fly back to the place from which they came, and light with dreadful vengeance on the heads of those who profaned their Maker's name, and gave scope to their own malice in uttering them; for as they delight in cursing, they shall have cursing for their portion, and unless the pardoning mercy of God prevent, their curses will enter into them like water, and like oil into their bones.

Groundless fears are real torments, for no passion is more distressing than fear; whether it has a just cause or not, its present effect is the same, and therefore God in mercy has given us antidotes against every needless and unprofitable kind of fear. The curses which bad men sometimes pour forth from their vindictive spirits, have such a dreadful sound, that they strike an impression of horror into the tender spirits of the innocent and conscientious, although they know they have not deserved them ; but if our consciences do not condemn us, we need not be afraid of the blasphemous imprecations of the wicked, although they were expressed in the coarsest language of hell. The curses of a conclave of cardinals, or the excommunications of an assembly of divines, could do no prejudice to one whom his own heart does not reproach. They may open their mouths wide, and speak great swelling words of terror, but their arm is short, and God has not entrusted them with his thunderbolts. Their curses, instead of being prejudicial, will be very useful to us, if we are wise enough to imitate the conduct of David, whose meekness was approved, his prayers kindled into a flame of desires, and his hopes invigorated by them *.

But we have just reason to fear the curse that is not causeless. Although persons when they meet with ill usage, are not warranted to wish a curse upon those that wrong them, yet the curses that are extorted by anguish from their spirits, will not fall to the ground †.

The most just curse in the world is the curse of God, that lies upon all the children of disobedience ; and we cannot escape the execution of it, but through Christ who was made a curse in our stead ‡.

Ver. 3. *A whip for the horse, a bridle for the ass, and a rod for the fool's back.*

A fool is more brutish than the horse or the ass ; for the horse, as well as the ox knoweth his owner, and the ass his master's crib, but foolish sinners are insensible of the obligations they are under, both to God and man. The horse needs the lash to chastise it when it is unruly, and to urge its speed when it is dull. The

---

*2 Sam. 16:10-12, Ps. 109:28   †Exod. 22:27   ‡Gal. 3:10,13

ass, when it was used for riding, needed the bridle to govern its course (or the spur to push it on its way, *Sept.*) The rod is equally needful for the fool's back. Are you the unhappy fathers of foolish children? you must make use of the rod and reproof to give them wisdom. Are you authorized to bear rule in the church? the rod of church discipline must be applied to offenders, that they may be reclaimed, and others warned. Are you magistrates? the rod which God has put into your hands may be a means of preserving young malefactors from the gibbet at a more advanced period of life. Are you wise? beware of turning aside unto folly, that you may never need the rod. Are you fools? learn wisdom, or do not blame those whom duty and charity will oblige to use the rod for your correction. Is it not better that you should be treated by your superiors with love, and in the spirit of meekness, than to be beaten with the rod *? Are you obliged, for your faults, to undergo the pains of church censure, or criminal law? Kiss the rod, and sin no more, lest a worse thing come unto you. Have you formerly endured the rod? Let the impressions and effects of it abide with you for life, lest the sword of divine vengeance be unsheathed against you, because you refused to hear the voice of the rod and him that hath appointed it†.

Ver. 4. *Answer not a fool according to his folly, lest thou also be like unto him.*

There are many cases in which a fool is to be heard, and not answered at all. When a scorner reviles us, it is needless to reprove him for it; for he is a dog, and the best way you can deal with him, is to let him bark till he ceases of his own accord: if you cast a stone at him, he will only follow you the longer and bark the

---

*1 Cor. 4:21   †Prov. 29:1

more furiously. When Rabshakeh railed at Hezekiah, and blasphemed the God of Israel, the servants of Hezekiah were expressly forbidden by their master to answer him a word, for he knew that an answer would only produce some blasphemous reply. Our Lord himself often kept silence when impertinent questions were asked at him. He was well acquainted with all the secrets of wisdom, and, if he had spoken, his words would have been the fittest that could be spoken in these cases ; but silence was, in his infallible judgment, fitter than any answer that his perfect wisdom could make.

But must this be a rule for us in every case? Should not the multitude of words be answered, and when the fool mocks shall no man make him ashamed? In many cases it is very fit that a fool's words should be answered, only you must take care in answering not to imitate him. If he speaks unreasonable, profane, peevish, or passionate words, you must not answer him in his own style. You are angry at him for his folly, and reprove him for the extravagance of his behaviour, and therefore you cannot but confess that yourselves are worthy of a very sharp reproof, if you behave like him at the very time that you are testifying your displeasure at his conduct. You cannot allege that his passionate manner of speaking and acting will justify you in behaving passionately ; for if one fire kindled from hell burns so fiercely, and threatens to devour every thing that comes in its way, why should another fire be lighted from it to do still greater mischief? It becomes not the followers of Jesus to return railing for railing, or one angry reflection for another, but in whatever manner others talk, our tongues ought still to be governed by the law of meekness and charity.

There are no cases in which this rule is more frequently transgressed than in religious disputes. Passion and railing, when they are employed in the support of truth, appear to many to be just expressions of Christian zeal; and that noble and necessary grace of the spirit has been brought into suspicion, and regarded with a very jealous eye, by reason of those who have substituted ill nature in its place, and called it by a name to which it is as well entitled as the prince of darkness is to be called an angel of light. The scripture enjoins ministers to instruct opposers in meekness *. It declares expressly that the wrath of man worketh not the righteousness of God; and it informs us that Michael, that great prince among the heavenly hosts, durst not bring a railing accusation against Satan †.

Ver. 5. *Answer a fool according to his folly, lest he be wise in his own conceit.*

When we answer a fool, we must give him the answer which his folly deserves and requires. If you do not answer him at all, other men may believe that he is in the right, and where there is any danger of that, the edification of your neighbours calls upon you to shew the folly of what he has said. Besides, if he is not answered, he will conclude that you cannot answer him, and his vanity and self-conceit will be increased by your silence. When Job's friends were all silenced in the course of their dispute with him, the next speech which the good man delivered is called a parable, or commanding speech ‡; for he spoke like one that had gained the victory, and claimed a right to be believed in what he said. And the fool when he is not answered, will conclude more naturally than such a man as Job, that his cause is good; for although prudence bind up your tongue from speaking in the ears of a fool, yet there is no man that reckons himself less a fool than he, or

*2 Tim. 2:26, Gal. 6:1   †Jude   ‡Job 27:1

has less conception of a man's holding his peace, when he is not baffled in argument.

It will be doing a good piece of service to the world, and to the fool himself, if you can answer him according to his folly, so as to humble his vanity, and make him ashamed of himself. Our Lord triumphed by his wisdom over his insolent enemies. When they blamed him for curing distressed persons on the Sabbath day, he exposed their self-inconsistency and inhumanity, to the conviction of the people, and their own shame. When Pilate insolently pretended to a sovereign power of life and death, and thereby entrenched on the prerogatives of the God of heaven, our Lord (who did not open his mouth, because he knew it was to no purpose, to vindicate his own injured character,) gave his assuming judge an answer which reminded him that he was but a man.

Let us seek wisdom from God, that we may know when we should speak, and when we should be silent; and that we may be preserved from speaking such things as are improper for the mouths of saints, and taught to give an answer with meekness and prudence to the words of wise men or fools, as occasion requires.

Ver. 6. *He that sendeth a message by the hands of a fool, cutteth off the feet, and drinketh damage.*

It would be very ridiculous in a man when he sends a servant on an errand, to cut off his feet, and disable him from doing that business in which he was employing him. It is equally foolish to employ an unwise or unfaithful man in a business of importance; for he is like a man whose feet are cut off, for any good he can be expected to do, and his employer not only meets with damage in his affairs, but he drinketh damage in great abundance, losing his reputation for sense, and suffering great loss in his important interests.

This proverb, like many others of them that were copied out by Hezekiah's men, is instructive chiefly to

princes and other great men; but it is not without its
use to us also in the management of our less important
concerns, which we ought for our credit and comfort to
manage with prudence; and one great branch of prudence, consists in employing those to assist us in any
affair, who will discharge that trust like wise and honest
men.   Have we a vote in the election of the legislative
body? We are accountable for the use we make of it.
If we choose for our representative, one that is likely to
betray the interests of the nation, for serving his private
interest, or the purposes of a faction, we concur, in his
person, in all the public mischief that he does.   Do we
choose a minister to take the oversight of our souls?
We must beware of fixing our choice upon an ignorant,
or erroneous, or graceless man, otherwise we cut out
the tongue, (to use Solomon's style,) and bring great
damage, for ought we know, not only upon our own
souls, but upon the souls of thousands of our fellow
men.

Ver. 7. *The legs of the lame are not equal; so is a parable in the mouth of fools.*

A lame man is very untowardsome in his manner of
walking.   But a fool appears with a still worse grace
when he presumes to talk of subjects beyond his reach,
or to speak in praise of those virtues to which he is a
total stranger in his practice. A clown would be laughed at, if he were to talk about Greek and Hebrew, and
navigation, and court breeding; but it would fill a person with indignation, to hear a thief speak in praise of
justice, a drunkard commend temperance, or a hypocrite
talk in praise of the uprightness of David. Our tongues
and our lives must be of a piece, otherwise all our professions will serve no other purpose but to condemn
ourselves, and to procure us a portion in the other world
with hypocrites.   A grave and wise sentence becomes
the mouth of a wise and holy man.   It is very unbe-

coming in a Christian to be silent on occasions when he is called to glorify God or edify men, and it is still more unbecoming in a saint, to allow himself on any occasion in foolish and vain talking; but when open sinners profane the scripture and religion, by their unhallowed mouths, they are like an ass dressing himself in a lion's skin, or a devil transforming himself into an angel of light.

There must be a conformity between every part of our character and conduct, if we wish to be upright in the way of the Lord, and like Caleb and Joshua to follow the Lord fully. No man in this world is perfect in wisdom and goodness, but an uniformity of conduct in the general course of life is attainable. Although we cannot all run in the way of God's commandments, or mount up with wings as eagles, yet we may walk on with an even course in the way of holiness, shewing an equal respect to those precepts which regard our speech, and to those which regulate our heart and conversation. God denounces vengeance upon those hypocrites that take his covenant into their mouths, whilst they join with the wicked in their sinful courses ; but to him that ordereth his conversation aright, he promises to shew the salvation of God *.

Ver. 8. *As he that bindeth a stone in a sling, so is he that giveth honour to a fool.*

Honour is not seemly for a fool, and he that gives him honour is himself a fool, for he acts like one that means to sling a stone at some mark, and yet binds it up in the sling that it cannot get away from it. He disappoints his own intentions by taking the most absurd means in the world to accomplish them. When we give our applause to foolish persons, expecting their favour, or hoping that our praise will induce them to

---

*Ps. 50:16-23

respect their own honour in their manner of conduct, we only make them more self-sufficient and domineering, and swell that pride in their hearts which makes them insufferable to all about them. If those that have the disposal of high offices bestow them upon undeserving men, they are only preparing disgrace and repentance for themselves; as king Ahasuerus found to his great vexation, when he was deceived so far by that wicked minister whom he had foolishly advanced, that he ignorantly signed a death-warrant for his much loved queen and her whole nation. Men cannot search the hearts of their fellow-creatures, and if they are the means of advancing some to public offices who disappoint the hopes that were entertained of them, they cannot help it. But we can form some probable opinions of the dispositions of men from their behaviour, and ought to do so, before we take any share in placing them in those stations where they are likely to do much good or much hurt. Besides, we should pray to the Searcher of hearts to direct our judgments on all such occasions, as we find the disciples did in the choice of an apostle. Without consideration and prayer, we run a great risk of sharing in other men's sins, when we contribute to the elevation of men to places, where, if they be fools, they will find great scope for their folly.

But does not God himself often give honour to fools? Yes. But who art thou, O man, that settest thy heart like the heart of God? God is the absolute sovereign of the world, and is not bound to give an account of any of his matters. He is the judge of nations, who has a right to punish men by subjecting them to the power of fools. He is the infinitely wise God, who brings good out of evil. We must be holy, as God is holy; but we must not pretend to claim the prerogatives of sovereignty, because God is the sovereign of the world. Our business is to acquiesce in the disposals of God, to adore where we cannot comprehend him, and to regu‧late our conduct not by his secret, but his revealed will; and we are thereby taught that bad men ought to be despised in our eyes, and that we must honour them that fear the Lord *.

Ver. 9. *As a thorn goeth up into the hand of a drunk‧ard, so is a parable in the mouth of fools.*

Wise and holy sayings, especially on deep and mys‧terious subjects, are not only improper for the mouth of fools, but often hurtful to themselves and others. They are like thorns, or sharp-pointed weapons in the hands of drunkards, which wound the hands that hold them, and may be used to wound others that happen to be in company with them.

Proverbs have sometimes been hurtful even in the mouths of wise men, through the imperfection of their wisdom. Job's friends dealt much in parables, which they had learned by tradition from their wise ancestors, but they misapplied them to the case of Job; and al‧though they meant to plead the cause of God, yet they displeased him so much by their uncharitable speeches against Job, which they drew, by unjust inference, from undoubted truths, that he told them they had not spo‧ken the thing that was right concerning him as his servant Job had done. If Job had not been a strong believer, their management of truth must have sunk him into despondency.

If wise and holy men have done hurt to themselves and others, by meddling with parables beyond their capacity, or by unjust comments upon them, what mis‧chief may a fool do by dealing in them! When he speaks of the wonderful mercy of God, he will praise it at the expence of divine justice, and maim the at‧tributes of God by dashing them one against another.

---

*Ps. 15:4

When he speaks of the necessity and beauty of holiness, he will bestow on it a part of that glory which is due to Christ: When he speaks of the efficacy of the atonement, he will insinuate encouragements to sin into the minds of his hearers. Every doctrine will be perverted by his management; or, if he speaks correctly and properly on any religious subject, yet the inconsistency of his life with his words, will bring suspicions to the prejudice of truth into the minds of those that converse with him. And if he shews the true way to heaven, and yet takes the road to hell, those who pay any regard to him, will be disposed to think that the way in which he chooses to walk is preferable in his eyes to that of which he only talks.

From this proverb we learn, that all ministers of the gospel must be men of knowledge, soundness in the faith, and a pious conversation. Without the former qualities, they cannot handle the word of God in an edifying manner, and may pervert precious souls. Without the latter, their conversation will do more evil than their sermons can do good.

Christians ought to have their speech seasoned with salt. Knowledge of the form of sound words is necessary to furnish their lips with this kind of discourse; and their practice must correspond with their words, otherwise they make themselves, and, perhaps, their profession likewise, to be abhorred.

Ver. 10. *The great God that formed all things, both rewardeth the fool and rewardeth transgressors.*

Sinners shall in due time be punished, whether their wicked courses are the effect of folly and inconsideration, or of stubborn and hardened dispositions. Fools will not be excused, because they did not know, or did not think upon the evil of their courses; for men are accountable not only for the knowledge they possessed, but likewise for that which they might have got, if they had not wickedly neglected to make use of the means of grace, and to improve those talents which were given them ; as our Lord clearly shows in the parable concerning the talents, where he tells us, that the man who had received but one talent was punished, not for spending it in riot and dissipation, but for hiding it in a napkin.

Those that have been eminent transgressors, that have rebelled against the light, and stifled the loud clamours of their consciences, and led others in the way of sin, shall be rewarded in proportion to the greatness and aggravations of their offences. Every sinner that continues impenitent shall receive from God that recompense of his error which is meet ; and divine omniscience and justice shall shine in proportioning the severity of punishment to the nature and number of the offences that have procured it *.

The judge of all the earth is the great God, who is clothed with terrible majesty. His greatness shews the greatness of the evil of sin, for the greater that any superior is, the more aggravated is any instance of disrespect shewed to him. God is infinitely great, and therefore we are under infinite obligation to obey him ; and if we transgress his laws, that grandeur which was insulted by our disobedience, must be vindicated and glorified by inflicting a vengeance worthy of itself. It is a terrible thing to provoke the wrath of a prince, but who knoweth the power of God's anger ? According to his fear so is his wrath.

God is the former of all things, and he made all things for himself, and will not suffer his creatures to frustrate his purpose of glory to his own name. Rational creatures may abuse the gifts of reason and free will to the dishonour of the Almighty ; but if he is not

---

*Luke 12:47,48

glorified in the obedience of his laws, he will be glorified in the execution of the penalties denounced in them
against transgressors, who shall be punished with everlasting destruction from the presence of the Lord, and
from the glory of his power. Revenging justice belongs
to the great Creator. He punished sin even in his own
beloved Son, who never knew sin ; for the Lord made
the iniquities of all his people to meet in Christ, and
he was oppressed and afflicted, and bruised, and put to
unspeakable grief. He pardons no sin to any man,
that was not first punished in Christ ; and if the great
God dealt in this awful manner with his own Son, and
with his chosen people in the person of their surety,
how can impenitent and hardened sinners escape the
damnation of hell? They sometimes indulge hopes that
the God who made them will not finally destroy them;
but their obligations to God as their Creator and preserver, make their sins inexcusable, and therefore he
that made them will not have mercy upon them. It is
true he gives them space for repentance at present, and
loudly calls them to turn and live, and swears by his
own life that he has no pleasure that they should die *.
But the words of this gracious oath are a plain evidence
that the glorious mercy of the Lord will not exempt
from punishment the obstinate sinner who goes on still
in his trespasses. To those that are found unbelieving
and impenitent, the precious displays of grace will at
last be like rivers of oil to enrage those flames in which
they are tormented.

This text has a very different translation in the margin, which appears agreeable enough to the original :
*A great man grieveth all, and he hireth the fool, he hireth
also transgressors.* This makes it a political instruction,
teaching us what mischief a prince does to the country

*Ezek. 33:11

by employing foolish and wicked ministers. This was exemplified in the administration of Saul, who did great hurt to the nation, and grieved the hearts of all lovers of their country, by employing such ruffians in his service as Doeg the Edomite. We are accountable not only for the mischiefs which we do with our own hands, or by the orders which we give, but likewise for those which we do, by enabling persons of corrupt dispositions to gratify them, to the hurt of other men. If one puts a sword into the hand of a drunkard, or madman, he deserves to be punished for all the mischief that follows upon it.

Ver. 11. *As a dog returneth to his vomit, so a fool returneth to his folly.*

Sin is called by the worst names in Scripture, and the vileness of it is represented by comparisons taken from the most loathsome objects. It is folly, it is the vomit of a dog, it is the poison of asps, it is the superfluity of naughtiness; but no words are sufficient to describe, no images are sufficient to represent, the malignity of sin.˙ The worst thing that can be said of any sin is, that it is exceeding sinful. Sinners are fools and dogs. All sinners are unclean beasts; and some have so much of the temper of a surly dog, that Christ forbids us to admonish them, lest they should turn and rend us.

When sinners hear of the vengeance of the great Creator against themselves, they are sometimes startled, and in some degree convinced of the necessity of reformation; and therefore they will stop short in their wicked course, and forbear those gross sins which press hard upon their consciences, and, like Herod, do many things which they are commanded to do, that they may obtain some ease to their minds, and reputation among saints; but, unless their nature is renewed by the grace of the Spirit, which turns dogs into sheep, their hearts are still much the same as formerly. Their awakened consciences resist sin; but their love to it is not diminished'; and for the most part their corruptions obtain the victory over their consciences, and they return to their former course of life with redoubled eagerness.

The sight of a dog returning to his vomit is very loathsome; but it is much more detestable for sinners to return to their former wickedness. Nothing is more dishonouring to God, or insulting to his majesty; nothing is more hurtful to the souls of men, and especially of the sinner himself; for if any man draw back, it is to perdition of the most terrible kind. Impenitent sinners, that never shewed any disposition to repent, shall be severely punished; but not so severely as those who, after they have known and tried the way of righteousness, have turned aside from the holy commandment delivered unto them. The reproach which they cast upon God, as if iniquity were to be found in him, is intolerably provoking; and God, in righteous judgment, suffers the devil, when he returns into these wretches, to take with him seven devils, and the last state of that man becomes worse than the first.

Turn, O ye fools, at the reproof of wisdom; but if ye will return, return unto the Lord, and put away all your abominations; make to yourselves a new heart, and a new spirit; and if ye cannot perform this great work, (as indeed ye can no more make to yourselves a new heart than a new heaven and earth) give the Lord no rest till he perform his great promise of making you a new heart and a new spirit. A dog chained, and silenced from barking, is a dog still, and cannot find entrance into heaven*. You must be created anew in Christ Jesus, otherwise your partial reformations will only tend to your greater security in your present con-

---

*Rev. 22:15

dition, to your greater reproach, when your convictions are stifled by the rage of your corrupt passions, and to your greater condemnation in the day of the Lord.

Ver. 12. *Seest thou a man wise in his own conceit? there is more hope of a fool than of him.*

When a man has left some of his follies, he thinks himself a new man ; old things, he imagines, are passed away, and all things are become new ; for there is nothing in which the power of folly appears to a greater degree, than in the judgment which a fool passes on himself. For this reason those fools are in the most dangerous condition of all others, who persuade themselves, either from some change in their conduct, or from any other cause, that they are become wise. Many of the publicans heard with pleasure the sermons of John Baptist, and of Christ, concerning repentance ; whilst the self-conceited Pharisees and scribes rejected the counsel of God against themselves. The Gentiles in like manner were made to see the folly and wretchedness of their former course of life, and to receive with thankfulness the offer of a better righteousness than their own, whilst Israel, trusting to their own righteousness, did not submit to the righteousness of God.

There is some hope of a fool and a sinner, if you can make him really to believe that he is what he is. The first lesson to be learned in the school of wisdom, is our own folly *. And when we are deeply sensible of this truth, the revelation of Christ, as our wisdom, and our salvation, will be pleasant to our ears ; but if we still think ourselves wise, when we are fools, we shall despise Christ as much as the pharisees did, and the discoveries of the Gospel will be either idle tales, or tasteless stuff, in our apprehension.

---

*1 Cor. 3:18

Woe to them that are wise in their own conceit, and prudent in their eyes. They depend on wind and vanity; or if they really possess some of that kind of wisdom which a fool may have, they lean on a broken reed, which will go into their arms and pierce them, and rend their souls with eternal remorse, because, in their vain opinion of their own understandings, they rejected the light of the world. "For judgment," says our Lord, "am I come into this world, that they which see not might see, and that they which see might be made blind." None are more blind than those who are readiest to say, with the Pharisees, "are we blind also?" They say that they see, and take away all excuse from themselves, and shall have the mortification, at the great day, to find that God has revealed those things unto babes which he has hidden from the wise and prudent*.

Ver. 13. *The slothful man saith, there is a lion in the way, I shall be slain in the streets.*

Solomon published many proverbs against slothfulness in his own edition of this book. The men of Hezekiah repeat some of them, and join some others to them on the same subject.

The slothful man is reduced to such pitiful shifts for excusing his conduct, that he saith, contrary to all reason and experience, that there is a lion in the way, and that he may be killed in the very streets of the city if he should go forth to his work. This sign of sloth is in nothing more observable than in the excuses that people make for excusing themselves from the duties of religion. The first Christians never minded lions, when they were in the path of duty†, for they were deeply impressed with the love of Christ, who regarded neither the bulls of Bashan, nor the lions of the pit, in

---

*Matt. 11:25, 1 Cor. 1:26,27   †Acts 20:24, 2 Tim. 4:17

working out their salvation; but when we make religion our smallest concern, a frown, or a jeer, or a few drops of rain, will be a sufficient reason to us for declining the most important services. We should remember that our consciences are God's deputies in our bosoms, and not bribe them to sustain any plea that will be rejected by our Judge*.

Ver. 14. *As the door turneth upon his hinges, so doth the slothful upon his bed.*

How dearly does the sluggard love his sleep! but, to his great vexation, he cannot sleep always. When he finds himself half awake, and wearied with lying so long, he tries to get a little more sleep by changing his posture. As the door turns upon its hinges, but still continues in the same place, so the sluggard turns from one part of his bed to another, and from his right side to his left, and then he turns himself on his back, and on his face; for to put on his clothes is a dreadful and intolerable toil. But when every part of his body is wearied with the fatigue of lying and turning, he slowly draws to his clothes, and with great difficulty gets them thrown about him, and perhaps necessity or weariness drives him to some kind of work; but still he is like a door moving upon its hinges, for he only trifles about the most serious affairs, and the night finds his work in much the same state as the morning.

In this manner do sluggards trifle and sleep, not only in the things that concern their present happiness, but in things of awful and eternal consequence. As if they could work out their salvation with faint wishes, and spiritless endeavours, their hearts sleep when they are calling on God for the pardon of their sins, and when they come to church, the words of the preacher are forgotten almost as soon as they are heard; and it is ten to one but their pew serves for a bed, and the book-board

*Chap. 22:13

for a pillow to them; and, as if the devil had given them some opium on the Sabbath morning, they can scarcely be awakened out of their sleep by the united voices of the congregation in the praises of God.

Alas! how do men loiter and doze away their time, which can never be recalled, whilst their grand adversary is ever busy and watchful for their ruin. Awake, sleepers, and call upon your God. Who knows but God may think upon you, that you perish not!

As drunkards and gluttons enjoy less pleasure in eating and drinking than the sober and temperate, so the sluggard never enjoys that sweet and delightful sleep by which the labourer is refreshed; for his excess in this bodily indulgence, makes his slumbers broken and interrupted; nor can he taste that pleasure in eating which other men enjoy, for although he could procure meat without work, eating is a toil to him.

Ver 15. *The slothful hideth his hand in his bosom, it grieveth him to bring it again to his mouth.*

This is a strong expression of the power of laziness, and yet it is literally true of the spiritual sluggard, who will not put forth his hand to receive the richest blessings, nor open his mouth to eat that which is good*.

But when laziness is so prodigiously foolish, and productive of such mischiefs, may not the sluggard be reasoned into another kind of behaviour?

Ver 16. *The sluggard is wiser in his own conceit than seven men that can render a reason.*

He reckons himself wiser than all the seven wise men of Greece put together. The wisdom of Chalcol and Darda, and Ethan and Heman, and Solomon, in one man, could not convince him of his folly. "What," says he, "if I should go forth to work in such a sultry day, I might catch an headach; and an headach cost the Shunamite's son his life. If I should expose myself to the terrible cold of winter, I might catch a cold

_____

*Chap. 19:24

that would bring on a fever or a consumption; for cold is the beginning of almost all diseases; and what is a little worldly gain compared to one's health or life? Is not a life of ease and tranquillity incomparably better, though attended with poverty, than a life of toil and anxiety with riches?"These and the like reasons for his behaviour, appear to him demonstrations, and his disease is incurable, because he cannot be made to believe that he is sick.

Self conceit never fails to attend spiritual sloth; for it prevents the receiving of those instructions that tend to the humiliation of the soul. Kings were commanded by Moses to read the Bible with care, that their hearts might not be lifted up above their brethren; for truths abound in the Scripture, of sovereign efficacy to mortify pride; but the sluggard never learned them, or will not take the trouble of thinking upon them. He has perhaps heard or read, that wisdom's ways are pleasantness, and from thence concludes that they are fools who are at the pains to enter into the strait gate, or walk in the narrow way. He expects, by the gift of grace, to obtain heaven, as well as the most laborious Christian; and thinks himself a far happier and wiser man, than those who work out their salvation with fear and trembling.

None are more foolish than those who have the highest opinion of their own wisdom. Those only are truly wise, whose understandings and wills are regulated by the wisdom and will of God, revealed in his word.

Ver. 17. *He that passeth by, and meddleth with strife, belonging not to him, is like a man that taketh a dog by the ears.*

He that takes a dog by the ears, can scarcely escape without a wound, for the enraged cur will be sure to leap at him as soon as it finds itself at liberty; and he that interests himself in quarrels that he has no business with, can as little expect to escape unhurt.

It is foolish for us to quarrel about our own concerns if we can possibly avoid it; for contention is like an unfathomable gulf, into which a man may easily leap, but will find it a great difficulty to get out; but it is the height of folly for men to engage in quarrels where they have no interest, for we cannot derive any advantage, and are very likely to get much damage from it. If we can make peace, by interposing between contending parties, and persuading them, in the spirit of meekness, to compose their differences, we are doing a very good work, and are in little more danger than a man that is casting a piece of bread to a dog; and yet, if either of the parties have a contentious spirit, his angry passions may lead him to say very disagreeable things to the most friendly mediator, as the quarrelsome Israelites did to Moses in a like case. But if we become a partner in the dispute, by taking one of the sides, we will either receive blows, or hear something to inflame our passions into rage, or suffer some mischief on another occasion, from the person whom we have offended. The apostle Peter insinuates to us that men are very liable to suffer by this means, and that sufferings of this kind do not become saints. ' If any man suffer, let him not suffer as a thief, or as a busy body in other men's matters."

Let us therefore study to be quiet and to do our own business, and this will keep us from thrusting ourselves into the business of other men.

Ver. 18. *As a mad man who casteth fire-brands, arrows, and death ;*

Ver. 19. *So is the man that deceiveth his neighbour, and saith, Am not I in sport ?*

The apostle forbids all that kind of jesting, which is not convenient. A jest is not in every case unlawful ; but it is unwise and wicked, under pretence of jesting, to expose our friends and neighbours to scorn, or to say something that will inflame their passions, and kindle up strife and contention. It is still worse to deceive and flatter them into something that will prove hurtful to their interests, or prejudicial to their souls, and then to pretend 'that we were only amusing ourselves with a little harmless diversion! No diversion is harmless that puts an honest man to the blush, or wounds his spirit or his interests. He that sports himself in this rude and unchristian manner, is like a real or pretended madman, that amuses himself with casting about at random firebrands, and arrows, and other instruments of death.

Let those that would be wits at the expence of friendship and charity, consider in what class of men Solomon so justly places them, and be ashamed. He counts them not only fools but madmen, and ranks them with the worst kind of madmen, in the height of their rage.

But may not a man use freedoms with a friend ? Yes. But such freedoms only as cement friendship, and not those freedoms that turn a friend into an enemy.

To carry on a scheme of imposition, under the mask of friendship, is the worst kind of wickedness, and places a man in the same black list with Joab and Judas. There are some men with whom it is safer to be at variance than to possess their friendship. From such friends may the good Lord deliver us ; for open enemies are far less dangerous.

Ver. 20. *Where no wood is, there the fire goeth out, so where there is no tale bearer the strife ceaseth.*

A tale bearer is one who tells stories that ought not to be told, whether true or false, whether fairly or unfairly represented ; and the worst kind of tale bearers are those who tell their stories to those who are most likely to be provoked by them, and at the same time do not wish to be mentioned as authors of the story, or witnesses in it.

There is sometimes a propriety in telling secret sto-

ries; and Gedaliah lost his life by carrying his contempt
of this mean vice to excess ; but the most part of those
that carry tales of their neighbours are to be numbered not only with the basest, but with the most pernicious of mankind. They are serpents in the way, and
adders in the path ; they are firebrands kindled from
hell, that kindle a fire among men, which spreads from
one to another, till parishes and counties are in danger of being set on fire.

He that listens to tale-bearers, is like a man that
sees a house ready to be set on fire, and uses no means
to prevent it. He that turns an angry countenance to
the back-biter, is the friend of mankind, who carries
water to quench the burning.

It were happy for society if such pernicious members could be banished from it, for they are like madmen that cast around firebrands ; but as we live in a
world where such incendiaries are still going about, we
should do what we can to prevent them from carrying
any coals from our own houses, or fetching them within our walls.

Tale bearers little consider the evil they are doing,
and the extent of that mischief which may be justly
charged upon them, or the misery they are heaping up
for themselves, for they shall (unless pardon interpose)
be cast into a deep pit, and a fiery furnace, from whence
they shall never get out *.

Contentious men are the brethren and friends of the
tale bearers, and merit the same censure and condemnation.

Ver. 21. *As coals are to burning coals, and wood to
fire, so is a contentious man to kindle strife.*

Men of proud, and passionate, and selfish spirits,
give scope to their corrupt dispositions in kindling
strife and debate, which seem to be as agreeable to

*Ps. 141

them as a fire to one who is ready to perish with cold. We ought to avoid the society of such persons. If we are cast into their company, it is absolutely necessary for us to keep a strict guard over our hearts and our tongues; for their provoking or seducing words, have the same tendency to kindle strife, as burning coals have to kindle dry wood into a flame. The conflagration that was raised by Korah, and that which was kindled by Sheba the son of Bichri, soon spread itself through all the armies of Israel.

Let none who calls himself a Christian give any occasion to call him a contentious man, for Christ is the prince of peace; his gospel is the gospel of peace, and all that believe it in truth are the sons and the lovers of peace; but the lovers of strife are children of the wicked one.

Ver. 22. *The words of a tale bearer are as wounds, and they go down into the innermost parts of the belly.*

This proverb was inserted by Solomon himself, chap. xviii. 8. but the men of Hezekiah annex it to the former proverbs about contention; for they wished if possible to banish tale-bearing, that grand engine of mischief, out of the world.

Ver. 23. *Burning lips, and a wicked heart, are like a potsherd covered with silver dross.*

Every thing that glitters is not precious metal. You may sometimes observe a piece of metal that you take to be silver, and yet, when you examine it, there is nothing but a thin surface of silver dross, which conceals a worthless piece of potsherd below it. Like to this is a wicked disposition concealed under the mask of a tongue that flames with holy zeal, or burns with professions of the most ardent friendship.

The Pharisees, in the time of our Lord's humbled state, were men of this disposition, and therefore he compares them to whited sepulchres. They were enemies to all goodness, and yet their zeal for religion was so great that Christ himself was a profane person, if their testimony was of any worth. These abominable hypocrites are a smoke in God's nostrils, a fire that burneth all the day.

There are some that practise the like hypocrisy towards their fellow men, and they are the most dangerous members of society that can be found in the world. Absalom was a perfect master in both these kinds of hypocrisy, and therefore his name will be infamous whilst the world stands*. Against those who cover their malignity with professions of kindness, we are warned in the following verses.

Ver. 24. *He that hateth, dissembleth with his lips, and layeth up deceit within him.*

Ver. 25. *When he speaketh fair, believe him not ; for there are seven abominations in his heart.*

A passionate man is dangerous ; but, if you are on your guard, the danger will soon be over ; the malicious man is far worse, and much more dangerous, for his hatred ferments in his heart, and his head is, in the mean time, projecting methods for wreaking it in such a manner as will be safest to himself, and most stunning to its object. He is not like the dog that barks before it bites, otherwise you might stand to your own defence ; but he is a dog that fawns upon you, and, when you are never dreaming of it, falls upon you, and inflicts an unexpected and dangerous wound. Solomon warns you that your safety lies in refusing to trust him, even when he makes the largest professions of friendship. When he speaketh fair, believe him not, although he should swear to the truth of all he says. If you have any reason, from your knowledge of a man's disposition, or from his former behaviour, to think that he is one of this stamp, and capable of such wicked conduct, his ardent professions of love should rather confirm than remove your suspicions of him ; for the dark-

_____

*2 Sam. 13:22-26, 14:3

est designs are always covered under the greatest shows of virtue and friendship. You may as safely believe the devil himself as one that joins malignity of heart with flattery and caresses, for he is a man after the devil's own heart. His character is a compound of all those vices of the blackest and the meanest kind, that make a consummate villain, and render a man a disgrace to human nature, by his exact resemblance to those infernal fiends who are to be dreaded equally for their malice and subtilty. Abner and Amasa lost their lives by believing a man of this character.

But the providence of God will not always bear with such abominable wretches.

Ver. 26. *Whose hatred is covered by deceit, his wickedness shall be shewed before the whole congregation.*

He is ashamed or afraid to discover his malice, but God shall bring it to light in the view of all men, and make him the object of universal abhorrence. This is often done by his own agency, for malice ordinarily discovers itself sooner or later. When Saul could not destroy David by the hands of the Philistines, or by his javelin in private, his hatred became too violent to be smothered by his prudence. Sometimes God, by a strange train of providences, exposes the wicked purposes of men's hearts, and if it continues hid through the whole course of this life, there is a day that will declare it. Let us never harbour any thing in our minds that we would be ashamed if all the world should know it; for all the world shall certainly know it, in the day when the secrets of hearts shall be judged; for,

God will not only discover, but punish the malignity of men; for,

Ver. 27. *Whoso diggeth a pit shall fall therein, and he that rolleth a stone, it will return upon him.*

" Whatsoever ye would that others should do unto you, do ye even so to them," says our Lord, " for this is

the law and the prophets." But if neither Moses, nor
the prophets, nor Christ himself, can prevail upon us
to observe this golden rule, our own interest may be expected to work us to a compliance with it; for the mischief that we do to others, must at last recoil upon
ourselves, with a heavy aggravation of remorse and
self-condemnation attending it. When Haman was
hanged on his own gallows, his miserable end must have
been attended with anguish and self-reflections a thousand times more grievous than any thing that Mordecai
could have felt if Haman's malice had been accomplished on him.

Here is encouragement for the faith and patience of
the saints. Here is ground for the highest praise to
the righteousness of God*.

Ver. 28. *A lying tongue hateth those that are afflicted
by it, and a flattering mouth worketh ruin.*

It might be expected that when a man has wronged
his neighbour, by his lies or flatteries, he would be
filled with remorse, and try to make some reparation;
but the loss is, that he judges of other men from himself; he does not believe that there is enough of generosity in any man to forgive him, and therefore per-
sists in his hatred. It is not easy for us to forgive the
injuries we receive; but it is far more difficult to forgive the injuries we do.

Flatterers are the worst kind of liars, and the most
likely to be believed, because self-love favours their
deceits. Flatterers are commonly men that intend to
betray with a kiss; but, although they should only design to gain our favour by their fair speeches, yet they
are very pernicious, because they are the friends of
our pride, which is the worst of our bosom enemies.

---

*Rev. 13:10, 16:5,6

Proverbs 27

Ver. 1. *Boast not thyself of to-morrow, for thou know-est not what a day may bring forth.*

In God we live, and move, and have our being; but we too often forget this important truth, and speak, and act, and think, as if we lived, and moved, and had our being in ourselves. We boast of what we will do, or of what we shall enjoy at the distance of days, and months, and years. This presumption is forbidden in this and in many places of Scripture; and a reason is given for the prohibition that every person must ac-knowledge to be a true and good one, that we cannot tell what a day may bring forth; for every new day brings forth the accomplishment of some decree of the Most High; but these decrees are written in a sealed book, and no man can loose the seals, nor open the book, nor read what is written therein.

We know that the sun will rise to-morrow; but we cannot tell whether he will rise to us, or to our survi-vors. We can guess what the weather will be; but we cannot say whether we shall be rich or poor, sick or in health, left in the possession of our friends, or bereav-ed of them that are dearest to our hearts. In the morn-ing Haman went forth from his magnificent palace, expecting to be gratified before the evening came with the blood of his hated enemy, which would have been sweeter to him than wine; but, before the evening came, he was hanged like a dog, and went to the place appointed for him.

We ought to boast of nothing; for what is our life but a vapour? What are our bags of gold but a glittering nothing ? * What are our honours but a puff of wind ? Or what are our earthly hopes, when their basis is a shadow that fleeth away, and never returneth ? But the hopes that are founded upon the rock of ages can never fail us, and the believer in Christ can, upon so-lid ground, triumph in the expectation of eternal joys, and unfading crowns. He boasts not of himself, but glories in the Lord, whose promises are more stable than the everlasting hills, or the pillars of heaven.

The same reason that should check our boasting of to-morrow, may preserve us from desponding fears. It may be stormy weather to-day; but storms do not last all the year. We are filled and tormented with fears of some impending evil; but we often give ourselves real pain by the prospect of calamities that never were ap-pointed to us by the providence of God. This is now the spring of the year, (1785,) and within the last twelve-month, the country has been three times alarmed with anxious fears, all of which have been most agreeably disappointed.

Ver. 2. *Let another man praise thee, and not thine own mouth ; a stranger, and not thine own lips.*

For a man to search his own glory is no glory ; and when a man publishes his own praises, it is a sign that he has none else to do it for him, and that there is only one fool in the world, and no wise man that knows his merit. Suppose a man has really done some good things, yet when he boasts of them, he destroys all their credit; for no man will think himself obliged to praise the man that has face enough to publish his own praises ; and every one will believe that he did those ac-tions which are the subject of his talk, not from any principle of love to God or man, but merely with a view to his own honour. The Pharisees had but a poor reward for their alms and prayers, in the praise of men, but the vain boaster has a poorer reward, for

---

*Chap. 23:4

he is his own paymaster, and must be content to want the praise of other men as well as of God.

But we ought to do those things which deserve praise. Our hands, and not our tongues, must be employed to publish our worth, and thus we shall comply with the precept*, and follow the example of our Lord. He had a good title to praise himself, for he was not a mere man, yet his right to bear testimony to himself was excepted against by his enemies; but he could appeal to his works, which bare witness continually on his behalf, and published his praise through the world, in spite of all the rage and cunning of his adversaries.

In some cases a man is at liberty, and has a call to speak to his own praise; but these cases are few. When Paul was laid under a necessity of this kind, he often reminds us that he speaks like a fool; and blames the Corinthians that they had reduced him to this necessity, by neglecting to interpose in the behalf of his injured character; for although we must be very cautious how we praise ourselves, yet when we are called to speak in the praise of another man, we are not only at greater liberty, but may expose ourselves to just blame by unseasonable silence.

Ver. 3. *A stone is heavy, and the sand weighty; but a fool's wrath is heavier than them both.*

Ver. 4. *Wrath is cruel, and anger is outrageous; but who can stand before envy?*

The wrath of a wise man is sometimes very heavy. If David had not been prevented, he would have massacred the whole family of Nabal; but the grace of God, and a principle of conscience and charity, disposed him to calm his resentment at Abigail's remonstrances. A wise man endeavours to live under the influence of that meekness so strongly recommended, and so wonderfully exemplified by our Lord; but a fool has no

---

*Matt. 5:16

government over his passions, and it is better to meet a bear bereaved of her whelps, than a fool in his folly ; for his wrath is heavier than the sand of the sea, it is fiercer than the rage of tigers, it is more stubborn and inflexible than the rocks. May we never come within the reach of a fool when his passions are roused ; for they must be gratified and satiated if they should bring him to a gibbet. May we ever possess our souls in patience and calmness ; for boisterous passions are a whirlwind in the soul, that threaten to rend it in a thousand pieces.

But terrible as wrath is, envy is a great deal worse. Envy is the grief that a man feels for the prosperity of another person ; it is a compound of pride and malice it derives misery to a man from his neighbour's happiness. The blessings and mercies of God are turned by it into curses ; and the life of another man is the envious man's death. As the devil fell by pride, so he wrought the fall of man by his envy ; and when envy takes possession of a man, it makes him a devil to his neighbours. The envious man is far blacker than the passionate man ; for the outrageous behaviour of an angry person sounds an alarm to his neighbour to be on his guard ; but the envious man conceals his malignity, till he has a fit opportunity to strike a mortal blow without danger of missing his aim. The one is a dog, that barks before he bites, the other is an adder in the grass, that stings the traveller when he is dreading no hurt ; for the malice of the envious man is generally unsuspected, because no occasion was given for it. It is the good and happiness of the envied object that excites his malignity, and he does not so much as pretend (unless he adds lying to envy,) that he has received any provocation. Anger may generally be appeased ; but envy is the vice of a dark and hellish spirit, that has not the least spark of generosity to give any hope of pacifying it. The only way you can take to soothe envy is to be miserable; for it makes a man such a perfect devil, that evil is his only good.

The fall of man, the murder of Abel, the slavery of Joseph, the persecutions of David, the crucifixion of our Lord, are monuments of the rage of envy, and the danger incurred by being objects of it. But the curse of the serpent, the miserable end of Saul, the horrors that pursued Cain, the desolations of Jerusalem, and the torments prepared for devils, are terrible proofs that envy is infinitely worse for the person that harbours it, than for the innocent object of it.

Ver. 5. *Open rebuke is better than secret love.*

There are two qualities very requisite in a friend, love and faithfulness; the last as necessary as the first to make our friendships really beneficial to us. There are some that love us with sincerity and warmth, and yet want the courage that is necessary to make them faithful in reproving us when we deserve to be reproved. But reproof, although it should be severe and cutting, is better than love which does not discover itself in needful rebukes. A true friend will not disclose our faults to the world, but he will not justify them to save our credit; for virtue is the soul of true friendship, and must not be entrenched upon, out of regard to our dearest friends; and therefore that friend is to be valued, who makes his reproofs as public as our faults are, and who does not spare to tell us roundly to our faces, wherein we have erred; for he gives good evidence that he esteems our real welfare above his own interest in our regard. A friend that loves, but is afraid to reprove us when we deserve it, does not discover a very high esteem of our sense and temper; for he seems to think us incapable of bearing reproof, and rather chooses to enjoy our smiles than to do us an essential service. Our Lord loved his Apostles with a tender regard;

and with admirable prudence and kindness he rebuked them when they spoke or behaved amiss. He would
never suffer sin upon them, and yet he reproved them
in such a manner as to increase and not diminish their
love to himself. Let us learn, from this proverb, to
exercise the fidelity of friendship to those whom we
love, and to thank our friends when they discover the
sincerity of their regard in their concern for our souls.
We ought to value honesty above politeness, and to excuse a little defect in the last quality, for the sake of
the first.

Ver. 6. *Faithful are the wounds of a friend; but the
kisses of an enemy are deceitful.*

Friends are not to be loved chiefly on account of the
pleasure they give us, although nothing earthly is more
pleasant than a true friend. Their integrity and faithfulness is their most valuable quality, and they will sometimes have occasion for them, by speaking to us things
that are a great deal more useful than pleasant. David esteemed a friend that would wound and smite him to his
profit, as much as a wise man values a chirurgeon that
makes needful but painful incisions in his flesh, for the
restoration of his lost health. Abishai, who discovered
such zeal for his honour, was not dearer to him than
Nathan the prophet, who reproved him, in the plainest manner, for the murder of Uriah*.

All men allow that the kisses of an enemy are deceitful and detestable. " An enemy speaketh sweetly with
his lips, but in his heart he imagineth how to throw
thee into a pit: he will weep with his eyes, but if he
find opportunity, he will not be satisfied with blood.
If adversity come upon thee, thou shalt find him there
first, and though he pretend to help thee, yet shall he
undermine thee. " The caresses of an enemy are very

---

*Ps. 141:5

base and dangerous; but it deserves to be considered whether we have not a greater quantity of revenge than generosity in our temper, when we hate the kisses of an enemy more than we value the wounds of a friend. If we value the image of Christ, it is certain that faithful reprovers express a friendship that resembles his love to his people to a greater degree than those who withhold from us this plainest token of real regard.

Ver. 7. *The full soul loatheth an honeycomb; but to the hungry soul every bitter thing is sweet.*

The poor generally reckon the rich a great deal happier than themselves, because they are clothed in fine apparel, and dwell in elegant houses, and feed upon the richest dainties; but the envy and discontent of poor men is very ill founded, for the rich, being accustomed to these things, receive no more gratification from them than the poor derive from their homely fare, and mean raiment, and poor accommodations; or, if the sight of a well furnished room, and of fine paintings, could give any considerable pleasure to those that are accustomed to see them, the poor might enjoy as much pleasure by looking at the verdant clothing of the earth, and the glorious canopy of heaven.

The man that fares sumptuously every day, has no more relish for honey and wine than the poor man has for bread and water, for he seldom experienceth hunger, and so he wants the best sauce that any food can have; or, if he denies himself so far as to be hungry, he puts a force upon himself, because he has the means of gratification always at hand, and therefore it costs him more pain to prepare himself for relishing his ordinary food, than it costs the man to whom necessity renders abstinence habitual, and hunger easy to be endured.

When a man's appetite is excited by hunger and labour, every kind of food is welcome and pleasant to him, and whilst the rich are exposed to weariness and listlessness in their abundance, the poor have strong excitements to be cheerful and thankful although scanty meals are all they can afford.

The children of Israel loathed the manna, although it was bread given them immediately from God, and was called the food of angels. They wished to be in Canaan, and eat common bread in the sweat of their brows; for the plenty of manna made them to despise it. If we have fulness of bread, we ought to be cautious lest we despise the mercies of God, and the giver of them.

We ought especially to be on our guard against despising our spiritual privileges, which we enjoy in so great abundance without molestation. Estates have been given in former days for a few leaves of the Bible, and gospel ordinances were attended at the hazard of life; for those that know what spiritual hunger means, will break through stone walls for the bread of life; but those who are full in their own apprehension, will despise the riches of divine goodness, and God will send them empty away.

Ver. 8. *As a bird that wandereth from her nest; so is a man that wandereth from his place.*

When a bird wanders from her nest, and flies about at random, she is in danger of becoming the prey of the fowler, or the hawk; and when a man abides not at home, when he ought to be employed in his business, or when he leaves his calling without a sufficient reason, he exposes himself to great inconveniences, and sometimes to dangers. He loses his good name, and his estate is likely to go to ruin; he learns habits of idleness and dissipation, and gets into company that may very probably corrupt his morals.

Let every man abide with God in that calling wherewith he is called, endeavouring to perform the duties of it conscientiously, that the doctrine of God our Saviour may be adorned. God assigns to every one of us our station in life, and we ought to keep it till the call of Providence warrant us to make a change in it. When our health, or the necessities of our families, or a well-grounded respect of doing greater service to God, or some other important consideration, will justify our change of place, we come not under the censure of the wise man, nor do we run the risk that others do who wantonly and causelessly change their place. We are safe in following Providence, although it is dangerous to run before it, or to attempt to set ourselves free from it, as Jonah did, who sought to flee from the presence of the Lord by wandering from his place, but soon found that the way of duty is the only way of safety and comfort.

Paul joins with Solomon in testifying against those that abide not in their place to fulfil the duties of it*.

Ver. 9. *Ointment and perfume rejoice the heart; so doth the sweetness of a man's friend by hearty counsel.*

Ointments and perfumes diffuse their fragrant odours around, by which men's spirits are refreshed, and their hearts cheered; but the sweetness of a well chosen friend cheers the soul better than the sweetest flowers, or the most precious odours prepared by the art of the apothecary. His amiable virtues, and his affectionate fondness beaming from his eyes, and breathing in his words and actions, make him the joy of our hearts, and diffuse the sweetest sensations of delight into our bosom.

Friends are at all times useful. They give a relish to the pleasures of life, and their society makes the labours of it delightful; but at the times when we need advice, or meet with perplexities, the advantage of

---

*2 Thess. 3:11,12, 1 Tim. 1:7

their friendship is best understood. Other men often give us such advice as suits their own interest or humour; they cannot, at least, enter into our interests, and judge what advice is most proper to be given to us, so well as the friends of our bosom, who are acquainted with our business and our dispositions, and whose fidelity will dispose them to give us advice, according to the best of their understanding. In many cases advice is necessary for us, as Solomon frequently tells us; for a man perplexed with difficulties, or surprised by some unexpected accident, is not so well qualified to judge what is fit to be done, as another person would be that has no superior degree of wisdom, but has the advantage of more composure and sedateness. To have a bosom friend at such a time to take a share of our sorrows, to direct our behaviour, to assist us in our time of need, is a great relief to the mind, and a restorative to the disquieted heart.

We ought to value a wise and faithful friend more than gold and silver; for how small a part do they contribute of our comfort in life, in comparison with our friends who turn even our days of sorrow into joy, and lighten our heaviest burdens?

If we expect the pleasures of friendship in their full extent, let us remember that our friends have the same claims upon us, and the same grounds for them, that we have on the other side, and we ought to take the same pleasure in giving as in receiving happiness. For this end we must be furnished, not only with an honest and a feeling heart, but with such a measure of wisdom as will qualify us for conversing with our friends to our mutual improvement, and for giving them counsel in the time of their perplexity. He that hath friends must show himself friendly, and must continue to do so till the end of his life.

Ver. 10. *Thine own friend and thy father's friend,*

forsake not ; neither go into thy brother's house in the day of thy calamity: for better is a neighbour that is near, than a brother far off.

Clothes and houses are valued for being new, but old friends, like old wine, are entitled to the greatest share of our esteem, and we must not forsake them when they give us no good reason for it. To exchange an old friend for a new is to betray a fickle disposition, unfit and unworthy to enjoy the blessings of friendship. Some persons cool in their friendships through an instability of mind, and can give no reason for it but their own humour ; others are no less unfit to taste the pleasures of a cordial and lasting friendship, because they are so peevish that they can bear with no manly freedoms, or so credulous that they give ear to every whisper, and so unforgiving that they cannot love those by whom they think they have been offended. The son of Sirach gives us a good advice on this point, "Admonish a friend ; it may be he hath not done it, and if he have done it, that he do it no more. Admonish thy friend ; it may be he hath not said it, and if he have, that he speak it not again. Admonish a friend ; for many times it is a slander, and believe not every tale. There is one that slippeth in his speech, but not from his heart, and who is he that hath not offended with his tongue ? "

The faults that we ourselves have been guilty of towards our friends are more likely than any thing to cool our affections to them, through an apprehension that they must stick in their breasts ; but if we can forgive the trivial offences of our friends, why may we not believe that they can forgive ours also ? Do we imagine that all generosity is confined to ourselves ? Let us hear what the same wise author says on this point. " Whoso casteth a stone at the birds frayeth them away; and he that upbraideth his friend, breaketh friendship. Though thou drewest thy sword at thy friend, yet despair not, for there may be a returning to favour. If thou hast opened thy mouth against thy friend, fear not, for there may be a reconciliation, except for upbraiding or pride, or disclosing of secrets, or a treacherous wound ; for, for these things every friend will depart ." But those who are capable of such unpardonable faults were never fit for being friends to any man.

If the faults of our friends, or the differences that may take place between them and us, will not justify us in giving up with them ; it is a scandalous thing to desert them in the time of their distress, when they have most need of our friendship. A brother is born for adversity, and a friend loveth at all times; and he is no genuine friend who proves to us in our time of calamity like a broken tooth or a foot out of joint. "A friend cannot be known in prosperity, and an enemy cannot be hidden in adversity ."

We must not forsake our own friend, for that would be to forsake our second self; and we must not forsake our father's friend, for that would make us guilty of a double ingratitude of the basest sort that we can practise towards men. Our father's friends, if they are honest, are the best possessions that they can leave us, and if Naboth would not sell, for any price, the inheritance left him by his fathers, but kept it in spite of an Ahab and a Jezebel, till he was stoned, shall we show such irreverence to the memory of our fathers, as to give up, without any price, the most precious possessions which they have bequeathed to us. Solomon carried on his father's friendly intercourse with Hiram, and spared a traitor to his crown and dignity, because he had shared with his father in all his afflictions. Rehoboam would have been a wiser and happier man, if he had followed the example and precept of his father.

Trust in our friends is a duty which we owe them, as well as fidelity, and our confidence will be made to appear in the use we make of their kindness in the time of our distress. The house of a constant and warm friend is then preferable to that of a cold and inconstant brother. Brethren by birth, have, for the most part, less attachment to one another than those friends who single out one another, not from accident, or relation of kindred, but from the harmony of their minds, and their mutual kind affections. Greater acts of heroism have been performed by those who have been knit by such voluntary and endearing ties, than by any kind of relations for one another. There is a friend that sticketh closer than a brother, and we do him honour by placing an entire confidence in him when we need his assistance. At his house we shall meet with a more cordial reception than we can expect from a brother, and shall hear none of those upbraidings which the unfortunate too often hear in the houses of their near relations. When David's brethren of the tribe of Judah proved treacherous, his gallant friend, the son of his great enemy, maintained his cause against his own father, when he was persecuted by him for the sake of Jonathan himself.

If we must not forsake our own and our father's friend, shall we ever forsake our own God, and the God of our pious father, who is infinitely the best of friends, and disdains not to call us by the endearing name of friends to himself*.

---

*John 15:14, 1 Chron. 28:9, Ps. 90:1

Ver. 11. *My son, be wise, and make my heart glad, that I may answer him that reproacheth me.*

Wise children are not only the joy but the crown of their parents. Foolish children are their disgrace as well as their torment. How unnatural are those children that bring grief and dishonour on those to whom they are under obligations that can never be cancelled!

As is the mother, so is her daughter, was a very ancient proverb *. As some vices, like some diseases, run in the blood, the father will be liable to the suspicion of those vices which disgrace his son, or if his character is so clear that there is no room for this, yet it will be judged that the father is in part accessory to his son's faults, by neglecting his education, by imprudent rigour, or foolish indulgence, or by carelessness in the example which he set before him. Although men are frequently guilty of great injustice, by making a whole family accountable for the behaviour of those who are the blemishes of it, yet there is often too much reason for concluding that some neglect or mismanagement of the father has afforded scope for the irregularities of his family. David was justly chargeable on this account, in his behaviour towards the three eldest of his sons, of whom we have any particular account. God himself ordered that the harlot who imposed herself as a virgin upon an husband, should be stoned before the door of her father's house † ; and under the New Testament none are to be admitted into holy offices, that have disorderly children, because a man must be unfit to rule the house of God that cannot rule his own house.

Parents ought to inculcate wisdom on their children for their own credit, as well as the benefit of their children ‡.

---

*Ezek. 16:44   †Deut. 22:21   ‡Chap. 17:6

Ver. 12. *A prudent man foreseeth the evil, and hideth himself: but the simple pass on, and are punished.*

Ver. 13. *Take his garment that is surety for a stranger, and take a pledge of him for a strange woman.*

These instructions were already given us by Solomon *. Perhaps there is a new motive to enforce them implied in the connection of them with the foregoing verse ; that the wisdom by which men are preserved from these mischiefs will tend to the comfort and honour of our parents, and if we are so foolish as to run into needless dangers, or to ruin our substance by our connection with strangers or harlots, the comfort of our parents will be ruined, and their credit impaired, as well as our own. If we are wise, we are wise for ourselves, and if we are foolish, we alone must bear it ; and yet by consulting our own happiness, we give happiness to those whom we ought to love, and by our own voluntary misery we bring down sorrow and dishonour upon those grey hairs and hoary heads which are well entitled to our reverence.

Ver. 14. *He that blesseth his friend with a loud voice, rising early in the morning, it shall be counted a curse unto him.*

We cannot tell whether morning levees were in use among the Israelites in Solomon's time, as they afterwards were among some other nations. If they were, there is no doubt that persons who wished to thrust themselves into favour with their superiors would take the opportunity to appear among the first to pay their court.

The blessing or praising of one's friends is not here absolutely condemned. When praises and blessings are a proper expression of gratitude, when they are a probable means of exciting to virtuous conduct, when they

---

*Chap. 22:3, 20:16

are needful to vindicate a character unjustly attacked, and when they are needful to revive a spirit over- whelmed with a false humility and groundless terrors, they deserve no blame *.

But he that blesses and praises his friend in high swelling words, and seeks opportunities for that pur- pose, letting no time pass, however unseasonable, for loading with commendations the person whose friend- ship he affects, is to be suspected of flattery and base designs, and therefore his blessings shall be counted for a curse either to his friend, or to himself, or to both.

If his friend is wise, he will be as much displeased with these blessings as if they were curses ; for they are an evidence that the fulsome flatterer has a very mean opinion of the person whom he hopes to gratify by such methods, and that he looks upon him to be a man so weak and self-conceited as to swallow gross flattery without knowing it.

If those whose favour is thus solicited have their judgments so much biassed by self-conceit as to relish it, every one of their vices is strengthened, their pride in particular is swelled, and their character is ruined by it, for all men will look upon them to be fools over- run with vanity and self-esteem.

Such flatteries will be a curse to those that utter them ; for they are guilty of spreading a net for their neighbour's feet, and whether they are entangled or not, the crime is the same.

Ver. 15. *A continual dropping in a very rainy day, and a contentious woman, are alike.*

Ver. 16. *Whosoever hideth her hideth the wind, and the ointment of his right hand which bewrayeth itself.*

" The contentions of a wife," saith Solomon, in one of his former proverbs, " are a continual dropping." He

*Chap. 31:22, Josh. 22, Luke 22:28

goes farther in this passage, and tells us that they are like a continual dropping in a very rainy day. When a man is exposed to the weather in a very rainy day, he finds his situation very unpleasant, only he has this great comfort that an house is not far distant, and therefore he will soon find a shelter; but how much is the man to be pitied who is joined for life to a contentious wife! His ears must be stunned, and the whole time of his life, for ought he knows, embittered by clamour and noise beating constantly upon him like a tempest. He may sometimes obtain a respite, by absence from his house; but a man cannot be always from home without leaving behind him the means of his subsistence, and his beloved children, and every thing dear to him; and when he is in the field, or in the house of some friend, yet the noise he has heard, and is still doomed to hear within his own walls, rings constantly in his ears.

But may not a man subdue the haughty spirit of a vexatious wife? He may as soon tame the fierce spirit of a lion. The grace of God, and nothing of less power, can do this great work. May he not then conceal his dishonour from the world? He may as soon shackle the wind, and command it to blow where he pleases, or hinder the ointment which is poured on his right hand (which is almost constantly in motion) from spreading its fragrance through the whole room where he sits. The clamours of an imperious wife will be heard, not only in the house, but in the street, and through every corner of the town. It is impossible to force into her so much sense, as to make her regard either her own honour, or the credit of her husband; for if she had the least degree of common understanding, or if she were capable of receiving any advice, she could never bear the thought of being the scourge and torment of that man to whom she is bound by every motive of duty and interest to be a comfort and a crown.

The uninspired sages of ancient days concur with Solomon in condemning the behaviour of bad wives with great severity. " I had rather," says the son of Sirach, " dwell with a lion and a dragon, than to keep house with a wicked woman. An evil wife is a yoke shaken to and fro, he that hath hold of her, is as though he held a scorpion. A loud crying woman, and a scold, shall be sought out to drive away the enemies ." And nothing better can be said of a tyrannical husband. If a king deserves to be branded with the most odious names when he oppresses his subjects, what words can paint the baseness of that man who tyrannizes over the wife of his bosom, his other self.

We wish for comfort in our various relations; but to obtain it, we must in the first place mind the duties of them, and endeavour to be a comfort to those with whom we are connected.

Ver. 17. *Iron sharpeneth iron, so a man sharpeneth the countenance of his friend.*

When iron tools were blunt, it seems they used to be whetted and sharpened by files or some other instrument of iron. In like manner, when the heart is dull, and the countenance overcast with melancholy, the pleasing society of a friend infuses gladness and new life into the heart, and scatters the gloom that sat upon the countenance.

" A faithful friend is a strong defence, and he that hath found such an one, hath found a treasure. Nothing doth countervail a faithful friend, and his excellency is invaluable. A faithful friend is the medicine of life" . The intercourses of friendship cheer the spirit, brighten the understanding, and inspire us with alacrity and vigour for every useful employment of the mind. If we are dejected with grief, their kind attentions, and seasonable discourse, have an happy effect in alleviating our distress, and softening our sorrows. They keep the soul from sinking into despondency, and enliven it with hopes of better days.

What reason have we to be thankful that this evil world affords some that are qualified to afford such pleasure and advantage to us ; but in choosing our friends, we ought to consider religion as one thing necessary to be regarded, for that alone, attended with the blessing of God, will effectually serve all these valuable purposes, and others of equal importance. A religious friend will be of great use to animate our souls in the service of God, to assist us in combating the difficulties that meet us in our Christian course, and to warm our souls with holy zeal. " They that fear the Lord shall find him. Whoso feareth the Lord shall direct his friendship aright ; for as he is, so shall his neighbour be also *."

Ver. 18. *Whoso keepeth the fig tree shall eat the fruit thereof; so he that waiteth on his master shall be honoured.*

It is the business of a servant to wait on his master with respect, to obey his orders with cheerfulness and fidelity, to promote his interest and happiness by all proper means, and to prevent, as far as he can, every thing that may tend to his prejudice.

But perhaps those who are in this humble station may think that they have very little encouragement to perform the duties of it, because the meanness of their condition places them below the hope of any valuable reward. In answer to this, the Spirit of God tells them that they shall have a very good and honourable reward for their service however mean. Who planteth

---

*1 Sam. 23:16

a vineyard and eateth not of the fruit, or who takes care of the fig trees, and is not allowed to share in their delicious product? And if the care of fig trees be thus recompensed, shall not that servant be honoured who shows a zeal for every thing that concerns the comfort and interest of his master? Certainly: he will be respected by all wise men who know him; his master especially will show him that respect which his fidelity deserves, and will find occasions perhaps to serve him more than he expected. Servants are indeed often unnoticed by their masters, when the time of their service is over; but that is owing, perhaps, as much to the want of merit in the servants, as the want of gratitude in their masters.

Masters are bound by the law of God, to behave not only justly, but kindly, towards honest servants; but if they should prove ungrateful, there is a master and Lord in heaven, who shall recompense with divine liberality those servants that performed their duty, not as eye servants, but as the servants of Christ, adorning the doctrine of God their Saviour by the religious performance of their duty to men*.

Ver. 19. *As in water face answereth to face; so the heart of man to man.*

The water is nature's looking glass, in which we discern our faces; and the face which is seen in the water has a resemblance, though not an exact and perfect image of that face which looks into it. So likewise there is a resemblance in one man's soul to another. As God hath fashioned the bodies of men like one another, so the soul of every man has the like faculties and passions, and none of the human race is born a brute or an angel. There is, indeed, a difference of faces, although in water that difference is

---

*Deut. 15:13, Col. 4

not well discerned, and there is likewise a natural difference in the tempers and understandings of men.
And yet none of us have reason to be proud or insolent, for we are but men, and our neighbours are
men also. Some of them have miserably disgraced
the human nature, but they have only improved upon
that corruption of human nature which is common to
them and to us, and instead of triumphing over them,
we ought to mourn over the ruins of our condition,
and to adore that mercy which has kept us from sinking down, by our natural weight of corruption, to
the same deplorable depth of wickedness. When
the holy martyr Bradford heard of any person that had
been guilty of an atrocious act of guilt, he used to strike
his hand upon his breast, and say, " here is the seed
of all that wickedness."

There is a mighty change made upon the heart by
the grace of God creating it anew in Christ Jesus.
But the saints will not boast on this account, for they
well know what they once were, and who made them
to differ from others, and from their former selves.
They still feel the body of death within themselves,
and heartily sympathize with them who are yet nothing
but flesh.

As the corrupt heart in one man is like to the same
heart in another man, so there is a resemblance in one
Christian to another. There is a difference between
Christians, as there is a difference of stature and
feature and understanding among men. But there
are the same outlines of character among all real
Christians, so that the representations made of the
hearts of David, and Paul, and other good men, in
Scripture, are of great use to us, not only to direct
our course of life, but to assist us in searching our own
hearts. We have not the same degrees of faith in
Christ, and love to God, and delight in his word, as

these holy men; but if we are true saints, the same dispositions, though with less vigour, will rule in our lives, for every Christian has the same sanctifying Spirit, though his operations in all are not equally signal *.

Ver. 20. *Hell and destruction are never full, so the eyes of man are never satisfied.*

Although heart answereth to heart, yet there are such varieties in the hearts of men, that we cannot search out the secret workings of the hearts of our fellow men, and it is a happy thing that we cannot do it; but because it is of importance to us to know in some degree the thoughts, and wishes, and designs of others, we have some means of discovering them. They can inform us by their tongues what is in their hearts, and when they think proper, for reasons of their own, to dissemble with their tongues, their eyes often betray them, for in the eyes love, and anger, and envy, and desire, often paint themselves so visibly, that they cannot but be perceived in spite of every endeavour to conceal them.

One of the many things in which men agree with one another is the insatiableness of the desires of the heart, (which are discovered in the eyes.) The invisible world is never full of souls, and the grave is never satiated with the carcases of men. After the innumerable millions that have been buried in death, they are still crying, give, give, and will continue their importunate demands till that day when death and hell are to be cast into the lake of fire and brimstone. The heart of the sons of men is equally clamorous for something to satisfy it. They enlarge their desires as hell, and cannot be satisfied. If you should give them a world, they will weep for another world. They

---

*Rom. 8:9

think if they had this and the other object of their wishes they would be happy; but they find that the gratification of their desires, is but like drink to one in a dropsy, which does not allay, but increase his thirst.

The improvement of this truth is taught by Solomon himself, at great length, in the book of Ecclesiastes. The insatiableness of men's desires is one of the arguments by which he proves the vanity of the world, and the unsatisfactory nature of its richest enjoyments. Man's chief end is to glorify God, and to enjoy him for ever, and he will never be happy till his heart is suited to his end. To seek happiness in this world, is to seek the living among the dead. It is to seek to be happy in opposition to the irreversible determination of the author of happiness, who framed our souls with such large and boundless desires that they never can be filled, but by him that filleth all in all. The only way of being happy is to comply with the gracious invitation of our Redeemer, " If any man thirst, let him come unto me and drink*."

Ver. 21. *As the fining pot for silver, and the furnace for gold; so is a man to his praise.*

The fining pot tries silver, and the furnace discovers whether gold be genuine and pure, so praise bestowed upon a man, discovers the reigning temper of his mind. If a wise and humble man is praised, he will not be thereby elevated in his own mind. If the praise conferred upon him is not just, he will not think himself warranted to lay any stress upon it, for it is an evidence of pride when a man despises undeserved reproaches, and yet piques himself on commendations which are equally groundless, and therefore equally vain; and if it is a piece of meanness to be dejected by the one, it is a piece of vanity to be puffed up by the

---

*John 7:37, 4:14, Prov. 8:21

other. But if a wise man is commended upon good grounds, he does not consider himself as entitled to the chief praise of those good qualities which he is possessed of, or those good actions which he hath performed, because it is God alone that makes him to differ from other men, and every thing that is of him, and through him, ought to be ascribed to him *.

When a bad man is praised for those qualities that he has, or those actions that he has done, he spoils all their value and credit by the greediness with which he swallows the commendations; he does not ascribe the praise of them to God, but like Herod wishes to appropriate all the glory to himself, or if he gives it to God, he does it only in words and professions, like the self-conceited Pharisee. But when a fool receives praise that is founded only on falsehood, or on flattering misconstructions of his actions, he is so fond of every thing that tends to his own advancement, whether right or wrong, that he is well pleased; and as if other people knew him better than himself, he can prevail on himself to believe every thing they are pleased to say in his favour. Darkness will be light, and vice will be virtue in his eyes, when it serves to nourish his self-esteem.

There is one good effect which may arise out of undeserved commendations to a wise man. They will be a motive to him to deserve them, that men may not run into mistakes by their good opinion of him; but praise ought to be administered with great caution to the best of men, for as it discovers some men to be nothing but dross, so it shews good men to have too much dross in their composition. The compliments of the ambassadors of Babylon were prejudicial to no less a man than Hezekiah. But to Herod the praise of men proved pernicious.

*I Cor. 15:11, Acts 12:21-23, Hos. 14:2,3

Ver. 22. *Though thou shouldest bray a fool in a mortar among wheat with a pestle, yet will not his foolishness depart from him.*

How deplorably perverse are the hearts of fallen men! Let favour be shewed to the wicked, yet will they not learn righteousness; in the land of uprightness they will deal unjustly, and will not behold the majesty of the Lord. Let them be afflicted, and bruised, and crushed under the judgments of God, or punishments inflicted by the hand of men, as wheat is bruised in a mortar, or between the upper and nether millstones, yet they will refuse to part with their folly. Pharaoh was broken by the terrible plagues which God inflicted upon him, and sometimes he confessed his folly, and promised amendment, and yet he returned to his folly, like the dog to his vomit, till he was utterly destroyed; for when God fights against a man he will be sure to overcome. Ahaz had the sermons of the prince of the later prophets to enforce the language of the rod. Isaiah preached with celestial eloquence. God smote him with a succession of the most alarming judgments, yet in the time of his distress did Ahaz sin more and more against the Lord. This was that king Ahaz; and multitudes walk in his paths, refusing to receive correction, and thereby exposing themselves to tenfold condemnation.

To what purpose then serves the rod for the fool's back? Does not the rod of correction drive foolishness away from the heart? It does when the blessing of God accompanies it, and it must be used with a dependence upon him that has appointed it. Without the concurrence of divine grace, the rod will not drive away folly from the hearts of young persons, and far less from the hearts of those in whom corruption receives double strength, from the superadded force of custom *.

---

*Jer. 13:23

The judgments of God against sinners tend greatly to aggravate sin, when they have not a reforming effect ; and therefore when they are in the earth, we ought to pour out fervent supplications to God that he may subdue, by his almighty grace, the stubbornness of the hearts of men, and make them to learn righteousness.

If we are under the rod, let us consider the design of it, and the intolerable load of guilt which we must contract by continuing unhumbled ; and under a sense of the hardness and instability of our spirits, let us turn unto the Lord with those supplications which God himself puts into our mouths *.

Ver. 23. *Be thou diligent to know the state of thy flocks, and look well to thy herds.*

To the precepts so often given us about diligence in the business of our calling, some will object that they have plenty of servants to manage their affairs, and they have no occasion to toil their own bodies, or fatigue their minds with them. But Solomon tells them that they may soon come to poverty, if they will not take the trouble of minding their own affairs, and inspecting their servants. Every man ought to be acquainted with the state of his own business, and look to it with his own eyes.

I am in affluent circumstances, you will perhaps say. But if you will not mind your business you may soon be as poor as Lazarus.

Ver. 24. *For riches are not for ever, and doth the crown endure to every generation ?*

You have not the riches of a crowned head, but if you had, they might be wasted and scattered by carelessness, which has often turned princes into beggars or bankrupts. Although there was never a richer king than Solomon, yet he was sensible of the necessity

*Jer. 31:18, Hos.14:2,3

of attending to his affairs, and acquired a part of his reputation for wisdom from the management of his domestic concerns.

Solomon tells us in another place, that the instability and uncertainty of earthly things, after all our care, is a motive to draw off our hearts from them, and to fix our eyes upon nobler objects ; but he tells us, in this place, that the perishing nature of earthly things is likewise a reason for bestowing a moderate and lawful share of our attention upon our temporal interests.   Let us do what we can, the world cannot be secured to us, and therefore we must choose a more durable portion ; but by the blessing of God upon our honest labours, we may in most cases expect to enjoy a competency of earthly blessings ; whereas negligence in our earthly business will in all probability reduce us to those straits which would embitter our days, and those shifts which would prejudice our credit and our consciences.

God's bounty is a great encouragement to our industry.

Ver. 25. *The hay appeareth, and the tender grass showeth itself, and the herbs of the mountains are gathered.*

God has given us great testimonies of his goodness, in giving us rain from heaven and fruitful seasons. By his kind providence the springing of the earth is blessed, and the mountains are covered with herbage, which may be gathered for the use of those beasts that serve for the use of man.   Does God stretch out his hand with blessings, and shall man, ungratefully and foolishly despise the bounty, and lose the benefit of it by his own neglect and sloth ? If God puts a price into our hands, to get either heavenly wisdom or the needful blessings of life, we are fools if we have not heart to employ it for the intended purpose.   The valleys and the mountains, which rejoice and sing to God, cry out against sluggish men. The necessity and advantage of industry and care are very visible;

Ver. 26. *The lambs are for thy clothing, and the goats are the price of the fold.*

Ver. 27. *And thou shalt have goat's milk enough for thy food, for the food of thy household, and for maintenance for thy maidens.*

By industry you shall have clothing, and food, and rent for your fields, or money to buy new possessions. You shall not perhaps be able to procure the luxuries of life, but these are not to be sought after; you shall have a comfortable maintenance for yourselves and your families; your maid servants shall have plenty of that food that is proper and convenient for them. On the other side, if you neglect your business, you bring want not only upon yourselves, but upon those for whom you are bound to provide. " If a man provide not for those of his own house, he is worse than an infidel," or even a robber in the Arabian desert *.

But how does our Lord say, " Labour not for the meat that perisheth, but for that which endureth unto everlasting life?" His meaning is, that we are to labour in the first and chief place, for that enduring bread. If we must not be careless about our bodies, and the interests of this life, which passes away like a cloud, what care can be too great about our everlasting interests †?

If men must look well to the state of their flocks and herds, they are guilty of insufferable negligence who have some of Christ's flock committed to their care, as masters, or parents, or teachers, or pastors, and yet thoughtlessly suffer them to perish ‡.

---

*Job 24:5   †1 Cor. 9:25, 2 Cor. 4:18   ‡Ezek. 34:4

Proverbs 28

Ver. 1. *The wicked flee when no man pursueth : but the righteous are bold as a lion.*

The wicked are so desperately hardened that they have no fear of the most horrible dangers, at least they have not such an apprehension of them, as to flee to that sure and only refuge which Divine grace has provided. At the same time they are so wretched that that they are never in security, and are liable to the most distressing terrors, when there is no reason for them. The Syrians that besieged Samaria heard the noise of chariots and horsemen, which threw them into such a panic that they fled away, and left their bread and clothes behind them. In like manner, sinners are liable to terrors which sometimes encompass them like waters, when no reason can be given for them ; for the objects which ought to alarm transgressors, and have a tremendous reality in them, are not the things that take hold of their minds. They are like madmen who fear not a drawn sword, but tremble at the shaking of a leaf, as if it were a devil ready to hurry them away to the bottomless pit. No passion is more tormenting than fear, and a sense of guilt producing it. It was a punishment threatened against the people of Israel, if they revolted from God, that they should flee before their pursuing enemies ; but it is a sign of the utmost wretchedness, when men flee away through terror when there are no enemies, but such as are conjured up by a timorous fancy.

Sinners have great reason after all to fear, even when the objects of their fear are mere fancies. God is angry

with them every day, and their anxious alarms are a
part of the punishment of their sins *. They cannot
expect tranquillity and happiness of mind but in Christ,
by whom we are delivered from the guilt of sin, and
enjoy that peace which passeth all understanding.
Those who are justified by his righteousness, and led
in the paths of righteousness by his Spirit, are bold as a
lion, the most courageous of creatures upon earth ; for
they are delivered from all danger of condemnation ;
they are at peace with God, and a league is made for
their safety with the stones of the field, and the beasts
of the earth, and the serpents of the dust. They may
have many enemies, but God is their friend, and no
weapon formed against them shall prosper. They
may meet with adversities and deaths, but they shall
meet with nothing to separate them from the love of
God, with nothing that was not designed for them by
an all wise and gracious providence, with nothing but
what shall contribute to their good.

The righteous are sometimes timorous like doves,
but they have reason to be bold as lions ; they have
that spirit which is a spirit of power; they are partakers of those graces which have a native tendency
to expel tormenting fears, and to produce quietness
and assurance for ever. Their natural constitution,
their remaining corruptions, their unhappy falls, their
numerous enemies, may counteract their principles of
holy courage, but they are commanded to be always
strong in the grace that is in Christ Jesus ; and the
day is coming when every fear shall vanish away, and
be succeeded by eternal triumphs.

What effect righteousness has to produce boldness,
and to banish fear, appears from the history of the
elders who obtained a good report through faith †, and

---

*Job 15:21   †Heb.11

of the apostles and first Christians, who triumphed in the midst of daily deaths, and in the face of bloody tyrants; nor have later ages been destitute of testimonies to the truth of this proverb. Martyrs have rejoiced in flames, as if they had been beds of roses; and Christians on a death bed have often said, " O death, where is thy victory! Thanks be unto God who giveth us the victory through our Lord Jesus Christ."

Ver. 2. *For the transgression of a land, many are the princes thereof: but by a man of understanding and knowledge shall the state thereof be prolonged.*

The providence of God suffereth not a sparrow to fall unnoticed to the ground; how much less is it to be supposed that the affairs of men, and of societies consisting of millions of men, are unobserved by the great God, whose kingdom ruleth over all.

We often rejoice, and often mourn, when we observe the occurrences of public governments, but we attend too little to the justice of God concerned in them. When frequent changes happen in the administration by the deaths of princes, or by those revolutions which seat a new family on the throne, God is carrying on his purposes of mercy or judgment; and although the same princes continue sitting on the throne, when the ministry is in a fluctuating state, and public measures continually changing, we may see the justice of Providence, and the provocations of the land calling down that vengeance which is executed in the miseries brought upon a land by these means. For the transgressions of Israel and Judah we find many princes, sometimes cut off in a very short space of time; and even the good Josiah was removed from an earthly to a heavenly kingdom, to make way for that punishment which was due to the guilt of the land *.

---

*Isa. 5:7, 2 Kings 15:24,25, Zech. 11:8

But a man of wisdom and piety is a great national blessing. A private man of such a character may sometimes be a happy instrument of rescuing a nation from destruction, or establishing its peace and happiness *. But a prince furnished with skill to govern a nation, and with religion to govern himself, is an inestimable gift of God. His wise choice of counsellors and magistrates, his good example, his just and vigorous administration, the countenance he gives to virtue, and the checks he gives to wickedness, concur to establish the land in peace and prosperity, and the blessing of God attends his government.

The history of the good kings of Judah, and of almost all the good kings with which any nation has been blessed, are confirmations of this truth. Lord, give thy judgments to our king, and thy righteousness to the king's son.

Ver. 3. *A poor man that oppresseth the poor, is like a sweeping rain which leaveth no food.*

One would naturally think that poor men, though exalted to high stations, would, through their knowledge of the heart, and experience of the hardships of a poor man, look down with tenderness upon the poor, and use their newly acquired authority for the protection of those who are left in that state out of which they were raised ; but experience tells us that the worst of all oppressors have ordinarily been the poor, when they were advanced to rule. The poor that oppress the poor, are like a sweeping inundation that carries every thing along with it, and scarcely leaves any thing in the ground to be the seed of a future crop.

When poor men are exalted to power, their new dignity too often turns their brain. They know not

*Eccles. 9:13, 2 Sam. 20:16, Job 22:30

770 / *Exposition of Proverbs*

themselves, and they cannot be expected to know their former brethren.

Their experience of the hardships of poverty meeting with a selfish heart, disposes them to guard against its return, by oppressing those below them, and dragging every thing into their own possession, that they may set their nest on high, and be delivered from the power of evil. It is therefore very improper to place the poor in stations where they may have an opportunity to enrich themselves at the expense of others, unless they are well known to be men, like Joseph, of inflexible integrity. Those that might behave well in private stations, are often tyrants when temptation and opportunity concur to make them so; and history is full of the mischiefs which arise from the unwise neglect of the instruction given to nations and kings in this text.

How lovely is the character of our Redeemer! He made himself poor for our sakes, and he is now exalted to an heavenly throne; but his heart is not exalted above those poor men on earth, whom he vouchsafes to call his brethren. He knows the heart of a poor man, and he will deliver the needy when he crieth, the poor also, and him that hath no helper.

Ver. 4. *They that forsake the law praise the wicked, but such as keep the law contend with them.*

Sinners not only destroy their own souls, but contribute to the ruin of other men, by praising their wicked courses, and encouraging them in sin. No wicked man wishes to be called wicked, and therefore he puts false colours upon his own and other men's sins, baptizing them with the names of those virtues to which they seem to have most resemblance. Drunkenness is called good fellowship, covetousness is called prudence and frugality, courage in sin is called bravery, and peevishness has the name of honesty and plain dealing.

If no good quality can be found to put a gloss upon their sins, then the wicked will flatter one another by praising them for good qualities to which they have no shadow of a title, and at the same time extenuating their faults, as if they had no proportion to their good qualities. To forsake the law of God is a very bad thing; but to take pleasure in those that do the same, and to strengthen their hands in wickedness, is to walk in the ways of Jeroboam, the son of Nebat, who made Israel to sin.

The practice of sin is praise to evil-doers. Our example is of itself an encouragement to those who are like us in their behaviour; and when those who have fallen into sin through temptation, and resolve to reform, see others continuing in the practice of iniquity, they will be emboldened to go on in the same path; they see that they are no worse than other men.

Of all sinners, those that have left off to be wise and to do good are the most pernicious enemies to holiness, and give the most effectual encouragement to sin. The language of their practice is, we have tasted of the new wine of religion, and we find that the old wine of the pleasures of sin is better. Why should I leave my present practices, says the wicked man, to take the yoke of religion on my neck; others have tried it, and they find they are not able to bear it, and have been obliged to shake it off. They that forsake the law, are living infections to all around them, and little consider what loads of guilt, their own and other men's, lie upon them.

But they that keep the law contend with sinners; for they love God, and hate every thing that provokes and dishonours him. God promised Abraham to be a friend to his friends, and an enemy to his enemies. All the children of Abraham are heirs of this promise, and can they forbear to hate those that hate God, and to be grieved with those that rise up against him? But their hatred to them that hate God has no ill-will to their persons in it. They wish well to their best interests, and are zealous against their sins for the mischief which they do to their souls, as well as the provocation they give to God. Those that keep the law are in very different stations, and have very different degrees of influence. Magistrates and ministers, parents and masters, if they have a zeal for God, contend each in their places against sin; but even those pious persons that are in the meanest rank of life have an opportunity of striving against it, by their practice and prayers, and in many cases by their admonitions.

God is well pleased with those that rise up for him against the workers of iniquity. Great were the honours bestowed on the tribe of Levi for their impartial zeal against sin *. Yet we must remember that we ought to strive against sin with God's weapons, and in our proper ranks, under the banner of him that was manifested to destroy the works of the devil, and in the imitation of that example which he left us, that we might follow his steps.

Ver. 5. *Evil men understand not judgment, but they that seek the Lord understand all things.*

Evil men may have great talents, and much learning, but they understand not judgment, and therefore they cannot be said to understand any thing that is worth the knowing. Their corrupt affections spread a dark cloud over their judgments, that they cannot understand the way of wisdom and holiness. Their eyes are disordered and darkened by the malignant influence of sin, and therefore their whole course of life is full of darkness. It is true, they know their duty in many cases better than they practise it; but the knowledge which they have is at best a learned ignorance, for they

---

*Deut 33:9-11

are unacquainted with the necessity and excellency of doing their duty, and with those means that would be effectual for enabling and disposing them to do it.

The understandings of sinners are perverse as well as their will. Some error is mingled with the knowledge they have, which, unknown to others, and undiscerned by themselves, misleads them continually. They cannot receive the things of the Spirit of God, but their minds and hearts are both sensual, and therefore there is no judgment in their goings *.

They that know not judgment, know nothing at all; they are more brutish in their knowledge than the stork, and the crane, and the swallow †. But they that seek the Lord know judgment, and therefore they know every thing that is needful to be known by them. They are acquainted with the method of salvation, and with the way of being holy and happy. And what knowledge can be compared with this ? All the things that we can desire, all the things that are accounted precious on earth, are but loss and dung, compared with the excellency of the knowledge of Christ Jesus our Lord, and of the way of salvation through his blood, and of being conformed to him in his death and life.

The persons blessed with this excellent knowledge, are those that seek the Lord. They are set in opposition to evil men ; for they are all wicked who call not upon the name of the Lord, and who do not seek his favour as their chief happiness ; but they that seek the Lord with the desire of their souls, are haters of evil, and lovers of goodness, and have their portion with the saints. Perhaps they dare not say that they have found him whom their souls love, but their desires shall not be always disappointed ; for those relishes which the Spi-

---

*Matt. 6:22,23   †Jer. 8:9

rit of God has excited in their souls shall be gratified in due time.

They that seek the Lord search the Scriptures, and make them the subject of their meditation ; and God blesseth their diligence by giving them wisdom through his statutes. They pray with great fervency for the promised spirit, and God gives the Holy Spirit to them that ask him : this spirit is a spirit of wisdom and re-velation to them, leading them into all necessary truth; and therefore the spiritual man is said to judge all things. If he is sometimes at a loss to know his duty in particular cases, yet he has sure promises to plead with God, and to encourage his own soul in the hope that God will be pleased to reveal those things that he knows not unto him *.

Ver. 6. *Better is the poor that walketh in his integrity, than he that is perverse in his ways though he be rich.*

We had the sense of this proverb in the beginning of the 19th chapter; but it is here repeated because of the important instruction contained in it. Gold and silver glitter in our eyes, and dazzle our sight to such a degree, that a rich sinner appears more respectable than a saint in rags ; and the fatal consequence is, that men labour rather to be rich than holy. To direct our practice aright, it is necessary to have our unreasonable judg-ments of things corrected, and to esteem the poorest saint above the most prosperous transgressor. Upright-ness is so valuable in itself, that it gives a lustre to the possessors of it beyond what all the dignity and wealth of the world can do ; but double-mindedness and in-sincerity are so vile, that they stain the glory of th highest man on earth. Let us therefore choose the por-tion of God's people, however mean they are, and pray that we may not have our portion with the men of the

*Ps. 25:8, 1 Cor. 2:15, 1 John 2:20,27, Phil. 3:15

world, although their bellies should be filled with God's hidden treasure *.

Ver. 7. *Whoso keepeth the law is a wise son, but he that is a companion of riotous men, shameth his father.*

Let us suppose that two men have each of them a son. The son of the first is polished in his manners, has his understanding adorned with every liberal science, and is placed in a way of life, wherein he has the prospect of making a large fortune ; but, after all, wants the grace of God, and has no deep impressions of religion : the other man's son has none of these advantages, but is so deeply impressed with a sense of religion, that he shews a respect in his behaviour to all God's commandments. Which of the two parents has most comfort and credit in his son? Solomon would answer,— the second, because he is a wise son.

This wisdom will make a young man to choose good company, and to avoid the society of riotous persons, and every thing that might reflect disgrace upon himself or his father ; but he that is unrestrained by a principle of religion, is in great danger of associating himself with riotous and dissolute companions. And he that is a companion of riotous persons, shameth his father, for he will soon imitate those whose company he loves; or, if he preserves himself from their vices, (which can scarcely be expected,) he at least exposes himself to suspicions, and loses his character.

Do you wish to have credit in your children? Let your first and great care be to train them up in the nurture and admonition of the Lord ; for the wisdom in a son whereby he honours his father, lies mainly in keeping the law. Do you wish to give comfort to your parents, and to reflect honour upon them ? Let religion be your great business, and choose for your companions

---

*Ps 17:14

those that fear the Lord. But have no fellowship with dissipated youths. Let not their mirth and humour allure you into their company; for you may as soon touch pitch and not be defiled, as have fellowship with bad men, without being in a lesser or greater degree corrupted.

Ver. 8. *He that by usury and unjust gain increaseth his substance, shall gather it for him that will pity the poor.*

The reason why men grind the faces of their poor neighbours, by usury and unjust gain, is, that they expect to make themselves rich by such means. The reason why men are averse from pitying the poor is, that they fear poverty will be the consequence. These hopes and fears are equally groundless. Solomon, in many places of this book, teaches us, that oppression and unmercifulness is the surest road to poverty, and that liberality to the poor is the surest and shortest road to riches; because God maketh men rich or poor at his pleasure, and by his secret methods of providence makes the money of the wicked to find its way into the purses of the righteous and merciful. This is a truth which experience often verifies. If it is not constantly, it is generally the case, and when things appear to be otherwise ordered, we ought to acquiesce in the sovereignty of God, and to believe that his word has, or will have, its accomplishment, though in a manner as yet unknown to us. Job was reduced to extreme poverty, after all his wonderful acts of generosity to the poor *, and never expected to enjoy any more happiness in this world, yet he never doubted of this truth. Though he heap up silver as the dust, and prepare raiment as the clay;—he may prepare it, but the just shall put it on, and the innocent shall divide the silver †.

---

*Job 29   †Job 27:16,17

Let us not be afraid of bringing poverty upon ourselves by well-doing. Do we not see multitudes of men endeavouring vainly to enrich themselves by unjustifiable means? Do these men trust to the dictates of the devil and the flesh, and shall we refuse our confidence to the God of truth? These men are the stewards of merciful men. They squeeze the poor to bring money into their own pockets, but God will distrain upon them, and bring their unjust gains into the possession of them that are good in his sight *.

Ver. 9. *He that turneth away his ear from hearing the law, even his prayer shall be an abomination.*

If a subject refuses to grant the requests of his prince, which have the force of commands in them, what face can that subject have to appear with his own requests before his royal master, or what hopes can he entertain that they shall be granted? How strange then is it that sinners can expect any favour at the hand of the King of heaven, when they are provoking him to anger every day to his face!

The law of God signifies the whole revelation of his mind, concerning our faith and practice. When we reject the salvation revealed in the gospel, we are guilty of the most ungrateful disobedience to God, and by refusing an interest in Christ, we render all our prayers unacceptable and abominable to God, who hears no prayers but those which are presented in the name of Christ. When we live in a wilful disobedience to any of God's commandments, we declare all our professions to be insincere, and our faith to be a dead faith, and therefore we only impose upon ourselves, and we cannot impose on the hearer of prayer, if we hope that any of our requests will be acceptable to him. If we have the genuine and living faith of God's people, and trust

---

*Eccles. 2:16

in God as the hearer of our prayers, we will surely hear
what the Lord God will say unto us, and regard every
one of his precepts as the apple of our eye .

When the wise man tells us that even the prayer of
the sinner is an abomination, he plainly insinuates, that
no act of devotion or charity can find acceptance from
such a person. He that disobeys the law of God may
be in some cases liberal to the poor, and in many things
he may gain the praise of men, but every thing that he
does is detestable to God, who sees how corrupt his
principles and views are. Such a man is without Christ,
and can have no happy intercourse with God. His
heart is under the reigning power of sin, and the best
thing that he does is sinful; he is a rebel to God, and
God is an enemy to him for his wicked works.

Ver. 10. *Whoso causeth the righteous to go astray in
an evil way, he shall fall himself into his own pit; but the
righteous shall have good things in possession.*

He that digs a pit for any man shall fall into it †.
How then can they escape who dig a pit for the favourites of God, or by their artful persuasions, and deceitful misrepresentations, seduce the people of God into
those pits which have been digged for them by others?
The Lord is the protector of the righteous, and the
avenger of the injuries that are done to them by violence or deceit. Their enemies are considered by Christ
as his own enemies; and he must reign till he hath put
all enemies under his feet.

Those who contrive and execute mischievous designs
against the righteous, are contriving mischiefs for themselves, and drawing a sword out of its scabbard to be
sheathed in their own bowels ‡; for every event in the
world is over-ruled by a righteous providence. They
may indeed meet with success at first, for the righteous

---

*1 John 3:22   †Chap. 26:27   ‡Ps. 37:15

falleth sometimes into the pits prepared for him, but they have no reason to triumph ; for if the righteous should fall seven times in a day, yet he has an Almighty helper present with him, who will not suffer him to perish, but will raise him up, and put him in possession of all those good things which are promised by that faithfulness which never could deceive. The wicked man may soon bring abundance of mischief upon himself, by his malignity to those whom God supports; but he can bring no evil upon them, that shall not be made to work together with other things for their good, and he shall not be able to keep from them any of those good things which are the sure portion of the heirs of God. Earth and hell may rage against the righteous—all the force and cunning of the old serpent and his seed may be exerted against them ; but they have constant encouragement to trust in God, and have no reason to despond, for God withdraweth not his eyes from the righteous, but with kings are they on the throne. Yea, he doth establish them for ever, and they are exalted *.

Ver. 11. *The rich man is wise in his own conceit, but the poor that hath understanding searcheth him out.*

Riches are good in themselves, and are very useful in the hands of a wise and good man ; but the greatest part of rich men, in the judgment of Solomon and of Christ, are the worse men for their riches; because they are a means of making them more proud and self-conceited than they would otherwise be. They think themselves men of greater abilities than poor men, because they attribute their wealth to their own skill in business ; or, if they possess it by inheritance, they take to themselves airs of importance, as if they were men of a superior species to the rest of the human race. The

---

*Job 36:7, Mic. 7

respect which is shewed them by discretion, and the court paid them by flattery, they consider as a tribute of praise to their great merit.

The importance which they assume, and the respect which they exact, render them the objects of scorn or pity to many of their poor neighbours. God has imparted his gifts variously. To some he has given much wealth and little understanding. To others, he has not given riches, but what is of incomparably greater value, a sagacious and comprehensive mind ; and, therefore, no man ought to be proud on the one hand, or dejected on the other hand. Let each of us be thankful for the bounties of God to ourselves and others ; but it would be a great presumption to grudge other men what God has thought fit to bestow on them, or to be displeased because he has not given us every thing.

The poor that hath understanding sees through the weakness and folly of his rich neighbour that boasts of his wisdom, and despises him, not so much for his want of sense, as for his groundless pretensions to it. No man would make himself the object of laughter, if he would be content with his due ; but when one exacts more respect than he is entitled to, he loses that respect which he would otherwise have.

Let rich men consider, that much of that regard which they think is paid to themselves, is in reality paid to their purses ; and that a horse might, with as much justice, be valued according to the splendour of its trappings, as a man by the extent of his possessions. Let them take care lest they expose themselves to the censure and scorn of their inferiors, by exacting respect, and, what is worst of all, lest they make the gifts of providence an instrument of their own destruction, by turning them into nourishment to their vanity, and obstacles in their way to the kingdom of heaven. Paul enjoins Timothy to charge the rich not to trust in riches ; pointing out to us that rich men are too much disposed to trust in riches, and that trust in riches is a very dangerous vice.

Ver. 12. *When righteous men do rejoice there is great glory ; but when the wicked rise a man is hidden.*

When righteous men are exalted to power in a nation, the state of it is happy and honourable ; for they punish wickedness, and encourage virtue ; they protect the liberty and property of their inferiors ; and all men rejoice in their administration.

But when the wicked enjoy the places of power, no man thinks himself sure of his life and property. Villains may rejoice, because their crimes are countenanced, but honest men run into corners to hide themselves ; for many are oppressed, and all the rest are afraid. Such was the situation of our own country an hundred and fifty years ago. Let us bless God that things are now on a very different footing : and let us pray that our judges may be always peace, and our exactors righteousness.

How valuable is a righteous man ! If he is not a blessing to all around him, the reason is because the sphere of his influence is narrow. How much is wickedness to be abhorred ! It is the ruin of a man's own soul, and it makes him a plague to all that are connected with him. Bad men themselves hate wickedness, when they find it pointed against themselves ; and tyrants have been execrated by all nations.

Ver. 13. *He that covereth his sins shall not prosper ; but whoso confesseth and forsaketh them shall have mercy.*

Sin is the source of misery and ruin : It has turned angels into devils, and peopled the regions of horror with those that once dwelt in the abodes of perfect bliss. It has brought misery and woe into our world, that might have been a lower heaven, if we had not revolted from God, and destroyed ourselves by our iniquity.

But, blessed be the Lord, our condition is not desperate, like that of the angels who kept not their first habitation. God looked upon our race with an eye of compassion, and provided us effectual relief. The Son of God is our great atonement, and we are called to the enjoyment of pardon through faith in his blood. Under a deep sense of our guilt and danger, we are warranted to claim salvation from sin and wrath from that mercy that reigns through righteousness unto eternal life, by Jesus Christ our Lord.

But such is the folly of many sinners, that they would rather hide their sins from their own eyes, and, if possible, from the eyes of God, than receive mercy under the character of sinners. They will allow themselves to be sinners, but they will not confess their sins ; or, if they cannot altogether deny them, they endeavour to save their honour, or rather their pride, to the ruin of their souls, by excusing and extenuating them, or by transferring, like our first parents, the blame of them to others. How foolish is it for those that pine away under a mortal disease to conceal it from the knowledge of the world, rather than seek a cure from the physician ?

Those who cover their sins shall not prosper ; for it is impossible to cover them from the eye of our Judge, and to endeavour to shelter ourselves under coverings that are not of his spirit, is an additional provocation to the eyes of his glory. If we would judge ourselves we should not be judged ; but if we cover our sins with excuses, and will not suffer ourselves to be sensible of our absolute need of sovereign mercy, how can we expect to share in that salvation, which is bestowed on men to the praise of the glory of the grace of God ? If we will not acknowledge our disease, we refuse to the physician the praise of a cure.

There are some who expose themselves to the censure of this text, by hiding their sins from men, when providence, by bringing them to light, calls for a public confession as one evidence of repentance. Such persons think it would be a dishonour to them to confess their faults; but the dishonour lay in committing them, and confession, with other proofs of repentance, is the only possible means of wiping it away. They stand upon a false point of honour, and expose themselves to disgrace and misery; for they shall not prosper, because they refuse to give glory to God by taking shame to themselves *.

Those that hide their sins shall not prosper, because they reject that mercy without which they must be miserable. They prefer their own fig-leaf coverings to that covering of sin by pardoning mercy which is the ground of blessedness to the guilty†. But if we confess our sins, God is faithful and just to forgive us our sins, and to cleanse us from all unrighteousness. Under the law, the offerer of an atoning sacrifice was appointed to lay his hands upon the head of the victim, as a token of the translation of his guilt unto his sacrifice. In like manner, we are to confess our sin, with a dependence on that blessed sacrifice which takes away the sin of the world, claiming the pardon of our iniquities through the Messiah, whose soul was made an offering for sin; and through him all that believe are justified from all things from which they could not be justified by the law of Moses.

But what shall we say of those who confess their sins, like Pharaoh, and again return to the practice of them ? These persons are not partakers of mercy, for their

---

*Josh. 7:19   †Ps. 32:1

confessions were never sincere. They were never produced by a genuine humiliation, nor mingled with faith in the atonement, and therefore they are not accompanied with reformation. They are provocations to God, because he is mocked and insulted by such deceitful professions. But he that confesseth and forsaketh his sins shall have mercy. It was divine mercy that wrought in him such a happy temper. The sincerity of his repentance is an evidence of his interest in the blessings of saving mercy. That mercy which he has already experienced shall still follow him, till he is crowned with loving-kindnesses and mercies*.

Ver. 14. *Happy is the man that feareth alway ; but he that hardeneth his heart shall fall into mischief.*

" The righteous is bold as a lion," says the wise man. How then does he pronounce a blessing upon the man that feareth alway ? Christian courage is very consistent with an holy and child-like fear of God, although it is opposite to that slavish and dispiriting fear which often possesseth the hearts of the children of disobedience.

The believer in Christ trusts in God as a father; but his confidence is mingled with a deep veneration of the holy name of God, which makes him to dread the thoughts of sinning against him more than death, and to tremble at the word of God, lest he should break any of its precepts, or deserve the execution of any of its threatenings, or seem to come short, through unbelief, of any of its promises. Paul was a triumphant believer, who feared neither men nor devils, and reckoned himself perfectly secure against every charge that might be produced against him ; and yet he lived in the constant exercise of holy fear, which disposed him to bring down his body, and keep it in subjection, lest when he

---

*Ps. 32, Luke 15

had preached the gospel to others, he himself should be a castaway.

He is not an unhappy but a blessed man whose heart is continually governed by this fear. It has a happy influence upon his soul, to guard it from the temptations of satan and the world, and to keep it close to the Redeemer. It tends not to obstruct, but to promote the exercise of faith, and hope, and joy in the Lord. Thus fear is a fruit of the Holy Spirit, and a blessed means of establishing the heart in the love of God. It is a happy sign of an interest in the everlasting covenant of mercy, and in that special favour of God which is the source of all our joys *. Josiah's heart was made tender by this fear ; and judgment could not light upon that land where he reigned, till he was removed out of it to a better kingdom.

But wretched is the man who is not afraid to sin against his maker and judge. His heart is hard as the nether millstone. He thinks himself a man of courage, but his courage is the bravery of an infernal fiend. He is not impressed with the awful authority of God, nor melted with the astonishing declarations of his mercy, nor terrified at the tremendous thunders of the threatening law. Shall such a man escape the vengeance which he defies? or, in other words, is he stronger than the Lord?

Let Pharaoh's ruin in the Red Sea, and the destruction of Israel in the desert, and the misery of that nation which rejected our Saviour, be considered by stupid sinners, that they may judge whether a man can harden himself against God and prosper. Wherefore, as the Holy Ghost saith, " to-day, if ye will hear the voice of Christ, harden not your hearts †." Do you find your hearts stubborn and insensible, after all God's dealings

---

*Jer. 32:40, Isa. 66:2   †Heb. 3:7-11

with you by his word and providence; put them into the hand of God, that he may take away from you the hearts of stone, and give you hearts of flesh *.

Ver. 15. *As a roaring lion and a ranging bear, so is a wicked ruler over the poor people.*

The lion and the bear are two of the fiercest kinds of animals; but they are doubly dreadful when the one is roaring, and the other ranging about for prey, seeking in the rage of hunger whom they may devour. No less dreadful is a tyrant who spreads desolation and terror through the country, by oppressing his poor subjects. He is a general enemy'; but his cruelty is felt most by the poor, who have no means of resistance in their power, and who can least bear his exactions.

Oppressors are called benefactors by their slavish flatterers, but they are called wild beasts in Scripture. The fiercest of animals, at the time when they surpass themselves in fierceness, are used by Solomon as emblems of their savage nature. But these emblems were insufficient to represent the monstrous barbarities that have been often exercised by those that were at the head of the Roman empire in its pagan or antichristian state; and, therefore, Daniel and John represent them under the figure of monsters more dreadful than any that were ever beheld by the eyes of men †. The language of inspiration could not furnish out more terrible images for the devil himself, than those which have been used to represent the wickedness of tyrannical and persecuting powers.

We ought to be thankful for the wounds that have been given to the beast with seven heads and ten horns, and for the civil and religious liberties which we enjoy; and to pray with fervency, that those nations which groan under the oppressions of civil or spiritual tyranny,

---

*Jer. 31:18   †Daniel 7:10, Rev. 13

may be rescued from their bondage, by that great king of whom it was promised, that he would judge the poor and needy, and break in pieces their oppressors.

Ver. 16. *The prince that wanteth understanding is also a great oppressor : but he that hateth covetousness shall prolong his days.*

Those princes are cursed with a blind mind as well as an iron heart who oppress their subjects ; for otherwise they could not, for the gratification of a senseless lust of having, make themselves the plague and curse, the abhorrence and execration of thousands and millions, and expose themselves to those plots from men, and that vengeance from heaven, which seldom suffer a tyrant to fill a throne for many years.

Want of understanding is the root of covetousness in any man, especially in a sovereign prince, whose proper treasure lies in the breasts of his subjects. A wise prince not only abstains from oppressive exactions, but hates covetousness, and would far rather deny himself the pleasures and splendours of royalty, than impose excessive burdens on his subjects. Happy is the prince who is possessed of this disposition. He shall live and reign for many years. He has a throne in the heart of every subject; and there is not one in his dominions, who has any sense of gratitude and generosity, that will not venture his life in his defence.

Ver. 17. *A man that doth violence to the blood of any person shall flee to the pit, let no man stay him.*

As he that digs a pit falls into it, so the murderer of his neighbour is his own murderer, God commands his blood to be shed by men, and his providence seldom suffers a murderer to escape. The pit of destruction is prepared for him, and he is driven to it by vengeance which will not suffer a murderer to live.

Let no man conceal the destroyer of his fellow-men; let no man plead for him ; let no man solicit a pardon for him; let no man do any thing to hinder his just punishment; but let every man contribute his endeavours to bring the assassin to the gibbet. Whatever have been his merits in other respects, whatever excuses he may plead for his crime, whatever connections you may have with him by relation or friendship, you make yourselves sharers in his guilt, if you help him to escape justice. The land is defiled with blood, if the murderer (when he can be found, and the crime can be proven,) escapes unpunished; how deeply then must they be defiled, who stay him from fleeing to the pit! Justifying the wicked is a crime of the same nature with condemning the righteous; and saving the life of a murderer has the same relation to the guilt of slaying the innocent.

Is God so severe in his laws and providence against murderers; let us give no indulgence to any of those passions or dispositions, that lead to such a black and atrocious crime. Hatred and wrath do not always end in blood, but blood commonly begins with hatred and wrath. These malignant passions are viewed as murder by the holy eyes of God; and the man who indulges them has committed murder already in his heart *.

Ver. 28. *Whoso walketh uprightly shall be saved; but he that is perverse in his ways shall fall at once.*

He that walketh uprightly walketh surely. But may he not stumble and fall into calamity? Solomon never meant to deny that he may; but although he fall, he shall not be utterly cast down. He shall be preserved and rescued by the power of God, who looketh upon the upright with complacency, and glorifies his power and faithfulness by the salvations which he bestows on them. The upright are exposed to the same calamities with other men, and sometimes they meet with special hardships and dangers for the sake of their uprightness;

*Matt. 5:21,22

but if they should die for the sake of a good conscience, they are safe, for Christ hath assured us, that he who loses his life for bearing an upright testimony for the sake of Christ shall save it.

The double-minded man expects safety from his pliable temper. He is not like the inflexible oak, but like the pliant osier, which bends with every wind, and therefore he thinks that no tempest shall blow him down; but God hath said it, and his word will stand that he shall fall at once. His arts may succeed for a time to spin out an infamous life, or to preserve his property and credit; but the ruin which he endeavours to avoid, shall seize upon him when he is not expecting it, and to his great mortification, he shall find himself ruined by those very arts which he employed for his security. He is cast into a net by his own feet, and he walketh upon a snare, and his destruction, when it comes, shall be complete and irremediable. It may be delayed for a time, but when it comes it shall not need to rise up the second time *.

Ver. 19. *He that tilleth his land shall have plenty of bread, but he that followeth after vain persons shall have poverty enough.*

We must seek from God our daily bread, but we must not expect to have it rained down like manna from the clouds without any labour of our own. Let us join industry to our dependence upon God, and we shall have bread enough for ourselves and our families, and something to give to the poor.

But the man that loves idle company has no relish for the business of his calling; he learns habits of idleness and dissipation, which will soon bring him to poverty. He behaves as if he were hungering and thirst-

---

*Nah. 1:9

ing after poverty, and he shall soon be filled with that which he is so eagerly seeking after *.

Ver. 20. *A faithful man shall abound with blessings, but he that maketh haste to be rich shall not be innocent.*

He is a faithful man that prefers his duty and his conscience to his interests, and would rather suffer poverty and disgrace a thousand times, than obtain riches as the reward of iniquitous compliance with the wicked, or any violation of his duty to God or man. Covetousness is absolutely inconsistent with faithfulness ; for when men are more eagerly solicitous to be rich, than to be approved of God, their ruling passion will on some occasions hurry them over the belly of their consciences to iniquity ; and by a course of bad actions their consciences will be hardened, and they will be reconciled to every thing, however unfair and unjustifiable, that promises to put money in their pockets. As the men that love God with a supreme affection will displease their dearest friends, and mortify their most eager desires rather than offend God, so those that are determined to be rich will venture on every danger, and displease all the world and God himself, rather than want that shining metal which darkens the splendour of every other excellency in their eyes.

The faithful man, like Job, shall abound with blessings, for men will bless him, by applauding his integrity, and by prayers in his behalf; and the blessing is not causeless, but shall come upon him. His faithfulness, when it is a fruit of the spirit †, is an evidence that he is blessed of God, and an heir of blessings of the richest kind.

But the man that loads himself with guilt, by endeavouring to lade himself with thick clay, shall be heavy

---

*Chap. 12:1   †Gal. 5:23

laden with well-earned curses, that shall sink him deep in perdition and destruction *.

Ver. 21. *To have respect of persons is not good, for, for a piece of bread that man will transgress.*

When judges are first perverted from integrity, it is owing to some powerful temptation addressed to them, which they think irresistible; at the same time, they think that they will never transgress the rules of justice for any paltry consideration. If justice is to be violated, said Julius Cæsar, it is to be violated for the sake of empire. Few of the covetous or ambitious hold their integrity at such a high price, but they must have some valuable consideration in exchange for their conscience and honesty. Some will sell justice for an estate or a title, that would scorn to barter it away for a trifle of money, or to sell their souls at such a pitiful price as that which Judas Iscariot had for his master.

But there is great danger in yielding to any temptation, however great; for besides that it is the sign of a corrupt heart, the conscience that is once violated, will, in time, be prostituted and debauched, and the most trifling temptation will become a sufficient motive for the greatest iniquities. The second step in wickedness will not raise such a conflict in the soul as the first, and the third will be easier than the second; and the most detestable villanies will appear less horrible to a man hackneyed in iniquity, than the slightest deviations from justice once did to the same person. He that would not transgress without the offer of thousands, will at length transgress for a piece of bread; and he that once refused a whole estate, if he suffer himself at last to be perverted, will become so degenerate, that he will sell the righteous for a few pieces of silver, and the needy for a pair of shoes.

---

*1 Tim. 6:9

792 / *Exposition of Proverbs*

Oppose the beginnings of sin, and give no place to the devil. If he can prevail upon you to comply now and then with his temptation, he will expect to bring you by degrees into such a compliant humour, that he will have no occasion to put himself to the trouble of tempting you at all.

Ver. 22. *He that hasteth to be rich hath an evil eye, and considereth not that poverty shall come upon him.*

They that will be rich fall into temptation and a snare. An evil eye is one of the products of a heart governed by the love of riches. A man of this temper is so tenacious, that every thing he can catch sticks to his fingers, and he cannot look with a bountiful eye upon the distresses of the poor, or stretch forth his hands for their relief. It is an eye-sore to him to see any man prospering but himself, or to behold any fish coming into the net of his best friend. He is so thoroughly immersed in selfishness, that he can hear no good news, except of some profitable bargain for himself, or of some deceased friend, who has left him a sum of money.

Such a man shall be baffled in all his labours, and all his hopes will be disappointed; for poverty shall come upon him. He lies under the curse of God; and since it is the blessing of God that maketh rich, poverty must be the fruit of his curse. He makes both God and men his enemies; and if either the injustice of the one, or the just vengeance of the other can rifle his stores, he must be reduced to want.

The covetous man will not believe that poverty is coming upon him, for he imagines that he is taking the most effectual way to become rich; but it will bring upon him so much the greater distress and pain that he was not expecting it. Those calamities, which are afflicting if they are expected, are shocking when they were unlooked for. Saints themselves find great dif-

ficulty in bearing sudden reverses of fortune ; but what
a terrible impression must they make upon wicked
men, who have none of those consolations that mitigate
every distress to the people of God !

If the covetous man does not feel the assaults of poverty whilst he lives, death will turn him out naked
and stript of every thing, to another world. His sins
alone shall cleave to him, and the curses which he was
collecting to himself in greater quantities than gold,
shall cleave to him through eternal ages.

Ver. 23. *He that rebuketh a man, afterwards shall find
more favour than he that flattereth with the tongue.*

A desire of enjoying the good graces of our friends
and neighbours, is the reason that we are so averse to
give them faithful admonitions when they do amiss,
and so ready to flatter them with our tongues. But is
the neglect of faithful reproof, or a fair and flattering
tongue, the true way of gaining the favour of our
friends ? By no means ; God has declared otherwise,
and God turns the hearts of men at his pleasure. If
our ways please the Lord, we have reason to hope that
he will turn the hearts of our enemies to love us ; but
if they displease him, he will make those to become
our enemies whose favour we courted by unworthy
means.

Flattery may gain us a transient flow of kindness,
and faithful reproof may excite a temporary disgust ;
for the unbridled self-love of men makes them unwilling to hear any reflection on their own conduct, and
disposes them to swallow down their own praise, without examining whether it is just or not. But the force
of truth and reason will in time appear, and flattery
will render the person that presented it odious, when
the bad effects of it are found by bitter experience. On
the other side, the faithful reprover is still esteemed,

when he is not loved so well as formerly ; and in time it will be found that his faithfulness will procure him a greater measure of that good-will and friendship which he seemed to forfeit. If we wish to enjoy a permanent interest in any man's love, we should make it our first point to secure his esteem by deserving it.

But, that we may experience the truth of this proverb, we ought to administer needful reproofs in a friendly manner ; for if we behave like enemies in doing the office of a friend, we must not think it strange if we are taken for enemies.

Ver. 24. *Whoso robbeth his father or his mother, and saith it is no transgression, the same is the companion of a destroyer.*

Some graceless youths imagine there is little harm in robbing their fathers ; and would take it very much amiss if you should class them with common thieves, for applying to their own use their father's money, without his knowledge or consent. They say in their hearts, that they are guilty of no transgression ; but the corruption of their principles is no extenuation of the badness of their practice. In the judgment of God they are to be ranked with the worst sort of villains, for they are guilty of violating, in a gross manner, the strongest bonds of nature. They waste the estate, and wound the spirit of one whom they are bound to love and honour, by the greatest benefits that one man can receive from another. And their relation to their parents is not an extenuation, but a grievous aggravation of their crime.

Parents should take care not to tempt their children to this sort of behaviour, either by withholding from them what is meet, or by foolishly indulging them in expences which they may find themselves afterwards obliged to restrain.

To say that we did not look upon a thing to be a transgression, will be no just excuse for any piece of conduct that we might have known to be criminal. It will only shew us to be so depraved, that even our minds and our consciences are defiled.

Ver. 25. *He that is of a proud heart stirreth up strife; but he that putteth his trust in the Lord shall be made fat.*

Only by pride cometh contention, and pride never comes without contention. The proud man has an high opinion of his own merit, and cannot bear with those who have not the same respect for him, that he has for himself. When he finds a man that does not cringe to him, or submit implicitly to his opinions, he is instantly alarmed as if an attack were made on his honour, and by his angry words and overbearing behaviour kindles up the fire of contention.

The proud man trusts in himself, and not in the Lord. He that trusts in the Lord is not high-minded and insolent. He has a low opinion of himself, and although he is not careless about his own reputation, yet he trusts God with his honour, as well as all his other concerns; believing that if his righteousness should be eclipsed, God will in due time bring it forth to the light. The weapons he uses for the support of his character, are the meekness and gentleness of Christ; and the consequence is, that he lives at peace, and rather pacifies than stirs up strife.

The proud are much to be pitied, for they have a poor wretched life. They can scarcely enjoy one day's tranquillity, because there are never wanting some to mortify their pride, and cross their ambition. But they that trust in the Lord enjoy an inward tranquillity and outward peace. The God whom they trust takes care of all their concerns, so that every thing which they do shall prosper ; or if any thing happens to cross their wishes, they know that it is agreeable to the appoint-ment of God whose will they prefer to their own. Their souls are like a watered garden, and like a well of water, whose waters fail not, for they are refreshed with the manifestations of the love of God, and the communications of his grace, and their hopes are full of immortality. O Lord God of Hosts, blessed is the man that trusteth in thee ! But miserable are the proud, and they that trust in their own hearts.

Ver. 26. *He that trusteth in his own heart is a fool ; but whoso walketh wisely shall be delivered.*

We must not trust our own prudence, even about our worldly business, without acknowledging God in it, for it is a piece of folly to neglect him in whom we live and move, and whose blessing is absolutely neces-sary for our daily labours, and our daily bread.

It is still more foolish to trust our own hearts in our spiritual concerns ; and yet we are guilty of this folly in a thousand instances. When we consult with our own judgment what worship we ought to give to God, instead of consulting with implicit submission of heart the oracles of God, who best knows what service will please himself—when we form our apprehensions about the doctrines of religion, without searching the Scrip-tures, and supplicating God to send forth his light and truth to direct and fix our judgments—when we try some other way of salvation than the way revealed in the gos-pel—when we form resolutions in our own strength, or persuade ourselves that we are able to keep them in opposition to temptation—when we endeavour to purify our own hearts, by closely applying to them moral per-suasions, or even divine truths, without a sense of our absolute need of Christ as our sanctification :—In all these cases, and in many others, we are chargeable with this folly ; and how gross the folly is may appear upon a slight examination of it. If any cheat had deceived us an hundred times, we would certainly deserve the character of fools if we trusted him any more ; and we are great strangers at home, if we are not sensible that it has been the common practice of our hearts to impose falsehoods on us from our youth up. The idolatrous heathens and Roman Catholics, the falls of saints, and the general wickedness of mankind, might be adduced as proofs of the danger and folly of this carnal confidence.

The only way of walking wisely is to have no confidence in ourselves, but to trust in the Lord with all our hearts, and to follow his counsels whithersoever they lead us. They that trust in their own hearts lean upon a broken reed, which will soon fail under them, and they will fall into mischief. Those that trust in the Lord and walk wisely, may fall into calamities and temptations ; but, for their comfort, they have a sure promise of deliverance. Their distresses are the trial of their faith, and they shall end in joy and happiness *.

Ver. 27. *He that giveth to the poor shall not lack ; but he that hideth his eyes shall have many a curse.*

Look upon the distresses of the poor, and your hearts will be melted into tenderness. If the sight does not affect your hearts, listen to their complaints and petitions ; if you disregard the voice of the poor, hear the voice of God commanding you to give to the poor. Do you grudge to give a little at the command of him that gave you all ? God has answered every objection against his precepts in his promises. He condescends to assure you that you shall be no losers but great gainers, by a

---

*Verse 18

cheerful compliance with his will. The poor cannot recompence you, but God will do it liberally. Are you afraid of bringing poverty upon yourself by your bounty ? Many have been ruined by withholding, never any by giving according to the will of God. Giving to the poor is the best preventive of poverty, for it is putting your money into the bank of heaven, which can never forfeit credit. The best securities on earth will not hinder your money from making wings and fleeing away. But he that giveth to the poor lendeth to the Lord, and shall surely receive it again when he needs it, with abundant increase.

The uncharitable man hides his eyes from the poor, lest his eyes should melt his hard heart, and tempt him to sin against his god, the unrighteous mammon. He is as much afraid of any thing that might excite him to goodness, as a saint is of temptations to sin*. But shall he save his money by his unrighteous withholding? Will this procure him the blessing of God, which maketh rich ? He can expect nothing but curses as his reward. The curse of him that is ready to perish shall come upon him. The curse of God is upon his hardened soul, and upon his basket and his store. He is miserable upon earth, in the hatred of God and men, and he takes the way to be cursed at the last day, and to secure himself an abode in that place where judgment without mercy shall be executed upon them that show no mercy.

Ver. 28. *When the wicked rise men hide themselves ; but when they perish the righteous increase.*

The reign of wicked princes is a general calamity, more dreadful than war and pestilence. Those that are not cut off, or stripped of their property, live in con-

---

*Job 31:1

tinual terror, because they know not how soon the overflowing scourge may reach themselves. These enemies of mankind are like ranging bears, or roaring lions whilst they live, and when they die their end is no more regretted than the death of a mad dog; for it is a deliverance to the nation, and a blessing to the church. The righteous are then freed from their restraints, and take courage to themselves, to support and spread the interests of religion and virtue. It is well known what happiness was caused by the death of Ahaz in the kingdom of Judah, and how Christianity was advanced in the Roman empire by the death of Julian; and how the death of Queen Mary of England, and the abdication of James II. tended to the restoration of happiness and religion in our own island.

How wretched are wicked rulers! They are hated whilst they live above the ground, and the curses of a nation pursue them to their long homes. They are accountable for the wickedness of thousands whom they draw or drive into sin; and they lie down in the dust loaded with innumerable iniquities of other men. The mercy, as well as the justice of God, is engaged to chace them out of the world; and those who are perverted by their influence upon earth will load them with execrations through eternity.

Proverbs 29

Verse 1. *He that, being often reproved, hardeneth his neck, shall suddenly be destroyed, and that without remedy.*

Asa, king of Judah, was a good man, and yet when he was reproved by a prophet, he stormed instead of repenting. This piece of history shews us that we must not despair of reforming those that depart from the path of duty, although they are not reclaimed by the first admonition. Perhaps they may relent at the second or third admonition, and then we are richly recompensed for our trouble *.

But woe to that man that is stubborn and obstinate after many reproofs. He despises a merciful appointment of God for his recovery, and tramples upon precious pearls †. He refuses to bow before the Lord, and he shall be dashed in pieces like a potter's vessel. He perhaps designs to reform at some other time ; but he is hardened in sin, and puts off his intended repentance till judgment comes upon him unexpectedly, and he is ruined for ever. The reproofs which he received will then be like hot thunderbolts to him, and the remembrance of them will feed the worm that never dieth.

All of us meet with many reproofs from God. The warnings of his word, and the addresses made to sinners by the ministers of Christ ; the kind advices of ministers and friends, the crosses which providence brings upon men in the way of sin, and even the favours which are showered down from heaven upon transgressors, are admonitions to them to leave the

*Matt. 18:15   †Matt. 7:6

ways of sin; and how shall they escape the most aggravated condemnation who continue impenitent? All
God's dealings with them are aggravations of their
guilt, and they are not to expect that the day of God's
patience will continue for ever, or that he will strive
with them for so long a space as he did with the old
world. To day, O sinners, if ye will hear the voice
of God, harden not your hearts as in the provocation. Those that fell in the wilderness are ensamples
unto you; your guilt will be heavier than theirs if you
harden your hearts, when such a monument of vengeance is placed before your eyes in the word of God.
The oath of God still stands in force against those that
always err in heart, and refuse to know God's ways;
and unless God can lie, they shall never enter into his
rest.

Ver. 2. *When the righteous are in authority the people
rejoice; but when the wicked beareth rule the people mourn.*

Like the ointment that was poured upon the head of
Aaron, and flowed down to the skirts of his garments,
is the administration of a wise and pious prince. He
diffuses peace and happiness around him. He is blessed, and he is a blessing to thousands.

But the people groan under the oppression of a wicked prince, and all the comfort they have is, that he is
not immortal, and that either a kind providence will
cut him off, or some provoked stroke of violence will
rid the world of such an intolerable burden. Let us
bless God for the establishment of our happy constitution of government, by which princes are at liberty to
do much good, and have their hands bound up, in a
great measure, from mischief, if they were disposed to
do it; and let us rejoice in that blessed administration
of grace, under which it is promised that the mountains shall bring forth peace to the people, and the little
hills by righteousness.

Ver. 3. *Whoso loveth wisdom rejoiceth his father ; but he that keepeth company with harlots, spendeth his substance.*

It is not the youth who has got much knowledge; it is not he that complies with the precepts of wisdom in many instances, but he that loves wisdom, and takes more pleasure in it than in all the delights of sense, that is truly a wise son, and gives joy to the hearts of his parents ; and he that loves wisdom will regard the happiness of his parents as his own, and he will have no greater joy than in giving them pleasure.

The love of wisdom will be a preservative from those dissolute courses to which young men are too much disposed *. But he that follows them discovers himself to be under the reigning power of folly. He spends his father's substance, and grieves the hearts of those who are the means of his existence. There are indeed stronger motives than the loss of substance, but this is a consideration fitted to work on the minds of the thoughtless, unless they are so deeply plunged in sensuality as to be almost beyond hope of recovery. The everlasting world is at a distance, and, therefore, it appears to young men a piece of superfluity to think much about it at present, but poverty, and the unhappiness of those that love you, are miseries that follow hard upon a dissolute course of life. You are double fools, fools for time and fools for eternity, if neither present nor eternal punishment can convince you of the danger of lewdness and bad company †.

Ver. 4. *The king by judgment establisheth the land; but he that receiveth gifts overthroweth it.*

Would you practise integrity, take heed and beware of covetousness ; for the love of gifts is sufficient to pervert even a king from the paths of judgment.

The prince that hateth covetousness shall prolong

---

*Chap. 7:4,5   †Chap. 24:24,25

his days; but that is not all his happiness. He has the pleasure of seeing millions made happy by his means, and rejoicing under the shadow of his government. He establishes a land, and bears up the pillars of it : for religion and righteousness, which are the safety and honour of a nation, are effectually promoted and encouraged by him. His authority and influence, his example, and his proper choice of inferior magistrates, are unspeakable advantages to his people, and a race yet unborn shall rise up and call him blessed *.

But the fountains of justice are poisoned, and the pillars of it subverted by a prince that is too fond of money. He perverts law into oppression, and makes his subjects unhappy. He destroys the foundations of his own throne, and plunges himself and his people into inexpressible miseries. He brings down the judgments of God upon a land, and is himself one of the greatest judgments that an angry God can inflict upon a nation.

Ver. 5. *A man that flattereth his neighbour spreadeth a net for his feet.*

Solomon was a great enemy to flattery. He tells us that the flatterer worketh ruin †; that he is as bad as the man that curses his friend ‡; and here he illustrates the mischief which he does, by comparing him to a fowler that catches the unwary birds with his net. The flatterer sometimes intends to ensnare the person whom he praises, and to persuade him to serve the flatterer's interest to his own damage. You are a man of a generous and friendly disposition, says the fawning hypocrite, and I am sure that you will serve me in this matter. Such arguments win upon a man's vanity, and seduce him to do himself the greatest hurt, or to expose himself to very great dangers that he may not disap-

---

*Ps. 75   †Chap. 26:28   ‡Chap. 27:14

point the expectations that are formed of him. Many have been cheated into poverty, and many have been cozened into sin and hell by such artifices.

But although the flatterer has no other selfish design but to insinuate himself into the friendship of the person whom he caresses, he may be justly said to spread a net for his feet, by betraying him into the hands of his worst enemy. We all flatter ourselves; and our self-flattery makes the praises of other flatterers welcome, and these gratify and feed our pride, so that we are in double danger of falling into the condemnation of the devil.

If flattery be a net, we ought to be on our guard against it, and to keep a suspicious eye upon those that praise us to our faces. Birds are silly animals, and there is no wonder that they suffer themselves to be catched in the snare of the fowler; and yet when they find themselves fast in the snare, they flutter, and use every possible effort to escape. Men are like silly birds when they are caught in this net, and they are sillier than birds, when, after all, they make the flatterer welcome to their houses, and his fair words welcome to their ears.

Ver. 6. *In the transgression of an evil man there is a snare; but the righteous doth sing and rejoice.*

Wicked men are ensnared, either when they are seduced to sin, or when they are involved in miseries from which they cannot deliver themselves, and in both these senses they find a snare in their transgression. One act of sin makes way for another act, and the second for a third; and the repetition of many sinful acts produces a settled habit, which gains an irresistible power over the soul, so that the sinner who meant to repent after he had indulged himself for a time in the pleasures of sin, finds himself quite indisposed to put his resolutions in practice, and walks on in his trespasses till destruction comes upon him without remedy. Besides this, one kind of sin prepares the way for another that is worse, because the natural effect of sin is to stupify the understanding, and harden the heart; and he that entered into the way of the ungodly, proceeds, in the next place, to stand in the counsel of the wicked, and then sits down in the seat of the scorner.

Wicked men find the thorns and snares of inevitable and irremediable calamity in the way of sin, and this will make them at last to curse themselves for their folly, in drinking down the delights of sin, which they find, too late, to be sugared poison. They think that they walk at liberty, because they have broken the bands of the Lord, and cast away his cords from them, but they will groan at the last, when they find themselves entangled in the cords of their own sins.

But the righteous are free from these snares, and cannot but sing and rejoice, and praise the name of the Lord, when they think of that sovereign grace which hath delivered them, like a roe from the hunter, and a bird from the snare of the fowler. They walk in a safe way, and the sins and miseries which others meet in the way of destruction, excite at once their sorrow for the miserable creatures that expose themselves to such tremendous dangers, and their joy at their own happiness in escaping them all *.

The way of sin is broad: the way of holiness is narrow; but those have reason to mourn that are travelling to the gibbet, although their path should be strewed with flowers. And those have reason to sing and rejoice who are walking over a rugged path to take possession of a throne.

---

*Ps. 138:4

Ver. 7. *The righteous considereth the cause of the poor ; but the wicked regardeth not to know it.*

The wise man does not say that a righteous judge will countenance a poor man in his cause, for that would be to respect persons in judgment, and to consider his poverty rather than his cause ; but he tells us that a righteous man will endeavour so to investigate and ma-nage the cause of a poor man in judgment, that he shall not lose it, for his inability to defend himself. Such a man was Job. The cause which he knew not he searched out. He delivered the needy when he cried, the poor also, and him that had none to help him. He broke the jaws of the wicked, and plucked the spoil from his teeth. Thus he put on righteousness as a breast plate, and his judgment was as a robe and a dia-dem. All just magistrates will endeavour to follow the example of that venerable prince, for this is one article of the commission which they have from the great king who entrusts them with this power. Lawyers, and people in every station, as opportunity offers, are bound to testify their righteousness and charity in like man-ner, as far as it consists with the station in which they are placed *.

But the wicked regardeth not to know the cause of the poor. It is the person that he regards and not the cause. He considers which of the two parties will give him most money, and passes such a decision, if he dares, as he thinks will tend most to his own interest ; or, if he is not yet so far gone in the ways of sin as to pervert justice in the most open manner, yet he will not be at the trouble of searching out the cause of a man that has no money to pay for it, and if his sentence should happen to be right, he is entitled to no thanks for it.

---

*Ps. 82, Prov. 24:11,12

Let judges remember that they must give an account of every act of their administration to him by whom kings reign. Let the poor that suffer oppression comfort their souls by considering the grace of the Redeemer's administration. He shall spare the poor and needy, and he shall save the souls of the needy. He shall redeem them from deceit and violence, and precious shall their blood be in his sight.

Ver. 8. *Scornful men bring a city into a snare* * ; (or rather, *scornful men set a city on fire*,) *but wise men turn away wrath.*

The proud in heart stir up strife ; and the fire which they kindle is not confined within the narrow circle of their own immediate connections, but often spreads with fury through every part of the city where they dwell. They are public incendiaries, that must have every thing done in their own way, or, if their pride and honour is not gratified, they excite universal disorder, drawing over as many as they can to their own party, by all the methods of fraud and villainy, and provoking other men by their conduct, till there is a kind of civil war raised within the bowels of that society to which they belong, and the city or country is in great danger of destruction.

These proud and scornful men are the bane of the place where they live ; but divine providence has scattered some wise men through many places, who counteract their mischiefs, and by prudent management, keep under or extinguish the flames of contention; to such persons, the places where they dwell are under the greatest obligations, and they ought to be respected as much as the haughty and insolent deserve to be abhorred.

---

* פחים certainly means burning coals. Josh. 11:7

There is another sense in which this proverb is verified. Men that despise God and goodness, and laugh at instruction and admonition, kindle the wrath of God against the country to which they belong; for they not only provoke the displeasure of God against themselves, but their example corrupts their neighbours, and those that do not follow their pernicious ways are in a lesser degree sharers in their guilt, when they do not mourn for the abominations of the land, nor bear a proper testimony against them, and thus the whole community is involved in guilt, and exposed to punishment *.

But wise and holy men turn away wrath by their fervent prayers, and by the success with which their endeavours are sometimes blessed, to stem the torrent of corruption. Such men stand like Moses in the gap, and prevent the execution of deserved indignation, and they justly deserve that glorious character of the chariots and horsemen of the nation. The wicked may call them the troublers of the land, but that is no strange thing, for Ahab reproached Elijah in such words.

The holy seed are the substance and strength of a land. The wicked of a land are its most dangerous enemies. Have we any love for our native country? Let us discover our patriotism by endeavouring to turn away wrath. If this cannot be done, it may be we shall be hid in the day of the Lord's anger; and it is certain that we shall in no wise lose our reward.

Ver. 9. *If a wise man contendeth with a foolish man, whether he rage or laugh, there is no rest.*

They that keep the law contend with the wicked;

---

*Ezek. 9

and prudence must direct us in what manner we should contend with them. Men have very different dispositions; some must be addressed with severe and sharp reproofs, that they may feel the iniquity of their conduct, but others are to be addressed in the language of mildness and gentleness, and will be won to goodness, although they could not be driven to it *.

We find that the prophets sometimes thundered, and sometimes wept, and sometimes allured men by the language of love to repentance. God, who is well acquainted with all the springs of conduct in human nature, taught them to deal with men in these various ways; but experience proved how generally this proverb agreed with the temper of foolish men; for the prophets seldom had much success in their exhortations, though diversified with all that wisdom and prudence in which God abounded towards men. The forerunner of our Lord, who was greater than the former prophets, lamented unto the people of his generation, and yet they did not mourn. Our Lord himself piped unto them, and the people wondered at the gracious words which proceeded out of his mouth. But they only wondered and did not generally repent.

Let us endeavour to turn sinners to the wisdom of the just by all the prudent methods competent to our station. If we do not succeed in our charitable endeavours, our reward is with the Lord, and obstinate sinners must give an account to the Judge of the living and the dead.

This proverb teaches us to avoid all personal contentions with foolish men; for whether we are angry at them, or endeavour by gentle means to reason or laugh them out of their folly, they will give us no rest, but

---

*Jude 22,23

behave in such a manner as may throw us off our guard, and deprive us of the possession of our own souls. When conscience and charity do not oblige us to enter into disputes with them for their own good, it is best to let them alone, except when the object of strife is sufficient to compensate our loss of peace.

The last words of the verse are by some interpreters understood of the fool, who is so intractable, that he either storms against the wise man that contends with him, or laughs him to scorn, and treats him with contempt. If we enter into dispute, we ought to behave with temper. Fury and scorn are the fool's weapons of warfare, but a wise man scorns to make use of them. As he wishes to do all things with charity, so he can carry on a necessary dispute, either about religion, or property, or any thing else that will justify a dispute, with that meekness of wisdom which becometh saints. The enemies of our Lord were remarkable examples of the fool's method of managing disputes. Our Lord himself is the great example whom Christians are to imitate in this and in every other point.

Ver. 10. *The blood-thirsty hate the upright ; but the just seek his soul.*

" If the world hate you," says our Lord to his disciples, " ye know that it hated me before it hated you." If God's people are conformed unto Christ in suffering the hatred of men, they need not think it a strange thing, nor suffer themselves to be dispirited on that account. There are some men whose hatred is better than their love, and such are the haters of the upright. They are blood-thirsty men, the successors of those who have been drunk with the blood of the saints, and with the blood of the martyrs of Jesus. Every man that hates his brother in his heart is a murderer, and those are murderers of the worst kind who hate men for that which is good. They are the true children of him that was a murderer from the beginning; for the just are of an opposite disposition. They seek his soul, (or care for it, as the word is translated*,) and it is a comfort to the upright to consider who they are that hate, and who they are that love them, and care for their welfare.

" Hereby know we the children of God and the children of the devil. Whosoever doth not righteousness is not of God, neither he that loveth not his brother ;" and he that loveth his brother will be zealous for his welfare, and will endeavour to screen him from the malice of the wicked. It is the duty of all men, and the disposition of the just, to deliver them that are drawn unto death, and those that are ready to be slain. Justice is not a lazy inactive virtue ; it does not rest satisfied with doing no evil, but it will dispose men to do good, and to prevent evil to the utmost of their power.

Do we profess to be just ? We must remember that love is a debt which we owe to men, and especially to the upright ; and that we must love, not in word and in tongue, but in deed and in truth.

Ver. 11. *A fool uttereth all his mind ; but a wise man keepeth it in till afterwards.*

There are many people who boast of their honesty in telling what they think, and concealing nothing that comes into their mind. Such persons may call themselves by any honourable names they please, but Solomon calls them fools. Some things come into our minds that we should never speak, but suppress the very thought of them ; and other things may be very fit to be spoken at a fit season, and yet very improper to be spoken at present.

---

*Ps. 142:4

The fool's thoughts lie at the tip of his tongue; and there is no door at his mouth to keep them in. The thoughts of the wise man lie in his heart; and there is a door upon his tongue, which he keeps close barred, that nothing may get out of his mouth that may prejudice himself, or other men. Some things occur to him, which he will never utter to the wife of his bosom, because they could do no good; other things he thinks proper to be spoken at a fit time, and then he keeps in his thoughts till afterwards. He will never speak against his mind, but he will not always speak his mind; and when he speaks it, he does not think that honesty obliges him to speak all that is in it. Samuel told the elders of Bethlehem a part of his design in coming to their town; but he concealed the principal part of it by divine direction. There is a time to be silent, and a time to speak; there is a time to be silent even from good, because the wicked are before us; there is a time to speak a part of our mind, and a time to declare all that is in our hearts; and the wise man's heart knoweth both time and judgment.

When a fool is in a passion he pours forth all his mind in a torrent of ill language, and speaks words which afterwards cut him to the heart. Does he mean to reprove? he will do it at the most improper season, and inflame with rage the person whom he reproves. He may shew something of the temper of the dove; but he imitates it rather in silliness than harmlessness. The wise man is sensible that it is as much his duty to practise the wisdom of the serpent as the harmlessness of the dove; he will take care what he says, when he finds himself or sees others under the influence of passion, and will abstain from speeches wherewith he can do no good *.

---

*Job 15:3

Ver. 12. *If a ruler hearken to lies, all his servants are wicked.*

Great is the account which rulers must give; for they are accountable for thousands of actions which they never committed, and of which it is possible they never heard. Their behaviour has such a mighty influence, that we find, in the history of the kings of Israel and Judah, the nation behaving well or ill according to the example and influence of their sovereign.

If a ruler take pleasure in flattery, the greater part of his servants will be so wicked as to poison him with their fulsome and ill-grounded praises. They will make him glad with their lies, but at the same time they make him more wicked, whilst they are polluting their own hearts, and debauching their consciences, by prostituting themselves to such base means of ingratiating themselves with their prince.

The servants of a ruler are still more wicked, if he hearken to slander and false accusations ; for some of them through fear, and others of them to gain his favour, will join in persecuting the innocent, and encouraging that pestilent vermin of a nation, called informers or spies. The reigns of those princes who gave an easy belief to accusations, are stained with the most atrocious crimes. Tiberius Cæsar put to death the greater number of his own privy councillors, by giving ear to lies, and encouraging his servants to be wicked; and it is probable that the worst action that ever was committed since the fall of Adam, the murder of the Prince of life, was occasioned by Pilate's wicked and cowardly regard to the temper of that tyrant, and his fear of being accused as an encourager of treason, if he had suffered our Lord to escape.

It is a mean and unmanly vice in any person to hearken to idle tales, that may very likely turn out to be lies, or misrepresentations of truth. The man that encourages people to tell him what this or the other person says of him, can never live in peace and friendship with his neighbours ; and he makes other people wicked, by the countenance which he affords to slander, and whispering, and evil speaking in all its different kinds.

Ver. 13. *The poor and the deceitful man meet together ; the Lord lighteneth both their eyes.*

The word which we translate *deceitful,* is not found in any other place of Scripture, and therefore the meaning of it cannot be exactly ascertained. The most ancient interpreters render it *creditors ;* and if we take it in this sense, the meaning of the proverb is the same with that which we have in the second verse of the xxii. chapter.

The poor too often look with an envious eye upon the rich, especially those to whom they are in debt, and the creditor looks with an eye of contempt upon his poor debtor. But what has the rich more than the poor, or why should the poor grudge at the riches of another man ? The Lord is the maker of them both, and gives them equally the light of understanding. He bestows comfort upon the poor as well as the rich ; and although they have not the pleasure of looking at splendid ceilings, and fine furniture in their dwellings, yet the cheerful light of day shines upon his eyelids, and he beholds those wonderful glories of the firmament, which darken the lustre of all earthly pomp.

If the rich man has acquired his fortune by deceit, he has no advantage from it above the poor to put in the balance against that guilt with which he has loaded his soul. The light of life, and reason, and comfort, is granted to the poor, at least as much as to himself. And the light of grace, which is enjoyed by the poor, is hid from his eyes. He cannot think that the poor man is hated by God, because he is not worth so great a sum of money as himself, nor can he flatter himself, unless he is sunk in stupidity, that God loves him because he is worth a thousand a-year. God continues with him the light of life, for his patience and mercy is very great, and he waits for the repentance of sinners; but the impenitent must soon have their eyes closed in darkness, and their souls shut up in the place of utter darkness, when the poor of this world, that were rich in faith, shall no longer meet with the deceitful man, because they are admitted to that world of light into which no deceitful man, without pardoning and converting grace, shall be permitted to enter.

Ver. 14. *The king that faithfully judgeth the poor, his throne shall be established for ever.*

All kings are anxious to have their thrones established, and their crowns transmitted to the latest posterity. But by what means shall they establish their thrones? By forming alliances, by fortifying their cities, by providing powerful navies, and by supporting great armies? These things may be useful; but good government is the best and surest way of establishing their thrones, for that will secure them the love of their subjects, and render their kingdoms prosperous. And what is of still greater consequence, the blessing of the Lord of hosts will attend that administration, which is managed according to his own directions.

Kings are obliged to do justice to all men; but the God of mercy gives them a special charge of the poor, who are most liable to oppression and insult. The Lord looks down from heaven with an eye of compassion to the poor and needy, and commands the princes and judges of the earth to be very merciful to them, and will not suffer the justice and kindness that is showed them to pass unrewarded.

The poor may expect good at the hands of all that

regard the word of God; but if they are treated with scorn by men, they may safely commit themselves unto him that testifies so much kindness to them in his promises and precepts.

Ver. 15. *The rod and reproof give wisdom; but a child left to himself bringeth his mother to shame.*

"Though you should bray a fool in a mortar among wheat with a pestle, yet will not his folly depart from him." This is true, especially of old fools that are hardened by a course of foolish conduct. But the rod of correction is a means appointed by God, and often blessed by him, for driving away folly from the hearts of young persons. God never prescribed any vain or unprofitable precepts; and he would not have insisted so much on the duty of correcting children, unless he had designed in general to give a blessing to it.

But the rod of correction is of no use without the concurrence of God, the great and only author of wisdom; those, therefore, who desire the blessing of God to attend it, must administer correction in the manner appointed by him, and he requires reproof to be joined to the rod, that the child who is corrected may be made sensible of the evil for which he is treated with severity. Some parents follow the dictates of their own passion in correcting their children, and strike without mercy, when they use no means to make them sensible that they deserve the rod. They deal worse with their children than shepherds with their dogs, who beat them when they have done something that displeases their masters; but do it in such a manner, or at such a time, that these animals may perceive the fault for which they are punished.

The rod, joined with reproof, is a means of giving wisdom, and of making a child to behave in such a manner that he may be a credit to his parents; but a child left to behave as he pleases, will never, in all pro-

bability, be a comfort or an honour either to his father
or to his mother. Men are naturally corrupt, and those
that are left to follow the propensities of nature will be
a grief to their fathers, and bring their mothers to shame.
Their mothers deserved much blame for the indulgence
so foolishly given them, and when they feel the torment which the bad behaviour of their children cannot fail of giving them, they must see their sin in their
punishment.

Ver. 16. *When the wicked are multiplied, (or possess
authority *,) transgression increaseth, but the righteous
shall see their fall.*

When the pestilence rages in a country, multitudes
are infected with the dreadful distemper, and there is no
disease more fatal or more infectious than sin. When
the generality of men are profane, the restraints of
shame are removed from sin; wicked men gain credit,
and they must possess a spirit like that of Noah or
Lot, who are untainted by the spreading contagion.

When wicked men possess authority the danger is
extreme. The countenance which they give to sin is
a dreadful temptation, which few have the resolution
and courage to resist. One Obadiah in the court, and
seven thousand worshippers of the Lord in the kingdom of Ahab, were more than Elijah dreamed of. The
abundance of wickedness in such evil times is very distressing to the eyes of the righteous, but they have the
comfortable prospect of seeing the fall of the wicked.
God is their enemy, and although he bears with them
for a time, yet he has doomed them to destruction. Their
iniquity shall come into remembrance with the Lord,
and when the measure of it is full, they shall be swept
away with the besom of destruction. The righteous
shall see their fall and shall rejoice, (not that they en-

*Verse 2

tertained hatred to the wicked, for they ardently desired their repentance, but) because their fall is a check
to wickedness, and an evidence that there is a God who
reigneth in the earth, and has an invariable love for
righteousness *.

Ver. 17. *Correct thy son, and he shall give thee rest :
yea, he shall give delight unto thy soul.*

Why does Solomon so often press this duty of correcting children ? Because it is a necessary duty ; and
yet many parents are very averse to the practice of it.
When there is a great drought in the ground, it requires many showers to make it fruitful, and when
there is a violent aversion to any duty, precept must
be upon precept, and line upon line, before we will
practise it.

But correcting of children gives great pain to the
parent ? On the contrary, it gives great pleasure. The
pain is transient, the pleasure is lasting. The rod and
reproof give wisdom ; and how delightful to a parent is
wisdom in a child !

But what if a child still continue obstinate ? This
is not ordinarily the case. Correct like a parent and
a friend, and your child will learn at length the duty
of a child. Join prayer with your corrections, to that
God who has appointed them. He never said to any
of the seed of Jacob, seek ye me in vain, and he never
appointed useless and unavailing means for any end.

But God is sovereign ; perhaps he will not be pleased to communicate wisdom by the rod to my child ?
Make the trial. If you should be unsuccessful, you
shall be free of those tormenting stings of remorse which
thousands of parents feel.

Isaac was the beloved son of Abraham, and never
did a parent taste such pleasure in a son as the venera-

*Ps. 58:11

ble patriarch, except the Virgin Mary; but Abraham did not refuse to sacrifice his son with his own hands, when God gave the order; and shall we refuse to administer a little salutary correction to our children at his command? Abraham never found so much pleasure in his son, as when he shewed that he feared and loved God above his son, in not withholding him from God; and other parents may look for greater or lesser degrees of comfort in their children, as they observe or neglect the commandments of the Lord, about the management of them. Eli honoured his sons above God, and they proved the greatest of his crosses; "for them that honour me," says God, "I will honour, and they that despise me shall be lightly esteemed."

Ver. 18. *Where there is no vision, the people perish* : but he that keepeth the law happy is he.*

It is a distinguishing mercy to us that God has made known in our land the great things of his law and covenant. There are nations that never heard of the name of a Redeemer, and under the influence of corrupt traditions or false prophets, they are serving those gods that are no gods, with detestable ceremonies, or at least do not worship the God and father of our Lord Jesus Christ. They are born, like ourselves, in a sinful and wretched condition, but are left in utter ignorance of that great Saviour in whose name our help lies. They are left naked and exposed to the assaults of their spiritual enemies, who are still walking about seeking whom they may destroy.

Where there is no vision, the light of philosophy cannot supply its place. The Greeks were admirably enlightened by science, and yet Paul tells them, that before the gospel of their salvation was preached among them, they were strangers to the covenant of promise;

---

*Or, are made naked.

without God, without Christ, and without hope in the world *.

Blessed be God who made light to arise in darkness to us. Britain was, in ancient days, one of the darkest places of the earth, but through the tender mercies of our God, the day spring from on high visited us. By the cruelty of the Popish clergy, the key of knowledge was almost taken from us in later ages ; but through the good hand of our God upon us, we have now great plenty of Bibles and sermons. Let it be our daily prayer, that all the nations of the world who are perishing through lack of knowledge, may be made to share in our privileges.

But what will unimproved privileges avail? He is not the happy man who has a Bible, but the man is blessed who delights in it, and meditates upon it day and night ; who believes the doctrines of it, trusts in the Saviour whom it reveals, and respects all the precepts of it in his practice.

" Not every one that saith unto Christ, Lord, Lord, shall enter into the kingdom of heaven, but he that does the will of Christ's heavenly father." If those that sin without the law perish without the law, there must be a deeper perdition, and more intolerable torments for those that despise both law and gospel.

Ver. 19. *A servant will not be corrected by words : for though he understand he will not answer.*

The Seventy translators apply what is here said to a stubborn servant only ; and it is plain, from fact, that Solomon meant this proverb only of such, for there are many hired servants every way equal to their masters in every generous quality, and the character of those servants that must be corrected by blows does by no means belong to them. There have been even slaves

*Eph. 2:12

who have shewed a noble disposition, and have not only served their masters with fidelity, but performed acts of heroism that might have done honour to any station. But it is very probable, that in Solomon's days, when servants were commonly bond slaves, the greatest part of them had their spirits sunk and debased, so far as to be of the temper here represented.

The loss of liberty is often the destruction of every thing good and noble; and servants that were treated like cattle would need a strict hand to govern them; because words would not be much regarded by those that had neither attachment to their masters, nor any sense of honour.

The proverb teaches us that masters ought to keep up their authority in their families. Without this every thing must be in a state of confusion, and go to ruin, and if they have servants that will not yield obedience, they must either be compelled to do it, or dismissed from the house.

But it teaches us likewise, that methods of severity are not to be used by heads of families, when milder means are sufficient to answer the end. It is only when servants, though they understand the wishes of their masters, will not answer by respectful words and due obedience, that masters are warranted to use harsh methods of dealing with them.

Let servants learn from this passage, how much God is displeased with them, when they are sullen and disobedient to their masters. God commands masters to give unto their servants that which is just and equal; at the same time he gives them commission to support their authority over stubborn servants, by such means as are sufficient to answer the end. If servants are reproved with sharpness for their faults, they must blame themselves and not their masters. The apostle Peter tells them, that they deserve no thanks, if they are patient, even when they are buffeted for their faults. If they deserve no thanks for their patience under just buffetings, they deserve very great blame when they are impatient of merited reproof.

Ver. 20. *Seest thou a man that is hasty in his words* ? there is more hope of a fool than of him.*

" Seest thou a man wise in his own conceit ? there is more hope of a fool than of him." But how shall we know the man that is wise in his own conceit when we see him ? This text gives us a sure mark of such a person. When a man speaks rashly and inconsiderately, every thing that strikes his mind, or when he is rash and headstrong in the management of his business, disdaining to take any advice from others, and so confident of his own wisdom and abilities, that he takes little time to consider the most important undertaking, but pushes on in the way that seems best to his own unadvised mind, hoping to command success by his own power, it is evident that he is wise in his own conceit; and he that is wise in his own eyes, is the greatest and most hopeless of fools in Solomon's estimation.

If rashness in the things of this life is a sign of great folly, it is a great deal more dangerous to make too much haste in matters of religion. The Bereans are commended because they candidly examined Paul's doctrine by the Scriptures of the Old Testament. The apostle condemns those that are heady, and joins them with the high minded ; and it is certain, that persons of that character have been the authors of those heresies and divisions which have plagued the church of God, and are still the fire-brands of Christian societies.

There is another kind of rashness in religion forbidden by Solomon as a token of great irreverence to God ; I mean rashness in vowing or in praying. God is in

---

*Or matters, (the same Hebrew word signifying both.)

heaven, and we are upon earth, and therefore our words before him ought to be few and well considered *.

Ver. 21. *He that delicately bringeth up his servant from a child, shall have him become his son at the length.*

The greatest part of masters cannot be blamed for too much indulgence to their servants, and yet some err on that side; and Solomon, who wished us to stand perfect and complete in all wisdom, guards us against it. Men must condescend to them of low degree; but they ought at the same time to respect their own place and station, and not to debase it, by such familiarities towards their inferiors as may expose themselves to contempt, and tempt their inferiors to forget their distance. Joab, by the indulgence of David, became such a great man, that he presumed to kill the commander in chief of David's army, at the head of his troops. As an officer in the army would deserve to lose his place, if he did not oblige his soldiers to obey him, so the man shews himself unworthy of his station in the family, or church, or nation, who does not know the authority which God has given him, and uses no care to preserve it.

Servants are taught by this proverb, to respect, as well as to obey their masters. The apostle Peter enjoins servants to obey their masters with all fear, whether their masters are froward, or good and gentle. Whatever condescensions our superiors use in their behaviour towards us, we must not forget our distance, but give fear to whom fear, and honour to whom honour is due. Job was a prince of extraordinary goodness to his servants and all his inferiors, yet he never, till the time of his severe trials, forfeited, or lost any part of that respect which was his due †.

---

*Eccles. 5   †Job. 29:24,25

Ver. 22. *An angry man stirreth up strife, and a furious man aboundeth in transgression.*

Solomon has told us already, that the wrathful man stirreth up strife *.   His anger pushes him on to bitter contentions, and makes him the incendiary of the place where he lives.   But strife is not the only evil produced by anger, for when it is roused to fury, it becomes a fruitful source of every iniquity.   We read in the 24th chapter of Leviticus, that a man in his passion cursed the name of the God of Israel, and was stoned for it. David, although he was a meek man in the general course of his life, swore a very rash oath, by the name of the Lord, when he was incensed at Nabal.   Railing, and reviling, and backbiting, and evil speaking, and lies, and wars, and duels, and murders, are only a few of the transgressions to which men have been a thousand times tempted by their unbridled anger.   He that indulges anger gives place to the devil.   He puts that malignant spirit in possession of the throne of his heart, and commits to him the direction of his heart, and tongue, and hands.   The wrath of man never works the righteousness of God ; it utterly disqualifies him for praying, or doing any other holy action ; but it works the will of the devil with both hands earnestly.   Many volumes of history might be written in proof of this point ; but the evidences of it are every day before our eyes.   Cease from anger, and forsake wrath, and let the meekness and gentleness of Christ be still before your eyes.

Ver. 23. *A man's pride shall bring him low : but honour shall uphold the humble in spirit.*

Pride raises a man as high as heaven in his own apprehension, but it shall bring him as low as hell.   All men are the enemies of the proud, and proud men them-

---

*Chap. 15:18

selves are the bitterest enemies to one another ; for other
vices unite men in confederacies and friendships, but
pride has often set fathers and sons, husbands and wives,
at variance. God is the enemy of the proud, he looks
upon them with disdain and abhorrence, and will abase
them. Pride itself is the enemy of the proud, and will
bring them down from the highest honours to the deepest pit of disgrace. What was it but pride that brought
Haman to the gallows, and made angels devils ?

But those whose hearts are humble enjoy true and
solid honours. The honours of the proud are feathers
and wind. They soon fly away and never return; but
honour shall uphold the man of an humble spirit. His
crown consists, not of such corruptible things as silver
and gold, but it is a crown of life and glory which
never fades away. He is exalted to safety, and shall
reign with angels for ever and ever.

Let us all beware of the devil's first born sin, and
learn humility from him who was meek and lowly in
heart. There are remainders of pride even in believers,
which, if left unmortified, will do them great hurt ; for
any man's pride (were he as good as Hezekiah) will
bring him low, till his spirit be effectually humbled.

Why does the wise man insist so much on this point ?
Not because he wanted new matter for instructing us,
for his soul covered the whole earth, and he filled the
world with dark parables. But because humility is a
lesson which we must learn, and yet are very backward
to learn. Our Lord frequently repeats this proverb in
other words. " He that exalteth himself shall be abased,
and he that humbleth himself shall be exalted."

Ver. 24. *Whoso is partner with a thief, hateth his own
soul ; he heareth cursing and bwrayethe it not.*

Stealing is an abominable crime. It was to be se-

verely punished by the law of God, and is still more
severely punished by our own laws. Thieves, and all
that are partners with thieves, are haters of their own
souls, for they love money more than salvation. They
are the enemies of all men ; but they are worse enemies
to themselves than to those whom they plunder. How
poor a recompense do they obtain by their ill-gotten
gains, for the mischiefs which they bring upon themselves here, and in another world.

There are some who would be afraid to steal, and yet
they venture to partake with thieves in their crime, by
receiving a part of what is stolen as the price of concealment, or by buying commodities which they have
reason to suspect for stolen goods, because they can have
them at a low price. If we are but underworkers in
any good action, we will not fail to obtain our share of
the praise ; but we are very unwilling to sustain any
blame for dishonourable actions unless we are principal
agents. The Scripture however assures us, that men
may bring much guilt upon themselves by partaking
of other men's sins ; and that he who is a partner with
a thief is a hater of his own life and soul, as well as the
principal thief.

The devil is not content with drawing men to single
acts of sin ; but he makes one evil thing the preface to
another. Julius Cæsar was more celebrated for improving than gaining victories ; for he never thought
that any thing was done whilst any thing remained
undone. The devil is a conqueror of this sort ; he
makes one transgression a snare for leading the sinner
into another ; and he that joins with a thief is prepared
for lying and perjury. He heareth cursing, (being laid
under a curse by the magistrate that puts him on his
oath, though he will not conceal any thing he knows
about the crime,) and yet he does not make a discovery,
and thus he adds to the guilt of stealing the greater

guilt of falsehood and concealment, when he is upon his oath.

Those that are under examination upon oath should consider this text. If they swear that they will tell every thing they know about the affair before the judge, or if they are required, by proper authority, to bear witness about a crime which ought to be punished, they are enemies to justice, and haters of their own souls, if they do not give a faithful and honest declaration of the truth. Men may partake of other men's sins, not only by countenancing them, but by refusing to concur in proper endeavours to have them punished, for a warning to others.

Ver. 25. *The fear of man bringeth a snare: but whoso putteth his trust in the Lord shall be safe.*

When men are more afraid of offending their fellow men than of sinning against God, they are in great danger of being drawn or driven into some of the worst of sins. It was this fear which made David sometimes to lie, although that good man hated lying. It was the fear of a woman that made Peter to deny his gracious master; and the same passion afterwards induced him to behave in a very unedifying manner at Antioch, that he might not give offence to his bigoted brethren.

If the fear of man has sometimes misled such men as David and Peter, (and we may add, the father of the faithful, and Aaron the priest of the Lord,) how ensnaring must it be to those who are entirely destitute of faith in God. Many are kept by it from performing necessary duties, like those that believed Jesus to be the Christ, and yet durst not confess him, lest they should have been excommunicated. Many are driven to rebel in many things against the light of their judgments, to gratify masters, or parents, or princes, or friends, whom they wish not to displease.

It will be no sufficient excuse for sin that the fear of men led us into the commission of it. Who are we that we should be afraid of men that shall die? Are men more worthy of fear than the Almighty? Was it right in our first parents to obey the devil rather than God? Do we not imitate their conduct when we prefer the pleasing of men to the pleasing of our Maker? If we rather choose to venture on the wrath of God than the wrath of men, can we complain if we have our choice?

The great antidote against the fear of man is confidence in the Lord. The true believer, acting like himself, goes on in the path of duty, without fearing the wrath of men or devils. " The Lord," says he, " is my light and my salvation, whom shall I fear? The Lord is my helper, what can man do unto me * ?" In our tormenting and ensnaring fears, our Lord teaches us to discern the weakness of our faith †.

He that trusteth in the Lord shall be safe from the snares of sin ; for his faith is a shield to quench all the fiery darts of temptation. He shall be safe from every danger which timorous men apprehend in the way of duty. He shall find that there is no lion, nor any ravenous beast in the way of holiness ; or if there are, that they are chained, and cannot do him any evil which shall not turn out to his advantage in the end ‡.

Ver. 26. *Many seek the ruler's favour, but every man's judgment cometh from the Lord.*

Confidence in men is no less dangerous than the fear of man, and there is a dreadful curse pronounced upon those who trust in man, and make flesh their arm, and whose heart departeth from the Lord. Princes are the idols of those who are honoured with their

---

*Ps. 27:1, Heb. 13:6   †Matt. 14:31, Luke 22:32
‡Ps. 91, Dan. 3

friendship ; and men in lower stations make idols of those who are most likely to do them any service, and solicit their kindness oftentimes with greater earnest- ness than the favour of God.

This behaviour proceeds from a secret disbelief of the providence of God. Men seem to think that earth- ly things are managed by a train of inferior causes, without any superintendency of the Most High. If they have the favour of great men they are happy for this life, whether they have an interest in the favour of God or not.

But we ought to believe and remember this great truth, that every man's judgment cometh from the Lord. It depends upon his sovereign pleasure whether we shall be prosperous or unsuccessful in any particu- lar business ; whether we shall be rich or poor ; whe- ther we shall enjoy the favour of men, or suffer the effects of their displeasure. Riches, and honours, and friendship, and hatred, are under the controul of the Ruler of the world, and not a hair can fall from our heads, nor can the least addition to our comfort be made, without his pleasure.

A sense of this truth would dispose us to acknow- ledge God in all our ways ; to make our requests in all things known unto him with fervency of spirit ; to thank him with greater cordiality for every happy event, than those who were the instruments of his kindness. It would be a strong antidote against the ensnaring fear of men, and every fleshly confidence. It would keep us from sinking under adversity, and from abusing prosperity into provision for the flesh, to fulfil the lusts thereof.

A persuasion of this truth disposing us to cleave unto God, is the best means of ensuring success in all our undertakings. Esther prayed more earnestly to God than to Ahasuerus for the safety of her nation, and her success is celebrated by the Jews unto this day.

Nehemiah acted upon the same principle, when he petitioned his master for the place of his father's sepulchres ; the Lord gave him great favour with the king of Persia, and his fame shall live for ever.

All who place that confidence in any creature which is due to the Sovereign of heaven and earth, are reproved by this precept, and directed to expect every thing they want from God as the first cause, although the warrantable means of obtaining our wishes, are not to be neglected *.

Ver. 27. *An unjust man is an abomination to the just ; and he that is upright in the way, is an abomination to the wicked.*

That an unjust man abhors the just, we have already heard †, and find no cause to doubt it. But how can the just abhor the wicked ? Christ commands us to love our enemies, although our enemies, in all appearance, must be the enemies of God also ; and we are required to love our neighbours as ourselves, although we know that great multitudes of them are unrighteous men. How then will the law of God permit us to hold the unrighteous in abhorrence ?

The just man wishes no evil to the wicked, for he would have them all to be saved. Paul could have wished that he was accursed from Christ for his brethren, his kinsmen according to the flesh, although they were the worst enemies of the gospel in the world. But the unjust man is detested by the just, as a rebel against God, although, as a man, he is the object of charity. The just man abhors the sins of the wicked, and shuns their company, and testifies by every regular method against their iniquities, and joins his influence to bring them under the salutary rod of discipline. His abhorrence of them is a part of his conformity to Christ, who

*Jer. 17:5-8   †Verse 10

exposed hypocrites, and spoke with a voice of thunder
against the wickedness of men, and yet called all to
repentance, and prayed for the wicked when they were
crucifying him.

Hatred to sin in ourselves and other men, is one
necessary branch of the Christian temper*. If we are
the friends of Christ we shall be determined enemies
to that which brought him to a cross.

The proverbs of Solomon, the son of David, are
ended.

Proverbs 30

Verse 1. *The words of Agur the son of Jakeh, even
the prophecy: the man spake unto Ithiel, even unto
Ithiel and Ucal.*

Agur was honoured, like Obadiah and Jude, to write
a very small portion of the Holy Scripture; but every
part of the word of God is precious, however small.
The words of Agur are not a prediction of things to
come, yet they are called a prophecy or burden, for
they were indited by the Holy Ghost, and are profitable for our correction and instruction in righteousness.
This prophecy is added to the proverbs of Solomon,
because they treat on the same subjects, and are written in a like form. The name of Agur is not given to
a distinct book of the Bible, but his memorial shall be
everlasting, for he was furnished with that wisdom
which is from above.

---

*Heb. 12:4

We can give no historical account of this wise man; we only know the name of his father, and his two chief disciples, who were doubtless men of credit in their generation; but their names only live in our days, for the current of time swallows up the names of the greatest part of men, and leaves little or nothing but the names of the rest. It is an honour to these men that their names are mentioned in the book of God as the disciples of Agur. If we are diligent learners at the school of Christ, and of those men that were inspired by the Spirit of Christ, although our names be not recorded in this blessed book, yet we may rejoice that they are written in heaven.

In this prophecy, Agur expresses his humble sense of his own ignorance, and tells us what need we have of a divine teacher to explain the glories of God to us. He recommends the word of God to us, and calls us to the exercise of that faith for which we have so sure a foundation in the word of God. He directs us by his own example how to pray. He warns us against several dangerous sins, and makes several instructive observations on the manners of men, and the nature and qualities of many of God's creatures. These are perhaps a summary of what he spoke to Ithiel and Ucal whilst he lived; and although he is now dead he speaks them to us.

Ver. 2. *Surely I am more brutish than any man, and have not the understanding of a man.*

One of the best proofs of wisdom is a sense of our own ignorance and folly. Pythagoras would not suffer himself to be called a wise man, but a lover of wisdom; and Socrates, who far exceeded him in wisdom, said, that he knew nothing, but that he knew nothing. Agur goes still further, and calls himself a brutish man. All men are naturally brutish in respect of spiritual things; and Agur calls himself more brutish than any man. He was well acquainted with the fallen and degenerate condition of men, and deeply affected with his own particular share in it. Man is born like a wild ass's colt; and a humble man is ready to acknowledge that there is none to whom this debasing comparison can be so justly applied as to himself.

But did Agur speak truth, or was he sincere in speaking so humbly of himself? No doubt he uses very strong language, but he was perfectly sincere in it; for he thought about God and eternal things, but felt so much difficulty in understanding them, he found himself naturally so much indisposed to the most important duties, and was filled with such grief at the darkness of his mind, and the perverseness of his heart, that he could not find words strong enough to express his inward sense of his own vileness and darkness.

It is a literal truth concerning the wisest of us, that we are more brutish in relation to the noblest objects that can occupy our minds, than any man is about the affairs of life. Men have retained their wisdom about things of small consequence; but surely every man is brutish in his knowledge of divine things, till his mind is opened by the Holy Spirit to receive the knowledge of them. " Surely there is a vein for the gold, and a place for the silver where they fine it;" and the sons of men have found methods of forcing their way through mountains and rocks, and of binding up floods that they may fetch out these shining metals, and bring out to the light of day the stores of darkness and of the shadow of death. " But where is wisdom to be found, and where is the place of understanding ? Man knoweth not the price thereof, neither is it found in the land of the living."

None are so ignorant, and so likely to continue so, as those who are wise in their own eyes, and prudent in their own sight. None are so wise, and so likely to increase in wisdom, as the humble souls who are deeply conscious of their folly and ignorance. They will open their mouths, and pant for God's commandments. They will rejoice to hear that Christ is made of God unto us wisdom, and will sit at the feet of Jesus, and receive from him the words of eternal life.

Ver. 3. *I neither learned wisdom, nor have the knowledge of the holy* (ones.)

Perhaps Agur means the same thing with Amos, when he says, " I was not a prophet, neither was I a prophet's son." He was not trained up in the schools of the prophets; but God lays up sound wisdom for the righteous, and dispenses it with or without the ordinary means, as he pleases; for although he has required us to make a conscientious use of these means, yet he has not restricted himself to them in the distributions of his favour.

Paul was of the same humble temper with Agur. He counted himself less than the least of all saints ; and Agur accounts himself inferior in divine knowledge to other saints. The spirit of Diotrephes is in those men who court the pre-eminence among the brethren, but the lowly temper of a true saint will dispose us in honour to prefer one another.

When Elihu began to speak, in the dispute carried on between Job and his friends, he prefaces his discourse with high, though just encomiums on the wisdom that God had bestowed on him. Agur introduces his discourse with confessions of his own ignorance; but their situations were very different. Elihu was afraid that his friends would despise him for his youth, and lose the benefit of his speech; Agur thought he had reason to be afraid of the contrary extreme. When Ithiel and Ucal applied to him for instruction, they discovered a high opinion of his understanding. We ought not to affect too great a name for knowledge and learning, nor to encourage men to expect too much from us, lest they should be disappointed to our own shame; or lest they should place too great a dependence upon us, and too little on the Author of wisdom. A good name is valuable, but a great name is dangerous; and a wise man would rather decline than desire it.

" As the fining pot for silver, and the furnace for gold, so is a man to his praise." A fool swells with vain conceit, if he finds his wisdom admired. A wise man is humbled to find how far he falls short of the opinion that is entertained of him. A fool, when he is praised, seeks more praise, for the wind after which he hungers cannot fill him. But a man of Agur's spirit will endeavour to moderate those high opinions that are entertained to his advantage. Herod was destroyed by worms, for the vain joy which he felt in the ungodly applause given to his wisdom and eloquence. Agur is recorded in Scripture as a pattern of humility to those men whose wisdom is admired.

As Agur himself was insufficient to satisfy his friends' thirst of knowledge, so he directs them to look above all men for instruction.

Ver. 4. *Who hath ascended up into heaven, or descended? who hath gathered the wind in his fists? who hath bound the waters in a garment? who hath established all the ends of the earth? what is his name, and what is his son's name, if thou canst tell?*

It is just as impossible for men, without divine illumination, to discover God, and to reveal him to their fellow-creatures, as to ascend into heaven, or descend from it; to bind up the waters in a garment, or to gather the winds in their fists, or to establish all the ends of the earth. Has any man ever been able to achieve such wonders? where did he live? what was his name? or what is the name of any man that has the honour to spring from such a wonderful ancestor? If you can tell me the name of such a man as this, or his son, then I will confess that he is possessed of treasures of wisdom sufficient to supply all your wants, and to satisfy all your desires of knowledge.

The God, whose name is beyond our comprehension, and whose Son's name is Wonderful, does all these things. Heaven is his throne, and the clouds are his chariots, and the earth has often felt his awful presence. " He makes a weight for the winds, and weigheth the waters by measure. He hangeth the earth upon nothing. With him is wisdom and strength ; he hath counsel and understanding ;" and from him, the Father of lights, every ray of useful knowledge comes.

It deserves to be observed that our great Teacher makes use of the truth delivered in this verse to prove his absolute perfection as our instructor *. " No man hath ascended up to heaven," to fetch down the knowledge of God to men, " but he that came down from heaven, even the Son of man who is in heaven." He shewed his mission, by issuing forth his commands to the winds and the waves, which instantly obeyed him. He establishes all the ends of the earth, and by him all things in heaven and in earth consist. " He is the Lord our God, who teacheth us to profit ; and the Lord God and his Spirit did send him." Let us therefore acknowledge with Agur that we have no knowledge of our own, and wait for his instructions as the earth for the latter rain.

All the treasures of wisdom and knowledge are laid up in him, and these treasures are not sealed up, but spread before us in the word of Christ, which we ought to read with an humble dependence on him for his

---

*John 3:13

light and truth, that we may learn to set our hope on God.

Ver. 5. *Every word of God is pure ; he is a shield unto them that put their trust in him.*

There are no superfluities in the word of God, as we are too ready to imagine. Every word of God is useful and holy, righteous and true. When we hear the words of men, our reason must try them, as the mouth tasteth meat, for any man may be a liar, or deceive us by his own misapprehensions ; but the words of God are all worthy of himself. As the power of the Creator shines in all the works of his hands, his inviolable truth and untainted holiness, give dignity and credit to every thing that he speaks ; and the Bible has the same impression of divinity upon it that appears in the sun and the stars.

Because the word of God is very pure, we ought to love it, and to believe it with all our hearts, and to trust in God, as he is revealed to us in it ; for it discovers him to be for ever possessed of all those infinite excellencies that make him the proper object of confidence to creatures, of all that mercy and grace, and plenteous redemption, which are sufficient to encourage the confidence of guilty creatures.

Blessed are all they that put their trust in him. The world is full of mischief and miseries sufficient to destroy or embitter our lives, and of invisible enemies, who seek to destroy our souls ; but they that trust in the Lord, are completely safe and happy. His mercy is their refuge from condemnation, through that atonement which his word reveals. His power will shield them from every enemy, and they shall be kept in perfect peace whose mind is stayed on him, because they trust in him. " Fear not," said the Lord to Abraham, " I am thy shield, and thine exceeding great reward." All that walk in the steps of the faith of Abraham, enjoy the benefit and comfort of this promise. They shall travel in safety through armies of enemies, and at last inherit the better country, where the father of the faithful now dwells.

But our trust must be in the name of the Lord, as it is represented to us in the word of God ; the seed and the ground of our faith in him. To alter or to add to it is very dangerous.

Ver. 6. *Add thou not unto his words, lest he reprove thee, and thou be found a liar.*

It is strange, but true, that men have been often disposed to add to the words of God, by establishing some rule of faith beside the Scripture, or intruding into the secrets of God, and devising religious doctrines not taught in the Scripture, or means of divine worship, which never came into his mind. Surely such presumption shall be reproved and punished by the Most High. Princes would require the blood of those daring subjects that presumed to insert some additions in their laws of grants, and God will add unto them that add to his words, all the plagues contained in the last and most dreadful book of the Scripture.

To add to the true meaning of the Scripture, in order to accommodate its doctrine to our own prejudices or taste, is a sin of the like kind. If we do so, we shall be reproved by God, and found liars, by saying that God has taught things which he never taught.

Errors and sin are incident to man in his corrupted state ; but we ought to guard against the former as well as the latter, by perusing the Bible with diligence and humility, and praying for that unction from the Holy One, which is truth and is no lie, and will effectually preserve us from every dangerous mistake.

Ver. 7. *Two things have I required of thee, deny me them not before I die.*

Agur has taught us faith in God. He now teaches

us by his own example, to pray, although he does not mention, by name, the object of prayer. He never dreamed that any person who professed to believe the word of God, would think of any other object of prayer than God himself; but, since his days, men have found means to jumble together, in their systems of religion, the most incompatible truths and errors.

Two things comprised the objects of his petitions.— David had one thing that he chiefly desired, and our Lord sums up every necessary request in six petitions. The great blessings that we need from God should be habitually present to our minds, that when we have occasion to appear before the Lord, without time to premeditate, we may, in our requests, present the meditations of our heart in the words of our mouth.

The wisest of the heathens were at a great loss to know what blessings they should ask from God; but God in mercy has instructed us what we should pray for, and hath promised the Spirit to help the infirmities of our understandings and souls, in this duty. When we observe the directions of the Scripture about our prayers, we know that we ask things agreeable to the will of God. The gracious Hearer of Prayer never said unto any of the seed of Jacob, " seek ye me in vain ;" and he will not refuse hearing to those prayers that are dictated by his own Spirit.

But when we pray, we must pray in faith, nothing doubting. This holy man used great boldness at the throne of God. He insisted for these two things, and requires them, and pleads against a denial.

The revelations of the New Testament give us greater encouragements than Agur had, to exercise boldness in the presence of God, and to plead with unceasing earnestness till we obtain the blessings that we need.— God sits on a throne of grace, and we have a great High

Priest, who is passed into the heavens, and there appears in the presence of God for us. Therefore let us come boldly to the throne of grace. This great High Priest is also our instructor, and teaches us to pray always, and not to faint, assuring us that our importunity shall at length prevail. The most glorious name of any mere man spoken of in the histories of the world, was obtained by such importunate supplications. Jacob wept and made supplication at Bethel ; yea, by his strength, he had power with the angel and prevailed, and his name was called Israel, because as a prince he had power with God, and received the blessing for which he wrestled.

Agur prayed to God with proper impressions of his frailty and mortality upon his mind. He spoke like a dying man to the eternal God, and requested that he might enjoy the blessings of God whilst he lived. Spiritual blessings were the grand object of his wishes ; and if we duly considered the uncertainty of our lives, and the approaches that death is constantly making to us, we should never ask these blessings with such coldness as if we desired a denial. Thoughts of death would inflame our desires after heavenly things, and moderate our exorbitant desires for the blessings of the present life.

Ver. 8. *Remove far from me vanity and lies ; give me neither poverty nor riches, feed me with food convenient for me.*

His first petition is for deliverance from sin. Whether he means particularly the sins usually known by these names, or the sin of idolatry, or sin in general, he no doubt desired freedom from all sin. The best of men need preservation from the worst sins, for they are conscious that they might fall into the deepest mire of iniquity, if God withheld his mercy*. But all kinds of

---

*Ps. 19:12

sin may be justly called vanities and lies, because it is
empty and unprofitable*, and imposes the most mischievous falsehoods upon men, promising them pleasure and gain, and giving them nothing but disappointment and death. An impression of the unprofitable-
ness and danger of sin would make us very earnest in
our prayers for the removal of it from us. " O Lord,
the Gentiles shall come unto thee from the ends of the
earth, and shall say, surely our fathers have inherited
lies, vanity, and things wherein there is no profit†."

The removal of sin includes in it both pardon and
sanctification, and therefore the petition may include
both the fifth and sixth petition of the Lord's prayer.
When God pardons sin, he removes it far from us as
the east is from the west, and casts it into the depth of
the sea. When he sanctifies a soul, he removes sin from
its throne, and gradually drives it out of its residence
in the soul. Both these blessings are absolutely necessary for us. They are to be the subject of our most
earnest petitions, and we have great encouragement to
plead for them, because they are graciously promised
in his word ; and these rich promises are yea and amen
in Christ, who purchased them for us by his blood, and
gives us all possible assurance of obtaining them from
God.

We are not only to pray for the removal of sin, but
for the removal of it at a great distance from us. As
God removes it far away in pardon, the soul that abhors sin desires to have it far removed from the heart
and life. Our Lord teaches us not only to pray against
sin, but against temptation ; for there is a strong inclination in the hearts of men to comply with temptations when they are presented to the soul. If a man

---

*Job 33:27   †Jer. 16:19

has a bag of powder in his hands, he will certainly wish to keep at a distance from the fire.

We must seek first the kingdom of God, and the righteousness thereof; but we are not forbidden to seek also those things that are needful for the body. We are forbidden to seek great things for ourselves, but directed to seek daily bread; and accordingly Agur prays for it in these words, " Give me neither poverty nor riches."

Poverty is a very disagreeable thing to all men, and none will wonder that Agur prays against it. Yet our Lord, for our sakes, endured extreme poverty. If Providence should appoint poverty to us as our lot, we ought to be content with that situation in which Christ himself lived among us; yet such is the kindness of God to us that we are warranted to pray against it, as a state of sore temptation.

Had Agur prayed against poverty only, we would have all joined with him; but few men would choose to have him for their chaplain, because to poverty he adds riches, as a thing equally undesirable to him.— Riches are the desire of all men, except those who know the weakness of their own hearts, and believe what our Lord tells us of the danger of riches. Riches are good if they are rightly used, and have been the instrument of much good when they were in the hands of very good and wise men ; but there are few even of the saints that have a sufficiency of wisdom and grace, for using, without abusing them. Agur desired to have nothing, however agreeable to the natural and ordinary wishes of men, if it might prove injurious to his soul.

What then would this good man have from God, if he desires neither poverty nor riches ? He prays that God would feed him with food convenient for him; bestowing on him whatever was needful for his support and conveniency, and suitable to the station in which he was placed.   Having food and raiment, and all that is commonly included under the name of bread in Scripture language, he would be content and thankful, and ask no more.

Agur teaches us, in this account of his prayers, to look upon God as the dispenser of the good things or life, who gives riches or poverty at his pleasure ; from whom we receive our food and raiment ; on whom we ought to depend for the supply of all our necessities ; to whom we should pray for every good thing, and render thanks for every blessing.

We are taught likewise to offer our most fervent petitions for the blessings of God's salvation.   Agur did not think that vanity and lies could be removed too far from him ; but he thought that poverty might soon be too far removed.   How opposite was his spirit to the spirit of the world !

The greatest part of men seek earthly blessings with all the desire of their hearts, and the blessings of salvation with more moderate desires, and only so far as they may consist with the main objects of their affection.   But Agur desires outward conveniences for the good of his soul, and only in such a measure as might consist with his best interests.

Ver. 9. *Lest I be full and deny thee, and say, Who is the Lord ? or lest I be poor, and steal, and take the name of my God in vain.*

He prays for daily bread, that he might not be led into temptation ; and for the same reason he prays against riches.   If his riches increased, he was afraid that, through the depravity of his nature, they would tempt him to the dangerous sin of luxury, to impiety, presumption and arrogancy.   Such are the effects of riches upon men of corrupt minds.   According to the pasture of the people of Israel, so were they filled : They were filled, and their heart was exalted.   Riches

are the gift of God, but they are too often improved to
the prejudice of the giver; and those who receive those
common gifts in the greatest abundance, are generally
the most ungrateful of all men to him from whom every
good gift comes. They do not perhaps deny the Lord
in words, or say with their tongues who is the Lord ?
but deeds speak louder than words. When men wilfully transgress the laws of God, they say in effect, "who
is the Lord that we should serve him ?" When they neglect prayer to God, they say that they are lords, and
will come no more unto him. Such was the practical
language of a great part of rich men in former ages,
and it is the same at this day. " They spend their days
in wealth," says Job, " Therefore they say unto God
depart from us ; what is the Almighty that we should
serve him ; and what profit shall we have if we pray
unto him ?"

But are real saints ready to be ensnared into such
sins by the influence of riches ? Saints have flesh as
well as spirit ; and riches are a powerful temptation to
them as well as other men. It requires more than a
Solomon's wisdom and grace to preserve men from the
corrupting influence of prosperity. Job was the best
as well as the richest man in the East. But where is
the saint who has received such rich communications of
grace as Job ? God grant that we may never be so rich
as Job, unless he is pleased to make us as good and
upright.

Some persons think they are in no danger of making
a bad use of riches, if they could but obtain them, because they feel no disposition to make a bad use of any
thing they have; " but he that trusteth in his own heart
is a fool." Is there a greater fool in the world than
the man that thinks himself wiser than Solomon or
Agur, or Christ himself, who tells us, that those who
have riches shall hardly enter into the kingdom of God ?

A wise man will not choose to leave a country of ordinary fertility, for another whose soil is far richer, but the air very pestilential, although his constitution of body is at present very healthful ; nor will he choose to walk in a flowery path where there are secret pits, and where the country is infested with robbers, if he can find another path, that is less pleasant and more safe.

But poverty is not without its temptations also. Pinching necessity may tempt a man to use unlawful shifts for his subsistence, and even to steal. And therefore this wise man prays that he might be kept from poverty as well as riches, for he had no confidence in his own heart, which he knew to be so foolish and treacherous.

But what made him so much afraid of stealing ? Did he think he would be disgraced and punished for it ? That was not the thing for which he chiefly abhorred stealing ; but he knew that this sin brings a great guilt, and a deep stain on the soul, and besides is a snare to the soul, which brings it into the devil's power, and gives him advantage for drawing on men to sins of greater guilt. One sin needs to be supported by another sin, and lying and perjury are the common refuges to which thieves have recourse for screening themselves from shame and punishment *.

Agur abhorred all sin ; but the sin of profaning the name of the Lord was one of the most dreadful wickedness in his apprehension, because the Lord was his God.   He believed in God, and loved him with all his heart, and he earnestly wished to be kept at the utmost distance from every thing that might lead him to dishonour or profane the name of his God.

Ver. 10. *Accuse not a servant unto his master, lest he curse thee, and thou be found guilty.*

---

*Chap. 29:24

Agur teaches us not only to keep a good conscience in the things that relate immediately to the worship and service of God, he enjoins us, likewise, to exercise ourselves to have a conscience void of offence towards men, not excepting the meanest of them. We must not hurt the meanest slave on earth; for although he is not able to revenge the injury, yet God will do it with severe justice.

As we must do no hurt to a poor servant, so we must not tempt any other person to hurt him. Agur forbids us to accuse him to his master, lest we should expose him to severe treatment at his hands. But is accusing a servant to his master in every case unlawful? Did not Abraham accuse the servants of Abimelech to their master for robbing him of his wells? He did; but there was no danger in that case, for Abraham knew that Abimelech was too selfish a man to punish his servants because they exceeded the bounds of justice in their zeal for his service. There are other cases in which we may lawfully accuse servants to their masters, but they are not common. Men are too ready to take too much liberty in this point; and Agur does not think it necessary to mention the excepted cases, because any man can see them, and most men would take too great a license in applying them to particular cases.

But what is the evil of accusing a servant to his master? It is inhumanity and cruelty. It is adding to the distress which we should rather relieve if it were in our power, (for servants in those days were generally slaves.) It is a sowing of discord in families; and it may provoke the poor man to curse thee. And what if he does? It is his sin to curse me. It is your own sin; or if the sin be his, you are the devil that tempts him to it; and the weight of his curses, aggravated with the guilt of them, may come down from a just God upon your head. You may be found guilty of bringing a false accusation against him; guilty of the poor man's revengeful curses; guilty of his master's tyranny, through the bad opinion of his servant that you infuse into his mind. Men by their indiscreet and sinful conduct, do often bring upon themselves the guilt of many more sins than they ever think about.

Ver 11. *There is a generation that curseth their father, and doth not bless their mother.*

Many of Agur's sayings are better remembered than many other things, by his method of classing his observations into a certain number of particulars. His petitions were two; and his observations on the manners of men, and the qualities of creatures, are four on each subject. He begins at this verse to speak of four sets of men, that deserve a particular remark on account of their extreme wickedness.

" There is a generation of men that curseth their father." It is the disgrace of human nature that ever one man was found that could be guilty of this sin. Will a man curse the instrument of his existence? This is the next degree of guilt to that of cursing the author of it. The prophet Isaiah pronounces a wo upon him that striveth with his Maker, and proceeds next to pronounce a wo against him that saith to his father, " what begettest thou; or to the woman, what hast thou brought forth."

But there is a whole generation of men upon whom this atrocious guilt may be justly charged, and therefore we find a law in the writings of Moses appointing the punishment of it; and the punishment is the same which was to be inflicted on the blasphemers of God himself.

Although men do not expressly make use of their tongues to curse their fathers, yet they are to be ranked with this cursed generation, if they do not bless their mothers. Mothers are to be honoured as well as fathers ; and the neglect of duty to parents is criminal, as well as the commission of offences against them.

But perhaps you will say, my mother deserves not to be blessed. Is she not your mother ? Then she deserves your good will and tender affection, and prayers; and if you cannot praise her, you have no call to say any thing to her prejudice.

Ver. 12. *There is a generation that are pure in their own eyes, and yet is not washed from their filthiness.*

No man is truly pure unless he is washed from his filthiness ; for all men are naturally polluted with sin, and rendered abominable by it ; for nothing on earth is comparable to sin for vileness, and no creature on earth is so abominable and filthy as man, who drinketh iniquity like water *.

We cannot be washed from our filthiness but by the blood and Spirit of Christ. The blood of Christ is the fountain opened by God for sin and uncleanness, and it is the Spirit of Christ that applies it to our souls, and purifies our hearts by the faith of it †.

But there are many who are strangers to Christ, and yet reckon themselves pure. They never saw their pollution, because they are unacquainted with the law of God, or with themselves; or they have taken to themselves nitre and much soap, and flattered themselves that they could wash away their own filthiness by it ; or they are mistaken about the way of making use of Christ, for the cleansing of their souls ; or persuade themselves upon false grounds, that they are cleansed by his grace.

Seest thou a man that is clean in his own eyes, although he is yet impure in the sight of God, there is

---

*Job 15:14   †1 Cor. 6:11, Acts 15:9

more hope of a publican or a harlot than of him. He says unto Christ, " Depart from me, for I am not a sinful man." He is covered, like the leviathan, with scales that render him impenetrable by the sharpest pointed arrows. No sinners do worse things than those who do whatsoever is right in their own eyes, (Judges xviii. &c.) and none are farther from righteousness than those who are righteous in their own eyes. They are a smoke in God's nostrils, a fire that burneth all the day. Christ found such self-conceited men his greatest enemies whilst he was tabernacling among us, and spoke some parables, and denounced many heavy woes against them.

Let us examine our hearts impartially, lest we should deserve to be classed with this wretched generation, which, we have reason to fear, is more numerous than the generation of them whose hands are clean, and their hearts pure. We all profess to be Christians, but Christ will deny us if we belong to this set of men; for he hath declared, that except he wash us we have no part in him. Men are unwilling to class themselves with the impure, lest their consciences should fly in their faces; but those that falsely pretend to purity are the persons whose consciences shall lash them with greatest severity at last. Why should we seek to cover our nakedness with fig leaves? Why should we exclude ourselves from the fountain, through a pernicious shame of confessing our vileness? The promise of God stands upon record: " I will sprinkle clean water upon you and ye shall be clean." Is it best, sinners, to claim the benefit of this promise, or to allege that you have no need of it? Men are generally ashamed to be thought poor; yet who would not confess himself to be poor, if the king should offer great wealth to every poor man in the town and to none else?

Ver. 13. *There is a generation, O how lofty are their eyes! and their eye-lids are lifted up.*

There is a generation of men that are swelled with pride and vanity, and yet put on the dress of humility. Such are a great number of the generation last mentioned ; but God knoweth their hearts; and the fruits of their pride often discover them to men.

But there are some men who seem to be proud even of their pride. They do not hide their sin, but declare it as Sodom ; and the shew of their countenances witnesses against them. Agur was surprised how the sons of Adam, who are but worms, should put on such arrogant airs, and behave with so much insolence.

Solomon likewise speaks of this race of men as a generation abhorred by the Lord *. The prophets, in their predictions against Moab, and Ezekiel, in his prophecies against Tyre and Egypt, give us a striking picture of their manners, and a terrible description of the vengeance of God against such insolent despisers of God and men; for God will save the afflicted and lowly people, but will bring down the high looks.

Ver. 14. *There is a generation whose teeth are as swords, and their jaw-teeth as knives, to devour the poor from off the earth, and the needy from among men.*

By these monsters of men, the inspired writer means false accusers, extortioners, oppressors, bloody tyrants, and their wicked instruments, who are the common enemies of men, but plunder and destroy especially the poor and needy, because these cannot resist them.

To what kind of creatures does Agur compare these wretches ? Not to lions or tigers, for neither these nor any other kind of animals are so fierce and brutal. These men are brutes with iron teeth, sharp as knives,

---

*Prov. 6:17

to cut off, and to destroy. Whilst they grind the faces
of the poor, and rob them of their means of subsistence,
they do in effect eat the flesh of the poor, and flay their
skin from their bones ; and they break their bones, and
chop them in pieces, as for the pot, and as flesh for the
caldron.

To what wickednesses are men driven by the cursed
love of gold ! The horse-leech sucks till it bursts. The
grave, and the barren womb, and the parched earth,
and the fire, can never be satisfied ; but the hearts of
wicked men are still more insatiable. They are still
crying, give, give. Hell is evidently set forth before
them, and flaming with tremendous fury ; and yet the
insatiable lust of having, drags them on to purchase
for themselves one of the chief places in that burning
lake, by heaping one horrid instance of inhumanity and
cruelty upon another. Had Job reigned among this
generation of men, he would have broken their jaws,
and forced the spoil from their teeth *. But punishments inconceivably more dreadful, are appointed to
them by the just Lord, who will not do iniquity, nor
suffer it to pass unrevenged.

Ver. 15. *The horse-leech hath two daughters, crying,
Give, give. There are three things that are never satisfied, yea, four things say not, it is enough.*

Agur had been speaking of the dreadful effects of the
lust of covetousness, which still cries, give, give. Some
think that he intends, in the two following verses, to represent the insatiable nature of this lust, by comparing it
with the most craving and unsatisfied things that men
are acquainted with. He does not expressly draw any
moral instruction out of the account he gives of the
four things that cannot be satisfied, only he teaches us
to make observations on the works of God, and the na-

---

*Job 29:17

ture of things that we see or hear of. Such observations enlarge our minds, lead us to admire the Creator, and to raise religious meditations in our minds. Besides, the Scripture makes use of such observations to illustrate the important instructions which it gives us about the things that we are to believe or do.

The horse-leech is a blood-sucker. It will suck the blood of other creatures till it bursts, but covetous men will suck the blood of their fellow-men till they are damned.

It is very usual in the eastern languages to call one thing the son or daughter of another thing, on account of some resemblance or relation in the one to the other. Thus arrows are called the sons of the bow; and the friends which attend a bridegroom, are called his children. In this sense, Agur calls any thing remarkable for its greediness, a daughter of the horse-leech. Covetousness of spiritual and eternal blessings, deserves to be exempted from this humiliating comparison; but an heart set upon earthly treasure, is more like the horse-leech than any of its daughters; for there is no satisfying of a covetous man; with shame he loves, give ye. And if you should give him whole rivers of blood to drink, he will still cry for more; as you see in the example of those tyrants, whom providence in wrath to men, permitted to gratify their lust without restraint *.

Ver. 16. *The grave, and the barren womb, the earth that is not filled with water, and the fire that saith not, It is enough.*

"Hell and destruction" says Solomon, "are never full, so the eyes of man are never satisfied;" but because the invisible world is never full, it is folly to be greedy of earthly things; for the grave will soon receive us, and then what will all earthly treasures avail us? The in-

---

*Hab. 2:5

visible world keeps its gates wide open for us, and therefore we should be laying up our treasure in another world.   If the grave were full, or if we could make a sure covenant with death, and obtain exemption from its power, we might have some excuse for living as if we were to live always.

The barren womb is unsatisfied in the want of children.   Rachel was led into much sin and sorrow by her passionate desire of children.   Let others in the like circumstances beware of following her example. Discontentment with our lot, in any part of it, is a tormenting and a dangerous sin.

The earth, when it is parched, can scarcely be satisfied with rain. It gapes for the showers; and although it be well refreshed at present, it will soon thirst for more.   This teaches us our entire dependence upon God, who has the key of the clouds in his hand, and could soon make the rain of our land powder and dust, and our earth iron under our feet.   As the thirsty land cries for rain, so let our souls thirst not for those blessings that spring from the ground, but for the salvation of the Lord from on high; then will he rain down righteousness upon us *.

The fire is more greedy than any of these things. Lay on fuel as long as you please, it will soon make an end of it, and seek for more.   There is a fiercer flame in the corrupt hearts and tongues of men, kindled from hell, and sufficient to set on fire the course of nature †.

Ver. 17.   *The eye that mocketh at his father, and despiseth to obey his mother, the ravens of the valley shall pick it out, and the young eagles shall eat it.*

Agur, as well as Solomon, insists much on the respect due from children to their parents.   Children that disobey or despise their parents are the kindred of those

---

*Isa. 45:8, Hosea 10:12   †James 3:6

that curse them, for the one sin is the natural introduction to the other. Such unnatural children were to be punished with death by the law of Moses ; and Agur represents the disgrace that attends this death, to affright men from the sin.

The ravenous fowls will pick out their eyes. Let children think of this, and let it be a motive to them, (if better ones are ineffectual,) to respect their parents. If human laws, or the carelessness of magistrates, free disobedient children from this punishment, God suffers them, by the violation of other laws, to bring themselves to the gibbet, or at least will find means to convince offenders by fatal experience, that his laws and threatenings are not vain *.

Ver. 18. *There be three things, which are too wonderful for me, yea four which I know not:*

Ver. 19. *The way of an eagle in the air, the way of a serpent upon a rock, the way of a ship in the midst of the sea, and the way of a man with a maid.*

An eagle is speedily out of our view when she soars aloft, and no trace of her flight is to be seen. A serpent slides over the rock, without leaving any slime like worms, or feathers like birds. A ship leaves no mark in the waves by which you can discern its track ; but the way of a man with one that calls herself a maid, is more indiscernible than all of them together. The companions in lewdness have a thousand arts to draw one another into this abominable sin, and to conceal it when it is committed.

Ver. 20. *Such is the way of an adulterous woman ; she eateth, and wipeth her mouth, and saith, I have done no wickedness.*

" Stolen waters are sweet, saith the foolish woman, and bread eaten in secret is pleasant ;" and secret bread

---

*Chap. 20:20

is so much the more pleasant, because, when it is eaten the theft cannot be found out. She wipes her mouth, and no marks of it are to be seen upon her lips.

The sweetness and the hiddenness of this sin make it very dangerous. Persons commit theft with fear and trembling, and they are often discovered ; and the reproofs and punishments they meet with are means of conviction and repentance. But adulterous persons taste a deceitful pleasure in their sin ; and they have a thousand ways of concealing their guilt; and so they add one sin to another, and contract those habits which become a second nature to them. The devil entangles them in strong twisted cords of a thousand folds ; and they are seldom recovered from his snares. They obtain, by their lying arts, a miserable deliverance from the means of repentance ; and by degrees they almost bring themselves to think that they have escaped the watchful eye of God.

Do not imagine that the secrecy of sin is your security from punishment ; it is the snare of your souls. By your arts to hide your wickedness you are only hardening your hearts, and twisting thick cords for yourselves, that you may be held fast in sin, and prevented from ever enjoying the liberty of the children of God *.

Ver. 21. *For three things the earth is disquieted, and for four, which it cannot bear:*

Ver. 22. *For a servant when he reigneth, and a fool when he is filled with meat ;*

Ver. 23. *For an odious woman when she is married, and an handmaid that is heir to her mistress.*

Pride is a sin detestable to God ; and its effects are such, that even men cannot bear them, especially when

---

*Prov. 5:22,23

it is raised to an high pitch, by a sudden and unexpected rise from a low and despised condition ; and therefore a wise man would not wish to be raised by God to a condition much above his present state, unless God would give him grace to bear it with moderation.

When a servant is raised to a throne, or to some high station in the government, he thinks himself almost a god ; and unless every one gives him homage he is filled with wrath and revenge. Haman was raised so high by Ahasuerus that he became giddy ; and he thought the offence of one man that would not bow the knee to him so grievous, that it required the blood of a whole nation to make atonement for it. Joseph and David were indeed raised by God to high places, and behaved well in them ; but God knew their hearts, and gave them such grace that they were still lowly when their condition was high. The greatest tyrants in the world have generally been those that never expected to reign ; such as Maximin the Roman emperor, who put to death all that knew him in his low condition, and, amongst the rest, those that had relieved his father and himself, that he might blot out the memory of his former meanness. Servants have not more seeds of pride in their nature than other men ; but they are sown in human nature, and are wonderfully cherished when the sunbeams of prosperity shine upon them with extraordinary warmth. Leave men of mean condition where you found them, and they will behave in their station as well as kings. Raise kings to an unexpected height of grandeur, and they will become Nebuchadnezzars and Alexanders.

This observation is of use in the affairs of the church as well as the state ; and therefore Paul forbids a novice to be made a ruler in the church, lest, being lifted up with pride, he fall into the condemnation of the devil.

A fool, when he is filled with meat, or furnished with riches sufficient to gratify his vanity and supply his extravagant desires, is another burden of the earth. A fool is troublesome at all times; but there is no bearing of him, when his lust of intemperance or greediness is fully satisfied. It is a blemish in David's character that he once broke out into such a violent rage, that he swore to destroy an innocent family; but we must remember that the provocation was given him by a fool when he was filled with meat. In ordinary cases David was the meekest of men.

For the like reasons an odious woman is intolerable when she is married. Women of meek and quiet spirits are a lovely part of the human race; but women of fretful spirits and unbridled passions are odious; and when they are married, it would require all the patience of Job, and the meekness of Moses to bear with them. Before marriage their pride was checked by neglect, and covered with the mantle of prudence; but when they come into their new state of life, they throw off every restraint, and their new situation is a means of increasing their vanity and ill nature, till neither their neighbours, nor their servants, nor their husbands, can endure them. If you are wise, when you intend to marry a wife, let her portion be the least part of your concern; but be sure that you know her real temper, and beware of those cheats that are doves in their virgin state, and vultures the week after they are married.

An handmaid that grows rich by the last will of her deceased mistress, or obtains her master in marriage, is another plague to all around her, as we may learn from the example of Hagar the Egyptian. Men should never marry their servant maids unless they are furnished with virtuous qualifications, and particularly with modesty and meekness to an unusual degree.

Ver. 24. *There be four things which are little upon the earth, but they are exceeding wise.*

God is to be admired in the leviathan and behemoth, and he is no less to be admired in the ant and the locust. The formation of these little creatures, and the instincts which God has given them, appear surprising to the wisest of men. They are not furnished with the noble gift of reason, and yet they have a degree of wisdom which may raise a blush in the cheeks of many who boast of the dignity of their rank in the scale of creatures.

Ver. 25. *The ants are a people not strong, yet they prepare their meat in the summer.*

The strength of ants has been admired by wise men, but their wisdom and industry make them strong; for they are a feeble nation, from the make and size of their bodies. Sluggards make inability to do their duty one of their excuses; but let them go to the ants and locusts, and learn to be ashamed of their frivolous pretences. These puny creatures do wonders by their exertions and perseverance; and men know not their own strength more than their weakness, till they have made a fair trial of it. But as to spiritual things, you will say, the Scripture teaches us that we have no strength at all: that is true, but it teaches you at the same time " to work out your salvation with fear and trembling, because it is God that worketh in you both to will and to do of his good pleasure." Are the ants and the conies so strong by the instincts which they receive from their Maker? what will not worm Jacob accomplish, when he goes in the strength of the Lord God?

The ants prepare their meat in the summer, that they may not starve in the rigours of the winter months. How despicable, compared with these insects, are the rational creatures, who suffer the thoughts of an end-

less duration to be pushed out of their minds by threescore and ten years?

Ver. 26. *The conies are but a feeble folk, yet make
they their houses in the rocks.*

Perhaps the wise man means some other kind of
creatures than those which we call conies. He tells
us that weak as they are, they find means to make habitations for themselves in the holes of the rocks, or in
rocky ground. As the ants teach sluggards to provide
food for themselves, these animals reprove those that
are careless about providing proper houses and means
of security from dangers. Few of us want due care
about houses for accommodating our bodies, but what
provision have we made for a dwelling-place to our
souls? Do we build upon the sand, or on the everlasting rock? If our place of defence is not the munition
of rocks, but some refuge of lies, the conies are wiser
than we, according to their kind. The high hills are
a refuge for the wild goats, and the rocks for the conies;
and has God provided no refuge for our souls? God
himself is our refuge and our strength, and those that
make him their habitation shall be secured from the
fear of evil.

Ver. 27. *The locusts have no king, yet go they forth
all of them by bands.*

The locusts, notwithstanding their weakness as individuals, are strong and terrible by their order and
agreement. They go forth by bands, and nations tremble, and countries are turned into desolate wildernesses.
The prophet Joel speaks of the armies of locusts in the
same style which other prophets use when they are
speaking of armies of Chaldeans or Persians; and history fully justifies the propriety of his language.

The Saracen enemies of Christianity are compared
by John to locusts, for their number and harmony, and
the destructive ravages which they were enabled by

these means to commit. Shall the enemies of religion
join so harmoniously in the service of the devil ? and
shall we that do not want a king, we that have Christ
and not Apollyon for our king, betray his glorious cause
by breaking our ranks, and violating that beautiful order which he hath appointed ? When the followers of
the Redeemer stand fast in one spirit, and with one
mind, striving together for the faith of the gospel, every one in his proper station, then the church is terrible as an army with banners ; and the locusts that
come out of the bottomless pit cannot prevail against
her.

Ver. 28. *The spider taketh hold with her hands, and
is in king's palaces.*

The spider does not say, there are servants in the
palace appointed to keep it clear from every nuisance ;
I shall be slain in the window. She provides herself a
dwelling in the houses of the great, as well as in the
cottages of the poor, for labour and wisdom conquer
every difficulty ; but to the sluggish soul every easy
thing is impossible.

Does God furnish these despised creatures with wisdom so admirable in their rank of being ? We are surely of greater value in his esteem than they are, and he
has provided treasures of better wisdom for us. Let
us have recourse to him, and he will furnish us with
that wisdom which is proper to rational and immortal
creatures. Our Lord seems to justify this inference, in
the instructions that he draws from the providence of
God in clothing the grass of the field, and feeding the
fowls of the air *. The locusts and spiders are hateful
and mischievous creatures to men, but they are not for
that reason useless. Those creatures that we despise

*Matt. 6:26-34

and abhor, are a part of the riches of the Creator. They
read lectures to us concerning his wisdom ; and if they
are well considered, they will instruct us in some articles of our duty.

Ver. 29. *There be three things which go well, yea four
are comely in going.*

If an heathen will not believe in Christ, he cannot
deny a God ; for the invisible things of God are clearly
seen in the things that he has made, and in those various endowments which he has bestowed on his creatures. As a garden is rendered pleasant to the eye
by the rich variety of fruits, and herbs, and flowers,
which it contains, so to the eye of the mind the world
is a beautiful scene, containing such a surprising variety of creatures, every one of them possessing qualities
peculiar to itself. Agur had spoken of those creatures
that are remarkable for their great wisdom in little bodies, and proceeds to mention some creatures that deserve admiration for their courage and spirit, and the
dignity that appears in their motions. " O Lord, how
manifold are thy works, in wisdom hast thou made
them all, the earth is full of thy riches."

Ver. 30. *A lion which is strongest among beasts, and
turneth not away for any.*

This celebrated animal is full of courage and fire ;
and no danger can subdue its valour, or force it to discover any sign of fear. God himself is pleased to use it
as an emblem of that majesty and resistless power
which he displays in the defence of his injured people *.
And Christ our king disdains not to borrow from it
one of his glorious titles. Christians are furnished
with such strength from their Redeemer, that they are
said to be bold as lions ; and by the courage of faith the
saints have sometimes stopped the mouths of lions, or

*Isa. 31:4

slain them outright. Wicked men have reason to flee although there is no pursuer, but Christians should learn, in the cause of truth and righteousness, not to turn aside for any adversary, or any suffering; for they shall be more than conquerors through him that loved them.

Ver. 31. *A greyhound, an he-goat also, and a king against whom there is no rising up.*

A greyhound discovers great agility and life in the chace of its prey, and gives great pleasure to the eyes of the hunter. The word, in the original, properly signifies, some creature that is girt in its loins; some take it to mean a cock, and others an horse; which last animal has the honour to be celebrated by God himself, in the sublimest strains of poetry, and is used by the prophet Zechariah as an emblem of that conquering strength which God conveys into the hearts of those that faithfully fight his battles against the enemies of religion. " The Lord of hosts hath visited his flock, the house of Judah, and hath made them as his goodly horse in the battle." They are weak as sheep in themselves, but furnished with the strength of war horses for maintaining his cause *.

An he-goat is an animal so remarkable for its strength and stateliness, when it marches at the head of the flock, that the Macedonian power which crushed the strength of the mighty Persian empire, is represented by it in the book of Daniel; and the prophet Jeremiah calls the delivered captives to imitate the he-goat, by setting an example of vigour and courage to one another, in improving the merciful providence of God; for we ought to go before one another in every good work.

Wonder not at Agur for insisting so long in his little performance, upon the excellencies of the irrational

---

*Zech. 10:4, Song 1:9

part of the creation.   The creation is a volume spread before our eyes, that we may read in it the perfections of the Creator, and the Scripture is a commentary upon some parts of it, which opens our mind to learn instruction from the rest.   Great use was made of this volume before the word of God was written, as you find in the book of Job *; and the Almighty was pleased to humble Job for his unguarded complaints, by manifesting his own excellencies in a discourse upon his creatures.

A king against whom there is no rising up, is another of those creatures that are stately in going ; for the God who has given courage and strength to lions, has given majesty to kings, and stamped on them such dignity that their subjects are awed by their appearance. Kings should therefore employ their authority and influence for the service of God ; and their subjects owe them reverence as well as obedience ; they are ministers of God, and are entitled to honour for the sake of their master and their work, and to obedience both for wrath and for conscience sake.

Ver. 32.   *If thou hast done foolishly in lifting up thyself, or if thou hast thought evil, lay thine hand upon thy mouth.*

Pride is a very bad thing when it goes no farther than the thoughts, but it is still worse when it swells and overflows by the lips. If any proud or injurious thought come into our minds, it ought to be immediately checked and suppressed. To discover it by our words is to declare our sin as Sodom, to give indulgence to those passions that ought to be mortified, and to add iniquity to iniquity. Besides, if we do not lay our hand upon our mouth, we shall rouse the pride of other men, and kindle up rage and strife that will not be easily allayed ; and thus we shall be accountable not only for

*Job 12:7 and etc.

our own sin, which is heavy enough of itself, but likewise for those iniquities that we occasion in others, by the temptations which we throw in their way.

Ver. 33. *Surely the churning of milk bringeth forth butter, and the wringing of the nose bringeth forth blood; so the forcing of wrath bringeth forth strife.*

Wrath is not only provoked, but forced by haughty and spiteful words; for such is our weakness, that we are as easily kindled into anger by the angry words that are directed to us, as one coal is kindled by another coal that is burning. We should be meek when our neighbour is angry; but, alas! we have too little of the spirit of Moses, or rather of Jesus; for Moses himself has been provoked to speak unadvisedly with his lips.

As the violent shaking of milk in the churn produceth butter, as the wringing of the nose makes blood to spring forth, so when we teaze our neighbours, and set their passions into a ferment by bitter and galling words, we are the authors of strife, and kindle up that destructive and devouring fire, which perhaps cannot be quenched till it has done a thousand times more mischief than we dreamed off. The command of our passions and tongues is an attainment of vast consequence to our happiness and the welfare of our souls. Many of the wise instructions of Solomon and Agur are designed to recommend this point of wisdom to our regard, and to assist us in learning it. Our Lord Jesus recommends it to us as one of the marks of a true Christian, and an evidence of our regard to his example. The apostles Paul and James insist very much upon it; and that love which John is for ever pressing upon us, will sweeten our tempers effectually into that calmness and meekness which are so absolutely necessary to our happiness and usefulness in the world, and will gradually extinguish those seeds of wrath and contention which lie in our corrupted natures. The apostle Peter re-

commends the calmness and meekness which is here
enjoined by motives of irresistible force, the example
which Christ left us when he was bearing our sin; the
pleasure that God takes in meekness, and the happiness
which he graciously confers on those who govern their
passions, and their tongues, according to his will. Men
of arrogant and outrageous tempers, murmurers and
complainers, are condemned by Jude in his short epistle with great severity. The whole scripture testifies
loudly against the contentious and ill-natured.

Proverbs 31

Verse 1. *The words of king Lemuel, the prophecy that
his mother taught him.*

Women have sometimes enjoyed the inspiration of
the Holy Spirit. Deborah and Lemuel's mother were
honoured to be the composers, under the direction of
God, each of them of a chapter in the Bible; and the
prophecy of Lemuel's mother will make every woman
who governs her life by it an ornament to her sex.

It is the duty of mothers, as well as fathers, to instruct
their children. Although Lemuel was a king, yet his
mother was directed by God to give him instruction
and admonition. Cornelia, the mother of the Gracchi,
was renowned for the pleasure she took in the education of her children; and the celebrated Cicero reckons
them as much obliged to her for their education as
their birth. When a certain Campanian lady was one
day shewing that illustrious lady her jewels, and desiring a sight of Cornelia's jewels, she told her that her
children were her jewels; and certainly the richest dia-

monds of Golconda cannot give so much lustre to a lady, as the proper discharge of this duty to her children. Cornelia was an unenlightened heathen, but why should Christian mothers blush in her presence?

If we were as great as kings, it would be a scandal to us to despise the instructions and counsels of a mother. King Lemuel remembered, and wrote the prophecy that his mother taught him, and transmits it to posterity. Whoever he was, we have reason to believe that he practised the instructions which he so much respected. Lemuel shall be for ever held in honour for the respect which he shewed to his mother, and his mother's name will be renowned for her part in forming her son to virtue, and religion, and public usefulness.

Ver. 2. *What, my son? and what, the son of my womb? and what, the son of my vows?*

When this venerable lady was instructing her son, her heart was overflowing with inexpressible tenderness of affection to him. Parents often take a very absurd method of expressing their fondness for their children; but when they gratify every one of their humours, and suffer them to live without restraints and admonitions, they do not truly love but hate their children. He that spareth the rod hateth his child. The love of parents to their children is best shewed by doing their utmost endeavours to make them good Christians, and useful to their generation; and for this purpose they ought to dispense their instructions and their reproofs in the language of love, and to let their children see that every thing they say to them is dictated by the warmest affection.

" What, my son? and what, the son of my womb?" This fond mother considered and pondered in her mind what way she should express her tender regard, and she could find no better way of shewing it than by teaching him that wisdom which became his station;

for what greater testimony of love can any mother give to the son of her womb ?

Every mother loves the son of her womb. If she does not, she is not a mother, but a sister to the ostrich, to which God hath denied understanding. The love of a mother to the son of her womb is so fervent, that God is pleased to use it as an illustration of his own love to his people. Although the love of a mother bears no proportion to it, yet that is one of the best emblems of it which the world can afford.

Lemuel was the son of her vows, as well as of her womb. Every son of the womb should be a son of the mother's vows and prayers. And the instructions of a parent must be joined with prayers for their success ; for mothers may plant, and fathers may water, but it is God who giveth the increase. When Monica was shedding tears for her beloved son Augustine, at the time that he was a debauchee, and an heretic, one of her friends told her that the child of so many prayers could not be lost, and perhaps no mother since the days of the Virgin Mary had in the end greater comfort in a son.

Ver. 3. *Give not thy strength unto women, nor thy ways to that which destroyeth kings.*

Whoredom, as Solomon tells us, is the ruin of any man ; but none are in greater danger of being ruined in their bodies and fortunes by this vice than kings, who have too often the misfortune to want a check or a reprover, whilst the temptations that lead to sensuality are ever surrounding them. David and Solomon involved themselves in great distress by the love of women ; and it is well known, that in later times, the kingdom of Spain was totally ruined, and the Saracens introduced into the possession of it, through the unbridled lust of King Roderick.

Ver. 4. *It is not for kings, O Lemuel, it is not for kings to drink wine, nor for princes, strong drink.*

Wine, as well as whoredom, takes away the heart when it is drunk to excess ; but other men cannot do so much hurt as kings or magistrates when they are drunk.

Ver. 5. *Lest they drink, and forget the law, and pervert the judgment of any of the afflicted.*

When Nadab and Abihu were destroyed by fire from the Lord, for their unhallowed incense, it is probable they were in liquor ; and therefore a law was made on that occasion that priests should drink no wine when they went in before the Lord, lest they should blunder in any part of the sacred service. The more important any man's work is, he is the more obliged to be temperate in all things ; and dunkenness, which is a damning sin in any person, is attended with prodigious aggravations in those men that dispense the mysteries of the gospel, or administer the public affairs of the nation. The most oppressive and execrable laws that Scotland was ever plagued with, were made by a parliament called the drunken parliament. Alexander the Great, when he was drunk, killed one of his best friends, who had, on a former occasion, saved his life in battle ; and when that prince recovered his judgment he had almost killed himself. His father Philip was less unfortunate. He once forgot the law in his cups, and passed an unrighteous sentence upon a poor widow ; but soon recovering his senses, he condemned himself to refund her damages.

Some think that drunkenness is an excuse for the faults that are committed by men under the influence of it. Lemuel's mother, under the influence of the prophetical spirit, was of another mind ; and even uninlightened heathens have been sensible how frivolous this excuse is. Zaleucus (I think) made a law among the Locrians, that if any person committed a crime when he was drunk, he should be punished for both crimes; for he did not judge that one crime was a proper excuse for another. If men are mad without any fault of their own, they are not accountable for their actions; but a voluntary madness has no excuse for itself, and will be no excuse for any thing else.

To pervert judgment in any case is not good. To pervert the judgment of any of the afflicted, is such a complication of injustice and inhumanity, that none but a man who is drunk, or is of a disposition that makes him perpetually like a man in liquor, will be guilty of it. The wise woman knew that her beloved son could never commit this unpardonable iniquity whilst he was sober.

It is not for ministers, or teachers; it is not for parents, or masters, or mistresses, to drink wine to excess, lest they forget their duty and commit some pernicious error, in the discharge of that trust which lies upon them, and corrupt their inferiors by their example.

But is wine useless? Why then did God create the fruit of the vine? It is not useless. Mahomet reproached his Creator, when he prohibited the use of it without restriction. It is useful for the refreshment of any man, when his labours, or the dejection of his mind, or the state of his body requires it. It is peculiarly useful to those that are oppressed with calamity and grief.

Ver. 6. *Give strong drink unto him that is ready to perish, and wine to those that be of heavy hearts.*

Ver. 7. *Let him drink, and forget his poverty, and remember his misery no more.*

We must not give wine in immoderate quantities to any person, however dejected, for sin is never to be chosen rather than affliction; but wine moderately used is of great use to revive the languishing spirits of the disconsolate ; and it may be a piece of as real charity, to bestow this generous liquor upon them, as it is to give bread to the hungry. The Psalmist mentions this among other instances of God's bounty, that he gives not only bread to strengthen us, but likewise wine to cheer our hearts, and oil to make our faces shine. Some of the persons that were present at the crucifixion of our blessed Lord, gave him wine mixed with myrrh to render his sufferings more tolerable to him ; but our Lord, who allows and requires us to bestow cordials on those who are ready to faint under their sorrows, refused-them in his own severest sufferings, for he was not disposed to decline the bitterest dregs of that cup of sorrow which was put into his hands by his father ; but when his people are made partakers of the sufferings of Christ, he puts the cup of consolation into their hands, and calls them to drink of that generous wine which goes down sweetly, and causes the lips of those who are in the deepest distress to sing. " As the sufferings of Christ abound in us," said one that was pressed with affliction above measure, " so our consolation also aboundeth by Christ."

We ought to be followers of Christ in the exercise of compassion to the sorrowful and the distressed. It is devilish to add to the sorrows of the afflicted ; but it is Christ-like to wipe away the tears from the eyes of the fatherless and widows, and to deserve the blessings of them that are ready to perish.

Ver. 8. *Open thy mouth for the dumb, in the cause of all such as are appointed to destruction.*

Ver. 9. *Open thy mouth, judge righteously, and plead the cause of the poor and needy.*

Job was an excellent pattern to all princes. He was eyes to the blind, and feet to the lame, and a father to the poor ; and no doubt he was a mouth also to the dumb. Such a prince the mother of Lemuel wishes her son to be. She exhorts him to do judgment and justice to all his people, but to regard with peculiar tenderness those unfortunate men that were in danger of losing their estates or lives, by reason of accusations brought against them. If they were unable, through ignorance, or awkwardness, or fear, to plead their own cause, she would have him to be their advocate, and to plead every thing that truth and equity would allow on their behalf. The appointment of advocates to plead for prisoners at the bar agrees with this instruction; and those who are appointed to this charitable office should open their mouths, and interest themselves in the cause of their distressed clients, with all the warmth that justice can admit, that none may be condemned, unless the evidence against them clearly overbalances every argument that can be adduced on their side.

It is certain that charity to the poor, and clemency to the accused, must not interfere with the due administration of justice; for a poor man is not to be countenanced in his cause; but there is less danger of erring in this than in the contrary extreme; and it is the business of princes to take care, that, in the administration of justice, the poor may not suffer by their unacquaintedness with law, or their want of ability to take the benefit of it when they are oppressed, or to defend themselves against their wealthier adversaries.

Our Lord Jesus Christ is at once our king and our advocate. He saves the poor and needy, and breaks their oppressors in pieces. He stands at the right hand of the poor and needy, to save them from those that would condemn their souls. Princes, as they have opportunity, should imitate him by whom kings reign, and princes decree justice.

The mother of Lemuel having instructed him in the virtues of purity and temperance, justice and mercy, proceeds next to instruct him in the choice of a wife.

As a bad wife is one of the worst, and a good wife one of the best things in the world, men cannot be too cautious about entering into the relation of marriage, which death only (or what is worse than death) can dissolve. Those who are in public stations have peculiar reason, for their own sakes, and for the sake of their connections, to consider well who those persons are whom they take into such close connexion with themselves. Paul gives directions about the wives of deacons * ; and the instructions about the choice of a virtuous wife are here addressed to a king. Although his instructor was his mother, yet she says nothing about high birth, or a large portion, or great alliances ; for these things were trifles to her view, compared with virtue. Besides, the spirit of God designed these instructions not merely for kings, but for all that have wives to choose, and for the whole female sex.

The last part of this chapter should be learned with great care by all women. The spirit of God was pleased, in the composition of it, to begin every verse with different letters, according to the order of the alphabet, like the 119th Psalm, which would render it more easy to be retained in the memory.

Ver. 10. *Who can find a virtuous woman ? for her price is far above rubies.*

Those that wish to have a good wife ought to consider that one who deserves this character is not easily to be found ; and therefore they ought to be cautious in their choice, to be well acquainted with the disposition and behaviour of those women who are to be their constant companions through life, and to address fervent supplications for the favour of him from whom alone a prudent wife is to be had. Abraham observed these rules in seeking a wife for his son, only he had

---

*1 Tim. 3:11

no personal acquaintance with Rebecca ; but not knowing of any virtuous woman in Canaan, he trusted God to provide him one in the land to which his obedience to God hindered him from returning.

But why are virtuous women so rarely to be found? Is the female sex more corrupted by the transgression of their first mother than her sons? This cannot be supposed. Solomon found fewer good women than good men ; but the experience of a man who conversed too much with the blemishes of their sex, will not establish a general rule. Women were so ill used in ancient times, that it is not to be wondered at if there were few virtuous women to be found. In our times, when the yoke of marriage is become much lighter on the woman, it may be reasonably supposed that it would be no dishonour to the female sex to be compared with the male, and that the virtues in which they are inferior, are abundantly balanced by those more lovely accomplishments in which they excel.

Men have no reason to reflect that virtue is rarely to be found in women. The imputation is not just, if it be meant to state an odious distinction between the sexes ; but if it were, the fault lies as much in men as in women. Virtue is not duly esteemed ; but riches and beauty are preferred to it. Who can find a wife that will bring a large portion? is the general question. Were the judgment of the princess by whom this character of a good wife was drawn, to be followed by the generality of men, parents would alter in a great measure their plan in educating their children ; and women would endeavour to recommend themselves, not by setting off their beauty to advantage, or giving themselves out for great fortunes, but by the practice of religion and of every praiseworthy qualification.

The price of a virtuous woman is far above rubies and diamonds. Although she has no portion but her clothes, she will be preferred by a wise man to one that is destitute of her qualifications, although she were possessed of all the riches of the east. He is a fool who marries the woman that is dressed in silk and rubies, if he would refuse the same woman in russet.

Ver. 11. *The heart of her husband doth safely trust in her, so that he shall have no need of spoil.*

She behaves in such a manner as to be above all suspicion of any thing inconsistent with strict virtue. When Cæsar divorced his wife, and was asked the reason of it, he said, that Cæsar's wife ought to be free not only of guilt but of suspicion. All Christians ought to walk so inoffensively, that the adversary that wishes to defame them may find no evil thing to say ; but wives in a special manner ought, for the sake of their husbands and themselves, to keep at a great distance from every thing that might sully their character, because it is easily stained and not easily cleared.

Some husbands will suspect their wives of indiscretions without the least shadow of reason ; but such brutes are so rare, that the prophetess takes no notice of them. She takes it for granted, that the husband of the virtuous woman will trust to her fidelity and prudence, when she merits it so well at his hands. To give cause of suspicions is bad in a woman ; to suspect without any cause is extremely ungrateful in a man. Confidence in a virtuous wife is a piece of duty to herself, and pleasant to her husband. The harmony of hearts arising from mutual esteem in husband and wife, affords the most delightful pleasure which any thing less than religion can give ; and when true piety in them both is added, it makes a kind of heaven upon earth.

The heart of the virtuous woman's husband rejoices not only in his present pleasures, but in his agreeable prospects of future happiness and contentment. He knows that his house is managed with such frugality and prudence, that he can entertain no apprehensions of poverty. He needs not leave his family, and betake himself to a military life, to be enriched by the spoils of war. He is under no temptation to injustice and rapine, to make up any waste in his substance; for every part of it is managed to the best advantage. The virtuous woman does good to the soul of her husband as well as to his body ; for her behaviour is a preservation from those temptations to iniquity, by which others, not blessed with the like happy connexions, have been drawn to sin, and to disgrace, and to a gibbet.

Ver. 12. *She will do him good and not evil, all the days of her life.*

There are some wives who are a constant plague to their husbands, vexing them with their ungodly and perverse behaviour, every day and every hour of their life.

There are others who do some good to their husbands, but at the same time do them so much evil that they cannot with any propriety be called virtuous wives. They take good care of their substance, and will not spend a penny without necessity ; but they teaze their husbands, and eat the very life out of all their comforts, by perpetual contentions, and by fretting at every trifle and every nothing.

But the virtuous woman doth good and not evil to her husband, and that not only at particular times, but every day. Some wives are like the days of April ; at one time they are serene and pleasant, but at other times they are all tempest and fury, and at another time they are like a continual dropping. The virtuous wife is as careful to please her husband, by an even and sweet temper, as she is to manage his affairs with discretion. She is the same to-day, and will be the same to-morrow, that she was yesterday. She is the same twenty or fifty years after marriage, as she was the first month. Neither sickness, nor poverty, nor old age, nor even the errors into which her husband may fall in managing the business of his family, will damp her love. The more he needs, the more he enjoys her tender sympathy. If he should sometimes, through the frailty of human nature, be so ungrateful as to speak harshly to her, she will bear with him, and forgive him. When he is dead, she will cherish his memory; and when the relation is loosed by the parting stroke, she will still do him good, by shewing kindness to his children for his sake.

Ver. 13. *She seeketh wool and flax, and worketh willingly with her hands.*

Some women will rather sit idle whilst they live, than seek wool or flax. If their husbands do not provide them proper materials for their work, they will consider it as a very sufficient excuse for idleness; but the virtuous woman abhors idleness, and loves her duty; and therefore she takes care to provide every necessary material and implement for work, that she may employ her time to the best advantage.

It is not enough for a wife to manage with frugality the fruits of her husband's industry, or to keep her servants at work; the virtuous woman works with her own hands; and it is not a burden but a pleasure to her to work with her hands. When Abraham's wise servant sought a wife for his master's son, he prayed to God to direct him to a woman that would give proof of her virtue, by her industry and politeness.

Men and women have different tasks assigned them, and each must employ themselves in their proper work. She is not a virtuous woman that neglects the work of a woman, and intrudes herself into her husband's affairs. The good wife employs herself with cheerfulness about her wool and flax, and leaves others to mind their own affairs; at the same time, if there is any thing necessary for the family which cannot be provided at home, she will take proper care that it shall not be wanting.

Ver. 14. *She is like the merchant ships, she bringeth her food from afar.*

She does not contract a mean and narrow habit, by her close application to labour, nor employ her endeavours to amass a heap of useless treasure. She grudges no expense that may contribute to the happiness of her family, but cheerfully exchanges the fruits of her own labour for those necessaries and conveniences that are fetched from distant countries. While slothful wives can scarcely provide necessary clothing for their own families, she provides by her labour and good management, something to sell, that the price may serve for the purchase of other commodities.

By the wise management of providence, distant countries are rendered useful to one another, by the supply of their mutual wants. No country enjoys every advantage; but there is no country where industry will not procure both the commodities which the soil affords, and those which must be fetched from afar. The virtuous woman enjoys the fruit of other people's labour, and the produce of other climates; for divine providence bestows its blessing on her industry, and there is no want of any good thing endured in her house.

Ver. 15. *She riseth also while it is yet night, and giveth meat to her household, and a portion to her maidens.*

Slothful women will not rise when day is come, but suffer the sun to run a great part of his daily race before they can think of shaking off their slumbers. The virtuous woman often prevents the dawning of the day, for she loves her duty more than her sleep. But it is to be remembered, that in the country where this inspired woman lived, the days and the nights were almost equal through the whole year, so that her meaning is, the virtuous woman rises before six in the morning.

But how is she employed when she is out of bed? David speaks of rising early to praise God; and no doubt the virtuous woman will not neglect her devotions, for she is a woman that fears the Lord; but she does not, under pretence of religion, forget what she owes to her family. She is a good and not a hard steward in the house of her husband, and takes care that none of her servants want their necessary portion of food. It is a happy thing to live under her roof; and her maidens are encouraged by her kindness as well as excited by her example, to perform with cheerfulness the tasks assigned them.

Ver. 16. *She considereth a field, and buyeth it; with the fruit of her hands she planteth a vineyard.*

Some of the female sex will consider every trinket that comes in their way, and spend more money than ever they gained by their work, in purchasing every trifle that can minister to their vanity, or gratify a capricious humour; but the virtuous woman employs her money in useful purchases. She will not, however, buy any thing without considering it, that she may judge whether it is worth the money demanded for it; but when she has considered, she buys; for she is not of a capricious and inconstant humour, like some whose mind changes more quickly than the wind.

What she buys she improves to advantage; for she has abundance of money, the fruit of her labour and good management, and with it she plants a vineyard in the field which she has bought, that her family may be well supplied with the conveniences of life in time to come.

Ver 17. *She girdeth her loins with strength, and strengtheneth her arms.*

As rust gathers on metals that are seldom used, so sluggishness of disposition contracts a rust on the powers of the body and mind; and idle persons by degrees realize those excuses for their conduct which were at first mere shams. The virtuous woman is of a very different temper. She declines not any part of her duty through aversion to toil; and by exerting her strength with a cheerful mind, she improves it. Her labours give her health and vigour, and alacrity for new labours; so that she can with great ease and tranquillity go through those businesses which appear impossibilities to other women.

Ver. 18. *She perceiveth that her merchandise is good ; her candle goeth not out by night.*

Notwithstanding her activity, she is never in such a hurry as to do her work in a slight and superficial manner. Her merchandise is known to be good, and brings a ready market and a good price; and her knowledge of this is a sufficient reward of itself for her toils ; for when the lazy are perpetually uneasy by their reflections on their own conduct, the consciousness of having done her duty, and the prospect of the advantages arising from it, are a constant source of satisfaction and cheerfulness to the virtuous woman.

She denies not to herself the necessary refreshments of sleep and rest. This would be a piece of vanity *. When the inspired moralist tells us that her candle goeth not out by night, her meaning is, that she never wearies of her labours, nor indulges herself or her maidens in sleep, beyond the call of reason and nature. In this sense Paul speaks of warning people day and night ; for no virtuous woman ever laboured so diligently for the good of her family, as the great apostle for the advancement of the kingdom of Christ.

---

*Ps. 127:2

There are some fashionable ladies who keep their candles burning almost the whole night; but they make up for it abundantly, by sleeping away the one half of the day, as if a candle were better than the sun. The virtuous woman rises early in the morning, but she can bear sitting late also, when her business requires it, although she would by no means spend her candles, or her time upon cards.

Ver. 19. *She layeth her hands to the spindle, and her hands hold the distaff.*

Very good employment for a servant maid; but will any lady spoil her white hands, and consume that time which might be employed so much more agreeably, in the vulgar trade of spinning? or did Lemuel's mother expect that his consort would employ herself in such work? Why not? She was to be a woman as well as a queen; and where is the law that forbids queens to be virtuous women, or to make use of their hands for those purposes for which the Creator designed them? At Abraham's desire, Sarah dressed a kid for her guests with her own hands, and Rebekah was so expert in household work, that she could impose upon her husband the flesh of kids for venison caught in the fields. Or if these examples are too ancient and sacred to be imitated by fine ladies in modern times, Alexander the Great, and Augustus Cæsar, wore clothes that were made by their own sisters; and our amiable queen is pleased to set a royal example of industry to her subjects.

If the female sex must not be idle, although their rank might seem to exempt them from the drudgery of working, how inexcusable is it in men, who boast superior strength, to trifle away their days without doing any thing; especially, considering that their sphere of labour is so much wider, and their opportunities so much greater, of choosing some profession suited to their dispositions. Do they allege that their patrimonies set them above the need of doing any thing ? This is the same thing with saying that God has been so good to them, that they are under no obligation of serving God, by serving their generation according to the will of God.

Ver. 20. *She stretcheth out her hand to the poor, yea she reacheth forth her hands to the needy.*

Although she is very careful of her family, yet she does not confine her attention to it. She labours with her hands, working that which is good, that she may have to give to him that needeth. Some wives are of such a perverse disposition that they have nothing for the poor, and will even grudge if their husbands bestow a little of the fruits of their labour upon them ; but virtuous wives do not think that any thing is lost which is bestowed in works of charity. They would not wish to encourage idleness, by extending their liberality to those impudent beggars who come to their doors when they might be earning their livelihood by some useful employment ; but they are kind to those whom they know to be really in want, and unable to work, and will bestow as much, at least, upon them, as some others of their sex bestow upon their own pride and luxury.

The husband of the virtuous woman has no reason to find fault with her for her goodness to the poor ; for she is serving her family as well as herself by it, and bringing down the blessing of God upon her labours, which could not be successful without it. They were happy women who had the opportunity to minister unto Christ of their substance ; and they enjoy the like happiness who take delight in relieving the distresses of the indigent for Christ's sake. Whatsoever is done unto the least of his brethren, in his name, he considers as if it were done to himself.

Ver. 21. *She is not afraid of the snow for her house-hold: for all her household are clothed with scarlet.*

She deserves not the character of a virtuous woman who is not concerned for the happiness and comfort of those who dwell under her roof. Although a virtuous wife attends, in the first place, to the happiness of her husband, as well as her own, and in the next place, to the welfare of her children; yet she extends her care to her servants also, and interests herself in their prosperity.

But her kind and feeling temper is not the source of vexation but pleasure. She takes care that every member of her happy family is well fed and well clothed; therefore she is not afraid that any of them will be hurt by the snows and cold of winter.

The care of providing clothes for servants does not come so much within the province of those who keep none but hired servants; yet a virtuous woman will still see to their welfare in every article of importance.

The scarlet clothes that are here spoken of, were not costly and fine ornaments, as they are with us, otherwise it cannot be supposed that all her household would be clothed with them. Some translators make them to signify double garments. Convenience and health are studied by the virtuous woman, far above ornament and fashion.

Ver. 22. *She maketh herself coverings of tapestry, her clothing is silk and purple.*

Although the virtuous woman is liberal to the poor, yet she is not impoverished. Some have been made poor by selfishness and narrowness; millions have been impoverished by pride and profusion; but none have been impoverished, and many have been enriched, by charity. The virtuous woman after reaching forth her hands to the poor, has enough remaining to provide proper and elegant furniture for her house, and a dress for herself suitable to her station.

There is no part of the character of a virtuous woman that will please some ladies so much as this part of it, which seems to allow some scope for finery. And it is not to be denied, that ornaments of a decent kind may very lawfully be used by those that can afford them ; but Isaiah and Zephaniah, Paul and Peter, testify against that vanity of dress which is too much coveted by some of the sex. The adorning recommended to women by the apostles, does not consist in gold, and pearls, and costly array, but in modest apparel, shamefacedness, sobriety and good works, and a meek and quiet mind. And Lemuel's mother says nothing inconsistent with this doctrine. If the virtuous woman has coverings of tapestry for her house, she makes them to herself ; *if* she is clothed with silk (or fine linen, as it may be rendered) and purple, she earns it by her labours and good management. She does not starve her charity by her finery, nor spend upon her dress that which might support a poor family ; and she does not reckon herself superior to the duties of a wife, nor exempted by wearing silk and purple, from using her spindle and distaff. From all this it appears, that the inspired writer allows the use of costly array to none but those that can afford it in a full consistency with the duties which they owe to their families, to the poor, and to all men.

Ver. 23. *Her husband is known in the gates, when he sitteth among the elders of the land.*

The character drawn in this passage is that of a virtuous woman, who is in such a station of life that her husband has a right to a seat in the gate, among the elders of the land, who meet in that public place to transact public business, or to decide in causes that are brought before them. The wife of such a man may be allowed to wear silk and purple; but she is as careful to have her husband, as herself, dressed in a manner suitable to their rank. A man that sees him in the gate may easily judge that his wife is a virtuous woman. His clothes are decent, though not gaudy; his looks are cheerful; and the happiness which he enjoys at home appears in his face abroad.

Women are for the most part jealous of their husband's honour, and it lies in their power to procure them a great deal of respect; for it is a greater honour to have it said that a man has a virtuous wife, than to be admired for riches and titles. Phocion's wife, when she was asked about her jewels, said that her husband was her jewel; and a man who is married to a virtuous wife has Solomon's warrant to say that he is possessed of a crown.

Ver. 24. *She maketh fine linen, and selleth it, and delivereth girdles unto the merchant.*

It is wonderful to think what industry will accomplish. We think that the virtuous woman has done great things, when she has provided her house and her family with every conveniency: but besides all this, she provides fine linen and girdles for sale; and when other women impoverish their husbands by buying, she enriches her husband by selling those valuable commodities for which there is a constant demand.

It is only modern pride and laziness which has introduced the idea, that it is inconsistent with the dignity of a fine lady to make profit of her own manufactures. This virtuous woman, although her husband sits among the elders, does not think it a discredit, but an honour to herself, to make fine linen and girdles for sale; and the wise will praise her on account of it.

Ver. 25. *Strength and honour are her clothing, and she shall rejoice in time to come.*

" The virtuous woman is clothed with silk and purple* ;" but she has much nobler ornaments than any
thing of that sort. She possesses a greatness of soul,
an inward vigour and resolution of mind, which sets
her above all those little and tormenting fears which
keep many of her sex in perpetual uneasiness. The
strength of her mind displays itself in her behaviour,
and gains her universal esteem from men ; and she
wears those ornaments which are of great price in the
sight of God himself.

Those ladies that wear gold and jewels, dazzle the eyes
and draw the regard of ordinary understandings ; but
how much brighter are the ornaments of a meek and
quiet spirit, of strength and honour, which are the constant dress of the woman of virtue ! Those that wear
costly array rejoice for the present, because they think
themselves the object of all men's admiration ; but they
are often preparing future sorrow for themselves by
their extravagance, and their neglect of those accomplishments which would gain them respect in old age.
The virtuous woman is not only cheerful at present, but
she shall rejoice in time to come. It is a pleasure to her
to reflect on her past conduct, and when she looks forward, she is not afflicted at the thought of the fading and
uncertain nature of all earthly enjoyments ; for, besides
that she has made all the provision that human wisdom
can reach against future contingencies, she can place a
quiet confidence in the providence of God, which will
not suffer the righteous to be moved. She knows that
her beauty must wither by old age; but the regard of
her husband, and the esteem of others, is founded upon
other motives that will never perish.

The virtuous woman is one that fears the Lord†, and

---

*Verse 22   †Verse 30

light is sown for such persons, and gladness for the upright in heart.

Ver. 26. *She openeth her mouth with wisdom, and in her tongue is the law of kindness.*

As a sandy hill is to the feet of the aged, so is a wife full of words to a quiet man; but the virtuous woman plagues neither her husband nor any other man with her talk. She has learned that silence and subjection which the Apostle Paul recommends to wives. She does not lock up her lips in a sullen silence, but when she speaks it is a pleasure to hear her, for she opens her mouth with wisdom. Besides her other labours already mentioned, she rises in the morning, and finds time to read the Bible, and other instructive books; she meditates and reflects, and receives instruction from what she hears, and prays to the Father of lights; and so she improves daily in knowledge and prudence; and when she opens her mouth, she says nothing but what is well worthy of being heard. She says nothing that savours of levity, or affectation, nothing that is unseasonable, nothing to gain herself the reputation of wit. All her words are expressions of that good sense which adorns her mind, and that virtue which warms her heart, and regulates her conduct.

There are some who gain a character for smartness at the expense of their reputation. They will speak the rudest things without provocation, and applaud themselves for it, as an evidence of their wit and boldness. But the virtuous woman abhors the thought of making any person uneasy, but when there is a necessity for reproving, and even then, she will be as gentle as can possibly consist with the efficacy of her admonitions. Kindness is painted on her countenance, and flows from her tongue; for it possesses the throne of her heart, and gives law to all her words and actions. She is a living explication of that beautiful description of charity which

the Spirit of God gives us by the pen of the Apostle
Paul *.

Ver. 27. *She looketh well to the ways of her household,
and eateth not the bread of idleness.*

She carefully inspects the behaviour of her maidens
and children. She is not idle when she is not working with her hands, but promoting the welfare of her
family, by doing the duty of her place as mistress of
the house; and her authority cannot fail of being respected in it, when she sets such a noble example of
diligence before them.

She will take care that nothing indecent or offensive stain the honour of her family; and when she is
served by the labour of her maidens, she will not suffer them to neglect the service of God.

She will be very careful of the behaviour of her children in their tender years, and will not see them trained up in idleness, or indulged in any vanity which
may afterwards grow up into a vice. Lying, and Sab-
bath-breaking, and evil speaking, and corrupt communication, are banished from every place where her influence extends.

Her bread is well earned by her labours; and therefore she eats it with pleasure and appetite, and derives
from it health and vigour to her body, and cheerfulness
to her mind. The bread of idleness has a very contrary effect; it is eaten without relish, and produces in-
digestion, and an innumerable train of lingering diseases. He that eats it sins against God, who commands every man to work at his business with quietness, and to eat his own bread.

Ver. 28. *Her children arise up, and call her blessed;
her husband also, and he praiseth her :* (saying,)

Ver. 29. *Many daughters have done virtuously, but
thou excellest them all.*

---

*1 Cor. 13

Were women to consider their own interest and satisfaction, they would all endeavour to be virtuous. Every person counts it a great happiness to enjoy the esteem of those whom he loves ; and the virtuous woman finds herself blessed in the tender affection and high esteem of her dear children, and her dearer husband.

Her children are constant spectators of her virtue, and experience the sweet fruits of it ; and they cannot forbear to express their sense of it by pouring out blessings upon her. A mother deserves the tender regard of her children, although she cannot lay claim to the character of a virtuous woman. Alexander the Great, having received a letter from the governor of Macedonia, complaining of his mother's conduct, was sensible of the justice of the complaints, but observed that Antipater did not consider that one tear of a mother would blot out a thousand such letters. If an imperious mother is entitled to respect, how can children express sufficient regard to one that is the ornament to them, and a happy instrument in training them up to piety and virtue ? If their tongues were silent in her praise, their dress, their cheerfulness, their good behaviour, when they follow her precepts and example, would be a constant encomium on her virtues.

The praises of her husband will be still more delightful to her ears than those of her children. What earthly happiness can a good wife desire, like the affection and approbation of the guide of her youth ? and this a virtuous woman can scarcely fail of possessing, for what heart has so much marble in it, as to be able to resist those virtues which every hour appear in his other self ? He cannot refrain from bestowing praise on one whom he finds the sweetener of all his cares, his faithful adviser in perplexities, his comforter in every distress, the instrument of a great part of his earthly felicity ; his best friend, his unceasing joy, and his brightest crown. No wonder if the experience of such goodness and happiness makes him eloquent in her praise, and draws commendations from his tongue, that must be understood in a restricted sense to make them true. He prefers her to every other wife that ever lived upon earth ; and he is sincere in doing it, for she ravishes his heart by the beauties of her mind and conversation. Piety will dispose a man to think meanly of himself, in comparison with other men, but highly of his wife, when he compares her with other women.

Ver. 30. *Favour is deceitful, and beauty is vain ; but a woman that feareth the Lord she shall be praised.*

Why is not beauty mentioned in the character of the virtuous woman ? Is not beauty a bright ornament to her virtue ? But there is no mention made of it in this description, because it is a mean quality in comparison of those which are here enumerated. It is but a flower that fades in a day ; and the love produced by it is but a transient passion. When beauty is not sweetened by virtue, the woman that possesses it is but like a sow with a golden jewel in its snout, as Solomon tells us. At the best, beauty cannot secure that love which it raises, for when it becomes familiar to the lover, it palls upon his sight ; and sometimes tempts him to curse that enchanting influence which blinded his eyes to more solid qualifications.

But a woman that fears the Lord, whether she has or has not beauty, shall be praised ; for true piety is the beauty of the soul, and excels that which lies in complexion and features as much as heaven is higher than the earth, or eternity longer than time.

The fear of the Lord is the beginning of wisdom, and the most essential part of the virtuous woman's character. It is this which sanctifies every other part of it, and makes her all glorious within. Its praise is not of men but of God ; yet the pleasant effects of it, which spread themselves into every part of her behaviour, cannot but excite the admiration of all beholders.

The flowers of poetry have been exhausted in dressing out beauty to the greatest advantage; but this one verse of Scripture is sufficient to give us just notions of its real value. It is indeed a lovely qualification when it is joined with piety and humility, but without them it is a snare and a trap. In choosing a wife, fools will follow their fancy, and the wise will act according to reason and the word of God.

Ver. 31. *Give her of the fruit of her hands, and let her own works praise her in the gates.*

Her children praise her, her husband praises her; and let every man join to commend her virtues, and to hold her up to public view, that she may be imitated by all her sex. There are multitudes who never fail to trumpet abroad the faults of their neighbours; but it would be much better to conspire in spreading abroad the virtues of those that are an ornament to human nature, and models for the behaviour of all their neighbours.

She is entitled to honour; and if no tongue should give it to her, the works of charity and wisdom, which she is constantly practising, will be a monument to her name. She is praised by all the wise that know her, and she shall have praise of God on the day when the seal shall be set to every character.